Human
Resources
Management

Human Resources Management

Fifth edition

PROF P S NEL (coordinating author)

Authors
PROF P D GERBER
DR P S VAN DYK
DR G D HAASBROEK
MS H B SCHULTZ
PROF T J SONO
MS A WERNER

OXFORD
UNIVERSITY PRESS

Great Clarendon Street, Oxford OX2 6DP

Oxford University Press is a department of the University of Oxford.
It furthers the University's objective of excellence in research, scholarship,
and education by publishing worldwide in

Oxford   New York

Auckland Bangkok Buenos Aires Cape Town Chennai
Dar es Salaam Delhi Hong Kong Istanbul Karachi Kolkata
Kuala Lumpur Madrid Melbourne Mexico City Mumbai Nairobi
São Paulo Shanghai Singapore Taipei Tokyo Toronto

Oxford is a registered trade mark of Oxford University Press
in the UK and certain other countries

Published in South Africa
by Oxford University Press Southern Africa, Cape Town

Human Resources Management
ISBN 0 19 571853 4

© Oxford University Press Southern Africa 2001

The moral rights of the author have been asserted
Database right Oxford University Press (maker)

Previously published by Southern Book Publishers (Pty) Ltd
and by International Thomson Publishing Southern Africa (Pty) Ltd
First edition published 1987
Fifth edition published 2001
Reprinted 2002 (twice)

All rights reserved. No part of this publication may be reproduced,
stored in a retrieval system, or transmitted, in any form or by any means,
without the prior permission in writing of Oxford University Press,
or as expressly permitted by law, or under terms agreed with the appropriate
reprographics rights organisation. Enquiries concerning reproduction
outside the scope of the above should be sent to the Rights Department,
Oxford University Press, at the address below

You must not circulate this book in any other binding or cover and you must
impose this same condition on any acquirer

The authors and publishers gratefully acknowledge permission to reproduce
material in this book. Every effort has been made to trace copyright holders,
but where this has proved impossible, the publishers would be grateful for
information which would enable them to amend any omissions in future editions.

Editor: Laurie Rose-Innes
Cover design: Mark Standley

Published by Oxford University Press Southern Africa
PO Box 12119, N1 City, 7463 Cape Town, South Africa

Set in 10 pt Plantin on 12 pt by RHT desktop publishing, Durbanville
Reproduction by RHT desktop publishing, Durbanville
Cover reproduction by The Image Bureau
Printed and bound by Creda Communications

Dedication

This edition is dedicated to the families and the students of the authors.

Special dedication

A special dedication is presented to Dr Pieter Stephanus van Dyk, an astute academic, who unwillingly in his prime retired from active knowledge creation owing to failing health. He was a co-author of the book since its inception in 1987 and participated in all editions, including the fifth.

Preface

With the advent of the new millennium, most people expected that the world would change radically and rapidly in all areas of life, including occupation, field of study or even just the affairs of their local community. Time will tell whether the rate of change will be as rapid as expected.

Business people and educationalists have also been led to believe that the new challenges ought to be vastly different from those which faced the previous century. Technological advances, electronic business and the way human resources are to be managed, to mention but a few fields, have not escaped the expectations of a changed approach, nor the increased competition and the sophistication of the way in which business is to be conducted in the new millennium.

With the aforementioned expectations in mind, it is clear that human resources management in general and this book in particular could not escape the future. The cliche that the future is not what it used to be is extremely relevant in this regard. The authors saw fit to take up the challenge at the start of the real new millennium (2001) and to write a new edition so as to be able to present the business and educational community with a completely revitalised book.

The authors themselves have, likewise, not escaped the winds of change. Prof. Gerber retired from the academic profession after a lifetime of service and elected to take on a less strenuous role in the fifth edition. Prof. Van Dyk's untimely retirement owing to ill health led to the reduction of his contributions to the book as well. On the other hand, new authors were introduced: Deon Haasbroek, Helen Schultz, Themba Sono and Amanda Werner. They all contributed to a greatly enhanced contemporary approach now prevalent in the book, as well as a comprehensive updating and repositioning aimed at maintaining its relevance and the prominence it enjoyed during the previous four editions over a 13 year period. This rejuvenation is obvious from a perusal of the various chapter topics and should take the book well into the new millennium and a number of further editions. Chapters which were added include 'Cultural diversity and change management', 'Organisational renewal', and 'International human resources management'. Each chapter in the book now includes an illustrative case, as well as an end-of-chapter case study.

It is extremely appropriate in the authors' opinion to thank Leanne Martini and Aleta Mostert for their perseverance and enthusiasm in seeing this edition through under trying circumstances for both the authors and the publishers.

The authors also wish to thank Elize Nel for typing a major portion of the manuscript including the updated Instructors Manual which accompanies the fifth edition.

As stated in the Preface to the previous edition, we wholeheartedly continue to believe that this book will make a contribution to the enhancement of quality human resources management in Southern Africa. It will certainly enable students and practitioners to become truly conversant with the variety of challenges facing the management of human resources as they will rapidly unfold in the new millennium.

Prof Piet S Nel
Coordinating author
October 2000

Abridged table of contents

PART I Managing human resources in organisational context — 1
1. Definition and scope of human resources management — 3
2. The human being as an employee — 28

PART II Approaches to human resources management — 43
3. The functional, systems and efficiency approaches to human resources management — 45
4. The quality assurance approach to human resources management — 75

PART III Human resources and the legislative environment — 89
5. Employment law impacting on employment relationships — 91
6. Interdependency between employment relations and human resources management — 131
7. Employment equity and affirmative action — 174

PART IV Staffing the organisation and maintaining people — 193
8. Job analysis — 195
9. Workforce planning and recruitment — 217
10. Selection — 240
11. Induction and staffing decisions — 259
12. Compensation management — 279
13. Health and safety management — 301

PART V Behavioural aspects of human resources management — 323
14. Motivation — 325
15. Leadership — 348
16. Groups and teamwork — 372
17. Cultural diversity and change management — 394

PART VI Employee, group and organisational empowerment through human resources interventions — 409
18. Job design and organisational design — 411
19. National level skills development issues — 434
20. Training and development of employees and career management at organisational level — 465
21. Performance management — 514
22. Organisational renewal — 536

PART VII Strategic and international human resources management — 551
23. Interdependency between organisational strategy and strategic human resources management — 553
24. Human resources information systems — 574
25. International human resources management — 591
26. The future of human resources management — 610

Index — 624

Handwritten note at top: NB concentrate on → 8, 9, 10, 11, 18, 20, 21

Contents

Handwritten note in margin: study chapters that are circled

PART I		**Managing human resources in organisational context**	1
①		**Definition and scope of human resources management**	3
	1.1	Introduction	4
	1.2	The relation between human resources management at organisational level and economic prosperity	4
	1.2.1	General	4
	1.2.2	How can human resources management contribute towards improving this state of affairs in South Africa?	7
	1.3	Human resources management: a historical perspective	8
	1.3.1	General	8
	1.3.2	The end of the previous century	8
	1.3.3	The growth phase in human resources management	11
	1.3.4	Summary	12
	1.4	Human resources management as a profession	12
	1.4.1	The Institute of People Management of Southern Africa	12
	1.4.2	Membership categories	13
	1.4.3	The South African Board for Personnel Practice	13
	1.5	Careers in human resources management	15
	1.6	Human resources management defined	16
	1.6.1	Clarification of concepts	16
	1.6.2	Approach to defining human resources management	19
	1.7	Challenges facing human resources management in South Africa	22
	1.7.1	Historical background	22
	1.7.2	Challenges for human resources management	23
	1.8	The focus and structure of this book	24
	1.8.1	General	24
	1.8.2	A human resources management model of the individual as an employee	25
	1.8.3	The structure of the book	26
	1.9	Conclusion	26
②		**The human being as an employee**	28
	2.1	Introduction	29
	2.2	The individual employee as a human being	29
	2.3	The authors' view of personality	31
	2.4	The psychological contract between the human being as an employee and the organisation (management) as employer	33
	2.4.1	Types of psychological contract	33
	2.4.2	The cooperative contract — pg 34 expectations	33
	2.5	The integration of personal goals with those of the organisation	37
	2.6	Attachment to the organisation and involvement with the goals of the organisation	37

Handwritten annotations in margins:
- exclude (next to 1.4–1.4.3)
- explain define (next to 1.6–1.6.1)
- NB Historical development (next to 1.7.1)
- diagram pg 30–32 factors (next to 2.1–2.3)
- NB examples expectations of co-op. (next to 2.4.1–2.4.2)

Handwritten note at top: Don't Study Chapters 4, 6, 13 (excluding tought) (notes), 14, 15, 16, 22, 23-26

CONTENTS   ix

2.6.1	Employees' attachment to the organisation	38
2.6.2	Involvement with the organisation	39
2.7	Conclusion	40

PART II   Approaches to human resources management — 43

3   The functional, systems, and efficiency approaches to human resources management — 45

3.1	Introduction	46
3.2	The role and functions of human resources management from a functional perspective	46
3.2.1	General	46
3.2.2	The development and maintenance of human resources management objectives	46
3.3	Traditional human resources management functions	48
3.4	Specific responsibilities and functions	48
3.4.1	General	48
3.4.2	Responsibilities of the human resources management department	48
3.4.3	The function of the human resources manager	49
3.5	The structural placement of a human resources department from a functional perspective	50
3.5.1	General	50
3.5.2	A typical structure for a human resources management department within an organisation	50
3.6	The systems approach	50
3.6.1	General	50
3.6.2	Description of a system	51
3.6.3	A systems model for human resources management	55
3.6.4	Human resources management and the success of the organisation	67
3.7	Conclusion	71

Handwritten margin notes: "activities + functions of a HR manager"; "systems approach"; "but pg 56 is NB."

4   The quality assurance approach to human resources management — 75

4.1	Introduction	76
4.2	Quality assurance	76
4.3	Human resources management as a process	78
4.3.1	General	78
4.3.2	Human resources management: a process in itself	78
4.4	The process approach to quality assurance and human resources management	82
4.4.1	General	82
4.4.2	Defining the concepts	82
4.4.3	Process management and human resources operations	84
4.5	Conclusion	86

CONTENTS

PART III Human resources and the legislative environment — 89

5 Employment law impacting on employment relationships — 91

5.1	Introduction	94
5.1.1	Government policy and the Constitution	94
5.2	Employment Equity Act No. 55 of 1998	95
5.2.1	The purpose and scope of the Act	96
5.2.2	Commencement dates of provisions	97
5.2.3	Human resources impact of the Act	97
5.3	Basic Conditions of Employment Act No.75 of 1997	97
5.3.1	The purpose and scope of the Act	98
5.3.2	Work time and rules	98
5.3.3	Payment of remuneration and deductions	100
5.3.4	Termination of employment	101
5.3.5	Administrative obligations	101
5.3.6	Prohibition of employment of children and forced labour	101
5.3.7	Variation of basic conditions of employment	101
5.3.8	Monitoring, enforcement, and legal proceedings	102
5.3.9	Possible amendments to various Acts	102
5.4	Labour Relations Act No.66 of 1995	103
5.4.1	The purpose and scope of the Act	103
5.4.2	Freedom of association and general protections	105
5.4.3	Collective bargaining	106
5.4.4	Strikes and lock-outs	110
5.4.5	Workplace forums	113
5.4.6	Trade unions and employers' organisations	113
5.4.7	Dispute resolution	114
5.4.8	Unfair dismissals	116
5.5	Occupational Health and Safety Act No.85 of 1993	120
5.5.1	The purse and scope of the Act	120
5.5.2	The duties of employers concerning health and safety	121
5.5.3	The duties of employees concerning health and safety at work	121
5.5.4	The Advisory Council for Occupational Health and Safety	122
5.5.5	Penalties for offences	122
5.6	Skills Development Act No.97 of 1998	122
5.6.1	The purpose and scope of the Act	123
5.6.2	Application of the Act	124
5.7	Compensation for Occupational Injuries and Diseases Act No.130 of 1993	124
5.8	Unemployment Insurance Act No.30 of 1966	125
5.8.1	The purpose and scope of the Act	125
5.8.2	Employers' duties	125
5.8.3	Unemployment benefits	126
5.9	Conclusion	126

6	**Interdependency between employment relations and human resources management**	**131**
6.1	Introduction	133
6.2	The individual contract of employment	134
6.3	The focus of the interdependency	136
6.4	The rights and duties of employers and workers	137
6.4.1	The rights of management	137
6.4.2	The rights of workers	138
6.5	The relation between company, human resources, and employment relations policies	140
6.5.1	Company policy and human resources policy	140
6.5.2	Employment relations policy	141
6.6	The major components of employment relations of concern to the human resources manager	143
6.6.1	The essentials of employer-employee communication	143
6.6.2	The relationship between employer and trade union	145
6.6.3	Relationships with employers' associations	147
6.6.4	Dispute-handling procedures	147
6.6.5	Strike handling	151
6.6.6	Importance of grievance and discipline handling	153
6.7	Workplace forums	158
6.7.1	Setting up a workplace forum	158
6.7.2	How workplace forums work	158
6.7.3	Consultation	159
6.7.4	Joint decision-making	159
6.7.5	Effectiveness of workplace forums in practice	159
6.8	General employment practices that affect employment relations	160
6.8.1	Recruitment	160
6.8.2	Selection and induction	161
6.8.3	Training and development	162
6.8.4	Job evaluation	162
6.8.5	Compensation	163
6.8.6	Fringe benefits	163
6.8.7	Employee promotion	163
6.8.8	Industrial health and safety	163
6.8.9	Retrenchment	164
6.8.10	Termination procedures	164
6.8.11	Codes of employment	165
6.8.12	Quality of work life and social investment	165
6.8.13	The monitoring of employment relations	166
6.9	Employment equity	167
6.10	Implications of the Basic Conditions of Employment Act	169
6.11	Future perspectives	169
6.12	Conclusion	170

xii   CONTENTS

7	**Employment equity and affirmative action** *learn notes only*	**174**
7.1	Introduction	175
7.2	Meaning of affirmative action	176
7.3	Employment equity	178
7.3.1	Unfair discrimination	178
7.4	Why the need for employment equity	179
7.5	Prohibition of discrimination	180
7.6	Affirmative action according to the Employment Equity Act	180
7.6.1	Five steps to employment equity	181
7.6.2	Employment equity plan	181
7.6.3	Reporting to the Director-General	181
7.6.4	The Department of Labour	182
7.6.5	Designated employers	182
7.6.6	Compliance costs and maximum fines for contravening the EEA	182
7.7	Arguments for affirmative action: The McWhirter Thesis	182
7.8	Arguments against affirmative action: The Zelnick Thesis	183
7.9	Weaknesses of affirmative action: The Sono Thesis	183
7.10	International affirmative action and employment equity experiences	183
7.10.1	The Malaysian experience	184
7.10.2	The USA experience	184
7.10.3	The Namibian experience	185
7.11	The views of Business South Africa on affirmative action	186
7.12	Conclusion	187

PART IV	**Staffing the organisation and maintaining people**	**193**
8	**Job analysis** — *adv + disadv of job analysis.*	**195**
8.1	Introduction	196
8.2	Job analysis – the basis of human resources activities	196
8.3	The components of a job	198
8.4	The process of job analysis	198
8.4.1	The systematic process of job analysis	198
8.4.2	The implications of job analysis for human resources practitioners	200
8.5	Job analysis methods	200
8.5.1	Job-orientated methods of data collection	200
8.5.2	Worker-orientated methods of data collection	202
8.6	Problems in job analysis	203
8.7	Job descriptions	204
8.7.1	The job description debate	204
8.7.2	Developing a job description	207
8.8	Job specifications	208
8.8.1	Developing the job specification	208
8.9	Job analysis and quality assurance	208
8.10	Conclusion	209

9	**Workforce planning and recruitment**	**217**
9.1	Introduction	218
9.2	Workforce planning as part of strategic organisational planning	219
9.2.1	The benefits of workforce planning	220
9.3	Factors that influence workforce planning	220
9.3.1	Internal factors influencing workforce planning	220
9.3.2	External factors that influence workforce planning	221
9.4	Steps in the workforce planning process	222
9.4.1	Forecasting labour demand	222
9.4.2	Estimating labour supply	223
9.4.3	Implementation of the workforce plan	223
9.4.4	Control and evaluation of the workforce planning system	223
9.5	The role of staff members in workforce planning	224
9.6	Recruitment policy	226
9.7	Factors that influence recruitment	226
9.7.1	External factors	226
9.7.2	Internal factors	226
9.8	Recruitment sources and methods	227
9.8.1	Internal and external recruitment sources	228
9.8.2	Internal recruitment methods	228
9.8.3	External recruitment methods	228
9.9	Current and future trends in recruitment	232
9.10	Legal considerations in recruitment	234
9.11	Workforce planning, recruitment and quality assurance	234
9.12	Conclusion	235
10	**Selection**	**240**
10.1	Introduction	241
10.2	Factors that influence the selection decision	242
10.2.1	Factors in the external environment	242
10.2.2	Factors in the internal environment	243
10.3	The selection process	243
10.3.1	Initial screening	244
10.3.2	Application blank	244
10.3.3	Interviews	246
10.3.4	Employment tests	249
10.3.5	Reference checks	251
10.3.6	Medical checks	251
10.3.7	Offer of employment and appointment	251
10.4	The selection decision	252
10.5	Selection and quality assurance	252
10.6	Conclusion	253
11	**Induction and staffing decisions**	**259**
11.1	Introduction	260
11.2	The objectives and benefits of induction	261
11.3	The responsibility for induction	262

11.4	An induction model	262
11.4.1	The stages of induction (process)	262
11.4.2	Fostering organisational culture	263
11.5	Planning, designing and implementing the induction programme	264
11.5.1	Planning the induction programme	264
11.5.2	Designing the induction programme	266
11.5.3	Implementing the induction programme	266
11.6	Follow-up and evaluation of the induction programme	270
11.7	The importance of good staffing decisions	271
11.8	Staffing strategies	272
11.8.1	Internal staffing strategy	272
11.8.2	External staffing strategy	272
11.8.3	Workforce pool strategy	272
11.9	Approaches to internal staffing	272
11.9.1	Promotions	272
11.9.2	Transfers	273
11.9.3	Demotions	273
11.9.4	Resignations	273
11.9.5	Retrenchments	274
11.9.6	Layoffs	274
11.9.7	Dismissals	274
11.9.8	Retirements	274
11.10	Induction, staffing decisions and quality assurance	274
11.11	Conclusion	275
12	**Compensation management** *learn with Basic conditions Act UIF*	**279**
12.1	Introduction	280
12.2	The objectives of a compensation system	280
12.3	The design of a compensation system	281
12.3.1	The elements of total compensation	281
12.3.2	The principles of value-chain compensation	282
12.3.3	A model for designing and implementing a new compensation system	283
12.4	Conventional job evaluation methods	283
12.4.1	Conduct a job analysis	284
12.4.2	Identify compensable factors	284
12.4.3	Develop a job hierarchy	285
12.4.4	Construct job grades	285
12.4.5	Carry out a compensation survey	285
12.4.6	Establish a final pay policy	287
12.5	Emerging pay systems	287
12.5.1	Pay for knowledge and skills	287
12.5.2	Pay for competencies	288
12.5.3	Performance-based pay	289
12.5.4	Incentive pay systems	290
12.6	Broadbanding	291
12.7	Employee benefits	292
12.7.1	Types of benefit	292

12.8	Benefits planning	295
12.9	Calculating the costs of employee benefits	296
12.10	Compensation systems and quality assurance	296
12.11	Conclusion	297
13	**Health and safety management**	**301**
13.1	Introduction	303
13.2	Job and personal stress	303
13.2.1	Environmental stress factors	303
13.2.2	Personal stress factors	304
13.2.3	Consequences of stress	304
13.3	Burnout	305
13.3.1	The victims of burnout	305
13.3.2	Workaholism	305
13.4	Mechanisms for stress reduction	306
13.4.1	Reducing job stress	307
13.4.2	Spirituality in the workplace	307
13.5	Holistic healthcare programmes	308
13.6	The causes of accidents	312
13.6.1	Unsafe conditions	312
13.6.2	Unsafe acts	312
13.7	Promoting safety	312
13.7.1	Reducing unsafe acts through selection and placement	313
13.7.2	Reducing unsafe acts through propaganda	313
13.7.3	Reducing unsafe acts through training	313
13.7.4	Reducing unsafe acts through positive reinforcement	313
13.7.5	Reducing unsafe acts through top-management commitment	313
13.8	An ergonomic approach to combating occupational injuries	314
13.8.1	Situational and individual variables in accident occurrence	314
13.8.2	Stress as a source of accident behaviour	314
13.9	Legal requirements in health and safety management	314
13.9.1	The Occupational Health and Safety Act No.85 of 1993	314
13.9.2	The Mine Health and Safety Act No.29 of 1996	316
13.9.3	Safety and first aid training	316
13.10	National Occupational Safety Association of South Africa (NOSA)	316
13.11	Health and safety issues and quality assurance	317
13.12	Conclusion	318
PART V	**Behavioural aspects of human resources management**	**323**
14	**Motivation**	**325**
14.1	Introduction	326
14.2	The meaning of motivation	326
14.3	Motivational theories	327
14.3.1	Maslow's needs hierarchy	327
14.3.2	Herzberg's two-factor motivation theory	331
14.3.3	The job characteristics model	332

14.3.4	The expectancy theories	334
14.4	The role of goal setting in motivation	338
14.4.1	Why do goals motivate?	338
14.4.2	Practical application of goal setting	339
14.5	Money as a motivator	340
14.6	Motivating contingent employees	341
14.7	A holistic approach to motivation	342
14.8	Motivation and quality assurance	342
14.9	Conclusion	343
15	**Leadership**	**348**
15.1	Introduction	349
15.2	What is leadership?	349
15.3	Leadership versus management	350
15.4	The qualities or traits approach to leadership	350
15.5	Participative versus autocratic leadership behaviours	351
15.6	Power and authority	351
15.7	McGregor's X and Y theory	352
15.8	Schein's theory of human assumptions	353
15.9	The leadership grid of Blake and Mouton	356
15.10	The leadership continuum of Tannenbaum and Schmidt	358
15.11	The situational leadership theory of Hersey and Blanchard	360
15.12	Revised model of situational leadership by Nicholls	362
15.13	Transformational leadership	364
15.14	Charismatic leadership	365
15.15	Leadership in a virtual workplace	365
15.16	Quality assurance in leadership	366
15.17	Conclusion	366
16	**Groups and teamwork**	**372**
16.1	Introduction	373
16.2	What is a group?	373
16.3	Comparing and contrasting formal and informal groups	374
16.4	Group development	376
16.4.1	The five-stage model of group development	376
16.4.2	The punctuated-equilibrium model	377
16.5	Effective group functioning	379
16.5.1	Group leadership	379
16.5.2	Roles	380
16.5.3	Group norms and conformity	381
16.5.4	Status	382
16.5.5	Group size and composition	383
16.5.6	Decision-making in groups	383
16.5.7	Communication	384
16.5.8	Conflict	385
16.6	Work teams	386
16.6.1	Characteristics of successful work teams	387

16.6.2	Types of work teams	387
16.7	Groups and teams and quality assurance	389
16.8	Conclusion	390

17	**Cultural diversity and change management** *nice SA ques.*	**394**
17.1	Introduction	395
17.2	Diversity: a definition	396
17.2.1	Role of culture	396
17.2.2	Cultural diversity *Factors, adv, /*	397
17.3	Change management	400
17.3.1	Forms of change	400
17.3.2	Scope of change	400
17.3.3	Resistance to change	401
17.3.4	Managing resistance to change	402
17.4	Principles (or the how to) of managing change	404
17.5	Strategic change management	405
17.6	Conclusion	406

PART VI	**Employee, group and organisational empowerment through human resources interventions**	**409**

18	**Job design and organisational design** *learn with job analysis.*	**411**
18.1	Introduction	412
18.2	Job range and job depth	413
18.3	The specialised approach to job design	413
18.3.1	Designing job range	414
18.3.2	Designing job depth	417
18.4	Team-based job designs	417
18.5	Strategy and organisational design	418
18.6	Approaches to organisational design	419
18.6.1	The bureaucratic organisation	419
18.6.2	The flat organisation	419
18.6.3	The boundaryless organisation	420
18.7	Emerging trends in organisational design	420
18.7.1	Shamrocks, doughnuts and vineyards	421
18.7.2	The virtual organisation	425
18.8	Reengineering the organisation *notes aswell*	427
18.9	Job and organisational design and quality assurance	428
18.10	Conclusion	428

19	**National level skills development issues** *notes only Skills devel. Act*	**434**
19.1	Introduction	435
19.2	Macroeconomic context	436
19.2.1	The new world economy	436
19.2.2	The changing working environment	436
19.2.3	Productivity and flexibility	437
19.2.4	Investment in training	437

19.2.5	Economic and social policies	438
19.2.6	State intervention	438
19.3	A national perspective	438
19.3.1	The broad political, social, and economic scene	438
19.3.2	Human resources development	439
19.3.3	Tertiary education	439
19.3.4	Science and engineering	440
19.3.5	School education	440
19.3.6	The labour market	441
19.3.7	Vocational education and training	442
19.4	Funding of training	443
19.4.1	Who is responsible?	443
19.4.2	Cost and benefit of training	443
19.4.3	Sources and application of training funds	445
19.4.4	Alternatives for generating training funds	446
19.4.5	Funding mechanisms in South Africa	447
19.5	Certification of training	450
19.5.1	A qualification structure	450
19.5.2	Certification in South Africa	450
19.6	Training legislation	454
19.6.1	Introduction	454
19.6.2	The background to the current training legislation	455
19.6.3	Skills Development Act	455
19.6.4	Skills Development Levies Act	457
19.6.5	South African Qualifications Authority Act	458
19.7	Possible training policy options for South Africa	458
19.8	Conclusion	462
20	**Training and development of employees and career management at organisational level** — adv & disadv.	**465**
20.1	Introduction	466
20.2	Clarification of concepts	467
20.2.1	The concept of education	467
20.2.2	The concept of training	467
20.2.3	The concept of development	468
20.3	Outcomes-based education and training	468
20.3.1	Distinguishing between objectives and outcomes	470
20.4	The place and role of the training function in an organisation	471
20.5	Strategic human resources development	472
20.6	A strategic training approach	472
20.7	Training and development policy	473
20.8	Training and development models	476
20.9	Application of various models to training and development	477
20.9.1	Identify training needs	478
20.9.2	Devise instructional objectives	479
20.9.3	Prepare test items based on the objectives and desired outcomes	480
20.9.4	Select or design instructional content	480

20.9.5	Choosing delivery methods	480
20.9.6	Offering instruction	480
20.9.7	Transferring learning back to the job	480
20.9.8	Evaluation	483
20.10	Training and development methods	484
20.10.1	Off-the-job training	484
20.10.2	On-the-job training	490
20.10.3	Learnership training (previously apprenticeship training)	492
20.10.4	Vestibule training	492
20.11	Issues inherently applicable to training and development in the South African context	493
20.11.1	Adult learning	493
20.11.2	Diversity training	493
20.11.3	Recognition of prior learning	494
20.11.4	The training of supervisors in South Africa	494
20.11.5	Benefits of training and development to an organisation	497
20.12	Career management	499
20.12.1	The importance of career management to employers and employees	501
20.12.2	Career stages and choices	502
20.12.3	Career planning	503
20.12.4	Career development	505
20.12.5	A practical approach to career management	508
20.12	Conclusion	509
21	**Performance management**	**514**
21.1	Introduction	515
21.2	Achievement of organisational effectiveness through performance management	516
21.3	The performance management process	516
21.3.1	Launching the process	518
21.3.2	Coaching and mentoring	519
21.3.3	Performance evaluation	520
21.4	Methods of performance evaluation	521
21.4.1	Who should evaluate performance?	521
21.4.2	Performance evaluation techniques	523
21.5	Rater errors	527
21.6	The feedback interview	528
21.6.1	The nature of the feedback interview	528
21.6.2	Scheduling the feedback interview	529
21.7	Legal considerations in performance management	529
21.8	Performance management and quality assurance	529
21.9	Conclusion	530
22	**Organisational renewal**	**536**
22.1	Introduction	538
22.2	What is an organisation?	540
22.3	Critical factors for renewal	541

22.4	Characteristics of organisational development and organisational renewal	542
22.5	Environmental factors and renewal	542
22.5.1	Globalisation	543
22.5.2	Technology	544
22.6	Failure of organisations to renew themselves	544
22.6.1	Conditions for successful change	545
22.6.2	What to avoid	545
22.6.3	What is organisational learning?	545
22.6.4	In summary: organisational renewal strategies	545
22.7	Goals and values	546
22.8	Conclusion	547

PART VII Strategic and international human resources management 551

23 Interdependency between organisational strategy and strategic human resources management 553

23.1	Introduction	555
23.2	Explanation of concepts	556
23.3	The relation between strategic planning and human resources management	557
23.4	Strategic business planning	557
23.4.1	Step 1: Determination of the organisational mission	558
23.4.2	Step 2: Assessment of the organisation and its environment	559
23.4.3	Step 3: Setting of specific objectives or direction	560
23.4.4	Step 4: Determination of strategies to accomplish objectives	560
23.5	Strategy and levels of planning	561
23.5.1	Grand strategy	561
23.5.2	Business strategy	561
23.5.3	Strategic business unit	561
23.5.4	Functional strategy	561
23.6	Strategic management	562
23.7	Strategic human resources management	563
23.7.1	Formulating human resources management strategy	563
23.7.2	The view of Cascio	564
23.7.3	The view of Van Dyk	565
23.8	Strategic human resources development	568
23.9	Conclusion	569

24 Human resources information systems 574

24.1	Introduction	575
24.2	Components of a human resources information system	576
24.3	Myths of human resources information systems	576
24.4	Application of human resources information systems to human resources management	577
24.5	The human resources information system as a diagnostic and decision-making tool	581
24.5.1	Areas of human resources related research	581

24.5.2	The application of human resources information	582
24.6	Human resources information systems and quality assurance	587
24.7	Conclusion	588

25	**International human resources management**	**591**
25.1	Introduction	592
25.2	Factors affecting human resources management in global markets	593
25.2.1	Culture	593
25.2.2	Education/human capital	594
25.2.3	Political/legal system	595
25.2.4	Economic system	595
25.3	The stages of international involvement	596
25.4	The mix of host-country and expatriate employees	597
25.4.1	Approaches to managing an international subsidiary	597
25.4.2	Using parent-company and host-country employees	598
25.5	Problems faced by the expatriate	599
25.6	Problems faced by the repatriate	600
25.6.1	Common repatriation problems	600
25.6.2	Guidelines for dealing with the repatriate	601
25.7	International human resources management policies	601
25.7.1	Recruitment and selection	602
25.7.2	Training	603
25.7.3	Remuneration/benefits issues	603
25.7.4	Managing the performance of expatriates	603
25.7.5	International labour relations	604
25.8	International human resources management in the twenty-first century	605
25.9	Conclusion	606

26	**The future of human resources management**	**610**
26.1	Introduction	611
26.2	The employee and the organisation of the future	612
26.2.1	Employee values	612
26.2.2	Drivers for change	612
26.2.3	Forces shaping the future	612
26.3	An evolving role for human resources management	613
26.4	Adding value in the knowledge-based economy	615
26.5	Strategic customer orientation	618
26.5.1	Developing strategic customer orientation	618
26.6	Quality assurance in the future role of human resources management	619
26.7	Conclusion	620

Index	624

part one

Managing human resources in organisational context

1

Definition and scope of human resources management

P S van Dyk

Learning outcomes

At the end of this chapter the learner should be able to demonstrate the following outcomes:
- Explain how human resources management can contribute to the new South Africa.
- Weigh up the concepts of human resources management and personnel management against each other.
- Give an overview of the history of the human resources function within the organisation.
- Define the sphere of responsibility of human resources management.
- Explain the study layout of this book.

Key words and concepts

- components of human resources management
- definition of human resources
- human resources
- human resources careers
- human resources effectiveness
- human resources profession
- human resources management
- human resources registration categories
- Institute for Personnel Management
- organisation
- personnel management
- world competitiveness

Illustrative case

Stevan Motsi was promoted to Grade 11 at the beginning of 1994. The country was facing its first democratic election and buzz words like empowerment, RDP, equality, equal opportunity, and affirmative action were discussed over the national news, at political gatherings, in the newspapers, and at home.

Stevan was unsure what he was going to study when he completed

Grade 12 and, amid all the political activity, he realised that if a new Government was elected, this would open doors to exciting careers that remained 'reserved' for only a certain section of the population. He often heard of the concept of human resources development and the importance that politicians and trade unionists placed on it as the keystone to national economic success and an increase in the quality of life for all South Africans.

One day he decided to discuss his future with his vocational guidance teacher. Because Stevan was a people orientated person, he was convinced that a career in human resources management would fit him like a glove. After a few more discussions with his teacher (who had given Stevan a lot of reading material on career opportunities in human resources) he finally discussed it with his father, who thought it was an excellent idea for his son to study human resources. He requested his son to identify the different careers in the human resources management field during the upcoming winter school holidays, and undertook to arrange a few interviews for his son with human resources managers in the local industrial area. Consider the career opportunities that exist for Stevan and pupils like him.

1.1 Introduction

It is rightly said that labour (human resources) is the only resource in an organisation that reacts when acted upon. This means that, with the exception of human resources, all resources of an organisation are static. Other resources derive their dynamic character from human resources.

In the South African context, the efficient and effective management and utilisation of human resources cannot be overemphasised. South Africa has a shortage of skilled and professional human resources, and its labour market is characterised by an imbalance between skilled and unskilled human resources. In 1999 South Africa was rated second last out of 59 countries in this regard (see Table 1.1). Coupled with this, South Africa also has a very low productivity ratio that inhibits natural growth in employment opportunities. As successful human resources management plays a key role in rectifying this situation, it should be given its rightful place in the management of an organisation.

In this introductory chapter, the following relevant aspects are examined:
- the contribution that scientifically based human resources management can make to the success of the South African national economy as a whole;
- micro-aspects of human resources management such as definition of concepts, a historical perspective of human resources management, human resources management as a profession, and the human resources management department; and
- the layout of this book.

1.2 The relation between human resources management at organisational level and economic prosperity

1.2.1 General

It is important for the authors to offer you, whether you are a student, human resources manager, other functional

> manager or interested party, a general overview of the important contribution that South Africa's human resources management departments can make in the creation of the new South Africa and the real experience of an African Renaissance.

In a competitive environment, the softer side of competitiveness reflects the shift towards a knowledge-based economy. In the industrialised world of today, only 15 per cent of the active population physically touches a product. The other 85 per cent are adding value through the creation, the management, and the transfer of information. The human dimension of competitiveness has, therefore, become a key success factor in modern economies of the world.

The World Competitiveness Organisation (WCO) aims at comparing countries all over the world with regard to their competitive position. Only countries that fulfil certain requirements are included in the survey. In 1992, South Africa was included for the first time, under the so-called Group II countries known as 'newly industrialised economies'. In the 1999 report, there are eight general competitiveness factors:
- openness;
- government;
- finance;
- infrastructure;
- technology;
- labour management; and
- institutions.

The report ranks each country in terms of the eight competitive factors in its particular group and also gives reasons why a country has a specific ranking. The term 'country competitiveness' refers to a country's ability to create and maintain long-term added value in comparison with its competitors.

As the subject of study is management in general, and specifically human resources management, South Africa's position in comparison with the other countries, thirty-third out of fifty-nine, is of particular importance (WCR 1999:197).

Management as a competitiveness factor is regarded as the extent to which enterprises are managed in an innovative, profitable, and responsible manner. Examples of criteria for evaluating the competitiveness of management are the following:
- management competence, which is reflected in the competitiveness of products with regard to price and quality;
- the long-term orientation of a country's management cadre, which increases the country's competitiveness over time;
- the efficiency of a country's economic activities, together with the ability to adapt to a change in a competitive environment, which are decisive management attributes for an organisation's competitiveness;
- effective entrepreneurship, which is decisive for economic activities during the establishment phase; and
- in more advanced organisations, corporate management skills required for the integration and differentiation of business activities.

Let us now focus our attention on South Africa's position, as presented in Table 1.1, in terms of assets and liabilities.

If we probe deeper into South Africa's National Competitiveness Balance Sheet, the evaluation of management and of human resources, shocking statistics are revealed (see Table 1.1). The contents of this report are an attempt at a more scientific yet pragmatic approach to the management of human resources in Southern African organisations.

Table 1.1 South Africa's competitiveness balance sheet

Assets			Liabilities		
Criteria		*Rank*	*Criteria*		*Rank*
1	**Openness**		**1**	**Openness**	
1.06	Exchange rate and exports	12	1.04	Export position	45
1.13	Index of misalignment of real exchange rate	13	1.03	Foreign exchange	46
			1.11	Average tariff rate	47
2	**Government**		1.05	Exchange rate alignment	47
2.19	Pension indicator	17	1.10	Cross-border ventures	50
3	**Finance**		1.12	Index of capital controls	52
3.11	Stock markets	9	1.07	Exchange rate volatility	54
3.10	Bond markets	11	1.08	Access to foreign capital markets	54
3.13	Venture capital	14	**2**	**Government**	
3.12	Hostile takeovers	14	2.11	Composition of government spending	41
3.01	Sophistication of financial markets	14	2.10	Tax evasion	42
3.06	Soundness of banks	16	2.03	Administrative regulations	43
3.07	Entry into banking industry	18	2.18	General government surplus	43
3.14	Financial regulation and supervision	19	2.08	Civil service independence	48
3.21	Share of domestic credit to private sector	19	2.05	Public sector competence	54
			2.20	Government savings	54
4	**Infrastructure**		**3**	**Finance**	
4.16	Cost of domestic air travel	1	3.20	Change in gross domestic savings	40
4.04	Railroads	17	3.09	Interest rates	41
4.06	Ports	18	3.19	Gross domestic savings	42
4.05	Air transport	19	3.22	Financial sector risk rating	48
5	**Technology**		3.17	Gross domestic investment	51
5.13	Email	14	**4**	**Infrastructure**	
5.17	Internet and information	14	4.12	Number of telephone lines	44
5.10	Technology licensing	15	4.02	Infrastructure investment	45
7	**Labour**		**5**	**Technology**	
7.10	Collective bargaining	7	5.19	Tertiary education enrollment	50
7.06	Unemployment insurance	15	5.03	Scientists and engineers	56
8	**Institutions**		5.02	Math and science education	59
8.11	Litigation against government	18	**6**	**Management**	
			6.10	Customer orientation	50
			7	**Labour**	
			7.17	Wage adjusted for productivity differences	46
			7.15	Unemployment rate	56
			7.08	Strikes	57
			7.03	Minimum wage regulations	58
			7.01	Average years of schooling	58
			7.04	Hiring and firing practices	59
			7.02	Work ethic	59
			7.05	Labour regulations	59
			7.09	Labour/employer relations	59
			8	**Institutions**	
			8.13	Government commitments	43
			8.04	Additional payments	46
			8.02	Government favouritism	46
			8.23	Public sector contracts	46
			8.01	Institutional stability	47
			8.15	Organized crime	58
			8.14	Effectiveness of police force	59

SOURCE: World Competitiveness Report: 1999:197.

> The ranking reflects South Africa's performance with regard to each criterion in comparison with the rest of the countries. It appears that the liabilities exceed the assets: this state of affairs is worrying and requires human resources management interventions on both a national and an organisational level. The challenge is in your hands!

1.2.2 How can human resources management contribute towards improving this state of affairs in South Africa?

South Africa was placed very low or last in all the criteria on the liability side of the labour balance sheet. Human resources management interventions on both a national and an organisational level can, if effectively managed, change the situation to a large extent. South Africa requires:
- a highly skilled worker corps;
- a motivated worker corps;
- a satisfied worker corps;
- a worker corps that is free from discrimination based on race, sex, religious conviction, etc.;
- a criminal-free workforce, especially at the blue collar level, and a corruption-free management cadre; and
- improved labour regulations and employer relations which are more business-friendly.

The question then arises how this may be brought about. Some thoughts in this regard are given here:
- The creation of a highly skilled worker corps is primarily a matter of national education. From secondary school level onwards, schooling should take into account the needs and demands of the labour market. In other words, it must be practically orientated. However, the chaos in education over the past years points to a gloomy future.
- Uniform standards must be set and standardised national curricula must be developed for all occupations.
- At an organisational level, management must attempt to develop in-house training programmes in such a way that an increase in productivity is a clearly recognisable outcome.
- Pay increases can only be linked to productivity growth.
- Programmes for uplifting the underprivileged must be developed by organisations as a social responsibility initiative. This refers to human resources educational interventions such as programmes to address:
  - Literacy
  - Basic mathematical skills
  - Computer literacy
  - Economic literacy
  - Health education programmes in respect of HIV/AIDS, hygiene, alcohol and drug abuse. (These aspects are discussed later.)
- Sound management practices and particularly sound human resources management practices can relieve many of the existing problems. A motivated and satisfied worker corps can only exist if sound human resources management practices are adhered to, especially with all the new legislation in this regard.
- The technology used by an organisation is also decisive for the improvement of the competitive position of both the organisation and the country as a whole. Management must decide what is best for uplifting the organisation and the national economy. The link between the technology used and productivity is obvious.
- Finally, but certainly most importantly in South Africa, organisations should

pay particular attention to the implementation of employment equity. This is discussed in detail in Chapter 7.

The words of Peter Wrighton (1993), ex-Chairman of the Premier Group, are still a good summary of the South African position in this regard:

> It is then the third category, 'people', which will pose the greatest challenge! This is of course the most important category as 'people' make all the other things happen. Let me remind you that we came bottom in this category. It is important that we analyse why this is so, because in the final analysis it is the quality of people which determines a country's competitiveness: skilled, motivated people are the factors upon which success depends, before machines and money.
>
> The key to South Africa's success lies in creating an environment where people strive to do their best, where opportunities are equally distributed, where initiative is encouraged – business can't run an economy, but we can create the conditions for success.

The role of the human resources manager discussed in the following sections of this chapter is thus of cardinal importance.

1.3 Human resources management: a historical perspective

1.3.1 General

In informed circles, it is often stated that problems with people as employees began just before the Industrial Revolution, when cottage industries became so large that owners were obliged to employ strangers in addition to family members. This was the beginning of the problem with which contemporary managers still have to contend today, i.e. how does an employer or manager motivate an employee or subordinate to perform in an optimal manner?

In this section, brief attention is given to:
- an historical perspective of the course of development of the applied behavioural science of human resources management; and
- the status quo of human resources management in South Africa.

The aim of this section is to orientate the newcomer to human resources management with regard to the origin, development, application, and career practices in South Africa of this applied behavioural science.

> South Africa's competitiveness factor 'labour' was rated overall last among 59 countries by the WCR in 1999.

1.3.2 The end of the previous century

At the end of the previous century, there was a large-scale influx of workers to the manufacturing industry. This forced 'management' to decide on some kind of management practice to accommodate the new generation of 'employees'.

In this case, the human resources management question (Bendix 1956:254) dealt with the following:
- the relative position of management as compared with employees; and
- the obligations of management towards employees.

The general management practice during this period was based on the principle of 'social Darwinism', i.e. survival of the fittest.

The application of this scientific principle to human resources management amounted to the following:

> The weak (the employees) were thought to have lost the struggle for dominance and so were expected to submit to the successful competitors (the managers).

This management philosophy, which was associated with strict religious convictions during the 1800s, is illustrated by the following utterance (Litwack 1962:67):

> The rights and interests of human labouring man will be protected and cared for, not by labour agitators, but by the Christian men to whom God in his infinite wisdom has given the control of the property interests of the country.

This management philosophy was strengthened by state and judicial practices which amounted to the business world of the time being responsible for its own welfare.

Despite the above, there was no consensus among the management cadre of organisations about the best management philosophy regarding human resources management practice. In fact, there were two dominant approaches:
- the commodity approach; and
- the so-called paternalistic or social welfare approach.

Litwack (1962:64) reports the following in this regard:

Under the commodity approach, employees represented a factor of production to be performed as cheaply as possible and discarded when no longer useful. The human factor was at best irrelevant in employment decisions. Some employers, for example, viewed employees' desire for education as harmful, spoiling these people for the realities of hard work.

The paternalistic or social welfare approach was based on strong moral grounds, closely linked to social Darwinism. Many organisations employed so-called 'welfare secretaries'. Paternalism, or fatherly protection of employees, took the form of company services, schools, shops, and company housing. It has been said that this paternalistic approach was used to manipulate employees through kindness. Another opinion is that a paternalistic policy was followed because employers thought that employees could not think for themselves, and were unable to plan for the future and to arrange their own affairs.

With regard to the welfare function, Rowntree (Farnham 1990:21) has the following to say:

> As representatives of the employees it is the duty of the social helpers to be constantly in touch with them, to gain their confidence, to voice any grievances they may have either individually or collectively, to give effect to any reasonable desire they may show for recreative clubs, educational classes, etc. and to give advice in matters concerning them personally.

During the period 1910 to 1930 (Holley and Jennings 1987:27), two movements arose which began to bring employers to the realisation that employees are people with unique capabilities. The two movements can be described as:

- the psychological reform approach; and
- the effectiveness approach.

The psychological reform approach amounts to the fact that, in as far as is possible, every person wants to be a normal human being, but is at the same time also an employee. It was realised that people have certain needs with regard to family, work and justice, and that the human being is creative. Successful managers realised that workers are complicated beings as a result of their intelligence and are, thus, susceptible to stress in the work environment.

The effectiveness approach is the second approach of this era, which motivated management to realise that the employee is a unique being. One distinctive development that arose from this movement is Taylor's well-known scientific management approach. Taylor stated that, if an employee is not performing well, this was not the employee's fault but that of management. In 1937, Taylor published his famous book, *The Principles of Scientific Management*.

The publicity obtained from the abovementioned two approaches stimulated research with regard to personnel affairs. Among other things, research was conducted into subjects such as personnel services, recruitment and selection, training, salaries, and wages. Two professional personnel journals were also published in this era: *Personnel* and *Journal of Personnel Research*. Many of the research articles that appeared in these journals dealt with the association between employee characteristics and work performance. Research dealt with aspects such as hair colour, weight and height profiles, sex, marital status, and ethnic and religious background. Personnel departments were established in about 1912.

The outbreak of the First World War emphasised the importance of the personnel function as an essential organisational activity. The demand for products increased tremendously. Many employees were drafted into the armed forces, which led to the remaining employees getting far more attention from the management cadre. People as employees became so important for the company that legislation was introduced in the USA to force companies to establish personnel departments to ensure efficient functioning in the production of weaponry and implements of war.

Furthermore, the American government established a committee called 'Committee on Classification of Personnel' to determine soldiers' capabilities and to allocate them in accordance with the job requirements of the various military tasks. The personnel techniques that arose from this exercise were later adapted for industry. These wartime efforts also changed the dominant management philosophy with regard to the personnel function.

During the build-up to the Second World War, personnel management took another leap forward with its establishment as a full-fledged organisational function.

Niven (in Farnham 1990:23) defines personnel management in this era as follows:

Personnel management is that part of the management function which is primarily concerned with the human relationships within an organisation. Its objective is the maintenance of these relationships on a basis which, by consideration of the well-being of the individual, enables all those engaged in the undertaking to make their maximum personal contribution to the effective working of that undertaking.

Niven uses the word 'undertaking' when referring to a company or organisation, and his reference to 'effective working' is derived from the building blocks of organisational success.

Cascio (1995) is of the opinion that human resources management developed from nine related sources or fields. From a study of the evolution of human resources management it is clear that it originated largely in the USA. The box below, as adapted by the present author, supports this view.

> **The evolution of human resources management**
> - Rapid technological progress facilitated the specialisation of labour associated with the Industrial Revolution;
> - The emergence of free collective bargaining, with restrictions on both trade unions and employers;
> - The scientific management approach;
> - Early industrial psychology;
> - The government's personnel practices which emerged from the establishment of the Public Service Commission;
> - The rise of personnel specialists and the grouping of such specialists in personnel departments;
> - The human relations movement;
> - The behavioural sciences;
> - The social legislation and court rulings in the 1960s and 1970s in the USA.
>
> SOURCE: Adapted from Cascio (1995:43–45).

1.3.3 The growth phase in human resources management

Cascio (1995) identifies four phases in recent developments in the field of human resources management. The first phase originated in the mid-1960s, and Cascio calls this the 'file maintenance phase'. He puts it as follows (1995:39):

> 'Personnel' was the responsibility of a special department. Its responsibilities included screening applicants, conducting orientation for new employees, collecting and storing personnel data on each employee (date of birth, years of company service, education), planning the company picnic, and circulating memos 'whose impertinence was exceeded only by their irrelevance'.

This, therefore, merely involved keeping up-to-date personnel records and other administrative functions.

Cascio calls the second phase the 'government responsibility phase'. In the light of the many new pieces of legislation regarding labour matters, basic conditions of service etc., South Africa can now be placed in this phase to a large extent. The implications (as in South Africa at present) are that management has begun to take note of the fact that human resources management policy and practices can seriously harm organisations.

The third phase took shape in the 1970s. Cascio calls it 'the organisational responsibility phase'. This phase originated in poor economic and financial business circumstances, which made management realise that they needed to account for company expenditure in all functional fields of the organisation to a greater degree. Cascio (1995:40) puts it as follows:

> Although methods of assessing the costs and benefits of human resource programs are available, they are not widely known. In addition, social trends (more women in the workforce, as well

as more minorities, immigrants, older workers and poorly educated workers) accelerated demands for improving the quality of work life, for managing cultural and ethnic diversity, and for continual training and retraining.

The fourth phase manifested itself in the 1990s as the 'strategic partnership phase'. The origins of this phase lie in ever-increasing competition in the business world and the continual effort to maintain a competitive edge. Cascio (1995:40) is of the opinion that today:

> Top management look to the human resources department, as it does to line managers, to control costs, to enhance competitiveness, and to add value to the firm in everything it does.

This phase is linked to the integration of strategic human resources management and organisational strategy. This is discussed in Chapter 23.

1.3.4 Summary

The above gives a brief historical overview of the course of development of human resources management. Today the human resources management function is certainly one of the most essential functions for South African organisations in placing South Africa on the road to success.

1.4 Human resources management as a profession

1.4.1 The Institute of People Management of Southern Africa

The information in this section is reproduced with the permission of IPM (SA).

The IPM is an organisation dedicated to the human resources profession and is committed to the effective management and development of human potential, in accordance with its values statement. It provides effective leadership, appropriate knowledge and technology and the opportunity to network. Effectiveness is measured by: quality of output, growth of and participation by its membership and its contribution to the nation. Hence, IPM aims to influence and assist in the development and utilisation of human resources in South Africa in the interests of the South African community as a whole, including the promotion and development of the highest standards of competence and ethical conduct amongst the members of the Institute.

To achieve the above, the IPM aims to:
- promote the professional development of members and other interested persons;
- actively cooperate and liaise with organisations on relevant human resources issues and with professional human resources management locally and internationally;
- play a leading role in the field of promoting effective affirmative action strategies;
- supply specialised, formal, and professional training to members, and to see that provision is made for professional education;
- provide and disseminate specific, applicable, and current information on developments and trends in the field of human resources management and in the Institute;
- assist the human resources practitioner and profession in playing a strategic role in the areas of social investment, quality of work life, unemployment, etc.; and
- provide an appropriate infrastructure that includes a sound organisational structure and a healthy financial

resource base to implement and manage the above goals.

1.4.2 Membership categories

The membership of the IPM can be subdivided into two main categories: members with voting rights and members without voting rights.
- Members with voting rights include the following sub-categories:
  - honorary fellows, numbering 51;
  - fellows, numbering 45;
  - members, numbering 7 210; and
  - corporate members, numbering 1 283.
- Members without voting rights are the following:
  - students;
  - affiliates; and
  - group affiliates.

Allocation to a specific category or sub-category is determined by qualifications and experience.

1.4.3 The South African Board for Personnel Practice

The South African Board for Personnel Practice was established on 15 October 1982, but restructured in 1993. The Board serves as an instrument of the IPM to place professional practitioners of human resources management in organisations on a professional footing and to expand their sphere of influence in organisations.

The mission of the Board appears in the accompanying box:

Mission

To establish, conduct and maintain a high standard of professionalism and ethical behaviour in personnel practice.

The philosophy that underlies the reason for the existence of the Board is to enable those involved in personnel practice to make a meaningful contribution to:
- the organisation, its management and utilisation of human resources;
- the individual, in the fulfilment of his or her potential; and
- the broader society, in its striving for a better quality of life.

The Board follows this declared strategy:

To promote, guide and influence the development of the personnel profession; to set standards of competence for the education, training and conduct of those who practise the profession; to give the parties involved advice about the development and acquisition of such skills; and to evaluate their attainment.

The Board's objectives are to:
- promote the profession of personnel practice in South Africa;
- promote the standard of education and training of persons in personnel practice and to give recognition to the education and training that is a prerequisite for registration in terms of the charter;
- promote liaison in the fields of education and training;
- advise the Minister of Labour, or any other person, on any matters within the framework of the charter;
- communicate to the Minister of Labour information with regard to matters of public interest that has been acquired by the Board in the execution of its functions in terms of the charter; and
- exercise control over all matters regarding the standard of the professional conduct of persons in personnel practice, who are voluntarily

registered in terms of the Board's charter.

Every profession is characterised by a special behavioural code for its members. Personnel managers are no exception; the behavioural code of the Board for Personnel Practice is as follows.

A registered person shall:
- as far as responsibility to his or her employer, employee, client and profession is concerned, place public interest first, at the service of society;
- behave in such a way that the dignity, esteem and good name of the profession is honoured;
- carry out his or her duty towards the employer, employee or client to the best of his or her abilities;
- not accept work for which he or she is inadequately trained or has insufficient experience;
- not recruit or attract professional employment in an improper manner;
- not advertise professional services in a self-praising manner or in any other way that undermines the dignity of the profession;
- not compete for work in an unethical manner;
- neither maliciously nor recklessly, whether directly or indirectly, damage the good name, prospects or interests of any other person or organisation;
- not make public any information regarding any person or organisation which should not be made public and which is encountered when practising the profession (in a court of law, professional secrecy will only be violated under protest in accordance with a directive from the presiding officer of the court); and
- at all times and under all circumstances that affect personnel practice, act in accordance with the regulations as prescribed by the Board.

Registration categories

In terms of the Board's charter, a person is registered on one of the following levels:
- personnel practitioner (general or specialist);
- associate personnel practitioner (general or specialist);
- candidate personnel practitioner; or
- candidate associate personnel practitioner.

The registration requirements for the abovementioned levels are as follows:
- *Personnel practitioner.* A four-year qualification, accredited by the Board, in a discipline or disciplines relevant to the field of personnel practice is required, plus two years practical training in and experience of personnel work as a registered candidate under supervision of an approved mentor who will endorse the final application for registration (a candidateship); or another combination of appropriate qualifications and relevant practical training that is regarded as being of an equal standard by the Board, and that is acceptable to the Board. Under certain circumstances, the Board may give permission for a Board examination to be taken.
- *Associate personnel practitioner.* A three-year qualification after Grade 12, accredited by the Board, in a discipline or disciplines relevant to the field of personnel practice is required, plus two years practical training in and experience of personnel work as a registered candidate under supervision of an approved mentor who will endorse the final application for registration (a candidateship); or another combination of appropriate qualifications and relevant practical training that is acceptable to the Board.
- *Candidate personnel practitioner or candidate associate personnel practitioner.*

A candidateship programme of two years duration, the aim of which is to promote and structure the development of prospective professional personnel experts. The practical experience thus acquired by the individual is evaluated by a mentor and by the Board in the light of registration requirements set by the Board.

The following human resources functions are applicable to registration in any of the above categories:
- *Human resources provision.* This includes human resources planning, recruitment, selection, placement, transfers, promotions, and dismissals.
- *Training and development.* This includes induction, training, management development, and career planning.
- *Human resources utilisation.* This includes performance appraisal, productivity, and motivation.
- *Industrial welfare.* This includes safety, health, welfare services, housing, recreation, and advice.
- *Organisational development.* This includes organisational structure, job design, and organisational personnel planning.
- *Industrial relations.* This includes communication, negotiation, consultation, agreements, grievances, and disciplinary procedures.
- *Remuneration.* This includes job analysis, job evaluation, salary and wage structuring, fringe benefit schemes, and incentive systems.
- *Administration.* This includes personnel records, statistics about personnel, and information processing.
- *Research.* This includes the analysis of information, systems development, investigations, surveys, and applied personnel research.
- *Management.* This includes planning, organising, directing and controlling the personnel function, and coordination with other functions.

More information can be obtained at the address in the accompanying box.

> The Registrar
> South African Board for
> Personnel Practice
> P.O. Box 31390
> Braamfontein 2017
> Telephone (011) 482-4970

1.5 Careers in human resources management

There are many opportunities for people wishing to pursue a career in human resources management. In fact, any organisation, no matter how small or large, has a human resources component. Once an organisation becomes medium-sized, it certainly needs the services of somebody who has studied and is able to practice various facets of human resources management. The general ratio is one human resources specialist to every 200 employees in an organisation. Human resources management careers are more numerous in an organisation which is specialised and has various sub-departments or branches.

Depending on the nature and size of an organisation and the extent to which it specialises or outsources its human resources functions, various opportunities are available. Career opportunities are, for example: employment or staffing, compensation administration, training and development, and employment relations (Swanepoel et al. 2000:22–23). Indeed, the various chapters in this book broadly represent areas in which people can specialise as human resources practitioners.

It must also be noted that human resources generalists are in high demand where a range of aspects at organisational level must be addressed (recruitment, selection, induction, and employment equity, for example). This is particularly relevant where a single human resources officer must deal with all the aforementioned issues in an organisation which may employ between forty and a hundred employees.

Finally, it must be borne in mind that a high demand exists for human resources personnel who are qualified in both general human resources practice and employment relations, since these two fields are interdependent and currently of great importance in attempting to manage an organisation effectively and harmoniously as far as the productive employment of labour is concerned. This is due to the fact that trade unionism and employment law extensively protect employee rights in the employment situation, and employers must therefore ensure that they manage their labour within these constraints in order to be effective and survive.

1.6 Human resources management defined

The exact meanings of terms used in the field of human resources, for example, personnel management, the personnel function, human resources management, and personnel administration, are not always clear. To avoid confusion and uncertainty about the exact meanings of important terms in the field of human resources, they are explained in more detail in this part of the chapter.

1.6.1 Clarification of concepts

Holley and Jennings (1987:4) provide a general definition of the concept of human resources management in the following words:

> Human resources management refers to activities, policies, beliefs and the general function that relates to employees or the personnel department.

They describe the elements contained in the above-mentioned definition as follows:
- *Human resources activities.* Examples are activities carried out by the human resources department such as the training of a group of employees, or a recruitment campaign.
- *Human resources policy.* These are formalised official guidelines with regard to the manner in which personnel matters should be carried out.
- *Human resources beliefs.* These may be described as strong convictions on the part of executive personnel with regard to people as employees. These beliefs or convictions are one of the most important elements of organisational culture.
- *Human resources management function.* A function is a group of unique activities such as carrying out a job analysis, drawing up a job description and carrying out a salary and wage survey to create a remuneration structure for an organisation. The human resources management function indicates all human resources management activities within an organisation.
- *Human resources department.* This is the physical place where employees charged with carrying out human resources management activities are found.
- *Human resources official.* Employees, irrespective of their appointments, who deal with the execution of human resources activities, such as a human resources manager, training official or recruitment agent.

The British Institute for Personnel Management defines the concept of 'personnel management' as follows:

> Personnel management is that part of management concerned with people at work and with their relationships within an enterprise. Its aim is to bring together and develop into an effective organisation the men and women who make up an enterprise and, having regard for the well-being of the individual and of working groups, to enable them to make their best contribution to its success. (Graham and Bennett 1993:157)

Personnel management or human resources management?

In many organisations titles like personnel department, personnel director, and personnel manager are common. Traditional books about personnel management concentrate on how programmes for selection, training, compensation, and career planning are designed by members of the personnel department, and their audience is students who plan to specialise in personnel management. We have chosen to use the term 'human resources management' for two reasons.

First, we view it as a process much broader than designing personnel programmes; it also involves strategic planning and implementation.

Second, the expanded definition of human resources management includes responsibilities that can only be assumed by line managers.

Therefore, our audience is not only students who wish to become human resources professionals, but also business students who plan to become line managers.

According to the aforementioned institute, personnel management is concerned with the development and application of the following policies:

- human resources planning, recruitment, selection, placement and termination of service;
- education, training and career development;
- conditions of service and remuneration standards;
- formal and informal communication and consultation by the representatives of employers and employees at all levels of the organisation;
- negotiations and the application of agreements regarding wages and working conditions; and
- procedures for the prevention and avoidance of disputes.

Finally, personnel management is concerned with the human and social implications of internal changes in the activities of organisations, as well as with the social and economic implications of change within the community of the organisation.

The most important differentiation that must be made is between the terms personnel management and human resources management.

To obtain clarity on this difference, Hall and Goodale (1986:8) ask the question given in the accompanying box.

From an analysis of various writings in this regard it appears that the differences between the concepts personnel management and human resources management are as follows (Cascio 1995:34):

- Personnel management is practical, useful, and instrumental, and is generally concerned with the administration and implementation of human resources management policy. Human resources management, on the other hand, is concerned with strategic aspects and

involves the total development of human resources within the organisation.
- Human resources management is concerned with the broader implications of the management of change and not only with the effects of change on work in practice. Human resources management aspects are an important input for organisational development.
- Personnel management is both reactive and diagnostic in nature. Thus, for example, it reacts to changes in labour legislation, labour market conditions, trade union actions, and environmental influences. Human resources management, on the other hand, is prescriptive in nature and concerned with strategies, the introduction of new activities, and the development of new ideas.
- Human resources management determines the general policy for employment relations within the organisation. Its task is thus to develop a culture within an organisation that promotes employee relations and cooperation. Personnel management, on the other hand, is criticised because it is primarily concerned with the enforcement of company rules and regulations among employees rather than with bringing about loyalty and commitment to company goals.
- Personnel management has short-term perspectives, while human resources management has long-term perspectives and attempts to integrate all human aspects of the organisation into a coherent whole, thus encouraging individual employees to have an attitude of striving for high performance.

Human resources management as an applied management science is closely related to a sister science, industrial psychology.

From an industrial psychology perspective, human resources management may be regarded as the implementation of policies, customs, and procedures with regard to the human being as an employee on the basis of psychological principles.

Graham and Bennett (1993:158) put it as follows:

> Its purpose is not to make effective use of people at work and develop satisfactory relationships among them but to motivate them by providing them with jobs that are satisfying in themselves (if it is practically possible) and by offering them financial and other rewards.

To emphasise the psychological basis of human resources management, it is appropriate to redefine it as a management strategy related to one of the means of production of the organisation, i.e. its labour. From this perspective, human resources management consists of the following functions:
- human resources utilisation, which includes recruitment, selection, transfers, promotion, appraisal, training, and development;
- motivation of the human resources factor, which includes work design, remuneration, fringe benefits, counselling, participation, and equal rights; and
- protection of the human resources factor, which includes working conditions, welfare services, safety, and the formalisation of policy regarding the assurance of employee interests after retirement.

A clear distinction must also be made between human resources management and the management of people.
- Every functional manager (each departmental head, foreman, and supervisor) is responsible for the management of the staff. This means that every manager must provide guidelines for his or her

immediate subordinates. He or she must set objectives with and for them, delegate responsibility to them, measure their performance and provide them with feedback, and must encourage underachievers to improve – in short, must motivate immediate subordinates to do their best, and provide opportunities for them to make optimal use of their skills. This responsibility forms part of human resources utilisation.

- On the other hand, human resources management, like marketing and purchasing, is a specialised function that provides back-up services for other managers in the organisation to enable them also to make optimal use of their subordinates.

1.6.2 Approach to defining human resources management

The approach followed in this book is expressed in the definition of Hall and Goodale (1986:6):

Human resources management ... the process through which an optimal fit is achieved among the employee, job, organization, and environment so that employees reach their desired level of satisfaction and performance and the organization meets its goals.

Since this definition is a far more pragmatic approach than the traditional references that have been quoted above, for the purposes of this book it will be further elaborated upon. The discussion that follows refers to Figure 1.1.

It is clear from Figure 1.1 that there are four important components implied in the definition given by Hall and Goodale, namely:

- the external environment;
- the organisation;
- the work itself; and
- the individual or employee.

Nowadays, the focus of human resources management lies in the integration of the

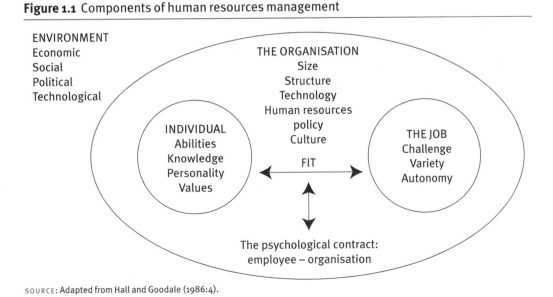

Figure 1.1 Components of human resources management

SOURCE: Adapted from Hall and Goodale (1986:4).

human resources management strategy into the global strategy of the organisation. This approach has been needed for a long time, since human resources are the only dynamic production factor an organisation has.

The external environment

Every organisation exists inside an external environment that consists of four primary sub-environments, namely:
- the economic environment;
- the social environment;
- the political environment; and
- the technological environment.

The economic environment must surely be the most important from a free market (capitalistic) point of view. In the general literature, the economic environment is taken to mean the external influences that have an effect on an organisation, such as:
- the availability of capital;
- the current interest rates;
- the rate of inflation;
- the strength (or weakness) of the competitors of the organisation; and
- the level of employment (whether it is above or below average).

The influence of the social environment of an organisation has been underestimated to a large extent in the past. Nowadays, it features much more prominently as far as the top management of organisations is concerned.

The social environment is shaped by the society in which the organisation features. Potential customers and employees of the organisation, with their attitudes and values concerning work, products, and business, their educational and skill levels, and their expectations, are integral parts of the social environment. To prosper, the organisation must achieve a fine balance between meeting the needs of the employees and customers, and meeting its own organisational goals.

The political environment is particularly important in the present South African context. Every organisation is run according to laws and regulations, whether they originate at central, provincial, or local levels. These laws and regulations influence any organisation from its external environment, no matter what the nature of the business is.

> In South Africa, labour legislation, affirmative action, as well as laws and regulations with regard to training and development, are currently of particular importance to the management of local organisations.

Now, more than ever before, the technological environment has an influence on management philosophy, not only in South Africa, but in the whole African context, since there is a positive correlation between the technology in use and the productivity of a community.

Technology essentially means the way in which an organisation changes the inputs (raw materials in whatever form is

> South African organisations (i.e. their management cadre) are, however, restricted in their ability to make optimal use of the country's raw materials because of the limited skills available on the South African labour market.

> Just consider the influence of the 'Green Movement' on pollution, and the subsequent reaction of top management.

available) into outputs (products or services) by means of an ongoing process.

The organisation

Before going on to discuss the role that the organisation plays in this regard, cognisance must first be taken of what constitutes an organisation. Schein (1980:15) says that:

> An organization is the planned co-ordination of the activities of a number of people for the achievement of some common explicit purpose or goal, through division of labor and function, and through a hierarchy of authority and responsibility.

According to Hall and Goodale (1986:5), an organisation has a number of characteristics. One obvious characteristic is size; some people have strong preferences about the size of the organisation they want to join. Organisations also differ in their structure. Some are hierarchical while others are structured according to certain functional preferences. Another key characteristic of organisations is the technology, which governs how work is done; this determines the profiles that employees must match. The organisation's human resources policies show its orientation towards people and play a major part in attracting and satisfying employees. Finally, the culture of the organisation is of particular importance. This indicates the way in which things are done in an organisation and is also known as the personality of the organisation. For the success of an organisation it is particularly important that the individual employee's personality and the 'personality' of the organisation are in tune with each other. A mismatch can hamper the attainment of both personal and organisational goals.

The work (job) itself

An individual employee joins an organisation by virtue of his or her potential for reaching personal goals in that organisation by supplying work and work potential. The basic motivation of a person (employee) in this context is that he or she sees the opportunity of satisfying his or her intrinsic and extrinsic needs (see Chapter 14).

Hall and Goodale (1986:6) comment in this regard that:

> Among the key characteristics of jobs that directly affect employee performance and satisfaction are the degrees of challenge, variety, and autonomy they offer to employees. Challenge is the level of difficulty of a job's tasks and activities. Variety refers to the number of different tasks and activities included in the job, and autonomy is the extent to which an employee works independently on a job.

The individual employee

The last, but undeniably the most important component in Hall's and Goodale's conceptualisation (Figure 1.1) is the individual in an organisation.

> Note that the term 'employee' is used not only to mean the employee at a low level – even though people in the management of an organisation and who are responsible for its functioning normally dissociate themselves from this designation.

The approach of Hall and Goodale (1986) now falls into line with that of the authors. As you get further into the book, the similarity will become more obvious.

Finally, each individual brings a unique combination of attributes to an employer. Some personal characteristics that cause people to succeed or fail on a job are their abilities, knowledge, personality, values and expectations. Abilities and knowledge determine an employee's potential to perform specific jobs successfully. Personality, values, and expectations are related to an individual's preference for different kinds of jobs and organisations and, therefore, determine the choice of a specific job or employer.

1.7 Challenges facing human resources management in South Africa

It can rightly be stated that human resources management in Southern Africa faces a long-term dilemma due to the types of organisation within the economic infrastructure, and the nature of the labour force.

1.7.1 Historical background

Traditionally, personnel management, or personnel administration, was conducted according to the functional approach to management. The personnel function was, and still is, practised on the basis of sound scientific research. Recruitment was carried out along traditional lines, and the selection decision was easy (the right person for the right job according to the fixed pay level). Compensation, rewards, and promotion were applied in a rigid manner. There was little room for any negotiations or manoeuvring outside the policy guidelines of the industry or organisation. The type of organisation was bureaucratic in nature with a tall organisational structure and many levels of command and control. A total top-down approach was the order of the day. Most employees were unskilled or semi-skilled, and stuck to the rules of the game as they were afraid to 'rock the boat'.

The evolution of management theory and practice brought the importance of human resources management to the fore. Management, especially in the USA and Europe, realised that organisations could become more profitable if some basic changes were introduced to their operating processes. The efficiency and effectiveness ideologies were born from this realisation, and many experiments were conducted in this regard. Management research was founded in this era and so many advances were made, that it would be hard to match today. One of these advances was the discovery that the human being is capable of achieving much more if managed properly.

Subsequently, a systems or efficiency approach to management appeared. This required that the individual employees, groups, departments, etc. within an organisation be considered as interrelated, with no part more important than another. It was also realised, as far as human resources are concerned, that in addition to the work environment, there are other environments in which employees exist and operate (the social, economic, or labour environments, for example) and that these environments can exert at least as much influence on an individual, group, or organisation's performance as the management environment which prescribes employees' work behaviour. The systems, efficiency, and effectiveness perspectives lead to another major breakthrough in this regard – the need for continuous change. Bureaucratic trimming started (bureaucracy-bashing, down-sizing, right-sizing, etc.) and flatter organisational structures with fewer command and control levels were instituted.

The nature of the workforce changed over time from unskilled, semi-skilled, and technically skilled, to skilled and professional employees. This does not imply that the earlier categories of labour vanished; it implies, rather, that 'newer organisations' accommodating the latter labour groups more intensively came into existence, while those organisations representing the former still exist.

In the past decade or two, the emphasis shifted to empowering organisations to become more competitive within industries, between industries, and in a global sense. With the tremendous advantages of technology and the realisation that competitiveness could only be achieved once an organisation was at least on a par with its competitors in terms of the quality of its products or service, the focus has shifted to empowering management, technical, and support personnel in organisations to continually deliver quality-assured outcomes. From a human resources management perspective, this required the empowerment of all involved in the different processes in an organisation to behave proactively in ensuring quality on a continuous basis. This change in focus to competitiveness, quality assurance, and empowerment as the bottom line of an organisation's operations has resulted in more attention being given to processes within a system. It is the bottom-line operations of an organisation which provide the reason for its existence. Most other functions, including human resources management, can be outsourced to organisations specialising in those fields of service. Thus, the ongoing movement towards down-sizing, re-design, etc., is alive and well, and poses the challenges facing human resources management in Southern Africa.

1.7.2 Challenges for human resources management

The existence of the human resources management function, as it is manifested today, is in jeopardy. With organisations specialising in sub-disciplines or specific applications of human resources management (such as recruitment and placement companies, labour relations firms, compensation management companies) together with the corporate trend of outsourcing all unnecessary overheads, the future of the traditional human resources management function within organisations looks bleak.

The human resources functional mix

The question or challenge here is how to apply human resources management in organisations. The national emphasis is on job creation, but because this goal's achievement is remote, there is an immense focus on job retention. This is in direct opposition to the trend in competitive, streamlined companies of delivering highly profitable quality products and services in local, national, and global markets. The huge effort made by government and organised labour with regard to employment equity, affirmative action, etc., is also the inverse of line of what global competitiveness requires. The changing nature of the workforce requires different approaches in recruitment, selection, placement, and compensation. Human resources management must find its niche in this dense forest of uncertainties if the function is to survive.

Job creation

Job creation is one of the biggest challenges facing the national economy. Organised business is of the opinion that the focus must be on job creation, whilst organised labour believes the focus should be on the protection of labour rights and existing jobs. Confrontation within the tripartite system is thus foreseeable. The question is how in-house human resources management deals with this ongoing, long-term dilemma.

Compensation management

Compensation management is also a huge challenge which confronts human resources management. The traditional practice worldwide is that wage, salary, and benefit increases must be based on productivity increases. Whilst organised business supports this view, irrespective of the nature of the labour force, organised labour is still pressing for the narrowing of the wage gap for previously disadvantaged groups, without taking productivity, profitability, or the demands of global competitiveness into consideration. Whether this divide in philosophy will be bridged in this decade remains to be seen.

Health and safety

Health and safety issues will become a greater challenge for human resources management. The degeneration of the national health service over the past years has led to a tremendous increase in medical assurance for the employees of organisations. Both organisations and employees suffer financially under the present conditions. With South Africa being number one in the world with regard to HIV/AIDS victims, and with the legislative requirements on employee organisations in this respect, it is difficult to predict what influence this will have on the future competitiveness of South African organisations.

Alternative work arrangements

The application of human resources management to 'intellectual companies', the virtual office, and alternative work arrangements seems, from the Southern African perspective, quite a few years away. However, the following examples illustrate the potential challenges:
- today less than 15 per cent of the American work force 'touches' the products or services their companies produce;
- millions of square metres of office blocks are presently converted into living areas; and
- thousands of people who are employed in high-tech companies, for example, do not know how to get to work.

The question arises: In the year 2020, will the human resources management function still exist in the way it is currently manifested in South African organisations?

1.8 The focus and structure of this book

1.8.1 General

The focus in this book is on human resources management from two viewpoints, namely:
- A macro-approach, which means that the management of labour as a resource is dealt with in broad terms from the point of view of national human resources management in Southern Africa, with special reference to the new South Africa's role in the Southern African Development Community (SADC).
- A micro-approach, where the focus primarily falls on the individual employee and the principles and techniques used by human resources management to improve the performance of individuals in organisations.

Other than in this chapter, the micro-viewpoint is discussed first.

1.8.2 A human resources management model of the individual as an employee

A step-by-step human resources management model of the individual as an employee is set out in Chapter 2. This is used to highlight those human resources management processes and principles that affect the individual as an employee, in an attempt to provide a visual representation of the variables that have a positive or negative effect on individual performance. From a quality assurance perspective, individual performance is regarded as the cornerstone of the success of an organisation; this is the focal point of this book.

The model is intended to explain the functioning of individual employees on the basis of the following theoretical principles.

- Each individual has a unique personality that is the result of environmental influences such as home, family, church, school, and field of experience.
- Individuals have certain expectations in life, particularly with regard to their careers.
- In most cases, individuals can only meet these expectations by joining organisations where they receive an income and are afforded the opportunity to meet career expectations or to satisfy needs.
- Individuals make inputs (energy, expertise, knowledge) into organisations, for which they receive certain outputs.
- Individuals translate their expectations into personal goals before they join the organisation, or during the negotiation process.
- Organisations have certain goals with which the individual has to identify and which must be pursued.
- The individual and the organisation have an equal responsibility towards each other for the achievement of both sets of goals (the psychological contract).
- At work the individual functions in three environments, namely the job content, the job context, and the external environment.
- The job content environment entails the work a person does or the job he holds. It relates to Maslow's higher-order needs and Herzberg's motivators. Theoretically, this environment has the following dimensions, among others: the degree of challenge in the work, the nature of the work, utilisation of training, knowledge and skills, goals and significance of the job, job satisfaction, feedback on the execution of the task (recognition), task standards and guidelines, and so on. These are dealt with in human resources management processes such as human resources planning, recruitment, selection, training, and development.
- The job context environment may be described as the task environment within which an individual functions, that is the organisation, the work group, other groups, leadership, etc., and which has an effect on individual employees' functioning within an organisation. Theoretically it relates to Herzberg's hygiene factors and Maslow's lower-order needs, and includes the following: leadership style, organisation structures and personnel policies, work conditions, service benefits, career planning, and quality of work life.
- The external environment represents factors outside the organisation that affect personal functioning. Theoretically, this environment includes the following: the effect of technological acceleration on individual employees, the effect of social and other groups outside the

organisation to which the employee belongs, such as labour unions, and the effect of the current economic climate on his or her participation in the organisation.
- According to the systems approach to organisations and the functioning of individual employees, these three environments always exert an influence on individual employees. These influences may be positive or negative.
- The individual employee constantly compares personal progress with personal goal achievement in a particular organisation, and the extent of progress determines his or her attitude towards the organisation.
- Individual employees' attitudes determine their personal functioning, i.e. it affects the way they identify with goals related to their job, their group, and the formal organisation.
- The sum total of individual employee outputs forms the basis of group efficiency, which in turn is the cornerstone of group performance.
- Group performance is the basis of the efficiency of an organisation, which is directly related to the success of the organisation.

1.8.3 The structure of the book

The book is presented in seven parts and twenty-six chapters:
- *Part 1.* Managing human resources in organisational context.
- *Part 2.* Approaches to human resources management.
- *Part 3.* Human resources and the legislative environment.
- *Part 4.* Staffing the organisation and maintaining people.
- *Part 5.* Behavioural aspects of human resources management.
- *Part 6.* Employee, group and organisational empowerment through human resources interventions.
- *Part 7.* Strategic and international human resources management.

1.9 Conclusion

This chapter discussed South Africa's relative position with regard to human resources management by comparing it to that of other countries. Attention was also given to the theoretical principles, points of departure, and conceptual base of this applied science. From the discussion it appears that individual employee performance is the basic building block of organisational success; this is then also the primary focal point of this book. Apart from the other relevant aspects contained in this chapter, it is essential that note should be taken of the structure and focus of the book, as this will be of help in studying and understanding it.

Chapter questions

1 Explain the difference between human resources management and personnel management.
2 Draw an organisational chart of an organisation that you know of. Use this chart to explain the different authority relationships that the human resources department has with the rest of the organisation.
3 Write an essay to demonstrate the critical relationship between strategic planning and efficient human resources management.
4 Write an essay (approximately 500 words) on the individual employee as the basic cornerstone of success in an organisation.
5 Describe the course of development of human resources management in not more than 500 words.
6 Motivate why it is essential to

professionalise human resources management.

7 What guidelines will you take into account before approaching a human resources consultant for advice?

Bibliography

BEER, M. 1980. *Organization change and development: a systems view.* Goodyear, Santa Monica, California.

BENDIX, R. 1956. *Work and authority in industry.* University of California Press, Berkeley.

CASCIO, W.E. 1995. *Managing human resources.* McGraw-Hill, New York.

FARNHAM, D. 1990. *Personnel in context.* Wimbledon, London.

GAVELLI, S. 1999. *World competitiveness report.* EMF Foundation, Geneva, Switzerland.

GRAHAM, H.T. & BENNETT, R. 1993. *Human resources management.* M & E Handbook Series, London.

HALL, D.T. & GOODALE, J.G. 1986. *Human resources management: strategy, design and implementation.* Scott, Foresman, Glenview, Illinois.

HOLLEY, W.H. & JENNINGS, K.M. 1987. *Personnel management: functions and issues.* Dryden, New York.

HOLLEY, W.H. & JENNINGS, K.M. 1987. *Personnel/human resources management: contributions and activities.* Dryden, Chicago and New York.

IPM (INSTITUTE OF PEOPLE MANAGEMENT OF SOUTHERN AFRICA). Brochure. Johannesburg.

LITWACK, L. 1962. *The American labor movement.* Prentice-Hall, Englewood Cliffs, New Jersey.

SCHEIN, E.H. 1980. *Organizational psychology.* Prentice-Hall, Englewood Cliffs, New Jersey.

SOUTH AFRICAN BOARD FOR PERSONNEL PRACTICE. 1993. *Bekendstelling van die Raad se riglyne vir registrasie.* Johannesburg.

SWANEPOEL, B.J., ERASMUS, B.J., VAN WYK, M. & SCHENK, H. 2000. *South African human resource management: theory and practice* (2nd edition). Cape Town: Juta.

VALCHANGES. 1996. In Gavelli, S. *World competitiveness report.* EMF Foundation, Geneva, Switzerland.

WRIGHTON, P. 1993. Reply to Stephane Gavelli's speech about South Africa's competitiveness. *Sandton Sun,* March.

The human being as an employee

P S van Dyk

Learning outcomes

At the end of this chapter the learner should be able to demonstrate the following outcomes:
- Explain the concept of personality in theory.
- Pragmatically describe the psychological contract between the employee and the organisation.
- Describe personal and organisational goal integration.
- Describe the attachment to and involvement in the goals of an organisation from personal experience.

Key words and concepts

- attachment
- expectations
- individual interaction
- involvement
- motivation
- organisational expectations
- organisational goals
- personality
- personal goals
- psychological contract

Illustrative case

Peet joined a motor car manufacturing concern at the age of seventeen in the capacity of an apprentice. He was a very steady worker and studied with commitment during his theoretical training periods. He finished his apprenticeship at the age of twenty-one and got married soon afterwards. His marriage was happy during the first few years and he and his wife stayed in a flat close to the factory where he got a permanent appointment after he had finished his apprenticeship.

When he was twenty-five years old they decided to start a family and a year later a baby son was born. The baby was not healthy at all and Peet soon used the money which his medical fund provided to its limit. However, a year later his wife gave birth to a baby daughter. With this addition to the family (although the baby daughter was healthy) and the extra financial expenditure, he could not replace his little sedan which had over 150 000 km on the clock. Furthermore, the flat became too small for the family of four. He and his wife got irritated with each other and they decided to buy a small house in an average suburb. Peet was thirty years old at that stage.

Their lives returned to normal, the boy developed into a healthy young lad who participated in sport. The children did well at school and they had the privilege of living a normal suburban life.

At the age of forty, Peet realised that he had to secure his future and that the best way to do so was to remain with the same employer, where he had been promoted to a foreman two years previously. However, during the next year the company experienced a huge drop in demand for their cars, due to economic and other circumstances, and Peet was in line for retrenchment.

What would you advise him to do to retain his job?

2.1 Introduction

This chapter focuses on the individual as an employee. In other words, the essence of this chapter is the inputs with which an individual joins an organisation as an employee. Discussions in this chapter will be presented in accordance with Figure 2.3. As each employee has a unique personality, this aspect is dealt with briefly without giving too much psychological detail. Nevertheless, the emphasis in this chapter falls on the psychological contract, and the personal expectations and goals with which an individual joins an organisation as an employee. As motivated employee behaviour is only possible when employee goals are integrated with the goals of an organisation, attention is also given to this most vital recipe for success. In recent literature, this integration is also referred to as the human resources approach. The success of an employee depends primarily on himself or herself. You should therefore study this chapter very well before continuing with the others.

2.2 The individual employee as a human being

Personality is certainly one of the most exhaustively researched concepts in the field of behavioural science. The relation between employee behaviour and personality requires knowledge and insight on the part of superiors to enable them effectively to guide their subordinates in their pursuit of the goals of the organisation. Personality can be defined as a characteristic way in which a person thinks and acts in an effort to adapt to his or her environment. This includes personal characteristics, values, motives, genetic factors, attitudes, emotional reactivity, abilities, self-image, and intelligence. It also includes a person's discernible behavioural patterns.

It is well known that cultural and social factors have a significant effect on personality. Psychologists agree on the following generalisations about the concept of personality:
- Personality is an organised whole, other-

wise the individual will have no meaning.
- Personality seems to be organised into patterns. These patterns can be observed and measured to a certain extent.
- Although personality has a biological basis, its particular development is a product of social and cultural environments.
- Personality has superficial aspects such as attitude towards taking the lead, and sentiments towards authority, among others.
- Personality involves both common and unique characteristics. People differ from each other in certain respects, and show similarities in other respects.

In view of this, personality is a relatively stable set of characteristics, tendencies, and temperaments that have been significantly formed by inheritance and by social, cultural, and environmental factors. This set of variables determines the commonalties and differences in the behaviour of the individual.

It has been shown that hereditary factors do play a role in the shaping of personality, but that this role differs from one characteristic to the next. Heredity usually plays a more significant role in temperament than in values and ideals. Culture, however, has a major effect on the shaping of personality. Gibson et al. (1976: 99) explain this effect as follows:

We do not clearly recognise the impact of culture in shaping our personalities. It happens gradually, and usually there is no alternative but to accept the culture. The stable functioning of a society requires that there be shared patterns of behaviour among its members and that there is some basis for knowing how to behave in certain situations. To ensure this, the society institutionalises various patterns of behaviour. The institutionalisation of some patterns of behaviour means that most members of a culture will have certain common personality characteristics.

This description poses many challenges

Figure 2.1 Major factors affecting personality

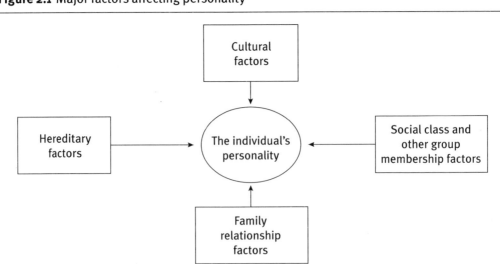

for the management of people and human resources. A diversified worker corps requires a more scientific human resources management practice than a homogeneous worker corps. The South African labour market is not only characterised by wide national diversity, but also by international diversity. This state of affairs results in human resources policies and practices having to be based on well-considered scientific principles.

Many authors conceptualise the influence of variables on personality as in Figure 2.1.

Social class is also important in the shaping of personalities. The environment in which a person grows up largely determines what he or she will learn about life. Social class affects a person's self-perception, perception of others, and perception of work, authority, and money. Such things as the nature of people's expectations of others, the way in which they try to achieve satisfaction, the way in which they express their feelings and solve emotional conflict, are acquired within interpersonal contexts. A key factor in this respect is the parent-child relationship which serves as a model of behaviour patterns for the child, and a frame of reference for its future.

The relation between an individual's personality and individual behaviour is shown in Figure 2.2.

This simple conceptualisation shows that the situations in which people are involved from time to time affect their perception of these situations, which in turn determines their behaviour as employees in the execution of a task or job.

When one considers the factors contributing to the shaping of personality (as set out in Figure 2.1) it seems that superiors within organisations have very little control over these factors. The significance of this will become clear in the following discussion of our view.

2.3 The authors' view of personality

Our view of the employee as a person with his or her own personality is set out in Figure 2.3.

Each individual has personal needs, expectations, and goals. Each individual also has a unique personality that differs from that of others. These differences mean that people are different and do not necessarily experience the same needs at specific times. Consequently, people also have different expectations in life, and this is shown in the way in which they pursue personal goals in organisations. In practice one finds that some individuals are happy if they can merely satisfy their basic needs and the minimum needs of the organisation, while others wish to satisfy social and status needs, and yet others are constantly trying to improve themselves and achieve self-actualisation. These behaviour pat-

Figure 2.2 The relation between personality and behaviour in organisations

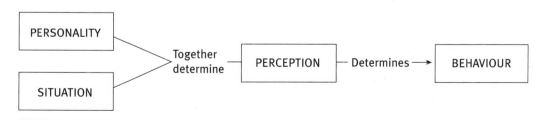

terns are the result of differences between individuals, as each individual constitutes a unique personality.

An individual's personality forms the basis of the expectations and personal goals with which he or she joins an organisation.

Personality is known to be the result of many factors, of which the most dominant are those shown in Figure 2.3.

An individual's personality is primarily the result of his or her personal environment from the day of birth until the day of joining the particular organisation with which he or she has entered into a psychological contract. Through personal envi-

Figure 2.3 Human resources inputs in organisations

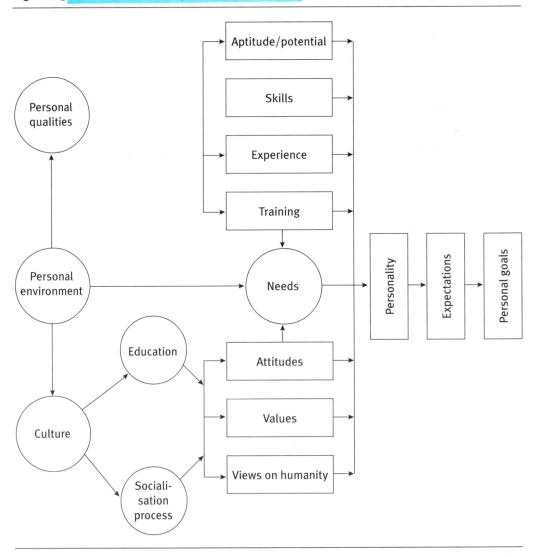

ronment an individual is exposed to a certain culture in terms of which he or she is educated. This culture influences the person through a process of socialisation during which certain behaviour patterns, values, attitudes, and views of humanity are acquired.

Individuals acquire certain personal qualities, such as skills, training, experience and ability within their personal environment, whereas the personal quality 'aptitude' is a physiological characteristic, the full realisation of which is the result of their personal environment. Certain needs are congenital (physiological needs) while others are acquired. In addition, it is characteristic of human beings that needs develop in the course of time and change in accordance with levels of development. All these factors together shape the personality of a person who has certain expectations of life and work, which are transformed into the personal goals with which the person joins an organisation.

2.4 The psychological contract between the human being as an employee and the organisation (management) as employer

Individual performance is the result of motivated employee behaviour. It is known that motivated employee behaviour is best achieved by integrating personal goals with the goals of the organisation. Personal goals can only be integrated with those of the organisation if employees' expectations of their employer, as well as the employer's expectations of individual employees, are clearly spelt out during the negotiation phase of the psychological contract. The psychological contract does, however, imply that individual expectations, and those of the organisation, change in the course of time. In other words, it is not a static agreement.

2.4.1 Types of psychological contract

Pearson (1992:142) differentiates between three types of psychological contract:
- *The coercive contract.* This is where individuals are held as organisation members against their will (e.g. in prison).
- *The calculative contract.* This is where the two parties discuss specific terms and all aspects of the contract are agreed and probably written down.
- *The cooperative contract.* This is open-ended and less clear-cut, the parties to it operating on the basis of mutual trust and interdependence and sharing the same broad goals and intentions.

2.4.2 The cooperative contract

The cooperative contract will be discussed from Schein's point of view.

In order to gain perspective on the important role of the psychological contract in producing motivated employee behaviour, we will now deal with:
- the nature of the psychological contract;
- the nature of the expectations of individual employees;
- the result of the needs of individual employees; and
- the nature of the expectations organisations have of their employees.

All these aspects have a positive or negative effect on the employee's quality of life.

The psychological contract is often referred to as the 'joining-up process' (Kotter 1976:93). The ineffective execution of this contract may result in numerous problems for the organisation, such as:

- dissatisfaction with the work;
- low productivity;
- poor attitude towards the organisation;
- low morale;
- increased labour turnover; and
- increased conflicts and tension.

When individuals join an organisation they have certain expectations about promotion opportunities, salary, status, office and decor, the amount of challenging work as opposed to the amount of boring work – things they expect to receive. They also have expectations about their technical skills, time and energy, involvement, communication skills, supervisory skills, and so on – things they expect to give.

The organisation (represented by management) also has certain expectations about what it will receive from the employee (in the same way as the employee expects to receive things from the organisation) as well as expectations about what it can offer the employee, examples of which are similar to what the employee expects to receive.

These two sets of expectations may therefore either correspond with or differ from each other. The psychological contract also differs from legal and labour agreements. In reality it could contain an indefinite number of items even though the employee may only be aware of a few expectations about his or her most pressing needs.

Kotter (1976: 93), who is a pioneer in this sphere, identifies two types of expectation. The first group of expectations represents what an individual expects to receive from an organisation and what the organisation expects to give the individual. In other words, for each item on the list an individual has expectations of what the organisation will offer and what he or she will receive. Similarly, the organisation has expectations of what it will offer or give the individual in that area:

- a meaningful job;
- opportunities for personal development;
- interesting work that will generate curiosity and excitement on the part of the individual;
- challenging work;
- authority and responsibility at work;
- recognition and approval for work of a high standard;
- status and prestige at work;
- friendly people and equality in the work group;
- compensation;
- the extent to which the environment is structured, for example general practices, discipline, or regimentation;
- security at work;
- promotion possibilities; and
- the amount and frequency of feedback and assessment.

The second group of expectations includes what an individual expects to offer an organisation and what the organisation expects to receive from employees. In other words, for each item on the list the individual has an expectation of what he or she is willing or able to offer or give the organisation. Similarly, the organisation has certain expectations of what it will receive from the individual in that area:

- the ability to execute tasks that are not socially related and that require a certain degree of technical knowledge and skills;
- the ability to learn to execute various aspects of a job in the work situation;
- the ability to invent new methods of task performance and the ability to solve problems;
- the ability to state an opinion effectively and convincingly;
- the ability to work productively with groups of people;
- the ability to present well-organised and clear reports orally or in writing;
- the ability to supervise and guide others in their work;

- the ability to make good, responsible decisions without assistance;
- the ability to plan and organise his or her own work as well as the work of other employees;
- the ability to use time and energy to the benefit of the organisation;
- the ability to accept instructions and requirements from the organisation that are incompatible with personal prerogatives;
- social interaction with other employees outside the working environment;
- conforming to the norms of the organisation applicable to the job in areas not directly related to the job;
- self-study outside normal working hours;
- maintaining a good public image of the organisation;
- accepting the organisation's values and goals as his or her own values and goals; and
- the ability to realise what has to be done and to take the appropriate steps.

The psychological contract may contain an infinite number of items. More important than these items, however, is an understanding of the nature of the psychological contract, and the communication of these mutual expectations.

Porter et al. (1975:109) refer to the psychological contract as the 'dynamics of organisation-individual interactions' and conceptualise it as in Figure 2.4.

As indicated by the arrows in Figure 2.4, the different requirements of the individual and the organisation represent a tapping of common resources. In other words, the communicated expectations of the organisation make demands on the skills and energy of individuals, while the satisfaction of individuals' needs depends on certain resources of the organisation. It seems obvious that if a working relationship is to be developed and maintained between the individual and the organisation, both parties will have to respond to mutual expectations and needs.

Schein (1980:77) makes the following remarks about the importance of the psychological contract:

> By way of conclusion, I would like to underline the importance of the psychological contract as a major variable of analysis. It is my central hypothesis that whether a person is working effectively, whether he generates commit-

Figure 2.4 The dynamics of organisation-individual interaction

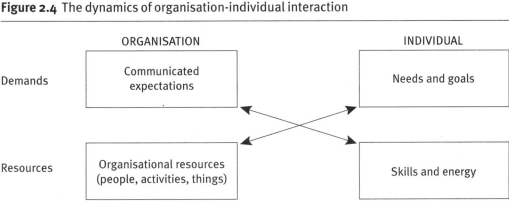

SOURCE: Porter et al. (1975:109).

ment, loyalty, and enthusiasm for the organisation and its goals, and whether he obtains satisfaction from his work, depends to a large measure on two conditions: (1) the degree to which his own expectations of what the organisation will provide him and what he owes the organisation match what the organisation's are of what it will give and get; (2) assuming there is agreement on expectations, what actually is to be exchanged – money in exchange for time at work; social-need satisfaction and security in exchange for work and loyalty; opportunities for self-actualisation and challenging work in exchange for high productivity, quality work and creative effort in the service of organisational goals; or various combinations of these and other things. Ultimately the relationship between the individual and organisation is interactive, unfolding through mutual bargaining to establish a workable psychological contract. We cannot understand the psychological dynamics if we look only to the individual's motivations or only to organisational conditions and practices. The two interact in a complex fashion, requiring us to develop theories and research approaches which can deal with systems and interdependent phenomena.

The psychological contract is dynamic and changes in the course of time. This change takes place in accordance with changed needs of both the individual employee and the organisation.

What an employee expects of an organisation or the employer at the age of twenty-five differs dramatically from what that same employee expects at the age of fifty. A newly married employee of twenty-five is primarily interested in career prospects and a good salary so that he or she may provide his or her family with housing and a good standard of living, while at fifty the same person would pay more attention to what the organisation can offer on retirement.

In the same way, the organisation's expectations of its employees differ from time to time. For example, the organisation may expect its members to do their very best and remain loyal and diligent in times of economic recession, or to promote the organisation's image in times of economic prosperity.

In most cases, the needs of employees starting a career revolve around 'self-testing'. Employees would like to determine whether they have all the skills needed to do the job for which they are appointed. Therefore they expect organisations to provide them with challenges to test their skills and knowledge in terms of goal achievement. This is where the problem of conflicting goals comes to the fore. Employees are usually disappointed if they are kept in meaningless training programmes for too long, or if they are occupied with tasks that bear no relation to the primary goals of the organisation. In such cases neither the organisation nor the individual employee is in a position to determine the employee's actual abilities in terms of the goal achievement of the organisation, and this results in a feeling of uncertainty.

During a later phase of employees' work life, their needs and expectations move into an area where they may feel that they are contributing to the organisation, and where they are enabled to develop in their area of speciality. At this stage employees expect the organisation to acknowledge their contributions. Most employees reach this position in the middle of their career, usually when they are at their most productive and, consequently, expecting the most recognition and remuneration. At a later stage, when the employee is doing less crucial work, his or her need for security increases and expectations in the psychological contract change to not wanting to be sidelined or sent into early retirement. Retired employees often complain that the psychological contract has been broken because they could still make a positive contribution to the organisation.

employees will tend to subordinate organisational goals to their personal goals for need satisfaction.

It should, thus, be clear that there is a critical link between the successful integration of personal goals and the goals of the organisation, as well as organisational success.

2.5 The integration of personal goals with those of the organisation

The expectations of both the employee and the manager are, among other things, the result of what they have learnt from others of prevailing traditions and norms and of previous experience. As needs and other external factors change, expectations also change, and this gives the psychological contract a dynamic character that requires constant re-negotiation. Although the psychological contract is unwritten, it remains the critical determinant of the work behaviour of employees.

The question then arises as to how the psychological contract can contribute to the process of motivation. In the following section, this important aspect is explained.

Individuals as employees have certain personal goals that are the result of the expectations contained in the psychological contract. In keeping with the nature and content of the psychological contract, it is also clear that organisations expect certain things from their employees. The individual and the organisation are thus in constant interaction with each other, with the aim of attaining their mutual goals.

An individual employee enters an organisation with a certain set of needs. If the organisation has an organisational climate that promotes need satisfaction, an employee should show positive employee behaviour. If such a climate is not present,

2.6 Attachment to the organisation and involvement with the goals of the organisation

An employee's behaviour within an organisation may be regarded as the function of his or her perception of the content of the psychological contract entered into with the organisation. Organisations expect their employees to accept the goals allocated to them, and to be motivated to achieve these goals. On the other hand, individual employees expect the organisation to fulfil its part of the contract too. Steers (1977:113) has the following view of the results of this interaction:

> The results of this interaction can be seen as leading to two equally important outcomes: (1) an individual's desire to maintain his membership in a particular organisation (termed here attachment); and (2) an individual's desire to perform on the job and contribute to organisational goal attainment.

An organisation can only expect its employees to be attached to the organisation and to be involved with their personal goals if it fulfils the following commitments:
- It must be able to attract (recruit) the workers required and retain them. This involves not only the recruitment, selection, employment, and induction of

workers, but ensuring that individual employees receive sufficient compensation, commensurate with their individual contribution and need satisfaction, in order to retain them.
- The organisation must also be able to ensure that each employee executes the tasks allocated to him or her. This implies that employees should not merely do their work, but should do it with responsibility.
- A third requirement, which is often neglected and which is not formally included in individual employees' goals, but which does promote the goal achievement of the organisation, is innovation and spontaneous cooperation on the part of employees.

Organisations must ensure that employees become involved and give their spontaneous and continuous cooperation.

The recruitment and maintenance of the required human resources are related to attachment to organisations. In other words, it has to do with why an individual joins a particular organisation, and what motivates him or her to stay with that organisation.

The second and third commitments on the part of the organisation, to ensure that employees are responsible and that their behaviour is spontaneous and innovative, are related to the quality of employee functioning or their performance level. Research has shown that in the study of human behaviour, as it relates to organisational effectiveness, employee attachment and performance emerge as the key variables to be examined. Although structure, technology, and environment contribute to and often constrain effectiveness, such variables are largely overshadowed by the role of employee behaviour. If employees are not motivated to remain with and contribute to an organisation, questions of effectiveness become academic.

This underlies the approach followed in this book. Therefore, it seems necessary to take a closer look at the concepts of attachment and involvement, as applied to organisations.

2.6.1 Employees' attachment to the organisation

Attachment to organisations may be divided into two components. The first is formal attachment. This refers to methods to reduce labour turnover, absenteeism and other forms of withdrawal from the work environment, and to increase time spent at work. A simple statement that employees are attached to organisations does not necessarily imply that they are strongly drawn to the organisation, nor that they have positive feelings about the organisation, but involves only the question of why they retain their membership of organisations. The second component, namely involvement, is discussed in Paragraph 2.6.2.

At this point one might well ask why individuals retain their membership of organisations. In general, it may be said that organisations can expect employees to be attached to them and less prone to withdrawal if the employees experience job satisfaction. This is related to the variables contained in the job content and job context environments.

From the literature (see Steers, 1977: 115, among others) the following reasons may be given why employees remain with a particular organisation:
- environmental factors, for example compensation and promotion policy and the size of the organisation;
- factors within the employee's immediate work environment, for example supervision and interpersonal and group relationships;
- job content factors; and
- personal factors.

Furthermore it should be noted that the employee's perception of these factors or sources will determine whether he or she will withdraw from the organisation permanently (which means labour turnover) or temporarily (for example absenteeism).

Another question arising at this stage is how it affects the success of an organisation if individuals terminate their membership of organisations permanently or temporarily. Withdrawal (in particular permanent withdrawal) often has specific consequences for organisations and eventually for their efficiency. Many studies claim that increased labour turnover often leads to the employment of more administrative personnel in proportion to production personnel. It can also have a negative effect on innovation and creativity. Labour turnover gives rise to undesirable outputs and is directly related to the success or failure of organisations. On the other hand, organisations do benefit from getting rid of unproductive workers. Some labour turnover is desirable as it ensures that new workers with new ideas join the organisation, thus preventing stagnation.

The withdrawal of performance-inclined employees, in particular, poses a difficult problem for management.

2.6.2 Involvement with the organisation

Involvement, the second component of attachment, represents a state where individuals feel strongly drawn to the objectives, values and goals of their employer. In other words, it goes much deeper than mere membership of an organisation, in the sense that it makes goal achievement possible by ensuring a positive attitude towards the organisation, as well as the willingness to make a bigger effort on behalf of the organisation.

Involvement in organisations and organisational goal achievement indicates

> Successful organisations are characterised by performance-inclined, innovative and creative employees. The 'price' that an organisation has to pay for the withdrawal of such an employee is irrecoverable. It is therefore a challenge to human resources management to retain such successful employees as well as less successful employees and to develop them further to the advantage of the organisation and its stake-holders.

the nature of the individual employee's relationship with the organisation. A performance-orientated employee generally shows the following work behaviour:
- a strong desire to remain a member of the organisation;
- a willingness to do more than is expected for the sake of the organisation; and
- a definite acceptance of the organisational culture and goals.

Involvement refers to an active relationship between employee and employer, where the employee is willing to make sacrifices in pursuit of the employer's goals. One might now ask how increased involvement with organisations would affect the success of the organisation, or in different terms, what the result of real involvement in organisations is? The authors are of the opinion that involvement is closely related to at least four effectiveness variables which are briefly discussed below.
- *Increased attendance.* Employees who are deeply involved with the goals and values of an organisation are more inclined to increase their participation in the activities of the organisation. In general, their attendance will only be prevented by events such as illness. With employees such as these, voluntary absenteeism will be lower than with employees who are less involved.

- *Employee retention.* A second variable related to increased attendance is reduced labour turnover (employee retention). This implies that employees who feel committed to an organisation have a strong desire to stay with that organisation, so that they may continue their contribution to goal achievement with which they identify.
- *Work involvement.* Increased identification with and belief in the goals of the organisation will increase employees' involvement in their work, as work is the key mechanism by which individuals contribute to the achievement of the goals of the organisation.
- *Increased effort.* This variable implies that individuals who are deeply involved will be willing to make a bigger effort on behalf of the organisation. In some cases such increased efforts will result in outstanding achievement.

2.7 Conclusion

In this chapter we have attempted to explain why individuals join a particular organisation and what motivates them to stay with that organisation. Organisations must, therefore, not only recruit, employ, and induct new individuals, but also ensure that they are attached to the organisation and in particular that they become involved in the pursuit of its goals. Employees will feel attached to or involved with organisations if factors such as their immediate work environment, job content, and so on are satisfactory. This will result in fewer resignations and reduced absenteeism with the resultant positive effect on the success of the organisation. Involvement also means that employees will identify with the overall goals of the organisation, and they will consequently make a bigger effort in their pursuit of the goals of the organisation.

The chapter also deals with the individual employee as a human being with a unique personality and his or her individual needs, expectations and personal goals. A person joins and enters into a psychological contract with an organisation on the basis of his or her personal needs and goals. Both the individual employee and the organisation have certain expectations that must be met in order to uphold this contract. The integration of personal goals with the goals of the organisation seems to be the best way to uphold this contract. This provides the basis for motivated employee behaviour, which is essential to the success of the organisation. Attachment to organisations and involvement with the goals of the organisation greatly contribute to the success of the organisation. In other words, the inputs with which an employee joins an organisation must be utilised by that organisation in order to achieve optimal employee functioning.

Case study

Bob was appointed MD of an engineering company which belonged to his father, who vacated the position at the age of sixty-two, when Bob completed his degree in mechanical engineering at Tukkies. Bob's father stayed on for a further six months before he gave him total control of the company, the registered name of which was SA Long Haul Manufacturers (Pty) Ltd.

Bob was more interested in designing, prototyping, testing and ultimately building new long and short haul trailers than he was in running the company. 'All I have to worry about is our bank balance, and for that reason I have employed a permanent auditor whose name is Smiley,' he said. 'Nella must worry about the day-to-day administration of the business. I do not have time for that,' he added.

Due to the quality of their trailers, SA Long Haul Manufacturers kept going for the following two years. All along Bob was replacing old people on their retirement with young mechanically skilled people. The business was still doing well, despite an economic slow-down.

Bob was approached by his auditor during a mid-year auditing inspection: 'Bob we have to talk. When can we put aside a hour or two?' asked Smiley. Bob was intrigued by this sudden request: 'Why?' he asked. 'Because things are not going as well as you might think,' Smiley replied.

Smiley and Bob eventually got together two days later where Bob was confronted with financial data which was not welcome or encouraging at all. 'These figures and numbers do not look good at all,' he reacted, 'what went wrong?' Smiley replied: 'Bob, I am only the auditor.'

Bob took the preliminary report home that Friday and analysed it thoroughly. The problem had to be somewhere else. On Saturday afternoon he phoned his secretary. 'Daisy, if at all possible, can you go to the office and prepare a break-down of our staff complement in the following categories: age groups (differentials, five years); marital status (unmarried, married, divorced, widow, etc.); qualifications (less than Grade 12, Grade 12 plus, diploma, degree); and years of service. If I can have that information by Thursday morning, when I return from my trip to the Fast Carriers Expo, you can take a long-weekend and I will see you again Monday-week.'

When Bob returned from the Expo, a neatly summarised document containing the statistics he had asked for was on his office desk. The information boiled down to the following:
1 Total work force: 180
   • Managerial: 20
   • Artisans: 40
   • Administrative: 15
   • Professional: 5
   • Labourers: 80
   • Miscellaneous: 20
2 Age groups
   • <20: 15
   • >20 – <25: 50
   • >25 – <40: 80
   • >40 – <55: 25
   • >55: 10
3 Marital status
   • Unmarried: 60
   • Married: 80
   • Divorced: 30
   • Widow(er): 10
4 Qualifications
   • Less than Grade 12: 140
   • Grade 12 plus diploma: 35
   • Degree: 5
5 Years of service
   • Less than 1 year: 30
   • Between 1-3 years: 50
   • Between 4-6 years: 60
   • Between 7-10 years: 25
   • 10 years and longer: 15

After Bob had studied the statistical data, he realised that something big was wrong. On the engineering side everything was OK, but something was not in place. Realising his shortcomings in the field of management, he phoned a management consultancy firm.

The next day he had lunch with a human resources specialist from the management consultancy firm, who suggested to Bob that a diagnostic survey be conducted by means of Nominal

> Group Techniques (structured brainstorming exercises) to diagnose the underlying 'illness(es)' of Bob's company. Bob agreed immediately, eager to get to the root of the problem.
>
> ## Question
>
> Write a report which would constitute the conclusions the consultants arrived at.

Chapter questions

1 How do you understand the concept of personality?
2 Critically discuss the authors' view of personality.
3 In not more than 500 words, explain what you understand by the psychological contract.
4 One of the key factors in individual motivation is achieving personal goals. Critically discuss this statement.
5 What do you understand by attachment to organisations?

Bibliography

CHARLTON, G. 2000. *Human habits of highly effective organisations.* Van Schaik, Pretoria.
GIBSON, J.L., IVANCEVICH, J.M. & DONNELLY, J.H. 1976. *Organizations: behavior, structure, process.* Business Publications, Dallas, Texas.
KOTTER, J.P. 1976. The psychological contract: managing the joining-up process. *California Management Reviews,* vol. xv, no. 3, pp. 91–9.
MCLAGLAN, P. 1989. *Training and Development Journal,* September, pp. 50–1.
PEARSON, G. 1992. *The competitive organisation.* McGraw-Hill, Berkshire.
PORTER, L.W., LAWLER, E.E. & HACKMAN, J.R. 1975. *Behavior in organizations.* McGraw-Hill, New York.
SCHEIN, E.H. 1980. *Organizational psychology.* Prentice-Hall, Englewood Cliffs, New Jersey.
STEERS, R.M. 1977. *Organizational effectiveness: a behavioral view.* Goodyear, Santa Monica, California.

part two

Approaches to human resources management

3

The functional, systems, and efficiency approaches to human resources management

P S van Dyk

Learning outcomes

At the end of this chapter the learner should be able to demonstrate the following outcomes:
- Illustrate the place of human resources management in a functional structure.
- Differentiate between human resources development, provisioning, and maintenance.
- Practically analyse the systems approach to human resources management.
- Compare line, staff, and functional responsibilities.
- Conceptually relate individual efficiency to organisational success.
- Distinguish between job content and job context factors.

Key words and concepts

- a system
- human resources department
- human resources development
- human resources maintenance
- human resources provisioning
- individual and group performance
- job content environment
- job context
- line function
- multiple goals
- organisational effectiveness
- organisational efficiency
- organisational success
- staff function

Illustrative case

Johanna was a second-year student in business management. During her first year, a compulsory study module was 'General Management' which she found very interesting; and from then on, applied the general management principles to her personal life. Of particular interest to her was the concept of the organisation as an open system.

Like all undergraduate students, she was quite keen to share the knowledge which she gained through her studies with friends and family.

One Sunday afternoon after lunch, her family, grandparents, and other extended family members were having coffee in the lounge. As most of her family stemmed from an agricultural background, her grandfather, a successful maize farmer, asked her how the theory she was learning could be used to improve his farming ability and skills. She was immediately motivated and told him, as well as the rest of the family, about the efficiency/systems approach to organisations.

Her grandfather listened attentively and, after his second cup of coffee, asked her to explain a few things she had said to him, namely: how his farm was a system; how each individual labourer of his was also a system; how his farm, as a system, differed from their church as a system; and what the difference was between efficient and effective farming.

If you were in Johanna's shoes, how would you answer her grandfather's questions?

3.1 Introduction

The purpose of this chapter is to provide a brief overview of different approaches to human resources management, excluding the quality assurance approach which is discussed in Chapter 4. We once again stress the need for the incorporation of these approaches - many organisations are still using the functional approach, while many others manage their employees from a 'best fit' (efficiency/systems approach) whilst making use of a functional human resources department. The quality assurance approach is in its establishing stage in South African organisations, and we are of the opinion that its acceptance and accommodation will accelerate in this decade.

3.2 The role and functions of human resources management from a functional perspective

3.2.1 General

From a functional perspective, human resources management is a staff function, with the aim of helping other functional managers to apply and utilise the most important production factor, human resources, as effectively as possible within the organisation. The people in an organisation essentially determine how successfully the other means of production will be applied.

Human resources management is a purposeful action of the human resources department aimed at assisting functional managers in the optimal application and utilisation of the human resources under their control, in accordance with official organisational policy as well as human resources management policy and application in practice, in order to achieve the goals of the organisation.

3.2.2 The development and maintenance of human resources management objectives

Like any other organisational function, the human resources department requires focal points or objectives to direct the diverse nature of the activities to be carried out. Three general human resources management objectives are universally accepted in this regard (see Holley and Jennings 1983: 6-7).

OBJECTIVE 1: *To establish the belief that the human resources of an organisation consist of unique individuals who can make a meaningful impact on the success of the organisation.*

This objective is usually reflected in the human resources vision or mission of an organisation. The vision of Toyota South Africa is a good example of this.

You might reason that this objective is an obvious one in modern organisations. This is, however, not the case; many organisations in South Africa, seen from a multicultural point of view, still disregard this important principle. Employees are still treated as "machines" and their contribution is regarded as unimportant for the success of the organisation. The contemporary view that the human being is the most important asset of an organisation is relatively new. The general acceptance of this principle, however, does give rise to individual employees having an optimally positive attitude towards performance.

> **Toyota SA Marketing**
> HUMAN RESOURCES DIVISION
> Vision
> 1 To unlock and unfold human potential.
> 2 To strategically align the organisation for change.

OBJECTIVE 2: *Establishing how employees and organisations can adapt to each other to the advantage of both parties.*

This objective is linked to the first objective. If employees are unique components of organisational success (see Figure 3.7) modern organisations should react in a flexible manner and adapt to the diverse needs of employees. The days of

Figure 3.1 The place of the human resources management function in an organisation

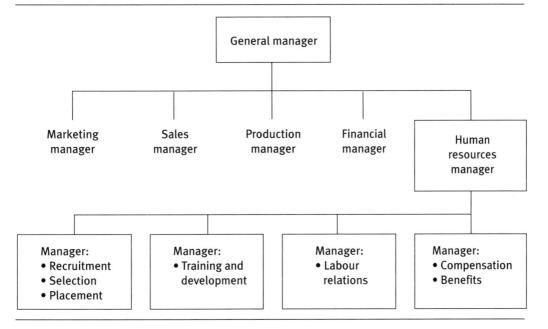

one policy for all employees are over. The divergence of individual employee needs may be seen in the conditions of service of modern organisations (see Chapter 2). Mutual adaptation of needs was also discussed in Chapter 2.

OBJECTIVE 3: *The support by human resources managers of other line and staff managers in the execution of their tasks related to human resources management and the management of people.*

The main theme of this book is to highlight the contribution to organisational success made by the human resources management function as well as the role of other managers in this regard. Figure 3.1 embodies this approach.

At the end of each chapter, we highlight the application of the relevant theories in increasing the performance inclination of employees.

implication, and the physical embodiment of this function depends on the nature of the organisation in terms of its size, products, services, and geographical location. The human resources function traditionally includes the following:

- human resources provisioning, comprising human resources planning, recruitment, selection, placement, induction, and career management;
- human resources maintenance, comprising the determination of conditions of service, remuneration structures, record keeping, personnel turnover, settlement of disputes, advisory services, employer-employee relations, social responsibility, affirmative action, and performance assessment; and
- human resources development, comprising training and development as its most important activities.

3.3 Traditional human resources management functions

Within the organisational framework of the organisation the human resources function manifests itself as a human resources department. The human resources function of an organisation refers to a number of functions carried out in order to achieve the goals of an organisation. The human resources function is carried out by a human resources department responsible for the organisation's human resources management activities. The department also gives advice and assistance to the rest of the organisation.

The human resources function is, therefore, a staff function aimed at providing the organisation with labour, and giving it specialised human resources services to help it to achieve its goals. The human resources function should be flexible by

3.4 Specific responsibilities and functions

3.4.1 General

The human resources management function in an organisation aims at producing certain outputs in order to achieve the organisation's goals. The responsibilities of the human resources function and the conditions for its success are briefly dealt with in the following paragraph.

3.4.2 Responsibilities of the human resources management department

The responsibilities of the human resources management department can probably best be outlined as follows (adapted from Graham and Bennett 1993:158):

- carrying out wage and salary surveys to ensure that the organisation's wage and salary levels are in line with those of other related organisations;
- the development of incentive schemes such as compensation systems to increase employee efficiency;
- implementing first-class pension schemes and advising employees with regard to their pension and other privileges;
- maintaining personnel details and statistics;
- preparing accurate job descriptions and other recruitment aids;
- implementing health and safety regulations, accident prevention, and first-aid facilities;
- management training, development, and succession planning; and
- employee communication, i.e. sending out important information to employees through newsletters, notice boards, and information sessions.

3.4.3 The function of the human resources manager

Theoretically, three functions of the human resources manager may be distinguished:
- a service function;
- a control function; and
- an advisory function.

The service function incorporates the everyday tasks of a human resources department, such as:
- recruitment;
- selection;
- remuneration;
- training; and
- health and safety activities.

The control function is of a strategic nature and incorporates activities such as:

- an analysis of key human resources management outputs such as labour turnover, productivity, absenteeism, and resignations; and
- the recommendation of appropriate corrective action by line managers, such as training and development, dismissals, and transfers.

The advisory function is associated with the expert advice given by the human resources department regarding human resources policy and procedures with regard to matters such as:
- which employees are ready for promotion;
- how a grievance procedure should be carried out; and
- how service contracts, and health and safety regulations should be carried out.

From the above it thus appears that the human resources manager must be a diplomat in the sense that he or she must act as a mediator between management and the employee, between management and management, and between various groups of employees. This role is of particular importance in contemporary South African organisations.

The human resources manager must also be a diagnostician who collects information, interprets it for various parties, and prescribes the best solutions.

Finally, Graham and Bennett (1993: 163) are of the following opinion:

> Thus a human resources manager has to be an effective planner, analyst, team worker and communicator, capable of presenting proposals and arguing a case at all levels within the organisation – from the board room to the employees' workplaces.

3.5 The structural placement of a human resources department from a functional perspective

3.5.1 General

The human resources management function is responsible for rendering a personnel service to both line and staff functions in an organisation. This function belongs to a department or section, which in turn forms an integral part of the total structure of the organisation.

3.5.2 A typical structure for a human resources management department within an organisation

A typical human resources management department with its different human resources management functions may be represented as shown in Figure 3.1.

A further subdivision of the organisational structure according to Figure 3.1 indicates that the human resources management function consists of various subfunctions. Each organisation will organise its human resources function in such a way that it will satisfy the unique requirements of the organisation.

The previously mentioned concept is the point of view of the authors. A further distinction must be made between line, functional, and staff authority.

- *Line authority* is the authority vested in managers to give their subordinates orders that they are expected to carry out. In other words, line authority is the direct authority of any manager or supervisor over immediate subordinates. For example, the general manager has line authority over heads of departments who have line authority over employees in their sections, and so forth. Line authority gives the human resources department the right to issue enforceable orders to its functionaries on any matter dealt with by the human resources department.
- *Functional authority* gives the human resources manager the right to issue enforceable instructions on human resources matters throughout the organisation, in order to fulfil duties and responsibilities outside his or her own department. The authority to ensure that human resources policy, regulations and procedures are correctly applied is an example of this functional authority.
- *Staff authority* is only advisory and cannot be enforced. A functionary of the department may, for example, advise a supervisor how to reprimand an employee who is regularly late for work.

Figure 3.2 illustrates the functional and staff authority of a human resources manager.

The dotted lines indicate the staff authority of the human resources department with regard to other line and staff functions. It is clear that the human resources manager may exercise functional authority over human resources matters throughout the organisation. Orders issued from the human resources department to the production department, for example on personnel matters, are binding and must be executed by the production department. Staff authority, however, means that the human resources manager may give advice but cannot enforce it. For instance, he or she cannot force a foreman to treat an underachieving factory worker in a specific way.

3.6 The systems approach

3.6.1 General

We shall discuss the systems approach to human resources management in broad

Figure 3.2 The functional and staff authority of the human resources department

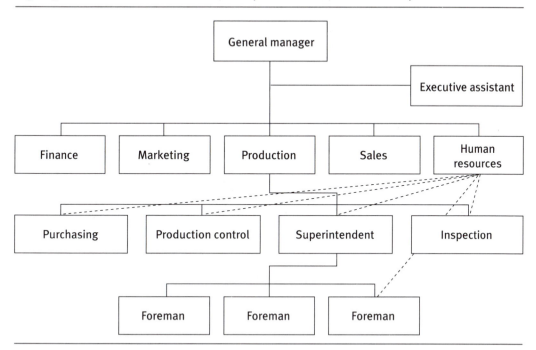

terms in this section. Attention will first be given to the definition of a system, and to the characteristics of a system. Then reasons will be provided as to why an organisation may be regarded as an open system. The model that is the focal point of this book will be provided against this background. We shall use this model as a point of departure for a discussion on the individual employee as a system in its own right. This will be followed by a brief discussion on human resources management processes affecting individual employees. The effect of these human resources management processes on individual employees will be explained throughout in terms of the model.

3.6.2 Description of a system

The question arises: 'What is a system?' A system is simply a number of interdependent components that form a whole and work together with a view to attaining a common goal. Thus, for example, you as a person are also a system in your own right (a biological system) and you come into daily contact with various types of systems:

- when you travel to work in the morning by car, bus, or train, you are part of a mechanical system;
- when you are at work, you are in a social system; and
- when you come home in the evenings, you are in a micro-social economic system, i.e. your family.

In the literature, a distinction is made between a closed and an open system. A system is closed when it is self-sustaining and independent of external stimuli or input. An example is the development of a test-tube baby from conception (fertilisation)

until it is implanted in the womb of a woman. An open system, on the other hand, requires certain input or stimuli from elsewhere, known in technical terms as the environment. A system is open if:
- it is dependent on the environment in which it operates;
- the environment depends on it; and
- there is interaction between the system and the environment.

Diagrammatically, an open system can be represented as in Figure 3.3.

The system takes input from its environment (which represents a larger system), processes them, and returns them to the environment in another form as output.

3.6.2.1 The most important characteristics of a system

Most authors identify the general characteristics in their work on the systems approach to organisations. Katz and Kahn (1966: 19), the pioneers in this field, describe the characteristics as:
- *Energy intake.* The first characteristic of an open system is that an organisation as a system is dependent on the intake of energy to activate the functioning process. Energy includes resources and information. Energy intake may also be described as the input process.
- *Throughput process.* All open systems transform the energy at their disposal by means of some throughput system. This throughput process differs from one organisation to the next, but it remains essential for the functioning of a system.
- *Output process.* Each open system has an output process for the very reason that it has an input process and a throughput process. Output may be regarded as the dependent variable in a system. Outputs usually take the form of finished products, services, and so on.
- *A system as a cycle of events.* The product released by means of the output process provides a source of energy for the repetition of the cycle of events. In a profit-seeking organisation making use of resources to produce a product, monetary returns are used to procure more resources for a repetition of the process.
- *Mutual dependence.* The components of a system are dependent on one another. If a change should take place in one part of the system, this will influence all the other components of the system, either directly or indirectly.

Figure 3.3 The basic elements of a system

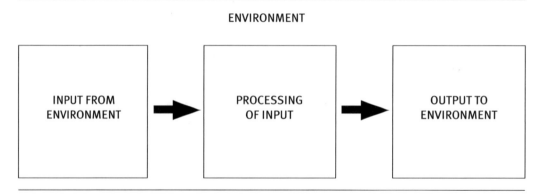

3.6.2.2 The organisation as an open system

Schein (1980: 228–9) expands on the above and defines an open system as follows:

- An organisation is an open system, which implies that it is continuously interacting with its environment. During this process it takes in resources, information, and energy which it transforms into products and services made available to the environment in the form of outputs.
- An organisation is a system with multiple goals or functions, which implies that there are multiple interactions between an organisation and its environments. Many of the activities of the sub-systems (see next point) will not be understood unless these multiple functions and interactions are taken into consideration.
- An organisation consists of a number of sub-systems in a state of dynamic interaction. It is becoming increasingly important to analyse the behaviour (functioning) of these sub-systems when focusing on the concept of the organisation, instead of describing individual behaviour.
- Change in one sub-system is followed by changes in other sub-systems because the sub-systems in an organisation are interdependent.
- An organisation functions in a dynamic environment which consists of other sub-systems differing in scope. The environment makes certain demands on an organisation, which inhibit it in certain respects. Therefore, thorough investigation of environmental problems and restrictions is essential to understand the overall functioning of an organisation.
- The multiple connections between an organisation and its environments complicate the delimitation of the boundaries of an organisation.

In the light of this, the organisation can be represented as an open system as shown in Figure 3.4.

Figure 3.4 shows the organisation from a systems perspective on the basis of the principles of organisational success. The reason for the existence of the organisation lies in the needs present in the organisation's external environment. For this reason, it is essential that the organisation should undertake environmental scanning to identify opportunities and threats in its external environment and to formulate its strategy accordingly. Even if an organisation identifies its needs, it will not automatically be successful, unless the external infrastructure is such that it favours the satisfaction of needs (or goal achievement).

> There is a great need for water to start agricultural production in the Sahara desert. However, there is no external infrastructure at all. Such an attempt would thus be doomed to failure from the start.

The external infrastructure of each organisation is unique, as is the nature of its activities. These aspects, which may be regarded as conditions for success, and can be classified as external success factors, are the inputs that activate the functioning of the organisation.

As will be discussed in this chapter, organisational efficiency refers to the internal functioning of an organisation, and according to Beer (1980: 29) there must be an optimal fit between the external environment and the internal components of the organisation as a system. The present authors refer to the internal components as the internal infrastructure that is used in the organisation's transformation process to render desirable output. They may also be regarded as internal success factors or prerequisites for efficiency.

Figure 3.4 The systems approach and organisational success

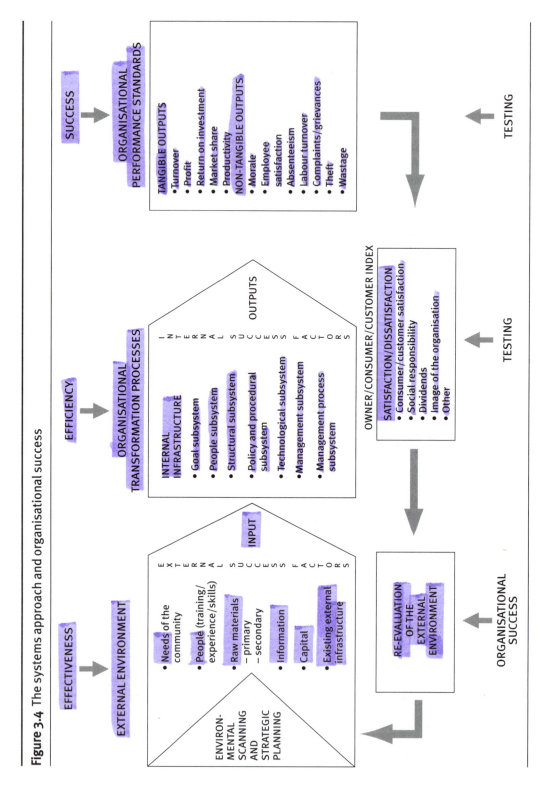

As far as organisational success is concerned, a distinction must be made between short-, medium-, and long-term success. This distinction will become clear during the course of the discussion below.

It was mentioned elsewhere that, according to the systems approach, an organisation strives for multiple objectives. The writers are of the opinion that these objectives can be divided into two main categories, i.e. tangible outputs and non-tangible outputs. The former refers to what organisations primarily pursue, i.e. profits, return on investment and an increased market share, while non-tangible outputs generally refer to the quality of work-life of the organisation's worker corps. This includes aspects such as morale, grievances, and job satisfaction.

For organisational success, management should set measurable objectives for those outputs, and the attainment thereof should be measured by a set performance standard.

An organisation that pursues tangible outputs at the cost of the human element (quality of work-life), will only be successful in the short term, as human resources, particularly in modern organisations, do not tolerate exploitation.

> The dilemma is that management is generally orientated towards the attainment of tangible outputs, and if it is kept in mind that tangible outputs are produced by the people in the organisation (who represent non-tangible outputs) goal achievement generally takes place at the cost of the human element.

An organisation will be successful in the medium term if there is a balance between management's focus on both types of outputs.

An organisation will only be successful in the long term if the owners, consumers, and other stake-holders are consistently satisfied with the outcomes, such as dividends and product reliability, which they receive from the organisation.

This double feedback loop, i.e. performance standards and owner/consumer satisfaction, is known in contemporary management as the cybernetic principle, which is a characteristic of the organisation as a social system. The aforementioned thus has important implications for human resources management and organisational success.

3.6.2.3 Summary

The above clearly demonstrates the necessity for an understanding of a system and its characteristics. An organisation must be managed in accordance with the characteristics of the systems approach if it is to be successful. The organisation as such consists of a number of sub-systems, including human resources management as a functional sub-system. Furthermore, an organisation consists of other types of sub-system, such as groups and individuals. The individual may be regarded as the smallest sub-system within the organisation.

3.6.3 A systems model for human resources management

3.6.3.1 General

A systems model (see Figure 3.5) is presented in this section and may be used for reference when studying the information in this book. This model has two main purposes:
- In the first place, it focuses on the employee as a sub-system within the organisation as a system, with specific reference to the inputs which an employee brings into an organisation, the throughput process, and the outputs produced

56 APPROACHES TO HUMAN RESOURCES MANAGEMENT

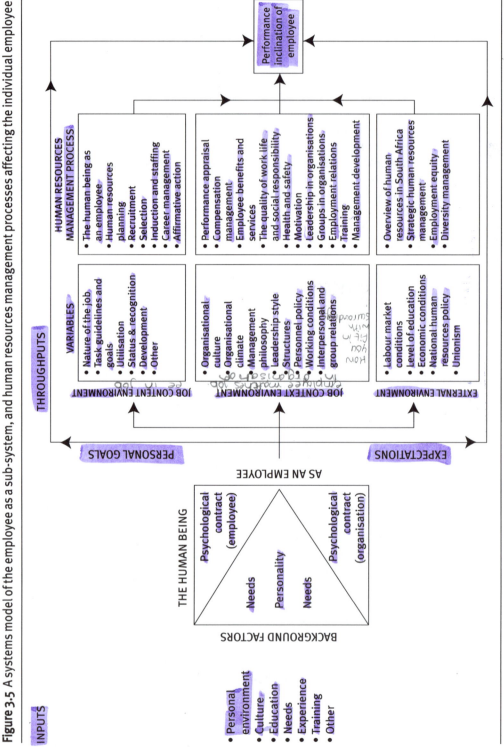

Figure 3.5 A systems model of the employee as a sub-system, and human resources management processes affecting the individual employee

by employees. This topic is discussed at length in Paragraph 3.6.3.2.
- In the second place, it focuses on those human resources management processes aimed at the management, maintenance, and development of an employee as a sub-system within an organisation. The purpose of these human resources management processes is to obtain optimal utilisation of the employee, as well as optimal outputs. There is a detailed discussion of this topic in Paragraph 3.6.3.3. This also provides the reader with a frame of reference when studying the information in this book.

3.6.3.2 The employee as a sub-system within the organisation

The individual employee is the smallest system within the organisation as a system. As can be deduced from the systems approach to organisations, there is a critical relationship between inputs, outputs, and throughputs in the organisation. As is the case with an organisation, individuals as a system also have certain inputs with which they join an organisation and which they release as long as they are part of the organisation.

These inputs are released mainly during the throughput phase where they are utilised and transformed by general and human resources management processes. The quality of application of these processes determines the individual employee's outputs. These phenomena will become clearer during the course of this discussion.

The input process of individual employee functioning within the organisation is discussed at length in Chapter 2, but a few clarifying remarks are deemed necessary here.
- Each employee has a unique personality, and employees' personalities differ from one another. These differences mean that employees are not the same and do not necessarily experience the same needs at the same times. An employee's personality is the result of numerous variables which have affected him or her since birth. These variables include aspects such as the personal environment in which the child grew up, the culture to which it was exposed, and its needs which, in turn, are the result of numerous other factors.
- Individuals' personality and needs constitute the basis of their expectations of their job and of life in general. Because individuals have different personalities they also have different expectations in life. This may be observed in the way in which individuals pursue their personal goals in an organisation.
- Individuals set certain personal goals they wish to achieve in life, on the basis of their unique personalities, needs, and expectations. To satisfy these needs and expectations, and to achieve these goals, individuals have to work and earn money. Therefore, individuals join organisations with the sole purpose of achieving their personal goals, as this results in need satisfaction. Individuals' personal goals, in turn, motivate them to behave in certain ways in the organisation. This behaviour is personal and is aimed at satisfying individuals' own needs and goals, irrespective of the group with which they identify. Therefore, individuals continuously interact with the organisation where they are employed in order to achieve their personal goals.
- Before an individual joins an organisation, a psychological negotiation process takes place, which takes the form of a psychological contract between the individual and the organisation. During this negotiation process, the individual states his or her expectations and personal goals, and the organisation similarly

states its expectations and goals. If this negotiation process results in an agreement, the individual is employed and joins the organisation as an employee.

An employee's personal goals, together with his or her aptitude, qualifications, ability, experience, and potential, constitute the input process of individual functioning within the context of the organisation. This input phase is indicated on the left-hand side of the model in Figure 3.5.

In terms of the throughput process of individual employee functioning within the organisation, we may say that individuals with unique personalities join organisations with certain expectations, and formulate personal goals on the basis of a negotiation process resulting in a psychological contract. They try to achieve their personal goals while also pursuing the goals of the organisation.

There are three environments that exert an influence on employee functioning within the organisation. These environments are the job content environment, the job context environment, and the external environment.

(a) The job content environment

The job content environment may also be referred to as the psychological work environment, and may thus be regarded as the most significant environment in terms of its relation to individual performance as the basic cornerstone of success in the organisation. The job content environment is related to the psychological satisfaction experienced by the employee while doing the job for which he or she applied and was appointed. This is related to the cognitive, affective, and conative functions of people. The cognitive function refers to the stimulus value of the job, that is the extent to which it creates interest. The affective function refers to the emotional aspect, the employee's feeling/attitude/inclination towards the job as such. The conative function refers to the volitional aspect of people. It, therefore, seems that the job content environment refers to personal job satisfaction.

Different authors use different terms for these concepts; however, what is important is that they concur to a large extent on the elements present in the job content environment, which exert an influence on the employee's inclination to perform.

One definition that may be closely related to what we term the job content environment, concerns Herzberg's so-called motivators.

Herzberg found that factors relating to the job itself can have a positive effect on job satisfaction and result in increased output. He called these motivators or satisfiers, and identified them as the work itself, recognition, advancement, the possibility of growth, responsibility, and achievement.

Ford (1969: 124) emphasises job characteristics rather than individual differences: jobs with opportunities for achievement, recognition, responsibility, promotion and growth in competence are jobs that will promote motivation and job satisfaction. Turner et al. (in Wanous 1974: 616) identify six attributes that jobs need to have (job content environment) namely: variety, autonomy, compulsory and optional interaction, required knowledge and skills, and responsibility.

In view of the aforementioned, an employee's job content environment consists of five important elements, i.e. the nature of the job, job guidelines and goals, utilisation, status and recognition, and development. These elements are now briefly discussed.

- *Nature of the job.* The nature of the job means what the job entails. Does it afford the employee the opportunity to utilise his or her abilities to their full potential? Does the employee find the opportunity for self-actualisation in the job? Does he or she have the opportunity to be creative and use initiative? Is the job interesting and in line with what he or she wants to do? Is there the opportunity for independent decision making? Does the job offer variety? The human resources management processes discussed in Paragraph 3.6.3.3 must address these questions if the organisation is to ensure motivated employee behaviour.

- *Job guidelines and goals.* This element entails directing an employee's work behaviour in accordance with the goals of the organisation. An important element often neglected is linking job goals to the goals of the organisation. Human resources management processes related to the job content environment need to answer the following questions: Do employees know what they have to do? Do they know how to do it? Do they know why they are doing it? Is there a logical relation between what employees do and the goals of the organisation? Do employees know what is expected of them? Do they know what they are accountable for and what standards they are to maintain? Job guidelines and goals not only enable the employee to assess his or her activities within the functioning of the organisation, but they also spell out how he or she should attempt to achieve personal goals.
- *Utilisation.* Vroom (1996: 143) states that the self-actualisation need is represented by the opportunity people are given to utilise their capabilities. We distinguish between qualitative and quantitative utilisation, however. Quantitative utilisation refers to the amount of time an employee actually spends on the job daily, whereas qualitative utilisation refers to the utilisation of an employee's potential such as intelligence, skills, and qualifications. Over- and under-utilisation may occur in both instances. Questions to be addressed in this respect in order to ensure optimal employee functioning are: Are employees busy every day, all day? Is the extent of an employee's job such that he or she can cope with what has to be done? Are employees utilised according to their abilities, qualifications, experience and training?
- *Status and recognition.* There is a causal relation between the type of job an employee has and the status enjoyed. Vroom (1996: 141) describes it as follows:

The job is a description or a tag which marks the person, both at his place of employment and in the world outside.

Status in this respect refers to the job content status, which means the relative status value linked to the job within a specific organisation by the organisation itself and by other employees of the organisation. Recognition in this respect comes from two sources. Firstly, it refers to the respect an employee enjoys among colleagues in the organisation, which is the result of the status value of the job; and secondly, it is the recognition the organisation affords an employee for good performance. The most critical question to be addressed by human resources management processes in this respect, is whether employees are proud of their jobs, as this is the best indication of the status and recognition they themselves give to the job.
- *Development.* Modern work life is characterised by technological and other changes placing increasing demands and pressure on employees. When employees are unable to meet changed job expectations or requirements, they become superfluous and redundant. In this respect, development refers to

development possibilities within a job or position for a specific employee, with reference to the employee's personal growth and personal goals. In our opinion, development has a number of dimensions applicable to any work situation within any organisation. Human resources management processes must assess the opportunities for training and development, whether the training offered is applicable to the execution of tasks and whether the work an employee is doing at present is preparing him or her for a higher position, i.e. whether there is career preparation.

Individual employee performance is the cornerstone of success in an organisation and takes place mainly in carrying out tasks given by the organisation. The extent to which employees experience psychological or personal job satisfaction within the job content environment determines to a large extent the quality and quantity of these employees' outputs.

(b) The job context environment

The second environment that has an extremely important influence on the throughput process is the employee's job context environment. This environment contains two important factors:
- The leadership element in the job context environment consists of the employee's superiors, and the management cadre within the organisation. The leadership element determines numerous aspects of the job content, for example the nature of the job. Therefore, the leadership element has a significant effect on the employee's job content environment.
- Those elements that Herzberg terms the hygiene factors (discussed in detail in Chapter 14) are primarily satisfiers of lower-order needs that include physiological, safety, and social needs.

According to Herzberg, examples of hygiene factors are salaries, promotion policy, and fringe benefits. These hygiene factors are an essential prerequisite for motivation to pursue the goals of the organisation, mainly because they are related to job content factors that can only come into prominence once job context aspects are such that lower-order needs are reasonably satisfied, so that the employee will look for the opportunity to satisfy his or her higher-order needs within the job.

We regard all the influences exerted on an employee (with the exception of the job content and external influences) because of his or her presence in the organisation, as job context influences affecting the employee in the job context environment. Porter et al. (1975: 211) emphasise the significance of these influences on individual employee behaviour as follows:

> Among the many influences on the work behavior of individuals in organizational settings, none is more important or more pervasive than the design of the organization itself. By "organization design" we mean primarily the particular arrangements of the structural factors that constitute the basic form and nature of the organisation.

In our opinion, the job context environment refers to the interpersonal as well as the intra-group job satisfaction individual employees experience because of their membership of an organisation. An employee derives interpersonal job satisfaction through interaction with peers, superiors, subordinates, and clients in the execution of the job. Schein (1980: 88) calls this an employee's interaction context. In other words, interpersonal job satisfaction refers to satisfaction experienced by an employee within the context of the formal organisation, i.e. within the formal execution of his or her tasks.

Intra-group satisfaction refers to the satisfaction an employee experiences through membership of informal groups.

Because humans are social beings, they will always try to establish informal interaction. Within the context of Maslow's theory, people are social beings and need to belong to groups and to be accepted by those groups. When a social need becomes dominant, a person will strive to establish favourable relationships with other persons. The need for social interaction may be satisfied in the work situation to a large extent, but it is very difficult to develop strategies that would translate this need into an incentive for improved performance.

We regard the following elements, that can have either a positive or a negative effect on the individual employee's functioning and his or her inclination to perform, as important within the job context environment: organisational culture, organisational climate, management philosophy, leadership style, structure and personnel policy, working conditions, and interpersonal and group relations.

- *Organisational culture.* We define the concept of organisational culture simply as 'the manner in which things are done in the organisation'. It is also known as the personality of the organisation. Irrespective of what it is called, the culture of an organisation develops over time and employees are often not even aware of its existence.
Organisational culture is, however, of particular importance to management because it helps them understand how employees feel about their work.
Culture involves general assumptions about the manner in which work should be done, appropriate goals for the organisation as a whole and for departments within the organisation, and personal goals for employees. It is particularly the latter that makes the nature of the psychological contract (discussed in Chapter 2) of special importance in the pursuit of organisational success.
- *Organisational climate.* In our opinion, organisational climate is an all-encompassing concept that could be regarded as the result of all the elements contained in the job context environment. For example, the climate within a specific organisation is the result of the management philosophy of that organisation as shown in the style of management practised in the organisation. In this respect, human resources management processes should be directed at monitoring the outputs of the organisation, such as labour turnover, absenteeism, grievances, complaints, and productivity, as there is a correlation between these variables and organisational climate.
- *Management philosophy.* The origin of management philosophy lies in the assumptions people make in respect of others, and the way in which they perceive and interact with others. Irrespective of whether they are aware of it or not, people's social behaviour is based on the way in which they believe other people behave. Managers, as human beings, do not differ from other human beings. All managers direct their behaviour and actions according to the way they believe others (employees) behave. Human resources management processes must use management and organisational development to determine the prevailing management philosophy and its effect on the work behaviour of the worker corps, and to change this philosophy if necessary.
- *Leadership style.* In our opinion, leadership style is the way in which management philosophy manifests itself in prac-

tice. The important relationship between leadership style and employee outputs should be emphasised. There is no doubt that managerial leadership and supervision have an important impact on the motivation, commitment, adaptability, and satisfaction of employees. The human resources manager must ensure that the leadership of the management cadre in the work situation is sound, as leadership behaviour has a significant effect on the functioning of individual employees.

- *Structures and personnel policy.* It is generally accepted that the structures of an organisation are related to the management style of its management cadre. Mintzberg (1992: 24) states that the structures of an organisation may be defined as the sum total of the way in which its labour is divided into specified tasks, and the degree of coordination achieved between these tasks. Gibson et al. (1976: 38) emphasise the importance of culture to organisational behaviour. They state that the purpose of management is to bring about an effective organisation. There are various examples of the way in which management may use structures in order to achieve desirable results. For example, management may design compensation systems, especially bonus systems, to promote performance and goal achievement; or they may implement job specialisation to promote closer supervision to counteract deviations from instructions. It is clear that all these aspects are related to human resources management processes. Personnel policy is a result of human resources management as a sub-system within an organisation. Therefore, personnel policy has a direct influence on employee functioning. Examples of this influence are: the effects of the compensation policy of the organisation, its promotion policy, and its labour relations policy on the individual employee. Numerous human resources management processes use these means to retain employees.
- *Working conditions.* Working conditions are created by the interaction of employees with their physical work environment. It is that environment which impacts on employees' senses and which is related to their lower order needs, which in turn affect their physiological functioning. Various sub-elements of working conditions should be distinguished.
  - The first sub-element is the physical working conditions. This aspect refers to the amount of work and the availability of facilities, such as production machinery and protective clothing, and to aspects of the physical environment in which the employee works, such as ventilation, lighting and space. There are, thus, two important considerations in the physical work environment, i.e. aids and the physical work environment per se. Aids refer to the equipment and appliances at the employee's disposal for the execution of a task, irrespective of its nature. What is important is the extent to which these aids enable employees to function effectively. The physical work environment per se refers to the attractiveness of the work environment - the aesthetic element and other aspects involved in the physical execution of tasks.
  - The second sub-element is the psychological working conditions. According to our view, this refers to the psychological effect of work pressure on individuals and groups. Psychological working conditions also include the psychological expectations of employees as to the psychological contract in respect of their working conditions, compared to what they actually experience.

– The last sub-element is the physical layout of the job, which refers to the neatness, organisation, convenience, attractiveness, and stimulus value of an employee's personal micro work environment. This affects the employee's physical interaction with these work aids, and this interaction affects physical and sensory functions.

It seems clear, therefore, that human resources management processes are faced with a number of problems which may affect employee functioning within the job context environment.

- Interpersonal and group relations. In our opinion interpersonal and group relations are a subsection of working conditions and, more specifically, social working conditions. Interpersonal relations can be defined as the whole range of human conduct between individuals who interact as they are involved in relationships of communicating, cooperating, changing, problem solving, and motivation. In these relationships, each employee tries to influence and adapt the behaviour of other employees in order to satisfy his or her own needs. Therefore, we should take a brief look at the role of the individual employee within the group context.

An organisation depends on groups for the achievement of its goals, therefore it is organised accordingly. Continuous interaction is a characteristic of groups within an organisation. The ideal state for each group is one of harmonious cooperation in order to achieve the goals of the organisation. In practice, however, groups are continuously in a state of conflict, mainly because they are often competing with one another. If this competition does not coincide with or follow the direction of the goals of the organisation, it will adversely affect the organisation. Competition should be in line with the goals of the organisation, and this means that group objectives need to be associated with these goals, bearing in mind that groups, as sub-systems of the organisation, have their own goals. In addition to the formal groups and the reasons they compete on a formal basis, there are informal groups within an organisation and these probably have the strongest influence on formal groups. Informal group formation determines group functioning and sets informal group goals which may either help or hinder the achievement of the goals of the organisation. Interpersonal and group relations present a great challenge for human resources management because of their effect on the functioning of an organisation.

To summarise, individual motivation and, therefore, individual performance, is either positively or negatively affected by the individual's job context environment. The philosophy of the management cadre or the leadership element determines to a large extent the nature and content of the influencing process within the job context. The leadership style of the management cadre in an organisation is a primary factor influencing employee functioning and performance. Structure and policies within an organisation must be such that they will not only promote the achievement goals of the organisation, but enhance the achievement of individual goals within the framework of the psychological contract. Physical, psychological, and social working conditions are important in any organisation. In this book we regard these conditions as even more important than is generally maintained among theorists. The quality of interpersonal and group relationships is equally important in view of the significant effect this has on the achievement of employee goals and the goals of the organisation.

However beneficial individual employees' job content environment may be to individual performances, influences from the job context environment, together with the external environment, are jointly responsible for their motivation and performance. The last environment in the throughput process of human resources management is the individual employee's external environment.

(c) The external environment

We shall discuss the external environment exerting an influence on individual employee functioning in broad terms only. The term external environment refers to areas outside the organisation that affect employees via the organisation, as well as areas within the organisation that affect individual employees. We refer specifically to the effect of labour demand and supply on an employee's period of service with a particular organisation. For example, an employee may be unhappy with his or her job content and job context environments in an organisation, but is forced to stay with that organisation because of labour market conditions. Such an employee will probably do just enough work not to be dismissed. In this respect, the economic conditions of South African organisations and the entire country are very relevant, as well as the effects of these conditions on individual employees. For example, the state of the economy has a direct effect on employees' compensation packages. Furthermore, technological change plays an important part. Owing to the lack of skilled employees in the Republic, organisations are sometimes forced to mechanise and this often leads to unemployment. These factors have an indirect effect on employees' performance inclinations.

Figure 3.5 indicates the three environments, i.e. an employee's job content environment, job context environment and external environment, as illustrated on the left-hand side of the model. The dotted line indicates the psychological contract, with specific reference to the extent to which an employee progresses towards the achievement of personal goals. The solid line at the top of the model is also related to the process of comparison mentioned above, with specific reference to the opportunity an employee perceives in an organisation to achieve personal goals while, at the same time, pursuing the goals of the organisation. If the opportunity is provided, the employee will integrate personal goals with the goals of the organisation, which will serve as a foundation for motivated employee behaviour. (This topic is dealt with at length in Chapter 16.) The extent to which personal goals coincide with the goals of the organisation determines the employee's inclination to perform. This inclination has a direct bearing on the employee's real outputs in terms of efficiency and effectiveness, which ultimately determine the success of the employee.

Attention will now be paid to those human resources management processes which may have a positive or negative effect on the employee's functioning within the three environments, and which are representative of the layout of this book.

3.6.3.3 Human resources management processes directed at employee functioning within the organisation

The input, throughput and output processes of an employee as a subsystem within an organisation have been discussed on the basis of a systems model of employee functioning. The next section will focus on those human resources management processes directed at improving individual employee functioning. This discussion will follow the systems approach towards human resources management, with reference to Figure 3.5.

(a) Human resources management input processes

An employee joins an organisation with certain inputs. A number of management processes may be classified as human resources management input processes, as they are directed at ensuring that the right employee holds the right job at the right time in order to contribute towards the functioning of the organisation by means of the throughput process. Figure 3.5 illustrates that these processes are related to ensuring that the right quality and quantity of employee inputs are released within the job context environment. These human resources management input processes are human resources planning, recruitment, selection, placement and induction, technology, training, and intrinsic motivation:

- *Human resources planning.* The human resources planning process is discussed in detail in Chapter 9. An organisation must conduct human resources planning according to the nature and composition of the labour market, and according to the needs of the organisation itself. Human resources planning is, therefore, aimed at obtaining the required human resources of the desired calibre.
- *Recruitment.* Recruitment (which is discussed in Chapter 9) as a human resources management input process, is aimed at providing a pool of potential employees from which the organisation can select the required number in accordance with job requirements.
- *Selection.* According to the systems approach, all sub-systems within a system are equally important. Selection plays an important part in providing suitable employees who have the aptitude, abilities, experience, etc., to meet the requirements of the job and of the organisation. This ensures that the right employee inputs are obtained. Selection is discussed in detail in Chapter 10.
- *Induction and staffing.* This ensures that new employees are appointed to positions which correspond with their abilities, whereas induction ensures that they will adapt to their new work environment as soon as possible. This will enable them to become productive without unnecessary delay. These topics are discussed in Chapter 11.
- *Training.* This human resources management input process is discussed in Chapters 19 and 20. Training is more applicable to an employee's job content environment. As a human resources management process it provides an employee with the opportunity to extend and improve skills in order to be more productive during the throughput process.
- *Intrinsic motivation.* An employee's will to perform stems mainly from the job. In other words, this stimulation comes from the job content environment. Motivation, which is discussed in detail in Chapter 14, also comes from the employee's job context environment, and this is termed extrinsic motivation. However, an employee's general motivation is extremely important with regard to the achievement of the goals of the organisation.

In our opinion, the effective implementation and application of these human resources management processes will ensure the optimal utilisation of the inputs with which employees join an organisation during the throughput phase of employee functioning.

(b) Human resources management throughput processes

The human resources management throughput processes are related to an employee's functioning in his or her job context environment. This entails numerous processes. The main purpose of these processes is to maintain the human resources of the organisation during the throughput phase of employee functioning.

- *Development* (discussed in detail in Chapter 19). This human resources management throughput process is aimed at preparing employees for further career development and progress.
- *Career development* (Chapter 20). Career development as a human resources management process has a significant effect on an employee's duration of service with an organisation.
- *Extrinsic motivation* (Chapter 14). Extrinsic motivation refers to motivational factors affecting the employee from the work environment outside the job content environment. This includes factors such as working conditions, leadership, and compensation.
- *Leadership* (Chapter 15). Although it is impossible to say which human resources management process has the most profound effect on employee functioning during the throughput phase, leadership is certainly one of the most important influencing factors.
- *Employment relations* (Chapters 5 and 6). The effect of current relationships between management and the labour force causes problems in many an organisation. Employment relations are becoming increasingly important, not only for human resources management, but for the management of the entire organisation. Employment relations are discussed in this book in view of the relevance and importance of the subject. We discuss employment relations from a human resources management point of view.
- *Employment equity and affirmative action* (Chapter 7). This is critical in South Africa today, and must be observed to comply with fair labour practice.
- *Performance appraisal* (Chapter 21). The importance of performance appraisal as a human resources management process in the throughput phase cannot be overemphasised. It is essential to the psychological contract that performance appraisal provides employees with formal feedback on their functioning within the job content and job context environments.
- *Compensation management* (Chapter 12). Theorists do not concur on the effect of compensation on employee attitudes. Our opinion is that it plays an extremely important part in employees' inclination to perform, as well as in their actual performance during the throughput phase.
- *Employee benefits and services* (Chapter 12). The benefits and services employees enjoy on the basis of their membership of an organisation are related to compensation administration.
- *Health and safety* (Chapter 13). Employee health and safety within the context of the organisation tie in with quality of work life and social responsibility. The importance of this human resources management throughput process is illustrated by the fact that organisations are forced by legislation to pay attention to health and safety.

An aspect that is as important as the management of an employee's input and throughput processes within the job content environment, is the positive influence of human resources management throughput processes on functioning within the job context environment. Every single human resources management process makes a positive contribution towards employee functioning, if it is effectively implemented.

(c) The effect of the external environment on employee functioning

Although the external environment falls outside the job context, it has an indirect and a direct effect on employee functioning within the organisation. For example, the state of a country's economy affects labour demand and supply: an oversupply of labour often forces employees to stay with an organisation even if the job content environment and the job context environment are not suited to their needs and preferences. Cultural diversity and organisational renewal (see Chapters 17 and 22) also play an important role in this regard.

(d) The management of the output process of employee functioning

As stated in Paragraph 3.6.3.2, the extent to which employees progress towards the achievement of personal goals due to the impact of human resources management processes, determines their will to perform. This, in turn, determines employees' outputs.

3.6.4 Human resources management and the success of the organisation

3.6.4.1 General

The success of an organisation means the extent to which it succeeds in achieving its organisational goals, as measured against set standards of achievement. According to the systems approach to organisations, organisations have multiple goals. To be successful, they must therefore work towards the optimal achievement of multiple goals.

3.6.4.2 Multiple goals in an organisation

The goals of an organisation are usually divided into three broad categories: long-, medium-, and short-term goals.
- *Long-term goals* focus on the organisation's ability to adapt to changes in the economic situation, technological development, social responsibilities, statutory and political responsibilities, human resources requirements, etc.
- *Short-term goals* are set, measurable goals with regard to production (for example, returns, sales, and market share); efficiency (for example, labour costs, unit costs, refuse, and waste); and employee satisfaction (for example, morale, attitudes, labour turnover, absenteeism, fatigue, and grievances).
- *Medium-term goals* are formulated to fill the gap between set long- and short-term goals; for example, to increase market share by 30 per cent over a period of three years, at a rate of 10 per cent per annum.

A question that might arise is how this relates to the study of human resources management. The relation between human resources management and the success of an organisation is now discussed in detail.

3.6.4.3 The cornerstones of organisational success

The success of an organisation is based on two cornerstones: efficiency and effectiveness. This is illustrated in Figure 3.6.

As may be seen from Figure 3.6, the success of an organisation is the result of its efficiency and effectiveness.

In simple terms, the efficiency of an organisation means doing things the right way and is closely related to ratios. Examples of ratios are the input-output ratios of individual employees, sections, and departments, in other words, the cost-effectiveness ratios in the production process and other processes within the organisation. The efficiency of an organisation also refers to the nature and quality of the interpersonal, inter-group, and intra-group relationships within the organisation. Beer (1980:29) defines organisational efficiency as follows:

Figure 3.6 The relation between efficiency and effectiveness and the success of an organisation

[Organisational efficiency] may be defined as the extent of fit between the internal components of the social system. The more congruity exists between these components the more the organisation will function smoothly, with relatively little dissatisfaction on the part of organisation members.

The definition of Beer (as adapted by the authors of this book) has many implications; among other things, it requires thorough internal management of the organisation.

Effectiveness means doing the right things, which is primarily determined by setting goals for the organisation. These goals are not set in isolation, but are directly linked to the demand for an organisation's product or service. A study of this demand must also be based on the systems approach with particular attention to the background of the organisation's suprasystem. Only thorough identification and analysis of the needs of groups interested in the organisation will enable top management to interpret the demand correctly, and formulate goals for the organisation accordingly.

Beer (1980:39) has the following view with regard to organisational effectiveness:

Effectiveness may be defined as the extent of fit between the organization's environment and all the internal components of the social system. The more congruity exists between the internal social system components and the environment, the more the organization is likely to exchange favorably with its environment.

Beer (1980:40) places organisational success in perspective, as follows (adapted by the current authors):

Organisational health (success) may be defined as the capacity of an organisation to engage in ongoing self-examination aimed at identifying incongruities between social systems components and developing plans for needed change in strategy (environment), structure, process, people, culture and the dominant coalition. Such a healthy organisation is likely to maintain organisational efficiency and effectiveness in the long term.

If organisational managers carry out the tasks assigned to them in an effective manner, and set aside organisational politics, they should be able to transform their organisations in the interests of their employees and shareholders, and to the benefit of South Africa.

However, these goals (and therefore the success of the organisation) cannot be

> Management in South Africa is rated 33rd out of 59 countries by the WCR (1999).
>
> Labour/employee relations are rated 59th out of 59 countries.

achieved of their own accord. Goals cannot be achieved without the necessary resources. Resources such as capital, raw materials, and machinery are static and can only take on a dynamic character through the intervention of labour resources (i.e. human resources). For this reason there is a causal relationship between the success of an organisation and the utilisation of its resources, in particular human resources, which activate the other resources. Therefore it seems essential that human resources management be studied from a management point of view, especially in the light of the purpose of human resources management, namely to provide the organisation with a more efficient and effective worker corps. Every organisation's worker corps consists of individual workers, groups, and management. In this respect, the task of human resources management may be defined as follows:

> Human resources management implies the proactive creation, maintenance and development of individual and group efficiency and effectiveness in order to improve individual and group performance (output).

Figure 3.7 The relation between the success of the organisation and individual and group performance

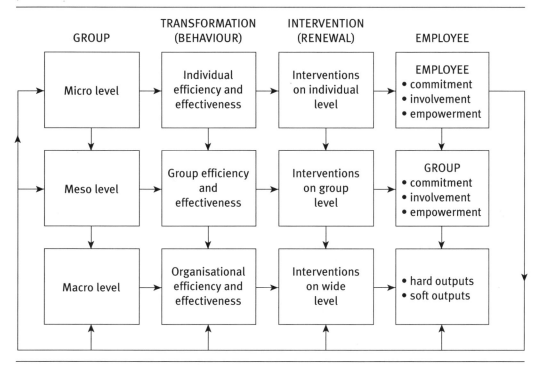

The integration of this with the concept of the success of the organisation is illustrated in Figure 3.7.

Figure 3.7 clearly shows that organisational success is the result of interaction between a number of variables. As mentioned, an organisation cannot be successful unless it accurately identifies the demand for the product or service within its external environment (effectiveness of the organisation). An organisation may accurately identify and define the demand for its product or service, and yet not be successful if it does not 'do things in the right way' (efficiency). This is illustrated in the following example.

Suppose the management of an organisation determined, on the basis of their strategic planning and market research, that there was a great demand for a less expensive version of a popular bicycle for children, and decided to produce it. They supplied according to demand, and sales forecasts were topped within a short period. Within the course of a few months, the organisation's management learnt from the media and through complaints from their outlets that their version of the bicycle had been responsible for many injuries among children using it. A thorough internal investigation found that the strength of the metal used for the bicycle was in accordance with the predetermined standards, but that the quality maintained during the assembly process was poor. As a result of these incidents the demand for this particular bicycle dropped sharply, and the organisation also became less successful with regard to the other products they marketed. On further investigation it was found that, for various reasons, the motivation of production personnel was very low, which resulted in a negative attitude towards their work and the organisation and its goals. In other words, although the management of the organisation was doing 'the right thing', they were not doing it 'in the right way'.

This example may also be approached from the point of view of the effectiveness of the organisation. Suppose the demand for that particular bicycle had indeed been identified, but the price was set so high that the greatest portion of the market (parents) could not afford it despite the fact that it was an example of exceptionally fine workmanship. In this case, the organisation would not have been successful either, as they were not 'doing the right thing' even though they were 'doing it in the right way'.

Figure 3.7 also shows that the efficiency of the organisation depends on group performance. Organisations consist of groups of employees, and employees are grouped on the basis of joint activities at work. For this reason organisations have different departments such as production, marketing and personnel, based on a functional approach. This implies that groups (whether departments, divisions, sections or plants) produce the organisation's product or render its service according to the demand as identified with a view to the effectiveness of the organisation. Group performance, however, is the result of group efficiency and effectiveness. Group effectiveness refers to the extent to which groups 'do the right things'. Here, the extent to which the formal activities of groups coincide with the goals pursued by the organisation is relevant (from the point of view of the effectiveness of the organisation). In other words, are they doing the right things in terms of the goals set for them by the management of the organisation?

Group efficiency refers to the extent to which groups carry out their tasks in the right way (i.e. in the most cost-effective way). This includes the quality and quantity of work produced.

The next point to be dealt with is the relationship between individual performance and the success of the organisation.

Figure 3.8 illustrates that individual performance (which is the result of individual efficiency and individual effectiveness) is the cornerstone of the success of an organisation. Therefore, the main responsibility of human resources management lies in this area. One might ask how human resources management is involved here.

> Human resources management is mainly concerned with establishing, maintaining and improving individual performance, as individual performance is the key to the success of an organisation.

Figure 3.8 also illustrates a number of different aspects of the efficiency of an organisation and its success. It also indicates that individual performance is the result of the interaction between an unlimited number of the elements of both individual effectiveness and individual efficiency. From this point of view, individual performance may be regarded as the cornerstone of the efficiency of an organisation and its success.

3.7 Conclusion

The above clearly shows that human resources management has an important role to play in establishing more successful organisations. Ensuring excellent individual performance largely depends on the application of sound human resources management principles. Furthermore, it is obvious that human resources management should be regarded as a scientific process to be implemented in full, and that every effort should be made to avoid focusing on only certain aspects of the

Figure 3.8 The relation between individual performance and group efficiency

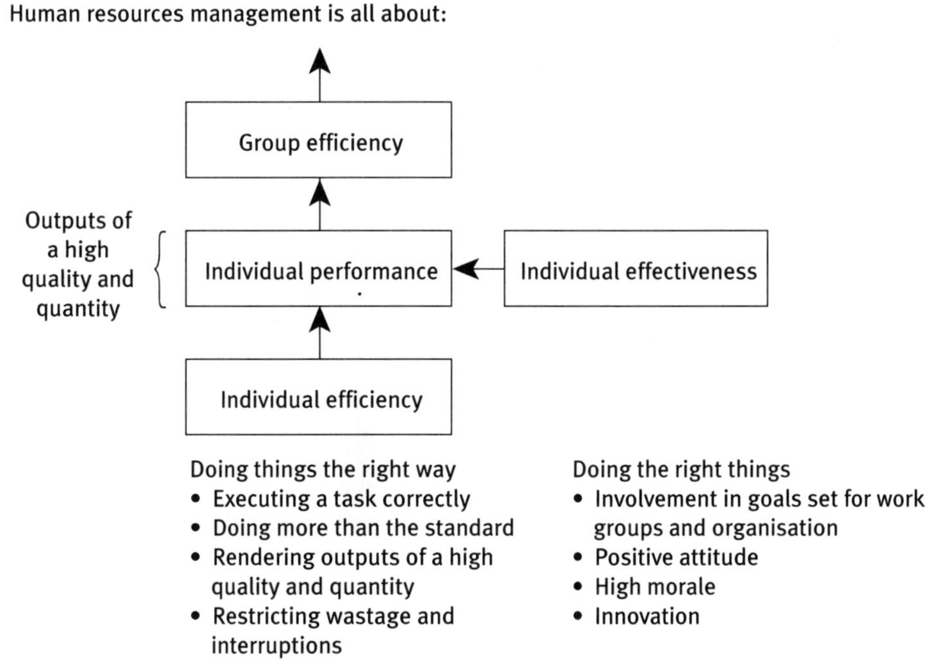

Human resources management is all about:

```
                    Group efficiency
                          ↑
Outputs of
a high        { Individual performance ← Individual effectiveness
quality and
quantity                  ↑
                  Individual efficiency
```

Doing things the right way
- Executing a task correctly
- Doing more than the standard
- Rendering outputs of a high quality and quantity
- Restricting wastage and interruptions

Doing the right things
- Involvement in goals set for work groups and organisation
- Positive attitude
- High morale
- Innovation

process. In other words, it requires a holistic approach.

This chapter is aimed at giving an overall idea of the systems approach to human resources management. We have discussed the systems approach as such, the characteristics of the systems approach, and the organisation as a system. To promote understanding, a systems model of employee functioning has been developed and discussed, and we have dealt with the employee's environments during the input, throughput and output processes. Problems affecting employee functioning within the job content environment, the job context environment and the external environment, were dealt with in broad terms. Human resources management processes influencing the employee within these environments were listed and placed within the model as a frame of reference to facilitate the study of this book.

Case study
The unorganised 'successful' company

Mabeni was a professional geologist. Whilst on holiday in Northern Natal he decided to pack a rucksack and spend some time under African skies. The second morning, while he was watching birds, he stumbled over a partially covered rock and fell. When he got up he saw some blood on another small rock. Looking at the rock, he noticed something strange. 'This is not a normal rock,' he said to himself, and took his archaeologist's hammer and chipped off a piece which he put in his pocket.

When Mabeni returned to his office the following Monday morning, he presented the piece of rock to a colleague who was a specialist in the natural resources of the Northern Natal/Eastern Mpumalanga area. Jeff (his colleague) got very excited and went directly to his laboratory. At about noon the same day, he entered Mabeni's office without even announcing himself. 'Where did you find this small piece of rock?' he confronted Mabeni, with a smile of excitement on his face. 'In a valley to the east of Ermelo – near Piet Retief,' Mabeni answered. 'Well, my friend, I think you have hit the jackpot, because I have never seen a piece of rock, in my entire professional career, which is so rich in minerals.'

Mabeni requested Jeff to keep the discovery a secret between them, and they arranged to meet that evening at Mabeni's house. They decided at the meeting that they should go back to the place where the rock was found and conduct more in-depth research. They submitted the research evidence to the Mineral Control Board, who commented on the high quality thereof. Then they approached a bank with a business proposal.

One year later, they both resigned, purchased the land where the rock was found, and started an open mine to exploit the mineral riches. Money flowed during the first year of operations, and their first financial report showed a nett profit which they never could have envisaged.

At the end of their second year of operations, the financial statements were OK, but could not be compared to the first year's report. They were then at a depth of approximately five metres. The results of the third year report were a warning to them. They had barely broken even and stood to loose money. At that stage, the same production process was still used, but the workforce had increased to 1 500 labourers, twenty heavy machine operators, and sixty 10-ton truck drivers, all employed to excavate the coal and transport it to coal dumps 10 km away from the plant, where it was sold to industry in 10 000-ton units. They then realised that, although they had professional mining skills, they were not doing the job in the right way.

You are approached by them, as a human resources consultant, and asked if you can help. 'Something is wrong and we just cannot pin-point it,' they say. You accept the challenge.

Questions

1 What would the outline of your research proposal be?
2 What would your findings be?
3 What would your recommendations be?

Chapter questions

1 List and discuss the characteristics of a system.
2 In about 500 words, give a practical explanation of the organisation as a system.
3 Critically discuss the input process of individual employee functioning within an organisation.
4 Which variables influence the employee in the throughput process? Critically discuss these variables.
5 Distinguish between the three environments in which the employee functions within an organisation. Discuss the influence of each environment on the employee's functioning.
6 What is the connection between management philosophy and leadership style?
7 Differentiate between long-, medium-, and short-term goals of an organisation.
8 Illustrate graphically the cornerstones of organisational success, and explain them briefly in practical terms.
9 Illustrate, and briefly explain, the relation between individual performance and group efficiency.

Bibliography

BACKER, W. 1979. *'n Kritiese evaluering van die motiveringshigiëneteorie van Herzberg.* TIMS, Pretoria.

BEER, M. 1980. *Organization change and development: a systems view.* Goodyear, Santa Monica, California.

CRONJE, G.J. DE J., NEULAND, E.W., HUGO, W.M.J. & VAN REENEN, M.J. (eds). 1999. *Introduction to management* (3rd ed.). International Thompson Publishing.

FORD, R.N. 1969. *Motivation through the work itself.* American Management Association, New York.

GIBSON, J.L., IVANCEVICH, J.M. & DONNELLY, J.H. 1976. *Organizations: behavior, structure, processes.* Business Publications, Dallas, Texas.

HODGETTS, R.M. 1979. *Management, theory, process and practice.* Saunders, Philadelphia.

HUSE, E.F. & BOWDITCH, J.L. 1977. *Behavior in organizations: a systems approach to managing.* Addison-Wesley, Boston, Massachusetts.

KATZ, D. & KAHN, R. 1966. *The social psychology of organizations.* Wiley, New York.

MILTON, C.R. 1981. *Human behavior in organizations: three levels of behavior.* Prentice-Hall, Englewood Cliffs, New Jersey.

MINTZBERG, H. 1992. *Structures in fives: designing effective organizations.* Prentice-Hall, Englewood Cliffs, New Jersey.

PORTER, W.W., LAWLER, E.E. & HACKMAN, J.R. 1975. *Behavior in organizations.* McGraw-Hill, New York.

SCHEIN, E.H. 1980. *Organizational psycho-*

logy. Prentice-Hall, Englewood Cliffs, New Jersey.

VROOM, V.H. 1966. *Work and motivation.* Wiley, New York.

WANOUS, J.P. 1974. Individual differences and reactions to job characteristics. *Journal of Applied Psychology,* vol. 59, no. 5, pp.616–22.

4

The quality assurance approach to human resources management

P S van Dyk

Learning outcomes

At the end of this chapter the learner should be able to demonstrate the following outcomes:
- Differentiate by definition between a holistic approach to quality assurance and a process approach to quality assurance.
- Identify five reasons why the quality assurance approach to human resources management has become more prominent.
- Explain, using a diagram, what is understood by human resources management as a process.
- Explain the difference between the human resources department's role as an internal supplier of quality service and as an internal customer of other functional areas.
- Briefly discuss the relationship between the human resources department and the internal supply chain.
- Describe human resources quality service assurance.

Key words and concepts

- continuous improvement
- human resources as a process
- internal supply chain
- key performance areas (KPAs)
- key performance indicators (KPIs)
- process management
- quality assurance

Illustrative case

A number of retired people formed a business with the capital they received from their pensions. They started a small manufacturing plant which produced PVC water tanks for the water supply of households in the rural areas of the Northern Province.

Jack, because of his financial background, managed the business, while Toby, a retired engineer, took charge of the manufacturing process. Dick, who was previously employed by the Department of Trade and Industry, was responsible for marketing and sales.

The business grew slowly and they employed only labourers, for the manufacturing process. Due to Dick's contacts at the Department of Trade and Industry, they landed a government contract to produce several thousand water tanks for distribution to additional areas. This created chaos, and since none of them had any experience in human resources management, they offered Toby's son, John (who had just completed his BCom degree in human resources management) the opportunity of managing the expansion of the company. John, aware of the legislation in this regard, realised that the company had to be restructured in order to make provision for an effective human resources department. How would you go about restructuring the business to assure quality?

4.1 Introduction

The quality assurance approach to human resources management endeavours to empower every manager throughout the organisation in human resources management practices and procedures, so as to obtain more efficient and better solutions to potential personnel or labour problems.

The survival of the human resources management function depends on the ability of human resources managers to decentralise, to delegate specific responsibilities to operational managers, to create a symbiotic relationship between organisation and work culture, and to foster an internal supplier and internal customer relationship.

We discuss quality assurance as a concept, the quality assurance approach to human resources management, human resources management as a process in itself, the process approach to human resources management, and the definition of specific process management concepts.

4.2 Quality assurance

Quality assurance is the key concept for the new millennium. If an organisation is not at least on a par with its competitors in terms of the quality of the products or services that it provides, it will cease to exist in the very near future. In the past, the South African consumer was somewhat complacent, and accepted an end-product or service as it was received. However, over the past decade or two, South Africans have become increasingly quality-minded, and products or services of inferior quality have been rejected, at great loss to their producers and providers. With the Internet, South African products and services are now marketed and sold directly to customers and consumers globally. Quality assurance must become the modus operandi of businesses throughout

Although there are many definitions of quality assurance, the authors view quality assurance from both a holistic perspective and a process perspective and, therefore, describe quality assurance as a behavioural inclination of the organisation as a whole (organisational culture dimension) and individual employee behaviour (motivation) as part of any process or sub-process used to pursue quality in the products or services of the organisation.

South Africa if they want to survive and succeed.

From a human resources management perspective, this requires of employees at all levels:
- total commitment to the products or services of the company;
- loyalty towards such products or services and to the company itself; and
- attachment to the goals and objectives of the organisation (see Chapter 2, Paragraph 2.6).

This demands exceptional input from the human resources department in the motivation and empowerment of employees.

The quality assurance approach to human resources management has become more prominent due to the following reasons:

Figure 4.1 Human resources management: a process in itself

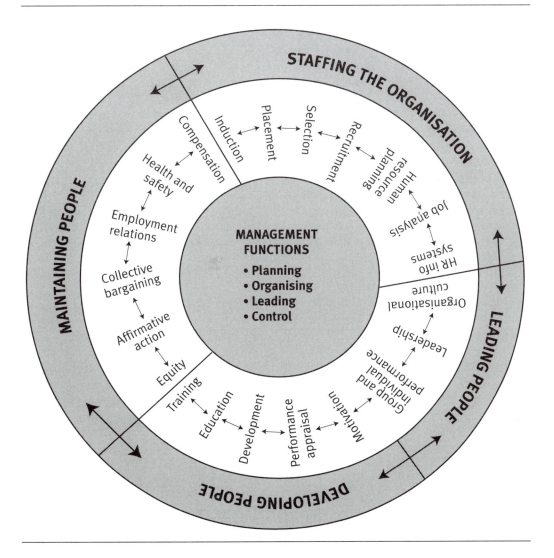

- the quality of products or services is a direct result of the quality of the human resources employed by an organisation;
- total quality management, of which quality assurance is the ultimate aim, requires different organisational structures and leadership styles to be successful;
- the accelerated pace of technological development requires organisations to adapt rapidly which, in turn, requires more flexible human resources policies;
- the changing nature of the workforce;
- the worldwide approach of providing line and other human resources managers with management practices and techniques, which empower them to respond more proactively to the challenges facing organisations with regard to their competitiveness position in the market place.

4.3 Human resources management as a process

4.3.1 General

The quality assurance approach to human resources management is not an approach on its own. It must be viewed as part of the evolution of human resources management. It cannot exist without a structure (the functional approach to human resources management). In the same way that finance, marketing, sales, etc., are all part of the organisation, so too is human resources management in terms of the quality assurance approach.

According to the definition provided earlier, an organisation is a system with inputs, throughputs and outputs. Based on this systems approach, this book has consistently adopted the efficiency and effectiveness approach to human resources management (in line with the views of leading experts in this field) according to which organisations pursue the best fit between the internal components of the system.

In the following sections, human resources management as a process in itself, as well as human resources management as a quality assurance intervention process, is discussed.

4.3.2 Human resources management: a process in itself

An interrelated chain of activities represents human resources management as a process. The efficiency and effectiveness with which these activities are carried out is indicative of the quality of the human resources of the organisation. The human resources management process is depicted in Figure 4.1.

The human resources department is responsible for delivering quality human resources potential to the various managers for deployment in work processes throughout the entire organisation.

An organisation is supposed to be designed, structurally and process-wise, to obtain the best fit between the various components present in every organisation i.e. people, structure, technology, process, policy, etc. Quality assurance begins with the effective design of jobs within the different processes that exist in the organisation. Underlying job design is job analysis, against which the requirements of the job and the personal qualities which an employee must possess (or have the potential to possess) are verified. If management fails to identify the job requirements accurately, including the necessary performance standards, and does not provide the human resources department with specific job and employee specifications, quality assurance throughout a potential employee's stay in the organisation is in jeopardy. To ensure quality, the human resources department can intervene by providing the necessary training to enable managers to develop accurate job descriptions and specifications, and to design jobs which achieve the best fit between the employee and his or her job environment. (Refer to Chapters 8 and 18).

Once the basics have been sorted out, the next step in assuring quality is to subject potential employees to valid and reliable selection procedures. The traditional view of selection was to ensure the best fit in terms of job specifications and job descriptions.

For this purpose, many different psychometric tests have been developed over the years; however, the days of lifelong employment are over and less importance is attached thereto in the contemporary South African business environment. Today, variables such as cultural fit, equity, affirmative action, and human potential play just as important a role in the selection process. However, ensuring the employment of quality people who are committed, attached, and loyal to the organisation, largely depends on those who have been recruited, and ultimately selected matching the job specifications as closely as possible.

Quality recruitment starts with the job specification. Recruitment is a costly exercise. To ensure quality assurance within the human resources department, the recruitment official must know where and how to advertise.

Organisations are forced to follow stringent guidelines according to the various labour relations laws. Decisions to recruit from within, or from the open labour market, must be taken in collaboration with all parties concerned, i.e. union representatives and management, and must be carried out in the fashion which is required by law (see Chapters 5 and 6) to ensure quality delivery in this regard.

Recently, it has become the practice to involve all relevant stakeholders in the selection process, irrespective of whether a policy of recruitment from within or from without is followed. There must be consensus amongst the stakeholders with regard to the steps applied in the selection processes for appointing applicants to the various jobs which exist on various levels in an organisation. To ensure quality in the selection process, the human resources department must empower stakeholders in matters such as interviewing, selection procedures, communication, and decision-making.

After a decision has been taken to appoint a specific candidate, an employment contract must be drafted. The employment contract formalises the work relationship between the company and the appointee. Quality assurance with regard to employee input starts here. The employment contract must specify the behaviour and performance standards required of the appointee. Normally, this is deduced from the job description in the form of Key Performance Areas (KPA's) and Key Performance Indicators (KPI's). The contract must also stipulate the performance assessment which will be applied to ensure quality performance, and the consequences of not reaching it. It must also include the empowerment which the organisation offers, such as training and development. It must further specify the compensation, employment conditions, and benefits the company offers in exchange for the delivery of the inputs required of the job incumbent. The human resources department and the responsible manager must induct the new appointment into the culture of the organisation and the internal work environment. The sooner an employee is socialised, the sooner he or she will be able to deliver inputs of a high quality.

Quality assurance implies a continuous commitment to service delivery. For this reason, compensation, conditions of service, service benefits, etc., must be based on the same principles for every new appointment or promotion. Differing standards cannot be allowed, as this consistently leads to dissatisfied employees. The human resources department must intervene by ensuring that all relevant stakeholders are familiar with the policy of the organisation and the relevant legislation.

Both the human resources department and management are responsible for the continuous delivery of organisation-wide quality assurance. As quality assurance is primarily a management responsibility, the human resources department can intervene by empowering management in the techniques of human resources planning and management succession planning. The success of the quality assurance approach is dependent on the ability of the human resources department to empower managers and employees. The education of managerial staff in human resources techniques, such as appraisal, employee guidance, objective setting, evaluation, corrective or remedial action, and counselling, will boost quality assurance tremendously, as the purpose of these human resources interventions is to change managerial philosophy and leadership style from passive or reactive to proactive and preventative. By empowering managerial and supervisory staff in employee behaviour, proactive interventions can be made to ensure quality employee behaviour in the various operational processes of the organisation.

Quality assurance, in the service delivery of the human resources department to the organisation, is under the spotlight, especially within the legal environment in which organisations function. This demands from the human resources department familiarity with the latest legislation regarding employment relations, affirmative action, basic conditions of service, equity, and collective bargaining. Not only must the human resources department be abreast of this legislation, they must ensure that each and every manager and supervisor is empowered in this regard. Quality assurance, on an organisation-wide basis, refers to the ability of the organisation to deliver quality products or services in a continuous, uninterrupted way. The sensitivity of employees and organised labour here cannot be overemphasised. Any infringement on the part of any stakeholder may spark off labour problems, which can halt an organisation's total operation. This poses a big challenge to organisations' human resources departments and all functional managers.

The goal of most organisations is to make profits in the long-term and to create wealth with such profits. This demands that the quality of an organisation's products or services be assured; if not, the organisation will cease to exist, especially in the global markets of today. One certain way of ensuring quality is to empower employees to meet the challenges which their jobs pose to them. The speed of technological change has resulted in jobs changing continuously, to such an extent that employees need to be retrained quickly in order to do the same job in a different way. As we advance into the new millennium, such job changes will become more frequent. This poses a major challenge to organisations and their human resources departments to remain profitable and competitive. Therefore, human resources departments and functional managers will be required to continuously assess the training and development needs of the various organisational processes, and to develop training and development programmes to fit the continuous discrepancies between what is required and how it is to be done. Herein lies the answer for ultimate survival.

As was mentioned earlier in this chapter, quality assurance must be viewed from both a holistic and process perspective.

From a process perspective, this means that line and other functional managers must:
- empower employees involved in the bottom-line operations of an organisation to continuously deliver quality products or services; and
- ensure a quality human resources management service to the total organisation.

From a holistic approach, and relating to the efficiency approach to human resources, quality assurance refers to a behavioural inclination, from an organisation-wide group and individual employee perspective, to accept quality as part of the organisational and work culture. This requires an attitudinal change, top-down and bottom-up, which must be vested in the mission statement, goals, strategy, and tactics of the organisation. Quality-mindedness must become 'the way we do things around here'.

However, the process and holistic (behavioural) approaches to quality assurance must be in a symbiotic relationship to be effective. The one cannot succeed without the other. The question remains as to how such a symbiotic relationship can be achieved. Figure 4.1 shows that management, as a process, is the pivot around which human resources management revolves. Management, and especially the management function of leading, is the principal vehicle through which such a symbiotic relationship can be achieved. In this modern area, transformational leadership (see Chapter 15) has become vital to the success of organisations. By empowering managerial and supervisory personnel in leadership practice, an organisation sets the scene for attitudinal changes towards a unified organisation and work culture, where quality is superimposed on all organisational activity. Further, the modern workforce has different needs and demands, which require different management styles and work arrangements. The human resources department can empower the organisation by educating managerial and supervisory staff in the management of groups, management development, and the management of diversity.

Quality assurance in human resources can be enhanced by using human resources management aids. The first of these aids is the application of the techniques of strategic management to human resources management. With what is known as strategic human resources management, both the human resources department, and line and other functional managers can assure long-term quality assurance by planning, recruiting, appointing, training, and developing human resources for the organisation in a proactive manner. The labour market, both national and international, is becoming more stringent and competitive. Professionally skilled people are in particular demand, and the global business world is competing for their scarce skills on an international basis. Only effective strategic human resources management can assure long-term quality employees. Another human resources management aid is the use of information management systems. The increase in accurate managerial decision-making can be directly attributed to the increase in management information effectiveness. No organisation can envisage survival without making use of the above aids.

In the next section the nature and scope of the process approach to quality assurance and human resources management is discussed.

4.4 The process approach to quality assurance and human resources management

4.4.1 General

It was mentioned earlier that the process approach to human resources management could be viewed as an evolution of the practice of human resources management over the past few decades. It was also emphasised that process management can only be practised within a structural and functional organisational set-up. The need for a process approach to human resources management stems from the need to empower line and other functional managers in human resources management practices. This is due to the fact that management (worldwide) has realised the value and benefits of an efficient and effective human resources management department in view of the realisation that organisational success depends mainly on the human potential of an organisation.

In this section the theory underlying process management and quality assurance within the realm of human resources management is discussed.

4.4.2 Defining the concepts

To understand process management learners have to acquaint themselves with certain concepts.

- *Process.* Interrelated activities that add value to the products or services of an organisation. Process activities have a beginning and an end, but constitute a never-ending cycle of events, unless the organisation or the specific products or services produced by the process cease to exist owing to economic factors (such as supply and demand).

- *Internal supply chain.* A network of major organisational events, directed at producing products or services, which represents an organisation's reason for existence or purpose.

A manufacturing concern, for example, must have a research and development department, a logistics department, a marketing department, manufacturing facilities, warehousing, quality control, distribution, and sales to enable it to deliver a product to the market place.

- *Internal customer.* A person, process, section, or department affected by the processes that contribute to the making of a product or the delivery of a service in the internal supply chain.

The quality of the raw materials that the logistics department delivers to manufacturing has a direct impact on the quality of the products produced by manufacturing.

- *Internal supplier.* The opposite of internal customer. The internal supplier delivers materials, products, technology, or information to some internal customer in the internal supply chain, to enable such an internal customer to further add value to the end product or service the organisation produces.

The marketing research department is expected to provide accurate information with regard to consumer quality expectations relating to the organisation's products or services. The accuracy of this information determines the sales volume achieved by a certain product or service.

- *Process flow chart.* A diagrammatic representation of the steps in a process, making use of standard process symbols.
- *External customer.* Those, irrespective of size, composition, market segment, etc., who purchase the products or services produced by an organisation.

In a manufacturing concern producing products in large quantities, especially in the food and beverage industry, important external customers are chain stores, such as Pick 'n Pay, Shoprite Checkers, and Spar.

- *External supplier.* Entities, institutions, and organisations who, on demand, deliver materials, technology, or information to an organisation to enable the organisation's internal supply chain to produce its products or services.

The typical external customers of a manufacturing concern are the producers of the raw materials the concern needs to produce the primary products which reflect its organisational purpose.

- *Continuous improvement.* Central to process management is the concept of continuous improvement, which refers to ongoing efforts to meet and exceed the expectations of stakeholders, by changing the way in which work is performed so that products or services are delivered sooner and at a lower cost than previously.

Within the realm of process management, this poses the biggest challenge to human resources management – the empowerment of managerial, supervisory, and ordinary employees involved in the organisation's different processes to continuously improve bottom-line results by applying human resources interventions at the points where they are required.

Table 4.1 Commonly used process symbols

Symbol	Description	Symbol	Description
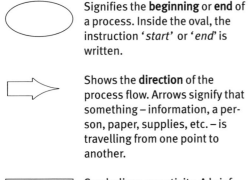	Signifies the **beginning** or **end** of a process. Inside the oval, the instruction '*start*' or '*end*' is written.		Major process steps should be written inside a double rectangle. A double rectangle should have one arrow flowing into it and one arrow flowing out.
	Shows the **direction** of the process flow. Arrows signify that something – information, a person, paper, supplies, etc. – is travelling from one point to another.		A diamond is used for those steps in a process where a decision must be made. A diamond will usually have one arrow flowing in, but two or more arrows flowing out. A question is written in the diamond and the number of 'out' arrows will depend on the question. Only 'no' or 'yes' questions must be asked.
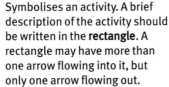	Symbolises an activity. A brief description of the activity should be written in the **rectangle**. A rectangle may have more than one arrow flowing into it, but only one arrow flowing out.		

- *Internal support chain.* This refers to other functional departments, such as marketing, sales, and merchandising, which are not directly involved with the internal supply chain.
- *Professional staff chain.* Those functional departments, such as human resources, corporate communications, social responsibility, labour relations, and legal services, which render services to the whole organisation.

4.4.3 Process management and human resources operations

Just like the functional and efficiency approach to human resources management, the quality assurance approach must operate within a structure which, in this case, is represented by organisational processes.

The process structure of the internal supply chain is depicted in Figure 4.2.

In traditional management terms, the internal supply chain represents the line function of an organisation. The inter-linked circles represent the inter-relatedness and interdependency of the main processes in the chain, emphasising the systems or efficiency approach to human resources management. The overlapping shackles imply the internal supplier and internal customer relationship. Both parties have certain expectations of each other with regard to the inputs and outputs each linkage requires. In managerial terms, these are called the Key Performance Areas (KPAs) and Key Performance Indicators (KPIs) of a process. The outputs (KPIs) of a shackle are the inputs (KPAs) for the next inter-related shackle. For example, the

Figure 4.2 Organisational structure from a process management perspective

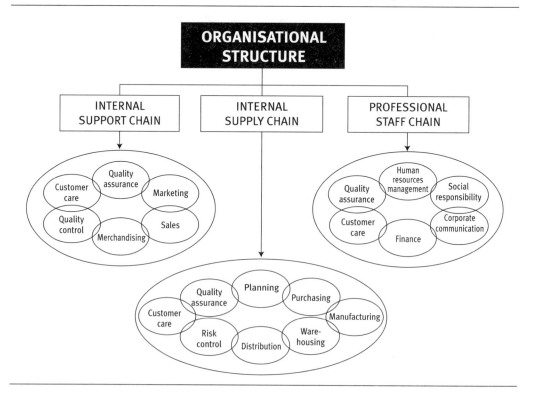

THE QUALITY ASSURANCE APPROACH   85

input of the sales department to manufacturing will determine whether inventory levels will match the sales forecasts.

Any discrepancy in terms of this example, whether from sales or manufacturing (underproduction or overproduction) triggers a red light and, in terms of human resources management, this indicates under-performance by the individuals involved in the process. This calls for the human resources department (which is part of the professional staff chain) to implement a continual improvement program. The nature of the intervention will depend on the diagnosis of the human resources professional and the process managers and may cover the entire spectrum of the human resources management function. In Figure 4.3, the human resources function is centrally depicted within the internal supply chain. This implies that a range of services can be offered to the relevant process operators to improve the quality of both their inputs (KPA's) and their outputs (KPI's) in order to assure quality service to their internal and external customers.

Ensuring quality service in the organisational processes requires the following range of products and services that the human resources department, as an internal supplier, can offer:

- improved job, process, and organisational design;
- improved job descriptions, job specifications, and performance contracts;
- improved human resources planning and management succession planning;
- more effective recruitment, selection, and placement;
- improving the quality of employee work life by continuously researching com-

Figure 4.3 Human resources management (internal supplier) and the internal supply chain (internal customer)

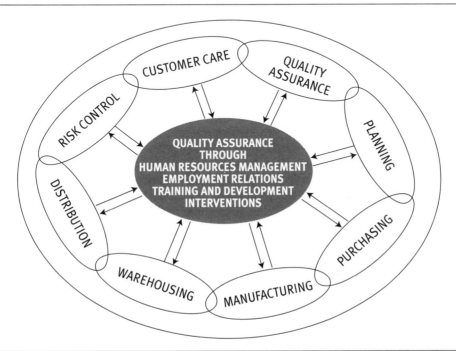

pensation trends, motivating experiences, and social life expectations;
- ensuring a labour-friendly work environment by applying and following the relevant legislation;
- empowering personnel by providing job-related education, training, and development;
- recognising and rewarding employees (process members) for attaining or improving on performance standards while, at the same time, disciplining under-achievers and providing remedial training intervention; and
- assisting managerial, supervisory, and other process employees with accurate human resources information.

This seems like one-way traffic, where everything is expected of the human resources department, which is not a true reflection of reality. The effectiveness of the human resources department, as an internal supplier of quality service, depends on the cooperation and accurate information it receives from its internal customers.

However, the shift from a traditional and efficiency systems approach towards a quality assurance approach can be directly attributed to the inability of other functional and process managers to exercise human resources management as part of their normal managerial duties. This has led to human resources management as an organisational unit being questioned and challenged by top management. No organisation can do without human resources management and, therefore, it is of the utmost importance to take human resources management (and not personnel management or personnel administration) to the bottom line of organisational processes. This is the only way it will survive, and also the only way that Southern African organisations will become efficient, effective, and successful in a very competitive global market.

4.5 Conclusion

The only way Southern African organisations can survive is to endeavour to practice what successful companies worldwide are practising; that is to ensure the quality of their services and products. South Africa's rating by the World Competitiveness Report (see Chapter 1, Table 1) is not acceptable at all and leaves much room for improvement. If management in Southern African companies can once and for all come to the realisation that the human resources they employ hold the key to quality and success, the sooner improved outcomes for the organisation and its stakeholders will be delivered. Of utmost importance is the creation by human resources managers of a symbiotic relationship between organisation and work culture, where quality assurance is the name of the game in all positions of employment.

- If a process manager is unable to, or does not, provide accurate job requirements for a certain position, the human resources department's efforts to recruit and employ the most suitable available person will be in vain.
- If a vacancy arises in the accounting department, and the financial manager cannot make a decision about whom to appoint, this cannot be laid at the door of the human resources department.

Case study
Supreme Corner Shops (Pty.) Ltd.

Background
The South African economy's isolation from the international evolution of business and innovations was broken after the democratic elections in 1994. Various industries, in particular the business sectors, have undergone major changes and adaptations since then. Furthermore, the entry of organisations like Macdonald's, Seven Eleven, and various others, have made their impact felt on the economy and consumers due to their professionalism and quality service.

Case detail
Vusi Pitjani completed a business degree in 1983 at Virginia Commonwealth University in the United States. This was after he left South Africa in 1978 because he was expelled from one of the local universities for his political convictions. He then started and managed a wholesale business successfully in Atlanta, Georgia, which he sold very profitably when he decided to return to South Africa in 1997.

He decided to apply his experience and start a new business venture in South Africa, but with a difference to what he did in the USA, in that he intended to integrate small businesses into one powerful organisation, while retaining a retail character. In fact, he was thinking of emulating Molopo foods, but with his own approach and niche market.

His idea was to integrate a number of independent, but currently small businesses into a chain of grocery outlets, under the combined ownership of one newly formed company. Owners of these businesses would become shareholders in the new company. The outlets would be located primarily in the suburbs and the micro shopping centres, which are being established throughout Gauteng in particular. He hoped to list this group on the Johannesburg Stock Exchange within eight years, to sell his shares at a handsome profit, and then become involved in community upliftment projects.

After many consultations with various retailers, Vusi convinced the following organisations' management to combine into one powerful corner convenience grocery store chain: Big Bun Pastries cc, Deli Meats and Butchery (Pty.) Ltd., Northern Tinned Meats (Pty.) Ltd., Pela Canned Fruits and Vegetables, Jabulani Supermarket cc, Sipho's Best Flamed Grilled Chickens cc, and Bob's Best Bread Bakery (Inc.).

He also entered into agreements with a number of manufacturers of well-known retail product brands to supply the various grocery outlets with the necessary products.

Vusi realised from his American experience that quality and service, as well as effective procurement, were key elements to making his business successful. He was also fully aware of the fact that qualified, experienced, and motivated employees form the core component of any business that wishes to be successful.

The number of personnel employed by the businesses listed above varied from seven to seventy-four. Needless to say, conditions of service, pension agreements, medical schemes, quality of service, working hours, benefits, length of service, etc., all varied extensively. To integrate them into an effective chain of grocers, and to provide a uniformly high level of service was to be a major issue for the group's success. Vusi realised that a quality assurance approach to human resources management would be essential. It would be the only way to beat similar outlets, based on the seven-eleven retail shop principle, which have recently established themselves in South Africa, and which he knew all too well from his experience in the USA.

You have been recruited and appointed as a knowledgeable and competent human resources manager for the group.

Question

Advise Vusi as to how to go about establishing a quality assurance approach to human resources management, by compiling a report to be presented to him. In the report, explain the principles and advantages of managing human resources from this point of view. Also ensure that your report includes the operationalisation of the process approach which is contained in Figures 4.1, 4.2, and 4.3 of this chapter.

Bibliography

CHARLTON, G. 2000. *Human habits of highly effective organisations.* Van Schaik, Pretoria.

RUMMLER, G.A. & BRACHE, A.P. 1990. *Improving performance.* Jossey Bass, San Francisco.

SPANGENBERG, H. (ed). 1994. *Understanding and implementing performance management.* Juta, Johannesburg.

STOREY, J. 1992. *Developments in the management of human resources.* Blackwell, Oxford.

SWANEPOEL, B.J., ERASMUS, B.J., VAN WYK, M. & SCHENK, H. 2000. *South African human resource management: theory and practice.* 2nd edition, Cape Town: Juta.

VAN DYK, P.S. 1998. *The development of a process management system to increase quality service in a large manufacturing concern.* Confidential research report, Pretoria.

WARNER, M. (ed). 1997. *The pocket international encyclopedia of business and management.* Southern Management, Johannesburg.

Chapter questions

1 Write an essay on the difference between the functional, efficiency, and quality assurance approach to human resources management. Explain why these three approaches cannot function in isolation.
2 Redesign an organisation with which you are familiar into an integrated functional and process design.
3 Identify and arrange the different human resources activities in your organisation to form a fluent human resources quality service process.

part three

Human resources and the legislative environment

5

Employment law impacting on employment relationships

P S Nel

Learning outcomes

At the end of this chapter the learner should be able to demonstrate the following outcomes:
- Explain the components of the employment relations system.
- Motivate and present arguments in favour of the effect of the Employment Equity Act.
- Explain the purpose, role, and function of the Labour Relations Act.
- Compile examples of how working hours are applied in terms of the Basic Conditions of Employment Act.
- Provide guidelines for effective skills development of employees.
- Consider the influence of the Skills Levy Act on employers' need for skilled personnel.
- Explain the role of compensation to employees for occupational injuries.
- Discuss the benefits of unemployment insurance for South Africa's workforce.
- Present arguments in favour of employment law on sound human resources management.

Key words and concepts

- bargaining councils and collective agreements
- basic conditions of employment
- CCMA
- closed shop agreements
- compensation for injuries and diseases
- constitution
- dispute resolution
- diverse workforce
- employment equity
- freedom of association
- hours of work
- occupational health and safety
- organisational rights
- political democracy
- skills development
- strikes and lockouts
- unemployment insurance
- unfair dismissals
- workplace forums

Illustrative case
Mafuta's Fast Food Diner

Mafuta Ncube started working as a chef, and ended up as manager after a number of years, at one of the largest fast food chain outlets in South Africa. He completed his hotel, catering and restaurant chefs' course at the Cordon Bleu School at the Gauteng North Technikon some twelve years ago. He accomplished this with a bursary he received for being the best soccer player in his school and region in Grade 12. In fact, at the time, he had an offer to join Morocco Swallow's junior team, which he declined. He opted out of soccer to indulge in his first love – good food, people-centred business, jazz music, and entertainment.

Mafuta's Fast Food Diner has expanded into a semi-franchised operation and consists of nine fast food diners (four of which were acquired during the course of last year) spread over Gauteng and the North West Province. Mafuta's ownership ranges from 51 per cent to 90 per cent in the various diners, because he begrudgingly had to sell off some ownership, as well as forming partnerships to get more operating capital to expand the business. Some of the diners started out as small shabeen-like operations which grew substantially; on the other hand, a recently acquired 300-seater Western Californian Diner nearly went bankrupt in Johannesburg. This diner was bought for a song as a going concern (including staff, equipment, etc.) by Mafuta and a consortium of partners. At the time, it was failing and nearly down and out, but is to be built up to become the flagship of Mafuta's Fast Food Diners chain.

All of Mafuta's diners are, however, still run as they were from their inception, lean and mean businesses, that are very profitable, and managed with a personal touch under the human resources slogan for staff of 'this is our business, we are all one big family'. Due to his business success, Mafuta also became friendly with a number of government officials in fairly senior positions, and he regularly entertains them at the different diners. This has become a status symbol for him, as well as a marketing opportunity to popularise and expand his business even faster. The public, thus, regularly gets the opportunity to meet high-profile people at Mafuta's diners. He is, however, cautious not to create any animosity by falling foul of the law and antagonising his friends who, amongst others, are Directors at the Department of Labour.

During last year, Mafuta obtained consultative advice from the small business and entrepreneurial unit of the Business Faculty of the University of Pretoria on how to expand and manage his business even better. The advice included that he should standardise all operations and mould his business on the American Macdonald's model, as far as simplification of management and controls throughout the group of businesses was concerned. He should also create a unique, classy African touch for his business. This approach would enhance his endeavours and ambitions to become a national player and ultimately an international tycoon in the food business. In fact, he secretly dreams of topping Macdonald's as the fast food chain in the world before he retires one day.

Part of the restructuring advice Mafuta received was that staff should work according to standardised employment conditions and standardised procedures

Conditions of employment, such as leave, sick leave, overtime rates, bonuses, travelling allowances, and commissions were different at every diner and this created major and recurring headaches for Mafuta. Some had conditions of employment which were much better than the prescriptions of the employment laws, while others were even below the requirements. He also had a few encounters with officials of the Bargaining Council via the trade unions, because some of the operations he had taken over did not comply with the Basic Conditions of Employment Act, the Labour Relations Act, the Unemployment Insurance Act, etc. At the start of the new year, all diners had to be standardised, and at least in line with the minimum requirements of the current South African employment laws. This would enable him to structure and implement integrated strategies for his future plans. Mafuta, therefore, informed every employee, at the end of October the previous year, by way of a personally signed letter, that new contracts would be negotiated and implemented from the beginning of the following year.

Mafuta contracted a human resources consultant specialising in employment relations to re-negotiate the conditions of employment, so that all staff would be employed on a full-time basis in future. Mafuta decided that the only exception would be waiters, who would operate as casuals on a part-time basis. This arrangement would provide him with staff who could be moved around to the various diners, as well as a well-qualified, experienced, committed, and regular source of human resources that would play a major role in stabilising and enhancing the future expansion of his business. All of the aforementioned aspects had to be in line with the applicable employment laws.

Cedric Mashege, a handsome, well-built young man, had worked for Mafuta as a permanently employed clerk in a mornings-only position at the Midrand diner for the last year and a half. All employee contracts at all diners were successfully re-negotiated, except Cedric's. He refused to give up a very lucrative part-time job he had as a stripper in three different strip clubs, where he performed every afternoon and evening, except on Saturdays and Sundays.

Cedric knew that the public easily tired of the same stripper and that he would have to move to another town or retire as a stripper within the next two years. He liked living in Midrand, as well as his job with Mafuta, and after he retires from stripping, would like to work full-time for Mafuta. He also had a very attractive girlfriend with a very well-paid job in Midrand who was not prepared to move should he resign or relocate and continue to be a stripper in another town. He decided to stick with matters as they were, because he was earning a very good income as a stripper, but wanted some occupational stability as well, which he received from Mafuta. With the knowledge he has as a shop steward at Mafuta's, he also thought he was acting fully within his rights, and that he could continue to work there mornings-only on a permanent basis.

After protracted negotiations between Cedric, Mafuta, and the consultant, he still refused to accept a full-day job and the new standardised conditions of employment. Mafuta listened to the advice from the consultant, but being an impatient, go-getting business man, he was still not sure what to do with regard to Cedric's case. Should he fire him, retain his half-day status, upsetting his plans for standardised service conditions at all diners, or discipline him? What about the Constitutional rights of the parties?

Mafuta was particularly concerned about his right to manage his business in terms of his future strategies to expand it into a national and, ultimately, an international operation. He was also afraid that the trade union might cause some interruptions at the various diners if he angered Cedric too much. On the other hand, he did not want to create a precedent by allowing exceptions to the new employment conditions of his staff, because he would then be just where he started, with chaos and headaches, and this was unacceptable in terms of his dreams and future ambitions.

What advice, in the context of employment law, sound human resources and effective business management practice would you give to Mafuta and Cedric to resolve this situation?

5.1 Introduction

Its own history and influences from other countries shape a country's labour/management system and its employment law. South Africa is no exception; the system in its broader context and employment relationships in particular have always been a reflection of the socio-political system and the development of the trade union movement, all of which is closely linked to the prevailing political dispensation.

Political and industrial democracy in South Africa evolved historically along racial lines, leading to the unique, but unfair, employment relations system, which came to an end with the April 1994 elections.

According to Swanepoel et al. (2000: 129) the employment relationship is also influenced by various sources of law, namely common law, the contract of employment, collective agreements negotiated by trade unions and management, guidelines of the international labour organisation in the form of conventions, and the South African Constitution Act No. 108 of 1996.

Readers must note that it is essential to understand the interdependence between human resources management and employment relations, as presented in this and the following chapter, which should be studied as a unit.

5.1.1 Government policy and the Constitution

It is important to take note of South Africa's Constitution (Act No. 108 of 1996) in that it is the supreme law of the country. The provisions of all South African statutes must conform to the basic principles contained in the Constitution. Parliament as well as the private and public sectors are all subordinate to the Constitution.

It is, for example, clearly stated in Chapter 2 of the Act that various rights are important to the peoples of South Africa, such as human dignity, equality, and freedom. The Constitution also provides very clear guidelines with regard to employment relations. Section 23, for example, stipulates the following provisions:
- Everyone has the right to fair labour practices.
- Every worker has the right to form and join a trade union, to participate in the activities of a trade union, and to strike.
- Every employer has the right to form and join an employers' organisation and to participate in the activities of an employers' organisation.

- Every trade union and employers' organisation has the right to determine its own activities, to organise, to bargain collectively, and to form and join a federation.
- Every trade union, employers' organisation, and employer has the right to engage in collective bargaining. National legislation may be enacted to regulate collective bargaining. To the extent that the legislation may limit a right in this Chapter, the limitation must comply with Section 36(1) of the Constitution Act 108 of 1996.

It is clear that the Constitution and Government policy set the scene for the practice for employment relations in South Africa in the emphasis that employment law should also facilitate worker participation and decision making in the workplace.

Roodt (1999:10) comments on how the Government ought to go about transforming South African society within the African renaissance and the focus on Africaness:

- Fundamental social delivery and transformation must be enhanced.
- A new understanding must be spread of what it means to live in a democracy in order to counter the myopic view that democracy engenders rights to citizens while responsibilities and duties reside with the government alone.
- The focus must be on effectiveness, efficiency, and delivery in respect of government initiatives and actions. This includes cuts to the civil service, which are linked to the need for economic growth as the engine for job creation. In other words, the fundamental base on which meaningful and sustainable jobs are created is by ensuring the economy grows in a way that creates jobs. This means that the number of people in the public service must be reduced.
- A tougher approach to dealing with law and order, including partnerships between state, communities, and business in preventing and combating crime and corruption is essential.
- Initiatives to stimulate job creation, in alliance with business and labour, must be accelerated.
- A world outlook is important for South Africa, on its position in the region, in Africa, and in the rest of the world and, in particular, in relation to bringing about an African renaissance.

However, Government policy and sentiment were reflected in President Mbeki's opening speech to Parliament in February 2000. He stated that government had to take strong action against irresponsible trade union behaviour such as strikes, since it could impact negatively on the economy and job creation. Furthermore, he spoke of the need for labour legislation to reflect fairness both to management and labour, and that adjustments should be made where necessary. These comments point to forthcoming changes in employment law in South Africa.

The applicable employment laws, which influence employment relations within the business context, are presented in Figure 5.1.

Readers must take careful note that the discussion of employment law in the following sections is in summarised form. It merely sensitises readers to the major provisions and focus, broadly applicable to the world of work in South Africa. Should readers require further detail, to the original text of the applicable law, signed by the President, should be referred to.

5.2 Employment Equity Act No. 55 of 1998

There was a long run-up to the signing of this Act on 12 October 1998. The Green Paper on Employment and Occupational Equity, which was published on 1 July 1996,

Figure 5.1 Statutes impacting on the employment relationship

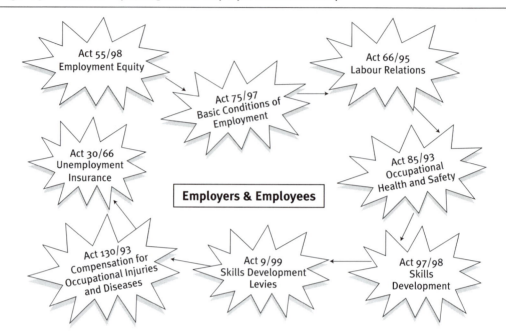

paved the way to the Act becoming the centrepiece of legislation doing away with all forms of discrimination in employment in South Africa. The preamble to the promulgated Act illustrates its focus and importance in promoting equity and non-discrimination in the employment sector in South Africa.

The preamble states that:
- as a result of apartheid and other discriminatory laws and practices, there are disparities in employment, occupation and income within the national labour market; and
- those disparities create such pronounced disadvantages for certain categories of people that simply repealing discriminatory laws cannot redress them.

Therefore, the Employment Equity Act was promulgated to:
- promote the constitutional right of equality and the exercise of true democracy;
- eliminate unfair discrimination in employment;
- ensure the implementation of employment equity to redress the effects of discrimination;
- achieve a diverse workforce broadly representative of our people
- promote economic development and efficiency in the workforce; and
- give effect to the obligations of the Republic as a member of the International Labour Organisation.

5.2.1 The purpose and scope of the Act

Section 2 contains the major purpose of the Act namely to achieve equity in the workplace by:
- promoting equal opportunity and fair treatment in employment through the elimination of unfair discrimination; and

- implementing affirmative action measures to redress the disadvantages in employment experienced by designated groups, in order to ensure their equitable representation in all occupational categories and levels in the workforce.

The Act excludes members of the South African National Defence Force (SANDF), the National Intelligence Agency (NIA) and the South African Secret Services (SASS). The anti-discriminatory provisions of the Act apply to all other employers and employees, but the affirmative action provisions only apply to 'designated employers' and members of 'designated groups'. This has a direct bearing on the anti-discrimination prohibitions outlined in Chapter 2 and the affirmative action provisions in Chapter 3 of the Act. The drawing up of employment equity plans and the achievement of numerical goals are also paramount aspects of the Act.

5.2.2 Commencement dates of provisions

The commencement dates of the various provisions of the Act are stipulated to be as follows:
- Establishment of the Commission for Employment Equity: 15 May 1999.
- Chapter 2 of the Act (anti-discrimination provisions): 9 August 1999.
- Chapter 3 of the Act (affirmative action provisions): 1 December 1999.
- Submission of employment equity plans for more than 150 employees being employed: The first report by June 2000.
- Submission of employment equity plans for less than 150 employees being employed: The first report by December 2000.
- Awarding of state contracts to employers who employ 150 or more employees: 1 September 2000.
- Awarding of state contracts to employers who employ fewer than 150 employees: 1 April 2001.

5.2.3 Human resources impact of the Act

The Act impacts greatly on employment policies and practices in all sectors of the South African economy. The impact includes, but is not limited to: recruitment procedures, advertising, and selection criteria; appointments and the appointment process; job classification and grading; remuneration, employment benefits and terms and conditions of employment; job assignments; the working environment and facilities; training and development; performance evaluation systems; promotion; transfer; demotion; disciplinary measures other than dismissal; and dismissal.

The Act is instrumental in breaking down the employment discrimination the country experienced previously, to propel it into the international community's acceptance of what an equal society stands for in the world of work. This includes how diversity and transformation in the workplace ought to be managed.

Further detail concerning employment equity and the application thereof, is discussed in this book in the context of cultural diversity and change management (in Chapter 17) and employment equity and affirmative action (in Chapter 7).

5.3 Basic Conditions of Employment Act No. 75 of 1997

Due to the importance of this Act, more attention is paid to it than other Acts in this chapter, except for the Labour Relations Act of 1995. The Act came into operation, replacing the Wage Act of 1957, on 1 December 1998 in respect of the private sector and became applicable to the public sector on 1 May 2000.

5.3.1 The purpose and scope of the Act

The purpose of this Act is to advance economic development and social justice by establishing and enforcing basic conditions of employment. The Act has two primary objectives:
- to ensure that working conditions of unorganised and vulnerable workers meet minimum standards that are socially acceptable in relation to the level of development of the country; and
- to remove rigidities and inefficiencies from the regulation of minimum conditions of employment and to promote flexibility.

The Act applies to all employees and employers except members of the National Defence Force, National Intelligence Agency, South African Secret Service, and unpaid charitable workers.

A further focus of the Act is to promote 'regulated flexibility' which is an attempt to balance the protection of minimum standards and the requirements of labour market flexibility.

The basic conditions of employment established by the Act form part of every contract of employment in South Africa, unless they have been replaced, varied, or excluded in accordance with the Act, or unless the employee has personally, or via a bargaining council agreement, contracted for more favourable terms of employment.

The working time of employees must be arranged so as not to endanger their health and safety, and with due regard to their family responsibilities.

The requirements with regard to remuneration, deductions, and termination do not apply to employees who work less than four hours a week.

5.3.2 Work time and rules

The aspects below are contained in Chapters 2 and 3 of the Act.

Ordinary hours of work

The maximum ordinary weekly hours for all employees are forty-five. The maximum daily hours that an employee may work are nine for employees who work on five days or less a week, and eight for employees who work six days a week.

According to Schedule 1 of the Act, there must be a progressive reduction of the maximum hours of work. It proposes a procedure to reduce working hours of employees to forty hours and an eight-hour working day. This is to be achieved by collective bargaining and the publication of sectoral determinations, having regard to the impact on existing employment and opportunities of employment creation, economic efficiency, and the health, safety, and welfare of all employees in South Africa. Furthermore, it must be noted that if a party to negotiations puts the reduction of working hours on the agenda, it must be negotiated.

Also, the maximum ordinary working hours of security guards must be reduced to forty-five hours per week by 1 December 2001, according to Schedule 3 of the Act.

The limits on hours of work do not apply to senior managers and travelling sales personnel. The Minister of Labour may exclude or vary the application of the provisions in Chapter 3 of the Act to employees earning above a certain amount.

Overtime

Overtime may only be worked by agreement. An employee may not work more than three hours overtime in a day, or ten hours overtime in a week. Overtime work must be compensated by paying the employee at 1,5 times the employee's normal wage or, if agreed, by granting the employee a period of paid time off, equivalent to the value of the overtime pay.

Extended ordinary daily hours of work

An agreement may permit an employee to work for up to twelve hours in a day without receiving overtime pay. The weekly limits continue to apply and the employee may not work on more than five days in a week. A collective agreement may permit the hours of work of an employee to be averaged over a period of up to four months. The average time worked over the agreed period must not exceed forty-five ordinary hours and five hours overtime per week.

The Minister of Labour, on grounds of health and safety, may make regulations setting shorter maximum hours of work for any category of employees.

Meal intervals

An employee must have a meal interval of at least sixty minutes after five hours. This may be reduced to thirty minutes by agreement. An employee required to be available for work or to remain on the employer's premises during the meal interval must be paid.

Daily and weekly rest period

An employee must have a daily rest period of at least twelve hours between ending work and starting work the following day. Every employee must have a rest period of at least thirty-six consecutive hours each week. The rest period must include a Sunday, unless otherwise agreed. An employee may agree to have a longer rest period (sixty hours) every two weeks.

An employee who works on a Sunday must receive double pay. However, an employee who normally works on a Sunday must be paid at 1,5 times the employee's normal wage. By agreement, an employer may compensate an employee for Sunday work by granting paid time off.

Night work

The Bill contains protection for employees who work at night. Night work is defined as work performed between 18h00 and 06h00. Employees must be compensated by the payment of an allowance or by a reduction of working hours. Transportation must be available for employees. Employers must inform employees who regularly work after 23h00 of the health and safety hazards of night work and, on request, provide employees with a free medical assessment.

Public holidays

All employees must be paid their normal wage for a public holiday that falls on a working day. An employee may not be required to work on a public holiday unless by agreement. Work on a public holiday must be remunerated at double rates.

Emergency work

The limits on ordinary and overtime working hours, and the requirements for meal intervals and rest periods do not prevent the performance of emergency work.

Annual leave

Employees are entitled to three weeks fully paid leave after every twelve months continuous employment. This may also be calculated as one day's leave for every seventeen days of employment. An employer must not pay an employee instead of granting annual leave. However, an employee whose employment is terminated must be paid out any pay due for leave that the employee has not taken.

Sick leave

An employee is entitled to six weeks paid sick leave for every thirty-six months of continuous employment. However, during the first six months of employment an employee is entitled to only one day's paid sick leave for every twenty-six days worked. An employer may require a medical certificate from an employee who is regularly away from work for more than two days, before paying the employee for sick leave.

An employee's daily pay for sick leave may be reduced by agreement, provided the number of days sick leave is increased. The pay may not be reduced below 75 per cent of ordinary pay.

Maternity leave

A pregnant employee is entitled to four months maternity leave. This leave may begin up to four weeks before the expected date of birth, unless otherwise agreed or, if required by the employee for health reasons. An employer may not require an employee to return to work for six weeks after the birth of a child; during this period, an employee may elect to return to work if a medical doctor or midwife certifies that she is fit to do so.

An employee who has a stillborn child or a miscarriage in the third trimester of pregnancy may remain on maternity leave for six weeks or, if a doctor certifies it necessary for her health, for longer. During pregnancy and for six months after birth, an employer must offer suitable alternative employment to an employee who works at night or whose work may endanger her health or safety or her child's.

Family responsibility leave

An employee is entitled to three days paid family responsibility leave. This only applies to employees who work on four or more days in a week. The employee may take this leave in the event of the birth of the employee's child, if the employee's child is sick, or if a member of the employee's immediate family dies. An employer may require reasonable proof of the purpose for which this leave is taken before paying the employee.

The provisions of Chapter 3 of the Act do not apply to leave granted by an employer in excess of the requirements of the Act; nor do they apply to employees who work less than four hours a week.

5.3.3 Payment of remuneration and deductions

These aspects are contained in Chapter 4 of the Act.

An employer must pay an employee according to arrangements made between them. Payment may take place daily, weekly, fortnightly or monthly and must take place at the workplace unless otherwise agreed and during, or within fifteen minutes of the end of the employee's working time. An employer may only deduct money from an employee's pay if permitted or required to do so by law, collective agreement, court order, or arbitration award.

A deduction for loss or damage caused by the employee in the course of employment may only be made by agreement and after the employer has established by a fair procedure that the employee was at fault. An employee may agree in writing to an employer deducting a debt specified in the agreement.

5.3.4 Termination of employment

These aspects are contained in Chapter 4 of the Act.

During the first four weeks of employment, an employment contract may be terminated on one week's notice. The notice period during the remainder of the first year of employment is two weeks. It is thirty days for employees with more than a year's service.

The notice period for a farm worker or domestic worker who has worked for more than four weeks is one month. The notice period may be varied by a collective agreement.

Notice must be given in writing. If the recipient cannot understand the notice, it must be explained to the employee in a language he or she can understand. An employer may pay the employee the remuneration for the notice period instead of giving notice. An employee who occupies accommodation situated on the employer's premises, or supplied by the employer, may elect to remain in the accommodation for the duration of the notice period.

The termination of employment by an employer on notice, in terms of the Act, does not prevent the employee challenging the fairness or lawfulness of the dismissal in terms of the Labour Relations Act.

5.3.5 Administrative obligations

In terms of Chapter 5 of the Act, the employer must:
- give the employee written particulars of employment when the employee starts employment;
- keep these particulars of employment for four years after the end of the contract of employment;
- give an employee information concerning remuneration, deductions, and time worked, with their pay;
- keep a record of the time worked by each employee and their remuneration; and
- display at the workplace a statement of employees' rights under the Act.

On termination of employment, an employee is entitled to a certificate of service. Simplified provisions apply to employers who have less than five employees, and to employers of domestic workers.

5.3.6 Prohibition of employment of children and forced labour

In terms of Chapter 6 of the Act, children under eighteen may not be employed to do work inappropriate for their age or that places them at risk. No person may employ a child under fifteen years of age, and the Minister of Labour may make regulations prohibiting or placing conditions on the employment of children over fifteen years of age.

The Minister of Labour may, further, make regulations concerning medical examinations for children in employment. The use of forced labour is prohibited, unless any other law permits it.

5.3.7 Variation of basic conditions of employment

This is dealt with in Chapter 7 of the Act.

A collective agreement concluded by a bargaining council or between an employer's organisation and a trade union may replace or exclude any basic condition of employment.

The Minister of Labour may make a determination, which varies or excludes any basic condition of employment. A determination that applies to a category of employers or employees must be made on the advice of the Employment Conditions

Commission. The Minister of Public Service and Administration must make a determination that applies to the public sector.

5.3.8 Monitoring, enforcement, and legal proceedings

These aspects are contained in Chapter 10 of the Act.

The Minister of Labour may appoint labour inspectors. Labour inspectors perform their functions subject to the direction and control of the Minister. The function of labour inspectors is to promote, monitor or enforce compliance with employment laws. Labour inspectors must advise employees and employers on their rights and obligations in terms of employment laws. They may also conduct inspections, investigate complaints, and secure compliance with employment law.

5.3.9 Possible amendments to various Acts

Regarding employment creation and the implementation of GEAR, the business community has lodged various objections against the restrictive nature of the Act. There are, however, overlaps with the Labour Relations Act, which are to be addressed.

Important matters which need to be considered are the impact of labour legislation on job security, job creation, and related issues. A number of specific areas may be identified that warrant re-evaluation in relation to the impact on job creation, which is restricted by the labour legislation. Such areas are: probationary periods; unfair dismissal procedures and compensation in respect of procedurally unfair dismissals; dismissals for operational requirements (retrenchments); retaining existing conditions of employment when organisations change hands; provisions in the BCEA on Sunday work and notice periods; and improving the efficiency of some of the institutions set up to assist in regulating the labour market, including the CCMA and Labour Court.

The Minister of Labour has made a number of suggestions which were debated in Parliament, and will probably be enacted as Amendments to the Basic Conditions of Employment Act and the Labour Relations Act towards the end of 2000 or early in 2001(Mdladlana 2000:19). The following issues, presented in a condensed format, may feature as future amendments to these Acts:

- A more flexible work week; this is currently restrictive and insufficient to enhance economic growth.
- A decrease in double pay for Sunday work; this currently stifles economic growth and job creation, and the fact that it comes into effect in June 2000 may threaten to derail Government's attempt to curb public service personnel costs. Government, itself, may have to apply for exemption from these provisions.
- Improved efficiency of the CCMA; disputes drag on for months and it is extremely detrimental to micro-level employers if they have to close shop and spend time at the CCMA.
- A redefinition of dismissal and retrenchment; business realities must be favourable for employers to improve international competition and flexibility.
- A halt to the decrease of the work-week from forty-five hours to forty hours; the cost of this may reduce employers' ability to compete internationally and should be revisited. It may be removed as 'a core right' to enable employers to negotiate the length of a working week with their workers.
- A more lenient approach to part-time workers and subcontractors; this will

enhance flexibility in the labour market.
- A redefinition of worker rights when an organisation changes hands; different rules may be necessary depending on an organisation's financial ability to accommodate employees.

Further details of the Basic Conditions of Employment Act, and applications thereof, are discussed in Chapter 6 and others of this book.

5.4 Labour Relations Act No. 66 of 1995

5.4.1 The purpose and scope of the Act

The purpose of the Act is to advance economic development, social justice, labour peace, and a democratisation of the workplace by fulfilling the primary objectives of the Act, which are to realise and regulate the fundamental rights of workers and employers under Section 23 of the Constitution.

The Act applies to all employment relationships between employers and employees and makes no distinction as to whether these relationships are in the private or the public sector. All previous exclusions of employees from the ambit of the Labour Relations Act have been removed, but the National Defence Force, the National Intelligence Agency, and the South African Secret Service are now specifically excluded (Section 2). This brings an entirely new dimension to the Labour Relations Act, as the public service, the South African police, the nursing and teaching professions, as well as agricultural and domestic employees now have virtually the same rights as other employees. However, in certain instances, specific procedures are established for these sectors.

The status of the Act is such that in the case of any conflict between the provisions of the Labour Relations Act and any other Act (except the Constitution) priority will be given to the provisions of the Labour Relations Act. The Labour Relations Act automatically supersedes the Basic Conditions of Employment Act. This, for example, enables bargaining councils to enter into agreements which contain conditions of employment less favourable than those provided for in the Basic Conditions of Employment Act.

The following schedules are contained in the Act, and greatly simplify the execution and understanding thereof:
- Schedule 1: The establishment of a bargaining council for the public service.
- Schedule 2: The establishment and constitution of workplace forums.
- Schedule 3: Aspects regarding the Commission for Conciliation, Mediation and Arbitration (CCMA).
- Schedule 4: Flow diagrams to enable users to determine how different disputes should be dealt with.
- Schedule 5: Technical amendments to the Basic Conditions of Employment Act and the Occupational Health and Safety Act.
- Schedule 6: Provisions of the Acts which have been repealed.
- Schedule 7: Transitional arrangements, e.g. those relating to residual unfair labour practices.
- Schedule 8: The Code of Good Practice: Dismissal, which is of cardinal importance to employment relations practitioners.

In order to gain a holistic perception of the South African system of labour relations a schematic presentation (technically not strictly accurate) adapted from Nel (ed.) (1999:77) is presented in Figure 5.2 to assist readers to understand how the components of the Act fit together.

Figure 5.2 Aspects of the employment relations system presented visually

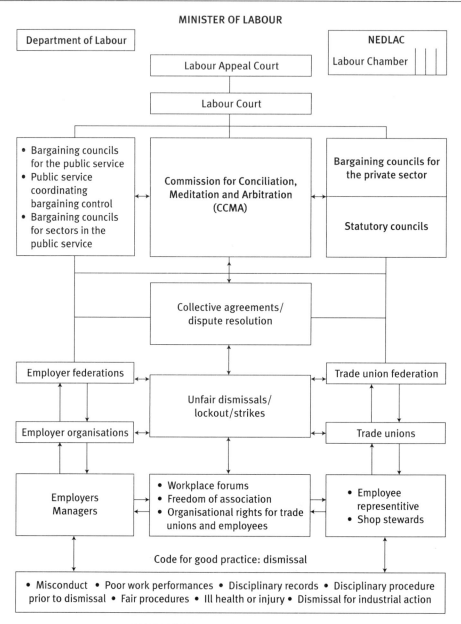

SOURCE: Nel (ed.) 1999:77.

Readers must also note that the presentation sequence of the LRA in this section is according to the chapters contained in the Act itself, namely Chapter 1 on the general provisions and scope, Chapter 2 on aspects of freedom of association, Chapter 3 on collective bargaining, Chapter 4 on strikes and lock-outs, Chapter 5 on workplace forums, Chapter 6 on trade unions and employers' organisations, Chapter 7 on dispute resolution, Chapter 8 on unfair dismissal, and Chapter 9 on general provisions. The focus will, however, be on the major issues only.

5.4.2 Freedom of association and general protections

Freedom of association and general protections are discussed in Chapter 2 of the Labour Relations Act.

One of the stated objectives of the Act is to give effect to the Constitution. One of the provisions contained in Section 23 of the Constitution is that workers have the right to form and to join trade unions, and employers have the right to form employers' organisations. This freedom of association is also enshrined in the International Labour Standards of the International Labour Organisation.

Union members, further, have the right to elect office-bearers, officials, or trade union representatives (shop stewards); to be elected and appointed as office-bearers or officials and, if elected or appointed, to hold office; and to be elected and appointed as trade union representatives. The functions of a trade union representative must be carried out subject to the union's constitution.

Protection of employees and persons seeking employment

Section 5 of Chapter 2 of the Act states clearly that no person may discriminate against an employee for exercising any right conferred by the Act. In addition, nobody may force an employee or a person seeking employment not to be or become a member of a trade union or workplace forum, or to give up membership of a trade union or workplace forum, for his or her omission or failure to do anything which the employer by law may not compel or allow him or her to do, for the publicising of information which an employee may lawfully give to another person, for the employee's assertion of any rights in terms of the Act, or for his or her participation in any activities of the Act. Furthermore, no one may offer or promise an employee favourable treatment if he or she waives any rights granted to him or her or desists from any activities in terms of the Act.

Employers' right to freedom of association

According to Section 6 of the Act every employer has the right to assist in forming an employers' organisation or a federation of employers' organisations and to join an employers' organisation. Their members have the right to participate in their lawful activities and in the election of office-bearers or officials.

Protection of employers' rights

No person, in terms of Section 7 of the Act, may discriminate against an employer by forcing an employer not to be or become a member of an employers' organisation, or to give up membership of an employers' organisation, or to take part in such an organisation's activities.

In any dispute regarding victimisation or interference with freedom of association, the complainant merely has to prove that he has been compelled, threatened, prohibited, or detrimentally affected in any manner, and it is then up to the defendant to prove that his action was not contrary to any of the provisions of the Act (Section 10).

Rights of trade unions and employers' organisations

Employers are granted essentially the same rights as employees in respect of freedom of association and freedom from victimisation. Trade unions and employers' associations likewise have the right to establish independently constituted bodies, to organise their own administration and activities, to take part in the establishment of federations, and to affiliate to other bodies, both locally and internationally.

Every trade union and employers' organisation has the right to determine its own constitution and rules and to elect office bearers, officials, and representatives, subject to the provisions of Chapter 6 of the Act.

5.4.3 Collective bargaining

The Act promotes collective bargaining, in particular sectoral level collective bargaining, as the desired method of settling wages and conditions of employment.

Although the Act does not contain a statutory right to bargain in the strict sense of the word, a duty to bargain is strongly promoted, given the statutory organisational rights now afforded trade unions.

Organisational rights

Unions are accorded 'sufficiently representative' rights, such as the right to access, to hold meetings with employees outside working hours (Section 12), to conduct an election at the workplace, and to be granted stop order facilities (Section 13). A majority union, or more than one union which together represent a majority of employees at the workplace, may also appoint shop stewards, may be given information necessary for the purpose of representation or collective bargaining and, in consultation with the employer, may establish thresholds for representation.

More attention is focused on access to the workplace, leave for trade union activities, and disclosure of information, since they have far-reaching implications for human resources managers.

Trade union access to workplace

A 'representative trade union' means any registered trade union, or two or more registered trade unions acting jointly that are sufficiently representative of employees employed. According to Le Roux (1995: 21) there is no definition of 'sufficiently representative' and if there is a dispute in this regard it should be resolved through arbitration undertaken by the Commission.

Any office-bearer or official of a representative trade union is entitled to enter the employer's premises to recruit, to communicate with its members, or just to serve its interests. Trade unions are entitled to hold meetings with employees outside their working hours at the employer's premises and, with members of a representative trade union, are entitled to vote at the employer's premises in any election or ballot in terms of that trade union's constitution.

The right of access to an employer's premises does not, however, include the right to enter the home of a domestic worker's employer, for which his or her consent is necessary.

Leave for trade union activities

In terms of Section 15 of the Labour Relations Act, an employee who is an office bearer of a representative trade union, or a federation of trade unions to which the representative trade union is affiliated, is entitled to take reasonable leave during working hours to perform the functions of that office and to be trained in any subject relevant to the performance of those functions.

The number of days leave, the number of days paid leave, and the conditions of leave may be agreed between the employer and trade union representative.

Disclosure of information

In terms of Section 16, an employer must disclose to a trade union representative all relevant information needed for the effective performance of his or her functions. Whenever an employer consults or bargains with a representative trade union, the employer must disclose all information necessary for the representative trade union to engage effectively in such consultation or collective bargaining.

The employer must notify the trade union representative or the representative trade union in writing if any information disclosed is confidential. An employer is not required to disclose information that:
- is legally privileged;
- cannot be disclosed without contravening a prohibition imposed on the employer by any law or order of any court;
- is confidential and, if disclosed, may cause substantial harm to an employee or the employer; or
- is private, personal information relating to an employee unless that employee consents to the disclosure of that information.

In a dispute about what information is required to be disclosed in terms of this section, any of the parties may refer the dispute in writing to the CCMA. The party that does so must satisfy the Commission that a copy of the referral has been served on all other parties to the dispute.

It is interesting to note that the right to disclosure of information (Section 16 of the Labour Relations Act) does not apply in the domestic sector.

The exercise of organisational rights

According to Section 21 of the Act, any registered trade union may notify an employer in writing at any time that it wishes to exercise organisational rights in a workplace. A certified copy of the trade union's certificate of registration must accompany the notice, which must specify:
- the workplace where the trade union seeks to exercise the rights;
- the representatives of the trade union in that workplace, and the facts that show that it is a representative trade union; and
- the rights that the trade union seeks to exercise and how they will be exercised.

The employer must meet the registered trade union within thirty days of receiving the notice and must attempt to conclude a collective agreement on how the trade union will exercise the rights in that workplace.

If a collective agreement is not concluded, either the trade union or the employer may refer the dispute in writing to the CCMA. The Commission must appoint a commissioner to attempt to resolve the dispute through conciliation.

An employer who alleges that a trade union is no longer a representative trade union may apply to the Commission to withdraw any of the organisational rights, by way of the conciliation and arbitration process, should there be a dispute.

Collective agreements

The Act defines a collective agreement very widely as a written agreement between, on the one hand, one or more regis-

Figure 5.3 Collective agreements

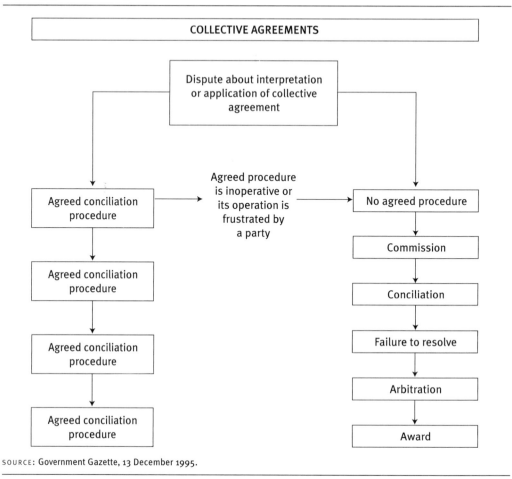

SOURCE: Government Gazette, 13 December 1995.

tered trade unions and, on the other, one or more employers, or one or more registered employers' organisations, or one or more employers together with one or more registered employers' organisations, concerning terms and conditions of employment or any other matter of mutual interest.

A collective agreement binds employees who are not members of the registered trade union or unions in the agreement if the employees are identified in the agreement. The agreement expressly binds them if the majority of employees in the workplace are members of the trade union(s).

Figure 5.3, contained in Schedule 4 of the Labour Relations Act, indicates how a dispute about the interpretation or application of a collective agreement should be executed.

Agency shop agreements

According to Section 25 of the Act, a representative trade union and an employer or employers' organisation may conclude an agency shop agreement, whereby the employer will deduct an agreed agency fee from the wages of employees who are identified in the agreement and who are not members of the trade union.

An agency shop agreement is binding only if it makes provision for employees not to be compelled to become members of the trade union, and the agreed agency fees are paid. The amount deducted must be paid into a separate account administered by the representative trade union, and no part of it may be paid to a political party as an affiliation fee, contributed in cash or kind to a political party or a person standing for election to any political office, or used for any expenditure that does not advance or protect the socio-economic interests of employees.

An employer does not need employees' authorisation to deduct the agreed agency fee from their wages. A conscientious objector may request the employer to pay the amount deducted into a fund administered by the Department of Labour (see Section 25(4)(b) of the Labour Relations Act).

Closed shop agreements

The reappearance of the closed shop agreement in the Act apparently violates the freedom of disassociation of an employee, in the sense that he or she is compelled to belong to a certain union on joining a certain employer in a certain industry.

A representative trade union and an employer or employers' organisation may conclude a closed shop agreement, requiring all employees covered by the agreement to be members of the trade union.

A registered trade union and a registered employers' organisation may conclude a closed shop agreement in respect of a sector and area.

Bargaining councils

Bargaining councils (Sections 27–34) were introduced to replace industrial councils under the old Labour Relations Act. Provision has been made for industrial councils to transform into bargaining councils. Registered trade unions and registered employers' organisations may establish a bargaining council for a sector and area.

The state may be a party to a bargaining council if it is an employer in the sector and area in respect of which the bargaining council is established.

Various other bargaining councils may also be formed, e.g. public sector and statutory councils, but these will not be discussed here.

According to Section 28 of the Act, a registered bargaining council, among other functions, may:
- conclude and enforce collective agreements;
- prevent and resolve labour disputes;
- perform the dispute resolution functions;
- establish and administer a fund to be used for resolving disputes;
- promote and establish training and education schemes; and
- establish and administer pension, provident, medical aid, sick pay, holiday, unemployment, and training schemes for the benefit of the parties to the bargaining council or their members.

A collective agreement concluded in a bargaining council binds to the bargaining council only those who are parties to the collective agreement. According to Section 32 of the Labour Relations Act, however, a bargaining council may ask the Minister in writing to extend such a collective agreement to non-parties to the collective agreement (within its registered scope and identified in the request) if at a meeting of the bargaining council:
- the members of one or more of the major registered trade unions in the bargaining council vote in favour of the extension; or

- the members of one or more of the major registered employers' organisations in the bargaining council vote in favour of the extension.

The Minister must extend the collective agreement within sixty days, as requested, by publishing a notice in the Government Gazette declaring that the agreement will bind the non-parties stipulated in the notice from a specified date and for a specified period.

5.4.4 Strikes and lock-outs

Industrial action, especially in the form of strikes, is discussed in Chapter 4 of the Act, and is a relatively common occurrence in South Africa. Most strikes occur as a result of wage disputes, followed by dismissal disputes.

In terms of the Act, every employee has a fundamental right to strike. This right is subject to certain limitations, which are mentioned below. This is also strictly in line with the letter and spirit of the Constitution. The definition of a strike in the Act is essentially similar to that in the old Act, with one major exception: voluntary or compulsory overtime bans are included in the definition.

Defining strikes and lock-outs

Section 213 of the Act defines a strike as:

The partial or complete considered refusal to work or the retardation or obstruction of work by persons who are or have been employed by the same employer or by different employers, for the purpose of remedying a grievance or resolving a dispute in respect of any matter of mutual interest between employer and employee, and every reference to 'work' in this definition includes overtime work, whether it is voluntary or compulsory.

Regarding a work stoppage itself, when a group of employees lay down their tools during working hours and decline to resume work, there is no question that their action amounts to a 'concerted refusal to work'. With one exception, a stoppage entails a refusal to do work which the employees are contractually obliged to perform. The exception is overtime, the refusal of which amounts to a strike if the overtime is compulsory in terms of a contract or collective agreement. There is no requirement as to the duration of the stoppage. Partial strikes, such as work-to-rules, go-slows, and 'grasshopper' (intermittent) stoppages also clearly amount to strikes. Joint action by employees, aimed against the employer and for a recognised purpose, or protest action, may also constitute a strike.

Section 213 of the Act defines protest action, which is different from strike action, as follows:

A partial or complete concerted refusal to work, or the retardation or obstruction of work, for the purpose of promoting or defending the socio-economic interests of workers, but not for a purpose referred to in the definition of strike.

Although the Act does not openly indicate that the purpose of a strike is to force an unwilling employer to do something, the definition does imply force: the joint action of employees must aim at remedying a grievance or resolving a dispute.

In terms of Section 213 of the Act, a lock-out is defined as follows:

Lock-out means the exclusion by an employer of employees from the employer's workplace, for the purpose of compelling the employees to accept a demand in respect of any matter of mutual interest between employer and employee, whether or not the employer breaches those employee's contracts of employment in the course of or for the purpose of that exclusion.

Strikes and lock-outs which are forbidden

In terms of Section 65, the Act forbids a person from engaging in strikes, lock-outs, and conduct aimed at or promoting them if:
- a collective agreement that binds that person prohibits a strike or lock out for the issue in dispute;
- a collective agreement or an arbitration award that binds that person regulates the issue in dispute, unless the collective agreement permits it;
- there is a collective agreement that became a determination by the Minister, unless the collective agreement permits it;
- an agreement binds that person to use compulsory arbitration on the issue in dispute;
- it is during the first year of a wage determination made in terms of the Wage Act that regulates the issue in dispute;
- a party has the right in terms of the Act to refer the issue in dispute to arbitration or to the Labour Court; or
- a person is engaged in an essential or a maintenance service.

Procedures to be followed to engage in protected strike action

According to Section 64, various procedures must be followed for an employee to embark on a protected strike action or for an employer to lock-out his or her employees.

The dispute must be referred to either a bargaining or statutory council (if there is one) or to the CCMA, and a certificate issued stating that the dispute remains unresolved. These institutions have thirty days, or any further period as agreed by the parties, to attempt to resolve the dispute.

If the dispute concerns a refusal to bargain (which includes a refusal to recognise a trade union as a collective bargaining agent, or the withdrawal of such recognition, or a dispute about appropriate bargaining units, levels, or subjects) then an advisory award by the commission is required in addition to the other requirements.

At least forty-eight hours written notice of either strike or lock-out must be given to the other party or parties.

Strikes or lockouts instituted after compliance with these procedures are referred to as protected strikes or lock-outs.

Strikes and lock-outs in compliance with the Act

According to Section 67, any person who takes part in a strike or lockout which complies with the required procedures, or conducts himself or herself in contemplation or in furtherance of such strike or lock-out does not thereby commit a delict or a breach of contract.

An employer is not compelled to pay employees not working as a result of a strike or lockout, whether protected or not, i.e. the 'no work, no pay' rule still applies. Where pay includes payment in kind, accommodation, food, etc., this shall not be discontinued at the request of the employee. The employer may afterwards recover the monetary value by way of civil proceedings in the Labour Court.

An employer may not dismiss an employee by virtue of the fact that the employee has participated in a protected strike. The following very important exceptions do however apply, in which case employees may be dismissed:

- for a fair reason connected with the employee's conduct during the strike, e.g. theft, wilful damage to property, assault, or endangering the safety of the employer, other employees, or the public; and
- for a reason based on the employer's operational requirements, in which case the normal consultation procedures for retrenchment must be followed.

The Act contains an indemnity that no civil legal proceedings may be brought against any person who participates in or for conduct in furtherance of a procedural or protected strike or lock-out. The indemnity shall, however, not apply to any act which is an offence. A contravention of the Basic Conditions of Employment Act (e.g. the non-payment of wages during a strike) does not constitute an offence for the purpose of this provision.

Secondary strikes (sympathy strikes)

A secondary strike is one which supports other workers who are on strike against their employer. In other words, the employees in this instance go on strike to pledge their solidarity with fellow unionists who are on strike, and their action has nothing to do with their own employer and is not even directed at their employer. However, a strike is not regarded as a secondary strike if it pursues a demand referred to a council as a dispute in which the striking employees have a material interest, and if they are employees within the registered scope of that council.

Picketing

According to Nel (ed.) (1999:197–198) rules for picketing are set out in Section 69 of the Act, to accommodate this phenomenon in the South African business environment. Provision is made for a registered trade union to authorise a peaceful picket by its members and supporters in support of a protected strike, or in opposing any lockout. Pickets under the authority of the Act may be held regardless of any laws regulating the right of assembly.

Employees participating in a picket are protected from any delictual action or breach of contract, from dismissal, and from any civil legal proceedings. The right to picket is now guaranteed in the Constitution. The Act extends this right further by making provision for picketing at the employer's premises. The picket may be at any place outside the premises of an employer to which the public has access, unless the employer has consented for it to take place inside the premises.

The employer may not withhold this permission unreasonably.

Essential and maintenance services

The Act also outlaws strikes in essential services or maintenance services in terms of Sections 71–75. Employers and employees engaged in essential services and maintenance services are prohibited from embarking on industrial action or socio-economic protest action. Both types of service are briefly discussed below.
- *Essential services.* Essential services are defined as those services whose interruption would endanger the life, personal safety, or health of the whole or part of the population. The Act does not provide a specific list of essential services to provide an element of certainty as to which services are essential. The only two exceptions are the South African Police Service and the parliamentary service.
- *Maintenance services.* The concept of maintenance services is also introduced by the Act, in terms of which a service is a maintenance service if its interruption has the effect of the material physical destruction of any working area, plant, or machinery.

The need to contain industrial action, which goes beyond the infliction of economic harm alone to the complete destruction of the wealth-generating capacity of the working area, plant, or machinery, is the justification for this prohibition.

Protest action

Section 77 of the Act grants the right to every employee, except those in essential or maintenance services, to take part in protest action to promote or defend the socio-economic interests of workers. This type of action is more commonly referred to in South Africa as 'mass action'.

The Labour Court has jurisdiction to grant an interdict or restraining order in respect of protest action not in conformity with the Act. The Labour Court, further, has the power to lift the protection of the Act, depending on circumstances such as the nature and duration of the protest action and the conduct of the parties.

Readers must refer to the relevant sections of Chapter 6 of this book where the management of strikes is also discussed.

5.4.5 Workplace forums

Workplace forums, introduced in Chapter 5 of the Act, are structures that are made up of representatives of workers and junior management employees. In terms of the Act, the role of a workplace forum is to promote the interests of all employees in the workplace (irrespective of whether they are trade union members) excluding senior managerial employees (whose contracts of employment or status authorise them to hire and fire, to formulate policy, to represent the employer's interests in interactions with workplace forums, and who may thus make decisions that may be in conflict with the representation of employees in the workplace). The term 'employee' in Chapter 5 specifically precludes senior managerial employees, who are viewed as 'employers'. Workplace forums must strive to enhance efficiency in the workplace. They have to be consulted by the employer with a view to reaching consensus about certain issues and they must be respected as joint decision-making structures in respect of specific matters.

In terms of Section 79, the functions of a workplace forum are to:
- promote the interests of all employees in the workplace, whether or not they are trade union members;
- enhance efficiency in the workplace;
- be consulted by the employer, with a view to reaching consensus, about the matters referred to in Section 84; and
- participate in joint decision-making about the matters referred to in Section 86.

In terms of Section 80, only a majority union can initiate a workplace forum. The employer cannot impose such a forum.

5.4.6 Trade unions and employers' organisations

In Chapter 6 of the Labour Relations Act, the registration and regulation of trade unions and employers' organisations are discussed.

For the purpose of this book, the readers' attention is drawn only to stipulations regulating the registration of trade unions and employers' organisations. For more detail, Sections 95 to 111 are to be consulted.

A trade union is independent if it is not controlled (directly or indirectly) by an employer or employers' organisation and is free of any interference or influence from an employer or employers' organisation.

The constitution of any trade union or employers' organisation, which intends to register, may not discriminate directly or indirectly against any person on the grounds of race or sex.

Every trade union and employers' organisation has the right to determine its own constitution and rules and to elect office bearers, officials, and representatives, subject to the provisions of the Act.

Readers should refer to Chapter 6 of this book for details regarding the actual functioning of employers' organisations and trade unions (including those of shop stewards).

5.4.7 Dispute resolution

In Chapter 7 of the Act, some of the most dramatic changes from the old dispensation are legislated. The Commission for Conciliation, Mediation and Arbitration (CCMA) referred to as 'The Commission', is introduced into the Act.

Because of the human resources function focus of this book, only the most important elements with regard to dispute resolution are discussed as they provide guidance to human resources and employment relations officials.

Commission for Conciliation, Mediation and Arbitration (CCMA)

The Commission for Conciliation, Mediation and Arbitration (CCMA) is an independent body with jurisdiction in all the provinces of South Africa.

The CCMA's functions are to:
- attempt to resolve, through conciliation, any dispute referred to it in terms of the Labour Relations Act;
- arbitrate the dispute if the act requires arbitration or if it remains unresolved after conciliation, or any party has requested that the dispute be resolved through arbitration;
- assist in the establishment of workplace forums; and
- compile and publish information and statistics about its activities.

The CCMA may give advice or provide training on matters relating to the primary objectives of the Act, which are among others:
- establishing collective bargaining structures;
- designing, establishing, and electing workplace forums and creating deadlock-breaking mechanisms;
- the functioning of workplace forums;
- preventing and resolving disputes and employees' grievances;
- disciplinary procedures;
- procedures in relation to dismissals;
- the process of restructuring the workplace;
- affirmative action and equal opportunity programmes; and
- sexual harassment in the workplace.

The CCMA must attempt to resolve disputes either through conciliation or arbitration. These approaches are briefly outlined below.

Resolution of disputes through conciliation

When a dispute has been referred to the CCMA, it must appoint a commissioner to attempt to resolve it through conciliation (Section 135). The commissioner must attempt to resolve the dispute within thirty days of the CCMA receiving the referral. However, the parties may agree to extend the thirty-day period.

The commissioner must determine a process to attempt to resolve the dispute, which may include mediating the dispute, conducting a fact-finding exercise, and making a recommendation to the parties (e.g. an advisory arbitration award).

At the end of the thirty-day period or the period agreed between the parties:
- the commissioner must issue a certificate stating whether or not the dispute has been resolved;

- the commissioner must file the original of the certificate with the CCMA; and
- the CCMA must serve a copy of that certificate on each party to the dispute or his or her representative.

Arbitration of disputes

If the Act requires a dispute to be resolved through arbitration, the CCMA must appoint a commissioner to arbitrate that dispute. The commissioner may decide on the most appropriate way to conduct the arbitration in order to resolve the dispute fairly and quickly, but must deal with the substantial merits of the dispute with the least legal formality.

A party to the dispute may give evidence, call witnesses, question witnesses of any other party and address concluding arguments to the commissioner.

If all the parties consent, the commissioner may suspend the arbitration proceedings and attempt to resolve the dispute through conciliation. A party to the dispute may appear in person or be represented only by a legal practitioner, a co-employee, or a member, office-bearer, or official of that party's trade union or employers' organisation or, in the case of a juristic person, by a director or an employee.

Within fourteen days of the conclusion of the arbitration proceedings, the commissioner must issue and sign an arbitration award with brief reasons.

If a dispute about a matter of mutual interest proceeds to arbitration and any party is engaged in an essential service (Section 139), the commissioner must, within thirty days of the date of the certificate or within a period agreed between the parties to the dispute, complete the arbitration and issue and sign an arbitration award with brief reasons.

If the dispute being arbitrated is about fairness of a dismissal (Section 140 of the Labour Relations Act) and a party has alleged that the reason for the dismissal relates to the employee's conduct or capacity, the parties are not entitled to be represented by a legal practitioner in the arbitration proceedings unless:

- all the other parties and the commissioner consent; and
- the commissioner concludes that it is unreasonable to expect a party to deal with the dispute without legal representation, after considering the:
  - nature of the questions of law raised by the dispute;
  - complexity of the dispute;
  - public interest; and
  - comparative ability of the opposing parties or their representatives to deal with the arbitration of the dispute.

If a dispute remains unresolved after conciliation, the CCMA must arbitrate the dispute if any of the parties would otherwise be entitled to refer the dispute to the Labour Court for adjudication but, instead, all the parties agree to arbitration under the auspices of the CCMA.

An arbitration award is final and binding and may be made an order of the Labour Court, unless it is an advisory award. Any party to a dispute who alleges a defect in any arbitration proceedings under the auspices of the CCMA may apply to the Labour Court within six weeks to set aside the decision. The Arbitration Act No. 42 of 1965 does not apply to any arbitration under the auspices of the CCMA.

Readers are also referred to Chapter 6 of this book for more detail regarding the conciliation and arbitration of disputes via means additional to the CCMA.

The Labour Court

In relation to matters under its jurisdiction, the Labour Court is a court of law and a superior court with authority, inherent powers, and standing equal to a court of a provincial division of the High Court. The proceedings in the Labour Court are open to the public, but it may exclude people in any case where a court of a provincial division of the Supreme Court could have done so.

Any party may appeal to the Labour Appeal Court against any final judgement or final order of the Labour Court. If the application to appeal is refused, the applicant may petition the Labour Appeal Court for leave to appeal. Leave to appeal may be granted subject to any conditions that the court concerned may determine.

Readers are also referred to Chapter 6 of this book for further detail regarding dispute resolution by the labour court.

The Labour Appeal Court

In terms of Section 167, the Labour Appeal Court is a court of law and equity, and also the final court of appeal in respect of all judgements and orders made by the Labour Court on matters within its exclusive jurisdiction. The Labour Appeal Court is a superior court and has authority, inherent powers, and standing in relation to matters under its jurisdiction, equal to that of the Appellate Division of the High Court.

The Labour Appeal Court has the power to receive further evidence, either orally or by deposition before a person appointed by it, or to remit the case to the Labour Court for further hearing, with any instructions on the taking of further evidence or otherwise, as it may consider necessary. The Labour Appeal Court may further confirm, amend or set aside the judgement or order that is the subject of the appeal, and give a judgement or make an order according to the circumstances.

5.4.8 Unfair dismissals

In Chapter 8 of the Act (as well as in Schedule 8, Code of Good Practice: Dismissal) the question of dismissal is dealt with. While the intention of the Act is to deal with all aspects of individual labour law, anti-discriminatory measures are dealt with in the Employment Equity Act.

It is important to note that the definition of an unfair labour practice is wide ranging and includes any unfair act or omission that arises between an employer and an employee.

Dismissal, according to Section 186, means that:
- an employer has terminated a contract of employment with or without notice;
- an employee reasonably expected the employer to renew a fixed-term contract of employment on the same or similar terms, but the employer offered to renew it on less favourable terms, or did not renew it;
- an employer refused to allow an employee to resume work after she:
  - took maternity leave in terms of any law, collective agreement, or her contract of employment;
  - was absent from work for up to four weeks before the expected date, and up to eight weeks after the actual date, of the birth of her child;
- an employer who dismissed a number of employees for the same or similar reasons has offered to re-employ one or more of them, but has refused to re-employ another; or
- an employee terminated a contract of employment with or without notice because the employer made continued employment intolerable for the employee.

In terms of Section 187, a dismissal is to be regarded as automatically unfair if the employer dismisses an employee for any of the following reasons:
- the employee participated in or supported or indicated an intention to participate in or support a strike or

protest action that complies with the provisions of Chapter 4 of the Act;
- the employee refused or indicated an intention to refuse to do any work normally done by an employee who at the time was taking part in a strike that complies with the provisions of Chapter 4 or was locked out, unless that work was necessary to prevent an actual danger to life, personal safety, or health;
- to compel the employee to accept a demand in respect of any matter of mutual interest between the employer and employee;
- the employee took action, or indicated an intention to take action, allowed by the Act, against the employer;
- the employee's pregnancy, intended

Figure 5.4 Unfair dismissal (automatically unfair reasons)

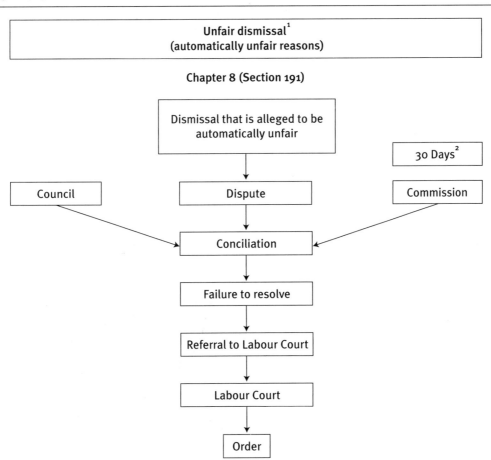

1 Examples of dismissals that are automatically unfair include dismissal for participation in a protected strike, dismissal on account of pregnancy and dismissal that amounts to discrimination.
2 The time limit is designed to ensure that disputes are dealt with as soon as possible. Condonation can be granted if there is a good cause to do so.

SOURCE: Labour Relations Act (1995:245).

pregnancy, or any reason related to her pregnancy; or
- unfair discrimination against an employee, directly or indirectly on any arbitrary ground, including, but not limited to race, gender, sex, ethnic or social origin, colour, sexual orientation, age, disability, religion, conscience, belief, political opinion, culture, language, marital status, or family responsibility.

In this regard, see the flow diagram in Figure 5.4, contained in Schedule 4 of the Act, which indicates the procedure to be followed.

A dismissal may be fair if the reason for the dismissal is based on an inherent requirement for the job or the dismissal is based on age, which is fair if the employee has reached the normal agreed retirement age for persons employed in that capacity.

The Act indicates in Section 188 that a dismissal that is not automatically unfair will be unfair if the employer fails to prove that:
- the reason for the dismissal is a fair reason and is related to:
  - the employee's conduct or capacity;
  - the employer's operational requirements;
- the dismissal was effected in accordance with a fair procedure.

Any employer, or for that matter, the relevant official, in considering whether or not the reason for dismissal is a fair reason, or whether or not the dismissal took place in accordance with a fair procedure, must bear in mind the contents of the Code of Good Practice: Dismissal, in Schedule 8 of the Act.

The Code of Good Practice: Dismissal provides detailed guidelines, which ought to be followed to ensure that a dismissal is fair. Guidelines in this regard include:
- fair reasons for dismissal;
- misconduct and the disciplinary procedures that should be followed prior to dismissal;
- what a fair procedure would entail;
- a review of disciplinary records;
- dismissal for industrial action;
- dismissal for misconduct;
- incapacity based on poor work performance;
- dismissal based on incapacity due to ill health or injury;
- dismissal for poor work performance; and
- dismissal based on ill health or injury.

The handling of discipline in terms of procedures, penalties and so on is discussed in Chapter 6 of this book.

Implications for employers

Human resources and employment relations officials must take note of the following, which could also be regarded as unfair practices in terms of Schedule 7 of the Act. Points to consider are:
- an employee includes an applicant for employment, who therefore falls under the Act for all intents and purposes when dealing with unfair labour practices;
- affirmative action is not regarded as unfair discrimination;
- discrimination based on an inherent requirement of a particular job does not constitute unfair discrimination;
- unfair conduct relating to the promotion, demotion, or training of an employee or relating to the provision of benefits to an employee certainly falls under the Act;
- the unfair suspension of an employee or any other disciplinary action short of dismissal in respect of an employee will probably lead to a dispute and action being taken; and
- the failure or refusal of an employer to reinstate or re-employ a former

Figure 5.5 Unfair labour practice

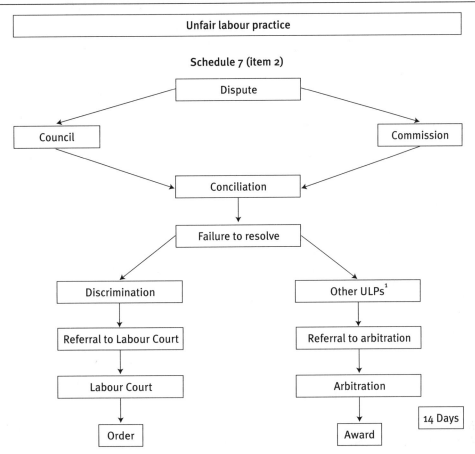

1 Other unfair labour practices include unfair conduct by the employer relating to promotion-demotion, training or the provision of benefits, unfair suspension, the failure to reinstate or re-employ an employee in terms of any agreement.

SOURCE: Labour Relations Act (1995:249).

employee in terms of any agreement will undoubtedly also be regarded as an unfair labour practice.

Human resources and industrial relations officials should note that because the unfair discrimination provision extends to work seekers, it will impact on recruitment and selection procedures, in other words, on advertising of vacancies, screening and testing of applicants, and selection of candidates for employment. Employee specifications should therefore focus solely on the inherent requirements for the job.

Figure 5.5 is a flow diagram in Schedule 4 of the Act, showing the procedure to be followed.

Limits on compensation for dismissal

It is important for human resources and employment relations officials to take note of the penalties for an unfair dismissal, since it could have far-reaching financial implications for an organisation, over and above severance pay.

In terms of Section 194, if a dismissal is unfair only because the employer did not allow a fair procedure, compensation must be equal to the remuneration an employee would have been paid between the date of dismissal and the last day of the hearing of the arbitration or adjudication, as the case may be, calculated at the employee's rate of remuneration on the date of dismissal. Compensation may not be awarded, however, in respect of any unreasonable period of delay caused by the employee in initiating or prosecuting a claim.

The compensation awarded to an employee whose dismissal is found to be unfair because the employer did not prove that the reason for dismissal was a fair reason related to the employee's conduct or capacity, or based on the employer's operational requirements, must be just and equitable in all the circumstances, but not less than the amount specified above and not more than the equivalent of twelve months remuneration calculated at the employee's rate of remuneration on the date of dismissal.

The compensation awarded to an employee whose dismissal is automatically unfair must be just and equitable in all the circumstances, but not more than the equivalent of twenty-four months remuneration calculated at the employee's rate of remuneration on the date of dismissal.

An award of compensation made as above is in addition to, and not a substitute for, any amounts to which an employee is entitled in terms of any law, collective agreement, or contract of employment (for example, overtime pay which is due, or performance bonuses).

Further details of the Labour Relations Act and applications thereof are discussed in Chapter 6 and other chapters in this book.

5.5 Occupational Health and Safety Act No. 85 of 1993

The Occupational Health and Safety Act ensures that no party can agree to work being conducted in unsafe conditions. The Act applies to all workers, including agricultural workers, domestic servants, public servants, and students. The general public who may be affected in terms of their health or safety are also included in the Act. The ambit of the Act is much wider than that of the other Acts, since it covers everybody in South Africa, except those in the mining industry and merchant shipping, which are separately legislated.

5.5.1 The purpose and scope of the Act

The Act covers all areas of employment and the use of machinery, which means that employees such as designers, suppliers, and installers of machinery and equipment are included. Others are also protected from hazards to their health and safety caused by the activities of persons at work. The Act further establishes an Advisory Council for Occupational Health and Safety.

Persons in any form of work activity, except for one-person businesses, are included in the definitions of employer and employee. Included are unpaid helpers, employees paid by some other agency, and independent contractors or sub-contractors.

The Act may be extended in terms of Section 1(2) which states that: 'The Minister may by notice in the Gazette declare that a person belonging to a category of persons specified in the notice shall for the purposes of this Act or any provision thereof be deemed to be an employee, and thereupon any person vested and charged with the control and supervision of the said persons shall for the said purposes be deemed to be the employer of such person.' The definition of 'employer' and 'employee' in this Act are thus the same as those contained in the Labour Relations Act and in the Basic Conditions of Employment Act.

Victimisation is forbidden in terms of Section 26 of this Act, in that no employer shall be allowed to dismiss an employee, or reduce the rate of his or her remuneration, or alter the terms or conditions of his or her employment because the employee has supplied information to the Minister, inspector, or any other party, regarding accidents, threats to occupational health and safety, and so on.

The Act makes provision for an advisory council on occupational safety, the duties of employers, employees, and safety representatives. It furthermore focuses attention on safety committees, the reporting of incidents, enquiries, the prohibition of victimisation, and stipulations regarding offences and penalties. Only the major aspects are focused on here.

5.5.2 The duties of employers concerning health and safety

The duties of employers are as follows:
- to ensure that systems of work, plant, and machinery are reasonably safe and without health risks;
- to initiate steps to eliminate possible health and safety hazards or risks before resorting to the use of protective equipment;
- to ensure, as far as is reasonably practicable, that the production, use, handling, storage or transport of articles and substances does not endanger health and safety;
- to establish which hazards or risks are involved in any type of work and in the handling of any substance, and what precautionary measures should be taken;
- to provide the necessary information, instruction, training, and supervision;
- to ensure that precautionary measures and the requirements of the Act are implemented;
- to ensure that work is performed, and plant or machinery is used, under the supervision of a trained person with sufficient authority to ensure that safety measures are implemented;
- in the area of 'listed' work (so declared by the Minister) to ensure not only that all safety measures are taken, but also that occupational hygiene and biological monitoring programmes are undertaken;
- to inform safety representatives of the steps taken to identify the hazards and evaluate the risks entailed in 'listed' work, and of the monitoring and occupational hygiene programmes and their results;
- to inform all employees of the danger involved in their work;
- to provide facilities, assistance, and training to health and safety representatives;
- to inform health and safety representatives beforehand of inspections, investigations, formal inquiries, and applications for exemption;
- to inform representatives of any incident which occurs at the workplace ('incident' is defined as an occurrence as a result of which a person dies, becomes unconscious, loses a limb or part of a limb, becomes so ill that he is likely to die or be disabled, or will not be able to work for a period of more than fourteen days); and
- to see that the safety committee performs its functions.

5.5.3 The duties of employees concerning health and safety at work

Employees themselves have a duty to care for their own health and safety, to obey the safety regulations, to cooperate with the employer in this regard, to report any unsafe situation to the safety representative of the employer, and to report to the employer, his mandatory or a safety representative any incident which has caused an injury to himself. Thus the maintenance of safety is the joint responsibility of the employer, the safety representative, the employees, and (if one exists) the safety committee. The greater responsibility, however, still falls on the employer.

The general duties of employees at work are set out in Section 14. These are that every employee shall:
- take reasonable care for the health and safety of himself and of other persons who may be affected by his acts or omissions;
- as regards any duty or requirement imposed on his employer or any other person by this Act, cooperate with such employer or person to enable that duty or requirement to be performed or complied with; and
- carry out any lawful order given to him, and obey the health and safety rules.

5.5.4 The Advisory Council for Occupational Health and Safety

The functions of the Council are to:
- advise the Minister of Labour concerning matters of policy in relation to the application of the Act and any matter relating to occupational safety and health;
- perform other functions referred to it by the Minister of Labour;
- conduct research and investigations which it considers to be necessary;
- make rules concerning the conduct of meetings of the Council and technical committees established by the Council; and
- advise the Department of Labour concerning the formulation and publication of standards, specifications, and other forms of guidance, the promotion of education and training in, and the collection of dissemination of information about, occupational health and safety.

5.5.5 Penalties for offences

No one may tamper with, discourage, deceive, or unduly influence somebody who is to give evidence, and no one may prejudice or precipitate proceedings, tamper with or misuse safety equipment, or wilfully or recklessly do anything which endangers health or safety. These offences are subject to fines of up to R50 000 or one year's imprisonment, or both. Finally, anyone who commits or omits to do an act and thereby injures another person in such a way that, if he were to die, the perpetrator would have been guilty of culpable homicide, can (irrespective of whether or not the person dies) be subject to a fine of up to R100 000 or two years' imprisonment, or both.

Further details of the Occupational Health and Safety Act, and applications thereof, are discussed in Chapter 6.

5.6 Skills Development Act No. 97 of 1998

Training is of critical importance in South Africa and a major overhaul has taken place in recent years. The forerunner to these adjustments was the South African Qualifications Authority Act No.58 of 1995 which put in place the South African Qualifications Authority and its functions, which have been executed by a board since 31 May 1996. The Authority is required to pursue the objectives of the National Qualifications Framework (NQF). The objectives of the NQF, according to Section 2 of the Act, are to:
- create an integrated national framework

for learning achievements;
- facilitate access to and mobility and progression within education, training, and career paths;
- enhance the quality of education and training;
- accelerate the redress of past unfair discrimination in education, training, and employment opportunities; and thereby
- contribute to the full personal development of each learner and the social and economic development of the nation at large.

This provided the backdrop for the Skills Development Act which came into effect on 1 February 1999, replacing the Manpower Training Act and the Guidance and Placement Act.

5.6.1 The purpose and scope of the Act

According to Section 2, the purposes of the Act are to:
- develop the skills of the South African workforce;
- increase the levels of investment in education and training in the labour market and to improve the return on investment;
- use the workplace as an active learning environment, to provide employees with the opportunities to acquire new skills, and to provide opportunities for new entrants to the labour market to gain work experience;
- employ persons who find it difficult to be employed;
- encourage workers to participate in leadership and other training programmes;
- improve the employment prospects of persons previously disadvantaged by unfair discrimination and to redress those disadvantages through training and education;
- ensure the quality of education and training in and for the workplace;
- assist work-seekers to find work, retrenched workers to re-enter the labour market, and employers to find qualified employees; and
- provide and regulate employment services.

These purposes are to be achieved by:
- establishing an institutional and financial framework comprising: the National Skills Authority, the National Skills Fund, a skills development levy-grant scheme as stipulated in Section 15(6) of the Skills Development Levies Act, Sector Educational and Training Authorities (SETAs), labour centres, and a Skills Development Planning Unit;
- encouraging partnerships between the public and private sectors of the economy to provide education and training in and for the workplace; and
- cooperating with the South African Qualifications Authority.

In regard to the further enhancement of skills development in South Africa, the Skills Development Levies Act was passed in 1999 to regulate the imposition and collection of levies for training purposes, the role of SETAs and the Commissioner, as well as the distribution of levies, recovery of levies by SETAs, etc. In terms of the Act, every employer must pay a skills development levy from 1 April 2000 at a rate of 0,5 per cent of the leviable amount (meaning the total amount of remuneration payable to an employee during any month as determined in the Fourth Schedule of the Income Tax Act, but excluding pensions, superannuations or retirement allowances) and 1 per cent from 1 April 2001 for the training and education of employees. The South African Revenue Services (SARS) is to be the national collection agency.

5.6.2 Application of the Act

According to Swanepoel et al. (2000:487) various managerial challenges and implications of the new Training Legislation should be taken note of. These are to:
- ensure that all stakeholders in the organisation are aware of the different Acts and the employer's responsibilities;
- participate in the bodies as set out by the South African Qualifications Authority (for example, standards generating bodies and Education Training Quality Assurers);
- participate in the process of establishing a SETA and in the planning thereof;
- align the organisation's human resources strategy, in particular the Education and Training strategy, with the overall business strategy; and
- make finances and personnel available to involve themselves in the NQF alignment process and for paying levies.

Further details the Training and Development Legislation and applications thereof are discussed in Chapters 19 and 20 of this book.

5.7 Compensation for Occupational Injuries and Diseases Act No. 130 of 1993

The Act allows for compensation to be paid to an employee who, as a result of his activities in the work situation, is partially or totally disabled, or contracts an occupational disease. In the event that the employee dies as a result of the accident, injury or disease, the compensation will be paid to his dependants. The Act is focused on all employees, including casual and seasonal workers, and directors who have a contract of employment. It must be noted that the Act also includes members of the Permanent Force of the SANDF and members of the SA Police Services while employed on service in defence of the Republic. It also applies to independent contractors and domestic workers.

The Act utilises a system of no-fault compensation for employees who are injured in accidents that arise out of and in the course of their employment or who contract occupational diseases. This means that employees are compensated whether their injuries or illnesses were caused by their own fault or due to their employer's negligence or that of any other person. At the same time, the employee may not institute a claim for damages against the employer or any other person for the injury or illness suffered.

The duties of employers under the Act are as follows:
- they must register with the Compensation Commissioner and provide details regarding their business and employees;
- they must keep records of wages, time worked, as well as payment for overtime and piecework, and retain these records for four years;
- by 31 March of every year, the total salary bill for the previous financial year must be submitted to the Commissioner in the prescribed form;
- they must report accidents within seven days and any occupational disease within fourteen days of its coming to their attention;
- they must pay an assessed amount into the Compensation Fund, since no contributions may be deducted from an employee's pay.

The Act requires provision for the payment of medical aid for the temporary or permanent disablement of an employee. A further obligation is that employers must pay employees who are temporarily disabled their compensation for the first three months of absence from work. A claim for compensation must be lodged within twelve months after the accident or illness has occurred or the employee has died.

A Compensation Commissioner administers the Act. A Compensation Fund consisting of payments and contributions made by employers is used for compensation and administration costs. The Compensation Board comprises sixteen members who represent the state, employers, employees, and two mutual associations operating in the mining and building industry, and the medical profession. The Board advises the Minister and decides on the minimum and maximum amounts to be paid in compensation for temporary or permanently disabled employees.

Benefits are paid to three categories of claimants:
- employees who suffer temporary disability;
- employees who are permanently disabled; and
- the dependants of employees who have died as a result of their injuries or an occupational disease.

5.8 Unemployment Insurance Act No.30 of 1966

This Act provides for the payment of benefits to contributors towards the Unemployment Insurance Fund (UIF) who become unemployed.

5.8.1 The purpose and scope of the Act

This Act does not contain a definition of an employee; it rather operates on the concept of a contributor. Contributors who qualify must pay 1 per cent of their remuneration to the UIF, and their employers the same amount.

The UIF provides financial assistance to contributors and their dependants whose services have been terminated through staff reduction, illness, or pregnancy, for example. Such persons may possibly have long periods of unemployment and that is where the UIF becomes operative.

All workers contribute to the fund except, for example:
- certain migrant workers from outside South Africa;
- people who work less than one day or eight hours per week;
- seasonal workers (as defined in the Act);
- people who execute work given by an employer on the premises, but who are not under the employer's control;
- the husband or wife of an employer when they are working for such an employer;
- civil servants, employees of provincial administrations, and members of Parliament who contribute to the government service pension fund;
- people who are officers in terms of the Public Service Act No.111 of 1984;
- people whose income consists only of a share of an income, or is calculated purely on a commission basis, including out-workers and those whose income consists solely of a share in takings;
- certain persons in the educational sector; and
- people who work in agriculture, the railways, and fixed establishments of Parliament.

5.8.2 Employers' duties

Employers have certain responsibilities under the Act. These are:
- Within fourteen days of starting an enterprise, an employer must furnish the Director-General of Labour with

certain information (as outlined in Appendix UF 1 of the regulations of the Act).
- A monthly statement, indicating the number of contributors as well as the amounts due by workers and employers, must be forwarded to the Unemployment Insurance Fund.
- A full record of all payments made by the employer on behalf of his workers must be kept for seven years.
- All contributors must have a contributor's record card (UF 74). If contributors do not have these so-called blue cards, the UIF must be notified so that cards can be issued.
- Employers must keep the contributors' cards of the workers in their employ in safe custody and give them to the employees on termination of service. The employer's fund reference number and official stamp should be clearly indicated on the card. The employee, in turn, must give his UIF card to his new employer.
- The employer is responsible for the collection of contributions for unemployment insurance and must forward both the employees' and his contribution, not later than ten days after the end of each month, to the Unemployment Insurance Commissioner.
- If a worker does not take the contributor's record card upon leaving his employ or leaves no address, the employer must keep it for a reasonable period.
- If a worker dies on duty, the contributor's record card must be handed over to his next of kin.

5.8.3 Unemployment benefits

To qualify for unemployment benefits, the applicant must be available and able to work, and must furnish proof that he cannot find suitable work and has contributed to the fund for at least thirteen weeks in the fifty-two weeks prior to being unemployed. The contributor will not receive any benefits for the first week of unemployment unless the job lasted for less than nine weeks and the employee was unemployed before that. Benefits will also not be paid in the first two weeks of illness. If a contributor dies, the spouse and children under seventeen, or any other dependants may institute claims for benefits for a maximum period of twenty-six weeks. Note that regarding illness, additional conditions apply namely that the contributor must not be in a position to work due to a listed illness. The contributor will also be disqualified from claiming benefits if the illness was due to the employee's own misconduct, or if the employee refuses to undergo medical treatment, or refuses to carry out the instructions of a medical practitioner (Swanepoel et al. 2000:141).

Benefits are usually 45 per cent of the total weekly or monthly remuneration, based on the average earnings at the time the employee became unemployed, or ill, or died. Benefits apply for a period of twenty-six weeks per fifty-two consecutive weeks of unemployment. Applications for an extension of the period may be made on form UF 139. Naturally, it is a condition that the unemployed will apply for work as soon as a suitable job opportunity presents itself.

The Act may change in due course, and readers are cautioned to compare aspects contained in this chapter with possible amendments.

5.9. Conclusion

It is essential that readers understand that a complete break with the apartheid past, to which South Africa's labour force was subjected, has been made and that an approach of participation by labour in the affairs of organisations has been enacted in various employment laws.

Current employment law in South Africa is structured according to the spirit and prescriptions of the Constitution. It also includes directives from the international community, particularly the International Labour Organisation, for a modern and acceptable set of laws in line with the global practices of today.

The background to the promulgation of the current employment law is discussed in this chapter. Other labour legislation in South Africa is also covered as it supports the Labour Relations Act, and facilitates employment equity, basic conditions of employment, compensation for occupational injuries and diseases, and skills development for employees.

It is evident from the discussion in this chapter that the Labour Relations Act, in particular, has been made as accessible and understandable to as many members of the population as possible. This is achieved by using straightforward and non-legalistic language. It is augmented with various schedules, flow diagrams, and so on, to describe the procedures and mechanisms in a clear and concise manner.

The Labour Relations Act focuses on issues such as freedom of association, the registration and constitutional requirements of trade unions and employers' organisations, and organisational rights. Further attention is given to bargaining councils, statutory councils, bargaining councils in the public service, collective agreements, and the CCMA. The Labour Court and Labour Appeal Court are also discussed. Various structures such as workplace forums and the CCMA were instituted to ensure participation by both management and labour in seeking solutions to workplace conflict. Dispute resolution and dismissal are also dealt with.

Once readers understand the context of employment law, which forms the basis of effective human resources management which is fair an equitable, it is appropriate to continue with human resources practice as it impacts on employment relations, and vice versa. Only then can a study be made of the staffing and other functions of human resources management, which follow in subsequent parts of the book.

Case study
Zap Instant Cash Loans

Bradley Tanazalki has worked in Genubi Strand, East London, during the last year as office manager for a micro lending business called Zap Instant Cash Loans. The business was established four years ago and makes lucrative profits. Bradley's duties include the supervision of the functions of a bookkeeper, two clerks, and three client assistants. Sonny Jones, the ex-bookkeeper, is Bradley's step-cousin.

Due to the nature of the business, operating primarily in the thirty-day short-term cash loans niche, large amounts of cash are generally in circulation. They do not make any long-term loans. The main job in the business is, therefore, to keep track of the cash loaned to clients and to make sure that it is returned on time, with interest. Trustworthy people and good accounting systems are the key to success in a business of this nature.

Records are kept of the cash loans via a computerised client contract system called Fanagalo Magic Accounting Systems, which was developed in the Eastern Cape by some slick up-town programming and computer experts, who advertised that they were creative self-made millionaires, despite the fact that they had limited knowledge of the micro lending business and accounting systems. It is rumoured that there are loopholes in the system, but this is denied by the system's programming designers, who claim that it is foolproof. The marketing of the system is extremely well done by very attractive, well-spoken, and mainly female staff.

When a client applies for a loan, in addition to a screening, he or she has to present the past three months' pay slips, ID number, and authenticated employers' address. This is usually verified within three days by the bookkeeper. If the client's application is successful, a loan contract is drawn up. The contract stipulates the repayment date, the capital amount of the loan, and the interest accrued, which has to be repaid thirty days after obtaining the loan.

The owners manage the company at an arm's length, because they live 500 km away, and leave all decision-making and administrative controls to Bradley. Bradley is in possession of the codes necessary to enter the contract details of any client and to check repayment details on the computer.

Some time ago, Bradley convinced his step-cousin to 'roll-over' some smaller client loan contracts by recalculating 'new interest' and 'new loan amounts' on so-called repaid accounts. Sonny would screen 'new' clients, and contracts would be provided against existing clients who would 'pay off' their loans. This was then logged in on the contracts, which existed on the computer, using the codes Bradley controlled. They were, therefore, old clients, but with new contracts superimposed by the 'roll-over' system Bradley devised. He craftily pocketed the difference and gave Sonny a small commission on the 'roll-over' contracts. Office staff also got commission on turnover and profits generated via any increased client loans for the business. Everybody in the office thus gained at the end of the month from 'increased' profits, but actual profits started declining a few months later.

Two weeks ago, just before the end of the month, the owners made an unprecedented spot check on the cash in hand, interest due, capital employed, and contract amounts reflected on the computerised system. A friend of the owners had tipped them off that the staff appeared to be living well and that profits must be very high in the business to enable such lifestyles.

Sonny was found guilty on a charge of dishonesty, and dismissed that very day. He did not spill the beans on Bradley, his step-cousin. Bradley also testified at the impromptu disciplinary hearing that he knew nothing of the 'fiddling' of names and contracts, nor that client contracts had been 'rolled-over'. When questioned about such a possibility by the owners, Bradley claimed that 'fiddling' was impossible, because the Fanagalo Magic Accounting System was advertised as foolproof, and he was convinced that this was the case in the way he applied the system. Sonny did not query any of these statements. The owners, however, were not convinced that Bradley had managed Sonny adequately, and gave Bradley a first written warning. None of the other staff received any warning.

Questions

1 Were the owners fair in dismissing Sonny when the discrepancies were discovered? Explain your view.
2 How should a disciplinary procedure operate in terms of Act No. 66 of

1995? Explain the detail thereof.
3 What measures should be designed and implemented to prevent corruption at Zap Instant Cash Loans?
4 In terms of the Constitution, what rights do Sonny and Bradley have separately and jointly regarding the above affair?
5 If you were a consultant, explain the nature of the employment law advice you would give to the owners?

Chapter questions

1 Explain the importance of the role of the labour legislation you have read about in this chapter in promoting the comprehensive protection of employees in the workplace.
2 Explain your view regarding the effectiveness of the Skills Development Act promoting the training and development of employees.
3 Explain what freedom of association entails.
4 Explain the concept of organisational rights, and indicate how workplace relationships between shop stewards and management will be influenced.
5 Discuss the protection that employees and persons seeking employment have. How will this influence the recruitment practices in an organisation with which you are familiar?
6 Are protected strikes beneficial or detrimental to the relationship between labour and management? Evaluate critically.
7 Illustrate and discuss, with the aid of a diagram, the main elements of the Labour Relations Act No. 66 of 1995.
8 Does the Labour Relations Act serve its purpose of dealing effectively with labour disputes? Explain how you would resolve industrial disputes.
9 Do you think that an institution like the CCMA will lead to the faster resolution of the previously high levels of conflict between employers and employees?
10 Can you distinguish between agency shop and closed shop agreements? Thereafter, motivate your view regarding the impact these agreements have on freedom of association.
11 Do you know the functions of the CCMA? List the problems you foresee in the execution of the CCMA's functions.
12 Evaluate the approach to dealing with dismissals followed in the Code of Good Practice: Dismissal, contained in Schedule 8 of the Act. Also comment on whether the prescriptive nature of dismissal procedures enhances or restricts the decision-making powers of human resources and industrial relations officials in enterprises.

Bibliography

BACKER, W. & OLIVIER, M. 1996. *Gids tot die nuwe Wet op Arbeidsverhoudinge.* Bactus Personeel, Pretoria.
DU PLESSIS, J.V., FOUCHÉ, M.A. & VAN WYK, M.W. 1998. *A practical guide to labour law.* 3rd edition. Butterworths, Durban.
DU TOIT, D., WOOLFREY, D., MURPHY, J., GODFREY, S., BOSCH, D. & CHRISTIE, S. 1996. *The Labour Relations Act of 1995.* Butterworths, Durban.
FINNEMORE, M. & VAN DER MERWE, R. 1996. *Introduction to labour relations in South Africa.* 4th edition. Butterworths, Cape Town.
GROGAN, J. 1999. *Workplace law.* Third edition. Juta, Kenwyn.
LANDMAN, L. 1995a. The closed shop born again. A surprise from the new Labour Relations Act. *Contemporary Labour Law.* Vol. 5, No. 2, pp. 11–17, September.
LANDMAN, L. 1995b. Unfair dismissal: the new rules for capital punishment in the workplace (Part One). *Contemporary Labour Law.* Vol. 5, No. 5, pp. 41–50, December.
LANDMAN, L. 1996. Unfair dismissal: the new rules for capital punishment in the

workplace (Part Two). *Contemporary Labour Law.* Vol. 5, No. 6, pp. 51–58, January.

LE ROUX, P.A.K. 1995. Organisational rights: the Labour Relations Act, 1995. *Contemporary Labour Law.* Vol. 5, No. 4, pp. 21–29, October.

LE ROUX, P.A.K. 1996. Statutory councils: their powers and functions. *Contemporary Labour Law.* Vol. 5, No. 7, pp. 61–72, February.

LE ROUX, P.A.K. 1999. Affirmative action and the individual employee. *Contemporary Labour Law.* Vol. 9, No. 4, November.

LE ROUX, P.A.K. 2000. Mass action, strikes and lock-outs. A review of some important cases. *Contemporary Labour Law.* Vol. 9, No. 7, pp. 61–67, February.

MDLADLANA, M. 2000. Labour pains. *Sunday Times*, 13 Feb, p.19.

NEL, P.S. (ed.) 1999. *South African industrial relations: theory and practice.* 3rd revised edition. Van Schaik, Pretoria.

NEL, P.S., ERASMUS, B.J. & SWANEPOEL, B.J. 1998. *Successful labour relations – guidelines for practice.* 2nd edition. Van Schaik, Pretoria.

REPUBLIC OF SOUTH AFRICA. 1995. South African Qualifications Authority Act No.58 of 1995. *Government Gazette*, Government Printer, Pretoria.

REPUBLIC OF SOUTH AFRICA. 1995. Labour Relations Act No. 66 of 1995. *Government Gazette*, Vol. 366, No. 16861. December. Government Printer, Pretoria.

REPUBLIC OF SOUTH AFRICA. 1996. Labour Relations Act No. 66 of 1995 (Regulations). *Government Gazette*, Vol. 366, No. 17516. November. Government Printer, Pretoria.

REPUBLIC OF SOUTH AFRICA. 1996. Labour Relations Amendment Act No. 42 of 1996. *Government Gazette*, vol. 375, No. 17427. September. Government Printer, Pretoria.

REPUBLIC OF SOUTH AFRICA. 1996. The Constitution of the Republic of Soth Africa Act No. 108 of 1996. *Government Gazette*, Vol. 367. Government Printer, Pretoria.

REPUBLIC OF SOUTH AFRICA. 1997. Basic Conditions of Employment Act No. 75 of 1997. Government Gazette, Vol. 390, No. 18491. December. *Government Printer*, Pretoria.

REPUBLIC OF SOUTH AFRICA. 1998. Employment Equity Act No.55 of 1998. *Government Gazette*, Government Printer, Pretoria.

REPUBLIC OF SOUTH AFRICA. 1998. Skills Development Act No. 97 of 1998. *Government Gazette*, Vol. 401, No. 19420. November. Government Printer, Pretoria.

REPUBLIC OF SOUTH AFRICA. 1999. Skills Development Levies Act No.9 of 1999. *Government Gazette*, Vol. 406, No. 19984. April. Government Printer, Pretoria.

REPUBLIC OF SOUTH AFRICA. 1999. Employment Equity Act 1999. Commencement Notice, Regulations and Code. *Government Gazette*, Regulation Gazette, No. 6674, Vol. 413, No. 20626. November. Government Printer, Pretoria.

ROODT, A. 1999. The leadership challenges of Thabo Mbeki. *Management Today.* Vol. 15, No. 5, pp. 6–11.

SLABBERT, J.A., PRINSLOO, J.J., SWANEPOEL, B.J. & BACKER, W. 1998. *Managing employment relations in South Africa.* Butterworths, Durban.

SWANEPOEL, B.J., SLABBERT, J.A., ERASMUS, B.J. & BRINK, M. 1999. The management of employment relations. Conceptual and contextual perspectives. Butterworths, Durban.

SWANEPOEL, B.J., ERASMUS, B.J., VAN WYK, M. & SCHENK, H. 2000. South African human resource management. Theory and practice. Juta, Cape Town.

VAN NIEKERK, A. & LE ROUX, P.A.K. 1995. Worker participation – sharing the right to decide. *Contemporary Labour Law.* Vol. 4, No. 6, January.

VAN NIEKERK, A. 1995. Workplace forums. *Contemporary Labour Law.* Vol. 5, No. 4, pp. 31–39, November.

6

Interdependency between employment relations and human resources management

P S Nel

Learning outcomes

At the end of this chapter the learner should be able to demonstrate the following outcomes:
- Explain the importance and the complex role of employment relations in human resources management.
- Explain the role of a policy on employment relations in an organisation.
- Explain why employment relations and human resources matters are interdependent and promote general human resources stability and progress in an organisation.
- Explain which policy components are essential to limit labour unrest and strikes.
- Consider the influence of the primary aspects of employment relations on the role of the human resources manager and vice versa.
- Provide guidelines to demonstrate the effect of general employment practices on employment relations in the context of applicable personnel law.

Key words and concepts

- compensation
- contract of employment
- dispute handling procedures
- employer/employee communication
- employers' association
- employment relations policy
- fringe benefits
- workplace forums
- grievance and discipline
- human resources policy
- individual, legal, informal, and collective dimensions
- AIDS
- recruitment and selection
- strike handling
- termination procedures
- training and development

Illustrative case
Jabulani Community Health Care Centre

Priscilla is Joan's sister and is only eleven months older than she is. They come from a broken home; in their tender teens, their alcoholic father used to beat his family in his drunken spells, and this ultimately led to a divorce. They are now in their late twenties and still unmarried, albeit with a walkout by Joan's husband-to-be, a week before she was to be married two years ago. They have a keen interest in care-giving services. Both are qualified community welfare workers, with qualifications obtained locally and from the Royal College of Community Health in London.

For the last three years they have been working at the Jabulani Community Health Care Centre, a Non-Governmental Organisation (NGO) providing welfare, counselling, and community health advisory services. The pay is below standard, but they believe in the cause. The employees there work in close collaboration, as the services provided overlap, and staff often have to stand in for each other when somebody is ill, on leave or there is a staff shortage immediately after a resignation.

Dr. Joseph, a very friendly and jovial person, aged thirty-seven, heads the centre. His bother, Moses, who is only a few years younger than he is, works in town as a pharmacist, and was widowed early last year after his wife died when his 4 x 4 was violently hijacked. Both Priscilla and Joan have attempted to win Moses's favour by visiting him and, whenever necessary, taking care of his disabled 7-year-old daughter and 5-year-old son with a learning disability. In this process, both have fallen in love with him and are now in serious competition to woo him into marriage. They are very concerned about becoming spinsters, because all their friends are already married. Everybody knows about the love triangle the sisters are involved in, but discreetly stay out of it. This state of affairs has spilled over into the work situation and is of concern to all staff.

Priscilla has a slightly more senior position than Joan and has started bossing her around by, for example, regularly making her work the 16h00 – 24h00 shift, to allow herself time to visit Moses and his children. This has built up to regular arguments at home and at work during the last few months. A very serious war of words, as well as an apparent attempt of assault by Joan on Priscilla, erupted last Wednesday afternoon. This happened in the laundry section when Priscilla, just before knock-off time for day shift at 16h15, was on her rounds to ensure that staff were present and doing their jobs. Joan was helping out in this section because someone was ill. There were no eyewitnesses, but other staff heard the loud argument when Priscilla accused Joan of not doing her job. This erupted into a serious altercation between the two sisters, with banging noises and things being thrown around.

After the incident, the supervisor on duty, Sipho Dlamini, received a complaint from Joan that Priscilla had been trying to manipulate her and was unnecessarily strict and 'catty' with her. She alleged that Priscilla had attempted to assault her. When Priscilla was called in for an explanation, she accused the supervisor of being prejudiced because last year he had taken Joan out on a few occasions. Priscilla had not been out with him, although he had asked her, because he was engaged.

Priscilla made it clear that she would oppose any action instituted by him against her, because she thought he was in no position to reprimand her owing to his vested interests. The supervisor thought this was a threat to his authority, and immediately suspended Priscilla indefinitely, because he believed that the conditions of employment and the centre's code of conduct were being transgressed. Sipho, afterwards, thought that he had not made a very wise judgement, but was not going to lose face by withdrawing it, and referred the case to Dr. Joseph for his decision.

What do you think are the major employment relations issues to consider in this scenario? How should it be approached so as to have the least negative effect on all the participants, bearing in mind the interdependency between human resources management and employment relations?

6.1 Introduction

It is common knowledge that without taking cognisance of people, no organisation can be effective. In this regard, Swanepoel et al. (1999a:1) state that the 'human dimension' is critical. To improve an organisation's effectiveness requires an improvement in both the work that people do and the relationship which exists between people and the organisation.

The area of employment relations is, thus, focused on how organisations manage the relations between themselves and their human resources regarding the effectiveness with which the production of goods and services takes place. According to Nel et al. (1998:4) three parties are, in fact, involved in this relationship; directly the employee and the employer and, indirectly, the State.

- Workers sell their labour to the producers of goods and services. Workers may be organised into trade unions, which regulate all matters on their behalf, or they may operate by means of the workplace forum system, or on an individual basis in their organisations.
- Employers are compelled to ensure an acceptable return on investment for shareholders. This means that they must ensure the most effective application of the scarce resources at their disposal.
- The State is both master and servant of the other two participants. On the one hand, the State holds legislative power and, on the other, it is expected to give assistance to both the other participants in satisfying their respective needs.

This relationship has existed for thousands of years, but it is only during the last few hundred years that the discipline called 'industrial relations' or 'labour relations' has evolved. In modern use, this relationship is known as the 'employment relationship' since it primarily focuses on the notion of work and labour.

Furthermore, the study of this relationship from a managerial perspective has become a focal point in the modern day business environment. A cornerstone of employment relations, therefore, is the employment relationship. This is so because as soon as one person works for another, various dimensions of the employment relationship become operative. There are four such dimensions: individual formal, individual informal, collective formal, and collective informal.

The *individual dimension* is that each individual worker is in daily contact with the employing body, with different managers at various levels, and with workers as individuals. There are, therefore, individualised interpersonal or human relationships.

The *collective dimension* is that workers can organise into groups that can interact with management as a group or with groups of employers. This is what is generally referred to as the labour-management or union-employer relationship. Labour mostly organises in groups such as trade unions, who act as representatives of the individual member-workers. Inter-group relations between management and trade unions are involved here. The role of trade unions is discussed elsewhere in more detail.

In practice these two dimensions occur in combination with a formal dimension or an informal dimension.

The *formal dimension* refers to certain rights and duties that the parties have due to official agreements between themselves, irrespective of whether these are individual or collective. An example of this is the contract of employment entered into between an employee and an employer, which creates a legal relationship between them.

Whether the individual-formal contract of service is written or verbal, it involves a formal agreement being entered into between the parties, which formalises the employment relationship. Swanepoel et al. (1999a:14) state that the employer therefore has a duty 'to pay remuneration for work done, to provide the employee with leave, to provide safe working conditions and many other duties – such as to respect and honour the employee's right to freedom of association and not to victimise or unfairly discriminate (directly or indirectly) against the employee on the basis of (for instance) race, gender, colour, religion, marital status or sexual orientation.'

The employee, on the other hand, has duties such as to obey lawful and reasonable instructions with regard to his work, and not to be dishonest.

There is also an informal dimension, which revolves around dynamic human behavioural aspects. This can be human behaviour within a group context (informal-collective dimension) or within the context of the individual dimension. It includes those aspects and consequences of relationships arising from what various parties feel and think about each other, what their needs and views of life are, their attitudes and perceptions towards each other, and so on. It, thus, revolves around the day-to-day interaction between employees.

It is clear that the employment relationship with these dimensions is anything but simple. The individual contract of employment also plays a major role in this relationship.

6.2 The individual contract of employment

The contract of employment is usually entered into between one person (the employer) and another person (the employee). In this regard Grogan (1999:23–24) states that:

A contract of employment is an agreement between two legal personae (parties) in terms of which one of the parties (the employee) undertakes to place his or her personal services at the disposal of the other party (the employer) for an indefinite or determined period in return for a fixed or ascertainable wage, and which entitles the employer to define the employee's duties and (usually) to control the manner in which the employee discharges them.

The contract must comply with the requirements set for all valid contracts, i.e. it must be a voluntary agreement between two legal personae (parties); the parties must have contractual capacity; performance of the contract must be possible (in other words, a person professing to be a welder should be able to do welding according to a certain standard); the contract may not be contra bonos mores (against public moral values); the contract must comply with any formalities which may be prescribed (for example, all apprenticeship contracts must be in writing); and the parties must intend to be bound by the contract.

The contents of the contract usually include the following terms to clarify the duties and obligations of both employer and employee:
- job description;
- remuneration – basic pay, overtime, and bonuses;
- hours of work per day and week;
- annual leave, sick leave, maternity, compassionate, and study leave;
- benefits – pension, provident fund, medical aid, and housing;
- protection of the company's interests – confidentiality, and restraint of trade;
- the period of the contract, retirement age, and period of notice required;
- closed shop or agency shop requirements;
- occupational health and safety rules;
- disciplinary rules; and
- any applicable procedural or substantive agreement between employer and union.

The parties may not agree to terms that are less favourable than those provided for in the Basic Conditions of Employment Act No. 75 of 1997, bargaining council agreements, or conditions required by the Occupational Health and Safety Act No. 75 of 1993. The contract of employment is, therefore, subordinate to the various labour laws in South Africa.

Under the collective dimension of employment relations, employment contracts could also be entered into via collective bargaining agreements concluded in terms of statutory collective bargaining mechanisms (for example bargaining council agreements) between employer organisations and trade unions.

Contracts can be entered into by employees at any level in an organisation, from a wage labourer to a top manager. The contract of employment can be terminated in a number of ways, such as the expiry of a fixed period, insolvency of the employer, dismissal, and termination by notice. However, under the new Labour Relations Act specific guidelines are laid down in, for example, Chapter 8 and Schedule 8 of the Act where the Code of Good Practice: Dismissal deals with how to terminate a contract by means of dismissal. It is important to note that Section 186 of the Act defines dismissal in such a way as to embrace common law forms of termination and other forms of termination not recognised by common law. Organisations must, therefore, take careful note of these guidelines prior to terminating an employee's contract of employment, and human resources managers, in particular, are advised to pay attention to the detail of the Act in this regard. For example, it is unacceptable in South Africa for an employer to terminate a contract of employment by notice without giving a reason.

From the above approach it is clear that the management of the employment relationship is influenced by both the collective and the individual dimensions. Therefore, an interdependency in the management of these elements exists. Consequently, human resources managers, as well as those managers dealing with the collective and formal dimensions of this relationship, must understand the interdependency in order to manage the relationship successfully (Swanepoel et al. 1999b). In the rest of this chapter we focus on those general aspects of employment relations with which a human resources manager should be familiar. Today, employment relations are so specialised that most organisations employ a labour relations officer or manager to deal with this aspect of employment relations.

6.3 The focus of the interdependency

The material presented in this chapter presupposes that the human resources manager has access to an employment relations officer or manager in the organisation. He or she should nevertheless be familiar with some employment relations issues, specifically in the private sector in South Africa. This chapter is, therefore, not addressed to the labour relations elements the specialist would focus on, and such information is not provided.

Employment relations are of special importance for human resources managers in South Africa, particularly because of the rapid changes that are taking place. Human resources managers, especially in large organisations in South Africa, however, have handed over this new facet of human resources management to employment relations managers. Developments in employment relations are so rapid that the task of the employment relations manager has become just as important as that of the human resources manager.

Not all organisations (particularly smaller ones) are lucky enough to have the services of an employment relations manager or officer, and many do not have a separate employment relations section or department. Here, employment relations are the human resources manager's responsibility, and it would be detrimental to the progress of the organisation if he or she neglected this responsibility. He or she needs to know the functions of employment relations, and should be willing to do the work of an employment relations officer, should one not be employed by the organisation. Employment relations are crucial in South Africa, and as more specialists in this area become available, human resources managers will become less involved. However, they should remain familiar with the general functioning of employment relations in an organisation.

What, then, should human resources managers know about employment relations and how should they go about integrating this function with the broader context of human resources management in an organisation?

In the modern business world it is essential that organisations have a company policy, a human resources policy, and an employment relations policy. An organisation that neglects to synchronise all three policies or draws up, for example, a human resources policy that is not in line with the company policy, commits a grave error. Human resources managers should be aware of the effect that conflict between employees and managers could have on the organisation. They should know the various trade union groupings or federations in South Africa and how the organisation should cope in the event of a strike. They should know that collective bargaining is an integral part of the interaction with trade unions, that employment relations training should be continually carried out in the organisation, and that supervisors, in particular, should be trained in human relations to interact with employees on the shop floor. Finally, they should know that an organisation should have specific procedures to deal with grievances and disciplinary matters. These issues form the nucleus of the discussion in the rest of this chapter. Human resources management issues (such as recruitment and selection) that have a bearing on employment relations will also be discussed, because the application of the new Labour Relations Act necessitates an integration of the functions which deal with broader human resources issues such as the prohibition of discrimination (Section 187 of the Labour Relations Act is an example in this regard).

6.4 The rights and duties of employers and workers

There is a division between the ownership (shareholders) and control (management) of capital, and management (or employers) need a certain amount of freedom in their management of organisations if they are to assure an acceptable return on the owners' investment. This means that they have certain rights (and responsibilities) in managing the organisation successfully.

Employers and workers are completely interdependent and need to cooperate if the running of the organisation is to be successful. Managers and workers, however, have different roles in the organisation and this means that they have different rights and responsibilities.

6.4.1 The rights of management

Managers have a right to manage an organisation to execute their task successfully. There are, however, two kinds of management rights: exclusive and shared rights. With the advent of worker participation in the affairs of organisations, a rearrangement of rights has taken place and is outlined below.

Management has the exclusive right to determine the objectives of the organisation, determine product policies, plan and implement policies, provide financial and material resources, establish and expand facilities, determine the quality of products, determine work standards, determine the composition of the workforce, direct and organise the workforce, belong to an employers' association, and manage the organisation. At best, employees could be consulted concerning the implications of these rights on them. Many attempts have been made by workers to take over these rights, but it has never been adequately shown in the Western democratic system that these rights should not be exclusive to management. In South Africa, according to the view held by Swanepoel (1996), certain rights belong indisputably to management and must be considered within the context of management prerogatives.

The following rights are shared with workers through the introduction of worker participation and in the spirit of industrial democracy introduced by the new Labour Relations Act. These rights are to recruit and appoint workers, assign them to jobs, promote or demote them, transfer them, increase or decrease their salaries or wages, discipline them, discharge or lay them off, establish hours of work, grant or refuse leave of absence, and determine overtime required.

What is important is not so much management's prerogative regarding these rights, but the way in which these rights are exercised. The exercising of shared rights has been dramatically changed with the introduction of the new Labour Relations Act. Managers are now compelled to share information on issues which affect workers. This is detailed in the issues relating to the functions of workplace forums. In particular, Section 84 prescribes matters for consultation between management and workers, e.g. restructuring of the workplace, job grading, criteria for merit increases, education, and training. In Section 86, matters for joint consultation are outlined, e.g. disciplinary codes and procedures, matters regarding the conduct of employees not related to work performance, and measures designed to protect and advance persons disadvantaged by unfair discrimination.

It is, therefore, clear that participation in the affairs of the organisation and the extent of shared rights has taken on a totally new approach in South Africa – which is in line with international views on the re-arrangement of the rights of management in the workplace.

Rights are never without obligations. Management represents the employers (and therefore the shareholders) of the organisation, and management's obligations to the organisation are to take calculated risks and to render an acceptable return on investment to the shareholders.

The general modern-day duties of management towards workers

Management has the responsibility of facilitating contact with workers and their respective representative bodies. This means management should:
- arrange regular meetings with the aim of establishing sound relationships with workers;
- discuss matters of importance with all parties;
- positively share important information, such as human resources statistics, human resources turnover, absenteeism, safety arrangements, and production targets and achievements; and
- promote the quality of work life, help with housing, implement the RDP, assist with education and training, etc.

Aspects such as vacation leave, pension, and sick leave are usually left to the human resources manager or the employment relations manager, who keep relations between management and workers smooth by negotiating with unions or workplace forums, or in the absence of any formal worker representative body, with the workers themselves.

6.4.2 The rights of workers

Workers have six internationally recognised categories of rights, namely the right to work, the right to freedom of association, the right to collective bargaining, the right to strike, the right to protection, and the right to training.

- *The right to work.* In South Africa the right to work is not a legal right, but rather the democratic right of a worker to find employment and to perform the job willingly. Employment possibilities are determined by the free market economy, which dictates the job market and the rate of remuneration.

  In its constitution and labour laws South Africa does not recognise either the right of a citizen to be placed in employment or the duty of the state to provide work. Section 46 of the Unemployment Insurance Act (No. 30 of 1966) makes provision for unemployment pay for a specified period, which is at most an indication of the state's interest in the continued existence of employment relations between employers and workers.

- *Freedom of association.* This right is entrenched in the Labour Relations Act (No. 66 of 1995). It gives anybody in South Africa the opportunity to join an association, which will protect him or her and negotiate on his or her behalf with the employer for fair and acceptable remuneration and conditions of employment.

- *Collective bargaining.* This right is also protected by the Labour Relations Act. It enables trade unions to represent workers and to bargain on their behalf with representatives of employers about all aspects of the employment contract.

- *Strikes.* This right is also protected by the Labour Relations Act. A strike is usually effective only if it is undertaken collectively regardless of whether or not workers are unionised. Unionised workers usually stage the most effective strikes.

- *Protection.* The right to protection consists of a number of components: the right to fair remuneration and

conditions of service, the right to health, safety, and security, and the right to protection from unfair labour practices. There are various laws to protect workers in the work environment, for example the Compensation for Occupational Injuries and Diseases Act No. 130 of 1993, the Unemployment Insurance Act (No. 30 of 1966) and the Occupational Health and Safety Act (No. 85 of 1993).
- *Training.* This right is of paramount importance in South Africa today, and the Skills Development Act (No. 97 of 1998) gives training prominence. The scope of the Act is to provide an institutional framework to devise and implement national, sector, and workplace strategies to develop and improve the skills of employees in terms of the National Qualifications Framework contemplated in the South African Qualifications Authority Act, 1995, to provide for learnerships that lead to recognised occupational qualifications, and to provide for the financing of skills development by means of a levy-grant scheme and a National Skills Fund. For more information in this regard, see Chapters 19 and 20 of this book, where training and development is discussed in detail.

A further development, which needs to be focused on, is the question of employment equity and dignified treatment of all persons in the workplace. As far as employment equity is concerned, legislation has been passed which has far reaching effects as far as the rights of worker in the workplace are concerned. This is also discussed elsewhere in this chapter, as well as in Chapters 5 and 7.

The general duties of workers towards management

Management is responsible for planning, directing and controlling the organisation's human resources. On the other hand, workers are responsible for the implementation of management plans. Without this shared responsibility, an organisation cannot be effective. If workers are to fulfil these responsibilities towards management, they need a worker's representative body, which will undertake:
- to ascertain the views and feelings of workers towards the organisation, and brief management on workers' customs and cultures;
- to investigate grievances and resolve them if this is within their power, and to make recommendations to management regarding these grievances (if a grievance is not resolved, a formal grievance must then be lodged with the human resources manager, the employment relations manager, or the supervisor of the worker, depending on how the grievance procedure operates);
- to maintain regular communication with workers, transmitting decisions and information from management to workers and explaining the reasons, and to communicate business results to other workers;
- to explain workplace forums, trade union activities, and representative procedures and methods, to make the responsibilities and limits of authority of these bodies clear, and to teach workers about the business they are in;
- to contact new workers and participate in their induction into the organisation; and
- to help workers understand the importance of economic considerations and to convey to management how this has been understood, in order to ensure that workers make requests that are economically possible.

The specific modern-day duties of workers towards management

The duty to work implies that workers will not be unnecessarily absent from work, be late for work, leave the work station without permission, work under the influence of intoxicating substances, indulge in bad behaviour in the workplace, or strike for no good reason. Workers also have the duty to be subordinate: that is, not to ignore legitimate orders or stir up other workers. Workers must behave well, which means that they must not insult co-workers or become involved in a fight on the organisation's premises. They should never be dishonest or commit fraud. Workers must be loyal to their employer and not reveal the secrets or work methods of the organisation to the opposition.

It is clear from the above that employment relations is a complex field of study and that the relationships between managers and workers are of cardinal importance to the goals of an organisation. Many attempts have been made to establish structures and procedures to formalise the relationship between managers and workers. This can be achieved by drawing up company, human resources, and employment relations policies. The contents of these policies and the relation between them are discussed in the next section.

6.5 The relation between company, human resources, and employment relations policies

6.5.1 Company policy and human resources policy

Management and workers have different interests, objectives and needs. It is essential, therefore, that there should be written documentation in the form of a policy to regulate communication and interaction between them. Company policy forms the basis upon which other policies and procedures in the organisation can be drawn up. The various levels of management in an organisation have different policies, and depending on its size, these could vary from simple to very complex. Should an organisation be fairly small, it may combine such documents for its own needs and purposes.

Organisations must formulate short-term and long-term goals and strategies (corporate planning) if they are to achieve their objectives. After this corporate planning is done, the organisation can draw up formal policies.

The formulation of an employment relations policy or a human resources policy is never done by the employment relations manager or human resources manager alone. It is the end product of corporate planning and strategy formulation, and therefore it is a corporate responsibility, like corporate planning.

Policy formulation is top management's responsibility because the area of responsibility of the executive team is the optimum application and integration of resources. Policy is dependent upon this integration and application of resources and, at the same time, has a major effect on it. It must, therefore, be an executive responsibility, although the human resources or employment relations manager will assist in working out the details.

Once a policy is formulated and accepted, it is important to put it in writing and make it public, perhaps by publishing it in the in-house magazine. This step is, in itself, proof of commitment to the policy. It is easy to deny or reverse a 'policy' that is merely part of the organisation's culture. Such informal policies are also open to manipulation or misinterpretation, either accidentally or intentionally.

The failure of many organisations to develop formal human resources and employment relations policies could be one of the reasons why there is increasing labour unrest in South Africa. It is of cardinal importance for the human resources manager to ensure that his or her organisation has such policies and follows them.

A policy provides proof of commitment and of preparedness to declare views and attitudes, and it sets limits of behaviour. It shows the intention of the parties involved to honour these declarations. It implies that there has been conscious and rational consideration of the relationship between management and workers. It recognises the security needs of workers and the interdependence of workers and management in the organisation. It acknowledges that workers are indispensable and that they are more than mere production factors. At the same time it recognises the rights of workers and the obligations of managers.

Policy, therefore, forms the basis for the development of all other processes and procedures that determine the conduct of workers and management in an organisation. An effective disciplinary procedure, for example, can only be drawn up once an employment relations policy has been formulated.

An organisation therefore needs a policy statement that indicates its approach and business philosophy. The company policy statement could contain the following:

> The Adcorp Group's primary objectives are to maintain growth as one of the top companies in South Africa and to increase its return to shareholders. At the same time it acknowledges its corporate responsibility to contribute to the prosperity and progress of the people in South Africa.

Other terms in the company policy statement could, for example, provide incentives to ensure maximum productivity and encourage worker participation in decision-making that affects workers, and make provision for housing and for educational projects for employees and a statement of the organisation's right to manage these.

An organisation should also have a human resources policy. Its terms could include: the aim to assist each employee in developing his or her skills and to enable him or her to use these skills to the full, thus ensuring the employee's job satisfaction and ability to contribute to the organisation; the intention to promote and preserve at all times the dignity and self-esteem of each employee; and the aim to develop and maintain open lines of communication and personal contact between the organisation and each employee.

An organisation should also have an employment relations policy, but it is important to draw a distinction between a human resources policy and an employment relations policy. A human resources policy addresses the needs of the individual within the organisation; an employment relations policy, on the other hand, is intended to regulate the relationships between management and the workers, between management and organised labour, and between management and the several external agencies that play a part in employment relations.

In practice the distinction between these policies is not always clear, as many organisations combine them.

6.5.2 Employment relations policy

The employment relations policy of an organisation is the expression of top management's philosophy towards the human resources of the organisation.

It is a declaration of the fundamental values, beliefs, standards, and philosophies (principles) that underlie the behaviour of the organisation, but it is detailed enough to provide specific guidelines for the relationship between the people in the organisation.

According to IPM Fact Sheet No. 103, the employment relations policy statement of an organisation should contain the following:
- a statement of the organisation's responsibility to protect worker rights and to provide workers with the opportunity of participating in decisions that directly affect them;
- a commitment to the principle of freedom of association;
- acceptance of the rights of workers to collective bargaining in industrial disputes;
- acceptance of the principle of lawful withholding of labour as a result of industrial disputes; and
- a statement of the organisation's attitude to the available machinery for collective bargaining (for example, support of bargaining councils and the CCMA).

It is important to bear in mind that a policy reflects values. Therefore the policy objectives should cover the following: development of mutual trust and cooperation; prevention of problems and disputes through agreed procedures; reduction of labour costs; strengthening of managerial control; development of human resources skills and management of productivity. The policy standards should be universally acceptable to all departments or subsidiaries; they should be in writing, in broad terms and in clear language; they should be justifiable in terms of their impact on profit; they should be approved and authorised by the highest authority so that the policy carries the weight of a directive; and the terms must be inviolate.

Other important considerations in drawing up an employment relations policy are:
- The policy must be unambiguous.
- The policy must be positively phrased and not contain negative statements; for instance, it is preferable to say, 'the organisation intends granting equal pay for equal work', rather than 'the organisation will not engage in any discriminatory practices'.
- The policy statement must not require interpretation.
- The rationale behind the policy must be explained.
- The boundaries within which individual discretion may be exercised must be clear.
- A distinction must be drawn between policies (for example, equal pay for equal work) and procedures (such as grievance procedures).
- The use of such words and phrases as 'may', 'generally recommended', 'in most cases', should be avoided as they have a permissive tone.
- No statement of policy that is contradicted by any other confidential policy should be included. It is better to ignore a subject than to say one thing publicly and another privately.
- The policy should meet the relevant legal and government requirements.
- Management should avoid the expedient settlement of disputes that could prejudice long-term interests.
- Collective agreements must be for fixed periods and should set out prescriptions regarding disputes of interest (such as the percentage wage increase employees are bargaining for when they regard the employer's offer as too low) for the full duration of the agreement. During the period of an agreement there should be no dispute of rights (such as common law requirements, legal issues, or the interpretation of a clause in the agreement).
- The policy should contain a clause stating that management will not negotiate or make concessions under illegal or non-procedural economic coercion or the explicit threat of it.
- Management must state clearly that the organisation's employment relations practices will be made known and comprehensible to employees and their

representatives, and will always be consistent with the organisation's general human resources policy and company policy.

The employment relations policy statement should contain procedures and guidelines which provide for operational structures in the organisation. Management can then consolidate and strengthen the organisation's position by utilising the procedures set down in the policy for settling grievances, disputes, and disciplinary actions. This means that managers can distance themselves from the negative side of the relationship between employer and workers, in the sense that they no longer need to be seen as the source of discipline in their personal capacity, but merely as officials carrying out policy prescriptions. It also eliminates many negative emotions associated with employer-worker relationships because procedures have been agreed to by the participants in the employment relations policy. Conflict is reduced in the work environment because the implementation of policy is then seen as an integral part of the relationship between employer and workers, because it is formalised in writing and known by everybody.

The procedures and structures in the employment relations policy prescribe relations with trade unions, strike handling, grievance procedures, and general employment relations issues, such as recruitment, industrial safety, and training. These issues are discussed in the next two sections.

6.6 The major components of employment relations of concern to the human resources manager

An employment relations policy is a document that is instrumental in formalising the relationship between employers and unionised employees, in particular, in any organisation. The structures and procedures in the employment relations policy form a basis for the practical details that govern the day-to-day interaction between management and workers. Issues that need to be precisely spelled out in the employment relations policy include trade union and workplace forum relations, participation in employers' associations, dispute-handling procedures, methods of collective bargaining, strike handling, grievance and disciplinary procedures, and the channels and role of communication between management and workers.

These issues are discussed separately in the sections after the discussion on communication.

6.6.1 The essentials of employer-employee communication

Communication and the channels used for it are essential for the survival of any organisation. The communication methods and channels used in organisations usually determine the effectiveness of communication between the various groups such as supervisors and subordinates, employee groups and the employer. Effective communication at all levels in an organisation is, therefore, essential. In the employment relations context, the means of communication, such as telephones, memos, or even personally delivered messages, are not the most important. What is important is not what is said, but how it is said. If communication between trade union members and the employer is hostile, unfriendly, and based on incorrect assumptions, this will lead to conflict, and the relationship between these parties will be strained. The human resources manager should, therefore, pay attention to those issues of communication that are important to employers and employees and which, if not contained, could lead to disputes and even strikes.

Communication is indispensable in organisations. It is generally known and accepted that people spend 70 per cent of their day communicating, and of this 45 per cent is spent listening. It is also known that people normally have only 25 per cent efficiency when listening. It is, therefore, not surprising that something like 50 per cent of all communication attempts fail. Yet communication in any organisation is essential to reduce conflict to a minimum and to increase the effectiveness of employees in carrying out their daily tasks. Effective communication should be a top priority of the human resources manager, so that the full benefit can be derived from it. Effective communication results in higher productivity and greater cooperation in an organisation. People can give of their best only if they understand what they have to do, why they have to do it, and to what extent they are achieving their targets. If communication is not systematic, employees who are affected by change, for example, will not understand the reasons for these changes and will resist them.

So far in this chapter we have dealt with those issues that are important in effective communication between employers and workers. The employment relations policy provides the means to specify the relationship between employer and worker, and provides a structure for communication between them. It also sets procedures for collective bargaining and for dealing with grievances and disciplinary issues – it thus makes known aspects of employment relations within the organisation. The grievance procedure is a form of upward communication from the worker to the employer concerning problems and work-related issues. On the other hand, the disciplinary procedure is a form of downward communication from the employer to the workers about issues that are regarded as unacceptable behaviour on the part of the workers. The organisation can gain several advantages from employer-to-worker downward communication:

- *Commitment to the job is improved.* The provision of information helps to build trust and motivates workers. Trust and motivation improve the commitment of workers to the work group and cause them to strive to achieve the goals of this group and of their section, and ultimately those of the organisation.
- *'Grapevine' distortion is reduced.* 'Grapevine' distortion is inevitable in informal communication. Regular formal communication serves to reduce such distortion since workers come to expect an official version instead of giving credence to rumours.
- *Feedback is elicited.* Formal communication usually elicits a response from the receiver. This response provides valuable information and feedback to the sender, which enables him or her to assess the opinions and reactions of the interested parties.
- *The status of supervisors is improved.* To possess and to impart information confers status. If management wants its supervisors to enjoy status in the eyes of the workers, one way to achieve this is to make supervisors the bearers of management information to workers.
- *Workers are involved in change.* It is human nature to resist change. Advance communication of a proposed or pending change allows workers time to evaluate it and prepare for it. They are then more likely to cooperate in the proposed changes.
- *The disciplinary system is more effective.* Workers accept the authority of management and see the disciplinary procedure as a means used by management to eliminate unacceptable behaviour in the organisation.

The management of an organisation, in conjunction with the human resources manager, should evolve a definite policy as to what should or should not be communicated to workers. Not all the activities of the organisation should automatically be communicated to everybody. The rights and responsibilities of managers and workers should be taken into consideration when communication structures are established. The following serve as guidelines on what should be communicated to workers:

- *Progress of the organisation, branch or section.* Workers are directly concerned with the results, whether positive or negative, of their efforts in their immediate job environment (section) and they are concerned with the progress of the organisation as a whole. Such results should, therefore, be communicated to workers as it gives them feedback on their work performance, serves as an indication that management recognises their contribution to the results, and confirms their job security, which is very important in the present economic climate.
- *Movements of people.* Not every appointment, transfer, promotion, and resignation is relevant to every worker, but movements of people belonging to their work group, people to whom they report or people with whom they are in frequent contact should be made known to workers.
- *Policy or procedural decisions affecting workers.* All new or revised procedures affecting workers should be communicated to them. Employment relations decisions arrived at between management and union officials or shop stewards, such as bargaining council or workplace forum decisions, are of direct concern to workers. Worker representatives (shop stewards or workplace forum members) as a party to the decisions should, however, report back to the workers through their own channels.

It is clear that aspects of employment relations are major contributors to effective communication. The most important aspects of employment relations with which the human resources manager should be familiar are now described.

6.6.2 The relationship between employer and trade union

In South Africa freedom of association is guaranteed by the Labour Relations Act. Whether employers or human resources managers like or dislike trade unions is immaterial, since it is a violation of the Labour Relations Act to oppose the efforts of a trade union to recruit members from among the employees of an organisation. However, the human resources manager can, via the employment relations policy of the organisation, place certain reasonable restrictions on trade union officials regarding access to the premises, and so on. Unreasonable restrictions will lead to claims of unfair labour practices or victimisation of employees, and this may result in a dispute with the employer. In this section, the focus is on the general relationship that may exist between an employer (represented by the employment relations or human resources manager) and the relevant unions.

Relationships between organisations and unions vary between two extremes. Organisations may be apathetic, yet remain within the limits of the law, or they may be patronising towards any trade union that represents their employees. Neither attitude makes for good relationships. It is important for the organisation and the union to develop a working arrangement whereby their respective goals can best be achieved.

The relationship between the employer and trade union entails an acknowledgement of their conflicting interests and an appreciation of the need to compromise. Earlier, we described the relationship between the primary participants in the employment relations system in South Africa. Further aspects of the relationship are now highlighted.

According to Nel (ed.) (1999: 118–122) the objectives of trade unions are to protect and promote the particular goals or interests of individual workers or groups of workers. That is why workers' reaction to trade union membership will indicate the degree to which they believe such membership will decrease their frustration and anxiety, improve their opportunities, and lead to the achievement of a better standard of living.

It is in the employer's interest, on the other hand, to maximise return on investment for shareholders, which means making the maximum profit that seems fair and reasonable to all parties concerned (including workers).

The human resources manager should bear in mind that it is immaterial whether there is a formal relationship with a trade union operating in terms of the Labour Relations Act, or an informal relationship based on a recognition agreement. It is not so much the contractual nature of the relationship with the union that matters, as the development of an atmosphere of trust and cooperation between the parties and the establishment of a working arrangement to accommodate each other's needs. There is an apparent contradiction in that the acknowledgement of inherent differences between employers and trade unions actually increases their chances of achieving their respective objectives. In the day-to-day running of the organisation, the human resources manager should, therefore, ensure that all management and supervisory staff reconcile themselves to the reality of trade unions. Provision should be made for the accommodation of shop stewards. Their role in the organisation is of cardinal importance in the promotion of harmony between the organisation and the trade union. Nel (ed.) (1999:125) points out:

The primary role of the shop steward is to ensure and maintain the equilibrium in relations between management and labour within the framework of existing rules, regulations and customs, since it is precisely this that creates efficient liaison across the age-old gulf between the interests of management and workers.

It is the shop steward who represents workers and acts as the link between the workers and the trade union when grievances are lodged or disciplinary action is taken. It could happen that trade union officials who are not employees of the organisation might, from time to time, wish to enter the premises to communicate with workers. The human resources manager needs to be aware of this and know the organisation's policy on such visits. This should be spelt out in the employment relations policy, which should also clarify further practical issues with regard to access to the organisation's premises. It may be stipulated that trade union officials may enter the organisation's premises only if they meet certain requirements (unless they obtain prior consent from the employer to do otherwise).

Management could consider granting unions other facilities under certain conditions, such as an office at the disposal of trade union officials at certain times, the use of notice boards, and time off for the training of shop stewards (but subject to specific limits, normally five working days per year). Arrangements should be made for interaction with the union if a serious dispute should arise.

Concerning collective bargaining, it is generally not in the interests of management to conduct dual discussions and negotiations where more than one union represents the same group of workers. The unions should get together to define the issues that they wish to discuss, and should present a single submission to management where possible. The human resources manager should take note of all these issues and should formulate a policy on them, which can be incorporated into the employment relations policy.

6.6.3 Relationships with employers' associations

Workers can belong to trade unions, while employers can join employers' associations such as the Chamber of Mines, the Building Industries Federation of South Africa (BIFSA), and the Foundation for African Business and Consumer Services (FABCOS), and chambers can join federated chambers, such as the National African Federated Chambers of Commerce (NAFCOC). These associations also operate under the sanction of the Labour Relations Act. In this chapter, only the philosophy underlying employers' associations is dealt with. Employers' associations can consist of any number of employers in any particular undertaking, industry, trade or occupation, who associate for the purpose of regulating relations in that industry between themselves and their employees or some of their employees.

An important consequence of membership of an employer's association is that as soon as an employer becomes a member of such an association, it is automatically bound by the provisions of any agreements or awards that are binding upon that association. Employers' associations usually participate in the bargaining council system, and participate at this level in collective bargaining with representatives of trade unions in order to enter into agreements. Employers (and trade unions) remain bound to such agreements during their currency and even if an employer ceases to be a member of the association, it still remains bound to the agreement.

South Africa's employment relations system allows for the participation of employers and employees so that they regulate their own affairs as far as possible. Human resources managers must be aware that employers' associations serve a useful purpose. They collect and maintain statistics regarding their members and represent their members in a variety of bodies, such as bargaining councils, medical aid societies, pension and unemployment organisations, insurance companies, and apprentice boards, as well as other statutory and non-statutory boards, councils, commissions, and organisations. Employers' associations also provide guidelines to their members on how to cope with contentious issues.

The human resources manager should assess his or her particular organisation's position in the industry and then decide whether or not to join an employer's association. The criterion may be the degree to which the relevant bargaining council is representative of that industry. The organisation's relationship with the employers' association will have an influence on the organisation's employment relations profile both in the industry and in the eyes of the various trade unions that operate in that industry.

Participation in the employers' association and, consequently, in the bargaining council system means that collective bargaining can take place on behalf of the organisation by means of employers' representatives, and that specialists in negotiation and collective bargaining can perform this task on behalf of the organisation.

6.6.4 Dispute-handling procedures

The main aim of the new Act is to simplify the dispute resolution process and to enable resolution at the lowest possible level. In other words, mechanisms have been instituted to attempt to resolve disputes as close as possible to the level at which the conflict actually took place. It will, therefore, in future not easily occur that a general dispute is resolved in the Labour Court, since this would be the exception rather than the rule, depending on the type of dispute which is to be resolved. Some disputes can, however, only be resolved via the Labour Court. Mechanisms like the CCMA and bargaining councils are geared to attempt to resolve disputes speedily. The type of dispute will also determine its route for resolution as outlined in the Labour Relations Act.

It must be noted that a dispute procedure is distinct from a grievance procedure. A grievance procedure provides employees with a channel for expressing dissatisfaction or feelings of injustice in connection with the employment situation and acts as an in-house means for an organisation to attempt to resolve a dispute. (Grievance procedures are discussed later in this chapter). If a grievance procedure runs its course without any agreement being reached between the affected parties a dispute arises. Note that disputes can also arise during the process of collective bargaining, or during the normal course of interaction between management and employees, or between management and management, or between employees and other employees.

A dispute procedure prescribes the action to be taken by both parties during the interval between the start of a dispute and a possible work stoppage or, even worse, a strike. The dispute procedures that are briefly discussed below all operate under the sanction of the Labour Relations Act.

The various dispute resolution institutions are: accredited bargaining councils, the Commission for Conciliation, Mediation and Arbitration (CCMA), the Labour Court and Labour Appeal Court, and accredited private agencies.

It must, however, be noted that should a bargaining council exist and it is accredited by the CCMA, then certain disputes may not be referred to the CCMA, but an attempt must be made to conciliate such a dispute in the bargaining council first. Human resources managers must, therefore, know which avenue to follow should a dispute arise in their organisation. The Act makes provision for a two-step approach to resolving disputes: firstly, conciliation which includes mediation, fact-finding, or the making of a recommendation to the parties by the conciliator (who decides which is the more appropriate process); and secondly, either arbitration, adjudication, or industrial action, depending on the type of dispute.

Depending on the type of dispute, various time periods apply. For example, a dispute concerning an unfair dismissal must be referred for conciliation within thirty days, while there is no fixed time limit for other disputes.

The methods of resolving disputes are now discussed.
- *Dispute resolution via bargaining councils (including statutory councils).* The duty of a bargaining council is to maintain industrial peace between all employers and employees under its jurisdiction. Once a council is accredited by the CCMA it can proceed to resolve disputes. It must however be noted that the constitution of a council will determine the approach to be followed in an attempt to resolve a dispute.

Any person who falls under the jurisdiction of a council can refer a dispute to it to be conciliated. Even a non-party who falls within a council's registration must utilise the council to conciliate in a dispute. Should the dispute not be resolved, a council is entitled to arbitrate the dispute, should the Act and the council's constitution allow it to do so, provided all the parties agree to that.

Disputes which must be referred to a council for conciliation are, for example, disputes about what an essential service is, a dispute in essential services, what a maintenance service is, unfair suspension or disciplinary action, unfair conduct of an employer relating to promotion, demotion, training, or provision of benefits to an employee, and matters that may give rise to a strike or lock-out.

- *Dispute resolution via the CCMA.*
  The CCMA will only conciliate a dispute if there is no council covering the parties to the dispute, or the council is precluded from resolving the dispute, e.g. a dispute concerning the interpretation and application of collective bargaining, exercise of picketing rights, or disclosure of information to workplace forums.

  A Commissioner of the CCMA may also arbitrate a dispute should conciliation not be reached between the parties. Such an arbitration decision will be binding on the parties and no appeal against the decision of an arbitrator is possible, only a review of the decision. Within fourteen days of the conclusion of arbitration proceedings, an arbitrator must issue an arbitration award. Note, however, that in the case of a review as a result of a defect in the arbitration proceedings, the affected party may apply to the Labour Court within six weeks to have the award set aside.

- *Dispute resolution by the Labour Court.*
  Under certain circumstances, as outlined above, the Labour Court (or if a decision of the Labour Court is appealed against, the Labour Appeal Court) can adjudicate a dispute. Under certain circumstances only the Labour Court is entitled to resolve a dispute, e.g. breach of fiduciary duty arising from changes in the rules of social benefit schemes, and appeals against CCMA arbitration decisions.

- *Dispute resolution by private agencies or private arrangement.* The parties involved in a dispute may decide to have the dispute resolved via an accredited private agency, such as the Independent Mediation Service of South Africa (IMSA). All other rules as set out by the Act are then followed.

  Should parties to a dispute decide to resolve the dispute by private arrangement, they are free to follow their own approach, provided the dispute is resolved. If not, they must follow the normal approach as set out by the Act, via either a council or the CCMA.

- *Dispute resolution via industrial action.*
  The parties may embark on industrial action, including strikes or lock-outs, only if the Act does not provide that the dispute must go to arbitration or adjudication, and specific restrictions in terms of the Act do not apply. In this case, readers should refer to Chapter 4 and 7 of the Act for specific detail.

As outlined in The Star (1996:8) the following approach is recommended for a conciliation meeting when a dispute is to be handled by a conciliator (commissioner), regardless of whether it takes place at a bargaining council or is conducted by a commissioner of the CCMA. The process can be subdivided into eight steps, which are presented below and which will be of assistance to employment relations managers in dealing with matters of this nature in their organisation.

This eight-step process is relatively simple and straightforward and could be completed within one day. There is generally no cost involved for the services of the conciliator and the process is handled in a practical and non-legalistic way.

In the light of the information presented

Step 1: Introduction
The conciliator (commissioner appointed to facilitate a settlement of the dispute) opens the meeting by introducing himself or herself.

The parties introduce themselves and their representatives, if any. Only representatives employed by the company or organisation or from the relevant union or employers' organisation are permitted.

The commissioner also deals with "housekeeping" matters at this point, matters such as start and finish times, tea and lunch times, access to telephones and ablution facilities, smoking or no smoking, cell phones and other matters relating to interruptions.

Step 2: Process and ground rules
The conciliator explains the conciliation process and obtains agreement on the ground rules for the meeting. He or she briefly explains the conciliator's role and the steps of the process. Ground rules include, for example, confidentiality agreements, that compromises made may be cancelled if settlement is not reached, that the commissioner will direct the order of speakers, no-one will interrupt another and that parties will treat each other with respect.

Step 3: Opening statements
Each party makes a statement to the conciliator on their version of the dispute as regards the dispute's background, the issues they consider to be in dispute and their positions on each issue.

After completion of the opening statements, the parties get the opportunity to question each other for purposes of obtaining clarity on the opening statements. The conciliator also asks clarifying questions and begins considering whether and at what stage the parties should be separated for purposes of conciliation.

Step 4: Selecting an appropriate intervention
Based on his or her understanding of the nature of the dispute, the conciliator discusses the dispute with the parties and decides on the best intervention technique. That is, the procedure most appropriate to the problem is chosen from the alternatives of mediation, relationship building, factfinding, advisory arbitration and others.

Step 5: Dispute analysis
Here the conciliator, with the aid of the parties, develops an in-depth understanding of all the issues and of the parties' underlying needs and problems.

This step may take place with all parties present, or between the conciliator with each party in private or a combination of both separate and joint discussions.

Step 6: Option exploration
Particularly where the intervention approach of mediation has been chosen, the issues, problems and underlying needs are carefully summarised.
- Common ground is sought through the mediator's efforts in assisting the parties to understand each other's needs and through brainstorming mutually satisfactory solutions.
- Alternatives for solutions or settlements are identified.

Step 7: Choosing solutions
- Objective criteria against which to measure options are agreed.
- The alternatives identified in step 6 are measured against the agreed criteria.

Step 8: Finalisation of agreement
- A solution or combination of solutions are agreed, based on the common ground established and on the previously evaluated alternatives.
- The agreement is reduced to writing and signed. Any such agreement is binding on the parties who may not then take the matter further in any way or form.

Should an agreement not be reached the commissioner completes a certificate confirming this and the matter may then be referred to arbitration, which will take place within a further 30 days.

in this section, it is evident that the human resources and employment relations official must clearly know which avenues are best to follow in the interests of his or her organisation if a dispute with employees should arise. It is, therefore, of cardinal importance that the human resources manager knows how these procedures operate and what the qualifications and talents of mediators and arbitrators should be in order to resolve disputes in a way that will be in the best interests of the organisation and yet will satisfy the workers as well.

6.6.5 Strike handling

Strikes are a fact of life in South Africa and the world over. The human resources or employment relations manager must, therefore, be prepared for strikes, know what they are and how to handle them when they occur (in other words, there should be a contingency plan), as well as knowing what to do after a strike.

In its general preparation for strikes, and in the context of the new Labour Relations Act, management needs to obtain information about unions and strikes by asking the following questions:
- Who are the unions?
- How and where do they operate?
- Who are the leaders?
- How strong are they?
- What are their aims or strategies?
- How many members do they have altogether?

Management should then answer the following questions regarding the organisation:
- What are the organisation's labour costs?
- How lean is the staffing and how easily can workers be replaced?
- Which are the critical areas in terms of management and effectiveness and the key performance areas in the organisation's overall operations?

Management and the human resources manager can use the answers to these critical questions to prepare for possible strikes by taking proactive measures.

Strikes contain four elements that the human resources manager needs to be aware of. Firstly, a strike is a temporary work stoppage, because strikers plan to resume their work with the same employer. Employers, however, do not always view strikers in the same light. Many employers incorrectly regard strikers as people who have cancelled their employment contracts in an uncalled-for and unseemly manner. Secondly, a strike is a specific type of work stoppage. Contrary to popular opinion, striking is not easily used as a weapon, since it entails deprivation for the strikers and their families. This means that striking is the final weapon in a trade union's armoury. Thirdly, a strike is carried out by a group of workers; it is a joint action taken by the workers, as opposed to resignation, which is the individual withdrawal of labour. Fourthly, a strike is a collective action by workers to express a grievance, which may have been disregarded by management for a long time.

In the event of the refusal by a significant number of workers to start or continue working, management should react in the manner most likely to resolve the issues that caused the work stoppage:
- as speedily as possible;
- as near to the point of origin as possible; and
- without injury to personnel and damage to property.

To achieve such an objective requires planning, organising, and decision-making in advance to ensure appropriate and uniform behaviour on the part of management. This means that a contingency plan must be drawn up that will cover most of the issues discussed below.

Human resources managers are advised in the IPM Fact Sheet No. 106 to adopt the following procedures in the event of a strike:
- Maintain a chronological diary of events.
- There should be no police involvement if this is at all possible. However, the police are responsible for public law and order and it may become necessary to call them, should public order be threatened. The police will never become involved in the industrial action dispute as long it remains an internal affair between the organisation and its workers and public order is not threatened in any way whatsoever.
- A reliable two-way channel of communication should be opened with the striking workers. Mass meetings to negotiate the issues should be avoided and an attempt should be made to identify representatives with whom management can communicate. The options available to management are:
  - the existing channels of communication;
  - an acceptable and neutral party;
  - elected representatives who can speak on behalf of the workers; or
  - a body (such as a trade union) that claims to represent the interests of the workers.
- Report-back facilities and a time schedule should be agreed on. Where necessary, workers should be allowed to hold meetings with their representatives to facilitate the process of resolving the grievances. Management must listen to and address any expressed grievances or demands.
- The Department of Labour could be informed. Its role would only be to provide advice and information on legal procedures and not to intervene.
- A single spokesperson should be appointed to liaise with the press. The media should be kept informed as much as possible regarding the developments, and the information they receive should be factually correct. Incorrect reporting should be avoided.
- Normal facilities such as food, accommodation, and transport should be provided where possible, and any form of confrontation should be avoided.
- A strike develops a personality of its own and management should acknowledge this and not immediately attempt to suppress the strike. A request for striking workers to cease striking before negotiations can take place constitutes a contradiction, as it implies that the workers must forfeit their bargaining power in order to bargain, and as such the request is highly unlikely to be successful.

Once the workers return to work, management should see to the following:
- The promises that were made must be carried out.
- Managers and supervisors must be carefully briefed and requested to be tactful, without relinquishing essential controls such as promptness.
- Workers are to clock in, in recognition of legal and civilised norms. They must be treated tactfully yet firmly, otherwise all previous efforts may have been in vain and the strike may flare up again.
- Management should inform all non-strikers of what has happened, commend them on their responsible decision not to strike, and express appreciation for their loyalty to the organisation.
- Management should, at the earliest opportunity, give consideration to the following:
  - the time and cause of the strike;
  - the role communication played in causing and resolving the strike;
  - the role of shop stewards and members of the workplace forum, should it exist;

- current channels for handling grievances and for disciplinary action, as well as those used by line managers for communication;
- mistakes that were made and the lessons to be learned from them; and
- the adjustment of plans to handle strikes better in the future. This may include a change to the contingency plan.
• The employment relations policy may have to be reviewed. It is therefore important that all workers should understand the following:
  - current procedures for the handling of grievances and discipline;
  - the role of shop stewards and workplace forums; and the organisation's employment relations policy as set out in the employment contract.

It is clear that the human resources manager can do a great deal to prevent strikes, and can do even more once a strike is in progress. This is contrary to the general belief that there is little that can be done while a strike is in progress. The biggest task, however, starts when the strike is over, when management has to re-establish relations with the workers and the trade union, and investigate and eliminate the issues that caused the strike.

6.6.6 Importance of grievance and discipline handling

Effective grievance and discipline handling are essential tools of good human resources management practices in any organisation. Organisations not in possession of such procedures are bound to suffer continuous conflict with their employees. Fortunately, the new Labour Relations Act makes it easy for organisations to practice sound grievance and discipline handling by means of the guidelines provided in the Act (particularly Schedule 8), and human resources and employment relations officials should take careful note of its functioning.

Written grievance and disciplinary procedures obviate the need for management to become involved in skirmishes about relationship procedures with labour, thereby allowing management to get on with running the organisation. The grievance procedure will be discussed first, followed by the disciplinary procedure.

Handling of grievances

There is no doubt that grievance procedures are the most important institutional system that can be used to support an organisation's employment relations. This can be deduced from the definition of a grievance as an occurrence, situation, or condition that justifies the lodging of a complaint by an individual. In the usual context of an organisation's employment relations activities, a grievance would constitute a real, perceived, or alleged breach of the terms of the employment contract. While this refers, in most cases, to the formal collective contract between the employer and the employees, it could also include both the individual's conditions of employment and the psychological contract between him or her and the employer.

If a sound grievance procedure does not exist, managers will not be aware of grievances or sources of dissatisfaction. This does not mean, however, that there are no grievances. It only means that they simmer under the surface. When they eventually erupt, the effect on the organisation is usually out of proportion to the extent of the underlying causes. Managers who profess to "know the workers" and maintain that they follow an "open-door policy" that is adequate for meeting workers' needs, are living in a fool's paradise and will eventually reap the bitter fruits of this short-sighted policy.

Furthermore, managers who limit the scope of the grievance procedure to those grievances relating to the formal human resources policy, or to the items contained in the collective agreement, are ignoring the complexity and uniqueness of individual human beings. It should be recognised that because of the complexity of human nature and the behaviour resulting from it, many issues that could constitute grievances fall beyond the scope of a written company policy and employment relations policy. Such issues need to be assessed on merit and management must be flexible.

The grievance procedure starts when the worker raises a grievance with his or her immediate supervisor and should end at the highest authority in the organisation, the managing director or someone of similar rank. The roles of the employee representative and of the human resources department must be specified, as should the time limits within which grievances must be lodged and appeals heard. Employees need to be taught during their induction how to utilise the procedure, and employee representatives and supervisors need to be trained in the performance of their respective roles. Furthermore, records of proceedings must be kept and the human resources department, which should provide advice and assistance (when requested) on its operation, must monitor the execution of the procedure.

Human resources managers need to realise that the key to successful grievance resolution is prompt action. A neglected grievance, or a delayed response to it, is often the origin of a new grievance. If specific time limits are laid down in the procedure, workers will be prepared to allow the process to be completed, and will even wait longer if facts are difficult to establish. They must, however, be kept continually informed.

An effective grievance procedure is an integral part of the organisation's total communications system. It keeps both workers and managers aware of each other's needs, desires, attitudes, opinions, values, and perceptions. However, more important than handling grievances is preventing them. Being sensitive to potential causes of dissatisfaction and taking steps to eliminate them will obviate the need to apply the grievance procedure. This means getting rid of poor human resources practices, adjusting managerial behaviour, and improving worker morale.

Grievance procedures can consist of various stages, which will depend on the size and complexity of the organisation. However, their operation should be just and fair, from the employee's interaction with his or her supervisor (the first stage) to the point where the grievance is lodged with the managing director, which would be the final stage in the attempt to solve the grievance within the organisation.

Finally, it must be noted that if no solution to a grievance can be found, external intervention follows, for example by the CCMA. Various external sources up to the level of the Labour Court may be solicited to solve disputes of this nature, but the process should be according to the prescribed dispute procedure as set out in the Labour Relations Act.

Handling of discipline

Any organisation, irrespective of its nature, structure, or objectives, needs to have rules and a standard of conduct, and its members have to observe these if the organisation is to function successfully. It is important to realise that these rules determine permissible behaviour for all the employees in the organisation. The rules should apply to all personnel, from the highest to the lowest level, if they are to have maximum effect, although there would be some exemptions, such as exemption from clocking in and out and working shifts for some personnel in an organisation. Grogan (1999:90–92) states that discipline should contribute to the effectiveness and efficiency of the business, as far as employees' work is concerned. Production and the provision of services will certainly be slowed down if employees are free to stay away from work when they please, to work at their own pace, to fight with their fellow employees, or to disobey their employers' instructions. It is, consequently, the employer's right and duty to ensure that its employees adhere to reasonable standards of efficiency and conduct.

It is thus evident, in the context of current employment law, that discipline is regarded as a corrective rather than punitive measure. A disciplinary code endorses the concept of corrective or progressive discipline, which regards the purpose of discipline as a means for employees to know and understand what standards are required of them. It empowers employers to seek to correct employees' behaviour by a system of graduated disciplinary measures, such as counselling and warnings.

Human resources officials in organisations should, therefore, ensure that the approach to discipline is carefully described in the various policies of the organisation. Furthermore, it must be emphasised, as stated by Grogan (1999:90) that 'the employer has a right, indeed a duty, to maintain discipline in the workplace. (This is also highlighted in the Atlantis Diesel Engines (Pty) Ltd. v Roux & another [1988] 9ILJ 45[C])'. This duty is recognised in the Labour Relations Act in Schedule 8, The Code of Good Practice: Dismissal. In Schedule 8, broad guidelines for dismissal for misconduct are set out, but which are also relevant to the general maintenance of discipline which should be observed by human resources and employment relations officials in organisations.

It is obvious from the above statements that the power to prescribe standards of conduct for the workplace, and to initiate disciplinary steps against transgressors, is one of the most jealously guarded assets of managers everywhere, forming as it does an integral part of the broader right to manage. It must, however, be borne in mind that in the context of the participative spirit of the new Labour Relations Act, the exercise by employers of their power to prescribe standards and to impose discipline will invariably be challenged by individuals and the trade unions representing them.

Discipline can, consequently, be defined as action or behaviour on the part of the authority in an organisation (usually management) aimed at restraining all employees (including managers) from behaviour that threatens to disrupt the functioning of the organisation.

Disciplinary action is usually initiated by management in response to unsatisfactory work performance or unacceptable behaviour on the part of workers. This is downward communication. (When a worker has problems and initiates a grievance procedure, this is upward communication.)

In terms of the Labour Relations Act, Sections 187-194 and Schedule 8 are the point of departure for policy statements in an organisation regarding the approach to be followed for discipline and dismissal. (Dismissal is dealt with in detail elsewhere

---

Example of a policy statement on disciplinary procedures

To ensure consistent and fair discipline in the organisation and promote disciplined behaviour among all employees, it is the organisation's policy to vest disciplinary action and accountability in line management, to ensure that disciplinary action is immediate in response to the transgression of defined limits, to commence, and where possible, to settle disciplinary action at the lowest possible level, and to ensure that it is consistently applied.

in this chapter under the heading Termination Procedures). However, it is essential that human resources and employment relations officialls take cognisance of the detail proposed in the relevant sections of the Act. In the Code of Good Practice of the Labour Relations Act (Section 3.1– 3.6) it is stated that various procedures prior to dismissal should be followed. These are:

1. All employers should adopt disciplinary rules that establish the standard of conduct required of their employees. The form and content of disciplinary rules will obviously vary according to the size and nature of the employer's business. In general, a larger business will require a more formal approach to discipline. An employer's rules must create certainty and consistency in the application of discipline. This requires that the standards of conduct are clear and made available to employees in a manner that is easily understood. Some rules or standards may be so well established and known that it is not necessary to communicate them.
2. The courts have endorsed the concept of corrective or progressive discipline. This approach regards the purpose of discipline as a means for employees to know and understand what standards are required of them. Efforts should be made to correct employees' behaviour through a system of graduated disciplinary measures such as counselling and warnings.
3. Formal procedures do not have to be invoked every time a rule is broken or a standard is not met. Informal advice and correction is the best and most effective way for an employer to deal with minor violations of work discipline. Repeated misconduct will warrant warnings, which themselves may be graded according to degrees of severity. More serious infringements or repeated misconduct may call for a final warning, or other action short of dismissal. Dismissal should be reserved for cases of serious misconduct or repeated offences.
4. Generally, it is not appropriate to dismiss an employee for a first offence, except if the misconduct is serious and of such gravity that it makes a continued employment relationship intolerable. Examples of serious misconduct, subject to the rule that each case should be judged on its merits, are gross dishonesty or wilful damage to the property of the employer, wilful endangering of the safety of others, physical assault on the employer, a fellow employee, client or customer and gross insubordination. Whatever the merits of the case for dismissal might be, a dismissal will not be fair if it does not meet the requirements of Section 188.
5. When deciding whether or not to impose the penalty of dismissal, the employer should, in addition to the gravity of the misconduct, consider factors such as the employee's circumstances. These include the length of service, previous disciplinary record and personal circumstances, the nature of the job and the circumstances of the infringement itself.
6. The employer should apply the penalty of dismissal consistently with the way in which it has been applied to the same and other employees in the past, and consistently as between two or more employees who participated in the misconduct under consideration.

It is important to note that a fair procedure must be applied when disciplinary action is to take place. In terms of Schedule 8, the employer should conduct an investigation to determine whether there are grounds for dismissal should an offence of such a grave nature occur. However, this need not be a formal enquiry. Section 4.1 of Schedule 8 provides the following guidelines:

The employer should notify the employee of all the allegations using a form and language that the employee can reasonably understand. The employee should be allowed the opportunity to state a case in response to the allegations. The employee should be entitled to a reasonable time to prepare the response and to the assistance of a trade union representative or fellow employee. After the enquiry, the employer should communicate the decision taken, and preferably furnish the employee with written notification of that decision.

The following needs are to be observed when the employer considers the appropriateness of a penalty, namely:
- the seriousness of the misconduct;
- the nature of the misconduct;
- the employee's state of mind, both at the time of the misconduct and during the subsequent investigation;
- the employee's previous disciplinary record;
- the guidelines of the applicable disciplinary code;
- the employee's personal circumstances; and
- the consistency of the penalty in comparison with similar past cases.

Employers should keep records for each employee, specifying the nature of any disciplinary transgressions, the actions taken by the employer, and the reasons for the actions.

At the end of a disciplinary enquiry, the employer must tell the employee of its decision and should preferably confirm it in writing. If the employee is dismissed, the employee should be given the reason for dismissal and reminded of any rights to refer the matter to a council with jurisdiction or to the Commission or to any dispute resolution procedures established in terms of a collective agreement. In exceptional circumstances, if the employer cannot reasonably be expected to comply with these guidelines, the employer may dispense with pre-dismissal procedures.

Lastly, in the spirit of fairness and reasonableness, rules must be reasonable, since a rule that is not reasonable and which is impossible or illegal will not be tolerated, and since the broad principle is that disciplinary rules must be designed to promote the efficiency of the enterprise and must have an economic rationale. In this regard, Grogan (1999:93) suggests the following checklist to assess the validity of a work rule:

(a) Did the employer have the authority to make the rule in terms of the employment contract?
(b) Does the rule comply with the applicable statutes or regulations?
(c) Is the rule reasonably required for the efficient, orderly and safe conduct of the employer's business?
(d) Was the existence of the rule known to the employee or could/should the employee reasonably have been expected to know of its existence?
(e) Has the rule been consistently applied in similar cases in the past?

Only if the answer to each of these questions is in the affirmative will the rule be enforceable. Otherwise stated, if the answer to any one of the above questions is 'no' then the employee may not fairly be disciplined for a breach of that rule.

It must be borne in mind that disciplinary action entails various progressive levels, i.e. oral warnings followed by written warnings and final written warnings prior to dismissal. Other measures, which could be applied short of dismissal, are the denial of privileges for a short time, e.g. loss of a portion of discretionary bonuses. Another approach is demotion or suspension instead of dismissal. It goes without saying that where this method is used, the employee must have committed a dismissable offence.

Dismissal is considered the most serious disciplinary penalty that can be lawfully imposed by an employer on an employee.

The advantages to an employer of a consistent disciplinary procedure are threefold: firstly, it contributes to the stability of the workforce; secondly, labour turnover is minimised; and thirdly, it promotes productivity. The advantages to an employee of a consistent disciplinary procedure are also threefold: firstly, the people who are able to dismiss employees are competent to do so; secondly, those who are able to dismiss employees have a strong sense of responsibility; and thirdly, employees need not automatically distrust every manager and every dismissal and disciplinary measure.

Three components are necessary for the effective maintenance of a disciplinary procedure in an organisation: consultation or negotiation, communication with everybody concerned regarding the exact way in which the system operates, and training of the individuals involved in the disciplinary process.

Grievance and disciplinary procedures are primarily aimed at interaction between employees and their supervisors where they have contact most often, i.e. on the shop floor. It is at that level that the foundations of a sound employment relations policy should be laid. The fulfilment of the needs of both workers and management is made possible through the grievance and disciplinary procedures, because these structures minimise conflict between the workers and management.

In the following section, issues that the human resources manager manages and that have a pronounced influence on employment relations are discussed.

6.7 Workplace forums

This mechanism contained in chapter 5 of the Labour Relations Act is bound to make a great impact on employment relationships, since it aims to promote the interests of all workers and efficiency in the workplace. It was specifically introduced to replace the inefficient works council system.

Managers must realise that if South African businesses are to compete in the global economy, major restructuring of the workplace is required. Management and labour have to find new ways of relating to each other. Consequently, there needs to be a shift towards joint problem-solving and better communication on certain issues.

Therefore, human resources and employment relations officials need to take careful note of how workplace forums operate and how they can benefit their organisations.

6.7.1 Setting up a workplace forum

A workplace forum may be established in any workplace with more than 100 workers. Registered unions that have a majority membership in the workplace may apply to the CCMA for the establishment of a workplace forum.

6.7.2 How workplace forums work

Members of a workplace forum must meet regularly with all the workers in that workplace. The workplace forum must also meet regularly with the employer. At these meetings, the employer must present a report on its financial and employment situation, its performance since the last report, and its expected performance in the short term and in the long term. The employer must then consult with the workplace forum on any matters arising from the report that may affect workers at the workplace.

The employer must provide the workplace forum with facilities so that it can perform its functions.

Forum members are entitled to reasonable time off during working hours with pay, either to perform their functions or to undergo training so as to perform these functions. Union officials are entitled to attend meetings of the forum. The forum can also call on experts for assistance.

There are two ways in which a workplace forum provides for this shift in promoting participative management and improving relations between management and employees: consultation, and joint decision-making. Human resources and employment relations officials must ensure that they understand the magnitude and consequences of consultation and joint decision-making, both of which are briefly discussed below.

6.7.3 Consultation

The employer is obliged to consult and try to reach agreement with the workplace forum on particular issues.

Some examples of the matters on which an employer is required to consult are:
- restructuring the workplace;
- partial or total plant closures;
- mergers and transfers of ownership, where these affect workers;
- retrenchments;
- exemptions from any collective agreement or law; and
- education and training.

6.7.4 Joint decision-making

On other matters, the employer may not take a decision alone. The decision must be made jointly with the workplace forum. If no agreement can be reached between the workplace forum and the employer on joint decision-making issues, the issue must be referred for conciliation. If no conciliation is reached the issue must be referred for arbitration. Matters specified for joint decision-making include disciplinary codes and procedures, affirmative action, and changes to the rules of benefit funds.

6.7.5 Effectiveness of workplace forums in practice

Recent research by Kirsten and Nel (2000) investigated the empirical effectiveness of workplace forums three years after their introduction, in terms of their potential usefulness and value to organisations. The project involved 1 039 organisations employing more than 100 employees in the Gauteng Province during 1999. To date, only seventeen workplace forums have been established and are operating in South Africa. The objective of the project was to uncover the reasons for the limited use of this mechanism to improve participation and co-operation between management and employees. The research led to the conclusion that the value of workplace forums in promoting industrial democracy and participation is either underestimated or not pursued. In order to utilise workplace forums more effectively in industry, the following recommendations, based on the research results, were made:
- Workplace forums should not have to be initiated by majority representative trade unions. They should be worker-driven rather than trade union-driven.
- Workplace forums should be prohibited by statute from using strikes as the final solution, since this cannot be conducive to the process of participation.
- It should be possible to set up statutory workplace forums in organisations with fewer than 100 employees. The minimum number of employees should, therefore, be reduced so that smaller organisations can also enjoy the benefits of protected worker participation.
- Employers, employees, and trade unions should receive training regarding

the role of workplace forums. Workplace forum representatives should also receive specific training to enable them to carry out their task effectively.
- A supervisory council should be established to exercise control over important strategic decisions. All role-players should be represented on this council. These decisions should be incorporated into the constitution of the workplace forum. This will prevent decisions from being taken by workers who do not have the necessary knowledge, skills, and experience.
- Workplace forums should function completely independently of trade unions.
- The role of workplace forums, and that of collective bargaining, should be very clearly spelled out if workplace forums are to be successful.
- There should be trade union representation at board level. This would counteract the 'us-them' approach that is prevalent between management and trade unions in some businesses.

6.8 General employment practices that affect employment relations

In this section, human resources management issues that are commonly considered to be general employment practices are covered. The manner in which they are handled in an organisation can hamper harmonious relations between management and workers; therefore, their handling must feature in the employment relations policy to assist human resources and employment relations officials to effectively deal with workplace relations.

Readers must note that the Labour Relations Act includes various sections regarding workplace relations between the various parties, e.g. no unfair recruitment and employment practices are permitted. Transgression of these will constitute discrimination and, therefore, unfair labour practices. A further refinement of this is included in the Employment Equity Act No. 55 of 1998, where unfair discrimination is prohibited in Section 6(1) of Chapter 2:

> No person may unfairly discriminate, directly or indirectly, against an employee in any employment policy or practice on one or more grounds, including race, gender, sex, pregnancy, marital status, family responsibility, ethnic or social origin, colour, sexual orientation, age, disability, religion, HIV status, conscience, belief, political opinion, culture, language and birth.

Harassment of an employee is a form of unfair discrimination and is prohibited on any one, or a combination of grounds of unfair discrimination listed above. Furthermore, medical and psychological testing, and other similar assessments are also prohibited unless certain requirements are met.

It is, however, in terms of Sections 6(2), 7(1), and 7(2) of the Employment Equity Act, not unfair discrimination to take affirmative action measures consistent with the purpose of this Act, or distinguish, exclude, or prefer any person on the basis of an inherent requirement of a job.

Readers must note that some of the above provisions were originally contained in Schedule 7 of the Labour Relations Act, and were repealed but reappeared as provisions in the Employment Equity Act, No. 55 of 1998.

6.8.1 Recruitment

Recruitment has two stages: the defining of requirements and the attracting of candidates. Both are affected by the employment relations standpoint of an organisation. For example, if an organisation professes to offer equal employment opportunities to employees, it is unlikely that it will tolerate any prohibitions in the recruitment of certain employees.

Prejudices and preferences in an organisation show in the manner in which recruitment is conducted. An organisation also has an opportunity, through the recruitment process, to advertise its employment practices and state for individual employees its public relations policy.

There is a direct overlap of the employment relations policy of an organisation and its recruitment practices in the case of a closed shop agreement. In such an instance, an organisation is bound to employ only those individuals in certain occupations who are members of the appropriate trade union representing that occupation. This means that the organisation's recruitment criteria for that occupation include membership of the union; this gives a degree of co-operation between the two organisations. There is even more overlap between an organisation's employment relations policy and its recruitment policy if the organisation uses a trade union as a recruitment agent.

6.8.2 Selection and induction

The selection procedures practised by an organisation also reflect its employment relations policy.

Selection practices may be specified in an employment relations agreement with worker representatives. Organisations may make provision for shop stewards to witness any testing procedures to ensure that the process is objective and that no labour group's interests are being promoted or prejudiced. Affirmative action will manifest itself in the selection procedure.

Selection and promotion are closely intertwined, especially if the organisation

> **Typical policy statement on selection**
> The organisation undertakes to fill vacancies with the most suitable individuals, and such individuals will be selected in accordance with established criteria for each job. Each individual's suitability will be measured against the job requirements by means of tests, past performance, education and biographical data.

follows a policy of filling vacancies from within where possible. Worker representatives have an interest in such promotion of employees: unions might prefer seniority as a criterion for promotion rather than performance, since this furthers the interests of their long-term members. Other unions may attempt to restrict occupation of certain positions to a limited group of individuals defined in their constitutions and, as such, will oppose promotion from within of anyone who does not meet these requirements.

During induction, new employees should be informed of the employment relations policy of the organisation. They should be trained in the use of employment relations structures, such as grievance and disciplinary procedures. Furthermore, it is during the induction process that new employees are informed of all the specific conditions of employment. Many of these, such as working hours and holidays, have probably been negotiated by a union, and new employees will, therefore, be able to gauge the employment relations climate in the organisation.

The induction process provides the employer, and specifically the human resources manager, with an opportunity to sow the seeds for a harmonious working environment, and therefore contribute towards the maintenance of industrial peace in the organisation.

6.8.3 Training and development

Training serves a dual role in that it helps management meet its human resources requirements, while at the same time increasing the market value or marketability of those being trained, and hence their bargaining power. Training, therefore, is a matter of mutual interest to both workers and management. Policy statements on training may include that:
- employees are encouraged to develop to their full potential in the best interests of both the organisation and themselves;
- in the event of technological changes, retraining will be provided for affected employees; and
- training and retraining affecting union members will be implemented with the cooperation and support of the union concerned.

Employment relations training is necessary if the procedures and programmes outlined in the employment relations policy are to be successfully implemented. Employees who are to use such procedures and programmes must be trained in the actions required.

According to Van Dyk et al. (2000) personnel at the appropriate management and supervisory levels need to receive training in the application of policies and procedures. This would specifically include training in employment relations matters to promote management and labour harmony. Employee and employer representatives should be trained in the functioning of workplace forums, conducting meetings, and so on. Employees who are not involved in a workplace forum should also be informed about its functioning and made aware that it is a medium for communication. If employment relations training involves members of a trade union, management should consult with the union involved about training material and, where necessary, should conduct joint training.

6.8.4 Job evaluation

Job evaluation is a formal system for determining the relative worth of jobs in an organisation. Steps must be taken to ensure that all employees are familiar with the job evaluation system and that members of the job evaluation committee (including the worker representative) have received the necessary training.

In the sphere of employment relations, job evaluation provides information that could have a profound influence on an organisation's management style. This is because employees, in terms of the job evaluation structures available to them, can assess management decisions on things like remuneration. This highlights the employment relations issues subject to management prerogative.

In the negotiation process over salaries and wages, trade unions should acknowledge both phases in the job evaluation process. Phase 1 is the process of grading jobs according to a particular job evaluation technique, such as the Paterson or Peromnes systems. Phase 2 is the process of attributing a pay structure to the graded hierarchy of jobs established in phase 1. It is only in phase 2 that there can be flexibility and negotiation.

Today, it is critically important to realise that job evaluation has become a focal point in the unionised environment. This is so because union pressure on job evaluation skills is nothing other than an attempt to get more money, rather than a concrete objection to the scheme itself. According to Levy and Associates (1996: 14) pressure will arise regarding grade drift, changes in job content, disclosure of information, and so on. It should, therefore, be carefully managed to minimise conflict between management and labour.

6.8.5 Compensation

The following aspects of employment relations are relevant to compensation and, in particular, to salary scales:
- whether there is a common pay structure, based on an accredited job evaluation system, which applies throughout the organisation;
- a corollary to the above is whether employees are paid according to the value of the job performed;
- whether salaries of the lowest remunerated employees are pegged at the minimum living level or the supplementary living level; and
- that an employee's race or sex is no factor in determining that employee's salary.

Issues such as the cost of living, productivity, the skills gap, seniority and minimum wages also relate to the salary scales applied by employers and are likely to be raised during negotiations with unions.

6.8.6 Fringe benefits

Fringe benefits are compensation other than wages and salaries. Some fringe benefits, such as unemployment insurance and workmen's compensation are mandated by law. In other cases, benefits result from negotiations between management and labour, and are then specified in bargaining council agreements, wage regulating measures, private employment contracts, and so on. Leave arrangements, for example, are a benefit specified in this way.

Some employers voluntarily introduce other fringe benefits, such as a canteen, additional leave, parking, medical benefits, or club membership fees with the object of maintaining a stable and contented labour force.

6.8.7 Employee promotion

Promotion (assigning an employee to a job of higher rank) is an area of management where trade unions can actively promote the interests of their members since they now have the backing of the new Labour Relations Act to ensure that fair promotion procedures are followed for employees. Examples of the manner in which trade unions can assert themselves are:
- unions can press for seniority as the criterion for promotion;
- unions can insist that employees be promoted from within the organisation before outsiders are hired;
- unions can press for the promotion of a specific individual, subject to the grievance procedure; and
- unions can put pressure on employers to start applying broad banding to job evaluation for remuneration purposes, to give employees upward movement in their jobs, which is tantamount to a promotion.

6.8.8 Industrial health and safety

The health and safety of workers in the working environment are of cardinal importance. Trade unions, in particular, focus strongly on this point. If a union were to take an organisation to court on a matter of health and safety, the union would be on safe ground since there would be no question of the union's moral right to ensure that proper safety and health standards are maintained. Consequently, health and safety can play an important part in union-management relations.

On the other hand, showing concern for workers' health and safety is to management's benefit in employment relations because it enhances the image of the employer. The application and effect of the Occupational, Health and Safety Act No. 85 of 1993 should also be borne in mind in this regard.

Issues that might be the subject of union bargaining include the provision of protective clothing, protection from industrial diseases, first aid provisions, and the appointment of a safety official who represents the union's interests.

6.8.9 Retrenchment

Retrenchment (dismissal based on operational requirements) becomes necessary when there are redundant workers. It is the removal of an employee from the payroll because of factors beyond his or her control. Such factors might include loss of sales, shortages of materials, seasonal changes, economic fluctuation, production delays and technological change.

Numerous industrial court cases under the old Act (Act No. 28 of 1956) where unfair retrenchment as an alleged unfair labour practice was dealt with, provide many guidelines as to what fair retrenchment ought to be today. However, this aspect is now also covered in Section 189 of the new Labour Relations Act (Act No. 66 of 1995) where specific guidelines are provided. The Labour Relations Act specifically sets out how consultation to proceed with retrenchments, which are termed dismissals based on operational requirements, is to be executed. In this regard, an employer must try to reach agreement on the following:
- ways to avoid the retrenchments;
- ways to reduce the number of people retrenched;
- ways to limit the harsh effects of retrenchment;
- the method for selecting the retrenched workers; and
- severance pay.

The new Labour Relations Act further states that:
- an employer must provide all the relevant information relating to the proposed retrenchments;
- an employer must pay a retrenched worker severance pay in terms of the negotiated agreement; and
- an employer must select the workers to be dismissed according to criteria agreed to by the consulting parties, or if there are no agreed criteria, according to criteria that are fair and objective.

Trade unions can, therefore, negotiate with management to minimise reductions in the workforce, yet maintain the efficient operation of the organisation. Measures might include the restriction of overtime, training and retraining, transfers between departments, division of work, reduced working hours, rotation of appointments and dismissals, and spreading the retrenchments over a certain period.

How to deal with, and assist, those workers who are retrenched may also be negotiated. Issues in this regard include redundancy payments, reappointment with or without the retention of seniority, putting retrenched workers in touch with other employers, offering potential employers facilities to interview on the organisation's premises, waiving the notice period of retrenched workers who have found alternative employment, assisting workers in obtaining unemployment insurance benefits, helping workers compile a curriculum vitae in order to find employment, and giving redundancy counselling.

6.8.10 Termination procedures

The employment relations policy usually contains a disciplinary procedure and a disciplinary code, and these structures make provision for dismissal as a possible disciplinary step. There are, nevertheless, certain constraints on termination, which may be highlighted in an employment relations context. Proper legal procedures must be followed when a person is dismissed, and matters such as notice of the termination of contract, payment on termination, payment in lieu of notice, and commencement of the notice period must be handled with great care and preferably in consultation with the organisation's lawyers.

Termination of service is discussed in Chapter 8 of the Labour Relations Act under the heading Unfair Dismissal. The chapter covers issues such as: what is regarded as dismissal, the right not to be unfairly dismissed, what is regarded as an unfair dismissal, and so on. The Act sets out the Code of Good Practice: Dismissal in Schedule 8. Detailed guidelines are provided as to how fair dismissal should take place and includes what fair reasons for dismissal would constitute. Dismissals based on operational requirements were dealt with in the previous section in this chapter. Specific information regarding the following types of dismissal is included in Schedule 8:
- dismissal for industrial action (Section 6);
- guidelines in cases of dismissal for misconduct (Section 7);
- incapacity: poor work performance (Sections 8 and 9); and
- incapacity: ill health or injury (Sections 10 and 11).

Finally, the chapter also deals with the approach to be followed if there are disputes about unfair dismissals, as well as limits on compensation, severance pay, transfer of the contract of employment, and so on.

Human resources and employment relations officials should take careful note of Section 194 of the Act. It stipulates that if an employee was dismissed unfairly and the employer cannot prove that the dismissal was for a fair reason related to the employee's conduct, capacity, or based on the employer's operational requirements, the employee will have to be paid not more than the equivalent of twelve months remuneration, calculated at the employee's rate of remuneration on the date of dismissal. Furthermore, if an employee's dismissal falls under the category of Automatic Unfair Dismissals, the employee must be paid not more than the equivalent of twenty-four months remuneration, calculated at the employee's rate of remuneration on the date of dismissal.

Section 195 also states that an order or award of compensation made in terms of Chapter 8 is in addition to, and not a substitute for, any other amount to which the employee is entitled in terms of any law, collective agreement, or contract of employment.

6.8.11 Codes of employment

Various codes of employment have been designed to encourage organisations to promote the social and economic development of South Africa's people. They are a contribution to employment relations outside of the law.

It must be noted that a code of employment is not an employment relations policy in its own right. Subscribers or signatories to a code may well model their employment relations policy on the objectives laid down in their code, but the code itself is a policy statement with a much broader base, which merely expresses the organisation's intentions with regard to its labour force. A code of employment is sometimes used instead of a human resources policy.

6.8.12 Quality of work life and social investment

The quality of work life and social investment (also called social responsibility) are also important. In the application of employment relations to these issues, quality of work life is discussed first and then social investment.

Quality of work life reflects an organisation's concern for its employees. It is usually indicated by whether or not:
- recreation facilities are provided;
- precautions are taken to protect the health of employees;
- training facilities are provided;
- opportunities are provided for career advancement;
- security of employment is regarded as a priority;
- satisfactory working conditions are provided;
- ethical employment practices are maintained; and
- there is company commitment to the implementation of the RDP.

Whether they are motivated by altruistic intent or provided as a means towards increased profitability, such benefits contribute towards the fulfilment of employees' social needs.

If an organisation meets its obligations (as outlined above) to its employees, this will foster cooperation and trust, which are necessary for collective bargaining, as well as generally better relations between management and employees in the organisation. It may reduce mistrust and the threat of strikes, and increase both parties' chances of achieving their respective objectives.

Corporate social investment: Both social conscience and expedience motivate the organisation in its concern for the external environment. It is expedient in that by maintaining environmental conditions at a satisfactory level, an organisation safeguards its own future. An organisation may discharge its social investment towards the external environment in the following ways: through concern for the effects of ecological imbalances and pollution; through sponsorship of public recreation and entertainment; through research; by providing housing and electricity; and by promoting community development and welfare in the communities in which its employees live.

Trade unions are showing increasing concern for community affairs and are likely to monitor organisations' commitment in this regard. Such issues could be included in collective bargaining. Taking this process one step further, management and worker representatives in an organisation could jointly determine the allocation of corporate resources for social projects through joint committees. This would lead to better relationships between the organisation and the trade union, with resultant better employment relations.

6.8.13 The monitoring of employment relations

There are two dimensions to the monitoring of employment relations programmes and procedures: firstly, the assessment of whether employees are implementing the required procedures; secondly, an assessment of whether the procedures that are implemented are effective.

To determine whether an employment relations policy and all the procedures that accompany it are being effectively implemented, the human resources or employment relations manager can circulate questionnaires to staff, interview staff, or observe interpersonal relationships in the organisation. However, the responsibility for the practical implementation of employment relations policy lies with line management. This should be included in their job description, and their effectiveness in its execution should be reflected in their performance appraisals. If this approach is not used, employment relations procedures will not be effectively implemented. It should be remembered that the human resources or employment relations manager performs a staff function in the organisation and, therefore, can only advise management on how things should be done with regard to employment relations, but cannot mandate action.

It is equally important that grievances (their nature and number), written disciplinary warnings, etc. should be examined to determine whether the procedures and programmes that have been implemented are effective. Other indices of the effectiveness of the employment relations policy in its totality are rates of labour turnover, rates of absenteeism, the number of hours lost through work stoppages, the production rate for a certain period, exit interviews, and the attitudes of employees towards management and towards their employment conditions.

It is evident that the monitoring of employment relations in an organisation is of cardinal importance if the human resources or employment relations manager wishes to determine the effectiveness of this function. In fact, it is crucial to the survival of the organisation in the turbulent times South Africa is experiencing. The human resources or employment relations manager can make or break his or her career by the way he or she manages employment relations in the organisation, because of the direct effect it has on the profitability of the organisation.

6.9 Employment equity

A very important development, which has a major impact on employment relations, and which human resources managers should take careful note of, is employment equity. South Africa has a legacy of discrimination in relation to race, gender, and disability that has denied access to opportunities for education, employment, promotion, and wealth creation to most South Africans. Chapter 3 of the Employment Equity Act No.55 of 1998 became operational on 1 December 1999. Large companies must report on their equity plan for the first time by 1 June 2000 and others by 1 December 2000.

The Act has two main objectives, namely to ensure that the workplace is free from discrimination and that employers take active steps to promote employment equity. The purpose of the Act in terms of Chapter 1 is to achieve equity in the workplace by:
- promoting equal opportunity and fair treatment in employment through the eliminating of unfair discrimination; and
- implementing affirmative action measures to redress the disadvantages in employment experienced by designated groups in order to ensure their equitable representation in all occupational categories and levels in the workforce.

Human resources managers should furthermore note that the question of the prohibition of unfair discrimination is contained in this Act, and was outlined earlier in this chapter. The detail of the Act concerning diversity is discussed in detail elsewhere in this book.

A major aspect of applying employment equity in the workplace is the preparation of the employment equity plan. Detail in this regard has been published in the Government Gazette of 23 November 1999 and a Users Guide, which has been published by the Department of Labour. These plans must be in place by 1 June 2000.

Only the essentials concerning the compilation of an organisation's plan to meet the provisions of the Act, and which according to Botha (1999:31) must be addressed by employers, are listed below:
- objectives should be achieved each year;
- affirmative action measures should be implemented;
- numerical goals, timetables, and strategies should be achieved;
- a timetable for the achievement of the goals and objectives other than the numerical goals for each year should be established;

- procedures to monitor and evaluate the implementation of the plan should be in place;
- internal procedures for dispute resolution should be established;
- persons responsible for the plan, including senior management, should be identified; and
- any other prescribed matter should be included.

To comply with the provisions listed above, specific strategies should be selected, such as procurement (recruitment and selection) and maintenance interventions, like specific job competency training and development, career management, mentorship programmes, and formal training.

This should be followed by specific organisational development techniques for the facilitation and support of the process, like sensitivity training, survey feedback, process consultation, team building, intergroup development, management development, diversity management, and conflict resolution techniques.

In addition, top management must commit itself to an equitable system of employment; employment equity should form part of the organisation's strategic management plan. Line management should drive the project and human resources should support it.

Concerning the affirmative action elements of employment equity, in terms of the Employment Equity Plans of the Department of Labour (2000:4) and according to Chapter 3 of the Act, employers must:
- consult with unions and employees in order to make sure that the plan is accepted by everybody;
- analyse all employment policies, practices, and procedures, and prepare a profile of their workforce in order to identify any problems relating to employment equity;
- prepare and implement an employment equity plan, setting out the affirmative action measures they intend taking to achieve employment equity goals;
- report to the Department of Labour on the implementation of their plan in order for the Department to monitor their compliance; and
- display a summary of the provisions of the Act in all languages relevant to their workforce.

There is, however, another angle concerning Chapter 3 of the Act, which human resource managers must take cognisance of, and that is the emphasis on employment equity within a group context. Le Roux (1999:31) states that 'some individuals within a designated group may not have suffered disadvantages, or that some groups may have been exposed to lesser degrees of disadvantage, is irrelevant. The emphasis is on the representivity of the designated groups within the workforce.'

The dilemma is now that many employees, especially employees who do not fall within the designated groups, will certainly expect and demand that their needs and interests as individuals must be acknowledged. Le Roux (1999:31) makes the point that these 'individual interests are protected in Chapter 2 of the EEA, which prohibits discrimination against an employee in any employment policy and practice on the basis of a wide range of grounds, including race, sex, gender and disability.' The result is that human resources managers must take note of group and individual rights, which creates many potential pitfalls in the workplace, which could lead to unfair labour practices if care is not taken.

6.10 Implications of the Basic Conditions of Employment Act

A very important development, which plays a major role in relations in the workplace, is the Basic Conditions of Employment Act No.75 of 1997, which regulates conditions in the workplace. Its detail is discussed elsewhere in this book. Human resources managers must, however, take cognisance of the fact that working time, meal intervals, daily and weekly rest periods, night work, public holidays, leave, etc. are regulated by this Act. Any transgression of its stipulations constitutes an unfair labour practice and may result in strained relations between employers and their employees, which may even erupt in industrial disputes, such as go-slows or strikes.

Human resources managers must therefore monitor its effect and the adherence thereto very carefully, particularly since some issues are fairly contentious, e.g. working hours. It is so sensitive that there is a possibility of amendment to some of the stipulations during the course of 2000 or early in 2001. It is recommended that readers watch the press to stay abreast of these developments and their impact on workplace conditions and employment relations in general.

6.11 Future perspectives

Human resource managers need to understand that the world of tomorrow will be vastly different from the world of today. A myriad of challenges also faces South Africa's young democracy in its efforts to grow its economy and to provide jobs for the unemployed millions. Economic growth and job creation can, therefore, be regarded as the primary foci in this regard. Specific issues which human resources managers should, however, take cognisance of are:

- The current labour legislation and envisaged changes, particularly as far as the Labour Relations Act is concerned.
- The need for employment equity to be addressed in all its facets in the workplace and in the South African business community.
- New dimensions with regard to trade unionism are emerging; the first steps towards cooperation between employers' organisations and employees' organisations are already visible and will speed up in the future. This has a variety of implications for the management of employees in the workplace.
- Training legislation is rapidly going to change the education and development of employees in the workplace. Human resources managers will have to take careful note of these developments.
- Unemployment is still a major factor and job creation via GEAR and other means must be seriously investigated to alleviate this pressing problem.
- According to Yadavalli (1999:25) AIDS is also a major factor and could seriously hamper economic growth in the future. For example, AIDS may lead to skills shortages, absenteeism, and reduced outputs. Life expectancy in South Africa could drop from sixty-five to forty-five by 2010, whereas the population growth rate could drop to 0.4 per cent.
- Labour market flexibility ought to be enhanced to ensure better employment opportunities and more mobility. Human resources managers ought to take note of the restrictions currently being placed on labour flexibility by unions.
- Knowledge management needs to be addressed, as many organisations in future will have to focus sharply on human capital as their competitive edge. Human resources managers will have to ensure that this element of retaining business competitiveness is addressed fully in future.

6.12 Conclusion

In this chapter a review was provided of those employment relations issues that pertain specifically to human resources managers and with which they need to be familiar in order to perform their job effectively. It was stressed that human resources managers are subject to numerous pressures regarding employment relations because it is a complex and rapidly changing field in South Africa's business environment. This area of human resources management is a daunting one, and human resources managers have to be au fait with all the rapid developments in trade unionism and legislation in South Africa.

Human resources managers need to know how the components of employment relations, such as relations with trade unions and dispute-handling procedures, affect them. They should be able to manage these critical issues confidently, particularly if they have to make do without the services of an employment relations manager. However, human resources managers can manage these components of employment relations effectively only if they understand the value of organisation, human resources, and employment relations policies. They also need to understand that the relationship between employers and workers is based on their various rights and responsibilities.

As far as general employment practices are concerned, if issues such as recruitment, job evaluation, remuneration, and industrial safety are ineptly handled, this will have an extremely negative effect on the organisation. This will be compounded if the employment relations elements contained in all general employment practices are disregarded or underestimated by the human resources manager. The employment relationship should therefore be given special consideration if general employment practices that affect human resources management in the employment relations context are to be effectively managed.

Case study
Voluntary services at Maroela Voluntary Pet and Animal Care Centre

Cicero works for the Maroela Voluntary Pet and Animal Care Centre, an organisation in Thabazimbi which collects dead cattle, sheep, goats, and game, free of charge, from conservation conscious farmers in the vicinity. Just over a year ago, he injured his back, slipping a disc, while assisting in loading a big Kudu bull carcass onto the Centre's pickup truck. The Kudu had been caught in a snare and badly mutilated by hyenas before being discovered by a game ranger. After his back injury, Cicero was off sick for two weeks and had apparently recovered without any negative effects. Later, however, he regularly complained of backache and was not keen to assist in picking up any heavy loads.

At the centre a veterinary surgeon normally checks a carcass brought in from a farm, to ensure that it does not contain any harmful diseases, and then it is used as food for its injured wild animals, birds of prey, stray dogs, cats, etc. It is the only centre of its kind in the Western part of the Northern Province, and is acknowledged by the South African SPCA and the International Wildlife Foundation for the work its staff does regarding animal care and recuperation.

Cicero, who drives the pickup truck, has been disciplined on various occasions for unruly behaviour and aggressive driving during the three years he has been with the centre. He has received traffic tickets on various occasions, including two speeding tickets, one for R200 last year and one only a month ago for R400, both of which have been deducted by the supervisor from his pay in two instalments each. Cicero is a member of the Wild Life Protection and Allied Trade Union (WLPATU).

Last week he had to fetch a dead Brahman cow, which had apparently drowned in a dam during the weekend on the farm 'Creamy Hills'. He had bought two quarts of beer and a half-bottle of brandy from the local bottle store that morning. His co-driver James (who does not have a driver's licence) subsequently testified that later on that day Cicero had drunk both quarts of beer and all the brandy, and had given him nothing. This had apparently been during Cicero's lunch time. They had been in town to execute some errands, before fetching the dead cow. Shortly after lunch they had left on the 35-km journey to the farm. When they turned off to the farm, Cicero drove nearly as fast on the secondary dirt roads as he had on the tar leaving town.

On their return to town, Cicero drove into the back of the neighbouring farmer's tractor and trailer, which the farmer had left in the road just around a bend, obscured by a very big baobab tree. The centre's pickup truck skidded into the trailer and overturned as a result of the collision. The accident occurred at approximately 15h30 in the afternoon.

James testified at the subsequent disciplinary hearing that he had warned Cicero to drive slower on the dirt road, but he had not heeded the warning. James had also reminded Cicero about complaints they had made regarding braking deficiencies of the pickup truck, and had questioned whether this had been attended to by the Centre's mechanic. Cicero could not remember that part of the conversation with James. Furthermore, the service of the pickup truck was overdue as a result of cash flow problems at the Centre, and the pickup truck had two smooth tyres, one of which was the spare, replaced on their way to the farm following a puncture caused by a very large lowveld 'camel thorn'.

The management of Maroela Voluntary Pet and Animal Care Centre cc. summarily dismissed Cicero. They claimed, on James' testimony, that Cicero had been cautioned on his reckless driving, and that he had consumed two quarts of strong beer and the brandy while on duty (although over lunch time before driving to the farm) and that no mitigating circumstances were to be found. The farmer whose Brahman cow was collected wrote an affidavit stating that Cicero had been uncoordinated and had difficulty in assisting them when the cow was loaded onto the pickup. The farmer who owned the tractor and trailer also wrote a letter testifying that Cicero had smelled of liquor and had slurred speech when explaining his version of the accident to him at the scene.

Questions

1 What should the proper investigation procedure have been? Explain.
2 Would 'fact finding' be appropriate in this instance? If you were Cicero's trade union representative, what would your considered verdict be in this regard?

3 Can a person be summarily dismissed for alleged drunken driving? Motivate your answer.
4 What are Cicero's rights in this case? Outline the procedural and substantive principles, in particular, which are applicable to the case, to indicate that you understand disciplinary procedures in terms of Employment Law.
5 The case was not resolved after conciliation and was referred to the CCMA for arbitration. You have to defend Cicero as you are his trade union representative. What line of action would you take to end up with a fair result for all parties concerned?

Chapter questions

1 Describe the relationship between the state, employers, and employees in South Africa. Pay special attention to the primary participants in the employment relations system.
2 What obstacles exist to the effective utilisation of workplace forums in organisations in South Africa? List at least 5 such obstacles.
3 Does your organisation or one that you are familiar with have organisation, human resources, and employment relations policies? If not, draw up such policies to reflect your organisation's culture. These must be acceptable to both top management and the relevant trade unions.
4 Which general employment practices in your organisation have resulted in disputes? Why? What solutions can be suggested for human resources managers?
5 Does the Labour Relations Act enhance or complicate the task of human resources and employment relations officials in the workplace to promote participative management? Provide convincing arguments to demonstrate your point of view and understanding of the interdependency of these concepts.
6 Compile an approach your organisation could follow to ensure employment equity is effectively practised in terms of the Department of Labour's Employment Equity Plan.

Bibliography

BACKER, W.A. 1996. *Die bestuur van dissipline.* Bactas Personeel Konsultante, Pretoria.

BACKER, W.A. 1999. *Die dienskontrak. Perspektiewe vanuit die Wet op Basiese Diensvoorwaardes.* Bactas Personeel Konsultante, Pretoria.

BOTHA, E. 1999. The next revolution in organisations. *Management Today,* Vol. 15, No. 6, pp. 30–31.

DEPARTMENT OF LABOUR. 2000. *Preparing an Employment Equity Plan. User's Guide.* Department of Labour, Pretoria.

EDITORIAL COMMENT. 2000. So staan sake nou in SA. *Finansies en Tegniek,* 7 January.

GROGAN, J. 1999. *Workplace law.* 3rd edition. Juta, Kenwyn.

INSTITUTE FOR PERSONNEL MANAGEMENT. (undated). *IPM Journal.* Fact Sheet Supplements Nos 103–107 and 232.

KIRSTEN, M. & NEL, P.S. 2000. Workplace forums in South Africa: are they effective. *South African Journal of Labour Relations,* Vol. 24, No. 1.

LE ROUX, P.A.K. 1999. Affirmative action and the individual employee. *Contemporary Labour Law,* Vol. 9, No. 4, pp. 31–38, November.

LEVY, A. & ASSOCIATES. 1996. *Critical issues in job evaluation.* Unpublished paper, Johannesburg.

NEL, P.S., ERASMUS, B.J. & SWANEPOEL, B.J. 1998. *Successful labour relations: guidelines for practice.* 2nd edition. Van Schaik, Pretoria.

NEL, P.S. (ed.). 1999. *South African employment relations: theory and practice.* 3rd revised edition. Van Schaik, Pretoria.

REPUBLIC OF SOUTH AFRICA. 1999. Employment Equity Act. Commencement Notice, Regulations and Code. *Government Gazette*, Vol. 413, No. 20626. 23 November 1999. Government Printer, Pretoria.

REPUBLIC OF SOUTH AFRICA. 1997. Basic Conditions of Employment Act. *Government Gazette*, Vol. 390, No. 18491. 5 December 1997. Government Printer, Cape Town.

REPUBLIC OF SOUTH AFRICA. 1995. Labour Relations Act No. 66 of 1995. *Government Gazette*, Vol. 366, No. 16861. 13 December 1995. Government Printer, Pretoria.

REPUBLIC OF SOUTH AFRICA. 1996. Labour Relations Act No. 66 of 1995 (Regulations). *Government Gazette*, Vol. 366, No. 17516. 1 November 1995. Government Printer, Pretoria.

REPUBLIC OF SOUTH AFRICA. 1996. Labour Relations Amendment Act No. 42 of 1996. *Government Gazette*, Vol. 375, No. 17427. 10 September 1996. Government Printer, Pretoria.

REPUBLIC OF SOUTH AFRICA. 1998. Labour Relations Amendment Act No. 127 of 1998. *Government Gazette*, Vol. 402, No. 19542. 2 December 1998. Government Printer, Pretoria.

REPUBLIC OF SOUTH AFRICA 1998. Skills Development Act No. 97 of 1998. *Government Gazette*, Vol. 401, No. 19420. 2 November 1998. Government Printer, Pretoria.

REPUBLIC OF SOUTH AFRICA. 1999. Skills Development Levies Act No. 9 of 1999. *Government Gazette*, Vol. 406, No. 19984. 30 April 1999. Government Printer, Pretoria.

SWANEPOEL, B.J. 1995. *'n Strategiese benadering tot die bestuur van die diensverhouding.* Unpublished D.Com. thesis, UNISA, Pretoria.

SWANEPOEL, B.J. 1996. Managing an environment of democracy: conceptualising the real challenge of managerial prerogative. *South African Journal of Labour Relations*, June, vol. 20, no. 2.

SWANEPOEL, B.J., SLABBERT, J.A., ERASMUS, B.J. & BRINK, M. 1999a. *The management of employment relations.* Conceptual and contextual perspectives. Butterworths, Durban.

SWANEPOEL, B.J., SLABBERT, J.A., ERASMUS, B.J. & NEL, P.S. 1999b. *The management of employment relations.* Organisational level perspectives. Butterworths, Durban.

THE STAR. 1996. *How user friendly is new dispute resolution process?* 12 December.

VAN DYK, P.S., NEL, P.S., LOEDOLFF, P. VAN Z. & HAASBROEK, G.D. 2000. *Training management: a multidisciplinary approach to human resources development in Southern Africa.* 3rd edition. Oxford University Press, Cape Town.

YADAVALLI, L. 1999. Labour problems in the next century. *Management Today*, Vol. 15, No. 4, pp. 25–27, May.

7

Employment equity and affirmative action

T Sono

Learning outcomes

At the end of this chapter the learner should be able to demonstrate the following outcomes:
- Distinguish between affirmative action and employment equity.
- State the requirements of the Employment Equity Act.
- Discuss the pros and cons of affirmative action and employment equity programs.
- Identify the affirmative action measures.
- Discuss the employment equity plan.
- Define the issues in the McWhirter Thesis on affirmative action.
- Explain the Zelnick Thesis on affirmative action.
- Discuss the Natal Technikon court case.
- Outline the Sono Thesis on the weaknesses of affirmative action.
- Compare and contrast the international experiences of affirmative action.
- Describe the rule of law.

Key words and concepts

- affirmative action
- affirmative action measures/strategies
- affirmative action discrimination
- competitive workforce
- compliance costs/orders
- employment discrimination law
- employment equity
- Employment Equity Act
- employment equity plan
- empowerment (economic/political)
- equality before the law
- equal employment opportunity
- fair/unfair discrimination
- group rights
- McWhirter Thesis
- non-racial/non-racialism
- preferential policies/treatment
- previously disadvantaged groups
- protected categories of people
- race population register
- racial preferences
- racial privileges

Illustrative case
The Natal Technikon case

In a landmark judgement on affirmative action in April 2000, the Labour Court in Kwa-Zulu Natal ordered the Natal Technikon to reinstate a white lecturer and to grant two years' back pay after the Technikon failed to renew her contract. A decision to appoint a black applicant in her place led her to challenge the Technikon's decision to exclude her.

The court found that the white lecturer had been unfairly dismissed, as she had a reasonable expectation that her fixed-term contract would be renewed.

The dismissal was also found to be unfair in terms of the Labour Relations Act, in that the applicant had been unfairly discriminated against on the basis of her race. The court found that 'affirmative action discrimination' could not constitute a fair basis for dismissing, as opposed to appointing, an employee.

The Court further stated that it was clear that the applicant would have continued to be employed if she had been black rather than white, 'and her dismissal was the result of the purported application by the respondent of its affirmative action policy'.

Facts of the case: The applicant was initially employed by the Technikon on a one-year contract, from 1996 to 1997. Before the termination of the contract, she was requested to reapply for the position, whereupon she was reappointed to a position as a junior lecturer for another year. The renewal of the position was advertised a year later and she had to reapply. A selection committee approved her appointment over a black candidate; but the vice-principal overturned the decision and referred the matter back to the committee 'with a direction that it reconsider its recommendation in the light of the Technikon's affirmative action policy'.

The committee reconvened and decided to appoint a black applicant, despite reaffirming its preference for the white applicant. It later emerged that the new appointee was offered a much higher salary than the salary range for which the post had been advertised. His final salary was even more than that of the head of the department. Attempts were made to place the white applicant in another position but this move was not supported by the human resources department. (Source: Renee Grawitzky 2000:6.)

This judgement is expected to have important implications for the implementation of employment equity plans as required by the Employment Equity Act.

Please study the section on Employment Equity and answer the following questions: What is the moral of this case? What are the likely implications of the court's decision on the employment equity plans? Will these implications have a likely impact on affirmative action?

- rule of law
- societal discrimination
- Sono Thesis
- Sowell Thesis
- specific discrimination
- workforce diversity
- workforce harassment
- Zelnick Thesis

7.1 Introduction

In racially and culturally diverse societies, organisations and companies will ideally be similarly diverse because of their demographics. South African organisations have generally been skewed in terms of their workforce, especially at the middle to upper levels of management. For instance, white employees and managers have been the major beneficiaries of company and government policies in terms of hiring, promotion, employment conditions, and remuneration. It is the white workforce in companies, government institutions, and parastatals which has historically been advantaged. They enjoyed affirmative action programmes and policies of the apartheid government to the disadvantage of black and women employees.

Systematic policies favouring white over black workers were first developed in the 1920s by the National Party – Labour Party coalition government, the so-called Pact Government. The inappropriately named 'civilised labour policy' of the government was designed to uplift the newly urbanised poor whites, at the expense of black workers (Thompson 1993:22). The apartheid government granted racial privilege on the basis of the policy of job reservation which was repealed in 1979.

Afrikaners were, thus, the first South African workers to enjoy affirmative action benefits. Although the term 'affirmative action' was coined in the United States by President Lyndon B. Johnson in 1965, South Africa long had a tradition of affirmative action through various legislation dealing with labour, industrial relations, companies, and artisans' training. Black trade unions, following their proscription around 1919, were not allowed in South Africa until 1979, in accordance with the recommendations of the Wiehahn Commission.

The Commission was inspired by pressures following the 1977 Sullivan Code governing American companies that operated in the country at the time (Madi 1993:18). Some companies in South Africa began token and ineffectual affirmative action window-dressing, but many of the black faces lacked the skills and qualifications for the positions they occupied. The University of the Witwatersrand was one of the first private institutions to launch affirmative action programmes in the mid-1970s. The 1980s saw much industrial activism by black trade unions.

Equal employment opportunities became the central demand by black trade unions, and by the early 1990s, when apartheid was being dismantled, companies began to speed up their affirmative action programmes. However, workers and their unions had by then become militant, and companies were constrained to engage in new strategies to accommodate the changed situation. The post-apartheid government entered the affirmative action issue on the side of those previously disadvantaged. It reversed the affirmative action programmes of the previous white governments of the period 1920–1994. Thus, affirmative action for whites was replaced by affirmative action for blacks.

7.2 Meaning of affirmative action

Affirmative action in South Africa lacks appropriate defining concepts and terms (Nel & Brits 1998:154). Consequently, affirmative action means many things to many persons and organisations. It may 'refer to 'racial preferential treatment for good reasons'. It could mean the redistribution of resources and opportunities. It may also refer to preferential financial assistance by business to institutions of those communities which have been traditionally disadvantaged' (Sonn, in Adams (ed.) 1993: 28).

There are many other definitions of affirmative action, and central to all is the protection and advancement of the interests of persons disadvantaged by past discrimination (Le Roux 1999:33–34). Affirmative action is preferential favour of one group over another.

Such 'protection and advancement' are, however, not necessarily seen in a positive light by all analysts, nor by most organisations. A cabinet minister who once propagated affirmative action for Afrikaners, demurred in 1991 about affirmative action for blacks, though his reasons were nevertheless cogent: 'Affirmative action programmes which consist of preferential policies, might benefit only a fortunate few and not the less fortunate. The have-nots do not always benefit and might actually retrogress because of reduced economic growth brought about by inappropriate affirmative action programmes' (Louw, in Adams (ed.) 1993:153). The BMF Blueprint (1993:4–5) on the other hand, sees affirmative action as:

a planned and positive process and strategy aimed at transforming socio-economic environments which have excluded individuals from disadvantaged groups, in order for such disadvantaged individuals to gain access to opportunities, including developmental opportunities, based on their suitability.

However, Joubert (1992: 1) cautions that if we see affirmative action merely as the replacement of white labour with black labour to redress inequality and injustices, we have no chance of improving South Africa's competitiveness.

A year after his release from twenty-seven years in prison, Nelson Mandela wrote: 'To millions, Affirmative Action is a beacon of positive expectation. To others it is an alarming spectre which is viewed as a threat to their personal security and a menace to the integrity of public life.' (Mandela, cited in Madi 1995: 28). The 'positive' aspect of affirmative action was naturally echoed by Mandela's ANC, through its journal Mayibuye, in the same year:

Affirmative action is needed because social, political and economic inequalities do not spontaneously evaporate. A conscious programme is required to involve and empower the victims of oppression at all levels of society within a reasonable period of time. So affirmative action is a transitional method to redress the imbalances created by domination ... (Mayibuye 1991: 27).

Other ANC intellectuals and agencies have, in the past, emphasised the positive nature of affirmative action. Wrote ANC stalwart Albie Sachs, now Constitutional Court judge: 'Affirmative action could be constitutionally recognised as a legitimate complement to the general principle of nonracialism' (Sachs 1990: 22). In other words a race-based policy is actually non-racial.

In the same year as the publication of Sachs' book, the ANC Department of Economic Policy issued its Discussion Document on Economic Policy (ANC-DEP 1990) which advanced Sachs' argument even further: 'A future democratic, nonracial and nonsexist state would give top priority to applying affirmative action principles to black women.' Thus, to discriminate in favour of certain individuals because they are black and female is actually to be non-racial and non-sexist even though the bases of the preference are race and sex. This view has since become law, and organisations and their human resource managers have to act accordingly to meet the requirements of the law.

Affirmative action then is affirmative discrimination. All sides would be agreed on this. Supporters would, however, add that affirmative discrimination is not unfair discrimination, whereas its detractors would argue that discrimination that allocates privileges to one set of people and excludes another set, on the basis of the racial or gender characteristics of members of such groups, cannot be fair. Our consti-

tution, however, is all things to all people. For instance, Section 9 of the Constitution has several contradictory sections:
- Section 9 (1) is the clause on equality before the law.
- Section 9 (2) is the clause on affirmative action.
- Sections 9 (3), 9 (4), and 9 (5) are the anti-discrimination clauses.

Fair or not, affirmative action is the law and companies are constrained to observe it. Affirmative action (both under apartheid and after it) has always been a method by which those who lack the skills, or are uncompetitive, for certain positions, but are politically powerful, receive government support to obtain their positions. Organisations are, thus, compelled by force of law to practice preferential policies. During apartheid, poor Afrikaners used the power of government to keep Africans, especially, out of the competitive market to secure jobs and higher wages for themselves (Sowell 1990:38–39). Now the shoe is on the other foot. If affirmative action was wrong then, it is wrong now; but since affirmative action has become law, organisations will have to comply. Companies targeted in terms of affirmative action under the Employment Equity Act will have to employ the following strategies:
- identify and remove barriers;
- increase workforce diversity;
- adjust with reasonable accommodation;
- ensure equitable representation of suitably qualified people;
- retain, train, and develop skills; and
- include such other measures as preferential treatment and numerical goals.

7.3 Employment equity

Affirmative action and employment equity are two related concepts, now fully formulated as law in the Employment Equity Act No. 55 of 1998. As we have seen, affirmative action precedes employment equity both in time and legislative enactment. The Employment Equity Act (EEA) is largely a rehash of Chapter 23 of the Canadian Constitution. Nearly everything, from 'designated groups' to 'employment equity plans' to the concept 'employment equity' itself comes from Chapter 23 (2nd Supp.) of the Constitution of Canada.

Affirmative action seeks to correct past unfair discrimination while employment equity seeks to prevent future unfair discrimination. The EEA has become an ambitious social engineering workplace programme to determine the composition of company workforces. Its aim, as the South African government's Department of Labour puts it (Department of Labour 1997: 7) is to undo the huge disparities in the labour market brought about by apartheid. Although the EEA does not define equity, it may be defined as 'present "fair" discrimination to prevent future "unfair" discrimination'. Affirmative action, on the other hand, is 'fair' discrimination to correct past 'unfair' discrimination.

Both the EEA and affirmative action emphasise groups. Chapter 3 of the EEA emphasises employment equity in a group context. Unfair discrimination could be construed on several grounds.

7.3.1 Unfair discrimination

The Act prohibits direct and indirect discrimination on a number of grounds, including:
- race, ethnic or social origin, colour, and culture;
- gender, sex, pregnancy, and sexual orientation;
- disability and HIV status; and
- religion, conscience, belief, and language.

According to Section 10 of the EEA, discrimination on one or more of the above grounds is unfair unless it is established that the discrimination is fair. In other words, the burden of proof of innocence on a charge of unfair discrimination rests with the employer.

The following are regarded as forms of discrimination:
- harassment;
- medical testing if not permitted by law or justifiable in light of certain conditions; and
- psychological testing if not valid, reliable, and applied fairly to all employees.

The EEA regards harassment of an employee as a form of discrimination, and it is prohibited. This includes harassment based on sex, sexual orientation, race, and religion. If a worker is found guilty of harassment in the workplace, his or her employer may also be held liable. A perpetrator may face disciplinary action, while employers may be faced with claims for compensation by the victims for failing to ensure that the work environment is safe and non-hostile. It would be prudent for employers to develop clear policies and procedures regarding workplace harassment, and to publicise these broadly to all employees.

Discrimination is not unfair if it is:
- part of affirmative action measures which are in line with the Act; or
- an inherent requirement of the job.

Disputes in this regard are referred to the CCMA. In light of the above, the following observation could be made: It will be unfair to discriminate against blacks, for instance, in favour of non-blacks, but fair to discriminate against non-blacks in favour of blacks for the purpose of racial preferences.

7.4 Why the need for employment equity?

Employment equity, according to the authors of the law, the Department of Labour (1997: Preamble) is based on the following:
- disparities in the labour market in
  - employment,
  - occupation, and
  - income;
- pronounced disadvantages for certain categories of people; and
- repealing discriminatory laws is not enough to redress disadvantages.

The purpose of the EEA is, thus, to achieve equity in the workplace by: (a) promoting equal opportunity and fair treatment in employment through the elimination of unfair discrimination; and (b) implementing affirmative action to redress the disadvantages in employment experienced by designated groups, in order to ensure their equitable representation in all occupational categories and levels in the workforce in terms of the Act. Protected 'categories of people' are blacks (that is Africans, Indians, and Coloureds), women, and people with disabilities.

Test case

Challenges to affirmative action measures are beginning to be mounted, especially in the public service. For instance, in Public Servants of South Africa and Another v Minister of Justice and Others (1997) 18 ILJ 241(W) the applicant challenged the decision of the Department of Justice to reserve certain posts for affirmative action candidates.

Le Roux (1999:32–33) from whom this entire case is cited, states that the case revolved around the interpretation of various statutory provisions. The first was Section 212 of the Interim Constitution (1993) which stated that the Public Service should promote an efficient public administration, broadly representative of the South African community. The second was Section 8 of the Interim Constitution, which entrenched equality rights and prohibited discrimination. Section 8 (3) (a), which was of particular importance, stated that Section 8 did not 'preclude measures designed to achieve the adequate protection and advancement of persons or groups or categories of persons disadvantaged by unfair discrimination, in order to enable their full and equal enjoyment of all rights and freedoms'.

Le Roux points out that the court adopted the formal approach to equality, and accepted that affirmative action measures constituted discrimination but that they could, in the correct circumstances, be fair. Taking into account the above provisions, the Court formulated the following principles with regard to affirmative action measures:

- The affirmative action measures must be specifically designed to achieve the goal of the adequate protection and advancement of persons subject to past unfair discrimination. The action taken must not be haphazard or random.
- There must be a causal connection between the affirmative action measures that have been designed and their objectives.
- Although the affirmative action measures must be designed to provide adequate protection and advancement, the rights of others and the interests of the community should also be taken into account.
- The requirement that the Public Service must ensure an efficient public administration should not be compromised.

The Court found that these principles had not been adhered to and that the affirmative action measures adopted by the Department of Justice were, therefore, invalid.

7.5 Prohibition of discrimination

Chapter 2 of the EEA requires every employer to 'take steps to promote equal opportunity in the workplace by eliminating unfair discrimination in any employment policy or practice'.

'Eliminating unfair discrimination' leads, of course, to the inference that the under-representation of blacks, women and the disabled is evidence of discrimination in the past. This places the onus on the employer to justify the composition of his workforce.

7.6 Affirmative action according to the employment equity act

Chapter 3 of EEA deals with affirmative action. 'Designated groups', as we have seen, are black people, women, and people with disabilities, and 'designated employers' are the focus of this category of employers.

To achieve employment equity, every designated employer must implement affirmative action measures for people from designated groups in terms of Section 13 of the Act. These measures are contained in Section 15 and are designed to ensure that 'suitably qualified' people from designated groups have equal employment opportunities and are equitably represented in all occupational categories and levels in the workforce of a designated employer.

The measures implemented by a designated employer must include:
- measures to identify and eliminate employment barriers, including unfair discrimination, which adversely affect people from designated groups;
- measures designed to further diversity in the workplace based on the equal dignity and respect of all people; and
- making reasonable accommodation

for blacks, women and people with disabilities so that they enjoy equal opportunities and are equitably represented in the workforce of a designated employer.

7.6.1 Five steps to employment equity

The following steps should be taken to ensure employment equity:
- consult employees (consulting with employees is required by Section 16 of the EEA);
- conduct analysis (conducting an analysis is required by Section 19);
- prepare an employment equity plan (preparing an employment equity plan is required by Section 20);
- implement the plan (implementing the plan is required by Section 20); and
- report to the Director-General of the Department of Labour (reporting to the Director-General on progress made is required by Section 7).

7.6.2 Employment equity plan

A major requirement of the 'designated employer' by the EEA is an employment equity plan. Section 20 (i) states that a designated employer must prepare and implement an employment equity plan which will achieve reasonable progress towards employment equity in that employer's workforce. Such employment equity plan must, inter alia, state:
- annual objectives to be attained;
- affirmative action measures to be implemented;
- where under-representation of people from designated groups has been identified by the analysis, the numerical goals to achieve the equitable representation of 'suitably qualified' people from designated groups within each occupational category and level in the workforce, the time-table within which this is to be achieved, and the strategies intended to achieve those goals;
- the time-table for each year of the plan for the achievement of goals and objectives other than numerical goals, as well as the duration of the plan covering a period within five years but not less than a year;
- the procedures that will be used to monitor and evaluate the implementation of the plan, and whether reasonable progress is being made towards implementing employment equity;
- the internal procedures to resolve any dispute about the interpretation or implementation of the plan; and
- the persons in the workforce, including senior managers, responsible for monitoring and implementing the plan.

7.6.3 Reporting to the Director-General

Reports to the Director-General will be due as follows:
- First reports for organisations who employ over 150 employees: six months after promulgation of the Act, i.e. June 2000. For organisations who employ fewer than 150 employees: twelve months after promulgation, i.e. December 2000; and
- Subsequent reports: on 1 October every year for big employers, and every two years for small employers.

The report to the Director-General of the Labour Department must contain the information that is prescribed, and this report must be signed by the chief executive officer of the designated employer. The law prescribes that this report must be a public document. A summary of this report must be published in the designated employer's annual financial report.

7.6.4 The Department of Labour

The Department is required to:
- assess whether or not employers comply with the provision of the EEA;
- issue compliance orders to employers who do not comply; and
- issue guidelines on developing and implementing affirmative action plans, and say what the reporting requirements are.

7.6.5 Designated employers

According to Section 24 of the EEA, each designated employer (organisation) must:
- assign one or more senior managers to take responsibility for monitoring and implementing;
- provide the managers with the authority and means to perform their functions; and
- take reasonable steps to ensure that the managers perform their functions.

7.6.6 Compliance costs and maximum fines for contravening the EEA

Compliance costs of the Employment Equity Act are not inconsiderable. A major aspect of these high compliance costs emanates from policies that drive current South African legislation. That is, labour legislation too often proceeds from the apparent assumption that employees need protection from unscrupulous employers who, if the law did not prevent them, would exact maximum labour for minimum benefits.

Consequently, the compliance costs would be exorbitant for most organisations. For instance, the implementation of an employment equity plan would require not only additional staff of a company, but also staff highly qualified to undertake the complex requirements of the Act. Chapter V of the EEA, 'Monitoring, Enforcement and Legal Proceedings', makes explicit what the responsibilities of the designated company in terms of compliance are. Merely complying with the equity plan would require additional budgetary allocations for many companies. Bigger companies would easily meet the costs, simply including them as part of the cost of labour. Such costs would invariably be passed on to the consumer. Smaller companies could even be compelled to close down their businesses. The fines for contravening the EEA are more onerous, as Schedule I of the Act shows (see Appendix 1).

7.7 Arguments for affirmative action: The Mc Whirter Thesis

- The first and, in the minds of many, the most legitimate justification for engaging in affirmative action, is the need to compensate for specific instances of race and gender discrimination in the past by particular organisations. This is termed 'specific discrimination'.
- The need to remedy 'societal discrimination'. By this, McWhirter means that though some organisations may not have 'engaged in intentional discrimination in the past... [other] entities in society have'.
- The justification for affirmative action is the need to create more diversity in a particular organisation.
- Affirmative action programmes have increased the labour force participation rate for women and blacks (McWhirter 1996: 6–8).

7.8 Arguments against affirmative action: The Zelnick Thesis

- Zelnick regards affirmative action as a racially discriminatory practice against whites and other non-favoured ethnic groups. It favours the less qualified over the more qualified, and it is therefore a systematic attack upon objective merit selection criteria. Zelnick concurs with the view that while it increases black enrolment at selective universities and also expands somewhat the pool of black entrepreneurs, it has brought little employment, educational or income benefits to those most in need of help. He holds that it has 'distracted attention from the real causes of misery among [really poor] blacks'. He sees affirmative action more as an ideology than as a programme. As such 'it has proven impervious to overwhelming evidence'. Zelnick thus sees it as counter-productive: 'It legitimizes negative stigmas and panders to the darker instincts of racial animosity'.
- Affirmative action, argues Zelnick, 'has been broadened for political purposes to include beneficiaries who lack the historical claim of blacks for relief'. Zelnick concludes that affirmative action has not been successful in other societies. It is being challenged, and successfully so, in the courts as well as in the political arena (Zelnick 1996: 18).

7.9 Weaknesses of affirmative action: The Sono Thesis

- Every employee is now a representative of a group. Affirmative action is a contrived programme of preferential policies based on membership of a specific group.
- Specific individuals are conferred the rights of groups. There seem to be no more specific individual rights, but only generic group rights.
- Affirmative action is based on political empowerment and not on economic empowerment.
- Contrary to the ANC Department of Economic Policy (1991) view, affirmative action has no expiry date. It is without a cut-off date nor is it, so far, a 'transient method' as was once claimed by the ANC-DEP.
- It discriminates against one group and prefers another group. It is an employment discrimination law.
- It adopts the doctrine that the end justifies the means. It argues that if the intentions are noble, then the means to attain those ends must also be noble.
- The re-emphasis on race is also its strong point. A racial preference is termed a non-racial condition. That is, it is non-racial to prefer some people over others on the basis of race. Moreover, it would depend on a racial population register.
- It fails to accommodate the least privileged of blacks and women. It tends to increase the economic status among blacks and women of those already relatively advanced in comparison to the poorest of the poor.
- All forms of affirmative action violate the principles of equal opportunity before the law and thus contravene the rule of law.

7.10 International affirmative action and employment equity experiences

The report of the commission to investigate the development of a comprehensive labour market policy indicates that international experience, as far as equal opportunity and affirmative action is concerned, differs substantially from that of South Africa. Nearly all previous experiences in this area had to do with addressing discrimination against a minority. The situation in South Africa is the reverse. International experience, while valuable, will be of limited direct application to the South African situation. One possible exception is the experience of Malaysia, where bold steps were taken to reorganise public employment in favour of the majority Malays.

Where international experience has proved more valuable, is with regard to affirmative action as it relates to gender and disability and, therefore, the experiences of Malaysia, the USA, and Namibia are discussed in this chapter.

7.10.1 The Malaysian experience

Castle (1995:19–20) indicates that in Malaysia affirmative action is defined in ethnic rather than racial or gender terms. Statutory affirmative action policies favour the Malays, who constitute 55 per cent of the population of 17 million, over the 35per cent Chinese and 10 per cent Indian components. Emsley (1996: 7) is of the opinion that Malaysian affirmative action has been both the world's most extensive programme and one of its most successful.

Charlton & Van Niekerk (1994:41–42) are of the opinion that the Malaysian model is of particular interest to South Africa. Many parallels exist in terms of a majority benefiting from affirmative action programmes and religious differences coinciding with ethnic ones. Malaysia had made significant strides in implementing affirmative action when the minority Chinese and the Malay majority, anticipating a coalition government, set up a comprehensive plan to implement affirmative action while still maintaining economic standards. Although much credit must go to the political and economic bargain struck in Malaysia, it needs to be borne in mind that its affirmative action success was, in large part, due to a high economic growth rate, enabling resources to be distributed.

Emsley's (1996:102–103) view is that the lessons for South Africa of the Malaysian experience imply the overarching importance of economic growth. The Malaysian affirmative action programme had four aspects, and economic growth was critical to each. The same will be true for similar programmes in South Africa :

- *Poverty reduction.* The Reconstruction and Development Programme (RDP) will address workers by equipping currently excluded workers with much of what is needed to participate in the formal sector. The speed with which poverty is reduced will depend critically on the ability of the economy to create employment opportunities. But the RDP poverty reduction programmes have so far had minimal effects.
- *Increased racial representation across the economy.* This is not as big a problem in South Africa as it was in Malaysia, as much of the black population is urbanised and ready to work in the formal economy.
- *Equity ownership.* Any attempt to replicate the Malaysian scheme without exceptionally buoyant government revenues would surely constitute a grave misallocation of resources.
- *Black middle class.* Malaysia has followed a course of organic growth for Malays in the private corporate sector, where affirmative action had been largely eschewed.

7.10.2 The USA experience

There are essential differences between circumstances in South Africa and in the USA, but South Africa can learn a great deal from the American experience. The USA was the first country to make affirmative action, as an anti-discriminatory measure, compulsory by law.

In 1961, President Kennedy declared that specific affirmative action should be taken to counteract discrimination. President Johnson defined in more detail what was meant by affirmative action. To a large extent this coincides with the current approach to affirmative action in the Western world.

The Civil Rights Act of 1957 was amended in 1964 to make discrimination based on race, sex, colour, religious belief, or national origin, by both private and public employers illegal. This law may be regarded as the forerunner of modern affirmative action legislation.

Schmitt & Noe (1986:71) provide the most important stipulation of the Civil Rights Act, Title VII, which spells out equal opportunities as follows:

It shall be an unlawful employment practice for an employer... to fail or refuse to hire or discharge any individual, or otherwise to discriminate against any individual with respect to his compensation, terms, conditions, or privileges of employment, because of such individual's race, colour, religion, sex or national origin...

However, Sowell (1983:200) observes that 'while affirmative action results were impressive in gross terms, a finer breakdown shows disturbing counter-productive trends'. In his opinion, these counterproductive results include the following:
- The least privileged black people are even worse off with affirmative action than before, while the more privileged black people rapidly increase their economic status.
- Reverse discrimination takes place because the demand for qualified black people is higher than the demand for qualified white people. In 1980, graduated black couples earned more than graduated white couples.

It is, therefore, clear that South Africa can learn a number of lessons from the USA experience.

7.10.3 The Namibian experience

Namibia's legislation on affirmative action is of particular importance to South Africa, regardless that legislation on South African affirmative action has unexpectedly preceded its Namibian counterpart. The International Labour Organisation (1991: 113) states the following:

By virtue of their history, the issue of equality of opportunity and treatment is one to which the Namibians are particularly sensitive. Consequently, Article 23 of the Constitution, entitled 'Apartheid and Affirmative Action', provides for parliament to enact legislation to facilitate the advancement of those 'socially, economically or educationally disadvantaged' as a result of past laws or practices.

Swanepoel (1993:1) indicates that the Namibian government took a decision at the thirty-first meeting of Cabinet (held on 14 September 1993) to prepare and implement an affirmative action policy as soon as procedurally possible. The Namibian bill on affirmative action has now been promulgated into law.

The Office of the Labour Commission of Namibia published the following policy statement on affirmative action during 1995:

The Government of the Republic of Namibia (Ministry of Labour) has decided that the Legislation of Affirmative

Action in Employment will be based on the following principles:
1. The goal of affirmative action is to create equal employment opportunity.
2. The target groups of affirmative action are the disadvantaged groups of Namibian society: blacks, women and the disabled.
3. Employment quotas and any other measures which require the hiring of unqualified persons are rejected.
4. Preferential treatment under carefully planned affirmative action programmes should only be given to suitable qualified persons. A special concern of affirmative action is to benefit the least well off persons from the relevant target groups.
5. Affirmative action measures should not be used as an absolute bar on the employment or career prospects of those who are not members of target groups.
6. Legislation of affirmative action should cover both the public and private sectors.
7. Affirmative action should be administered by an independent agency which can further the dialogue between social partners and other stakeholders.

The Cabinet had instructed the Minister of Labour to:
- prepare a draft bill on affirmative action in employment which is consistent with the seven key principles listed above and takes into account the submissions to the Consultation Document; and
- carry out, where necessary, further consultations on the draft bill with the social partners and other stakeholders.

As already indicated, this bill has now become law. The office of the Labour Commission of Namibia had published a document on Affirmative action in Employment Consulting in September 1995 and it is this document which was sent to 'social partners' and stakeholders for their comments, which comments have subsequently been incorporated into law. Chapter 1 explains the concept of affirmative action, Chapter 2 sets out the constitutional and legal framework, Chapter 3 summarises the government's approach to affirmative action, and Chapter 4 focuses on specific issues regarding the implementation of affirmative action.

7.11 The views of Business South Africa on affirmative action

Jeffery (1996:27) is of the opinion that the concept of affirmative action has widely varying connotations for top business leaders in South Africa. The views of the following top business leaders illustrate this:
- Some see it as a means of making their staff more representative of the population as a whole. 'We aim,' says Mr Hancke Scheepers of the international accounting firm, Coopers and Lybrand, 'to have our human resources reflect the population of South Africa'.
- Others regard it as a way of making their staff reflect the demographic mix in the areas in which they operate. Says Mr Hans Smith of the steel-producing former parastatal ISCOR, 'We aim to align the profile of our staff complement more closely with that of the South African population in the various locations in which we operate.'
- Some shy away from applying the demographic approach, and emphasise that account must be taken of the skills available on the labour market. 'It is unrealistic for us to aim at being representative of the population at large,' says Mrs Helga van der Merwe, of

Denel, 'our aim thus, is to make our staff representative of the labour market.'
- Others see affirmative action mainly in the context of overcoming past inequalities. 'It is,' says Mr Walter Simeoni of the Frame Textile Corporation, 'an intervention applied to previously disadvantaged groups to give them opportunities to enhance their capacities.'
- Still others see affirmative action as an essential measure to overcome the skills shortage which has always threatened economic growth. White managers are in short and diminishing supply, says Mr Scheepers of Coopers and Lybrand, and 'the number of whites retiring from business each year is much more than 13 000' – the annual increase in the white population.

Jeffery (1996:28) believes that the reasons for embarking on affirmative action vary less widely. Most business leaders regard it either as a moral or a business imperative, or both. Jeffrey (1996:28–29) also states that some business leaders are categorical on what affirmative action means. 'It does not mean,' says Mr Pretorius, 'taking jobs away from whites and giving them to non-whites.' Nor, says Mr Newbury, does it mean 'putting people from lesser privileged groups into jobs they can't handle'. Not all business leaders share these views, however, and there is concern that in many organisations affirmative action is, indeed, being implemented in these ways.

Thomas (1996:37) and Brits (1996) are of the view that CEOs generally seem to play only a monitoring role in affirmative action programmes. The driving of this initiative is largely delegated to human resources departments (HRDs). The majority of CEOs and HRDs stated that affirmative action programmes make good business sense.

Thomas's (1996:57–58) research sees the following as the future affirmative action challenges for business in South Africa:
- top management in South African business has to undergo a painful change of mindset, involving the realisation that business in South Africa cannot carry on in the traditional and comfortable ways of the past;
- with the integration of the workforce, it is becoming increasingly clear that unchallenged Western management models are not appropriate if used exclusively to the point of ignoring alternatives; and
- a major area of attention should be the empowerment of women in South Africa.

7.12 Conclusion

Preferential policies – such as affirmative action – are always in conflict with a regime of the rule of law. Citizens and diverse forms of activity must be treated equally and impartially by the law. Some citizens should not be singled out for either preferential treatment or harsh treatment, merely because they are considered by the government to be of greater or lesser importance or for any other reason (Davie 2000: 59). Such even-handed treatment is absolutely necessary for the rule of law to prevail.

Davie continues: 'The rule of law requires that government should enact only such laws as are general in nature, are applicable to everyone including itself, and which do not attempt to bring about particular outcomes.' The 1982 Canadian Constitutional Charter provides a clear formulation of the rule of law: '15(1) Every individual is equal before and under the law and has the right to the equal protection and equal benefit of the law without discrimination and, in particular, without discrimination based on race, national or ethnic origin, colour, religion, sex, age or mental or physical disability.'

As we have seen, much of the Employment Equity Act of 1998 was taken from the Constitution of Canada. Similarly for affirmative action, the Canadian Charter also has its affirmative action, which was similarly adapted by the drafters of our affirmative action/employment equity laws:

15 (2) Subsection (1) does not preclude any law, programme or activity that has as its objective the amelioration of conditions of disadvantaged individuals or groups including those that are disadvantaged because of race, national or ethnic origin, colour, religion, sex, age or mental or physical disability.

The juxtaposition of equality (equal opportunity) and preferential treatment (i.e. inequality) would lead to problems in any law, but especially in one that deals with contentious issues such as race, colour, and sex or sexual orientation.

Affirmative action is, however, open to scrutiny and challenge on whether or not it goes too far or oversteps the limits allowed, which are to ensure equal employment opportunities and 'equitable' representation in the workplace. In other words, 'it could be unfair to prohibit absolutely the employment or promotion of able-bodied white males in the name of affirmative action, as there would be no 'equitable' representation' (Jordan, N.D. *The Star*).

Chapter questions

1 Compare the evolvement of employment equity in two countries presented in this chapter. What have you learned from it?
2 What is affirmative action? Discuss existing approaches and how they can be successfully implemented in South Africa.

Case study
Blue Chip Retail Group

	% Black	% White	% Black women	% White women
Unskilled	89.0	11.0	56.0	44.0
Semi-skilled	81.3	18.7	74.7	25.3
Skilled	63.6	36.4	42.5	57.5
Professional	33.9	66.1	17.5	82.5
Senior Management	8.5	91.5	5.3	94.7
Top Management	14.3	85.7	0.0	0
Trainees	87.5	12.5	58	42
Total	74.0	26.0	61.3	38.7

SOURCE: Human Resources Department, Blue Chip Retail Group, Group Human Resources Director, 3 April 2000.

This Blue Chip Retail Group is a public company with 12 000 employees and an affirmative action programme that is older than its employment equity strategy by several years. The Group has 'embarked on an affirmative action strategy as a means of creating employment equity and creating a competitive workforce. It is a strategy designed to correct past imbalances and systematic discrimination and is a pre-requisite in the broad process of transforming the culture to become conducive to diversity and is performance driven,' according to the Group's Employment Equity Information file.

The Group acknowledges that employment equity is a 'highly controversial and sensitive topic' and that 'affirmative action is a temporary strategy and is dependent on the pace with which a representative staff profile and a changed culture [are] achieved'.

The beneficiaries of the Group's affirmative action are:
- Africans;
- Indians;
- White women; and
- Disabled employees.

Despite having launched a process of employment equity, there are still no women in the 'top management' category, while black males in this category constitute only 14,3 per cent, compared to their white counterparts who number 85,7 per cent. The majority of blacks are in the 'unskilled' to 'skilled' categories, while the majority of whites are in the 'professional' to 'top management' categories. The Group has an overwhelming black workforce. It has, however, a large pool of black trainees. Women of all races remain terribly disadvantaged at the executive management level.

The Group's employment equity aims are:
- to ensure that all people who were discriminated against in the workplace in terms of race, gender, and disability are empowered to enable them to gain access to and compete for all posts including those at a high level;
- to ensure that the company is proactive in addressing the change to a new South Africa characterised by non-discrimination and fairness to all;
- to strive towards achieving a company that fairly represents the demographics of the country;
- to promote employment equity as a business imperative that addresses the shortage of certain skills people and projected management requirements in the company;
- to ensure that all discriminatory barriers that prevent employees from designated groups from enjoying the same benefits and privileges as all other employees, are eliminated; and
- to ensure that the company complies with all provisions and requirements of the Employment Equity Act.

Question

How does this organisation's situation compare to that of other companies that you know, and is it fully in line with the EEA?

3 Compile an affirmative action policy for your organisation to promote employee empowerment and equal job opportunities.

4 Evaluate the relevance of affirmative action and employment equity in terms of the International Labour Standards.

5 Audit your organisation's employee component. What adjustments would you make to reflect the spirit of the Employment Equity Act.
6 Compile and describe an employment equity plan for your organisation that will meet all prescriptions of the Act.

Bibliography

ADAMS, C. (ed.). 1993. *Affirmative action in a democratic South Africa.* Juta and Co. Ltd., Kenwyn.

AFRICAN NATIONAL CONGRESS. 1990. *Discussion document on economic policy by the ANC Department of Economic Policy.* DEP Workshop, Harare, 20–23 September. Mimeo.

BELZ, H. 1991. *Equality transformed: a quarter-century of affirmative action.* Transaction Books, New Brunswick.

BLACK MANAGEMENT FORUM (FMF). 1993. *Affirmative action blue print.* BMF, Johannesburg.

BRITS, J.J. 1998. IN GERBER, P.D., NEL, P.S. & VAN DYK, P.S. 1998. *Human resources management.* 4th edition. Oxford University Press, Cape Town.

CASTLE, J. 1995. Affirmative action in three developing countries, lessons from Zimbabwe, Namibia, and Malaysia. *South African Journal of Labour Relations.* Autumn 19(1), 6–33.

CHARLTON, G.D.E. & VAN NIEKERK, N. 1994. *Affirmative action beyond 1994.* Juta, Cape Town.

DAVIE, E. 2000. *Directors' report.* Free Market Foundation Documents, Sandton.

EMSLEY, I. 1996. *The Malaysian experience of affirmative action: lessons for South Africa.* Human & Rousseau, Cape Town.

DEPARTMENT OF LABOUR. 1997. *Employment Equity Bill.* Pretoria.

DEPARTMENT OF LABOUR. 1998. *Employment Equity Bill.* Pretoria.

GOVERNMENT OF SOUTH AFRICA. 1998. *Employment Equity Bill* B-60-98, Government Printer, Pretoria.

GOVERNMENT OF CANADA. 1988. *Constitution of Canada* (Chapter 23 – 2nd Supp.). Queen's Printer for Canada, Ottawa.

GRAWITZKY, R. 2000. Court reinstates white lecturer. *Business Day,* 6 April.

HUMAN, L. 1992. *Women in the workplace: a programme to counteract gender discrimination at work.* In Adams (ed.), 1993.

HUMAN, L. (ed.). 1991. *Educating and developing managers for a changing South Africa: selected essays.* Juta, Cape Town.

INTERNATIONAL LABOUR ORGANISATION. 1991. *Social and labour bulletin of Namibia.* Windhoek, Namibia.

JEFFERY, A.J. 1996. *Business and affirmative action.* South African Institute of Race Relations, Johannesburg.

JORDAN, N.D. *The Star,* advertisement supplement.

JOUBERT, D. 1992. Affirmative action is the solution to South Africa's skills crisis. In Gerber et al. 1999.

LE ROUX, P.A.K. 1999. Affirmative action and the individual employee. *Contemporary Labour Law,* Vol. 9, No. 4, November, pp. 31-40.

MADI, P.M. 1993. *Affirmative action in corporate South Africa.* Juta, Cape Town.

MANDELA, N. 1991. *Statement on affirmative action in a new South Africa.* University of the Western Cape, Cape Town.

MAPHAI, V.T. 1993. One phrase, two distinct concepts. In *Die Suid-Afrikaan. Special focus: affirmative action in action.* May/June, No. 44, pp. 6–8.

MAYIBUYE. 1991. August, Vol. 2, No. 7.

MC WHIRTER, D.A. 1996. *The end of affirmative action: where do we go from here?* Carol Publishing Group, New York.

NEL, P.S. & BRITS, J.J. 1998. Affirmative action and equal opportunity in South Africa. In Gerber et al. 1998.

NJUGUNA, M. 1992. *A Kenyan case study: focusing on a country where affirmative action has been introduced.* Juta, Cape Town.

PERON, J. 1992. *Affirmative action, apartheid and capitalism.* Free Market Foundation, Sandton.

SACHS, A. 1990. *Protecting human rights in a new South Africa.* Oxford University Press, Cape Town.

SCHMITT, N. & NOE, R.A. 1986. Personnel selection and equal employment opportunity. In Cooper, C.L. and Robertson, I.T. (eds.) *International Review of Industrial and Organisational Psychology.* Wiley, Chichester.

SONN, F. 1992. Afrikaner nationalism and black advancement as two sides of the same coin. In Adams (ed.), 1993.

SOWELL, T. 1983. *The economics of politics and race.* Quill, New York.

SOWELL, T. 1985. From equal opportunity to 'affirmative action', in Schaeffer, F. (ed.). *Is capitalism Christian?* Crossway Books, Westchester.

SOWELL, T. 1990. *Preferential policies.* William Morrow and Co. Inc., New York.

THOMAS, A. 1996. *Beyond affirmative action.* Knowledge Resources, Randburg.

THOMPSON, C. 1992. Legislating affirmative action: employment equity and lessons from developed and developing countries. In Adams (ed.), 1993.

ZELNICK, BOB. 1996. *Backfire.* Regnery Publishing Inc., Washington D.C.

Appendix 1

The following schedule which reflects the fines prescribed by the Act also emphasises the tone thereof and the extent to which it should be taken seriously.

Schedule 1
Maximum permissible fines that may be imposed for contravening this act
This Schedule sets out the maximum fine that may be imposed in terms of this Act for the contravention of certain provisions of this Act.

Previous contravention	Contravention of any provision of sections 16, 19, 20, 21, 22 and 23
No previous contravention	R500 000
A previous contravention in respect of the same provision	R600 000
A previous contravention within the previous 12 months or two previous contraventions in respect of the same provision within three years	R700 000
Three previous contraventions in respect of same provision within three years	R800 000
Four previous contraventions in respect of the same provision within three years	R900 000

part four

Staffing the organisation and maintaining people

8

Job analysis

H B Schultz

Learning outcomes

At the end of this chapter the learner should be able to demonstrate the following outcomes:
- Discuss job analysis as the basis of all human resource activities.
- Identify the components of a job.
- Explain the process of job analysis.
- Debate the advantages and disadvantages of job-orientated methods of job analysis.
- Examine worker-orientated methods of job analysis.
- Evaluate various problems in job analysis.
- Develop a job description and job specification.
- Briefly describe the influence of quality assurance in job analysis.

Key words and concepts

- job analysis
- strategic job analysis
- job-orientated approach
- worker-orientated approach
- systematic activity log
- Position Analysis Questionnaire (PAQ)
- Functional Job Analysis (FJA)
- job description
- job specification
- knowledge, skills, and abilities (KSAs)

Illustrative case
A lot of hot air

Consolidated Auto Air Conditioning is a subsidiary of a major international manufacturer and supplier of air conditioners to the automobile industry. Consolidated Aircon is situated on the East coast of South Africa and has contracts with three major automobile manufacturers in the region. The South African subsidiary was established fifteen years ago and has grown from the original ten employees to a workforce of 180. During the last six years, the company has invested heavily in the team concept. Self-managed teams perform all routine manufacturing functions.

However, two years ago, senior managers were in a quandary. They were finding it increasingly difficult to maintain consistent performance in a number of the teams. Production standards were falling and there seemed to be a general decrease in the motivation levels of team members. A firm of human resources consultants was called in to investigate the problem. The experts quickly discovered that there was no formal performance management programme, because the company's directors believed that the teams would be able to manage their own performance. They conducted interviews with team members, who agreed that morale was low, because they didn't really know if they were doing their jobs properly. Their managers only communicated with them if there were problems.

The consultant firm recommended that job analysis be carried out within the various 'cells', or teams, in order to produce formal job profiles that were then used to foster a culture of performance management. Senior management discussed the job profiles with team members, who drew up their own plans to maintain the required level of performance. Within three months, performance results were showing a 30 per cent increase, and an attitude survey indicated that team members were more motivated because they had been consulted in the process, and now had direction in their jobs.

8.1 Introduction

The concept of continuous improvement is accepted as a basic business philosophy in every developed country around the world. This philosophy has encouraged these countries to rethink the fundamental principles that underlie the design of jobs and the way they are carried out. Whether it is called job analysis, job review, or job classification, the systematic process of compiling a description of the work to be done, the skills needed, the training and experience required for various jobs, and a forecast of the future direction of the business, is essential in making intelligent decisions in the workplace.

This chapter commences with a discussion of how job analysis forms the basis of all human resources activities. We investigate the process of job analysis, before describing some of the popular methods of data collection. The nature of job descriptions and job specifications are examined, before we take a brief look at the impact of quality assurance on the job analysis process.

8.2 Job analysis – the basis of human resources activities

Most of the people-related activities that take place in every company would not be effective unless some form of job analysis is undertaken at the start of the exercise. Rapidly changing technology has meant that almost every existing job has had at least some changes during the last ten years. In many cases, jobs have ceased to exist, to be replaced by a totally new form of work. Cascio (1995:129) mentions that job analysis plays a major role in the defence of employment practices that are challenged in terms of labour legislation, as job analysis can provide proof that these practices are job-related. Some of the major uses of job analysis are discussed below and summarised in Figure 8.1.

- *Workforce planning.* Job analysis provides the foundation for forecasting current and future human resources needs through incorporation into a human resources information system (HRIS).
- *Job evaluation and compensation.* Jobs cannot be ranked or compared in terms of their overall worth to an organisation unless job descriptions and job specifications provide the basis for making these decisions.
- *Recruitment, selection, and placement.* A clear picture of the duties, tasks, and responsibilities of the job, job expectations, and skills, knowledge, and abilities required, all obtained through job analysis, offers a much greater chance of success in these human resources activities.
- *Orientation, training, and development.* A company cannot expect to train a person to perform a job unless the tasks and operations required for job success are known. Up-to-date job descriptions and specifications ensure that training programmes reflect actual job requirements.
- *Performance management.* An employee can set his or her level of performance according to the work standards identified through job analysis. It also allows a manager to effectively develop, assess, and maintain a subordinate's performance.
- *Career planning.* Through job analysis, the requirements of available jobs and those at succeeding levels make it possible to plan the career paths of employees.
- *Ergonomics.* Job analysis can aid in efforts to design a job or workspace for more efficient performance.
- *Safety.* Safety hazards and dangerous op-

Figure 8.1 The major uses of job analysis

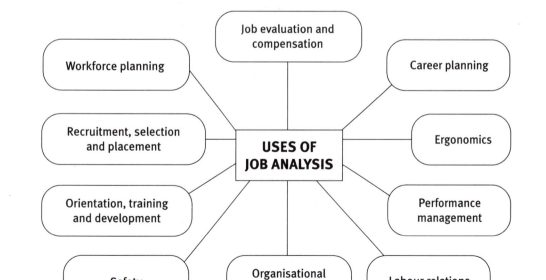

erating procedures associated with a job can be uncovered during job analysis.
- *Organisational restructuring.* Downsizing, rightsizing, delayering, decruiting, or just plain old retrenching, call for adaptations in the jobs people do and the way they do these jobs. Job analysis can be instrumental in rearranging and reorganising the jobs in a company.
- *Labour relations.* Job analysis is a useful tool for employers grappling with the implications of new labour legislation and, in particular, employment equity, which requires job descriptions reflecting the realities of the twenty-first century.

8.3 The components of a job

Jobs are important to individuals because they determine standards of living, places of residence, status, and one's sense of self-worth. From an organisational point of view, jobs are important because they are the vehicles through which organisational objectives are accomplished (Cascio 1995:127).

Jobs can be broken down into components and arranged in a hierarchy of work activities. This hierarchy is depicted in Figure 8.2.

8.4 The process of job analysis

Job analysis must always be conducted according to a systematic process. An example of this process is offered in Figure 8.3.

8.4.1 The systematic process of job analysis

The following steps form the basis of the job analysis process:

Step 1: Involve and empower employees in the process.

Job analysis must never be undertaken without consultation with employees. Certain

---

Figure 8.2 A hierarchy of work activities

- Job family – group of similar occupations
- Occupation – jobs grouped on the basis of skills, effort, and responsibilities
- Jobs – positions that are similar in elements, tasks and duties
- Position – combination of duties, tasks, and responsibilities required to perform a job
- Duty – group of tasks performed to complete a work activity
- Task – unit of work activity designed to produce a definite outcome
- Element – smallest practical unit into which a work activity can be subdivided

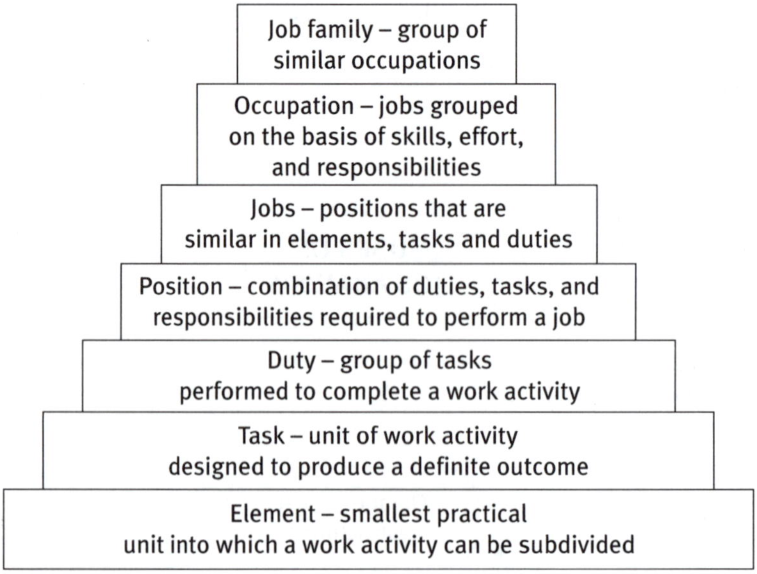

methods of data collection (for example, direct observation) could raise suspicions if undertaken without communication to the worker of the underlying reasons for the exercise. This could have a great impact on the quality of labour relations in the organisation. In addition, consultation affords employees the opportunity to 'buy into' and support the process.

The easiest way of ensuring consultation is to enlist the services of a job analysis committee, which normally includes representatives from trade unions, the major departments in the organisation, and members of professional bodies such as engineering, financial, and human resources associations. The latter would be representative of the jobs to be analysed.

Step 2: Investigate how all jobs fit into the organisation

The existing organisation chart offers an overall picture of how all the jobs combine to form the organisation's structure.

Step 3: Determine the reason for conducting job analysis

Job analysis should only be conducted for a specific reason. Is it for restructuring purposes; training and development; determining compensation structures; a combination of some of these; or possibly some of the other purposes of job analysis?

Step 4: Decide on the job/s to be analysed

It is often expensive and time-consuming to analyse every job in an organisation. To overcome these problems, a representative sample of jobs is chosen.

Step 5: Determine the method/s of data collection

The method, or methods, of data collection will depend on whether a job-orientated, worker-orientated, or combination approach to job analysis is chosen. The advantages and disadvantages of the methods available are then weighed against each other, before a final choice is made.

Step 6: Collect job information

Job data is obtained through the chosen collection method, or methods. This information is reviewed with employees and the job analysis committee to ensure that it is objective, factual, and easily comparable with analyses of other jobs.

Step 7: Process job information into job description and job specification

The information obtained is refined and used to compile job descriptions and job specifications. These documents are then used to accomplish the purpose of the job analysis exercise, as decided in step 3 of the process.

Step 8: Design or redesign jobs

Existing job descriptions and job specifications are compared to the revised documents. If there are extreme differences, the new documents are used to design a totally new job; smaller differences can result in redesigning the current job into a more up-to-date form. Where there is no existing job documentation, the newly processed job description and job specification are adopted as official company documents.

Step 9: Review and update the process

After the job analysis is undertaken and the resulting documentation used for the stated purpose, the value of the exercise must be assessed. For example, did the chosen data collection method yield adequate information, or might another method have been preferable?

8.4.2 The implications of job analysis for human resources practitioners

Schneider and Konz (in Lundy and Cowling 1996:231) state that a frequently overlooked assumption in job analysis is that the job in question is static. However, the business environment is changing so rapidly that jobs are unlikely to remain static for any period of time.

This assumption has two implications for human resource practitioners: firstly, rapidly changing jobs necessitate that job analysis, and the compilation of up-to-date job descriptions, becomes an exercise that is undertaken more and more frequently; and, secondly, to obviate having to undertake job analysis too frequently on one specific job, strategic job analysis is needed. Strategic job analysis is the specification of tasks to be performed, and the knowledge, skills, and abilities required for effective performance in a job as it is predicted to exist in the future.

8.5 Job analysis methods

Schultz and Schultz (1994:80) divide the approaches to job analysis into the job-orientated approach and the worker-orientated approach.

The job-orientated approach directs attention to the specific tasks and outcomes, or level of productivity, required by a job. In the worker-orientated approach, worker behaviours in the form of specific skills, abilities, and personal traits needed to perform the job, are the focus of analysis. Most job analyses involve a combination of the two approaches.

Strategic job analysis implies that most of the data collection methods referred to below are inadequate if used in their present form, as they focus only on the actual information which is currently available. Strategic job analysis also requires a process of brainstorming with job experts in which predictions are made regarding the kinds of issues in the job, the company, or the environment that may affect the job in the future (Lundy and Cowling 1996: 231).

8.5.1 Job-orientated methods of data collection

The following general methods of data collection follow the job-orientated approach and are frequently used in South Africa (Cascio 1995:135; Carrell et al. 1997:79–85).

Questionnaires

Most firms use the questionnaire method because, once the initial questionnaire has been compiled, it is the least time-consuming and cheapest of the methods. It usually provides standardised, specific information about the jobs in an organisation, but sometimes requires clarification by means of a follow-up interview. An unstructured questionnaire requires the job incumbent to describe the job in his own words. A structured questionnaire uses brief, unambiguous questions which can be answered in a minimum amount of time with the least disruption to the jobholder. Appendix 1 to this chapter offers an example of a job analysis questionnaire which can be used by organisations in various sectors.

Interviews

The interview is the second most frequently used method of job data collection. It is used with individual jobholders, or with groups of people who carry

Figure 8.3 The systematic process of job analysis

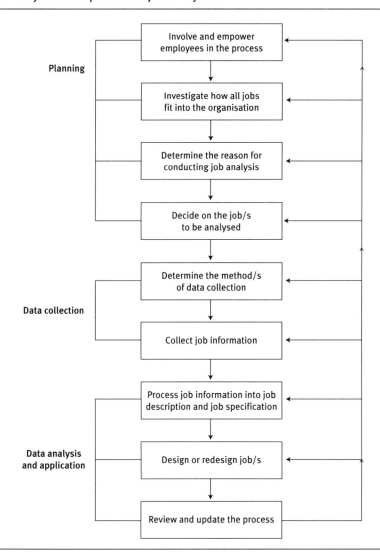

out similar tasks, functions, duties, and responsibilities. In many cases, it is simply not possible for the analyst actually to perform the job (such as that of an airline pilot), or it is impractical to observe the jobholder (such as an architect). Direct communication allows the job analyst to probe for clarity when answers are vague. It also allows the job incumbent to offer information which he or she believes is relevant, and which the job analyst may have overlooked. The interviewer normally uses a structured set of questions.

Direct observation

People often behave differently when they know they are being watched, so it is necessary for job analysts to remain as unobtrusive as possible when using the observation method. They also need to take into account changes in job behaviour caused by external factors such as fatigue. A variation of on-site observation is work sampling in which a job analyst randomly samples the content of a job, instead of observing all job behaviours. The sample must be representative of the entire domain of tasks, and not isolated acts. Jobs that are normally done by hand, that are standardised and have a short activity cycle, are best suited to analysis through observation.

Systematic activity logs

Also known as a jobholder's diary, this method of data collection requires the job incumbent to keep a diary of work activities which registers the content and frequency of duties. Although this method is cost-effective and offers the jobholder 'ownership' of the analysis process, it is the least reliable method. Employees may be negligent in completing diaries, due to forgetfulness, reluctance, or organisational obstacles, such as working conditions which make the recording of the information difficult. Sometimes employees try to maximise the importance of their jobs by adding more tasks and responsibilities than are required by the job.

Job performance

The job analyst can do repetitive jobs that are easily learned, and in this way obtains firsthand information of the job requirements.

The advantages and disadvantages of the most popular methods of job analysis are illustrated in Table 8.1. This knowledge assists the job analyst in choosing the most appropriate method of data collection.

8.5.2 Worker-orientated methods of data collection

Although worker-orientated job analysis methods concentrate on behaviours, skills, and abilities, they tend to be subjective. Some of these methods require special training and considerable time in learning how to apply and interpret them (Cascio 1995:135).

Critical incidents

This technique is based on the identification of those incidents or behaviours that are necessary for successful job performance. Subject matter experts indicate the behaviours that differentiate good from poor workers. A single critical incident is of little value, but hundreds of critical incidents can effectively describe a job in terms of the unique behaviours required to perform it well.

Position Analysis Questionnaire (PAQ)

The PAQ is a behaviour-orientated questionnaire consisting of 194 items that fall into twenty-seven job dimensions. These dimensions are further grouped into six general job categories, namely, information input, mental processes, work output, relationships, work situation and job context, and other job characteristics. A computer programme scores each job in relation to the job dimensions and the final score represents a profile of the job relative to standard profiles of jobs of a similar nature. The PAQ is a quantitative system that is widely used and produces consistent results when different analysts analyse the same job (McCormick et al. 1972:347–368).

Functional Job Analysis (FJA)

The FJA is commonly used to describe the nature of jobs, and to compile job descrip-

Table 8.1 Advantages and disadvantages of popular job analysis methods

Job analysis method	Advantages	Disadvantages
Job performance	Exposure to actual job tasks. Appropriate for jobs that can be learned in a short time.	Inappropriate for jobs that require extensive training or are dangerous.
Observation	Provides a richer, deeper understanding of job requirements.	Observations may reveal little useful information.
Interviews	Provides information about standard and non-standard activities, and physical and mental work. Worker can provide verbal information.	Workers may be suspicious of interviewer's motives. Interviewer may ask ambiguous questions. Information may be distorted.
Critical incidents	Focuses directly on what people do.	Takes time to gather, abstract, and categorise. May be difficult to develop a profile of average behaviour.
Structured questionnaires	Cheaper and quicker to administer than other methods. Can be completed off the job, saving productive time. Provides large breadth of coverage.	Time-consuming and expensive to develop. Impersonal approach between analyst and respondent may have adverse effects on cooperation and motivation.

SOURCE: Adapted from Cascio (1995:137).

tions and job specifications. Jobs are analysed in three work domains:
- data – such as working with information;
- people – such as in communicating;
- things – such as working with machines, tools and equipment.

The FJA is designed to measure the complexity of data, people, and things within each task in a job. The main drawbacks of the FJA are that it takes considerable time to learn to use, is time-consuming to apply, and is costly to the organisation.

8.6 Problems in job analysis

The various approaches to job analysis vary in their effectiveness. Unfortunately most job analyses are undertaken without specific goals in mind. Without a definite objective, much of the data collected in interviews, questionnaires, and by other methods of job analysis is wasted. In addition, unless the purpose of the job analysis is clear, the company cannot take informed decisions about which data collection technique to use or what kind of information to seek (Schultz and Schultz 1993:83).

Byars and Rue (1997:94–97) discuss some of the problems resulting from natural human behaviour and the nature of the job analysis process.

- *Top management support is missing.* Without communication from top management that they support and encourage the job analysis exercise, full and honest participation might not be forthcoming from the employees.
- *Only a single means and source are used for gathering data.* Very often a job analyst uses only one method of data collection, when a combination of methods could provide better data.
- *The supervisor and the jobholder do not participate in the design of the job analysis.* When a job analyst assumes exclusive responsibility for a project and excludes the supervisor and jobholder, distrust, suspicion, and a lack of cooperation are probable consequences.
- *No training or motivation exists for jobholders.* While jobholders are potentially a great source of job information and are called upon to share this information during job analysis, they are seldom trained to generate quality data. They are also almost never rewarded for providing good data.
- *Employees are not allowed sufficient time to complete the analysis.* Supervisors and managers often view the job analysis as a waste of time. The process is rushed through, and inadequate or inaccurate information is produced.
- *Activities may be distorted.* Without proper training and communication, employees may submit distorted data, either intentionally or not.
- *There is a failure to critique the job.* A common mistake made by job analysts is to accept reported job data without investigating whether the job is being done correctly or whether improvements can be made.

In addition, Carrell et al. (1997:89–90) mention the following problems associated with job analysis.

- *Employee fear.* In the past, job analysis was commonly used to expand jobs while reducing the total number of employees, to increase production rates and decrease employees' pay, and to determine minimum numbers of employees required when embarking on a downsizing programme. Employee involvement and representation will help overcome employee fears.
- *The need to update the information gathered.* As job content changes, it is necessary to keep track of those jobs that are affected by these changes. If this is not done, the job analysis information quickly becomes outdated and could result in undue costs for the company if incorrect and obsolete information is used in strategic organisational activities.
- *Only one or two employees hold the job.* This situation often results in an analysis of the person's performance and not of the job itself. The analyst must look at what the job should entail, not at how well or how poorly one employee performs the job.

8.7 Job descriptions

8.7.1 The job description debate

The traditional job description has been a subject for debate, especially during the final years of the twentieth century. Risher (1997:13–14) believes that it was the principles of scientific management formulated by Frederick W. Taylor nearly a century ago, that led to the development of job analysis and documentation practices 'that result in ten-page job descriptions'. It takes about ten hours for a trained job analyst to develop a traditional job description, which usually sets the parameters for a narrowly defined job, with specific duties, and limited expectations of a worker's contributions.

'The end of jobs' and 'a jobless society' have become euphemisms for new methods of organising work, geared to meet the business challenges of global competition and technological change. Modernists, such as Davis (1997:19) feel that there is no longer a place in our organisations for the rigid type of job that only requires specified work to be done and does not 'add value'. The demise of the traditional 'job' would, thus, also mean the end of the job description.

However, there are many human resource and business experts who believe that employees cannot contribute to organisational success without an awareness of the structures and limits imposed on a job by a specific job description. Figure 8.4 offers an example of a specific job description. This type of job description, with its detailed tasks, duties, and responsibilities best fits a bureaucratic organisational structure with well-defined boundaries, and allows the practitioner to undertake all the tasks previously discussed in Section 8.2 (Gómez-Mejía et al. 1998:68).

Not many companies are able to function entirely without job descriptions. Many companies use their own terminology (such as 'job profile') and design their own

Encounter 8.1 The status of traditional job descriptions in the twenty-first century

What is the status of job descriptions in the 21st century? In answering this question one needs to look carefully at the purpose of job descriptions. The traditional view from many employers is that the job description is a tool whereby employees can challenge management about the content of the job, and the compensation associated with the job. Employees on the other hand traditionally held the view that, 'if it is not in my job description why should I perform the work?' or, 'I am not paid to perform the work', and this obviously led to many disputes and disruptions.

The above are only basic examples and many more can be added to the list. The writer is of the opinion that the status of traditional job descriptions is outdated, and that they have no role to play in a post-apartheid, internationally competitive production environment. If South African companies want to survive and create jobs we must ensure that international standards pertaining to quality, productivity, and efficiency are achieved and maintained.

What does the above have to do with job analysis and job descriptions? The answer is 'everything'. It is believed that transparency holds the key to successful job analysis and accurate job descriptions. Where employees are involved, they have a full understanding of the Company's strategy, vision, operational methods, position within the market place, and most importantly, the Company's financial position. This involvement has two major benefits in that employees feel part of the process and it moderates unrealistic expectations. It ensures flexibility and adaptability to changing technology and business needs. Through this involvement, answers and solutions to questions such as skills development and utilisation, payment for skills utilised, etc, are to be found.

SOURCE: Leon Stoltz, Human Resources Manager, Hella (SA) (Pty) Ltd. Used with permission. The contents of this insert do not necessarily reflect the opinion of Hella (SA) (Pty) Ltd.

format of the written document. The need for greater flexibility has resulted in a number of organisations replacing the traditional job description with a general job description – a concise list of bullet points or accountability statements, often limited to one sheet of paper. Figure 8.5 shows an example of a general job description. This type of job description suits a flat or boundaryless organisational structure, where work-flow strategies emphasise innovation, flexibility, and loose work planning. In this way, the fluidity of job content is catered for and is, perhaps, the way of the

Figure 8.4 Specific job description

JOB TITLE: Senior computer sales assistant
LOCATION: Durban
JOB DESCRIPTION COMPILED BY: J Sibisi
JOB DESCRIPTION VERIFIED BY: P Jonas
DATE: January 2000

REPORTING STRUCTURE

JOB SUMMARY
To assist and advise customers in the selection of computer hardware and software.

JOB DUTIES AND RESPONSIBILITIES
1 Demonstrate equipment and software and advise customers on different payment methods in order to meet a sales target of R400 000 over a six-month period.
  Advise potential customers of additional software packages that can enhance their purchases and increase organisational sales.
2 Organise delivery of equipment sales to meet the customer's needs.
  Ensure that equipment is installed to the customer's satisfaction within 12 hours of delivery.
3 Answer after-sales customer queries immediately and provide technical care.
  Provide telephonic advice and, in an emergency, ensure that a technician provides personal service.
4 Develop and maintain a computerised stock control system.
  Control stock accurately, and interact with the sales manager regarding strategic requirements.
5 Monitor performance of junior sales assistant.
  Train, mentor, and assess the development of subordinate.

future (Dessler 1997: 110; Wright and Storey 1997:213).

8.7.2 Developing a job description

No matter what it is called, or what it looks like, a job description is a statement of the data collected in the job analysis process. A specific job description usually contains identification information, and a job summary, job duties and responsibilities.

Identification information

The first part of the job description offers:
- the job title;
- the location of the job (department, branch, etc.);
- reporting structure;
- the compiler of the job description;
- the date of the job analysis; and
- verification (name of the person authorising, or approving the job description).

Job summary

This is a short written statement that concisely summarises the purpose of the job.

Notes for the compiler of a job description

- Do not refer to a specific gender in the job title. For example, use 'Sales Person' rather than 'Salesman.'
- Update job descriptions regularly. A job description reflecting a date that is more than two years old has low credibility and may provide obsolete information.
- Insist that the supervisor, or department manager, verifies the job descriptions of jobs in his or her department. This will ensure that there is no misrepresentation of actual duties and responsibilities.

Job duties and responsibilities

This section must be comprehensive and accurate, as it influences all other parts of the job description. Job duties and responsibilities explain what is done, how it is done, and why it is done.

Some organisations, especially those who have a pay-for-skills compensation struc-

---

Figure 8.5 General job description

JOB TITLE: Senior computer sales assistant
LOCATION: Durban
JOB DESCRIPTION COMPILED BY: J Sibisi
JOB DESCRIPTION VERIFIED BY: P Jonas
DATE: January 2000
REPORTING STRUCTURE: Reports to sales manager; 1 subordinate (sales assistant)

ACCOUNTABILITIES:
- Equipment and software sales
- Sales deliveries and installations
- After-sales service
- Stock control system
- Performance of sales assistant

> **Notes for the compiler of a job description**
>
> - List the three to five most important responsibilities of the job, beginning with an action verb.
> - List one, or more, of the important job duties associated with each responsibility, also starting each with an action verb.
> - Write clearly, unambiguously, and concisely but do not omit any important responsibilities, or duties.
> - Any job performance standards, time limits, and abnormal working conditions are identified in this section of the job description.

ture, combine the job description and job specification, and list the skills required to do the job successfully, instead of the responsibilities and duties. The resulting document is not a job description in the true sense of the word, but rather a 'skills profile'.

8.8 Job specifications

Dessler (1997:107) states that the job specification takes the job description and answers the question, 'What human traits and experience are required to do this job well?'

8.8.1 Developing the job specification

The knowledge, skills, and abilities (KSAs) associated with a particular job can be obtained by allowing the present job incumbent to complete a form such as the one in Figure 8.6. As it is very easy for the employee to 'inflate' the person requirements, different workers doing similar jobs should all be requested to complete the document without access to each other. A knowledgeable supervisor or manager must also provide information for the specification. These different inputs and perspectives should provide a job specification which is as close to accurate as possible.

Knowledge, skills, and abilities that the incumbent possesses, but which are not related to the job, must be excluded. In terms of the Employment Equity Act, the job specification must only contain information regarding the essential person requirements. Stating the desirable requirements as well, would exclude certain future job applicants and could amount to an unfair labour practice.

Job experience, job training, and qualifications can be included in the job specification, but one must always be careful not to be too rigid in stating these requirements. The authors feel that the word 'well' should be deleted from Dessler's question quoted at the beginning of this section and that the emphasis should be placed on collecting information that specifies how the job should be done.

8.9 Job analysis and quality assurance

At the 1995 IPM (Institute of People Management) annual convention there were a number of debates regarding the nature and content of job analysis. These discussions brought to light the different modes of thinking of unionists and managers and indicated a need for quality assurance and consistency in this area. Although the discussion in this chapter has indicated that job analysis offers a starting point for all human resources activities, it is important to take a holistic view of people-related functions in an organisation. Van Wyk (1996:19–22) states that remuneration, industrial relations, and human resources development form more of a functional whole today than ever before. Policy

Figure 8.6 A sample job specification

JOB TITLE: Senior computer sales assistant
LOCATION: Durban
JOB SPECIFICATION COMPILED BY: J Sibisi
JOB SPECIFICATION VERIFIED BY: P Jonas
DATE: January 2000

KNOWLEDGE
All Microsoft Windows programmes; Internet ; DVD functions

SKILLS
Installation, set-up, trouble-shooting

ABILITIES
Problem-solving

QUALIFICATIONS
Three-year tertiary qualification in Information Technology or 4 years' relevant experience

TRAINING
No special training required

EXPERIENCE
Four years' relevant experience or three-year tertiary qualification in Information Technology

---

decisions on one aspect impact on another. It follows that job analysis efforts must contain the highest levels of quality throughout the process, starting with the involvement of employees, to the development of job descriptions and job specifications, and culminating with evaluation of the success of the process.

8.10 Conclusion

In a world where the only thing that is certain is change, job analysis is an anchor, which steadies the fast-moving organisational ship. It is clear from this chapter that all our dealings with people in the workplace are based on the jobs that they do, even if these jobs are continuously metabolising. Job analysis provides a platform from which we can manipulate the organisation through its jobs and in so doing, strive for effectiveness and success.

Summary

Although many jobs have become defunct over the past few years, new jobs have been created and existing jobs have been adapted to conform to the new technological order. Job analysis allows the practitioner to stay abreast of these changes in order to achieve success in the management of workforce planning, job evaluation, compensation, recruitment, selection, placement, orientation, training and development, performance management, career planning, ergonomics, safety, organisational restructuring, and labour relations.

Job analysis is a systematic process involving information collection by means of job-orientated or worker-orientated methods. Job-orientated methods include the use of questionnaires, interviews, observations, and workers' diaries. Worker-orientated methods include collecting information regarding critical incidents, and using the PAQ or the FJA. There are certain advantages and disadvantages to each of these data-collection methods.

Job analysis is an indispensable organisational tool, but the job analyst must be aware of the possible problems that can occur during the process.

Although the job description debate continues, most organisations cannot function without this document. The typical job description contains information on reporting structures, duties and responsibilities, standards of performance, and working conditions. Job specifications usually centre around the KSAs required to perform the job adequately.

Quality assurance is a non-negotiable requirement as job analysis impacts on every other human resources function in the organisation.

Related websites

This topic may be investigated further by referring to the following Internet web-sites:

HR Today (Canada) – http://www.hrtoday.com
The Center for Office Technology – http://www.cot.org
Innovative Practices Labs – http://www.iplabs.com/hr/index/htm
Research and practice in human resources management (Singapore) – http://www.fba.nus.edu.sg/rphr/Astart.htm

Case study
An ill wind blows no good

A number of tornadoes hit the Eastern Cape in South Africa during 1999. One of the most devastating struck the town of Umtata, and the State President at that time, Nelson Mandela, narrowly missed being gravely injured. Many businesses lost their roofs in the high wind, and torrential rain ruined their stock.

One of the companies that suffered little damage to its premises was Premier Furniture Works. This company produces high quality furniture for a number of leading retailers in South Africa. Although their building was intact, Premier's biggest problem was its staff, as many employees lost their homes and some even lost family members in the tragedy. These employees were more concerned with finding shelter for their families, and re-building their homes, than returning to work.

Premier guaranteed keeping their jobs for them for a period of six weeks, but in the meantime, their customers were clamouring for their orders and threatening to take their business elsewhere. Management hastily consulted with members of the trade union and they reached an agreement, which allowed Premier to hire new work crews for the next six weeks. They scouted around for available workers who possessed the skills that were needed, employed them on contract, and within 5 days were back in production. Or so they thought.

The factory manager and ten of the old staff members continued to report for work on a daily basis and no sooner had the new work crews joined them, than confusion reigned, as the new staff did not know what their jobs entailed. The factory manager asked some of the old staff members to list all their duties. Once he had taken a look at the lists, he tore them up in anger, as he felt they were exaggerating their responsibilities.

Conflict escalated; the old staff felt that there was no trust left between themselves and management, and the new staff still did not know what they were supposed to do. Irate customers demanding an explanation for overdue orders jammed the phone lines.

Questions

1 If you had been called in as an HR consultant, how would you have used the job analysis process to solve the problem?
2 What method, or methods, would you have used to collect job data?
3 Would you have developed job descriptions for the new work crews? Why or why not?

Experiential exercise 1

Purpose
To debate whether job descriptions still have a place in the organisation of the twenty-first century.

Introduction
Some people feel that job descriptions reduce organisational effectiveness by creating inflexible jobs. They claim that dynamic organisations must have the flexibility to redesign jobs and make job changes without the restrictions of a written job description.

Task

Step 1 (30 minutes)
Depending on the size of the class, form an odd number of groups, with a maximum of 11. Half the groups will discuss their arguments for, and the other groups will discuss their arguments against the debate topic. One person from each group (except the odd group) will be chosen to summarise the main points of the discussion. The remaining group will discuss both sides of the debate.

Step 2 (Maximum 30 minutes)
Each group will offer their arguments in a debate presentation of not more than 3 minutes.

Step 3 (10 minutes)
The odd group will discuss the arguments for and against the topic and decide on the winners.

(Steps 2 and 3 can be undertaken separately to step 1.)

Experiential exercise 2

Purpose
To produce a job description and job specification from job analysis data.

Introduction
Jabulani Mvubu is employed as a Chief Chemist in a tyre and rubber company. He has been asked to write a summary of his position requirements and has prepared the following document:

My job is to provide technical expertise to the production department and institute development of new rubber products. I work mainly in an air-conditioned office with access to a laboratory where tests are conducted. In my office I have a personal computer and a fax machine. After leaving school I attended the University of Port Elizabeth where I obtained a B.Sc. degree in Chemistry. I am currently studying for a Post Graduate Diploma in Management Skills which, I believe, will assist me in the supervision of my department.

I am involved in writing specifications for production manufacture and I set quality standards for these products. One of my main duties is to develop new products in response to customer requirements. It is essential that I remain healthy, as the chemicals that are used in the laboratory sometimes cause chest problems. Working closely with formulas demands good eyesight and accurate calculations.

I received my promotion to Chief Chemist after 10 years in a similar position although I believe it takes about 12 years' experience to perform this job to the best of one's ability. One of my tasks is to approve the purchase of raw materials for the company and I compile quality performance reports on a daily basis. I report to the Technical Manager of the Company, and there are two chemists and three laboratory assistants who work in my department. The Technical Manager sets specific time limits for the completion of all my duties. In addition, I must prepare and control departmental budgets on an annual basis. Good organisational skills are essential to the daily functioning of my position. I feel that it is also desirable to have a high level of problem solving and analytical abilities. My ability to communicate in English is essential although I sometimes use my knowledge of African languages to communicate with the laboratory assistants. I am 40 years old and live in Uitenhage.

Task

Develop a specific job description and job specification for the job of Chief Chemist. Use the guidelines contained in this chapter to ensure that the documents comply with all requirements.

Chapter questions

1. How can you make use of the information provided by a job analysis?
2. Which job analysis method, or methods, would you recommend for developing a job description of a computer programmer, and why?
3. Discuss the problems associated with job analysis.
4. Are there some business situations in which it is better to not use any job descriptions? Discuss.
5. Do you think a company can comply with the labour legislation of South Africa if it does not use job descriptions and job specifications in its human resources activities?

Bibliography

BYARS, L.L. & RUE, L.W. 1997. *Human resource management.* 5th edition. Irwin, Chicago.

CARRELL, M.R., ELBERT, N.F., HATFIELD, R.D., GROBLER, P.A., MARX, M. & VAN DER SCHYF, S. 1997. *Human resource management in South Africa.* Prentice-Hall, Upper Saddle River, NJ.

CASCIO, W.F. 1995. *Managing human resources: productivity, quality of work life, profits.* McGraw-Hill, New York.

DAVIS, J.H. 1997. The future of salary surveys when jobs disappear. *Compensation and Benefits Review.* 29(1), 18-26.

DESSLER, G. 1997. *Human resource management.* 7th edition. Prentice-Hall, Upper Saddle River, NJ.

GÓMEZ-MEJÍA, L.R., BALKIN, D.B., & CARDY, R.L. 1998. *Managing human resources.* 2nd edition. Prentice-Hall, Upper Saddle River, NJ.

LUNDY, O. & COWLING, A. 1996. *Strategic human resource management.* Routledge, London.

MCCORMICK, E.J., JEANNERET, P.R. & MECHAM, R.C. 1972. A study of job characteristics and job dimensions as based on the Position Analysis Questionnaire (PAQ). *Journal of Applied Psychology.* 56, 347-368.

RISHER, H. 1997. The end of jobs: planning and managing rewards in the new work paradigm. *Compensation and Benefits Review.* 29(1), 13-17.

SCHULTZ, D.P. & SCHULTZ, S.E. 1994. *Psychology and work today: an introduction to industrial and organizational psychology.* 6th edition. MacMillan, Englewood Cliffs, NJ.

VAN WYK, S. 1996. Levelheaded approach to job evaluation. *People Dynamics.* 14(2), 19-22.

WRIGHT, M., & STOREY, J. 1997. Recruitment and selection. In Beardwell & Holden (eds) *Human resource management: a contemporary perspective.* 2nd edition. Pitman, London.

Appendix 1:
A job analysis questionnaire

JOB TITLE:... DATE COMPLETED:..

NAME AND JOB TITLE OF PERSON COMPLETING THIS FORM:..
....

1 Complete the following reporting structure:

```
         ┌──────────┐
         │          │
         └────┬─────┘
              │
         ┌────┴─────┐
         │          │
         └────┬─────┘
              │
         ┌────┴─────────┐
         │ This job title│
         └────┬─────────┘
              │
         ┌────┴─────┐
         │          │
         └────┬─────┘
              │
         ┌────┴─────┐
         │          │
         └──────────┘
```

2 What are the main duties and responsibilities carried out in this job?

Duties/responsibilities	Percentage of time spent	Daily/weekly/monthly

3 What machines or equipment are operated during the course of the above duties?

Machines/equipment operated	Percentage of time spent	Daily/weekly/monthly

4 Are there any extreme or abnormal working conditions associated with this job (eg. extreme heat or cold, noise levels, etc.)?

....

....

....

5 What decisions are involved in carrying out the duties and responsibilities of this job?

Decisions	Percentage of time spent	Daily/weekly/monthly

6 What level of education is required to perform this job adequately?

....

....

....

7 What type of job training is required to perform this job adequately?

....

....

....

8 What special skills and/or experiences are required to perform this job adequately?
....
....
....

9 What unusual aspects about the job have not been covered in the previous questions?
....
....
....

THANK YOU FOR COMPLETING THIS JOB ANALYSIS QUESTIONNAIRE

9

Workforce planning and recruitment

H B Schultz

Learning outcomes

At the end of this chapter the learner should be able to demonstrate the following outcomes:
- Discuss workforce planning as part of strategic organisational planning.
- Examine the internal and external factors that influence workforce planning.
- Provide an overview of the steps in the workforce planning process.
- Briefly explain the role of various staff members in workforce planning.
- Explain the essentials of recruitment policy and the factors that influence recruitment.
- Evaluate internal and external recruitment sources and methods.
- Investigate current and future trends in recruitment.
- Offer some legal considerations in recruitment.
- Explain the impact of quality assurance on workforce planning and recruitment.

Key words and concepts

- workforce planning
- long-range, middle-range, and short-range planning
- labour demand
- labour supply
- forecasting techniques
- skills inventory
- management information system (MIS)
- contingent workers
- employee leasing
- flexitime
- job-sharing
- compressed workweeks
- telecommuting

Illustrative case
Man on the moon!

On 16 July 1969 at 9:32am, Apollo 11 was launched at Kennedy Space Center, Florida, from Launch Complex 39-A. The astronauts on board were Neil A. Armstrong – Commander, Michael Collins – Command Module Pilot, and Edwin E. Aldrin Jr. – Lunar Module Pilot. Their mission objective was to perform a manned lunar landing and return safely to Earth.

The Apollo 11 lunar excursion module landed on the moon on 20 July 1969 at 4:17pm, in the area of the moon known as the Sea of Tranquillity. It was the first manned lunar landing mission, and the first attempt was a complete success. The world will always remember Neil Armstrong's words as he set foot on the moon, 'One small step for man, one giant leap for mankind'. The United States flag was set upon the moon along with a plaque that stated, 'Here Men From Planet Earth First Set Foot Upon The Moon, July 1969 A.D. We Came In Peace For All Mankind'. This mission was the first to return samples from another planetary body. The spacecraft re-entered the Earth's atmosphere without mishap, and splashed down on 24 July 1969 after 8 days in space.

A deceptively simple story, clinically told and, fortunately, completely successful, but when one stops to think about the planning that went on behind the scenes, it is mind-boggling. Planning went far beyond just the logistics of the mission. Planning the workforce was a mission in itself; the numbers of scientists, engineers, medical and administrative personnel, to say nothing of technical ground staff, and even cleaners. It was a miracle that everything fell into place so smoothly, yet it was a real tribute to the planners of four decades ago. When it came to the workforce needed for this mission, from the astronauts themselves, down to the person who served the coffee, the recruiting techniques were fine examples of most of the methods that are still in use today. In the words of Neil Armstrong himself, 'It was one of the greatest shows of all time!'

SOURCE: http://www.nasa.org

9.1 Introduction

Workforce planning plays a central role in strategic human resources management. Planning for a firm's human resources is just as important as planning for its capital and financial resources. Managers have always been very concerned about planning for their capital and financial requirements, but only recently have they recognised the competitive advantage derived from a highly skilled and available workforce.

Horwitz (1991:113) states that workforce planning has begun to occupy an increasingly important role in relation to business plans and corporate strategy in South Africa. If the unique skills at the disposal of management are properly matched to the specific opportunities in the environment, the organisation will stand a better chance of being successful. Every organisation must be able to attract a sufficient number of job candidates who have the abilities and aptitudes needed to add value to the company. Recruitment supplies a pool of suitable applicants who can enter the selection process. Recruiting activities occur when someone in the organisation decides what kind of employees are needed and how many. If proactive planning has taken place, filling vacant positions is not a daunting task.

According to Van Clieaf (1995:55) an integrated and holistic resourcing and workforce planning process ensures that the right people are in the right roles to meet the current organisational profit plan.

We commence this chapter by introducing the reader to the concept of workforce planning as part of the strategic planning of an organisation. We explain the factors that influence workforce planning and the steps in the workforce planning process. We take a brief look at the role of staff members in workforce planning before we move on to investigate the basics of recruitment policy and factors that influence recruitment. Internal and external recruitment sources and methods are examined and an overview of current and future recruitment trends is provided. We conclude the chapter by discussing some legal considerations and the impact of quality assurance on workforce planning and recruitment.

9.2 Workforce planning as part of strategic organisational planning

Cherrington (1995:136) states that the importance of workforce planning is often overlooked. An organisation must have the proper number and mix of employees with the required knowledge, skills, and abilities to be able to reach its long-term goals. Workforce planning provides the foundation for personnel staffing, as Figure 9.1 indicates.

Effective workforce planning is an effort to find a possible or probable future scenario, rather than an attempt to provide definitive forecasts. Workforce planning cannot eliminate risk, but it offers planners the chance to understand the risks faced by an organisation. Rapid change and uncertainty demand that workforce planning involves a

Figure 9.1 A staffing model

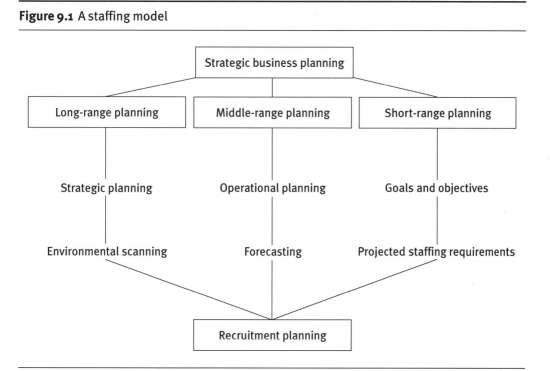

flexible process of systematically addressing the strategic fit of environmental and organisational variables (Horwitz 1991:115).

Workforce planning does not occur in isolation. The eventual size of an organisation's workforce depends upon its business plans. Organisations engage in long-range planning, which entails an examination of the organisational mission to determine what useful products or services the organisation should produce and an analysis of overall strengths and weaknesses. Middle-range planning consists of formulating organisational goals and objectives that the organisation expects to achieve within the next two to five years. Short-range planning typically involves developing annual operating plans and performance goals. Answers to these investigations help planners to establish comprehensive data on staffing requirements (Cherrington 1995:139-140).

Van Clieaf (1995:48) offers some final thoughts on strategic organisational planning. He states that there are notable common practices in benchmark companies:
- the chief executive officer owns the process;
- the process is designed to fit the culture of the organisation;
- the process is integrated with business and organisational planning;
- a competency-based approach is used to describe and assess the effective behaviours required for key jobs and key people; and
- benchmark companies build credibility with line managers through demonstrating that the workforce planning process adds value to the business.

9.2.1 The benefits of workforce planning

According to Horwitz (1991:115) the benefits derived from workforce planning include the following:

- improved understanding of the human and social implications of the business strategy;
- improved and more effective career management;
- employee development and succession planning;
- redundancy and retrenchment planning;
- ability to recruit experienced talent in advance of needs; and
- facilitating the achievement of corporate objectives.

9.3 Factors that influence workforce planning

Workforce planning is influenced by a number of factors. These may be internal or external (Gerber et al. 1992:168). The internal and external factors that influence workforce planning are shown schematically in Figure 9.2.

9.3.1 Internal factors influencing workforce planning

Goals of the organisation

The objective of workforce planning is to enable the organisation to react quickly to change. Change can take the shape of expansion of the enterprise, diversification, and downsizing, and directly influences the goals of the organisation.

Organisational style

The nature of the organisation determines the style and culture. 'Go-getters', people who are entrepreneurial and risk-takers, usually staff a dynamic, fast-paced environment. On the other hand, a traditional, slow-moving organisation (such as the conventional image of a banking institu-

Figure 9.2 Factors that influence workforce planning

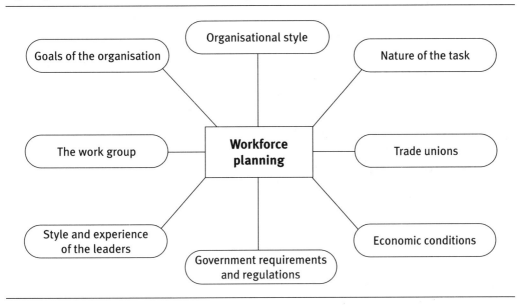

tion) is more often than not staffed by people who take very deliberate decisions and do not like departure from the norm.

Nature of the task

The nature of the task is closely linked to the type of organisation. The composition and requirements of tasks are determined by the organisational style.

The work group

In today's workplace, where teams are becoming the order of the day, the functioning of these work groups influences workforce planning, as the replacement of individuals in a team requires knowledge of the group's dynamics. Interaction between teams will also affect the planning process.

Style and experience of the leaders

Work experience very often influences the manager's style and behavioural characteristics. The way in which the leader manages his or her subordinates determines job satisfaction or job dissatisfaction. The latter can lead to high labour turnover and subsequent increases in recruitment efforts.

9.3.2 External factors that influence workforce planning

The three main external factors that influence workforce planning can be regarded as equally important.

Trade unions

The intervention of trade unions often disrupts an organisation's long-range planning. Unions insist on transparency in everything that management undertakes. This demand includes the number of people employed to do the same job in a specified area of the workforce. Unions will want to ensure that workers are not dismissed unfairly.

Government requirements and regulations

Recent legislation, in particular the Skills Development Act and the Employment Equity Act, impinges directly on workforce planning strategies.

Economic conditions

Labour market conditions such as a surplus or shortage of people with certain skills, also have an influence on workforce planning. The economic climate affects strategy, and the wages and salaries that employers can afford to pay will have an impact on the quality of staff they are able to hire.

9.4 Steps in the workforce planning process

We have already seen how important it is to integrate the plans of the human resources department with the strategic business plans of the organisation. Knowledge of where the company is heading is very important for planners, as firms that do not conduct workforce planning may not be able to meet their future labour needs (resulting in a labour shortage) or may have to resort to layoffs (in the case of a labour surplus). Armed with this strategic knowledge, the workforce planning process can begin.

9.4.1 Forecasting labour demand

The first activity in workforce planning entails forecasting labour demand, that is the estimated number of workers the organisation will need in the future. Gómez-Mejía et al. (1998:149) state that, in the past, many companies avoided planning the workforce, or developed superficial plans, because human resources staff were too busy doing administrative work, or they believed that planning is always a 'hit and miss affair', or they were not trained to use forecasting techniques. These days many computer companies offer sophisticated and powerful software packages that large and small companies can easily use.

Even if a company opts to use computer-forecasting techniques, the planners and users of these programmes should have a basic working knowledge of forecasting methods.

Forecasting techniques

Forecasting techniques can be categorised as quantitative and qualitative. Quantitative methods are used more often, probably because it is believed that forecasting is more accurate if one has figures to work with. However, quantitative forecasting models have two main limitations:

- They rely heavily on past data or previous relationships between staffing levels and other organisational variables.
- Most of the quantitative techniques were created between 1950 and the early 1970s, when the large firms of that era had stable environments and workforces. Quantitative techniques are less appropriate today, when relationships that held in the past may not hold in the future, and when firms are struggling with rapid technological change and intense global competition.

Qualitative techniques rely on experts' qualitative judgements or subjective estimates of labour demand or supply. These experts are usually top managers, who are involved in the strategic planning of the organisation and who are also familiar with the demands and requirements of the plant floor. They are flexible enough to incorporate any factors or conditions the expert feels should be considered. However, the results of these subjective methods may be less accurate than those obtained through quantitative techniques.

Quantitative and qualitative techniques are outlined in Table 9.1.

Table 9.1 Quantitative and qualitative techniques of labour forecasting

Quantitative techniques
- Moving average
- Exponential smoothing
- Trends projections
- Regression
- Linear programming
- Actuarial models
- Simulations
- Probability matrixes
- First-order Markov model
- Semi-Markov model

Qualitative Techniques
- Delphi Technique
- Nominal Group Technique

SOURCE: Gómez-Mejía et al. (1998:550–551).

9.4.2 Estimating labour supply

This activity entails estimating the availability of workers with the required skills to meet the company's labour needs in the future. The labour supply may come from existing employees (the internal labour market) or from outside the organisation (the external labour market). Estimations begin inside the organisation because the labour information is readily available and is more accurate than information obtained externally. Skills inventories and management information systems (MIS) are normally used to provide this information.

Skills inventories and management information systems

In both large and small organisations workforce information is often computerised. In addition to storing data, software packages can supply answers to many queries, such as: 'Which of our current staff members are due to retire within the next five years, in which departments are they currently employed, and what qualifications, experience, training, and competencies do they possess?'

The following is typical of information found in a skills inventory or a MIS:
- personal, or bibliographical data;
- education and qualifications (including degrees, licences, and certifications);
- service record (including significant work experience);
- results of performance assessments;
- language skills;
- training and development programmes attended;
- community and industry leadership responsibilities;
- disciplinary actions;
- awards received; and
- career prospects.

The Department of Labour also publishes initiatives for the provision of skilled workers and these can assist the employer when the organisation cannot completely provide the labour supply.

9.4.3 Implementation of the workforce plan

The results of the labour demand forecast and labour supply estimation determine the actions that must be planned. Gómez-Mejía et al. (1998:147) offer three scenarios and the responses the organisation can make to each scenario. These are listed in Table 9.2.

9.4.4 Control and evaluation of the workforce planning system

Exercising control and carrying out evaluation of workforce planning systems guides human resources activities, identifying

Table 9.2 Ways of implementing the workforce plan

Labour demand exceeds labour supply
Response
- Training or retraining
- Succession planning
- Promotion from within
- Recruitment from outside
- Subcontracting
- Use of part-timers or temporary workers
- Use of overtime

Labour supply exceeds labour demand
Response
- Pay cuts
- Reduced hours
- Work sharing
- Voluntary early retirements
- Inducements to resign
- Layoffs

Labour demand equals labour supply
Response
- Replacement of resignations from inside or outside
- Internal transfers and redeployment

---

deviations from the plan and their causes. Quantitative objectives make the control and evaluation process more objective and measure deviations from the plan more precisely. Quantitative measures are used more frequently in established planning systems, where key comparisons might include the following:

- actual staffing levels against forecast staffing requirements;
- actual levels of labour productivity against anticipated levels of productivity;
- actual personnel flow rates against desired rates;
- action programmes implemented against action programmes planned;
- actual results of action programmes implemented against expected results;
- labour and action programme costs against budgets; and
- ratios of action programme benefits to action programme costs.

In newly instituted planning systems, evaluation is more likely to be qualitative, because supply-and-demand forecasts are more often based on 'hunches' and subjective opinions (Cascio 1995:157).

9.5 The role of staff members in workforce planning

According to Cherrington (1995:136) the chief executive officer is ultimately responsible for the organisation's strategic management decisions. However, the responsibility for strategic business planning and workforce planning is shared equally between line managers and staff specialists. Once business plans have been established, human resource specialists generally develop and maintain the workforce planning system.

Swanepoel et al. (1998:275) explain that the responsibility for workforce planning depends to a large extent on the size of the organisation and the extent to which specialists perform human resources management or other levels of management. In large organisations, such as Eskom, Telkom, and in the mining industry, a specialist planning section usually undertakes workforce planning with inputs from line management. In smaller organisations, line managers can play a major role in planning activities. One question that plagues many organisational decision-makers in large organisations with numerous departments and/or geographical locations, is whether to centralise or decentralise workforce-planning activities. An example of a centralised planning system is offered in Encounter 9.1.

Encounter 9.1 Around the world in HR ways

A diverse group of HR professionals is bringing staff and organisational development issues to the top of the United Nations' list of concerns. A worldwide organisation with a staff of 8 500, representing the interests of more than 5.7 billion people in 188 nations presents unique challenges. But the United Nations Office of Human Resources Management (OHRM) has spearheaded a revolution in HR and planning practices.

In 1996, OHRM set up three new full-time posts to embody its HR priorities, one of which was to lead the workforce planning initiative. An HR Task Force for Reform was established, consisting of experts from the public and private sectors around the world. The Task Force identified various shortcomings in the personnel system of the UN. Inadequate human resources planning had impaired the UN's ability to identify short- and longer-term staffing needs, and complicated rules and procedures had discouraged the recruitment, advancement, and mobility of staff. This had affected the UN's capacity to move the right person into the right job at the right time – an essential requirement for a global organisation.

Since October 1997, Kofi Annan, the seventh secretary-general of the United Nations, and Rafiah Salim, the assistant secretary-general for OHRM has emphasised empowerment, responsibility, and accountability within the department. Part of the workforce plan is to have representatives from each member state employed somewhere in the UN Secretariat. Today, a South African representative might be an administrative officer at his embassy in Paris, next year he might be the cultural attaché in Bangladesh.

In 1998, the workforce plan of the centralised office of the OHRM predicted that 11 per cent of the Secretariat staff would retire by 2003. Everyone in offices around the world was asked to complete a detailed online survey of their skills and experience, setting up a new skills inventory. This skills inventory will assist in HR planning throughout the Secretariat, providing a clear analysis of what skills are being lost and helping to guide future recruitment. This doesn't mean that external recruitment is being ignored, but the many stakeholders in the organisation are now part of strategic workforce planning.

OHRM champions eight core competencies through the workforce plan. Communication, planning, organisation, teamwork, accountability, creativity, client orientation, commitment to continuous learning, and technological awareness are built into recruitment tactics developed as a result of HR planning. These strategies are all revolutionary for the United Nations, where even such core values as 'integrity' can be questioned by underdeveloped countries whose values are more likely to reflect those of basic survival.

The OHRM of the United Nations has been transformed into an organisation that prides itself on its new-found ability to plan strategically for the future.

SOURCE: Sunoo (2000:54–58).

9.6 Recruitment policy

Cherrington (1995:192) defines recruiting as the process of attracting potential job applicants from the available labour force. Every organisation must be able to attract a sufficient number of job candidates who have the abilities and aptitudes that will help the organisation achieve its objectives.

Recruitment policy reflects the organisation's general business strategy. Usually, a company's recruitment policy includes information on whether:
- internal or external recruitment will take place;
- relatives of existing employees may be hired;
- part-time, or any type of flexitime workers will be considered; and
- people over retirement age may be employed.

According to Brewster et al. (2000:150) the ultimate goal of an organisation striving towards obtaining and retaining a sustained competitive advantage is to have a workforce that possesses a unique knowledge base. This objective should be written into any recruitment policy, as the fulfilment of the intellectual capital requirement of a company is to obtain the right people. This can take place by means of external recruitment, but strategic policy-making demands that recruiters now first look within the organisation for those people who have a broad competency base as well as those who have the potential to create and expand their competency base.

Munetsi (1998:52) believes that recruitment policy must take into account the corporate philosophy, organisational mission, strengths, and weaknesses of the company. Corporate philosophy should be to promote from within and give chances to existing staff, while at the same time creating employment in the community. An example of a company recruitment policy is offered in Figure 9.3.

9.7 Factors that influence recruitment

A number of factors, which may be internal or external, influence the way in which recruitment is carried out. Gerber et al. (1992:176) discuss these, as outlined below.

9.7.1 External factors

Government or trade union restrictions

Government policy plays an increasing role in recruitment practice. The Labour Relations Act, and the Employment Equity Act, in particular, governs the way in which organisations may employ new staff. Trade unions are also seeking greater inclusion in the recruitment process and in many organisations trade union representatives participate in developing recruitment policy.

Labour market

Labour market conditions affect the availability of staff. If there is a surplus of skills, many applicants will be available; if there is a shortage of skills, few applicants will be available.

9.7.2 Internal factors

Organisational policy

The content of the organisation's recruitment policy determines the way in which this factor influences the recruitment process. The statements of intent in the policy dictate the parameters of the recruitment effort.

Image of the company

Many organisations are well known in the community, and the way in which the work-seeker perceives the company influences the calibre of potential staff. These days,

Figure 9.3 An example of a recruitment policy

RECRUITMENT POLICY OF DELHALL TYRE MANUFACTURING COMPANY (PTY) LTD

It is the intention of this company to develop a learning organisation by building a workforce of knowledge workers. Knowledge workers are defined as those who have a broad competency base, and those who have the potential to create and expand their competency base.

All permanent employees who have completed their probationary period are eligible to apply for any advertised positions, whether it would mean a lateral or a vertical move. Recruitment will always begin from within the company, providing the opportunity for internal promotions, before recruitment initiatives are expanded to include the external environment.

The following statements of intent have been agreed between management and the majority trade union:
- Relatives of existing employees may be hired, except where there could be a conflict of interests, such as in the financial department.
- Part-time workers may be hired in all areas.
- Flexitime workers may be employed in administrative departments, provided that staff members are on duty between the core times of 10h00 and 15h00.
- Retirement is mandatory at the age of 65 for males and 60 for females.
- The principles of affirmative action will be taken into consideration in all recruitment efforts.

---

companies cannot hide behind established names, or the length of time they have been in existence – the ease with which workseekers can obtain background information, particularly by means of the Internet, means that the company image must be able to withstand a multitude of tests.

9.8 Recruitment sources and methods

In the rush to fill a position, organisations sometimes lose sight of the fact that it may not be necessary to find a replacement or fill a new position at all. There may be other ways of dealing with the vacancy. It is important that other options are considered before the decision is taken to proceed with recruitment (Torrington and Hall 1995:213). Some of the options are to:
- reorganise the work so that the remaining employees do the total amount of work in a section without replacing the leaver;
- use overtime if it is a short-term problem;
- mechanise the work if the time has arrived to introduce new equipment;
- stagger the hours if flexible working arrangements can get the job done;
- make the job part-time by introducing job-sharing;
- sub-contract the work if possible; or
- use an agency to provide temporary personnel.

Some of the above options are becoming more prominent and are discussed in detail in section 9.9.

9.8.1 Internal and external recruitment sources

If none of the above options is feasible and the decision is taken to proceed with recruitment, the recruiter has various sources available. Internal recruitment takes place when current employees of the organisation are considered for a vacancy. External recruitment occurs when the employer uses a source outside of the company. The advantages and disadvantages of internal and external recruitment sources are compared in Table 9.3.

9.8.2 Internal recruitment methods

According to Gómez-Mejía et al. (1998: 153) the most prominent internal recruitment methods are:

Current employees

Internal job postings allow current employees to apply for more desirable jobs. The human resources department can also undertake computerised searches to identify existing employees who may possess the required job knowledge and competencies. However, an internal promotion automatically creates another vacancy that has to be filled.

Referrals from current employees

Referred employees tend to stay with the organisation longer and display greater loyalty and job satisfaction than other categories of recruits. However, current employees tend to refer people who are demographically similar to themselves, which can lead to complexities especially if the organisation has an affirmative action hiring policy.

Former employees

People who were laid off during economic downturns, or those who have worked seasonally, are easily recruited and become productive quickly. They tend to be very safe recruits, because the employer already has experience with these people.

9.8.3 External recruitment methods

Gómez-Mejía et al. (1998:148) also discuss the following external recruitment methods:

Advertisements

Advertisements can be used for local, regional, national, or international searches. Certain occupations, such as engineers and health care practitioners, are becoming increasingly specialized and difficult to fill. In such cases, the employer is targeting not the unemployed, but the currently employed person who will be tempted to change his or her job.

A non-discriminatory advertisement is a prerequisite. An advertisement must reach desirable candidates and supply enough information to unsuitable candidates to exclude themselves from the process. Other requirements are that the advertisement must enhance the image of the organisation and ensure demographic representation within the chosen media. The key selection criteria must be job-relevant, factual, and not arbitrary (Damoyi and Tissiman, 1997:33).

Experienced advertisers use the AIDA principle to construct their advertising copy:
- First, they attract *attention*, sometimes by using wide borders, or a great deal of empty space.
- Next, they develop *interest* in the job by using aspects such as the nature of the job itself, its location, or challenges.
- Thirdly, they create *desire* by amplifying the job's interest factors plus other

Table 9.3 The advantages and disadvantages of internal and external recruitment

Internal recruitment	
Advantages	**Disadvantages**
Provides greater motivation for good performance	Creates 'inbreeding' and stale ideas
Provides greater promotion opportunities for present employees	Creates political infighting and pressures to compete
Provides better opportunity to assess abilities	Requires a strong management development programme
Improves morale and organisational loyalty	Creates a homogeneous work-force
Enables an employee to perform the new job with little lost time	
External recruitment	
Advantages	**Disadvantages**
Provides new ideas and insights	Loss of time due to adjustment
The existing organisational hierarchy remains relatively unchanged	Present employees cease to strive for promotions
Provides greater diversity	The individual may not be able to fit in with the rest of the organisation

details such as job satisfaction, career development, and travel opportunities.
- Finally, they prompt *action*, encouraging the potential recruit to apply immediately.

Figure 9.4 provides an example of an advertisement created according to AIDA principles.

Employment agencies

Organisations often use employment agencies to recruit and screen applicants for a position. Typically, agencies are used when the company is too small to have its own human resources department that can carry out the recruiting process, or when the vacant position is one that will attract many applicants resulting in a time-consuming selection process. Employment agencies also sometimes 'head-hunt' talented candidates who are presently employed and not looking for a new job. Most agencies also assist with the recruitment of temporary workers.

Campus recruiting

Pre-screening programmes in universities, technikons, and colleges are designed to identify top students who are completing their final year of study and to introduce them to the organisation. Often these students will be offered a place on the company's graduate programme, which allows the organisation to fill vacant positions and mould the new recruit into a 'company employee' while exposing the graduate to a number of different areas.

Customers

One area that organisations have neglected to use in recruitment is the organisa-

Figure 9.4 An advertisement created according to AIDA principles

COMMERCIAL BANKER
- **Ceres** • **Vredendal**
- **Caledon**

BANK

THE GENERATION OF WEALTH.
FOR GENERATIONS.

INNOVATION – PROFESSIONALISM – COMMERCIAL BANKING – BUSINESS SOLUTIONS – CLIENT FOCUS

BoE Bank is in the process of targeting the financial world with an entirely new approach towards business and banking. This, then, is the reason why we need to appoint a dynamic, self-motivated professional to complement our team.

The incumbent will primarily be responsible for the development of the commercial market share of the Bank. This involves the procurement of new business and the sustained servicing of existing clients with regard to all banking products and services. In order to identify clients' needs and proactively manage their portfolios, the Commercial Banker must be thoroughly skilled in the analysis of financial statements.

This appointment requires possession of a tertiary qualification in Commercial Science, such as a B.Comm (or equivalent) in Sales or Marketing Management, and at least two years' marketing or sales experience. If you are an assertive person who thrives on challenges and can communicate effectively in English as well as Afrikaans and who focuses on professional service at all times, we would like to hear from you! A distinct negotiating flair is an asset for success in this position.

Your experience in relationship banking, preferably gained within the commercial or agriculture environment, will be a recommendation.

In return for your services, we offer a remuneration package that includes the normal large-company fringe benefits and could be structured to suit your personal needs.

If you would like to join our winning team, forward your latest CV, accompanied by a covering letter in which you motivate your application to Dirk Heydenrych on fax (021) 807-1816 or e-mail: dheydenr@boebank.co.za. Applications close on 1 December 2000.

Commencement of duties: January 2001

www.boebank.co.za The business division of BoE Bank Limited. Reg No 1951/000847/06

SAATCHI & SAATCHI 70298

tion's customers, who are already familiar with the organisation and what it offers. If these people have been satisfied with the company's products and service in the past, they will usually bring more enthusiasm to the workplace than other applicants who are less familiar with the organisation. Customers who may not wish to apply for vacant positions themselves, could offer valuable referrals for consideration.

Direct mail

Direct mail recruitment is aimed at gaining the attention of professionals who are generally employed and who would not normally be seeking employment through other media. Attractive advertisements can be included as loose-leaf flyers in professional journals, such as People Dynamics, the monthly publication of the Institute of People Management in South Africa (IPM). Alternatively, flyers can be handed out at conferences and trade fairs.

Radio, TV, and the Internet

Organisations sometimes use radio, especially local radio stations, to advertise vacant posts. Television offers another advertising medium, but costs are very high and with the specialised language channels on South African television, not everyone may have the opportunity of viewing the advertisement.

Internet recruitment is growing exceptionally fast as more and more of the population gain access to technology. Even those who do not possess their own personal computers are able to utilise this means for a job search by using 'cyber-cafes'. Organisations and employment agencies can display their vacancies, and work-seekers can get their CV's on the World Wide Web relatively inexpensively.

The advantage of Internet recruitment is that a large number of people can access this information at any given time. An example of this recruitment method is offered in the Case-in-Point.

> ### Case-in-point
> ### Texas Instruments –
> ### in front and at the centre
>
> Texas Instruments, with its headquarters in Dallas, Texas, is one of the biggest semiconductor and digital signal processing solutions companies in the United States. The HR department proudly states that they are in front and at the centre of the company's strategic table. That role is sustained through employee development efforts, succession planning, effective recruiting, and a landmark code of ethics.
>
> Although the company has had a succession-planning programme in place for about thirty years, only recently has it become focused and directed. Several years ago, all top executives completed an assessment process that identified the strengths and gaps in senior management. This led to a realignment of succession-planning objectives, no longer identifying the top performers and seeing where they would fit, but by listing the competencies needed for each job and seeing who has them.
>
> Texas Instruments' Internet recruiting page (http://www.ti.com/recruit) helps get those top people. In this 'cyber-centre', job seekers can find one-stop shopping not just for a career at TI, but for any career. Depending on which icon the person clicks on, this Web site can make him or her a better networker, interviewee, and job hunter. He or she can learn how to write a smart letter,

get suggestions on job resource materials and receive advice on developing a resumé, tracking the job hunt, and making a job decision.

SOURCE: Texas Instruments (1995:30–35).

9.9 Current and future trends in recruitment

Brewster et al. (2000:80) state that, in recent years, factors such as increasing economic volatility, competitiveness, and new technology have forced organisations to look for more efficient and effective ways of utilising their resources. The search for competitive advantage demands that management has the ability to flexibly adjust the available internal and external labour market resources in line with the supply and demand of the market. This new flexibility has resulted in a change of mindset for both employers and employees, and although South Africa lags far behind in the development of new work patterns, the time is rapidly approaching when flexible practices will become the norm.

For workers, flexible patterns of work mean:
- a wider range of tasks and abilities, and a willingness to offer them to a variety of purchasers (employers);
- a greater variety in the time periods of employment; and
- a greater capacity to be deployed, necessitating changed attitudes for all, and skills and time-management change for some.

Employers will seek ways of dispensing with certain workers when they are not strictly essential to the production process. This may lead to the replacement of traditional contracts of employment by franchise and subcontractor relations, and a greater use of part-time and temporary employees. Despite this, the South African labour market still displays a traditional employment structure, with almost 90 per cent of employees in permanent full-time employment and 78 per cent of employees working a standard working week between Mondays and Fridays (Brewster et al 2000:88).

Dessler (1997:141) and Leap and Crino (1993:194) discuss trends in recruitment that are currently finding favour in the United States and elsewhere and which South Africa can accept as possibilities for the future.

Contingent workers

Contingent workers are also known as temporary workers, part-time workers, and just-in-time employees. They are broadly defined as workers who do not have permanent jobs. Many companies hire contingency workers when they have absentee or turnover problems or when there are specific projects to complete. The contingency workforce is more productive and less expensive to recruit and train than permanent workers. However, they generally cost employers 20 per cent to 50 per cent more than comparable permanent workers, per hour or per week, particularly if they are employed via agencies, which also wish to earn a profit. Although contingents are usually flexible and adaptable, they experience real concerns in the way they are employed, for example:
- they are often discouraged by the dehumanising and impersonal way they are treated on the job;
- they feel insecure about their employment and are pessimistic about the future;
- they worry about their lack of insurance and pension benefits;
- they claim that employers fail to provide an accurate picture of their job assignments; and

they feel underemployed and express feelings of alienation and disenchantment towards the corporate world.

Employers can strengthen the relationship between themselves and contingency workers by:
- providing honest information about the length of the job assignment;
- implementing personnel policies that ensure fair and respectful treatment of temporary workers;
- using independent contractors and permanent part-time employees to complement the conventional temporary agency workforce;
- considering the potential impact of part-time workers on full-time employees; and
- providing the necessary training and orientation for temporary workers.

Hiring contingent workers may be appropriate under the following circumstances:
- when full-time employees experience downtimes;
- whenever there is a peak demand for labour;
- if qualified contingent workers are available;
- where jobs require minimum training; and
- when quick service to customers is a priority.

Employee leasing

Rather than employ workers themselves, some companies lease employees from a leasing company. The leasing company is responsible for hiring, record keeping, disciplining, paying, and terminating the services of the employees. Leasing allows a company to adjust the size of its workforce with greater ease and avoid the many responsibilities associated with hiring and terminating the services of employees. The organisation pays a management fee to the leasing company and expects the employee to carry out his duties as if he were part of the permanent workforce. Leasing is a method of reconciling supply and demand, as a company has more planning flexibility and is better able to manage the size and skill composition of its workforce. This type of recruitment is often used in so-called 'support services' such as catering, security, and health care, and allows a company to get on with its core business.

Other recruitment trends

Other programmes that bring flexibility to the workplace are flexitime, job-sharing, compressed work-weeks, and telecommuting.

Flexitime

Flexitime provides an alternative work schedule for employees who prefer to create their own starting and ending times on a job. The employer establishes a core time when all employees must be on duty. It is particularly beneficial to those employees who wish to schedule leisure activities and family responsibilities, and take care of personal business during working hours. Organisations report improved morale, increased productivity, and decreased absenteeism and turnover. The administrative implications can, however, produce a heavy workload.

Job-sharing

Job-sharing is a process of dividing a full-time job into two or more part-time positions. Two or more employees hold a position together and are either jointly responsible, or individually responsible only for the part of the job that they carry out. Job-sharing can provide the organisation with increased productivity and a greater pool of qualified applicants, and reduced costs. However, job-sharing can cause communication problems between the job-sharing partners and it is often difficult to assign responsibility to a particular individual.

Compressed workweeks

A compressed workweek is a schedule with fewer than the traditional five working days per week. An employee works an increased number of hours per day so that the total number of hours remains the same as it would have been, had the employee worked five days. Usually there are reduced transport costs for the employee and sometimes better utilisation of equipment. The Basic Conditions of Employment Act must be adhered to when an employer considers changing an employee's working hours.

Telecommuting

Telecommuting refers to the new trend for many employees to maintain an office at their homes and carry out all their normal duties while linked to the head office of their company by means of telephone, fax, personal computer, and electronic mail. Many people say that this is the office of the future, and that it will especially benefit working mothers who can be on hand when children return from school. There are however, certain problems that are inherent in such a work method. Employees have to be particularly disciplined to be able to work on their own without any supervision, and managers will find it difficult to evaluate performance if there are no objective factors that can be measured. Employees themselves may feel that they are not able to develop company loyalty if they are away from the organisational climate. In addition, they might feel cut off from their colleagues and even passed over for promotion if they are out of sight of the rest of the workforce.

9.10 Legal considerations in recruitment

The organisation's recruitment policy must reflect diversity issues and provide guidelines for the recruiter. Damoyi and Tissiman (1997:33) mention that the policy should state that job definitions must follow factual, job-relevant information. In order to comply with legislation, the policy should require the recruiter to make use of key issues such as:
- the purpose of the job;
- how it fits into the organisation;
- outputs required from the job;
- how these outputs are measured;
- levels of authority; and
- details of some of the activities to be performed to meet the outputs.

9.11 Workforce planning, recruitment, and quality assurance

For an organisation to be truly effective, each part of it must work properly together and seek continuous improvement of products and processes to satisfy customer requirements. Planning the workforce must be geared towards the skills and behaviours that support Total Quality Management (TQM) and recruitment methods should be designed to ensure that people understand the true nature of the job for which they are applying. Wright and Storey (1997: 261) offer the example of Diamond Star Motors (a Chrysler Mitsubishi company) which uses 'a realistic preview video that warns applicants that they must learn several jobs, change shifts, work overtime, make and take constructive criticisms and submit a constant stream of suggestions in improving efficiency'.

The conventional way of recruiting and selecting employees involves identifying and choosing from a pool of candidates the most competent individual to perform a certain job. The end result is that many skilled individuals are employed who perform reasonably well but are not necessarily contributing directly to attaining organisational goals. Meyer (1998:34) states that people who are well suited to perform in a quality environment will require additional competencies and characteristics over and above just the skills required to perform a certain job, if they are to be expected to add value to the organisation. Quality enforcement thus depends on the ability of the recruiter to seek and find those employees who already have the competencies of quality values, or who have the potential to cultivate them easily and readily.

9.12 Conclusion

In this chapter we have seen that workforce planning requires considerable time, staff, and financial resources. The return for this investment is the achievement of greater organisational effectiveness. Every organisation, whether large or small, must have a strategic plan in order to survive. The workforce plan must be based on, and linked to, this overall business plan.

Although line managers are often involved in the recruitment process, most of the recruitment process is the responsibility of professionals in the human resource department. Recruiters must be aware of the constraints and challenges offered in the organisation's recruitment policy. They must also be familiar with human resource and affirmative action plans, environmental conditions, job requirements, costs, and possible incentives that can be used to induce recruits to become applicants.

Summary

An organisation must have the proper number and mix of employees with the required knowledge, skills, and abilities to be able to reach its long-term goals. Effective workforce planning is an effort to find a possible or probable future scenario, rather than an attempt to provide definitive forecasts. The eventual size of an organisation's workforce depends upon its business plans.

Workforce planning is influenced by a number of internal and external factors. Internal factors are the goals of the organisation, the organisational style, the nature of the task, the work group, and the style and experience of the leaders. External factors are the intervention of trade unions, government requirements and regulations, and economic conditions.

The steps in the workforce planning process are: (1) forecasting labour demand by means of various quantitative and qualitative techniques, (2) estimating labour supply, (3) implementing the workforce plan, and (4) controlling and evaluating the workforce plan.

Recruitment policy reflects the organisation's general business strategy. The ultimate goal of an organisation should be to have a workforce that possesses a unique knowledge base while promoting the principles of affirmative action.

External factors that may influence recruitment are government or trade union restrictions, and the state of the labour market. Internal factors are organisational policy, and the image of the company.

Various advantages and disadvantages of using internal and external recruitment sources can be distinguished. Internal recruitment methods are job postings among current employees, referrals from current employees and applications and referrals from former employees. External recruitment methods include the use of advertisements, employment agencies, campus recruiting, customers, direct mail, and radio, TV, and the Internet.

Contingent workers, employee leasing, flexitime, job-sharing, compressed workweeks, and telecommuting are all either current or predicted future trends in recruitment.

The organisation's recruitment policy must reflect diversity issues and provide guidelines for the recruiter. Planning the workforce must be geared towards the skills and behaviours that support Total Quality Management (TQM) and recruitment methods should be designed to ensure that people understand the true nature of the job for which they are applying, if quality standards are to be upheld in the organisation.

Related websites

This topic may be investigated further by referring to the following Internet websites:

Texas Instruments' recruiting page – http://www.ti.com/recruit
Career Mosaic – http://www.careermosaic.com
Icarian Employment – http://www.icarian.com
Monster.com – http://www.occ.com
Workforce Dynamics – http://www.workdyn.com.au

Case study
Supa savers saves the best for last

In 1996, Supa Savers, a chain of franchised supermarkets opened a store in East London. The franchisee, Johan Pieterse, had waited for this opportunity for many years. He had fifteen years' retail experience in a chain of hypermarkets, the last six years of which he had spent in various departments, managing fresh foods, dry goods, the bakery, and the butchery. Franchise agreements are very expensive, and Johan and his wife, Anna, took their life savings and sold their house in order to raise the necessary finance to purchase the franchise.

Supa Savers was due to open at the beginning of November, in a new building located in Amalinda. On 7 October, Johan placed a written notice in the shop window. The notice made the following announcement:

This store will open on 1 November 1996!!!

We require the following staff:
- Bakers
- Butchery Blockman
- Shelf Packers
- Cashiers
- Storemen

If you are interested, please phone 4627983 before 15th October 1996 and ask for Johan.

Johan was very busy ordering stock for the new store, buying shelving units, arranging for the refrigerators to be delivered, and getting the bakery and butchery equipment installed. He was inundated by telephone calls for the vacant positions, and wrote down the callers' names and telephone numbers so that he could get back to them. Eventually he realised that it was 25 October and he had not yet conducted any selection interviews.

He hastily chose some numbers at random, phoned the applicants and arranged interviews for the following day. He had estimated the number of people he would require in each position and he was very lucky to be able to fill all the vacancies.

Opening day arrived and the doors opened for business. Most of the newly appointed people reported for duty but, before the end of the first week, Johan realised that he had problems. His cashiers were complaining about the long working hours and the fact that there was no relief staff. Some of the shelf packers approached him, explaining that they were concerned about the fact that there were very few previously disadvantaged workers on the payroll. He also received numerous customer complaints about the products supplied by the bakery.

Questions

1. Explain how Johan should have planned his workforce by providing an overview of the steps he should have followed.
2. Identify the mistakes that Johan made in his recruitment efforts, starting with the lack of a recruitment policy.
3. Discuss how Johan should have approached the recruitment process, indicating the methods he could have followed, and the trends that he could have taken into consideration.

Experiential exercise 1

Purpose
To evaluate the quality of various organisations' recruitment policies; alternatively, to develop a recruitment policy for an organisation.

Introduction
Most organisations have some kind of recruitment policy that lays down the framework for their recruitment efforts. In the interests of transparency, organisations should not keep their recruitment policies secret or confidential. However, some companies do not realise the advantages of regularly reviewing their recruitment policies, in order to ensure that they comply with revised company mission statements and strategic business plans.

Task
Obtain examples of three recruitment policies and evaluate them in terms of the theory contained in this chapter. If possible, try to obtain policies from a large company (over 200 employees) a medium-sized company (between 50 and 200 employees) and a small company (below 50 workers). Consider whether their policies meet the legal requirements. Offer any recommendations for improvement.

OR

Make contact with an organisation that does not have a written recruitment policy. Obtain the information you require, based on the theory in this chapter, and offer to develop a recruitment policy for the company.

Experiential exercise 2

Purpose
To evaluate a recruitment advertisement in terms of the AIDA principles.

Task
Obtain four recruitment advertisements, preferably from a weekend newspaper. Scrutinise these advertisements and evaluate them in terms of the AIDA principles discussed in this chapter. Use the following scale to rate the advertisements in terms of each of the principles:

1 = very poor
2 = below average
3 = average
4 = very good
5 = excellent

AIDA principle	Advertisement 1	2	3	4
Attract attention				
Develop interest				
Create desire				
Prompt action				
TOTAL				

Which advertisement rates the highest? Do you feel that the rating is a good indication of the best advertisement?

Chapter questions

1 Between the years 1946 and 1964 there was a noteworthy increase in the number of births worldwide. This phenomenon, known as the baby boom, was due, in part, to expressions of relief after the

end of the Second World War. How does such a change in the birth rate influence workforce planning?

2 This chapter concentrates on how an organisation should plan and recruit its workforce. Look at the topic from the other side of the fence. You have just been retrenched from your middle management position in an advertising agency. How will you look for a new job?

3 'As organisations become more global, workforce planning becomes more important and complex.' Discuss this statement.

4 Suppose you manage a restaurant in a holiday resort such as Plettenberg Bay. During the winter months it is profitable to keep the business open, but you need only half the number of cooks, table servers, and bartenders. Debate various flexible work practices you could utilise in order to ensure that the business remains effective.

5 In small businesses, managers usually handle their own recruiting. You own a small engineering firm in Gauteng. What recruitment methods would you use for the following situations? Motivate your choices.

  5.1 Your caretaker is going on holiday for three weeks.
  5.2 Your secretary has the flu.
  5.3 You need two more full-time salespersons: one to service local customers, and one to open a small sales office in Cape Town.
  5.4 You have only one engineer, who is due to retire in three months' time. He must be replaced with a highly skilled individual.

Bibliography

BREWSTER, C., DOWLING, P., GROBLER, P., HOLLAND, P. & WÄRNICH S. 2000. *Contemporary issues in human resource management: Gaining a competitive advantage.* Oxford University Press, Cape Town.

CASCIO, W.F. 1995. *Managing human resources: Productivity, quality of work life, profits.* McGraw-Hill, New York.

CHERRINGTON, D.J. 1995. *The management of human resources.* 4th edition. Prentice-Hall, Englewood Cliffs, NJ.

DAMOYI, T. & TISSIMAN, C. MARCH 1997. Structuring your recruitment, selection and placement process. *People Dynamics.* 15(3), 30–34.

DESSLER, G. 1997. *Human resource management.* 7th edition. Prentice-Hall, Upper Saddle River, NJ.

GERBER, P.D., NEL, P.S. & VAN DYK, P.S. 1992: *Human resources management.* 2nd edition. Southern, Halfway House.

GÓMEZ-MEJÍA, L.R., BALKIN, D.B., & CARDY, R.L. 1998. *Managing human resources.* 2nd edition. Prentice-Hall, Upper Saddle River, NJ.

HORWITZ, F. 1991. *Managing resourceful people: Human resource policy and practice.* Juta, Kenwyn.

LEAP, T.L. & CRINO, M.D. 1993. *Personnel/human resource management.* 2nd edition. MacMillan, New York.

MEYER, M. April 1998. Quality management: The essential component is teamwork. *People Dynamics.* 16(4), 30–35.

MUNETSI, W. May. 1998. Importance of the staffing process. *People Dynamics.* 52.

SUNOO, B.P. 2000. Around the world in HR ways. Workforce. 79(3), 54–58.

SWANEPOEL, B.J. (ED.), ERASMUS, B.J., VAN WYK, M.W. & SCHENK, H.W. 1998. *South African human resource management.* Juta, Kenwyn.

Texas Instruments: General Excellence Optimas® Award Profile. Feb 1998. 77(2), 30–35.

TORRINGTON, D. & HALL, L. 1995. *Personnel management.* 3rd edition. Prentice-Hall, London.

VAN CLIEAF, M. 1995. Executive resource and succession planning: reengineered for the twenty-first century. *American Journal of Management Development.* 1(2), 47–56.

WRIGHT, M. & STOREY, J. 1997. Recruitment and selection. In Beardwell & Holden (eds.) *Human resource management: a contemporary perspective.* 2nd edition. 210–276. Pitman, London.

10

Selection

H B Schultz

Learning outcomes

At the end of this chapter the learner should be able to demonstrate the following outcomes:
- Explain the internal and external factors that influence the selection decision.
- Construct a framework for carrying out the selection process.
- Develop an application blank.
- Prepare for a structured employment interview.
- Distinguish between different types of employment tests.
- Discuss the responsibility for making the final selection decision.
- Comment on the role of quality assurance in the selection process.

Key words and concepts

- selection decision
- Employment Equity Act
- standard application blank
- competence-based employment interview
- structured interview
- semi-structured interview
- unstructured interview
- stress interview
- group interview
- panel interview
- employment test
- test validity
- test reliability
- reference check

Illustrative case
Selection the Microsoft way

Bill Gates is considered by many sources to be the richest man in the world. There are some people who might not have heard of the co-founder of Microsoft, the software conglomerate, but Microsoft's reputation has grown as quickly as the company itself, and this was achieved through a deliberate strategy of hiring the smartest people for their workforce. Every year Microsoft screen 120 000 job applicants. And the cutting edge characteristic that is sought in every applicant is not job experience or qualifications. Instead, general intelligence or cognitive ability is the central feature that Microsoft uses in the selection process. Thousands of applicants with long resumés in the area of software development have been turned away in favour of people with an aptitude for mathematics or physics. This emphasis on general reasoning and problem-solving ability reflects the constantly changing world of software development, where yesterday's skills mean less than the ability to develop new skills.

The selection of personnel at Microsoft is such a central issue that Bill Gates makes himself available to both recruit and interview prospective job candidates. Gates has stated: 'Take our 20 best people away, and Microsoft would become an unimportant company.' This is, indeed, confirmation of the central role of staff selection to Microsoft's past success and its future competitive strategy.

SOURCE: Stross, R.E. (1996:159–162).

amounts of money. The problem in selection is to accurately predict who in the applicant pool will become capable, productive, and loyal employees. If the right applicants are identified, there is a saving; if not, there is a cost to the organisation. As can be seen from the following definition of Swanepoel et al. (1998:311) there is no guarantee in making a selection decision; we can only attempt to make it as successful as possible by utilising all the tools at our disposal.

> Selection can be defined as the process of trying to determine which individuals will best match particular jobs in the organisational context, taking into account individual differences, the requirements of the job and the organisation's internal and external environments.

Many tools are available to those making these selection decisions. The tools differ mainly in the amount and type of information they provide. Some, such as application blanks, collect information about an applicant's past. Such tools are based on the assumption that past behaviour predicts future behaviour. Others, such as tests, provide behavioural information about the present and are based on the assumption that present behaviour predicts future behaviour.

The selection process should not be undertaken without an awareness of the factors that influence the selection decision. This chapter commences with an overview of these factors before examining the steps of the selection process in detail. Various thoughts are expressed on who should take part in the selection decision, before we examine the importance of quality assurance in the entire process.

10.1 Introduction

Finding and hiring the best person for a job is a complex process of data gathering and decision making that does not occur through a flash of insight. How do you determine who among the job applicants is the best to hire? This question is the major concern of selection specialists and is crucial to the organisation because selection decisions can cost or save enormous

10.2 Factors that influence the selection decision

Before we discuss the actual process of selection, it is important to note that certain factors that are internal and external to the organisation, can have an impact on both the success of the selection decision, and the level of difficulty involved in working through the entire process. Various authors (Gerber et al. 1992:185–186; Torrington and Hall 1995: 233–234; Mondy and Noe 1996:181–182; Department of Labour: 4) suggest specific factors that may influence the selection decision. These are discussed below and summarised in Table 10.1.

10.2.1 Factors in the external environment

Legal considerations in selection

South Africa has a legacy of discrimination in relation to race, gender and disability that has denied access to opportunities for education, employment, promotion and wealth creation to the majority of South Africans. The Employment Equity Act was passed to address this legacy and has two main objectives:
- to ensure that our workplaces are free of discrimination; and
- to ensure that employers take active steps to promote employment equity.

Having a workforce that reflects the demographics of the country can improve market share, better understanding of markets, and the ability to service all current or prospective clients.

In order to achieve employment equity, employers have to take the following measures in terms of Chapter 3 of the Act:
- employers must consult with unions and employees in order to make sure everybody accepts the organisation's employment equity plan;
- employers must analyse all employment policies, practices, and procedures, and prepare a profile of their workforce in order to identify any problems relating to employment equity;
- employers must prepare and implement an employment equity plan setting out the affirmative action measures they intend taking to achieve employment equity goals;
- employers must report to the Department of Labour on the implementation of their plan in order for the Department to monitor their compliance; and
- employers must also display a summary, available from the Government Printer, of the provisions of the Act in all languages relevant to their workforce.

Table 10.1 The factors that influence selection

EXTERNAL FACTORS	INTERNAL FACTORS
• legislation • the labour market	• size of the organisation • type of organisation • speed of decision-making • applicant pool • selection methods

The nature of the labour market

The labour market from which an enterprise recruits its employees to fill vacancies is influenced by labour market conditions that affect the whole country. Labour market conditions in the city or district in which the company is situated also play an important part. The labour market, in turn, is influenced by labour conditions offered by the organisation, the content of the job itself, and the general image of the company.

10.2.2 Factors in the internal environment

The size of the organisation

The size of the company usually determines the level of formality of the selection process. In addition, different approaches to selection are generally taken for filling positions at different levels in the organisation. Extensive background checks and interviews are conducted when hiring someone for an executive position, while an applicant for a clerical position normally proceeds through the selection process quite quickly.

The type of organisation

The sector of the economy in which individuals are to be employed can also affect the selection process. Prospective employees in the private sector are screened with regard to how they can help achieve profit goals. In the public sector it is commonplace to allow a manager to select only from among the top three applicants for a position. Non-profit organisations may not be able to compete on the same salary levels as private or public sector companies; therefore, a person who fills such a position must not only be qualified but also dedicated to this type of work.

Speed of decision-making

The time available to make the selection decision can also have a major effect on the selection process. Sometimes, speed is crucial in the selection process, especially where production may come to a standstill if there is no one qualified to do a certain job. On the other hand, selecting a Chief Executive Officer may take a few months, with considerable attention being devoted to a careful study of resumés, intensive reference checking, and hours of interviews.

Applicant pool

The number of applicants for a particular job can influence the selection process. The process can be truly selective only if there are several qualified applicants for a job. However, if there are only a few people available with the required skills, it becomes a matter of choosing whoever is at hand.

Selection methods

The selection methods chosen can also affect the entire process. The choice of methods depends on a number of factors:
- the selection criteria, such as group selection methods and assessment centres;
- the acceptability and appropriateness of the methods;
- the abilities of the staff involved in the selection process;
- the complexities of administration; and
- the cost of selection methods chosen (for example, tests and assessment centres are expensive, interviews much cheaper).

10.3 The selection process

The selection process is a series of steps through which applicants pass. These steps represent the 'tools', or methods of selection. The steps are essentially a number of eliminators; as certain applicants drop out of the process at each step, so the applicant pool becomes smaller. A typical set of steps is suggested in Figure 10.1. Although the sequence of steps may vary from firm to firm, with some steps even taking place simultaneously, the process is designed to determine those candidates who are likely to be successful and eliminate those likely to fail. Within each step, multiple approaches help distinguish between performance-related and non-performance-related issues. The selection decision must focus on performance-related issues if the selection process is to contribute to the organisation's success (Werther and Davis 1993:231).

10.3.1 Initial screening

The first step in the selection process is a preliminary screening interview. Individuals who are not qualified for the job-opening should be immediately eliminated from the applicant pool. However, the criteria for deciding that someone is unqualified, need to be established carefully, especially in terms of South African legislation. Standards that have no relationship to an individual's ability to perform the job should not be used to disqualify an applicant. Lack of education, training, and job experience are legitimate qualifications, only if they relate to job performance. These factors may not be used to disqualify an applicant if he or she provides evidence of ability to perform the job (Cherrington 1995:226).

In most cases of initial screening, the applicant's first encounter with the organisation is via the telephone, or a personal appearance in response to a newspaper advertisement, or hearsay, or company information that there is a vacant position. It is thus quite easy for the company representative, for example the human resources officer, to reject the application immediately, if the minimum requirements are not met. Innovative technology is being used to shorten the selection process, especially at the initial screening stage. The Case-in-Point describes how a major footwear manufacturer used computer-assisted interviewing to conduct the first round of interviews and screen out inappropriate applicants. The company saved $2.4 million during a three-year period by reducing turnover from 87 to 51 per cent.

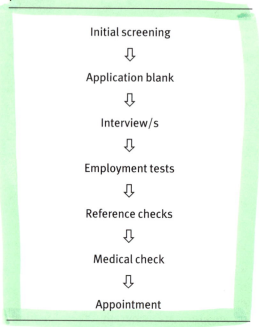

Figure 10.1 The steps in the selection process

Initial screening
⇩
Application blank
⇩
Interview/s
⇩
Employment tests
⇩
Reference checks
⇩
Medical check
⇩
Appointment

10.3.2 Application blank

The standard application blank has traditionally been used to evaluate the education and work experience of job applicants. In an effort to answer questions about the validity of the standard application blank, industrial psychologists have developed other techniques such as the weighted application blank, and biographical inventories. Because most companies develop and use their own application blanks without the expertise of industrial psychologists, only the standard application blank will be discussed.

Standard application blank

The standard application blank is used to gather routine information. Personal details of the job applicant are obtained from this document, including biographical information such as education completed, work experience, and general issues concerning the applicant's state of health. The questions on application blanks must comply with the requirements of the Employment Equity Act. Any questions about the applicant's race, nationality, religion, age, marital status, and any criminal record that may be regarded as discriminatory must be excluded. In fact, a general rule of thumb should be: if the question on the application blank is not relevant in terms of the position for which the applicant is applying, then it could be discriminatory and should be removed from the form.

Application blanks are used to screen applicants for minimum job requirements.

Case-in-point: Fleet of foot in the interviewing game

Nike is an example of a company using computer-assisted interviewing. At a recently opened store in Las Vegas, 6 000 people responded to advertisements for workers needed to fill 250 positions. Nike used interactive voice response (IVR) technology to conduct the first screening. Applicants responded to eight questions over the telephone; 3 500 applicants were eliminated immediately because they were not available when they would be needed or did not have retail experience. The rest had a computer-assisted interview at the store, followed by a personal interview.

The computer-assisted interview identified those candidates who had been in customer service environments, had a passion for sports and would make good Nike customer service representatives. Interviews were done in batches. As applicants completed the interview a printer in the next room printed their responses. Areas that needed to be probed further, and individual strengths were highlighted. The computer not only helped interviewers screen for people who lost their temper in work situations or who demonstrated other undesirable behaviours, but it also helped to determine where there were inconsistencies on the online application form, completed at the same time as the computer interview. Some applicants were offered jobs on the spot; others were called back for second interviews.

Brian Rogers, Nike's manager of human resources for the retail division believes that using computer-assisted interviewing has helped the organisation speed up the hiring process and reduce turnover in the retail division by 21 per cent in two years. Other areas of the company see the technology as promising, and Nike is exploring developing electronic profiles for manufacturing positions.

SOURCE: Thornburg, L. (1998).

This screening can be economical in that applicants who clearly are not acceptable are disqualified early. The expense and time involved in administering tests and conducting interviews can be saved in this way. Application blanks must be interpreted with care. Serumula (1999:32) states that certain 'red flags' should be noticed and investigated. These include:
- time gaps in employment;
- vague reasons for leaving previous jobs; and
- all employers listed being out of business.

Applicants who are rejected must be informed, either telephonically or in writing, that their applications will not be taken further. Candidates whose application forms or CVs closely match the requirements of the job are invited to the company for an interview.

Advances in technology have meant that application forms and CVs can also be faxed or e-mailed to companies to save time. Organisations are also able to widen their recruitment search by downloading CVs from relevant career websites on the Internet and responding electronically to these applicants.

10.3.3 Interviews

As Berry (1998:106) states, hardly anyone is ever hired for work without being interviewed at least once. A new employee may have been interviewed several times – by employment agency staff, company recruiters, human resources department interviewers, and the immediate supervisor of the job – before finally being hired.

The selection interview has two purposes: to get information from the applicant, and to judge the applicant on the basis of this information. The evaluation of

---

Encounter 10.1 Human resources recruiters build interactivity into websites

---

At least four interactive selection tools are appearing on the World Wide Web: website search engines, interactive job application forms, e-mail auto-responders, and e-mail mailing lists. These tools allow human resources departments to link their company databases with the web site and enable applicants to interact with a company more efficiently. Interactive job application forms are becoming extremely popular, because all of the data entry into the human resources database is done directly over the web by the job applicant, thus allowing the human resources department more time to analyse the responses on the electronic data forms.

Online application forms initiate a quick and easy dialogue between the two parties. Once they have filled out a form, applicants immediately become part of the human resources database and this can be manipulated to trigger an e-mail notification of a job opening for the applicant to complete. For the applicant, the benefits of web-based application forms are enormous. Many people want to apply for jobs from home in the evening. If currently employed, they may not have time to stop by in person to fill out a paper form or for the tedious work of requesting and waiting for forms to be mailed to them.

SOURCE: Dysart, J. (1999).

the interview can also be combined with other assessments of the applicant and used later to make a hiring decision. Interviews can be used to assess the applicant's social ease and confidence, speaking ability, and manner of interacting. However, many jobs are not reliant on these interpersonal skills and, in such a case, the selection interview is normally used to expand on the information obtained from the application blank, particularly if any of the details supplied need further probing. Cherrington (1995:244) adds that interviews provide an opportunity to sell the company and promote a good image by supplying information regarding the company's services, policies, and job opportunities. If nothing else, the interview should be a friendly, interpersonal exchange.

10.3.3.1 Traditional versus competence-based employment interviewing

The traditional view of organisations is built around the concept of a job for which the best-qualified individual is selected. Berman (1997:6) states that this works well in a traditional organisation, but the new organisational model is based on open communication and participation of all members. In the past, a job description was the basic document for ascertaining what dimensions were job-related. Now, an employee may be expected to perform a wide range of roles as a member of a team. Role description has replaced job description in many organisations. By adopting the concept of competences (such as the ability to make rational decisions under pressure) the

Encounter 10.2 Job-hunting in Japan

The Internet is supposed to help Japanese college students simplify their hunt for jobs in this country's complex labour market, but graduates wanting to apply for positions at Sapporo Breweries Ltd are telling a different story. Going on line, they have to crawl through a programme called the 'Passion-filled Sapporo Drama'. The 'drama' takes them into the lives of actual employees (a beer salesman, wine marketer, and brewery manager) and asks the applicant what he or she thinks of them. Then they answer a number of questions, including 'How do you deal with a customer angry about finding a scratch on his beer can?' Three hours later, an application form finally pops up on the screen.

Japanese companies are hiring fewer graduates in a weak economy, but the most popular companies are flooded with applications. To fight back, they are setting up Web roadblocks to make it more difficult to apply. They believe that graduates who have the patience to work through the maze of links, online exercises and questions just to get to the application form, are the kind of employees they encourage to apply. However, many students are trading information with others on how to shortcut the online recruiting systems of dozens of companies. At Sapporo, Mr Akahane, a human resources official, says the company has to periodically change questions it asks during the online application process, because students tend to rush out and 'spill the beans' to others.

SOURCE: Ono, Y. (2000).

human resources management function assesses a job applicant not only on his or her ability to perform certain tasks, but also on the ability to take on changes in work as they occur.

10.3.3.2 Types of interview

The interaction that takes place during an interview can occur in several different ways. The nature of the job vacancy usually determines the type of interview that will take place (Cherrington 1995:245–248).

Structured or patterned interview

In a highly structured interview the interviewer prepares a list of predetermined questions and does not deviate from it during the course of the interview. This is the best type of interview to use if the interviewer is inexperienced and if the answers to the questions will probably not need further elaboration. However, it does not allow the interviewer to explore incidental remarks that may be passed by the applicant, and which may have a bearing on his or her application.

Gómez-Mejía et al. (1998:163) offer examples of the three types of questions commonly used in structured interviews:
- situational questions, which try to elicit from candidates how they would respond to particular work situations;
- job-knowledge questions, which assess whether candidates have the basic knowledge needed to perform the job; and
- worker-requirements questions, which assess candidates' willingness to perform under prevailing job conditions.

In Table 10.2 we summarise some of the common interviewing mistakes that inexperienced interviewers often make.

Semi-structured interview

In the semi-structured interview, only the major questions are prepared in advance. Although these questions are used to guide the interview, the interviewer can also probe into areas that seem to merit further investigation. This approach combines enough structure to facilitate the exchange of factual information with adequate freedom to develop insights. Semi-structured interviews are easily used by interviewers who are more experienced, as they have a planned framework to work from, but can allow the applicant to digress from the plan if necessary.

Unstructured or non-directive interview

A non-directive interview is also known as an unstructured interview because the interviewer does not plan the questions or the course of the interview in advance. The interviewer may prepare a few general questions to get the interview started, but the applicant is allowed to determine the course of discussion. The process is built on the assumption that an individual will talk about things that are personally important if given the opportunity and encouragement to do so.

To conduct a successful non-directive interview, the interviewer should listen carefully and not argue, interrupt, or change the subject abruptly. The interviewer should ask questions sparingly, allow pauses in the conversation, and occasionally rephrase responses to encourage the individual to say more.

Only highly experienced interviewers, who have the ability to control the interview with a minimum of intervention, yet elicit as much information of importance as possible, should use unstructured interviews. One of the important requirements of any type of interview is that the interviewer should make brief notes during the course of the interview, which are expanded on as soon as the candidate has left.

Table 10.2 Common interviewing mistakes

- Making snap judgements or jumping to conclusions during the first few minutes of the interview.
- Allowing negative information to influence the outcome of the interview.
- Neglecting to obtain proper knowledge of the job, thus erroneously matching interviewees with incorrect stereotypes.
- Making an appointment under pressure to hire someone/anyone.
- Rating candidates in the order in which they are interviewed.
- Allowing the applicant's non-verbal behaviour to influence assessment.
- Telegraphing an expected answer by offering clues regarding the answer being sought by the interviewer.
- Talking too much or too little.
- Playing the role of a psychologist by probing for hidden meanings in everything the applicants say.

SOURCE: Gómez-Mejía et al. (1998:163).

This is even more important in the case of an unstructured interview.

Stress interview

Although most interview situations involve a degree of stress, certain jobs are performed under a great deal of pressure, and some interviewers believe that stressful conditions should be simulated in order to assess the candidate's reaction. However, stress interviews are mostly avoided because it is believed they are invalid, unpleasant, and unethical.

Group interview

A group interview allows an interviewer to collect information from several applicants simultaneously and obviates having to repeat the same information about the organisation to each individual applicant.

Panel interview

A panel interview involves the use of a panel or board of interviewers to question and observe a single candidate. The technique is especially useful in situations where an applicant's appointment depends on the approval of several people.

Whichever type of interview is used, it is at this stage of the selection process that only the top few candidates survive and proceed to the next step. A sample letter of rejection for those applicants who are rejected at this stage is shown in Table 10.3.

10.3.4 Employment tests

According to Dessler (1997:169) a test is basically a sample of a person's behaviour. The use of tests in South Africa is carefully regulated by the government, the Professional Board for Psychology, and the Test Commission of South Africa. Tests are classified by the Test Commission in terms of their legal requirements as follows:

- C tests – examples of which are intelligence and personality tests, which can only be used by registered psychologists;
- B tests – examples of which are aptitude tests, which can only be used by registered psychologists and psychometrists; and
- A tests – examples of which are elementary aptitude and skills tests, which can be used by registered psychologists, psychometrists, and psychotechnicians.

Certain concepts are extremely important when considering the use of tests. Test validity is the accuracy with which a test measures what it is supposed to measure. Test reliability is the characteristic that refers to the consistency of scores obtained by the same person when re-tested with the identical or equivalent tests.

10.3.4.1 Types of employment test

During the 1980s tests were widely used in the workplace to measure everything from personality to interests. However, during the 1990s, the use of tests, especially psychological tests, fell out of favour in South Africa mainly because many of the tests that were used did not incorporate the norms of the South African population as a whole. During the last few years tests have regained a great deal of popularity because numerous new tests, that are fair and unbiased, have been developed for South Africans.

Mondy and Noe (1996:198–99) discuss some of the types of employment tests that are used to measure individual differences in characteristics related to job performance.

- *Cognitive aptitude tests* measure an individual's ability to learn and to perform a job.
- *Psychomotor tests* measure strength, coordination and dexterity.
- *Job knowledge tests* are designed to measure a candidate's knowledge of the duties of the position for which he or she is applying.
- *Work-sample tests* require an applicant to perform a task or set of tasks representative of the job.
- *Vocational interest* tests indicate the occupation in which the person is most interested.
- *Personality tests* must be administered by

Table 10.3 Sample letter of rejection at the interview stage

5 September 2000

John Brown
678 Chelsea Street
Coega
6100

Dear Mr Brown

APPLICATION FOR EMPLOYMENT

Thank you for your application for the position of Sales Manager, and for taking the time to attend an interview at our company. It was very interesting meeting you and getting to know you a bit better.

I regret to advise that your application was not successful. Your qualifications are very impressive but it was decided that the company needs someone who has more experience in the field than you presently have.

I shall keep your application on file for the next six months and advise you immediately if another position arises for which you would qualify. In the meantime, I wish you every success for the future and hope that you found our meeting as stimulating as I did.

Yours faithfully
Karen Wilson
Human Resources Manager

a qualified psychologist. Due to their low reliability and low validity, they are not very useful as employment tests.

10.3.5 Reference checks

There are two key reasons for conducting pre-employment background investigations: to verify the accuracy of factual information previously provided by the applicant, and to uncover any damaging background information such as a criminal record or a suspended driver's licence. The actual reference check can take many forms. Most employers at least try to verify an applicant's current position and salary if he or she has agreed to this. Others call the applicant's current and previous supervisors in an attempt to discover more about the person's motivation, technical competence, and ability to work with others. Handled correctly, the background check can be useful. It is an inexpensive and straightforward way of verifying factual information about the applicant (Dessler 1997:186).

Letters of recommendation are not highly related to job performance because most are very positive. For this reason, most human resources managers do not have a great deal of faith in letters of recommendation. However, a poor letter of recommendation may be very predictive and should not be ignored.

Table 10.4 How to check an applicant's current employer

- Ask the applicant for permission.
- Ask the applicant for the name of someone who was associated with him at his current company, but who has left the company.
- Ask the applicant if he or she is willing to accept a job offer on the condition that a satisfactory reference will be forthcoming after the applicant has tendered his or her resignation.

10.3.6 Medical checks

In order to save money, usually only the person to whom a job offer has been made is required to undergo a medical examination. There are five main reasons for making a physical examination a pre-employment condition:

- to ensure that the applicant qualifies for the physical requirements of the position;
- to discover any medical limitations of the applicant;
- to establish a record and baseline of the applicant's health;
- to reduce absenteeism and accidents by identifying health problems; and
- to detect communicable diseases that may be unknown to the applicant.

Verster (1997:21) explains that unlike other grounds of unlawful discrimination, including race and sex, the disability or health status of an applicant may directly determine whether that applicant would be able to perform at least the essential functions of a particular position. It is apparent, therefore, that an employer is not required to compromise the integrity of the work in order to employ a person who is physically incapable of carrying out the duties of the job. It is also necessary to ensure that the safety of other workers is not compromised by the disability or ill health of others.

10.3.7 Offer of employment and appointment

If a candidate makes it all the way through the above steps, he or she has a very good chance of receiving a job offer. Job offers are usually made verbally and then backed up with a written job offer. A typical letter of appointment is shown in Table 10.5.

10.4. The selection decision

Having discussed the steps in the selection process, it is pertinent that we turn our attention to the issue of who should make the final decision in choosing a new employee. In many organisations, the human resources department routinely makes staffing decisions, particularly for entry-level jobs. There are two good reasons for this: the organisation must ensure that its employment practices comply with legal requirements; and it makes good sense to allow the human resources department to follow through the entire selection process from start to finish (Gómez-Mejía et al. 1998:152).

On the other hand, Torrington and Hall (1995:230) point out that employment decisions have long been regarded as a management prerogative for the following reasons:
- it appeals to managers because it underlines their authority;
- it is supported by academic research, which provides evidence that line managers make sound judgements about candidates; and
- job applicants believe that they have no influence in the selection decision, and put their faith in the choice made by management.

However, all the above authors advocate a more reciprocal approach to the selection decision. The human resources department should play both an active and a directing role in the whole process, sharing its expertise and supporting decisions made by line managers. The general feeling is that an organisation can decide to involve employees other than just departmental managers. In addition, the new employee's co-workers and, where applicable, his or her subordinates can take part in interviews and work sampling procedures. Offering all three sets of employees part ownership in the hiring process substantiates the final decision and is probably more effective than a decision made by the human resources department alone. After all, the newly appointed staff member will spend his or her working days with co-workers and subordinates, not with human resources staff.

Making personnel decisions where a large number of applicants is involved can be difficult and costly. Many organisations make use of external consultants such as Saville and Holdsworth South Africa (Pty) Ltd(SHL) to assist them with the selection decision. SHL is part of a worldwide group and they have designed three systems to aid organisations with their decision-making. These systems are briefly discussed in Encounter 10.3.

O'Connell (1999) states that various criteria should be examined when evaluating a company's selection system:
- how difficult is it to administer;
- how difficult is it to interpret the results;
- how many job positions are covered in testing for potential;
- are interpersonal skills, problem solving, and work ethic being tested for;
- how would the results generated stand up in court;
- is the selection system cost effective;
- is the selection system reliable and consistent; and
- are the tests used fair and unbiased?

10.5 Selection and quality assurance

Many companies have successfully used the various selection tools to hire above-average employees who have made a significant contribution to the firm's bottom line. However, for companies emphasising Total Quality Management (TQM), it is important that employees are able to perform effectively in a continuous-improvement, high-involvement environment. It is widely agreed that organisations that do not adopt the objective of seeking a competitive advantage, will not survive in the new millennium. This competitive advantage cannot be achieved without embracing the philosophy of a learning organisation, staffed with knowledge workers who add value to the company through the way that they perform. Quality issues are therefore exceptionally important throughout the selection process – decisions made in haste will be repented at leisure.

10.6 Conclusion

We have seen that the hiring process is filled with challenges: determining which

Table 10.5 Letter of appointment

5 September 2000

Eric Ntuli
20 Harebell Avenue
Coega
6100

Dear Mr Ntuli

APPLICATION FOR EMPLOYMENT

Welcome to Joyful Jumpers CC. This letter confirms the verbal employment offer for the position of Sales Manager at our company. You will commence your duties on 1 October 2000. There is a six-month probationary period and during your first year of employment, interim performance reviews will be conducted every three months. Your first month with us includes a structured orientation programme focusing on the managerial function and overall business of the company.

Your annual salary, including a flexible benefits plan, amounts to R150 000. You will be allowed to compile your own package within the benefits structure offered by Joyful Jumpers CC. You are entitled to 15 working days annual leave after completing 12 months' service, and all statutory public holidays will be paid in full.

The attached booklet tells you more about the benefits plan of the company. This should assist you in your choice of benefits. You will also receive a handbook during orientation , which will offer you additional information on company policies, rules and regulations.

This letter serves as an official contract of appointment. Its termination is conditional on 30 days' notice from either party, except in the case where company policy has been infringed.

You have made an excellent choice in selecting this job, and we are looking forward to having you on the staff. Please sign one copy of this letter and return it to me as soon as possible, to indicate your acceptance of your terms of employment.

Yours sincerely
Karen Wilson
Human Resources Manager

Employment offer accepted
Name ......:..
Date..

characteristics are most important to performance, measuring these characteristics, evaluating applicants' motivation, and deciding who should make the hiring decision, all play a part in determining the quality of the choice of a new employee. Because choosing the right person for a job can make a tremendously positive difference to productivity and customer satisfaction, it is important that each step of the hiring process be managed carefully. The key challenge that underlies the entire selection process is to ensure the validity of each step, taking into consideration the needs of the organisation, co-workers, and the new employee, and also complying with all legal requirements.

Encounter 10.3 Selection strategies from SHL

Based on inherent job/role requirements, and the candidate's selection data, these systems automatically match the applicant's potential to perform in the job/role.

- Person-job match software, which is attribute-based, and competency-based.
- Decision-making models, which use scores from selection data that are summarised and weighted according to job relevance and criticality scores derived from the SHL Work Profiling System (WPS).
- Decision-maker software, which enables users to match small and large numbers of candidates against the three competency models of Management Competencies, Customer Contact and Sales Competencies, and Graduate Competencies.

These systems generate reports that can be used by line management to make quick and effective selection decisions.

SOURCE: Saville and Holdsworth South Africa (Pty) Ltd.

Summary

Certain internal and external factors influence the selection process. These are: legal considerations, the nature of the labour market, the size and type of organisation, the speed of decision making, the applicant pool, and the selection methods used by the company.

The selection process is a series of steps through which applicants pass. The first step in the selection process is a preliminary screening interview, followed by an evaluation of the application form or CV. The questions on application blanks must conform to the requirements of the Employment Equity Act. Application blanks are used to screen applicants for minimum job requirements.

The selection interview has two purposes: to get information from the applicant, and to judge the applicant on the basis of this information. The traditional selection interview assesses the applicant on the basis of his or her ability to perform certain tasks; competence-based employment interviewing assesses the ability to take on changes in the work as they occur.

Various types of employment interviews can be conducted, depending on the nature of the vacant position. These are: the structured or patterned interview, the semi-structured interview, the unstructured or non-directive interview, the stress interview, the group interview, and the panel interview.

The use of tests in South Africa is carefully regulated. Test validity and test reliability are very important. Employment tests include cognitive aptitude tests, psychomotor tests, job knowledge tests, work-sample tests, and vocational interest tests. Personality tests are not very useful as employment tests.

Reference checks are carried out to verify the accuracy of factual information previously provided by the applicant, and to uncover any damaging background information. Medical checks ensure that the new employee is physically capable of carrying out the duties of the job, and that the safety of other workers is not compromised by his or her possible disability or ill health.

Ideally, the responsibility for the selection process should be jointly that of the human resources department and line employees, particularly line management. The line manager should make the final decision, after which a letter of appointment confirms the job offer.

Related websites

This topic may be investigated further by referring to the following Internet websites:
Saville & Holdsworth (SHL) – http://www.shl.co.za
SHL website for students – http://www.shldirect.com/shldirect-forstudents/SHL-Direct-2.asp
Society for human resources management (Links to: Employment Interviewing Training Course; Discriminatory Effects of the Face-to-Face Selection Interview; The Interview Coach; Interviewer's Edge) – http://www.shrm.org/hrlinks/recruit.htm

Case study
Spinning a selection tale at Beachview

Beachview Spinning Mills has relied on its first-line supervisors to recruit, interview, and select new employees for their own work units. Over the past few years it has become apparent that some supervisors seem to be far more successful than others at selecting employees who maintain high performance levels and who remain with the organisation for longer periods of time.

After a series of interviews with the supervisors, Andrew Hayward, the general manager, found that those who were most successful had carefully planned selection procedures; whereas those who were least successful were very casual in the way they approached the process, and based their decisions on their first impressions of the applicants and the results of their own favourite questions.

Andrew is now considering what should be done next. The current situation could be allowed to continue, but the turnover and low productivity caused by inefficient selection procedures is proving very costly. In addition, Andrew is concerned about the implications of the Employment Equity Act. Clearly something must be done.

Question
What do you recommend that Andrew Hayward does to improve the selection process? Be specific in your recommendations and explain your reasoning.

Experiential exercise 1
Purpose
To show that application blanks differ between companies, and to evaluate a number of application blanks according to legal requirements.

Introduction
Application blanks should be developed in a manner that enables the person responsible to gather as much information as possible from the answers to the questions. Application blanks should contain sections on:
- biographical details;
- secondary and tertiary education;
- previous working experience, including duties, positions held, dates of employment, and salary earned; and
- any other information that the applicant believes is relevant to the application.

Task
Approach at least four different companies and obtain a copy of their application blank. Evaluate each form in terms of current legislation and the questions posed. Make any recommendations necessary for improvements to the forms.

Experiential exercise 2
Purpose
To experience the roles played by the participants in the selection process, namely the job applicant and the interviewer. In this case the interviewer is a member of the human resources department and the interview is the candidate's first meeting with a company employee.

Introduction
The interviewer needs to achieve several basic objectives during the employ-

ment interview. It is important that at least the following objectives be successfully attained.
- Create an appropriate environment by making the candidate comfortable and ensuring that there is a climate of mutual trust and confidence.
- Obtain behavioural, job-related information from the applicant, clarify vague points on the application form, and uncover additional information.
- Provide information about the job and the company by presenting a realistic summary of job requirements, company policies, products, and services.
- Determine whether the candidate is suitable for the vacant position; if the conclusion is positive, the process continues, otherwise the candidate is eliminated from consideration.

Task

Team up with a partner and obtain a job description for any job from an organisation. Both partners receive a copy of the job description. Assume that this position is vacant in a company. One partner plays the role of a job applicant. This partner fills in an application blank and hands it to the other partner, who will play the role of the interviewer.

The 'interviewer' must scrutinise the application blank and make preparations for a semi-structured interview. The 'job applicant' must try to anticipate the questions that will be asked, and prepare the answers.

The role-play is presented in front of the class. It should not last longer than five to seven minutes, and will be videotaped, if possible. Facilitated by the lecturer, the class will give feedback on both roles. If the role-play has been videotaped, the tape will be made available for the role players to review and analyse.

Chapter questions

1. Some people believe that the human resources department should have the authority to decide who is hired because the department contains the experts on hiring. Others say that the immediate supervisor is responsible for employee performance and should have the final authority. Support one argument or the other and explain your reasoning.
2. If the employment manager asked you to develop a selection process for identifying and selecting internal candidates for job openings, how would you arrange the steps in the selection process?
3. Why is it important to conduct pre-employment background investigations? How would you go about doing so?
4. Interviewing unqualified applicants can be a frustrating experience and a waste of time for managers, peers, or whoever is responsible for interviewing. How can the human resources department minimise or eliminate this problem?
5. What type of interview would you recommend in the following scenarios? Motivate your answer in each case.
   5.1 A lawyer interviewed by the senior partner in a law firm, who is an inexperienced interviewer.
   5.2 A sales representative interviewed by the Sales Manager, who has some experience in conducting interviews.
   5.3 An applicant for the position of chief executive officer, to be interviewed by the board of directors.
   5.4 Twenty applicants for ten vacant positions as seasonal apple packers on a farm.
   5.5 A heart surgeon, applying for a position as head of the cardiac unit at a large hospital, interviewed by the experienced hospital administrator.

Bibliography

BERMAN, J.A. 1997. *Competence-based employment interviewing.* Quorum Books, Westport, CT.

BERRY, L.M. 1998. *Psychology at work: an introduction to industrial and organizational psychology.* 2nd edition. McGraw-Hill, Boston.

CHERRINGTON, D.J. 1995. *The management of human resources.* 4th edition. Prentice-Hall, Englewood Cliffs, NJ.

DEPARTMENT OF LABOUR. *Preparing an employment equity plan: a user's guide.*

DESSLER, G. 1997. *Human resource management.* 7th edition. Prentice-Hall, Upper Saddle River, NJ.

DYSART, J. 1999. HR recruiters build interactivity into web sites. *HR Magazine.* http://www.shrm.org/hrmagazine/articles/0399hrs.htm.

GERBER, P.D., NEL, P.S. & VAN DYK, P.S. 1992. *Human resources management.* 2nd edition. Southern, Johannesburg.

GÓMEZ-MEJÍA, L.R., BALKIN, D.B., & CARDY, R.L. 1998. *Managing human resources.* 2nd edition. Prentice-Hall, Upper Saddle River, NJ.

MONDY, R.W. & NOE, R.M. 1996. *Human resource management.* 6th edition. Prentice-Hall, Upper Saddle River, NJ.

O'CONNELL, M. 1999. Recruiting and hiring in a tight labor market: new practices in recruitment and selection. Paper read at a conference, May 5-6, 1999.

ONO, Y. 2000. Job-hunting in Japan means battling employers' web traps. *Wall Street Journal.* http://207.46.148.249/news/394285.asp.

SAVILLE & HOLDSWORTH SOUTH AFRICA (PTY) LTD. Publicity brochure.

SERUMULA, C. 1999. Employee selection needn't be a game of chance. *People Dynamics.* 17(10), 32–37.

STROSS, R.E. 1996. Microsoft's big advantage – hiring only the supersmart. *Fortune.* November 25, 159–162.

THORNBURG, L. 1998. Computer-assisted interviewing shortens hiring cycle. *HRMagazine.* http://www.shrm.org/hrmagazine/articles/0298rec.htm.

TORRINGTON, D. & HALL, L. 1995. *Personnel management.* 3rd edition. Prentice-Hall, London.

VERSTER, J.D. 1997. Medical screening of job applicants. *People Dynamics.* 15(10), 18–21.

WERTHER, JR, W.B. & DAVIS, K. 1993. *Human resources and personnel management.* 4th edition. McGraw-Hill, New York.

11

Induction and staffing decisions

H B Schultz

Learning outcomes

At the end of this chapter the learner should be able to demonstrate the following outcomes:
- Distinguish between the concepts of induction, orientation, and socialisation.
- Explain the objectives and benefits of induction.
- Examine the responsibility for carrying out the two levels of orientation.
- Describe the stages of induction and discuss how the process of acculturation can be fostered.
- Provide an overview of the planning, design, implementation, and evaluation phases of an induction programme.
- Compare and evaluate various staffing strategies.
- Examine the approaches to internal staffing.
- Briefly describe the influence of quality assurance in induction and staffing decisions.

Key words and concepts

- acculturation
- anticipatory stage
- buddy
- demotion
- dismissal
- employee handbook
- encounter stage
- induction
- induction kit
- internal, external, and workforce pool staffing strategies
- layoff
- orientation
- promotion
- realistic job preview (RJP)
- realistic orientation programs for new employee stress (ROPES)
- resignation
- retirement
- retrenchment
- settling-in stage
- socialisation
- transfer

Illustrative case
Disney show and tell

Walt Disney World, near Orlando, Florida, is the home of the Magic Kingdom Theme Park, Epcot Center, and Disney-MGM Studios. It is the largest single-site employer in the United States, with a current workforce of 50 000 employees. Recruitment challenges are enormous – filling 100 job vacancies a day, or 20 000 vacancies a year. These statistics include new hires, transfers, and promotions of current employees, and applicants previously interviewed and kept on file for six months.

The typical orientation session for new Disney employees is innovative, stimulating, and dynamic. The orientation slogan is: 'We don't put people in Disney. We put Disney in people.' Disney's approach to orientation seeks to engage new employees on an emotional, not just an intellectual, level. All new Disney employees, plus many other new employees from hotels and restaurants at Disney resorts, attend a day-and-a-half 'Traditions' class. Delegates at orientation are taught to be 'aggressively friendly', by offering to take photographs for people carrying cameras, and providing directions to people looking at Disney centre maps. Disney employees are taught to make guests happy. New staff members vary widely in their enthusiasm, ranging from the most nonchalant to the most fervent 'Disnoids'.

Orientation also includes a great deal of 'how-to' information – how to call for emergency first-aid help, how to help children who have lost their parents, and parents who have lost their children. About nine classes, averaging forty-five new employees, are held each week, with up to fourteen classes a week during peak seasons. About five employees arrive at every orientation class with haircuts, or wearing jewellery that infringes the personal appearance regulations. These are taken aside privately and gently told that they are in violation of the policy. They are then given the chance of attending to the problem and may reschedule their starting date and orientation.

New employees display an initial peak of excitement, followed by a decline in enthusiasm, and hopefully, a climb to a more sustainable level as the reality of the job sinks in. Recognition programmes and employee activities support this period. While Disney World does not pretend to be a perfect employer, their techniques provide plenty of food for thought. The company philosophy builds on the words of its founder, Walt Disney, who said: 'You can dream, create, design and build the best, the most wonderful place on earth, but it requires people to make that dream a reality.'

SOURCE: Rubis, L. (1998).

11.1 Introduction

Starting a new job is considered to be one of the most stressful life experiences and a proper induction process that is sensitive to the anxieties, uncertainties, and needs of a new employee is of the utmost importance. The impact of diversity in terms of age, language, and cultural background on South African organisations also makes it critical that proper attention be paid to induction.

At this point it is appropriate that we pause and take a look at some relevant terminology. Although induction means to introduce, or to initiate, it is only part of the process that endeavours to absorb an employee into the organisation and turn him or her into a productive worker.

Orientation means becoming familiar with, or adjusting to facts or circumstances. It is the process of informing new employees about what is expected of them in the job, and helping them to cope with the stresses of transition. Employees receive orientation from their co-workers, and from the organisation. The orientation received from co-workers is usually unplanned and unofficial, and it often provides the new employee with misleading and inaccurate information. This is one of the reasons why the official orientation provided by the organisation is so important.

Socialisation means to adapt to life in society. In the organisation, socialisation is the process of instilling in all employees the prevailing attitudes, standards, values, and patterns of behaviour expected by the organisation and its departments. Socialisation really begins with induction and is often informal. Unfortunately, informal can mean poorly planned and haphazard.

We can see from the above that the process is actually one of socialisation, incorporating induction and orientation. However, because most organisations refer to the entire process as 'induction', this term will be used throughout the chapter.

The start of this chapter focuses on the objectives and benefits of induction, and the responsibility for carrying out the induction programme. A comprehensive discussion of an induction model follows before an overview of the planning, design, implementation, and evaluation stages of the induction programme is offered. The debate proceeds to examine various staffing strategies and approaches to internal staffing before the chapter concludes with some thoughts on the relationship between induction, staffing decisions, and quality assurance.

11.2 The objectives and benefits of induction

The main purpose of induction is to assist the new employee in his or her integration into the organisation. Werther and Davis (1993:281) state that the induction programme helps the individual to understand the social, technical, and cultural aspects of the workplace, and speeds up the socialisation process.

Various authors (Werther and Davis 1993:273; Cascio 1995:239; Cherrington 1995:367; and Dessler 1997:247) agree that the following are the main benefits of a successful induction programme:

- It reduces reality shock and cognitive dissonance. Dissonance occurs when there is a psychological gap between what newcomers expect and what they actually find.
- It increases job satisfaction and reduces turnover and absenteeism. When employees meet their personal objectives, satisfaction tends to improve, which reduces turnover and absenteeism costs.
- It alleviates employee anxieties. Proper induction results in quicker acceptance by peers and less criticism from supervisors, as well-integrated newcomers need less attention from co-workers and supervisors, and perform better.
- It creates positive work values and reduces start-up costs. Fostering a sense of belonging in the organisation allows the new employee to become productive much more quickly.
- It improves relations between managers and subordinates. Improved relationships are the result of new employees settling in to the new environment as quickly as possible, without becoming too much of a burden on their managers and co-workers.

11.3 The responsibility for induction

The two broad categories of an induction programme are, firstly, general topics of interest to most new employees and, secondly, specific, job-related issues of concern only to specific jobholders. Some of the common topics of induction, categorised into these two tiers, follow.

General topics:
- company history;
- company structure;
- layout of physical facilities;
- products and services;
- company policies and procedures;
- disciplinary regulations;
- safety procedures;
- pay scales and pay-days;
- holidays; and
- employee benefits.

Job-related issues:
- introductions to supervisor and co-workers;
- job location;
- job tasks;
- job objectives; and
- relationship to other jobs.

These two distinct levels of induction are shared between the human resources department and the new employee's immediate manager (Werther and Davis 1993: 278; Byars and Rue 1997:206).

The human resources department:
- co-ordinates both levels of induction;
- trains line managers in conducting departmental and job induction;
- conducts general company induction; and
- follows up the initial induction with the employee.

The new employee's manager:
- conducts departmental and job induction.

A 'buddy' or co-worker who has been carefully selected and trained to carry out this responsibility sometimes conducts job induction.

11.4 An induction model

11.4.1 The stages of induction

According to Wanous (in Gómez-Mejía et al. 1998:170, 259) the entire process of induction can be divided into three stages:
- the anticipatory, or induction stage;
- the encounter, or orientation stage; and
- the settling in, or socialisation stage.

The basic ideas in this induction model are presented in Figure 11.1.

At the anticipatory stage, applicants generally have a variety of expectations about the organisation and the job, based on accounts provided by newspapers and other media, word of mouth, public relations, and so on. A number of these expectations may be unrealistic, and if unmet, can lead to dissatisfaction, poor performance, and high turnover.

A realistic job preview (RJP) is probably the best method of creating appropriate expectations about the job. For instance, at most Toyota manufacturing plants, job simulations and work samples are used to demonstrate to applicants the repetitive nature of manufacturing work and the need for teamwork.

In the encounter stage, the new employee has started work and is facing the reality of the job. Even if a RJP was provided, he or she needs information about policies and procedures, reporting relationships, rules, and so on.

An important function of orientation during the encounter stage is to provide new workers with the tools to manage and control stress. Organisations can use an orientation approach called Realistic

Figure 11.1 An induction model

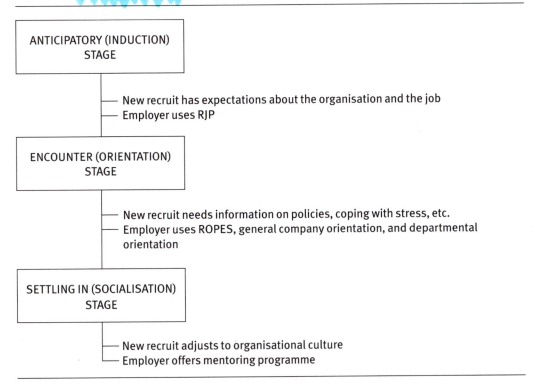

Orientation Programs for new Employee Stress, or ROPES. A good ROPES programme does all of the following:

- it provides realistic information about the job and the organisation;
- it offers general support and reassurance, informing employees that the stress they are experiencing is normal, and trains managers to support new employees;
- it demonstrates coping skills in how to deal with the stresses of the new job; and
- it identifies specific potential stressors that new employees might face.

During the settling-in stage, new workers begin to feel like part of the organisation. An employee mentoring programme, in which an established worker, or 'buddy', serves as an adviser to the new employee, may help ensure that settling in is a success.

Even the most extensive socialisation programme will not make new employees feel at ease if their immediate supervisors are not supportive during their settling in period. Although there is no universally effective set of practices for promoting the integration of new workers, certain actions that can be used with most people and in most situations are offered in Table 11.1.

11.4.2 Fostering organisational culture

Induction initiates the whole process of integrating employees into the organisation. Organisational values, beliefs, and traditions (commonly known as the organisational culture) are slowly absorbed as a

Table 11.1 Supportive actions for new recruits

- Offer constructive criticism laced with praise.
- Show confidence in the new recruit.
- Listen to self-doubts and share personal experiences.
- Acknowledge the value of past experience.
- Emphasise the new recruit's potential.

person is exposed to orientation, training, and his or her peer group. Anfuso (1995:70–77) calls this process 'acculturation'. The success of the induction process depends on the degree to which the new employee understands, absorbs and accepts the culture of the organisation. Long-serving employees often forget that the new incumbent has to deal with outside-life conflicts, inter-group role conflicts, the definition of his or her own role within the group, learning new tasks, establishing new interpersonal relationships, and learning group norms. Managers must be aware of these conflicts and offer support in resolving conflicting interests.

Open-door policies, and group and individual discussions, will assist new employees in understanding corporate culture. Individuals expect a hierarchical structure that emphasises status differences between subordinates and superiors. They also need to know the degree to which the company values personal goals, autonomy, and privacy over group loyalty, commitment to group norms, involvement in collective activities, and social cohesiveness.

Organisations operate efficiently when employees share values. The transmittal of values, assumptions and attitudes occurs from older to younger employees. Every organisation has its own personal symbols, language, ideologies, rituals, and myths, which form the basis of its culture, and these are often alien to the new employee. Organisations even develop their own jargon, or 'slang', which is incomprehensible to strangers.

A common failing of orientation programmes is to ignore this part of the socialisation process, concentrating instead on compliance with rules and regulations, benefits offered by the company, and what the organisation expects from the new employee. In this area, the 'buddy' system can achieve what individual managers often ignore or do not have time to offer. After all, the peer group is closer to the new employee than supervisors or managers.

Fostering company culture is an ongoing process, which is strengthened by the involvement of both co-workers and managers. South African managers must be made aware of the challenges demanded by an ethnically diverse workforce. The traditions and values of non-English-speaking employees, in particular, make it imperative that individual cultures are aligned, and not erased, in an attempt to make new employees conform to organisational culture.

11.5 Planning, designing, and implementing the induction programme

11.5.1 Planning the induction programme

Research has shown that in many organisations, 50 per cent of voluntary resignations occur within the first six months after organisational entry, often because employee expectations are not met (Boase 1997:50). Most organisations base their induction programmes on what the organisation believes the new employee needs to

know. However, the most common questions that new employees have should form the basis of induction. According to Cascio (1995:240) these questions are usually:
- what are the expectations of this company regarding the services I can offer;
- who is my boss and what is he or she like;
- what kind of social behaviour is regarded as the norm in this company;
- will I be able to carry out the technical aspects of my job; and
- what is my future in this company?

If one accepts the improvement and promotion of productivity as the ultimate goal of the induction process, it is important to note that there are other categories of employee who will benefit from an induction, or re-induction programme, namely: transferred or promoted employees, especially if the transfer or promotion involves a significant change of environment; indeed, all current employees, particularly if restructuring changes or mergers have taken place (for example, the recent formation and subsequent restructuring of the activities of the ABSA banking group in South Africa).

Based on these considerations, induction programmes are usually planned in accordance with common employee questions, targeted employees, and budget limitations.

Table 11.2 Induction at Gray Security Services (Eastern Cape) (Pty.) Ltd.

At Gray Security, induction is carried out in three phases:

Phase 1: Selected candidates are placed on a four-week training course that covers security training, basic fire fighting, a NOSA safety representative course, as well as first aid training. This includes an AIDS Awareness Programme (AAP), training in report writing, radio handling and telephone answering procedures. During this process, trainees are instructed in the company's specific procedures and documentation relevant to the specific day-to-day activities of a security guard. This phase is conducted by the Training Department.

Phase 2: The second phase of induction is a one-day induction programme presented by the HR department, and deals with the company's organisational structure, communication channels, HR policies, employee benefits and the terms and conditions of employment detailed in their employment contracts. On completion of this phase their line managers take the new employees to their workplaces.

Phase 3: On arrival at their sites, the employees are introduced to the site commander (supervisor)/shift leader and colleagues. At this point the third phase of site-specific induction is conducted. This phase is a formal aspect of the company's procedures. It is recorded on a site-induction checklist and includes introduction to key employees of the client, reporting procedures, site orientation (identifying layout, hazardous areas, alarms, fire equipment, patrol points, etc.) as well as familiarisation with the specific duties performed on site. This phase takes place over a period of between one and three days, depending on the nature and complexity of the services required by the client. Every employee is given formal site induction on transfer to a new site, or on promotion to a more senior position within the company.

SOURCE: Zola Mbulawa, Personnel Officer, Gray Security Services (Eastern Cape) (Pty.) Ltd. (2000). Used with permission.

11.5.2 Designing the induction programme

Byars (1997:207) believes that the induction programme must be based on a good balance between the organisation's and the new employee's needs. With this in mind, the designer must compile an induction programme that is comprehensive, concise, and to the point. This is achieved by reviewing the following:
- *the target audience* – current or transferred employees may require less information than new recruits;
- *essential and desirable information* – essential information cannot be omitted, desirable information can be summarised; and
- *the literacy level of the employees* – in South Africa, the large number of illiterate workers demands a visual rather than a written means of imparting information.

11.5.3 Implementing the induction programme

Byars (1997:207) states that it is desirable for each new employee to receive an induction kit, or package of information, to supplement the verbal and visual induction programme. This kit can provide a wide variety of materials. Care should be taken not only to ensure that essential information is provided, but also that not too much information is offered. Materials that might be included are:
- company organisation chart;
- map of the company's facilities;
- copy of a policy and procedures handbook;
- list of holidays and fringe benefits;
- copies of performance appraisal forms, dates, and procedures;
- emergency and accident prevention procedures;
- sample copy of the company newsletter or magazine; and
- telephone numbers and locations of key company personnel (e.g. security).

Some organisations even provide a T-shirt and pen with the company logo, as part of the welcoming kit.

Many organisations require employees to sign a form indicating they have received and read the documents in the induction kit. This is commonly required in unionised organisations to protect the company if a grievance arises and the employee alleges that he or she was not aware of certain company policies and procedures. It is equally important that such a form be signed in non-unionised organisations, particularly in the light of an increase in wrongful dismissal litigation. Whether signing a document actually encourages new employees to read the induction kit is questionable.

11.5.3.1 The employee handbook

Some of the most common and frequent mistakes employers make in preparing employee handbooks are related to legal issues. A recognised risk in having an employee handbook is that a court may interpret it as part of the contract of employment. It is generally recommended that the handbook includes a clear and conspicuous disclaimer, because deviations from the handbook may serve as fodder for litigation. While it is critical for employees to understand that the handbook is not a contract, supervisors need to be taught the importance of treating the handbook as though it were a contract.

Employees should not be required to acknowledge in writing that they will abide by the terms and conditions of the handbook. Instead, the certification they sign should be limited to acknowledging receipt of the handbook.

With regards to fringe benefits, the handbook should offer coverage of benefits, and not specific information related to particular benefits. The handbook should state explicitly that all statements relating to coverage are subject to the terms, conditions, restrictions and other eligibility requirements set forth in the benefits-plan documents. The employer should reserve its right to modify, amend, or terminate any benefit plan at any time and for any reason (Segal 1993).

The contents page of a typical employee handbook is shown in Figure 11.2.

11.5.3.2 Conducting the induction programme

Dessler (1997:247) believes that the actual implementation of the induction programme hinges around three considerations:

- the stage of induction;
- the information which needs to be delivered during the relevant stage; and
- the person, or persons, responsible for the relevant stage.

These parameters of implementation are summarised in Table 11.3.

Table 11.3 Implementing the induction programme

Stage of induction	Information	Responsible person(s)
1 Induction (anticipatory)	Basic organisational details and brief overview of benefits during recruitment and selection.	HR Officer
	Letter of appointment with job description, starting salary, job grade, terms and conditions of employment, probationary period, medical checks, etc.	HR department
	First day instructions.	HR department
2 Orientation (encounter)	Induction kit, tour of the workplace.	HR department
	Meeting new manager and co-workers.	HR department
	Basic job information, departmental goals and expectations.	Line manager
3 Socialisation (settling in)	Advanced job information, social activities.	Mentor or 'buddy'

Figure 11.2 Contents page of a typical employee handbook

Bakewell Biscuit Company Staff Handbook for Salaried Employees

Contents	Page	Contents	Page
Introduction	1	Study leave	4
Conditions of service	1	Refund of costs of study courses	4
Hours of work	2	Maternity leave	5
Occasional absence	2	Public holidays	5
Absence due to ill health	2	Religious holidays	5
Accumulated sick leave	2	Payment of salary	6
Absence without permission	2	Annual bonus	6
Medical aid	3	Long service bonus	6
Medical services	3	Social club	7
Compensation for accidental injury or death	3	Smoking	7
		Safety	7
Annual leave	4	Cleanliness	7
Unpaid leave	4	Communication	7

In Encounter 11.1 we read how Toyota Motor Manufacturing (USA) goes about conducting the orientation stage of its induction programme.

Encounter 11.1 Toyota Kentucky

At Toyota Motor Manufacturing in Kentucky, USA, orientation is called 'assimilation'. The main purpose of the assimilation exercise is to socialise new employees, by inculcating the firm's ideology of quality, teamwork, *kaizen* or continuous improvement, problem-solving, personal development, open communication, and mutual respect. It lasts four days and is undertaken before the new employee starts his duties for the first time.

Day One. At 6:30 a.m. the new recruits receive an overview of the programme, a welcome to the company, and a discussion of the firm's organisational structure and human resources department. Thereafter, an hour and a half are devoted to discussing Toyota's history and culture, and another two hours to employee benefits. The final two hours on day one are spent discussing Toyota's policies about the importance of quality and teamwork. The facilitator for this first day is the vice-president for human resources.

Day Two. A training officer takes the new recruits through a two-hour program entitled 'Communication training – the Toyota Motor Manufacturing way of listening'. The main emphasis of this training is on the organisational philosophy of mutual respect, teamwork, and open communication. Various other organisational specialists spend the rest of the day with the new employees, discussing general orientation issues including safety, environmental affairs, the Toyota production system, and the firm's library.

Day Three. This day also begins with two-and-a-half to three hours of communication training, emphasising 'making re-

> quests and giving feedback'. Again, departmental specialists spend the rest of the day covering matters such as Toyota's problem-solving methods, quality assurance, hazard communications, and safety.
>
> Day Four. The morning session is devoted to teamwork, stressing topics such as teamwork training, Toyota's suggestion system, and the Toyota Team Member Activities Association. The final coverage of teamwork allows the new employees to discuss what work teams are responsible for, and how to work together as a team. The afternoon session specifically covers fire prevention and fire extinguishers training, led by the safety officer.
>
> SOURCE: Dessler (1997:248).

Case-in-point
DuPont-Merck

The ongoing process of socialisation is illustrated in a case study of the merger between DuPont and Merck Pharmaceutical Co. in New Jersey, USA. Because 85 per cent of its workforce transferred from DuPont, the new company needed to synthesise and re-channel the talents and energy of these employees, as well as those who came from Merck.

The orientation programmes manager recognised a need for a comprehensive, consistent orientation process (DuPont Merck refer to the induction process as 'orientation'). A three-tiered approach to employee orientation was conceived. A process called orienteering, introducing new employees to their work units, divisions and the company as a whole, was developed.

Work-unit orienteering shapes an employee's perception of the company and his or her role in it. This first tier of the process begins when an employee is hired. Employees gain a clear sense of direction, define objectives, identify resources and assimilate company values. Their supervisor, a sponsor, and an administrative coordinator coach them.

An orienteering kit was designed which incorporates four posters associated with the company's mission and vision. The guide also serves as a training manual for the employee's supervisor. It summarises the advantages of an effective orienteering process, and explains how to customise the process for each new employee, how to form the work-unit orienteering team, and how to define each team member's role. In addition, it contains a master checklist that summarises team members' key actions. This checklist is organised by two criteria: who should provide the information, and when the information should be provided.

Company orienteering ensures that all employees adapt to DuPont Merck's culture. Through presentations, complemented by three videos, a workbook and handouts, the employees learn during this second tier how they, as individuals, their jobs, and their work units contribute to meeting the company's goals. This half-day segment is scheduled after the employee has been on the job for thirty to ninety days. By then, the employee has assimilated knowledge of the company's goals, mission, and shared values, and has enough work experience to understand the company message.

The company segment includes:
- pre- and post-programme assignments to ensure preparation and follow-up;
- a short welcome by a member of the executive management committee;
- an overview of company history, culture, product development, and the industry; and
- a one-hour Break-N-Learn, for which human resources managers at display booths provide take-away materials and informally answer questions about their groups' responsibilities and services.

A divisional segment follows company orienteering. Sometime between thirty to sixty days after the company segment, a new employee's supervisor schedules a half- to full-day division orienteering programme. The purpose of this third tier is to help employees to bring the company goals and vision into focus at the division level. The structure of this event is left open to each division, as long as they follow these guidelines:
- reinforce the company goals and vision;
- share and refine the employee's personal commitment statements; and
- incorporate division objectives.

This three-tiered process has ensured a work environment in which everyone knows the company values, vision and goals. The environment is built on quality, diversity, and performance, which allows the company to recruit, motivate, retain, and recognise its employees.

SOURCE: Klein, C.S. & Taylor, J. (1994:64–67).

11.6 Follow-up and evaluation of the induction programme

Many organisations make the mistake of believing that once a new employee has 'attended the induction programme', nothing more is needed from the supervisor or manager. This is almost as bad as an informal policy of 'Come and see me if you have any questions'. Instead, regular checks should be initiated and conducted by the line manager after the new employee has been on the job for a day and

Figure 11.3 A manager's induction checklist

Employee name ....

	Date attended to
Welcome from supervisors and co-workers	_____
Prepping co-workers for start of new employee	_____
Introduction to co-workers	_____
Introduction to other selected employees	_____
Overview of job setting and company tour	_____
Mentor or buddy assigned	_____
Employee handbook provided	_____
Specific job requirements discussed	_____
Outline of facilities: rest room, telephone regulations, eating arrangements, parking, day care centre, working hours, breaks, first aid facilities	

again after one week and, by the human resources representative, after one month (Cascio 1995:242). A typical manager's checklist is shown in Figure 11.3.

Very often, new employees have questions that remain unanswered because they do not wish to disturb the supervisor with something which may be regarded as trivial. Werther (1993:281) suggests that the human resources department can schedule a face-to-face meeting where the employee is asked to critique the weaknesses of the induction programme. Weaknesses are presumed to be topics about which the employee needs more information. This type of follow-up not only reinforces the content of the induction programme for the new recruit, but also serves to provide information for the human resources department regarding the strong and weak areas of the induction programme. Revision can then take place where necessary. Byars (1997:210) states that using the following methods can strengthen evaluation:

- unsigned questionnaires completed by all new employees;
- in-depth interviews of randomly selected new employees; and
- group discussion sessions with new employees who have settled comfortably into their jobs.

11.7 The importance of good staffing decisions

The allocation of people to jobs in an organisation is the result of a staffing decision. Not only new employees are allocated to jobs; movement also takes place within an organisation when an employee is assigned to a different job. Staffing decisions must be made even when people leave an organisation. Resignations, dismissals, and retirements force the company to consider the answers to various questions, such as:

- Do we need to fill this position?
- If the answer is yes, shall we try to fill the position from inside or outside the organisation?
- If the answer is no, how will we ensure that the job duties are still carried out?

Managers must calculate the costs of hiring a new employee who will possibly bring new ideas and enthusiasm into the

---

Encounter 11.2 Patagonia Inc.

Patagonia Inc. is an environment-friendly outdoor clothing company situated in California. The buddy system, or peer mentor scheme, is taken one step further at Patagonia, where new employees are teamed from the recruitment stage, with one human resources person who will look after their human resources needs. The human resources person is closely associated with the new employee through the initial training process and builds a really strong relationship so that the new recruit is not afraid or embarrassed to approach an official for assistance. Patagonia offers a three-day new employee orientation, which is taught by workers who have volunteered to become 'orientation trainers'. The human resources department offers 'brain food' in the form of time management, surfing, introduction to French culture, business, and communication, and other innovative classes.

SOURCE: Laabs, J. (2000:80–86).

organisation but who will require an extensive induction programme before he or she becomes productive. Filling a position with an existing employee might be less costly and might save time, but a current employee will have no new ideas and might not fulfil the hiring goals of an affirmative action programme.

11.8 Staffing strategies

A staffing strategy is the technique used by an organisation to place the right person in the right position. In their purest form, these strategies are categorised as either internal or external. A modification of an internal strategy is the workforce pool. These strategies will now be examined.

11.8.1 Internal staffing strategy

The internal staffing strategy only recruits new employees for entry-level positions. Existing employees fill all other vacancies in the organisation, whether through a transfer or a promotion. This means that current employees are assured of being considered for promotional opportunities and it is assumed that they will offer increased loyalty, dedication, and career orientation. The major disadvantage of this strategy is that individuals are expected to progress through all the levels of a job tree, even if they have the skills and ability to undertake a job at a higher level. Also, the company cannot consider using the services of an external applicant, even if highly recommended, except at entry-level.

11.8.2 External staffing strategy

External applicants fill all positions, at all organisational levels, and no provision is made for promotion opportunities. This ensures a constant flow of applicants with new ideas, but because there is no career planning, loyalty and dedication is low, and turnover is high.

11.8.3 Workforce pool strategy

The pool strategy appoints individuals to a pool of entry-level posts on a temporary basis, from where they are allocated to different positions as required. When a permanent position becomes available, the organisation will already have had the opportunity of observing the employee's performance and can more easily make a staffing decision. A pool strategy offers a company a ready-made staffing source in times of high labour turnover or absenteeism. However, the workforce pool is costly to maintain as, theoretically, the organisation is over-staffed.

Organisations very seldom use any of these strategies on their own, and are more likely to use a combination determined by situational variables, such as the supply of and demand for labour in various occupations, government legislation and requirements (such as the Employment Equity Act, and affirmative action) and the economic situation.

11.9 Approaches to internal staffing

Internal staffing decisions are applied mainly by way of promotions, transfers, demotions, and 'exits' such as resignations, layoffs, retrenchments, dismissals, and retirements. Werther and Davis (1993: 284–285) and Torrington and Hall (1995:260,267) discuss these staffing approaches.

11.9.1 Promotions

A promotion occurs when an employee is moved from one job to another that is higher in pay, responsibility, or organisational level. Promotions are usually based on merit or seniority.

According to Werther and Davis (1993: 284) merit-based promotions occur because of an employee's superior performance in his or her present job. Very often the promotion is a 'reward' for past efforts. Two problems may be encountered here. Firstly, 'superior performance' must be objectively distinguished from other grades of performance and those employees who are regarded as 'superior performers' must be treated consistently when it comes to promotional opportunities. Secondly, the *Peter Principle* states that people tend to rise to their level of incompetence in a hierarchy. Although this is not always true, the *Peter Principle* suggests that good performance in one job does not guarantee good performance in another. For example, an organisation might promote an engineer, identified as being a superior performer, to the job of engineering supervisor. The company might gain an ineffective supervisor and lose a superior engineer.

Seniority-based promotions are given to the employees with the longest length of service. This approach is very objective and one needs only to compare the seniority records of the candidates to determine who should be promoted. This approach can be used quite easily in blue-collar jobs, but is more difficult to implement when promoting from blue-collar to white-collar, or between white-collar jobs at different hierarchical levels. Again, the question of competency might arise in a seniority-based promotion decision. Usually, a combination of both approaches to promotion is considered to be most fair.

11.9.2 Transfers

Decision makers must be able to reallocate their human resources to meet internal and external challenges. Reallocation often takes place through transfer. A transfer occurs when an employee is moved from one job to another that is relatively equal in pay, responsibility, and organisational level. Transfers can thus improve the utilisation of human resources and provide a person with new skills and a different perspective. Often a transfer results in an increase in motivation and job satisfaction, particularly if there was little challenge in the employee's previous job. Technical and personal challenges in the new job can provide growth opportunities, and at the least offer variety and a change in routine (Werther and Davis 1993:285).

11.9.3 Demotions

Demotions occur when an employee is moved from one job to another that is lower in pay, responsibility, and organisational level. There are two main reasons for the use of demotions: in the case of an employee who is punished for an offence, and when an organisation offers redeployment to an employee in the form of a demotion instead of a retrenchment. Werther and Davis (1993:285) maintain that demotions are negative solutions to problems and can have serious consequences for motivation and performance. They should be used as a last resort and, if possible, other methods of discipline or redeployment should be sought.

11.9.4 Resignations

Torrington and Hall (1995:260) state that resignations represent an outward movement of staff and take place for various reasons. When there are no promotional opportunities, or better opportunities elsewhere, many employees take the option of leaving the company. Sometimes employees just do not fit into the company culture, or they find themselves in conflict situations from which they decide to withdraw. In the case of female employees, a resignation is sometimes the result of a decision to start a family, or spend more time with children. In the majority of cases, resignations are healthy events and allow the organisation to introduce new blood.

11.9.5 Retrenchments

A downturn in the economy, or business reasons such as the closure of a branch of a company, may dictate that employers ask employees to seek other work. One of the most difficult aspects of retrenchment for the employer is the selection of who should go. A long-standing convention is that of LIFO, or last-in first-out, as this provides for justice which is difficult to dispute and satisfies labour unions.

Retrenchments must always be carefully organised. Thorough consultation with all interested parties, including labour unions, is essential, and counselling should be made available to the affected employees. An increasing number of employers are using a range of other strategies, such as not replacing people who leave, early retirement, and voluntary redundancy (Torrington and Hall 1995: 267).

11.9.6 Layoffs

Layoffs take place for the same reasons as retrenchments, but are not as harsh as the latter because the employees are called back as soon as the economy improves. The psychological effects of a layoff can be severe, as the employee is not sure if, or when, he or she will be offered the position again, and must decide whether to start a job search in the interim. As in the case of retrenchments, employers try to use other strategies, such as cutting back on overtime, dismissing part-time workers, and not hiring new employees.

11.9.7 Dismissals

Dismissals are the result of employee misbehaviour and proper procedures must be followed when the employer takes this drastic action. Dismissals cause movement outside the organisation and invariably lead to an unplanned vacancy. Dismissals represent extreme disciplinary action and must not be taken lightly.

11.9.8 Retirements

According to Torrington and Hall (1995: 267) retirement has the advantage for the employer that there is usually plenty of notice, so that succession arrangements can be planned. Phased withdrawal from the organisation is encouraged so that the retiree adjusts gradually to being without stimulating employment and a lower level of income. Retirees, especially professional employees who can offer consulting services to the organisation, may continue to work part-time after retirement.

11.10 Induction, staffing decisions, and quality assurance

The effectiveness of all staffing decisions, including the entrance of new employees into the organisation, depends on a minimum of disruption to the employer and the employee. Appropriate induction procedures and relevant staffing decisions can help in relieving the pressures caused by these staff movements. Given the pace of change in modern society and technology, superior induction programmes and staffing decisions are necessary to achieve a high level of quality in the people who staff our organisations. Cascio (1995:223) believes that the evaluation of induction programmes and employer-initiated staff movements is crucial if one is to measure the impact on productivity, quality of work-life, and the bottom line.

11.11 Conclusion

Traditionally, induction programmes were rigid, generic, and completed over a limited period. However, as organisations begin to restructure their overall human resources practices to ensure continual growth and competitiveness, they need to refocus on the impact that initial employment experiences with an organisation have on a new employee. Induction can ease the entry process into an organisation, with positive results for new and repositioned employees, as well as for the company. Induction deals with technological and social change, and trends such as leased employees, disposable managers, and free-agent workers will make induction programmes even more important in the future.

Movement within and outside an organisation is healthy and challenging, provided that decision makers have the knowledge to be able to stimulate and control these changes. It is clear that all managers must come to accept the fact that organisational effectiveness depends, to a large degree, on the quality of staffing decisions.

Summary

Induction is only part of the process that endeavours to absorb an employee into the organisation and turn him or her into a productive worker. Orientation is the process of informing new employees about what is expected of them in the job and helping them cope with the stresses of transition. In the organisation, socialisation is the process of instilling in all employees the prevailing attitudes, standards, values, and patterns of behaviour expected by the organisation and its departments.

The main purpose of induction is to assist the new employee in his or her integration into the organisation. The two distinct levels of induction are shared between the human resources department and the new employee's immediate manager. Sometimes a 'buddy' or co-worker conducts job induction.

The entire process of induction can be divided into three stages: the anticipatory, or induction stage; the encounter, or orientation stage; and the settling in, or socialisation stage. Planning, designing and implementing the induction programme must be done methodically, and follow-up and evaluation of the programme is essential.

The allocation of people to jobs in an organisation is the result of new appointments and the redeployment of employees. Staffing strategies can be internal, external, or workforce pool, and these strategies are put into practice by means of promotions, transfers, demotions, and 'exits' such as resignations, layoffs, retrenchments, dismissals, and retirements. Well-planned induction programmes and staffing decisions contribute greatly to organisational effectiveness.

Case study
Biscuits in the Indian Ocean

Holdens Ltd is a biscuit manufacturing company located at Westmead, Pinetown in KwaZulu Natal. The Holden family had owned the company for over 100 years and recently sold the firm to a biscuit conglomerate. The new owners have plans to expand the export side of the business to the Indian Ocean Islands, in particular Mauritius, Madagascar, Reunion, and the Seychelles. They intend building a new factory at Port Louis in Mauritius, and opening sales branches in the other areas.

One of the decisions that top management has to take is how to staff the new plant and sales offices. The Westmead factory has well-qualified technicians and highly experienced sales personnel. Although it would cost a lot of money to relocate large numbers of people overseas, the expense of recruiting and training local nationals on the islands would negate these costs. Mauritius welcomes foreign investment, but a government policy prohibits more than a 5 per cent foreign component of the workforce for three years after setting up operations.

The human resources director has to take a decision as to how he will implement the staff movement, and has identified the following key personnel who could fill posts overseas:

Ross Watkins, Sales Manager, 58 years of age, 2 years from retirement, highly qualified, extremely competent in the past, beginning to slow down a bit.

Xola Mbenge, Sales Supervisor, 35 years of age, 10 years in sales, 4 years in present position, good performer, married, no children.

Jerry White, Production Supervisor, 40 years of age, 2 years with the company, good performer but doesn't get on with the Production Manager, unmarried.

Charlie Davis, Production Manager, 44 years of age, 20 years with the company, married, with two teenage children.

Jabu Sibisi, Sales Representative, 25 years of age, unmarried, 1 year's service, Sales and Marketing Diploma, enthusiastic performer, sometimes makes mistakes.

Joan Jarrett, Sales Supervisor, 30 years of age, married, no children, 5 years with the company, excellent sales record, intent on moving up the corporate ladder.

John Wilkinson, Sales Representative, 24 years of age, 6 months' service, unmarried, little experience but shows potential.

The human resources director must appoint a Production Manager, Production Supervisor, and Sales Manager in Mauritius, and Sales Supervisors in the other areas. Who would you advise him to appoint outside South Africa, and which approaches to staffing would be appropriate in each case? Motivate your answer.

Related websites

This topic may be investigated further by referring to the following Internet websites:
DisneyWorld – http://www.disney.com
HR Magazine – http://www.shrm.org/docs/Hrmagazine.html
Retirement Planning Associates, Inc. – http://www.insworld.com/Newsletter/index.html
Workforce – http://www.workforceonline.com/researchcenter/

Experiential exercise

Purpose
To investigate the application of an induction programme in an organisation.

Introduction
Many companies appoint new employees and want them to become productive as soon as possible. Often the new employee's introduction to the organisation is extremely brief and he or she is taken to his or her workstation after a very basic orientation. Although not all companies follow this route, those that do, need to be convinced of the benefits of a properly organised and well-designed induction programme.

Task
Working in a group of four or five students, make contact with a medium-sized to large organisation and investigate the elements of its induction programme. Use as much of the theory in this chapter as you can, when compiling the questionnaire for your investigation. Evaluate the quality of the organisation's induction programme in terms of the theory and make any recommendations for improvement that you believe are necessary.

Chapter questions

1 'All new employees, whether permanent or part-time staff members, should attend an induction programme.' Explain why you agree or disagree with this statement.
2 You must design an orientation programme for part-time sales assistants at Woolworths. Describe the issues that would be covered by the human resources department and the issues that would be covered by the first-level supervisor. Bear in mind the target audience, essential and desirable information, and the literacy level of the employees.
3 Why would a human resources department use seniority-based promotions, and what problems might result?
4 If you were a new first-year student at your institution, what information would you want to learn in an induction or orientation programme?
5 Compare and evaluate the staffing strategies at the disposal of South African managers. Bearing in mind issues such as unemployment, skills shortages, and global competitiveness, which of these strategies do you believe is most appropriate for South Africa at the beginning of the twenty-first century?

Bibliography

ANFUSO, D. Aug 1995. Creating a culture of caring pays off. *Personnel Journal.* 74(8), 70–77.
BOASE, N. Aug 1997. Induction – introducing new employees to the organisation. *People Dynamics.* 15(8), 50.
BYARS, L.L. & RUE, L.W. 1997. *Human resource management.* 5th edition. Irwin, Chicago.
CASCIO, W.F. 1995. *Managing human resources: productivity, quality of work life, profits.* 4th edition. McGraw-Hill, New York.
CHERRINGTON, D.J. 1995. *The management of human resources.* 4th edition. Prentice-Hall, Englewood Cliffs, NJ.
DESSLER, G. 1997. *Human resources management.* 7th edition. Prentice-Hall, Upper Saddle River, NJ.
GÓMEZ-MEJÍA, L.R., BALKIN, D.B. & CARDY, R.L. 1998. *Managing human*

resources. 2nd edition. Prentice-Hall, Upper Saddle River, NJ.

KLEIN, C.S. & TAYLOR, J. May 1994. Employee orientation is an ongoing process at the DuPont Merck Pharmaceutical Co. *Personnel Journal.* 73(5), 64–67.

LAABS, J. March 2000. Mixing business with passion. Workforce. 79(3), 80–86.

RUBIS, L. April 1998. Disney show and tell. *HR Magazine.* http://www.shrm.org.

SEGAL, J. Aug. 1993. Is your employee handbook a time bomb? *HR Magazine.* http://www. shrm.org.

WERTHER, W.B. & DAVIS, K.D. 1993. *Human resources and personnel management.* 4th edition. McGraw-Hill, New York.

12

Compensation management

H B Schultz

Learning outcomes

At the end of this chapter the learner should be able to demonstrate the following outcomes:
- Discuss the objectives of a compensation system.
- Investigate the elements of total compensation and describe the rationale behind value-chain compensation.
- Explain a model for designing and implementing a new compensation system.
- Examine the steps in a job-based compensation plan.
- Debate the pay-for-knowledge-and-skills, pay-for-competencies, pay-for-performance, and incentive compensation plans.
- Provide a brief overview of the concept of broadbanding.
- Compare mandatory and voluntary benefits.
- Discuss flexible benefits plans.
- Explain how the costs of employee benefits can be calculated.
- Describe the impact of quality assurance on compensation systems.

Key words and concepts

- broadbanding
- compensation survey
- incentive pay systems
- job evaluation
- job hierarchy
- mandatory benefits
- pay for competencies
- pay for knowledge and skills
- performance-based pay
- reward systems
- total compensation
- value-chain compensation
- voluntary benefits

Illustrative case
Making money in Mauritius

'Money makes the world go round.' 'Money is the root of all evil.' 'Money, money, money, it's a rich man's world.' Whatever way you describe it, money is an important element of most people's lives. Organisations have mostly taken the viewpoint that employees are dependent on the whim of managers for their pay packets, but at George du Maurier's company 'T-Squared' in Curepipe, Mauritius, the forty-five employees decide for themselves what they want to be paid. George du Maurier is an entrepreneurial Mauritian who has a thriving T-shirt factory, catering mainly for the tourist market. He has kept his prices low, but with a quick turnover of T-shirts to the tourist hotels on the east and west coasts of Mauritius, he has seen his company grow from a staff of ten in 1992.

George was innovative from the word go. Firstly, he staffed the factory with unemployed workers and told them they could name their own salaries. If the company made a profit, he would pay every worker an equal share of 20 per cent of the profits. At first, the employees decided on far too little pay, according to George. After three months they approached him and asked for an increase. 'Of course,' said George, 'it's your decision!' They still kept their wages below the going rate, but were very happy with their share of the profits at the end of the first year. Since then, the annual profits have been equally distributed amongst the workers, who still insist on not receiving more than the market average. George has never had any labour or performance problems since the day he opened his doors.

SOURCE: Personal communication with George du Maurier, Curepipe, Mauritius, 10 January 1998.

12.1 Introduction

An organisation's payroll can involve enormous sums of money. This is a major reason why pay systems must be part of organisational business strategy. The whole subject of pay has become increasingly complex; the impressive and sometimes confusing proliferation of compensation systems and trends of the twenty-first century can have a profound effect on new job and organisational designs and employee relationships. The pay debate – that is, the argument regarding the best way of rewarding people for their services – is far from settled. Some aspects of this pay debate are covered in this chapter.

A consideration of the objectives of a compensation system begins our studies in this chapter on compensation management. We proceed to discuss the design of compensation systems with an emphasis on the concept of value-adding designs. Conventional job evaluation methods and emerging pay systems are debated, before we take a brief look at employee benefits and services in an organisation. We close the chapter with some thoughts on the influence of quality assurance on compensation systems.

12.2 The objectives of a compensation system

Organisations spend a very large proportion of their gross income on paying the people who work for them, and a large amount of this goes to the senior people who direct the business. It is an accepted fact that people must be rewarded for the services they provide to our organisations, and it is also accepted that the majority of these rewards are monetary. Every organisation must be aware that the design of its rewards system rests on the objectives of compensation management, namely what the compensation system must achieve.

The system must attract good employees by structuring salary packages that tempt people to apply for the job in the first place; it must also be able to retain such workers, because many other employers in the marketplace will be seeking their services as well. Once a person is employed, the compensation system must provide all the support needed to keep the employee motivated to perform at his or her best (McClune 1997:76).

Boase (1997:61) points out that the achievement of these objectives is influenced by several external factors:
- labour market forces;
- collective bargaining;
- legislation;
- top management's philosophy regarding pay and benefits; and
- top management's willingness to recognise individual ability and effort.

12.3 The design of a compensation system

According to Risher (1997:14–15) our wage and salary programmes have been designed to reinforce bureaucratic structures. Traditional pay systems have focused on each job in isolation, ignoring the interaction of organisational members, and buying employees' time by the hour. There have rarely been any incentives to provide for rewards above the hourly wage. The new work paradigm argues that people are the only sustainable source of competitive advantage, and they really do want to contribute to the organisation's success. Risher proposes the hypothesis that employees who work in a rewarding environment often work very hard. What he is actually saying is that when people are rewarded for old behaviours they are less likely to adopt new behaviours. The reward environment is thus the starting point for adding value to the organisation. This environment should provide the opportunities to ask questions such as:
- how does this practice benefit the organisation;
- does the benefit offset the administrative costs; and
- if we discontinued this practice, would that adversely affect the organisation's performance?

When organisations turn to the development of innovative compensation approaches, some basic caveats should be considered. Firstly, companies must not assume that the latest and most popular compensation fad is the answer to their problems; secondly, a holistic, not a piecemeal approach to implementing a new compensation design must be followed (Hackett and McDermott 1999:37). McClune (1997:98) states that whatever type of compensation design is decided upon, the concept of total compensation must always be addressed. Total compensation is the sum of all the cash items and the annual value of non-cash benefits provided to the employee. The elements of total compensation are shown in Table 12.1.

12.3.1 The elements of total compensation

Direct compensation is the fixed pay an employee receives on a regular basis, either in the form of a salary or as an hourly wage. These days, direct compensation has expanded to include cash incentives and various share offers from employers, but the defining factor of direct compensation is that it has a cash value.

Incentives are programmes designed to reward employees for good performance. They come in many forms and can be monetary or non-monetary.

Benefits encompass a wide variety of programmes such as medical aids, pension

Table 12.1 The elements of total compensation

Direct compensation	Other direct compensation	Incentives
• cash compensation	• share options	• bonuses
• basic salary	• share ownership	• profit-sharing
• deferred cash	• restricted shares	• recognition
Employee benefits	**Perquisites/fringe benefits**	
• retirement benefits	• cars	
• death benefits	• holidays	
• disability benefits	• loans	
• medical benefits	• other	
• other		

SOURCE: McClune, D. (1997:73-101).

schemes or provident funds, unemployment insurance, and many others. Perquisites, or perks, are a special category of benefits and are available only to employees with some special status, such as upper-level managers.

12.3.2 The principles of value-chain compensation

Newman and Krzystofiak (1998:60) maintain that companies must look at compensation as a value-creating function in the organisation. There are two basic principles of this compensation approach:
- value-chain compensation creates value for both the organisation and the employee; and
- it balances the four major compensation objectives of sustaining membership, motivating performance, building employee commitment, and encouraging growth in employees' skills.

A compensation system becomes value-adding when its designers take into account the employees' priorities as well. The way in which the latter rank rewards at any given time determines the basis of the compensation structure. Rewards are ranked differently at different times, for example, job security ranks highly as a reward during times of high unemployment.

According to Hale and Bailey (1998:72-77) human capital gives a company its sustainable competitive advantage. Successful companies recognise seven principles of reward strategy that lead to superior business results:
- pay for performance, and ensure that performance is tied to the successful achievement of critical business goals;
- link rewards to other levers of organisational change, such as providing recognition when deserved, offering career development, and providing challenging opportunities;
- reward measurable competencies;
- match incentives to the company culture;
- keep group incentives clear and simple;
- over-communicate the reward strategy for best results; and
- recognise employees for the work they do and the contribution they make – the greatest incentive is the work itself.

12.3.3 A model for designing and implementing a new compensation system

Figure 12.1 shows the steps required to design and implement a new compensation system.

The first step requires a thorough analysis of the present compensation structure, current remuneration policies, pay procedures, and salary problems. Thereafter, the compensation system designer formulates new salary policies, based on the business strategy of the organisation, and incorporating the value chain.

The choice of a new compensation system follows. The nature of the business and its strategic plans will influence this decision. The new system could be skills- or knowledge-based, competency-based, performance-related, variable-based incorporating incentives, or based on broadbanding. If the organisation has decided to investigate the feasibility of a new compensation system, it probably means that it has become dissatisfied with the existing one which, in many cases, would be a job-based system. The organisation must not discard this system completely, as there is always the possibility that it might still be the best system if improvements are looked at

The next step is to develop the implementation plan, working closely with remuneration experts, consulting with trade unions, and communicating with all employees. Once the new system is in place, evaluation and monitoring should be carried out on an ongoing basis.

12.4 Conventional job evaluation methods

Gómez-Mejía et al. (1998:307) state that job-based approaches to compensation assume that work gets done by people who

Figure 12.1 A model for a new compensation system

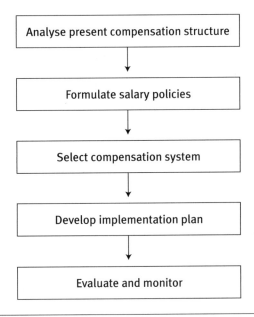

are paid to perform well-defined jobs. Because all jobs are not equally important to the organisation, and the labour market places a greater value on some jobs than others, the job-based compensation system aims to allocate pay so that the most important jobs are paid the most.

Most job-based plans follow a similar route in determining the value of jobs within the organisation, and the range in which the job should be paid. This route is depicted in Figure 12.2.

12.4.1 Conduct a job analysis

The concept of job analysis was discussed in Chapter 8, and you will recall that it includes the gathering and organisation of information concerning the tasks, duties, and responsibilities of specific jobs. In a job-based compensation system, the initial step of conducting a job analysis produces job descriptions and job specifications for the specific jobs of the organisation.

12.4.2 Identify compensable factors

Job descriptions allow the identification of factors that are deemed necessary for acceptable job performance. These factors could be certain mental processes, such as decision making, reasoning and planning, or know-how, which is the sum total of every kind of skill required to do the job. The practice of identifying compensable factors is known as job evaluation.

Job evaluation is a process of systematically analysing jobs to determine their relative worth within the organisation. This analysis is the basis of a job hierarchy and pay ranges. Job evaluation does not assess the value of the employees within a position but, rather, determines the worth of the job to the organisation. Popular job evaluation methods include job ranking, the classification method, the factor comparison method, and the point method.

The job ranking and classification methods are simple to use and do not need much prior training. They call for subjective decisions, usually with a benchmarked job as a starting point, and are often used by very small companies that do not possess the expertise to undertake more complex job evaluation methods.

Because it is impossible for one person to have a comprehensive knowledge of all jobs in an organisation, especially a large company, a job evaluation committee usually carries out the factor comparison and points methods of job evaluation. The committee members should have an adequate knowledge of all work areas in the organisation, and should have received basic training in the way that job evaluation is carried out. Job evaluation committee members typically consist of:
- a departmental head from the area in which the job to be evaluated is performed;
- a departmental head from another, neutral area in the organisation;
- a trade union representative; and
- a representative from the human resources department, who keeps the process moving forward and on track.

In some cases, an external compensation consultant may join the committee as an unbiased third party.

In South Africa, popular forms of the factor comparison and points job evaluation methods are:
- the Patterson method – based on decision making;
- the Hay method – based on factors such as know-how, problem-solving, and accountability; and
- the Peromnes method – based on the eight factors of problem solving, consequences of judgement, pressure of work, knowledge required, job impact, educational qualifications, training, and experience.

Figure 12.2 The job-based compensation plan route

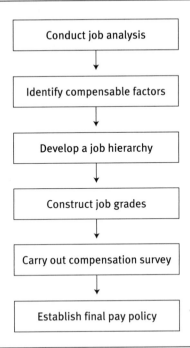

Computerised software packages have made the utilisation of these job evaluation methods much simpler and more accurate than they once were.

12.4.3 Develop a job hierarchy

Once jobs have been evaluated by means of one or other of the job evaluation methods, the value that has been established for each job allows it to be slotted into a hierarchy that will eventually paint a picture of the importance of each job to the organisation. In this way, the value of certain jobs can be compared to the value of other jobs in the organisation. A typical job hierarchy is depicted in Table 12.2.

12.4.4 Construct job grades

A job hierarchy allows an organisation to classify jobs into grades. All the jobs in a given grade are judged to be essentially the same in terms of importance and, therefore, it is logical that all the jobs in a specific grade should be paid relative to one another, and to the other jobs in the organisation. Job evaluation does not take into account the wage rates in the marketplace and organisations use compensation surveys to determine and fix pay rates to specific jobs.

12.4.5 Carry out a compensation survey

Nearly all compensation professionals use surveys to collect data for creating, adjusting, or updating a firm's pay system. Compensation surveys may be purchased from companies that specialise in collecting and interpreting pay data, outsourced to a consulting firm, or conducted by a company itself. Accurate data is extremely important

Table 12.2 A job hierarchy

General manager		
Production manager	Sales manager	Financial manager
Production supervisor	Sales supervisors	Accounts supervisors
Artisans	Sales representatives	
Machine operators	Creditors clerks	Debtors clerks
Receptionist		
Cleaners	Security assistants	

because inaccuracies can result in high labour costs and an increase in undesirable employee behaviours. Compensation surveys generally yield ranges of data for different salary grades. It must be borne in mind that this information refers to the value of the job to the specific organisation, not to the value of the person doing the job.

Werner et al. (1999:56) state that, before it is used by an organisation, the data obtained from compensation surveys should be assessed in terms of the answers to the following questions:
- How well does the survey describe the job being measured?
- If the job in the survey is a multilevel job, are all levels represented?
- What is the effective date of the data?
- What is the labour market for the job to be priced (geographic or industry-specific)?
- Who participated in the survey?
- Does the survey describe the methodology used to process the data?
- What was the methodology used to collect the data?
- How do the average, median, and twenty-fifth and seventy-fifth percentiles relate to each other?
- Does the survey provide non-weighted, as well as weighted averages?
- Do the survey participants vary significantly from year to year?

But what about gathering information for new, emerging compensation plans? McDermott (1997:57-58) maintains that none of the new approaches to compensation is neatly contained within the confines of traditional salary surveys. What is changing is the kind of data that is needed and the way in which it should be gathered. This does not merely represent a transition from one widely used means of information gathering, such as a broad-based salary survey, to another. Finding and using relevant compensation information requires different skills that encompass problem-solving, researching, and statistical analysis.

Using the traditional broad-based compensation surveys is a good starting point. However, drawing from a smaller, more focused sample of comparable companies, it is possible to glean data that includes information on the skills and abilities required in a certain job, the measures used to gauge performance in a particular position, and the relative worth of the skills and abilities. Finding new and better ways of obtaining the data to match a company's compensation approach, remains one of the biggest challenges of the new century. Organisations must rely less on broad-based annual surveys in favour of industry-specific and customised surveys geared towards a company's specific needs.

12.4.6 Establish a final pay policy

Because wages and salaries vary widely in the marketplace, a company must decide whether to take the lead, lag behind or pay the same as the majority of companies in an industry. The company's pay policy is, therefore, determined by how it chooses to position itself in the pay market. A number of factors will influence this decision, among them the wages and salaries it can afford to pay, and whether it wishes to attract above-average or mediocre workers. Those organisations that position themselves around the midpoint of wage and salary distribution are said to follow the going rate.

12.5 Emerging pay systems

Traditionally, people were paid primarily through base salaries, determined by the specific job, the need to maintain a certain level of internal pay equity, and the need to pay externally competitive salaries. Employees were not encouraged to develop skills other than those required by the job, nor were they rewarded for attributes such as flexibility, practical judgement, and the ability to work with others. While such programmes work well in functional organisations, they do little to advance many of the values of the newer work cultures.

Base pay does not motivate employees in a flatter, leaner organisation, where individual and organisational success hinges on performance and the lateral growth of the workforce (Flannery et al. 1996:83).

In many of our organisations, individuals have not changed as rapidly as have the cultures in which they are expected to work. Many employees cling to the belief that they are entitled to ever-increasing salaries, punctual and substantial raises, and luxurious benefits packages.

Old habits, however, can be broken, old behaviours changed, and old expectations replaced with more attractive new ones. The knowledge of new cultures and compensation strategies must not be the sole property of the compensation professional. Line managers must have a clear understanding of pay strategies, and the pay process must be made clear to both supervisors and employees. To be successful, pay strategies must add value to the organisation, but one must understand how they work, what values and behaviours they support, how they must be administered and communicated, and what their limitations are.

12.5.1 Pay for knowledge and skills

As employees acquire more skills, they become more flexible resources, developing a broader understanding of the work processes and of their contribution to the organisation. By rewarding the development of the new skills and knowledge needed in a value-added environment, an organisation sends a strong behavioural message to its employees: 'The world is changing quickly and you are expected to change at the same pace. But not to worry, we'll reward you for the necessary growth that change requires.' For those employees who can't, or won't learn new skills, the options are limited, unless the company tries to find new roles for displaced workers.

Various critical issues manifest themselves within a knowledge- and skill-based pay system:
- a scheme must be created for training employees and helping them develop the required new skills;
- the organisation must also address what skills and knowledge they will pay for, and the scope of development that will be rewarded; and
- the organisation must decide whether it is going to design a programme that works within a single job family, or whether it will utilise a plan that encourages true cross-training, or multiskilling.

Although skill-based and knowledge-based pay can rank and reward today's skill-driven jobs, and ultimately help change behaviour and advance performance, it is not a radical departure from current compensation practices. It is delivered in much the same manner as traditional pay systems and can transform a company into a more flexible, performance-oriented, team-driven organisation (Flannery et al. 1996:91).

12.5.2 Pay for competencies

Many organisations are discovering that they want to reward more than just the

---

Case-in-point
Safe in the arms of Armstrong

Armstrong Hydraulics, an automotive component manufacturer situated in Port Elizabeth, manufactures premium brand shock absorbers for the local as well as the export market. They are leaders in human resources strategy, moving from being one of the lowest paying companies in the sector, to one of the pioneers in hourly remuneration and job grading.

In order to attain the success that has been achieved, a paradigm shift in not only management-thinking, but in workforce perception and participation, was essential. To realise the required competitive advantage, an hourly grading system based on skills, and shrinking the number of grades from eleven to five, was critical.

The original proposal was met with distrust from both line management and the workforce; however, led by Tim Lane (now the managing director of Armstrong) acceptance was gained through a series of joint meetings between senior management and union representatives. After a day-long joint session, facilitated by a consultant from the Department of Human Resources Management at the P E Technikon, the six-month process started. A joint committee was set up to evaluate all hourly-paid jobs. The company team-feedback system was used to report on the progress of the joint evaluation committee. Weekly reports were presented to each team by the HR Manager and Chief Shop Steward. At these sessions, questions relating to evaluation issues were dealt with.

The process was not without its own unique problems. The most sensitive of these was the case of an employee's skills not measuring up to the grade or level of the previous position. Assurances were given that no individual would lose status or money. This, together with the rationale behind the system, was continually reiterated to the workforce, and the initial project was duly completed according to the agreed six-month plan.

SOURCE: Timothy Hutton, Human Resources Consultant, Armstrong Hydraulics SA (Pty) Ltd. Used with permission.

skills or knowledge necessary for a new role. Employees are needed who are not only skilled, but also energetic, service-conscious, and problem-solvers. The answer lies in the development of less obvious competencies – the ability to work in teams, to accomplish specific goals, to solve problems rapidly, and to understand the customer's perspectives and meet their needs in a way that really adds value.

Competencies are the sets of skills, knowledge, abilities, behavioural characteristics, and other attributes that predict superior performance. True competencies are those that add value and help predict success; these are the ones that should be rewarded, and this involves identifying which competencies are needed to support an organisation's strategy.

Certain problems manifest themselves when a company considers adopting a competency-based pay model. Firstly, how does one define a competency and, secondly, what competencies are appropriate in a specific organisation? Cira and Benjamin (1998:22-25) state that more than twenty-five years ago David McClelland, the renowned psychologist, defined competencies as those underlying characteristics or behaviours that excellent performers exhibit more consistently and more effectively than average performers. The actual selection of competencies depends on the nature of the business and of the job, and could include leadership, flexibility, initiative, and so on. Organisations can establish a competency model as a basis for determining competencies. These models are:
- *the core competency model*, which is used to capture the competencies required in the organisation as a whole and is often closely aligned with the organisation's mission, vision, and values;
- *the functional competency model*, which is built around key business functions, such as finance, marketing, information technology, and manufacturing;
- *the role competency model*, which applies to the specific role that the individual plays in the organisation – technician, manager, and so on; and
- *the job competency model*, which is the narrowest of the four models, only applies to a single job, and its relevance to pay applications is limited.

What sets superior performers apart from the more mediocre workers, what do the best performers do and what behavioural characteristics predict outstanding performance? Every organisation will find different answers to these questions. The decision to be made is how to find the answers. In Encounter 12.1 we read how two large American organisations handled this issue.

Competency-based pay should be implemented only as part of a broader competency-based human resources programme, and it must follow successful implementation of competency-based performance management.

12.5.3 Performance-based pay

The pay strategies described thus far focus on two primary issues critical to organisational success, namely people, and how they perform. Yet this alone does not drive the organisation forward. In searching for answers to the fundamental changes in business, organisations have rediscovered the value of variable, performance-based pay strategies.

Empowerment has followed the moving of incentive programmes beyond the executive suites, and has allowed employees to share in the organisation's risks and rewards. These pay strategies have slowly found favour, particularly in the United States, but it is extremely important that employees are told not only how the programme works, but what they must do to make it work.

> **Encounter 12.1** The Holiday Inn and LEGO Systems Inc. experience
>
> When Holiday Inn and LEGO Systems Inc. decided to implement competency-based pay systems, they took the route of using their employees to identify top performers and their competencies. They made sure that employees were trained to utilise only distinguishing competencies, that is, those competencies that not only set the best performers apart from the rest, but also add value to the results of the organisation. If this had not been done, they could have landed up paying for new behaviours, but not necessarily new results.
>
> These organisations found that tying the competencies to the base salary programme in the initial stages of the new system was the least painful way of achieving acceptance. Managers also ensured that their competency-based pay system was incorporated into the processes for selecting new employees and assessing employee performance. They realised that a 360-degree performance evaluation was the best way of assessing performance based on competencies.

SOURCE: Flannery, T.P. et al. (1996:92).

Some of the following strategies have been used in South Africa for a number of years but normally only in the domain of white-collar employees. The difference between international companies and South African companies is that our colleagues abroad are involving blue-collar workers, as well, in performance-based incentive schemes.

12.5.4 Incentive pay systems

Incentive pay systems may be either individual or group plans, and they are usually geared to measurable performance results, such as units of production, sales volume, cost savings, or profitability. A common type of individual incentive programme is the piecework plan in which the employee is paid for each unit produced. The more an employee produces, the more he or she receives. Sales commissions represent a common individual incentive, as do managerial and executive bonuses, and stock option plans. All these incentive pay systems are usually built upon a minimum base pay that remains standard no matter what the measured performance results are. Individual incentives are gaining popularity lower in the organisation, and are used to drive not only traditional financial goals, but also the more contemporary values of productivity, customer satisfaction, service, and quality.

Group incentive plans include profit-sharing, which involves all or certain groups of employees sharing in a non-deferred pool created by a percentage of the profits.

Gain-sharing is another type of group incentive and is usually tied to achievement of very specific goals for productivity, quality improvement, and cost effectiveness. A difficulty is how to measure the gains, and how to determine the role employees have played in achieving those gains (Leap and Crino 1993:424–427).

Small group incentives are often paid to specific career groups, project groups, or teams. They tend to be temporary, lasting only until the project is finished.

Long-term incentives and lump-sum payments are also used as part of variable pay programmes.

Whether the emphasis is on teams or individuals, it is clear that pay strategies, like the business strategies they support, are changing dramatically. Managers and leaders must understand five basic tenets of dynamic compensation:

- pay is first and foremost a people issue – it is about motivating them, reshaping and refocusing their behaviours and accepting new values;
- pay is a major organisational communication tool;
- no single pay strategy is right for everyone – even different employee groups in the same organisation may require different strategies;
- pay must support, not lead, the organisation's vision, values, and business strategies; and
- to achieve the first four points, pay must be aligned with the organisation's work cultures.

Taking the step to change a company's compensation strategies is not an overnight decision. What strategies have international companies selected and what is the success factor? Two examples of American companies that changed their compensation policies are offered in Encounter 12.2.

12.6 Broadbanding

If an organisation has reduced staff and cut management levels it must look for new ways to move people through the organisation. Tom Peters (1993:47) says, 'There's

---

Encounter 12.2 Whirlpool and Owens-Corning re-route their pay structures

Whirlpool Corporation, one of the world's largest automatic washer manufacturers, opted to institute a performance-based compensation system. The cornerstone of their gain-sharing programme is an approach that provides workers, especially those on the line, with the incentives and motivation to treat their work as if they're an owner of the company. Whirlpool places the money from all cost savings, business improvements and productivity gains into a fund for each specific facility, and workers receive a quarterly payout for their efforts.

Total cost savings for the company's Ohio plant recently measured $36.4 million, with payouts of $19.2 million. Managers say that employees are more knowledgeable, there is greater cooperation and involvement, and financial and quality-control benchmarks have reached all-time highs. The programme has helped narrow the culture gap between hourly and salaried employees, and payouts have alleviated pressure for base-wage increases.

Owens-Corning, a construction material manufacturer, scrapped its existing compensation and benefits programmes, and created a variable compensation and flexible benefits programme that is tied to performance.

Their *Rewards and Resources* programme is linked to company performance. Base rewards, such as salary and variable rewards, depend on performance. Resources incorporate a global stock plan, where each employee receives an annual bonus in stock; savings and profit-sharing; a cash balance plan which converts retirement benefits to an opening cash balance; and choice making, the handing over of benefits choices to individuals to encourage employee ownership and decision making.

SOURCES: Greengard, S. (1995:100) and Solomon, C.M. (1998:78–81).

not much of a pyramid left to climb. So how will people get their kicks – their bucks, their psychic compensation?'

Even the few organisations that remain fatter rather than flatter are adopting new organisational values and changing cultures. Their traditional pay strategies and delivery systems have become obsolete. The vertical system of grading is out of synch with the flatter, flexible, team-orientated cultures that many organisations are moving toward. To counter this misalignment, some are adopting the strategy known as broadbanding, in which a few relatively broad bands replace numerous grades.

Broadbanding is not another pay-for-strategy. It is a new pay platform on which a compensation strategy, such as skill- or competency-based pay, can be built and effectively operated.

Rather than climbing up through a series of grades, employees might spend most, if not all of their careers in a single band, moving laterally and getting more pay as they gain new skills, competencies, or responsibilities, or as they improve their performance. Unlike traditional pay grades, bands can be designed to overlap, adding flexibility to an already flexible pay programme. This overlap allows employees to continue to progress within the organisation without the elevation to another pay range or job title.

Broadbanding can be especially useful in the new 'boundaryless' organisations and in those team-based organisations that emphasise less specialised jobs and processes that cross departments, requiring more skills and individual or team authority. It also facilitates the growth and development of alternate career tracks.

Collapsing the old grading system without first changing the organisational culture, or deciding how people will move through the bands can only lead to failure in a broadbanding system. However, it can be very effective when tailored to an organisation's individual culture, values, and business strategy (Flannery et al. 1996:99).

12.7 Employee benefits

Employee benefits are items in the total package offered to employees over and above salary, which increase their wealth or well-being at some cost to the employer. Benefits can frequently add up to around one third of payroll costs. Items such as pensions, sick pay, holidays, and a range of other benefits are an integral part of every employer's conditions of employment.

Many benefits are interdependent, and an effective benefits policy generally relies on careful evaluation of the pattern and balance of benefit entitlements throughout the organisation. Many of the problems that arise over benefits occur because the effect of new or improved benefits on employee attitudes has not been properly assessed. Many benefits are linked with status and this can often be the source of discontent. No organisation should have to waste valuable time sorting out problems of this nature, which can usually be prevented by careful benefits policy planning and effective and detailed communication of entitlements to employees (Armstrong and Murlis 1994:140).

12.7.1 Types of benefit

Some employee benefits and services are regulated by the government, and employers are compelled to make these benefits available to their employees. These are called mandatory benefits. Other benefits are offered to the employees voluntarily.

12.7.1.1 Mandatory benefits

Unemployment insurance

The Unemployment Insurance Act No. 30 of 1966 makes provision for the establishment of a central fund to be utilised for the payment of unemployment, maternity, death, and sickness benefits. The fund makes provision for the insurance of employees contributing to the fund against the risk of loss of income through the termination of their services, illness, or pregnancy. In addition, provision is made for the payment of benefits to dependants of deceased contributors. The main purpose of the fund is to insure contributors against temporary loss of employment, and not to provide for those who leave the labour market.

Compensation for injuries and diseases

The Compensation for Occupational Injuries and Diseases Act, No. 130 of 1993, regulates the payment of compensation to persons who are injured or who contract a disease during the execution of their duties. All persons who employ one or more employees are required to register and to pay annual assessments to the Compensation Fund. The revenue of this Fund comprises mainly the annual assessments paid by the registered employers. Employees do not contribute to the Fund.

12.7.1.2 Voluntary benefits

Employees can rely on a number of benefits, which are non-mandatory or voluntary on the part of the employer. It should be noted, however, that some of the benefits discussed below do have a certain legislated minimum, such as the number of days vacation leave, the number of paid public holidays, the number of days sick leave, and maternity leave benefits. In South Africa, these minima are legislated in the Basic Conditions of Employment Act.

Vacation leave

Vacation leave serves primarily to improve employees' health, personal development and morale. Most companies offer their employees vacation leave with pay after a set minimum period of service, usually one year. Employees are entitled to three weeks fully-paid leave after every twelve months of continuous employment.

Paid public holidays

South Africans currently enjoy twelve paid public holidays per year as follows:

New Years Day	1 January
Human Rights Day	21 March
Good Friday	
Family Day	
Freedom Day	27 April
Workers' Day	1 May
Youth Day	16 June
National Women's Day	9 August
Heritage Day	24 September
Day of Reconciliation	16 December
Christmas Day	25 December
Day of Goodwill	26 December

Whenever one of the above public holidays falls on a Sunday, the following Monday is proclaimed a public holiday.

Time for personal matters

Employees may receive full pay for a number of personal absences, such as sorting out business matters, attending funerals, dental appointments, and weddings.

Sick-leave

The number of days sick-leave to which an employee is entitled depends on company policy regarding seniority and period of service. The minimum entitlement is six weeks paid sick-leave for every thirty-six months of continuous employment.

Maternity leave

Under the Basic Conditions of Employment Bill Act, a pregnant employee is entitled to four months maternity leave, which may be taken on full, partial, or no pay, according to the rules and regulations laid down by, or negotiated with, the company. It must be noted that where there is only partial, or no pay, the Unemployment Insurance Fund makes up the difference to an amount of 45 per cent of the worker's rate of pay, provided that certain requirements have been met.

Health and life insurance

Many employers provide insurance benefits as part of a group life insurance plan, which covers employees while they are in the employ of the company. Group life insurance allows the company and the employee to benefit from lower premium rates, and this insurance is often subsidised or paid in full by the employer. Such insurance also covers episodes such as trauma experienced due to a life-threatening disease, disability of the employee, and death of a spouse.

Medical aid schemes

Medical aid schemes are highly valued by employees because they provide medical coverage for both themselves and their dependants; this is especially so with the high cost of medical care in South Africa, and the perception that services at state-run hospitals and clinics leave a lot to be desired. Basic medical plans usually make provision for a restricted number of hospital, surgical, and medical services, or offer full services with a percentage levy paid by members, while general plans provide for the full cost of prolonged treatment for more serious conditions. Some organisations in South Africa also make provision for funding towards the costs of consulting traditional healers.

Pension funds

Although company pension funds have been around since the 1950s, many organisations have never taken the time to impress upon their employees the importance of managing their investment in retirement. As people have moved from one company to another they have drawn their pension contributions and then started contributing to a new fund as they enter new employment. If this trend continues throughout a person's working life, it is obvious that the provision for retirement will be totally inadequate. Moreover, since the notion of permanent employment for long periods of time in one company is becoming globally outdated, this trend towards spending retirement funds is likely to continue unless organisations take it upon themselves to do a great deal more counselling, or unless some kind of legislation is passed.

Be that as it may, most organisations provide a pension or provident fund, to which employees contribute a percentage of their wages, a portion of which is usually subsidised by the employer. There is usually a waiting period before an employee can join a pension fund, after which membership is compulsory.

Employee services

Employee services include the provision of various facilities that are non-mandatory but offered by employers because these additional services to employees are thought to have a positive impact on employee loyalty, and to decrease absenteeism and turnover. These services include cafeteria facilities, relocation expenses, social and recreational facilities, financial and legal services, educational facilities, child care programmes, transportation programmes, and housing subsidies or allowances.

12.8 Benefits planning

Research shows that employees prefer employee benefits that reflect the dynamic labour market. More that 75 per cent of all workers prefer health benefits; young workers state a second preference for a savings plan, older workers for a pension. The vast majority of all workers state a preference for the ability to make choices in order to shape the benefits package to their special needs (Salisbury 1997:74–75). In the past, most large private employers adopted a paternalistic approach in managing employee benefits. Today, although the tendency in bureaucratic-style organisations is still to dictate the terms of benefits packages, employers are starting to realise that the new deal in the employer-employee relationship demands much more flexibility. Table 12.3 suggests a framework for comprehensive benefit planning.

Dessler (1997:530) states that the terms 'flexible benefits plan' and 'cafeteria benefits plan' are generally used synonymously. The idea of cafeteria benefits allows the employee to put together his or her own benefits package, subject to two constraints: the employers must limit the total cost of each benefits package; and each benefits plan must include certain non-optional items, such as the mandatory benefits mentioned above. The philosophy behind flexible benefits plans is that no-one knows the employee's needs better than the employee; and as his or her needs change through the years, so can the benefits be altered. Software packages are available to assist employees in making wise choices under a flexible benefits programme. The advantages and disadvantages of flexible benefits programmes are summarised in Table 12.4.

Table 12.3 A framework for comprehensive benefit planning

1. Establish objectives.
2. Collect complete descriptive data on the current workforce.
3. Determine how much money is available in the budget.
4. Determine what programmes fit your objectives, your workforce, and your budget.
5. Determine what your employees need and want.
6. Decide what you will provide and what you will actually spend in total.
7. Determine options and costs of administration, management, and communication.
8. Plan how the above will be accomplished.
9. Implement all the above.

SOURCE: Salisbury, D.L. (1997:74–80).

Table 12.4 Advantages and disadvantages of flexible benefits programmes

Advantages
- The company can set the sum total of benefits for each employee.
- The changing needs of the workforce are catered for.
- Employees take ownership of their choice of benefits by satisfying their own unique needs.
- It is less costly for the organisation when an employee adds a new benefit.

Disadvantages
- Without proper assistance, employees can make bad choices and find themselves not covered for emergencies.
- Company administrative costs increase.
- The cost of some benefits may increase as a result of a majority of employees choosing the benefit.

The assessment of proposed additions or improvements to benefits provisions usually depends on the following factors:
- legal implications;
- tax implications;
- value to the individual in relation to cost to the organisation;
- the incidence of similar arrangements among competitors;
- employee demand for the benefit in question, either informally or by negotiation;
- whether the introduction of the benefit ahead of demand would earn valuable employee goodwill; and
- the extent to which it is appropriate and acceptable to limit entitlements to particular employee categories.

12.9 Calculating the costs of employee benefits

Gerber et al. (1992:477) offer four bases on which employers can calculate the costs of benefits and services, namely:
- total annual costs of benefits for all employees;
- costs of benefits per employee per annum (total costs divided by number of employees);
- percentage of the payroll (total costs of benefits divided by annual wages); and
- costs per employee per hour (costs per employee per annum divided by number of hours worked).

It is important to note that when management make certain decisions in respect of incurring costs for benefits and services, they have to take into account the following considerations:
- there is little evidence that benefits and services really encourage improved performance, or increase employees' job satisfaction;
- costs of employee benefits and services have increased dramatically;
- employers are required by law to introduce certain programmes; and
- so-called voluntary programmes are constantly under pressure from labour unions, competitors, and the industry to improve on employee benefits and services.

Calculating the costs of the benefits and services the company offers to its employees allows management to decide which benefits strategy the company will follow:
- the pacesetter strategy, which means that the organisation is the first to introduce the benefits employees want;
- the comparable benefits strategy, which means that the organisation puts its benefits on a par with those offered by similar organisations; or
- the minimum benefits strategy, which means that the organisation offers only those benefits required by law and demanded by employees.

12.10 Compensation systems and quality assurance

According to Boase (1997:61) certain future trends are likely to manifest themselves in South Africa:
- compensation practices will shift towards base rates with top-up incentives based on performance, such as gain-share and profit-share;
- increased flexibility will become evident in remuneration packages;
- remuneration packages will become more tax-effective; and
- remuneration will be linked to teams, rather than to individuals.

The whole question of whether an organisation's compensation plan is adequate or not, depends on the quality of compensation planning, design, and implementation. The external customers of the company are the ultimate winners in this game; well-designed benefits inspire motivated employees who, in turn, contribute towards the satisfaction of the customer.

12.11 Conclusion

Whatever the future holds in store for the way people are remunerated in an organisation, one thing which appears certain is that effective, well-motivated and appropriately rewarded employees are pivotal to a successful business. The technicalities of a compensation system are important because pay determination creates the climate of trust that is essential to building a sense of fairness and equity. Without this, it is difficult to see how a performance management system could be maintained.

Summary

The compensation system must attract good employees, it must also be able to retain good workers, and it must provide all the support needed to keep the employee motivated to perform at his or her best.

The reward environment is the starting point for adding value to the organisation. A holistic approach to implementing a new compensation design must be followed. Total compensation is the sum of all the cash items and the annual value of non-cash benefits provided to the employee.

Direct compensation is the fixed pay an employee receives on a regular basis, either in the form of a salary or as an hourly wage. Incentives are programmes designed to reward employees for good performance. Benefits encompass a wide variety of programmes such as medical aids, pension schemes or provident funds, unemployment insurance, and many others.

Value-chain compensation creates value for both the organisation and the employee, and balances the four major compensation objectives of sustaining membership, motivating performance, building employee commitment, and encouraging growth in employees' skills.

Seven principles of reward strategy lead to superior business results. A new compensation system could be skills- or knowledge-based, competency-based, performance-related, and variable-based incorporating incentives, and broadbanding could be used as a pay base. Job-based compensation systems aim to allocate pay so that the most important jobs are paid the most. Most job-based systems determine the value of jobs within the organisation, and the range in which the job should be paid.

Pay strategies must add value to the organisation, but one must understand how they work, what values and behaviours they support, how they must be administered and communicated, and what their limitations are. Emerging pay trends include pay for knowledge and skills, pay for competencies, performance-based pay and incentive pay systems. Broadbanding is not another pay-for-strategy. It is a new pay platform on which a compensation strategy such as skill- or competency-based pay can be built and effectively operated.

Employee benefits are items in the total package offered to employees, over and above salary, which increase their wealth or well-being at some cost to the employer. Mandatory benefits are regulated by the government and other benefits are offered voluntarily by employers. A cafeteria benefits plan allows the employee to put together his or her own benefits package.

There are four bases on which employers can calculate the costs of benefits and services: the total annual costs, costs of benefits per employee per annum, percentage of the payroll, and costs per employee per hour. Benefits strategies include the pacesetter strategy, the comparable benefits strategy, and the minimum benefits strategy.

Related websites

This topic may be investigated further by referring to the following Internet websites:
American Compensation Association – http//www.acaonline.org
Benefits Link – http://www.ifebp.org
Equity Compensation Strategies – http://www.fed.org/library.html
Retirement Planning Associates, Inc. – http://www.insworld.com/Newsletter/index.html
Kryslyn Corporation – http://www.krislyn.com/sites/hr/htm
Benefits and Compensation Solutions Magazine Online - http://www.bcsolutionsmag.com

Case study
More than exhaust fumes at Durapipe

Durapipe (Pty.) Ltd. is a 25-year-old company in Pietermaritzburg producing exhaust systems for motor vehicles and motor cycles. The firm was started by the three Rawlins brothers in a small garage and now has eighty employees. The firm's market share has expanded rapidly during the last five years, but in recent times certain problems have become evident. The Rawlins brothers, who are still directors of the company, feel that the organisation is losing its entrepreneurial spirit and that workers are not as enthusiastic as they once were. Low employee morale and commitment have become significant obstacles to the firm's continued success.

The directors realise that the firm is regarded as too bureaucratic, with many systems that were developed and implemented in the mid 1970s, when they first opened their doors, still in place. In particular, the compensation system is regarded as being out-dated and non-motivating. The pay system is an adaptation of the Patterson evaluation system, based on decision-making in the company. A new structure is envisaged as follows:

Level 3: Directors and Management.

Level 2: Supervisors, Foremen, and Artisans.

Level 1: Machine operators, Welders, Artisans' Assistants, Clerical staff, Sales Representatives and Cleaners.

The employee profile is as follows:
Level 3: highly experienced, mainly with tertiary qualifications;
Level 2: skilled workers; and
Level 1: semiskilled and unskilled workers.

Write a report in which you recommend a new pay system for Durapipe, based on the envisaged new organisational structure, and incorporating all you have learnt from this chapter.

Experiential exercise 1

Purpose
To show that benefits planning depends on the age, length of service, status in the company, and family needs of the employee.

Introduction
Many research studies have indicated that the use of flexible benefits plans will increase greatly in the near future. Flexible benefits plans allow employees to decide for themselves exactly which benefits are most appropriate for them, within the parameters laid down by their company. It is generally agreed however, that employees, particularly those with less education, need assistance and counselling from the organisation when making their benefits choices.

Task
Assume that you fit the profile of each of the following employees. Compile a flexible benefits plan that indicates the specific benefits you would choose in each case.
- Married male, 55 years of age, 20 years in the company, no dependant children.
- Single female, 28 years of age, 2 years in the company, 2 dependant children.
- Unmarried male, 22 years of age, no dependants, just started work.
- Unmarried female, 25 years of age, parents are pensioners, 6 years in the company, no other dependants.
- Married male, 40 years of age, 10 years in the company, 3 school-going children.

Chapter questions

1 You have been asked to evaluate whether your organisation's current pay structure competes with the pay structures of similar organisations. How would you go about conducting this comparison and what criteria would you use to determine if your data is valid and reliable?

2 The decision-makers in your organisation have agreed that the company is too bureaucratic and has too many layers of jobs to compete effectively. The company has decided to flatten the structure to not more than five levels, and you have been asked to suggest innovative alternatives to the traditional 'job-based' approach to employee compensation. Discuss and compare your suggestions in detail.

3 New legislation has allowed a number of multimillion rand casino complexes to be developed in South Africa. In Gauteng Carnival City and Caesar's Palace recently opened. In Cape Town and Port Elizabeth new casino complexes will be

opened by the end of 2000. Using the model for a new compensation system in Figure 12.1, make brief recommendations in terms of each step of the model regarding the compensation system you think would be most appropriate for the staff of a casino complex.

4 Most companies insist that their permanent employees belong to the various benefit funds such as medical schemes, pension funds, and group life assurance funds. Do you think this is a violation of human rights? Should employees be given the opportunity to decide for themselves if they wish to make use of the benefits plan? How would a company ensure that employees do not lose on their total remuneration package if they are allowed to refuse the benefits?

5 Although there are innovative pay systems available, many organisations believe that the traditional job-based pay system is still the best choice. Discuss the job-based compensation model and indicate which type of organisational structure it would match the best.

Bibliography

ARMSTRONG, M. & MURLIS, H. 1994. *A handbook of salary administration.* 2nd edition. Kogan Page, London.

BOASE. Sep 1997. Strategising the remuneration policy. *People Dynamics.* 15(9), 61.

CIRA, D.J. & BENJAMIN, E.R. Sept/Oct 1998. Competency-based pay: a concept in evolution. *Compensation and Benefits Review.* 30(5), 21–28.

DESSLER, G. 1997. *Human resource management.* 7th edition. Prentice-Hall, Upper Saddle River, NJ.

FLANNERY, T.P., HOFRICHTER, D.A. & PLATTEN, P.E. 1996. *People, performance, and pay: dynamic compensation for changing organizations.* The Free Press, New York.

GERBER, P.D., NEL, P.S. & VAN DYK, P.S. 1992. *Human resources management.* 2nd edition. Southern, Halfway House.

GÓMEZ-MEJÍA, L.R., BALKIN, D.B., & CARDY, R.L. 1998. *Managing human resources.* 2nd edition. Prentice-Hall, Upper Saddle River, NJ.

GREENGARD, S. 1995. Whirlpool build a performance-based strategy. *Personnel Journal.* 74(1), 100.

HACKETT, T.J. & MCDERMOTT, D.G. Sept/Oct 1999. Integrating compensation strategies: a holistic approach to compensation design. *Compensation and Benefits Review.* 31 (5), 36–43.

HALE, J. & BAILEY, G. July/Aug 1998. Seven dimensions of successful reward plans. *Compensation and Benefits Review.* 30(4), 71–77.

LEAP, T.L. & CRINO, M.D. 1993. Personnel/human resource management. 2nd edition. MacMillan, New York.

MCCLUNE, D. 1997. Managing reward strategy. In Tyson, S. (ed.). *The practice of human resource strategy.* 73–101. Pitman, London.

MCDERMOTT, D.G. Mar/Apr 1997. Gathering information for the new age of compensation. *Compensation and Benefits Review.* 29 (2), 57–63.

NEWMAN, J.M. & KRYSTOFIAK, F.J. May/June 1998. Value-chain compensation. *Compensation and Benefits Review.* 30(3), 60–66.

RISHER, H. Jan/Feb 1997. The end of jobs: planning and managing rewards in the new work paradigm. *Compensation and Benefits Review.* 29 (1), 13-17.

SALISBURY, D.L. Jan/Feb 1997. Benefit planning and management in a changing, dynamic labor market. *Compensation and Benefits Review.* 29(1), 74–80.

SOLOMON, C.M. 1998. Owens-Corning: Optimas ® Award Profile. Workforce. 77(2), 78–81.

WERNER, S., KONOPASKE, R. & TOUHEY, C. May/June 1999. Ten questions to ask yourself about compensation surveys. *Compensation and Benefits Review.* 31(3), 54–59.

13

Health and safety management

H B Schultz

Learning outcomes

At the end of this chapter the learner should be able to demonstrate the following outcomes:
- Explain the job and personal stress factors that can have a detrimental effect on an employee.
- Discuss the concept of burnout and differentiate between burnout and workaholism.
- Provide an overview of ways in which the employee and other organisational role-players can reduce job stress.
- Investigate the idea of spirituality in the workplace.
- Describe various programmes to which employers can subscribe in order to provide a holistic approach to health care.
- Investigate the causes of accidents in the workplace.
- Discuss ways in which unsafe acts can be reduced.
- Develop and explain a diagram that indicates how accidents are caused and how they can be avoided.
- Offer a brief overview of the legal requirements in health and safety management.
- Examine the work of the National Occupational Safety Association (NOSA).
- Discuss the impact of health and safety issues on quality assurance.

Key words and concepts

- burnout
- Employee assistance programmes (EAPs)
- HIV/AIDS
- holistic health care
- job stress
- karoshi
- NOSA
- Occupational Health and Safety Act
- smoking policy

- spirituality
- substance abuse
- unsafe conditions and unsafe acts
- wellness
- work overload and work underload
- workaholism

Illustrative case
Meltdown!

The explosion at the Chernobyl nuclear power station in the former USSR on Saturday 26 April 1986 was undoubtedly the world's greatest nuclear accident. At 01:00 on 25 April, the day before the disaster, the reactor was running at full power with normal operation. Slowly the operators began to reduce power in preparation for a test to observe the dynamics of the reactor with limited power flow.

Twelve hours after power reduction was initiated the reactor reached 50 per cent power. Under normal circumstances the reactor would have been reduced to 30 per cent power, but the Soviet electricity authorities refused to allow this because of an apparent need for electricity elsewhere, so the reactor remained at 50 per cent power for another nine hours. At 00:28 on 26 April the Chernobyl staff received permission to resume the reactor power reduction. One of the operators made a mistake. Instead of keeping power at 30 per cent, he forgot to reset a controller, which caused the power to plummet to 1 per cent.

Between 01:00 and 01:20 the operator forced the reactor up to 7 per cent. This was a violation of procedure and the reactor was not built to operate at such low power. The reactor was becoming increasingly unstable, but the operator disabled emergency shutdown procedures, because a shutdown would have aborted the test. At 01:23:44 disaster-point was reached when all the radioactive fuel disintegrated, and pressure from the excess steam, which was supposed to go to the turbines, broke every one of the pressure tubes and blew off the entire top shield of the reactor.

About thirty fires had to be extinguished, and when radiation levels began to reach extreme highs, the order was given to evacuate cities, towns, and villages near the damaged reactor. Radioactive particles had to be cleaned from buildings and roads, and a concrete and steel coffin was constructed around the radioactive reactor to prevent further contamination of the environment. The explosion at Chernobyl acted like a volcano, blowing radioactive particles far into the sky. Wind moved the cloud of particles all around the world; as the cloud passed several countries, it began to rain, and nuclear fallout hit the ground. Nearly fifteen years after the accident, many who survived the explosion are still suffering from the effects of radiation and manifesting symptoms of cancer and physical abnormalities.

Today, the area around Chernobyl is a wasteland, still highly radioactive, devoid of humans and animals, while children born from parents exposed to high radiation levels have frightening deformities. Were the operators of Reactor No. 4 over-confident in making decisions? Was the design of the Chernobyl RBMK-type reactor faulty? Why were the safety systems inadequate, and why weren't they implemented at the time of the accident? Was it human error, ignorance, or blatant disregard of safety procedures that caused this disaster?

SOURCE: http://www.osha.com

13.1 Introduction

Stress means different things to different people. Feeling tense, anxious, or worried are all manifestations of the stress experience. Most people can endure short periods of stress without serious consequences. However, when this acute type of stress becomes chronic or long-duration stress, the consequences can be devastating. Managing stress is only one aspect of the entire spectrum of health considerations in an organisation. The maintenance of good physical health standards in the workforce is of the utmost importance.

Safety issues are also critical from the point of view of both the employee and the employer. The employee has a right to expect a work environment that is free of unnecessary hazards, and the employer has the right to expect the employee to maintain a safe working area.

This chapter commences with a discussion on job and personal stress factors, including references to the modern phenomena of burnout and workaholism. Some thoughts are presented on the reduction of job stress and on the idea of spirituality in the organisation. Organisational health care programmes are investigated before the discussion proceeds to the causes of accidents and ways in which they can be reduced. Health and safety legislation in South Africa is examined briefly and an opinion is offered on the impact of health and safety programmes on quality assurance.

13.2 Job and personal stress

Job-related stress factors can put an employee under such stress that a pathological reaction occurs. Cherrington (1997: 640) states that the two main sources of job stress are environmental and personal.

13.2.1 Environmental stress factors

Environmental stress factors are external and include work schedules, revised work procedures, new workplace facilities, pace of work, job security, route to and from work, and the number and nature of customers or clients. A number of other environmental stress factors are discussed below.

Work overload and work underload

Schultz and Schultz (1994:413) indicate that both work overload and work underload can lead to a stressful condition.

Quantitative overload involves having too much work to do in the time available, and has been associated with stress-related ailments such as heart disease. It appears that the key factor is the degree of control workers have over the rate at which they work, rather than the amount of work they are required to do. Qualitative overload involves work that is too difficult. Many employees have found themselves in a position of having insufficient ability to perform a job. The threat of discipline and embarrassment caused by inability to perform, can lead to a high degree of stress.

Work underload, or having work that is too simple or insufficient to fill one's time and challenge one's abilities, is stressful and demotivating. A lack of stimulation leads to boredom, and can also result in mental health problems. This discussion suggests that somewhere between underload and overload an area of optimal stress must exist – an area where workers should be able to perform at their peak. Figure 13.1 represents this assumption on an underload-overload continuum.

Change

Change can be exciting and challenging to some workers while others view change as a threat. Those who see change as a chal-

Figure 13.1 The underload-overload continuum

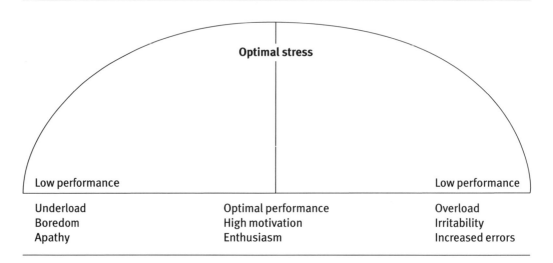

Low performance		Low performance
Underload	Optimal performance	Overload
Boredom	High motivation	Irritability
Apathy	Enthusiasm	Increased errors

lenge are less vulnerable to the consequences of stress, but those who resist change succumb more easily to stress because they prefer familiar situations where they know what to expect.

The changing mix of the workforce

Many older workers find the growing number of younger workers, more females (and female managers), and a culture of transformation and diversity stressful. In South Africa this is a particular problem amongst older white male workers.

Organisational requirements

The twenty-first century demands that workers take up new roles in the organisation. Changing structures lead to role ambiguity and role conflict as employees grapple to come to terms with the multi-skilling requirements of a learning organisation. Problems of career development, taking responsibility for subordinates, uncomfortable physical working conditions, and repetitive pacing of work all contribute to rising stress levels. Even rapid advances in technology have not succeeded in diminishing organisational stress – everyone has experienced the consequences of computers going off-line.

13.2.2 Personal stress factors

No two people react to the same job in the same way, because personal factors also influence stress. Type A personalities, who feel driven to always be on time and meet deadlines, often place themselves under greater stress than do others. Tolerance of ambiguity, patience, self-esteem, health and exercise, and work and sleep patterns also affect a person's reaction to stress. Non-job problems, such as financial troubles, divorce, and sickness intensify the susceptibility to stress.

13.2.3 Consequences of stress

Stress is not necessarily dysfunctional. A modest amount of stress may encourage a person to perform better, especially when working towards a deadline; it may lead to more creativity in a competitive situation and generate new ideas as a matter of necessity. However, when stress turns into distress it leads to negative consequences.

Psychological consequences of stress include anxiety, depression, and anger. Physical consequences can manifest themselves as cardiovascular disease, headaches, accidents, drug abuse, eating disorders, and poor interpersonal relations.

Organisational consequences of stress include reduction in the quality and quantity of job performance, increased absenteeism and turnover, increased disciplinary offences, and grievances (Dessler 1997: 640).

13.3 Burnout

Dessler (1997:642) defines burnout as the total exhaustion of physical and mental resources as a result of excessive striving to reach an unrealistic work-related goal, combined with an overload of job stress. According to Dessler, people are showing the signs of burnout when they:
- are unable to relax, emotionally exhausted, and bored;
- are less energetic and less interested in their jobs;
- identify so closely with their activities that when these fall apart they do too;
- feel that positions they worked so hard to attain are meaningless;
- are doing more work, but enjoying it less;
- are constantly irritable, apathetic, and depressed; and
- strive to achieve work-related goals, but exclude almost all outside interests.

13.3.1 The victims of burnout

Persons who are prone to burnout include those who are over-dedicated to achieving their goals. They don't lead well-balanced lives, often casting aside family and social involvement because they are so focused and intent on their work performance. It is not only executives who suffer from burnout. Workers at lower levels in the hierarchy, and even social-work counsellors are often burnout victims.

Victims of burnout can do a number of things to relieve a potential burnout situation:
- they can break their patterns by trying a variety of new activities, instead of doing the same things over and over;
- they should make time for occasional periods of reflection, preferably alone, in order to gain a perspective on the direction their lives are taking;
- they should reassess their goals in terms of whether they are really worth the sacrifices that are being made;
- they must consider whether they could perform as efficiently if they allowed time for the pursuit of outside interests; and
- they must reduce stress by organising time effectively, building better relationships, developing realistic deadlines, and making time for relaxation.

The problem of burnout has reached considerable proportions in Japan, where 'sudden death from overwork' is reported to be on the increase. This phenomenon of the late twentieth century is discussed in Encounter 13.1.

13.3.2 Workaholism

Workaholism is sometimes confused with burnout, although there is a subtle difference between the two concepts. Not all workaholics are driven by anxiety and insecurity to perform well. Very often, workaholics are happy, well-adjusted, and committed people who enjoy the satisfaction derived from putting more into their jobs than is required. They are likely to have supportive families and are able to balance the demands of their jobs with the demands of society.

Encounter 13.1 The fear of karoshi

The fabled workaholism of Japanese white-collar workers has taken its toll, as the Fukoku Life Insurance Co. reports. In 1993 surveys revealed that 43 per cent of 500 employees with more than fifteen years' work experience at the same companies in metropolitan Tokyo feared karoshi – death from overwork. Fierce competition among employees, as well as a strong sense of responsibility to their companies, leads many workers to stay at the office well into the night and to refuse to take all their vacation time.

Tetsuya Yonemori reports that karoshi is a new word in the Japanese language. It symbolises Japan's workaholic society, and is most often used in actions for compensation, especially in the case of cardiovascular disease brought on by extreme work and stresses from work. The Japanese government does not keep statistics on karoshi per se, but a survey by the Asahi Shimbun newspaper found that the Ministry of Labour recognised 196 cases of stress-related deaths due to overwork between 1987 and 1994. The National Defence Council for Victims of Karoshi argues that the figures are rather higher than that. In 1993, in its World Labor Report, the International Labor Organization (ILO) addressed the problem of karoshi for the first time. The report tabled the following comments:

- Japanese employees work longer hours than those in most industrial nations, much of which is unpaid 'service overtime';
- most karoshi victims are believed to have logged more than 3 000 hours a year on the job – roughly twice the annual working hours of people in France, Germany, and Sweden;
- the average Japanese businessperson takes only half of his or her paid holidays;
- ostensibly this is because he or she does not want to inconvenience fellow workers, and would like to save up a bit of a cushion in case of illness;
- the real reason is that people who use all their holiday allowance are seen as less committed to their jobs when personnel reviews are made; and
- in 1999 the total number of workers surveyed who fear karoshi had risen to 48 percent.

There are signs, however, that things may be changing. Some of Japan's leading firms, such as the Sony Corporation, have begun to insist that employees take vacations, whether they want to or not. More companies are closing on Saturdays, part of a national drive toward a five-day week. Traditions die hard in Japan, however, and no one believes fear of karoshi will disappear.

SOURCE: Yonemori, T. (1999).

13.4 Mechanisms for stress reduction

Berry (1998:442) states that although some stressors can be removed, it is not likely that we will ever live in a stress-free world. The results of uncontrolled stress are serious and costly to the individual and the organisation. It is therefore necessary that we learn how to cope effectively with the stress we experience. Ivancevich and Matteson (1999:277) agree that stress management seeks ways of coping with stress, while stress prevention focuses on controlling or eliminating stressors.

13.4.1 Reducing job stress

Making use of personal and organisational interventions can alleviate job stress. Simple common sense remedies, such as getting more sleep, improving one's eating habits, using relaxation techniques, changing one's job, getting counselling, and planning and organising daily activities all contribute to the reduction of stress. In the organisation, human resources specialists and supervisors can also play a role in identifying and monitoring symptoms of stress. The human resources professional can make use of attitude surveys to identify organisational sources of stress, ensure an effective person-job match in the selection and career-planning processes, and together with supervisors, can recommend job transfers or counselling (Cherrington 1997:649).

Research suggests that gender-related issues such as the threat of sexual harassment and the 'glass ceiling' phenomenon are distinct stressors for women. Although there is no general remedy for relieving stress caused by the threat of sexual harassment, certain factors can contribute towards achieving a balanced job state. The amount of control an employee has in the job, and the opportunity to discuss anxieties with managers without fear of victimisation assist in managing workplace stress.

In the first reported case of sexual harassment, the South African Industrial Court stated that an employer has a duty to ensure that employees are not subjected to sexual harassment within the workplace. There is no common ground for a definition of sexual harassment. Some perceive subtle, unwelcome sexual attention as harassment; for others, it is suggestive remarks, blackmail (such as promotion as a reward for sexual favours), or violent behaviour (such as attempted or actual rape). Sexual harassment can take several forms such as verbal, non-verbal, visual, and physical gestures (Boase 1996:88).

13.4.2. Spirituality in the workplace

'Spirituality at work' attempts to make organisations friendlier, and to develop a more creative environment by tapping into the spiritual side of employees. Many people believe the primary reason for the emerging trend in insecurity is the widespread feeling that workplaces have become vulnerable environments. The downsizing, reengineering, and layoffs of recent years have transformed company cultures into bases of uncertainty.

Those survivors who are left are emotionally scarred by the retrenchments of their friends and co-workers. There is less support staff, more difficult technology to master, and everyone is stretched thin trying to perform. Employees long for strength from within to help them do their jobs and live their lives despite fears and insecurity.

Many business people are growing away from the idea that science and technology can solve every business problem. Spirituality is seen as a mainstay for integrating and cementing corporate and employee values. Spirituality is not a religion. Its goal is greater personal awareness of universal values, helping an individual to live and work better and more joyfully.

Spirituality should not be seen as a business whim. Spirituality involves getting in touch with oneself and reaching a state of contentment in our everyday lives. Judi Neal (in Brandt 1996) a leading advocate of spirituality in corporations in America says:

> With corporate change at an all-time high and trust in corporations at an all-time low, human resource managers are clearly in the hot seat. Developing one's own spiritual side offers a source of

strength both on the job and off. Helping other employees to develop theirs can make the workplace a stronger, safer and much saner place to do business.

Eleven steps to a more spiritual organisation are offered in Table 13.1.

13.5 Holistic healthcare programmes

Occupational health practitioners are starting to adopt a proactive approach to managing employee health matters. Besides realising that prevention is better than cure, a holistic focus requires that care be taken of the broader social and domestic dynamics of employees – a focus that aims at achieving a well-balanced work and family life.

13.5.1 Wellness

Wellness programmes focus on the employee's overall physical and mental health. These programmes concentrate on preventing or correcting specific health problems, health hazards, or negative health habits. They include not only disease identification but also lifestyle modification such as hypertension identification and control, smoking cessation, physical fitness and exercise, nutrition and diet control, and job and personal stress management (Ivancevich and Matteson 1999:280). As Cascio (1995:55) states, the objective of wellness programmes is not to eliminate symptoms and disease; it is to help employees build lifestyles that will enable them to achieve their full physical and mental potential through health awareness.

Gómez-Mejía et al. (1998:508) point out that wellness programmes can be as simple and inexpensive as providing information about stop-smoking clinics and

Table 13.1 Eleven steps to a more spiritual organisation

1. Connect with nature by bringing as many natural features as possible, such as green plants, skylights, and fountains, into offices and factories.
2. Hold some meetings outdoors to refresh, revive, and improve productivity.
3. Promote physical and spiritual wellness by encouraging staff to take regular exercise breaks.
4. Stage frequent company celebrations to acknowledge milestones and achievements.
5. Honour and support creative expression by decorating the workplace with employee-made paintings, sculpture, craft work, and poetry.
6. Create an evolving mission statement by holding periodic open meetings to refine and improve the organisation's mission.
7. Encourage employee education in interesting, free or low-cost training, including non-business courses, from yoga and meditation to book discussion groups and assertiveness training.
8. Allow manufacturing workers, line managers, secretaries, accountants, and other 'unexpected' employees to represent the organisation at marketing initiatives.
9. Promote openness and equality by holding some meetings at a round table, or at a circle of chairs.
10. Support employees who want to get to know fellow workers as human beings, not just as co-workers.
11. Make all employees feel important and effective by allowing everyone a turn at answering customer correspondence or becoming involved in customer liaison.

SOURCE: Chappell, T. (1996).

weight-loss programmes, or as comprehensive and expensive as providing professional health screening and multimillion-rand fitness facilities. In South Africa, many companies subsidise their employees' subscription to a fitness centre, such as the Health and Racquet Club, in order to promote their general well-being.

According to Matlala (1999:24) organisations can promote wellness by:
- incorporating employee wellness or health promotion into the overall strategy of the organisation;
- adopting employee wellness into the culture of the organisation;
- encouraging involvement and support from all the role players such as labour representatives, management, and others; and
- developing and implementing health promotion policies, such as employee assistance programmes, a smoking policy, and a HIV/AIDS policy and programme.

Managers should be equipped to identify symptoms of diseases such as alcoholism, drug abuse, and HIV/AIDS, and must provide lines of referral to professionals who can assist with treatment. Whatever action is planned, the rights of employees must be taken into consideration (Sunday Times, Business Times, 10 January 1999).

13.5.2 Employee Assistance Programmes

According to Ivancevich and Matteson (1999:279) employee assistance programmes (EAPs) are designed to deal with a wide range of stress-related problems, including behavioural and emotional difficulties, substance abuse, family and marital discord, and other personal problems. EAPs tend to be based on the traditional approach of diagnosis, treatment, screening, and prevention. A prerequisite of EAPs is the element of trust. Employees must trust that the programme can and will provide real help, that confidentiality will be maintained, and that use of the programme carries no negative implications for job security or future advancement.

13.5.3 Substance abuse

Alcoholism is a serious and widespread disease. The effects of alcoholism on the worker and his work are severe. The quality and quantity of work decline sharply and the morale of other workers is affected as they are called upon to do the work of their alcoholic peer. On-the-job accidents do not increase significantly, because the alcoholic becomes more cautious, but off-the-job accidents can be three to four times higher than those in which non-alcoholics are involved. Labour turnover is not unusually high.

Recognising the alcoholic on the job can be difficult. It often takes a medical expert to be able to attribute early symptoms, such as tardiness, to alcoholism, as they could easily be related to other problems. Often, alcoholism is not detected until it has reached a problematic stage. However, once diagnosis has taken place, it is important that the organisation is able to deal with the problem in a systematic way.

A formal written policy on substance abuse must be developed and communicated to all employees. This document should:
- state management's philosophy and position on the use and possession of illegal drugs and alcohol;
- set standards for appropriate conduct both on and off the job;
- list the methods that might be used to determine the causes of poor performance; and
- state the organisation's views on rehabilitation including specific penalties for policy violations.

Traditional techniques for dealing with substance abuse problems include disciplining, discharge, in-house counselling, and referral to an outside agency. Often discipline is used in conjunction with counselling or referral; most companies acknowledge that addiction is an illness, but are strict when it comes to giving the employee an opportunity for rehabilitation (Ivancevich and Matteson 1999:280).

13.5.4 Smoking

Smoking has long been an issue in the workplace. Passive smoking, or smoke inhalation by non-smokers, is becoming more of a matter for concern as employers become aware of evidence of measurable health effects and possible legal implications. An increasing number of public places have demarcated areas for smoking and non-smoking, and most employers in South Africa have either introduced or have considered developing a smoking policy. Araujo (1996:39) suggests some general principles for formulating a smoking policy:

- establish a working party to develop basic guidelines;
- consult the workforce; and
- develop the policy as part of the total company health policy, and not as a management or subordinate issue.

Introducing a smoking policy in stages is most practical. The first stage could forbid smoking in certain areas, such as canteens, lifts, designated offices, and conference rooms. The next stage reinforces and extends the above and the final stage implements a total smoking ban, with the possible exception of a few areas allocated to die-hards for this purpose. When considering whether or not to introduce a smoking policy, companies should consider the following:

- Smoking leads to increased absenteeism, higher cleaning costs, medical retirements, premature deaths, and various other liabilities. If these consequences could be quantified, employees might see the desirability of introducing the policy.
- Smoking bans provide considerable health benefits for both smokers and non-smokers in the workforce, the organisation as a whole, and the community. It is a relatively inexpensive way of making a good health investment.

In the Case-in-point the successful introduction of a smoking policy in Telecom Australia is discussed.

Case-in-point
Telecom Australia's smoking policy

Telecom Australia opted for a total ban on smoking. The company introduced the ban by issuing a clear statement of policy with strong managerial support. This top management support was achieved by equipping managers with the skills to deal with the addiction and by furnishing information on the side effects of smoking. Occupational health nurses received training to deal with both physical and mental withdrawal symptoms.

Managers were prepared to listen to their subordinates' viewpoints on the new smoking policy. They followed an approach of openness and honesty with the employees so that there would be no misconceptions and this, in turn, resulted in the employees being more supportive of the policy. Employees passed a vote of confidence in their managers, who not only supported the implementation of the policy amongst the workers, but also provided evidence of adhering to the regulations of the policy themselves.

> Statistics were carefully monitored and eighteen months after the introduction of the policy, 81 per cent of all staff (including 53 per cent of smokers) approved of the ban. Smokers were smoking between three and four fewer cigarettes per workday and the number of smokers had decreased at about double the rate of the rest of the community.
>
> source: Araujo, J.P. (1996:39-40).

13.5.5 HIV/AIDS

The high incidence of ignorance and prejudice that still surrounds the issue of the Acquired Immune Deficiency Syndrome (AIDS) indicates that attempts to educate the general population have not been altogether successful. Managers must accept the burden of informing their workforces about the disease, although in Africa deep-seated tribal customs very often prevent a complete understanding of the social reality of AIDS.

Numerous issues present themselves for consideration, and organisations must make decisions and formulate policies on:
- whether to use pre-employment testing for AIDS;
- exclusions from medical funds;
- termination of employment due to HIV/AIDS; and
- confidentiality.

Bracks and Van Wyk (in Swanepoel et al. 1998:593) maintain that employers can play an important part in sponsoring AIDS awareness programmes and providing informative training.

The South African Business Council on HIV/AIDS was formed in February 2000 in an effort to fight the AIDS epidemic. Experts predict that one in five South African workers may have HIV by the year 2005, and the council aims to create universal strategies for fighting the disease in the workplace. AIDS could also prevent growth in the nation's economy, which is expected to expand by 3 per cent during the year 2000. In a statement, the business council noted that the epidemic has already taken its toll, with a loss of skilled workers, more absenteeism, higher health care costs, and higher labour turnover (CDC National Prevention Information Network).

At the time of writing, the 13th International AIDS Conference is scheduled to be held in Durban from 9 to 14 July 2000 – the first time it will be hosted in Africa. The theme is 'Break the Silence' and the conference is expected to draw thousands of delegates from first-world and developing countries across the globe.

13.5.6 Conflict and violence in the workplace

In South Africa, as in many other countries, violence against employees has become a serious safety problem in the workplace. Physical attacks, harassment, and intimidation have become a way of life. It is a sad but accepted fact that heightened security measures are an employer's first line of defence against workplace violence, whether that violence derives from co-workers, customers, or outsiders. With the number of cash heists on the increase, many companies are taking precautionary measures not only for the sake of the business, but for the protection of their employees as well. These measures include improving external lighting, minimising the amount of cash on hand, installing silent alarms and surveillance cameras, increasing the number of staff on duty, providing staff training in conflict resolution and non-violent response, and closing their establishments during high-risk hours.

13.6 The causes of accidents

According to Dessler (1997:628) there are three basic causes of workplace accidents: chance occurrences, unsafe conditions, and unsafe acts. Chance occurrences are more commonly referred to as 'freak accidents' and are usually beyond the control of employees and the employer. Unsafe conditions and unsafe acts can be controlled.

13.6.1 Unsafe conditions

Unsafe conditions include factors such as:
- improperly guarded equipment;
- a lack of protective equipment;
- defective equipment;
- hazardous procedures in, on, or around, machines or equipment;
- unsafe storage – congestion, overloading;
- improper illumination – glare, insufficient light;
- improper ventilation – insufficient air change, impure air source; and
- excessive noise, heat, or cold.

The correction and elimination of unsafe conditions is catered for in the Occupational Health and Safety Act No 85 of 1993, and through the activities of NOSA (National Occupational Safety Association). Both are discussed in a later section.

Other accident-causing factors may also be present in the workplace. The job itself may be inherently dangerous; overloaded work schedules, night shifts, fatigue, and a psychological climate of hostility caused by dissatisfaction among workers tend to increase employees' susceptibility to work accidents.

13.6.2 Unsafe acts

People cause accidents by continuing to take part in unsafe acts such as:
- throwing material indiscriminately;
- operating or working at unsafe speeds;
- making safety devices inoperative;
- using unsafe equipment or disregarding safety rules;
- using unsafe procedures in loading, placing, mixing, or combining;
- taking unsafe positions under suspended loads;
- lifting incorrectly;
- distracting, teasing, abusing, startling, quarrelling, horseplay, and fighting;
- alcohol or drug intoxication or abuse; and
- failure by supervisors to enforce safety rules.

What causes people to take part in unsafe acts? Dessler (1997:630–631) believes that a number of factors contribute to the problem. Certain personal characteristics serve as the basis for undesirable attitudes and behaviour, such as the tendency to take risks. The debate on 'accident-prone' people has not yet been resolved, but it appears that certain personality traits, coupled with specific job situations and a lack of motor skills also result in unsafe acts. Poor vision, youth, and workers with a perception level lower than the motor level have also been identified as contributing factors.

13.7 Promoting safety

Neither the presence of unsafe conditions nor unsafe employee behaviours necessarily mean that an accident will occur. Employees may manage to survive dangerous conditions or unsafe behaviours for months or even years without an accident. Even if an accident does occur, the employee may escape without injury. When an injury is sustained, its severity may range from minor abrasion to death.

According to Leap and Crino (1993: 527–529) the severity of an accident can

be assessed by considering:
- the medical expenses incurred;
- work time lost;
- costs associated with hiring and training new employees to replace those who are injured;
- the costs of decreased output of the injured worker after he or she returns to work;
- cost of damage to material or equipment;
- increased workers' compensation and health insurance costs; and
- pain, suffering, and mental anguish caused by the accident.

Reducing unsafe conditions is an employer's first line of defence. Safety engineers should use ergonomic principles to design jobs in such a way that physical hazards are removed or reduced. In addition to legislative requirements, supervisors and managers must develop a self-awareness of potential hazards and promote safe working areas.

Reducing the incidence of unsafe acts is more difficult because the human element always comes into play, but various actions can be taken.

13.7.1 Reducing unsafe acts through selection and placement

Identifying the human traits that might be related to accidents on the specific job can screen out so-called 'accident prone' individuals. Emotional stability and personality tests, measures of muscular coordination, tests of visual skills, and employee reliability tests, although not foolproof, can assist in making placement decisions. In terms of South African legislation, however, one should be cautious in allowing the results of any of these tests to exclude a potential employee from a job.

13.7.2 Reducing unsafe acts through propaganda

Safety posters, although not a substitute for a comprehensive safety programme, can be combined with other techniques to reduce the occurrence of unsafe acts. They serve as a visual reminder that safety rules must be obeyed, and should be changed often to stimulate interest in safety.

13.7.3 Reducing unsafe acts through training

Safety training is especially appropriate with new employees, although current employees should receive regular refresher training courses. Specialist safety organisations such as NOSA provide such training, and a number of pioneering organisations even have their employees engage in exercises such as callisthenics, before starting work.

13.7.4 Reducing unsafe acts through positive reinforcement

Pictorial graphs showing assigned safety goals, and the current and previous performance of departmental groups, coupled with supervisory praise for performing selected incidents safely, are a continuous encouragement to maintain safety levels.

13.7.5 Reducing unsafe acts through top-management commitment

Successful programmes require a strong management commitment to safety. Top managers must become personally involved in safety activities on a routine basis. They must give safety matters high priority in company meetings and production scheduling, and the company safety officer must have a high rank and respected status within the organisation.

13.8 An ergonomic approach to combating occupational injuries

13.8.1 Situational and individual variables in accident occurrence

The principles of ergonomics dictate that imbalances between the person and his environment must be eliminated, and the balance maintained. This is known as person – environment (P-E) fit. This approach to combating occupational injuries and illnesses focuses on two dimensions of fit. One is the extent to which work provides formal and informal rewards that meet or match the person's needs. The other type of fit deals with the extent to which the employee's skills, abilities, and experience match the demands and requirements of the employer. Neglecting these two aspects of P-E fit leads to an increase in occupational injuries (Ivancevich and Matteson 1999:277).

Accidents are caused by situational and/or individual variables. Situational factors include the failure to remove physical hazards, resulting in unsafe working conditions. This implies that a 'zero defect' situation is necessary in the general administration of the workplace. Other situational factors include inadequate job design, work schedules, and atmospheric conditions that are less than optimal.

Unsafe behaviours can be attributed to individual differences. Repeated investigations have been conducted into the reasons why people behave in an unsafe manner. The ergonomist's view is that it is a matter of user error. Each person experiences a comfort zone as a feature of interaction between his job and the job environment. When the tolerance limits of the comfort zone are exceeded the individual functions less effectively and this sets the scene for possible unsafe behaviour (Blignaut 1988:37).

13.8.2 Stress as a source of accident behaviour

The last decade of the twentieth century was a time of rapid technological change and increasing pressure on employees in the form of obscure and conflicting demands, limited guidance, unrealistic deadlines, unclear responsibility and information overload. Many employees perceive these demands and pressures as a threat and this results in stress which manifests itself in lack of concentration and physical and mental ill-health. This scenario leads the worker to place less emphasis on his job behaviour, resulting in a situation where accidents are likely to occur. Figure 13.2 offers a model in the form of a flow diagram, indicating how accidents are caused, and how they can be avoided.

13.9 Legal requirements in health and safety management

The two main pieces of legislation concerning employee health and safety are the Occupational Health and Safety Act (OHSA) 85 of 1993 and the Mine Health and Safety Act 29 of 1996.

13.9.1 The Occupational Health and Safety Act No. 85 of 1993

The OHSA provides for the health and safety of persons at work and for the health and safety of persons in connection with the use of plant and machinery. The following is a summary of some of the measures provided for in the Act in order to achieve its objectives.
- The establishment of an Advisory Council for Occupational Health and Safety.

Figure 13.2 A flow diagram of the accident process

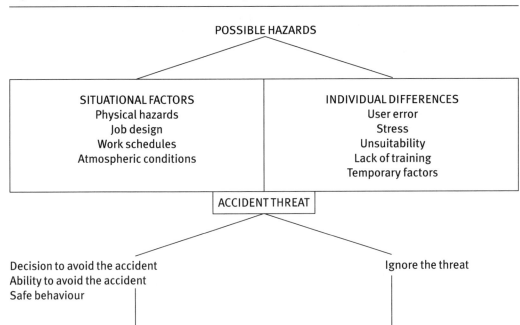

- Every employer must provide and maintain a working environment that is safe and without risk to the health of employees and other people affected by business operations.
- Suppliers and manufacturers must ensure that their products do not pose a safety or health risk in the workplace.
- Employers must inform their workforces of workplace hazards.
- Every employee must: take reasonable care of his or her own health and safety and of those persons who may be affected by his or her acts or omissions; carry out any lawful order given to him or her regarding workplace health and safety; and report any unsafe or unhealthy situations or incidents that affect his or her health.
- The appointment of health and safety representatives.
- The establishment of health and safety committees.
- Certain incidents must be reported to an inspector.
- Wide powers of inspection, entry, enquiry and seizure are conferred on inspectors.
- A wide range of acts of omission and commission are declared offences and can incur criminal penalties.

It must be remembered that legislation lays the foundation for the enforcement of good health and safety habits in an organisation. However, employers should take a proactive stance in the implementation of a holistic approach to wellness. Such an approach goes beyond being bound by the law, and if achieved, will ensure that optimal states of health and safety are maintained.

13.9.2 The Mine Health and Safety Act No. 29 of 1996

The Mine Health and Safety Act provides for the health and safety of all persons employed in the mining industry, through regulations governing the reporting of incidents and accidents, and for the appointment of health and safety representatives and committees. Mining is a very hazardous occupation, yet the South African economy is reliant to a great extent on the activities of local mines. For this reason, the Mine Health and Safety Act is an extremely important part of the statute book.

13.9.3 Safety and first aid training

The majority of organisations provide some sort of orientation to safety regulations and procedures in their induction programmes. Regular refresher training is vital so that safety practices can be applied consistently.

The Occupational Health and Safety Act No. 85 of 1993 requires that one in every fifty people employed in industry must be in possession of a Level O First Aid Certificate. The syllabus of this course is laid down by the Department of Labour. The Act also defines the minimum content of first aid boxes.

Many organisations make use of the St John's Ambulance First Aid Training for Industry (St John's Ambulance Home Page). Regular training programmes are offered at St John's twelve centres around the country, and on-site at many companies. The Emergency First Aid Safety Oriented Course (EFASO) is a modular course of basic first aid skills and other subjects needed to sustain life and manage the scene of injury. It meets industry, business, and legislative requirements. The minimum compulsory content of the EFASO Level 1 course covers the following areas:
- principles of first aid and safety;
- emergency scene management;
- artificial respiration;
- one-rescuer CPR;
- choking;
- wounds and bleeding;
- shock, unconsciousness, and fainting;
- fractures;
- burns; and
- head and spinal injuries.

13.10 National Occupational Safety Association of South Africa (NOSA)

The website of The National Occupational Safety Association of South Africa (NOSA) is an informative source on the details of the organisation. NOSA is a non-profit organisation that plays a prominent role in supporting quality health and safety standards in the workplace. Since its inception on 11 April 1951, NOSA has provided an exceptional service in educating, training, and motivating employees in the mining sector, industry, and commerce. NOSA aims to foster among workers and management alike an awareness of the need for safety in all work operations, in order to prevent industrial accidents and occupational diseases. NOSA's thrust for the twenty-first century is the promotion of new attitudes and approaches to occupational safety, health, and environmental risk management, by means of a programme known as SHE. These issues were the focus of NOSA's biggest international conference to date in 1999.

The training services of NOSA include in-house or on-site training, the NOSA Training Academy (NTA) and Occupational Hygiene Technologies (OHTEC). NOSA also offers consulting services in the form of baseline safety audits, legal compliance audits, occupational hygiene surveys, and environmental services.

Perhaps the most widely known aspect of NOSA's services is the Five Star Grading System. The system is based on the

HEALTH AND SAFETY MANAGEMENT

Table 13.2 The NOSA Five Star System

The NOSA Five Star System can be divided into three distinct phases of activity:

1 The preparation phase
Once a company has confirmed their full participation in the NOSA system the following actions are undertaken:
- formulation of a policy statement signifying the importance of health, safety, and environmental management in the business;
- development of an implementation plan emphasising employee participation, and defining responsibilities and accountabilities;
- establishing organisational health, safety, and environmental management needs;
- determining priority elements and establishing appropriate standards; and
- establishing a health, safety, and environmental training programme for the company.

2 The implementation phase
The following aspects are now implemented:
- identification and priority of standards; and
- furthering awareness and recommended training.

NOSA officials conduct a baseline audit to identify strengths and weaknesses in the development of safety element standards. The programme then commences using self-audits and external NOSA audits.

3 The sustaining phase
All additional elements and standards are developed and implemented during this phase. Self-audits and grading audits are conducted. Follow-up audits are dependent on the needs of the client. The concept of continuous improvement ensures that the process maintains its momentum, and that new innovations and further improvements are added.

SOURCE: NOSA Information brochure.

---

continuous application of the ISSMEC process, namely:
- I – identify possible causes of incidents;
- S – set standards of practice and procedures;
- S – set standards of accountability;
- M – measure performance against standards;
- E – evaluate compliance with standards; and
- C – control deficiencies and deviations.

An overview of the NOSA Five Star System is offered in Table 13.2.

13.11 Health and safety issues and quality assurance

Given the amounts of time and money invested in employees, especially highly skilled knowledge workers, many firms try to rehabilitate those with substance abuse and stress-related problems. Safety programmes target an accident-free and productive workplace. However, the competitive society and quality requirements of the twenty-first century demand that employers take a proactive stance in managing health and safety issues. Environmental issues also necessitate that strategic precautions are taken to safeguard communities from chemical spills, pollution, hazardous gases, and so on. Yet, in many of the less developed countries around the world, where labour unions are weak and corruption is often endemic, safety and health matters are at the bottom of the agenda. South African organisations must make a concerted effort not to allow this to happen.

13.12 Conclusion

Employee safety, health, and wellness are important issues. Managers have the responsibility of ensuring that workers are not unnecessarily endangered, and that they are fully aware of, and properly trained and prepared for, unusual workplace risks. As society has experienced such problems as chemical substance abuse, AIDS, and the ever-increasing stresses on the individual, so too have employees. There is a growing recognition that work is an important part of life and that organisations, by providing more than simply a safe place to work, can have a positive impact on the physical and psychological well-being of employees.

Summary

Environmental job stress factors include work schedules, revised work procedures, new workplace facilities, pace of work, job security, route to and from work, and the number and nature of customers or clients, work overload and underload. Changing organisational circumstances and personal factors can also contribute to negative consequences.

Burnout is the total exhaustion of physical and mental resources as a result of excessive striving to reach an unrealistic work-related goal, combined with an overload of job stress. Workaholics do not always manifest abnormal behaviour patterns.

Personal and organisational interventions can alleviate job stress. Human resources specialists and supervisors can also play a role in identifying and monitoring symptoms of stress.

An employer has a duty to ensure that employees are not subjected to sexual harassment within the workplace. There is no common ground for a definition of sexual harassment. Sexual harassment can take several forms such as verbal and non-verbal, gestures, visual, and physical.

Spirituality is seen as a mainstay for integrating and cementing corporate and employee values. Its goal is greater personal awareness of universal values, helping an individual live and work better and more joyfully. Wellness programmes focus on the employee's overall physical and mental health. They include lifestyle modification and job and personal stress management. The objective of wellness programmes is to help employees build lifestyles that will enable them to achieve their full physical and mental potential through health awareness. Wellness programmes include Employee Assistance Programmes (EAPs) that are designed to deal with a wide range of stress-related problems, including behavioural and emotional difficulties, substance abuse, family and marital discord, workplace violence, and other personal problems.

Unsafe conditions and unsafe acts cause accidents. Certain personal characteristics serve as the basis for undesirable attitudes and behaviour, such as the tendency to take risks. Reducing unsafe conditions is an employer's first line of defence. The incidence of unsafe acts can be reduced through proper selection and placement methods, the use of safety posters, training, positive reinforcement, and top-management commitment.

Accidents are caused by situational or individual variables. Many employees perceive the demands and pressures of the workplace as a threat and this results in stress. This leads the worker to place less emphasis on his job behaviour, resulting in a situation where accidents are likely to occur.

The two main pieces of legislation concerning employee health and safety are the Occupational Health and Safety Act No. 85 of 1993 and the Mine Health and Safety Act No. 29 of 1996. Safety and first-aid training are also legal requirements.

The National Occupational Safety Association of South Africa (NOSA) plays a prominent role in supporting quality health and safety standards in the workplace. The training services of NOSA include in-house or on-site training, the NOSA Training Academy (NTA) and Occupational Hygiene Technologies (OHTEC). NOSA also offers consulting services and the Five Star Grading System.

Related websites

This topic may be investigated further by referring to the following Internet websites:
National Occupational Safety Association – http://www.nosa.co.za
St John's Ambulance – http://www.stjohn.org.za
AIDS Conference 2000 – http://www.aids2000.com
CDC National Prevention Information Network – http://www.cdcnpin.org
AIDS in South Africa – http://www.redribbon.co.za
FAMSA – http://www.famsa.co.za

Case study
The grass isn't always greener on the other side

The time was 07:30 in the morning. Jeff Presley, the Packing Room Manager, walked to his office situated on the mezzanine floor above the packing floor of the chocolate factory. Already the night-shift supervisor had reported that a breakdown during the last shift had resulted in the loss of two hours' production. It was possible that user-error was the cause of the breakdown. It was not a good start to the day. 'And here comes Dan,' thought Jeff. 'It's going to get worse!'

Dan Parker, the Plant Manager, burst into Jeff's office and without even a 'Good morning', said, 'Come with me.' Jeff wondered what this was all about, as he followed Dan to the male changing room. When they entered the door of the changing area, Dan turned to Jeff and asked, 'What do you smell?' Jeff sighed. Now he knew what the problem was. 'It smells like someone has been smoking dagga,' he replied.

'You're right!' Dan said, 'and this isn't

the first time! What are you going to do about it?'

Jeff had known for quite a while that certain employees on the night shift were smoking dagga during their rest breaks. When he spoke to the night-shift supervisor about it, he was told that it helped the 'guys' to stay awake and gave them more energy to be able to exceed their production targets. Even though he realised it was illegal, the night-shift supervisor said he was prepared to over-look it, as long as those involved kept it quiet and didn't let things get out of hand. Jeff was confused. He knew the right thing to do would be to discipline the culprits and not allow this to happen again. If he turned a blind eye, he would be condoning the use of an illegal substance, and both he and the company could get into trouble with the law. But it wasn't harming anyone, and smoking dagga seemed to keep everyone happy on the night shift.

Questions

1 Which probable unsafe acts can you identify from the facts of the case?
2 There is no company policy on the matter. What does this tell you about the company's approach to health and safety matters?
3 How would you solve the problem?

Experiential exercise 1

Purpose
To investigate how a company manages organisational health and safety.

Introduction
Many companies have never been able to settle the debate concerning which department in the organisation should have the responsibility for health and safety programmes. The human resources department usually attends to health aspects, while safety typically falls within the domain of one of the engineering departments.

Task
Investigate the health and safety programmes in a selected company. Develop a questionnaire using the framework of this chapter as a guide, and analyse the information obtained so that you are able to compile a comprehensive report. Make recommendations for any improvements you believe the organisation should undertake.

Experiential exercise 2

Purpose
To assist a subordinate in defusing a stressful situation.

Introduction
Read the following background information and prepare to role-play the part assigned to you.

Role-play (Subordinate)
You are Phumeza, secretary to Siseko, the Marketing Manager of your company. Although you love your job, your relationship with Siseko has been worry-

ing you lately. In your opinion, he has sexually harassed you. Some of the things that have bothered you are:
- Siseko joking about women's breasts in front of you, which makes you feel uncomfortable;
- Siseko telling you that you should wear mini-skirts when he is entertaining clients, as it makes male clients 'feel good';
- on at least three occasions, Siseko suggesting that he will give you a lift home from work if you stay behind in the office after the rest of the staff have left. You have declined each time; and
- now Siseko is dropping hints that there may not be much of an increase for you this year.

You have decided to talk to Jane, the Human Resources Manager, about your problem. You are very shy and embarrassed about the matter, and you are not sure how much you will be able to tell her.

Role-play (Human Resources Manager)
You are Jane, the HR Manager. Phumeza has asked to speak to you about a personal problem. Although you are not sure what it is about, you have an idea that it might have something to do with Siseko, her boss. Two other ladies who work in the Marketing Department have already approached you for advice on what they call the 'sexual harassment problem' in their office. You know that Phumeza is very shy. If this is indeed the problem she wants to discuss, she is going to find it very difficult.

However, you are aware that you must get to the bottom of the matter. If Siseko's behaviour is out of place, you must be able to build up a case before you can confront him with any accusations. To do this you will need as much specific information as possible.

Prepare for your discussion with Phumeza.

Chapter questions

1. Karoshi, or death from overwork, is the second leading cause of death, after cancer, among Japanese workers. If you were a Japanese manager what would you do to reduce the risk of karoshi?
2. Besides work overload, a number of other environmental and personal stress factors can contribute to a pathological reaction in workers. Discuss these factors and include any other stress factors that you or a colleague may have experienced.
3. Explain how spirituality and wellness programmes can contribute to a holistic approach to healthcare in the workplace.
4. Discuss how an ergonomic approach to safety can be used in combating occupational injuries.
5. Sir Winston Churchill was a great statesman who led Britain to victory in the Second World War. He made the following comment: 'Most of the world's work is done by people who do not feel very well all of the time.' Do you agree or disagree with his statement? Motivate your answer.

Bibliography

ARAUJO, J.P. Jan. 1996. The introduction of a no-smoking policy. *People Dynamics.* 16(1), 39–40.
BERRY, L.M. 1998. *Psychology at work.* 2nd edition. McGraw-Hill, Boston.
BLIGNAUT, C.J.H. 1988. *Ergonomics for behavioural scientists.* RAU, Johannesburg.

BOASE, N. 1996. Dealing with sexual harassment in the workplace. *People Dynamics.* 14(11), 88.

BRANDT, E. April 1996. Corporate pioneers explore spirituality. *HR Magazine.* http//www.shrm.org.

CASCIO, W.F. 1995. *Managing human resources: productivity, quality of work life, profits.* McGraw-Hill, New York.

CDC NATIONAL PREVENTION INFORMATION NETWORK. Http://www.cdcnpin.org.

CHERRINGTON, D.J. 1995. *The management of human resources.* 4th edition. Prentice-Hall, Englewood Cliffs, NJ.

CHAPPELL, T. April 1996. Eleven steps to a more spiritual company. *HR Magazine.* http//www.shrm.org.

DESSLER, G. 1997. *Human resource management.* 7th edition. Prentice-Hall, Upper Saddle River, NJ.

GÓMEZ-MEJÍA, L.R., BALKIN, D.B., & CARDY, R.L. 1998. *Managing human resources.* 2nd edition. Prentice-Hall, Upper Saddle River, NJ.

IVANCEVICH, J.M. & MATTESON, M.T. 1999. *Organizational behavior and management.* 5th edition. Irwin McGraw-Hill, Boston.

LEAP, T.L. & CRINO, M.D. 1993. *Personnel/human resource management.* 2nd edition. MacMillan, New York.

MATLALA, S. 1999. Prioritising health promotion and employee wellness. *People Dynamics.* 17(6), 22–25.

NATIONAL OCCUPATIONAL SAFETY ASSOCIATION. http://www.nosa.co.za .

SCHULTZ, D.P. & SCHULTZ, S.E. 1994. *Psychology and work today: an introduction to industrial and organizational psychology.* 6th edition. MacMillan, Englewood Cliffs, NJ.

ST JOHN'S AMBULANCE HOME PAGE. http://www.stjohn.org.za

SWANEPOEL, B.J. (ED.), ERASMUS, B.J., VAN WYK, M.W. & SCHENK, H.W. 1998. *South African human resource management.* Juta, Kenwyn.

YONEMORI, T. 28 April 1999. http://www.miyazaki-mic.ac.jp/stu.

part five

Behavioural aspects of human resources management

14

Motivation

A Werner

Learning outcomes

At the end of this chapter the learner should be able to demonstrate the following outcomes:
- Explain the concept of motivation.
- Discuss the content theories of motivation and their application to the work context.
- Discuss the process theories of motivation and their application to the work context.
- Explain how goal setting serves as a motivational tool.
- Discuss money as a motivator.
- Analyse the motivational levels of employees in various situations.
- Indicate the relevance of quality assurance in motivation.

Key words and concepts

- equity
- expectancy
- hygiene factors
- instrumentality
- meaningfulness
- motivators
- self-actualisation

Illustrative case
Lighten up

Thomas Alva Edison (1847–1931) is best known as the inventor of the first electric light. In 1879, he discovered that if electric current is passed through a thin thread of carbon in a glass vacuum, it becomes white-hot, giving off a brilliant light. However, that was not his only invention. He patented over 1000 inventions, including the record player, 'moving pictures', and the quadruplex telegraph system. Edison received home-schooling, and only went to formal school for about three months in 1854.

> In 1877, he invented the record player, his favourite invention. It was called a phonograph, or gramophone. Once Edison set a goal for himself, everything else became less important. He often worked up to twenty hours a day. A well-known photograph of Edison was taken after he had worked non-stop for five days and nights to finish the phonograph. In 1878, he formed the Edison Electric Light Company, which enabled New York to become the first city lit by electricity.
>
> SOURCE: Jeffries, M. and Lewis, G.A. (1992:6–7).

14.1 Introduction

Motivating employees is one of the most important managerial functions. Success in this endeavour is essential in the quest to utilise the full potential of people in ensuring quality products and service. Motivation is a very complex issue due to the uniqueness of people and the wide range of internal and external factors that impact on it. Motivation can also not be separated from leadership, which is the ability to inspire people to voluntarily and enthusiastically work towards the attainment of organisational goals. But what is motivation? And how does one motivate people?

The purpose of this chapter is to provide a holistic approach to the question of employee motivation. Firstly, we explore the meaning of motivation, and investigate the practical application of various content and process theories in the workplace. Then the role of goal setting in motivation is examined, and the power of money as a motivator is considered.

14.2 The meaning of motivation

Employees function at one of three basic levels (Mol 1990:42):
- minimum level – doing less than is required;
- expected level – doing just what is required; and
- maximum level – doing more than is required.

The employee who does less than is required of him or her makes more errors, is more tardy, delivers poor quality work, and is disciplined more often. Employees at the in-between level do what is expected of them – nothing more, nothing less. They do enough not to get into trouble, but nothing more. The third group of employees performs at the maximum level. They are prepared to walk that extra mile, use their initiative, apply their skills where needed, and put in an extra effort to achieve goals. Employees who voluntarily and enthusiastically do more than what is required of them, are motivated.

Mol (1992:39) distinguishes between the words 'motivation' and 'movement'. When a person carries out a task just for the sake of being remunerated, the person is being moved rather than being motivated. Mol does not denounce the movement of employees. According to him, it has always been used as a strategy to get people to achieve goals. Yet, it cannot be considered as motivation. Only when a person carries out a task because he or she is enjoying it or is totally involved in it, is that person motivated.

Motivation can be described as intentional and directional. The word 'intentional' refers to personal choice and persistence of action. The word 'directional' indicates the presence of a driving force aimed at attaining a specific goal. A motivated person is always aware of the fact that a specific goal must be achieved, and continuously directs his or her efforts at achieving that goal, even in the face of adversity.

14.3 Motivational theories

The motivational theories that we are going to discuss in this chapter can be divided into content and process theories. Content theories focus on the needs and factors that motivate behaviour, the 'what' of motivation, while process theories focus on the origin of behaviour and the factors which influence the strength and direction of the behaviour, in other words the 'how' of motivation.

14.3.1 Maslow's needs hierarchy

Maslow's (1954) theory has a twofold basis: People are continuously wanting things. People always want more, and what they want depends on what they already have. As soon as one need is satisfied, another takes its place. People can therefore never be fully satisfied, and they behave in a particular way to satisfy a need or a combination of needs. A satisfied need cannot act as a motivator of behaviour.

Before reading on, complete Self-assessment 14.1 to identify your position on the needs hierarchy. The interpretation of this assessment is explained at the end of the chapter.

Self-assessment 14.1 What are your needs?

For each of the items below, circle the number that best describes you at this point in your life. Answer as honestly as possible.

How often do you:	Never	Seldom	Sometimes	Often	Always
1 wish you had more intimate friends	1	2	3	4	5
2 worry about your financial position	1	2	3	4	5
3 identify potential learning opportunities	1	2	3	4	5
4 feel your life is not worth much	1	2	3	4	5
5 think about your safety	1	2	3	4	5
6 feel lonely and unloved	1	2	3	4	5
7 feel good about yourself	5	4	3	2	1
8 experience personal growth	5	4	3	2	1
9 think others appreciate your skills	5	4	3	2	1
10 compare your income and expenses	1	2	3	4	5
11 feel you are in physical danger	1	2	3	4	5
12 feel that you are making progress in your life	5	4	3	2	1
13 feel perfectly safe and secure from personal harm	5	4	3	2	1
14 worry about how you are going to pay your bills	1	2	3	4	5
15 feel well accepted by others	5	4	3	2	1

People's needs are arranged in order of importance. Maslow divides human needs into five main categories according to importance. The lowest level contains the most basic human needs which must be satisfied before higher-order needs emerge and become motivators of behaviour.

The levels of needs in Maslow's hierarchy are as follows:
- *Physiological needs.* The satisfaction of these needs is essential for a human being's biological functioning and survival (for example the need for food, water, and warmth). These are the most prominent needs; if they are not satisfied, human behaviour will be mainly directed at satisfying them. If you are really hungry, you will risk your safety in order to find food.
- *Safety needs.* As soon as physiological needs are reasonably satisfied, needs on the next level emerge and the importance of the previous level of needs diminishes. Humans now use energy to satisfy the need for safety, which also has a direct bearing on their survival.
- *Social needs.* Once a person feels safe and in control of possible threats, social needs are activated. These include the need for love, acceptance, and friendship.
- *Ego needs.* These needs may be divided into two groups; self-respect and self-esteem, and respect and approval from others. They include the need for self-confidence, independence, freedom, recognition, appreciation, and achievement.
- *Self-actualisation needs.* Self-actualisation is the uninhibited expression of your true self and your talents. If all the above-mentioned needs are largely satisfied or can readily be satisfied, people then spend their time in search of opportunities to apply their skills to the best of their ability. Self-actualisation needs now become uppermost. Maslow (1954:92) describes these needs as 'the desire to become more and more what one is and to become everything one is capable of becoming'.

This theory has many implications for individual performance. The most common strategy used by management to motivate people (by means of money, service benefits, and job security, among other things) is aimed at the continued satisfaction of needs on the physiological and safety level. For most people these needs have been satisfied, either by themselves or through the country's social systems. Once satisfied, a need no longer acts as a motivator, so this strategy is not an incentive to perform. Performance bonuses often do not have the desired result.

Social needs may be satisfied in the work situation to a large extent, but it is difficult to develop a strategy that will translate these needs into an incentive for improved individual performance. The work people do, and the work environment, may be designed in a way that increases interaction between employees. The disadvantage is, however, that excessive socialisation may have a negative effect on employees' work output.

The needs that probably provide the best opportunities for employee motivation are the fourth- and fifth-level needs of Maslow's hierarchy, i.e. the ego and self-actualisation needs. Self-esteem and self-respect (as well as the esteem and respect of others) are functions of the type of work people do, rather than of working conditions such as free interaction and good remuneration. Interesting, challenging, and meaningful work provides a solid foundation for the improvement of performance.

A further implication of Maslow's theory concerns the control function. People need to control their environment in order to manipulate it according to their needs. If, however, people are controlled by the environment and thwarted in the satisfac-

Figure 14.1 Maslow's needs hierarchy

Self-actualisation needs

Ego needs

Social needs

Safety needs

Physiological needs

tion of their needs, they become frustrated and tense. If prevailing needs cannot be satisfied, the result is undesirable employee behaviour such as aggression, frustration, and resignations, which can hardly be described as healthy or productive.

If a person's work is, in itself, a source of need satisfaction, that person becomes self-regulating and the roles of external incentives, such as remuneration or punishment, become much less prominent as motivators. Systems relying on external mechanisms to motivate people usually also require a control system to ensure continued employee performance. The maintenance of mechanisms such as strict supervision, policy, rules, and regulations requires a great deal of effort on the part of the organisation. When people are motivated by challenging, interesting, and meaningful work, however, such control mechanisms are superfluous.

Maslow's theory provides a useful framework for the understanding of needs and expectations. It has had a significant influence on management approaches to motivation and can be related to Herzberg's two-factor theory of motivation.

Case-in-point
Winston Industrial Irrigation (Pty.) Ltd.

The manager at Winston Industrial Irrigation (Pty) Ltd was quite shocked when he studied the latest labour turnover report. He was aware of the fact that quite a few people in the design and quoting section had resigned during the last semester, but he did not really think the problem was that bad. A total of 17 per cent of the employees in this section had left the company. Translating this into a comparable yearly figure would give 34 per cent. No wonder the customers had complained lately about poor service and quality. Something had to be done.

The first task was to collect more information. Further investigation revealed that 80 per cent of the employees who left, had been with the company for three or more years. This implied that the problem did not lie with the selection process. After studying the exit-interview reports and conducting more detailed interviews with some of the leavers, the following were identified as the main reasons why these employees had decided to go:
- better job opportunities (advancement);
- supervisory positions at other companies;
- incompatible personalities at Winston that led to interpersonal conflict;
- favouritism at Winston;
- inequitable pay at Winston; and
- the supervisor at Winston always took credit for the hard work done by others.

The manager then decided to study the data of a published wage survey, to evaluate all the jobs in the design and quoting department, and to adjust the salaries accordingly. The supervisor and all the employees attended a three-day workshop on interpersonal skills, which everybody found very useful. The problem was solved. At least that is what the manager believed at first. However, after some time, it became clear that although the employees seemed to be no longer dissatisfied, they were still not motivated. The manager was baffled.

He contacted a management consultant he trusted, who gave him the following explanation: 'You have addressed some of the factors that caused dissatisfaction, and although I have to commend the actions you took to rectify the situation, you still have not addressed the factors that lead to higher motivation and improved performance. You have to redesign the jobs of the employees and your supervisor, to give them positive control and to make their jobs more exciting and challenging. Let me explain to you how it can be done.' The manager listened carefully and acted on the advice.

Within three months, performance results increased by 34 per cent, labour turnover decreased to 10 per cent, and job satisfaction indexes showed that employees were very happy with the new way in which their jobs were designed.

14.3.2 Herzberg's two-factor motivation theory

Herzberg used the critical incident technique to identify factors that made employees feel exceptionally good or exceptionally bad about their jobs. Responses were generally consistent, and based on them, Herzberg developed the two-factor theory of motivation, identifying two sets of factors that influenced motivation and job satisfaction; he called the one set of factors hygiene factors and the other motivators (Kreitner and Kinicki 1998: 200).

Hygiene factors are closely related to the working environment, and include:
- organisational policy and administration;
- equipment;
- supervision;
- interpersonal relationships with colleagues, superiors, and subordinates;
- salary;
- status;
- working conditions; and
- work security.

Hygiene factors, also called maintenance factors, do not motivate. If they are inadequately met, they cause dissatisfaction. If they are adequately met, the employee is neither dissatisfied, nor satisfied (not motivated), but feels neutral about his job. The opposite of dissatisfaction is not satisfaction but, rather, lack of dissatisfaction. A dissatisfied employee cannot be motivated. It is therefore important that management first give attention to hygiene factors before they introduce motivators into the employee's job. If a secretary's computer is out of order, she becomes dissatisfied and complains. On the other hand, you do not hear secretaries say: 'I really love my job, my computer is working well and not giving any problems.' Good work equipment is taken for granted; so are fair pay, equitable benefits, good working conditions, and so on.

Only motivators can motivate people. Motivated people exert a bigger effort than what is expected of them in achieving goals. Motivators, also called growth factors, are closely related to the nature and content of the work done, and include:
- achievement, for example successful execution of tasks;
- recognition for what has been achieved;
- the job itself (how interesting, meaningful, and challenging it is);
- progress or growth (learning and developing);
- responsibility; and
- feedback.

According to Herzberg, the answer to the motivation problem lies in the design of the work itself. Job enrichment is based on the application of Herzberg's ideas. Job enrichment is the vertical loading of an employee's job to make it more challenging and interesting, and to provide opportunities for responsibility, growth, and recognition. Job enrichment is an alternative to scientific management, also called Taylorism, where specialised and standardised jobs lead to monotony, boredom, and psychological stagnancy.

Herzberg's theory can be linked to the needs hierarchy of Maslow. The hygiene factors are similar to the lower-level needs in the hierarchy, while the motivators are similar to the higher-level needs. Figure 14.2 illustrates the relation between these two theories.

Although Herzberg's theory has elicited much criticism, his view that job satisfaction lies in the task itself is of value. According to Mol (1990:21) employees enjoy their work when they take pride in attaining a goal. If the work itself is not a source of pride for the employee, he or she will never be motivated, but will only be moved. This statement is based on the

Figure 14.2 A comparison of Maslow's needs hierarchy and Herzberg's two-factor theory

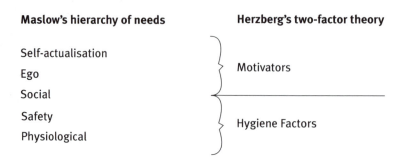

assumption that most workers have a basic need for self-actualisation and personal pride.

There are, however, theories that question this assumption. These so-called contingency theories emphasise the individual differences between employees and the necessity for managers to focus their approach to motivation on the individual characteristics of each employee. A supporter of these theories might reason that some employees are maintenance-seekers and others motivator-seekers. According to Mol (1990:15) the danger in holding this belief is that managers might have low expectations of some employees and, therefore, not create opportunities for them to learn and grow. By over-emphasising hygiene factors in the work place, employees are reinforced to become maintenance-seekers.

Mol (1990:12) says that his experience in South African organisations indicates that many managers are very successful in motivating their subordinates, particularly at the lower levels. They do this by concentrating on the task or job itself. One of the greatest mistakes made by management and trade unions is to think that fair treatment, pleasant working conditions, above-average remuneration, and outstanding fringe benefits will motivate employees.

There is no doubt that these aspects are important, but they seldom give rise to an increase in productivity, for the simple reason that they do not contribute towards an employee's enjoyment of the job.

14.3.3 The job characteristics model

The job characteristics model, proposed by Hackman and Oldham (in Kreitner and Kinicki 1998:202) and represented in Figure 14.4, is based on the idea that the task itself is the key to employee motivation. It provides a framework by which jobs can be redesigned to make their incumbents feel that they are doing meaningful and valuable work. Enriching certain elements of the job leads to altered psychological states in employees that influence both their work performance and satisfaction positively.

The five critical job dimensions are skill variety, task identity, task significance, autonomy, and feedback. The first three dimensions impact on the meaningfulness of the work, autonomy impacts on the responsibility experienced for outcomes, and feedback impacts on the employee's knowledge of the actual results of work activities.

- *Skill variety:* the extent to which a job requires a person to do a variety of tasks that require different skills and talents.

Instead of just feeding a machine with raw material, a typical machine operator can also become responsible for routine maintenance on the machine, calculating wastage, safety checks on the machine, and quality and quantity of production.
- *Task identity:* the extent to which a person is responsible for a completely identifiable piece of work. A person who designs a piece of furniture, buys the raw material, and does all the carpentry has high task identity.
- *Task significance:* the extent to which the job impacts on other people. Employees who really understand how their jobs impact on customer satisfaction, experience task significance. A computer technician who is responsible for maintaining the organisation's computer network experiences task significance.
- *Autonomy:* the extent to which the job allows a person to experience the freedom and discretion to plan, schedule, and execute the task. A mechanic who decides independently what repairs need to be done, who schedules his own day, and decides how to do the repairs, is working autonomously.
- *Feedback:* the extent to which the person receives factual information on how effectively the job is done. A credit controller who receives information on the amount of bad debts, number of 'bad' customers, average time it takes to respond to a credit application and number of queries outstanding, knows exactly how well the job has been done.

The critical psychological factors influenced by the core job dimensions are the following:
- *Experienced meaningfulness.* A meaningful job is one that is perceived by the employee as highly important, worthwhile, and valuable.
- *Experienced responsibility.* The employee feels that he is personally responsible for the successful completion of the job.
- *Knowledge of results.* Effective feedback helps an employee to understand the level of performance, and serves as a basis for goal setting and improved performance.

14.3.3.1 Applying the job characteristics model

The job characteristics model can be applied in three steps (Kreitner & Kinicki, 1998:204). The first step is a diagnosis of the work environment to determine whether a problem exists. This is done through a self-report instrument, called the job diagnostic survey (JDS), which is completed by the employee. The motivating potential score (MPS) is then calculated. This index represents the extent to which the job characteristics foster internal work motivation. Low scores indicate a low motivating potential and that job redesign should be considered. The MPS is computed as shown in Figure 14.3.

If the MPS is high and the employee is under-performing, the problem does not lie with the job itself, but with contextual

---

Figure 14.3 Computing the motivating potential score (MPS)

$$MPS = \frac{\text{Skill variety} + \text{Task variety} + \text{Task significance}}{3} \times \text{Autonomy} \times \text{Feedback}$$

Figure 14.4 The job characteristics model

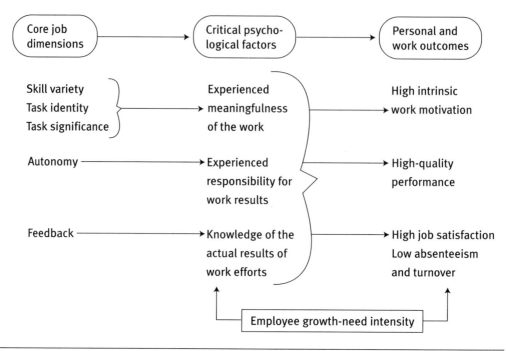

factors such as the condition of equipment, inability, stress, and conflict (Herzberg's hygiene factors). If the MPS is low, those aspects of the job which are inadequate must be determined.

The second step involves determining whether job redesign is appropriate for a given group of employees. According to Kreiter and Kinicki (1998:204) job redesign is most suited to a participative work environment where employees have the necessary skills. Greenberg and Baron (1995: 150) reason that job redesign will work better when employees have a strong growth-need. Mol (1990) reasons that all jobs can be redesigned, that training forms an integral part of the job enrichment intervention, and that most employees can develop a growth-need through effective goal-setting.

The third step involves the redesign of the job, starting with those job characteristics that are lower than the national norms. Including employees in the redesign of the job will lead to greater commitment.

According to Greenberg and Baron (1995:150) a South African study found that job enrichment led to significant improvements in internal motivation and job satisfaction. It also led to lower rates of absenteeism and labour turnover. An interesting fact is that no significant changes were found in job performance; employees in unenriched jobs performed just as well as those in enriched jobs. This is ascribed to the complexity of job motivation and job performance as explained by expectancy theory.

14.3.4 The expectancy theories

In this section we will introduce and examine two expectancy theories: Vroom's expectancy theory, and Porter and Lawler's expectancy theory. Both theories hold that people are only motivated to act in a specific way if they believe that a desired outcome will be attained. Expectancy theories view behaviour and motivation as a function of beliefs, expectations, perceptions, values, and other mental cognitions.

14.3.4.1 Vroom's expectancy theory

According to Vroom's theory, a person will exert a high effort if he or she believes that there is a reasonable probability that the effort will lead to the attainment of an organisational goal, and that the attainment of the organisational goal will become an instrument through which that person will attain personal goals. If an employee desires a promotion, and believes that through meeting certain organisational criteria he or she will get a promotion, the person will put in greater effort. The opposite is also true. If a person believes that no amount of hard work will lead to promotion, he or she will put in less or no effort. Figure 14.5 illustrates the key concepts of Vroom's expectancy model. Three key concepts in this theory are valence, instrumentality and expectancy.

Valence refers to how attractive a specific outcome is to an individual. It is the anticipated satisfaction of attaining a goal. It differs from value, in the sense that a person might desire a specific outcome, and when it is obtained, the person derives less satisfaction than anticipated from it. Valence is the anticipated satisfaction, and value the actual satisfaction. A person might desire a promotion (valence), and when it occurs, the person might not enjoy the new position, and might wonder why he or she actually desired it in the first place. Valence can be assessed on a scale ranging from −2 (very undesirable) to 0 (neutral) to +2 (very desirable).

Expectancy refers to an individual's belief that a certain level of effort will lead to a certain level of performance. This represents the effort-performance expectation. If an individual has a zero expectancy that effort will lead to performance, the person

Figure 14.5 Vroom's expectancy theory

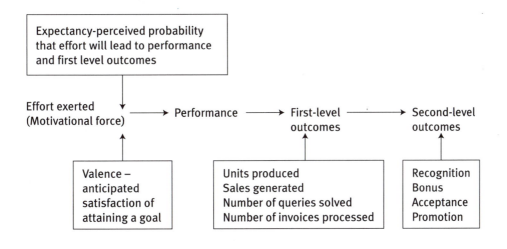

will not put in a remarkable effort. If a reward is offered to students who achieve 80 per cent or more for a test, and a student desires the reward (positive valence) but believes that it is an unrealistic goal and cannot be attained, he or she will not put in a big effort. However, if the student expects to be successful at achieving the desired level of performance, he or she will put in a bigger effort in order to perform.

According to Kreitner and Kinicki (1998:229) the following factors influence a person's expectancy perceptions:
- self-esteem;
- self-efficacy;
- previous success at the task or a similar task;
- support from others (supervisor, subordinates, colleagues);
- access to relevant information; and
- sufficient material and equipment.

Instrumentality is the perception that performance will lead to the desired outcome. Performance is instrumental when it leads to a specific outcome or outcomes. The first-level outcomes are performance-related and the second-level outcomes are need-related. People normally do not receive rewards for their efforts, but for achieving actual results. Instrumentalities range from −1.0 to 1.0. An instrumentality of 1.0 indicates that the attainment of an outcome is totally dependent on performance, an instrumentality of 0.0 indicates no relationship between performance and outcome, while an instrumentality of −1.0 indicates that high performance reduces the chance of obtaining an outcome, while low performance increases the chance. For example, the more time you spend at work to get a promotion (high performance), the less time you will have for your family; the less time you spend working for a promotion (low performance) the more time you have for your family.

14.3.4.2 The expectancy theory of Porter and Lawler

Lyman Porter and Edward Lawler III extended Vroom's theory into an expectancy model of motivation. This model, presented in Figure 14.6, attempted to:
- identify the origin of people's valences and expectancies;
- link effort with performance and job satisfaction;
- identify factors other than effort that influence performance; and
- emphasise the importance of equitable rewards.

Value of reward is similar to valence in Vroom's theory. People desire a combination of outcomes or rewards for what they put into their jobs. The content theories of motivation can be used to explore these values further.

The perceived effort-reward probability is the extent to which a person believes that his or her efforts will in fact lead to the reward. This is similar to the concept of expectancy in Vroom's theory. Both the desirability of the reward and the perceived probability that the effort will lead to the reward, impact on the effort the person will put into his job.

Effort does not lead directly to performance, but is moderated by *abilities and traits*, and *role perception*. A sales person can spend hours promoting a product without making a sale; this can be owing to using the wrong techniques, an unconvincing manner, or perhaps the belief that his or her role is only to demonstrate the product and not to persuade people to buy it.

Satisfaction is influenced by both *intrinsic* and *extrinsic rewards*. Intrinsic rewards are self-granted and consist of intangibles such as a sense of accomplishment and achievement. Extrinsic rewards include bonuses, public recognition, awards, and acceptance. Job satisfaction is influenced by an em-

Figure 14.6 The Porter and Lawler model

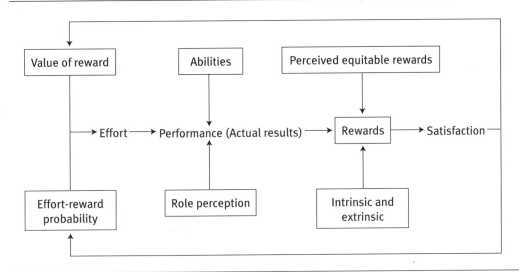

ployee's perception about the equity of rewards given. Employees expect rewards that are not only equitable to their own inputs, but also equitable to the rewards that other employees with similar inputs receive. If employees experience inequity, they direct their behaviour towards creating equity.

It is also important that some congruency exists between intrinsic and extrinsic rewards. Consider feeling very good about a job you have done, but nobody else notices your achievement. Also, consider receiving ample praise from others knowing that you do not deserve it.

The traditional organisation paid much attention to extrinsic rewards. Organisations do need systems that clearly and closely tie rewards to performance. Lawler (1996:57) uses the term line of sight, indicating the extent to which employees see that the extrinsic rewards they receive are a consequence of their performance. In the modern organisation, the emphasis is less on individual pay for performance, and more on gain sharing, profit sharing, and stock ownership, also linked to performance. Intrinsic rewards have a potent influence on performance and employee behaviour. Although individuals give themselves intrinsic rewards, organisations can influence the likelihood of those rewards being tied to performance by addressing job design. The complexity of the task, how challenging it is, and the kind of feedback people receive about their work have a huge impact on intrinsic rewards.

Managers can enhance the effort-performance expectancies by helping employees accomplish their performance goals. Specifically, managers can:
- communicate with individuals or groups to determine what personal goals and rewards they value;
- clearly link rewards to performance goals;
- train and guide employees to the required performance levels;
- make the individual and group responsible for goal attainment;
- provide equitable rewards; and
- foster a positive environment for intrinsic rewards through careful job design.

Lastly, employees' future effort-reward probability expectations are influenced by past experience with performance and rewards.

14.4 The role of goal setting in motivation

Any idea that is not translated into specific goals will stay an idea only. Objectives and goals dictate our purpose and direction. Motivation is described as a driving force aimed at attaining a specific goal. The importance of goal setting and goal attainment in performance management illustrates the role of goals in shaping and reinforcing the behaviour of employees. Management by Objectives (MBO) is a widely used management technique that fosters employee participation in goal setting, decision-making and feedback. A motivated person is always aware of the fact that he or she is working towards a specific goal, and continuously directs his or her efforts at achieving that goal, even in the face of adversity. The goal setting approach to motivation is based on the work of Edwin Locke.

14.4.1 Why do goals motivate?

Goal setting influences behaviour in four different ways:
- *Goals direct attention to what is most important.* The goal of the Ritz-Carlton Hotel Company is to delight their customers. The Ritz credo is to 'fulfil even the unexpected wishes and needs of our guests'. Good customer service is discussed every single day (Hays 1999: 1–4).
- *Goals prompt us into action.* At the Ritz-Carlton, employees address the needs of customers immediately. If a waiter overhears a customer complaining about a television's reception, the waiter addresses the issue immediately by reporting it to the engineering department and phoning the customer afterwards to find out if the problem had been resolved satisfactorily.
- *Goals increase our persistence.* An athlete whose goal it is to run the 100 metres in less than 10 seconds will practice more regularly and with more dedication than an athlete who just wants to stay fit.
- *Goals direct strategies and action plans.* The goal of a swimming pool construc-

---

Encounter 14.1 Microsoft South Africa

Terry Annecke, marketing director of Microsoft in South Africa:

'We hire smart people and then we manage them in the most effective way. One of the critical aspects is setting clear goals and managing performance against these goals. It must be a two way process though – the employee and the manager should discuss and set goals together. To me it is really important to have a meeting of minds and a common purpose. I believe you can get an astonishing amount from people if they know what is expected of them, what they need to accomplish and how it will contribute to the company's success.'

SOURCE: Management Today (2000:18).

tion company was to attract 25 per cent more customers during the following year. Once this goal was identified, marketing strategies (participation in exhibitions and fairs, sales specials, and intensive advertising) were formulated. For each strategy, specific action plans were identified.

14.4.2 Practical application of goal setting

To apply goal setting, the key performance areas of jobs must first be identified. The key performance area of a job refers to those areas in a job in which an employee must perform well in order to be successful. The key performance areas in any position must be aligned with the overall goals and strategies of the organisation. If excellent customer service is an organisational goal, then it should become the individual employee's goal as well.

In order to facilitate commitment, the manager and employee should set goals together. One of the most important considerations is that the employee must have control over the achievement of results. Goals should be quantifiable and specific.

Many authors accept that goals should be specific and difficult, yet attainable through persistence. Mol (1990:115) disagrees here. According to him, low goals are more motivating than high goals. Mol sees a low goal as a realistic goal where the likelihood of success is very high. A 'sense of achievement' is synonymous with 'an experience of success' and, by lowering the goals, the likelihood of success provides the motivating force. Mol also states that performance improvements should always be viewed in terms of the original baseline measure, and that the goalposts should not be moved, unless conditions change, such as an improvement in machinery. If the historical standard for performance is fifty units per hour, and management finds this acceptable, all improvements should be viewed against this acceptable standard of performance. All improvements, regardless

---

Encounter 14.2 South African Breweries

Norman Adami, MD of South African Breweries Ltd. since 1994:

'Three key strategic themes provide a frame of reference for the company going into the new century; growth, people and corporate reputation. Most growth achievements have more to do with motivation than pure technological performance – which is the relevance of our second key strategic theme, SAB's own people. It is why the company pays so much attention to its organisational culture. It constantly evaluates and reviews the overall effectiveness of the company, including leadership style and management practices such as fostering a culture of performance and reward, increasing employee participation and setting goals for individuals and teams. In SAB we strive to nurture a high-performance, high-involvement culture where there is a low tolerance for mediocrity and an openness to challenge, change and learning. Our Integrated Management Process (IMP) ensures that we align our people processes with our goals, and that our measures, rewards and incentives are effective in driving the right behaviour.'

SOURCE: Financial Mail Corporate Report (1999:8).

of their size, should be regarded as successful attempts. By continuously setting higher goals, while maintaining the baseline as the acceptable rate, quality will be improved in the organisation. Kreitner and Kinicki (1998:239) also acknowledge that different goals may have to be set for employees with different levels of skill and ability. Unfortunately, this practice might lead to perceived inequity among co-workers.

Managers must provide adequate support and feedback for employees to be successful. This includes ensuring that employees have the necessary skills and information to achieve their goals. Managers should also pay attention to employees' perceptions of effort-performance expectancies, self-efficacy, and valence of rewards. Feedback on performance should be timely, accurate, objective, and aimed at identifying performance areas that need further development. Feedback is an interactive process between an employee and the manager.

14.5 Money as a motivator

Whether you perceive money as a motivator or not depends on what you perceive as motivation. Both Frederick Herzberg and Arnold Mol perceive motivation as an internally directed desire to achieve a primary goal. An employee exerts a high effort to accomplish goals that will make him or her feel good. According to Mol (1990:59) money does not motivate, but moves a person to achieve a goal in order to obtain the reward. Herzberg's two-factor theory states that extrinsic rewards, such as pay, benefits, working conditions, or company policies do not motivate people, they merely bring performance to an acceptable level. Motivated people perform at levels that are higher than the acceptable standard. Intrinsic awards, such as responsibility, growth and opportunities motivate an employee to these high levels of performance.

According to Maslow's needs hierarchy theory, money can only serve as a motivator if it is a means to satisfy a need. Money can be used to satisfy many needs. People can buy food and clothes with money (physiological need), money provides physical and emotional security, increases your social capacity, gives status, and creates more opportunities for personal realisation.

Lawler (1996:207) reasons that if money as a reward can cause dysfunctional behaviour, it obviously affects behaviour and therefore also performance. According to him, the effect of money as a motivator depends largely on the pay system used in the organisation. When pay systems are not designed well, they either do not motivate or motivate the wrong behaviour, as in Illustrative Case 14.1.

> ### Illustrative case
> ### Money as a motivator – two studies
>
> **Sears Stores**
> At this group of stores, sales people developed a way to allocate customers on a rotating basis, so that each employee had a relatively equal chance to earn sales commission. Once contact was made with a customer, the employee 'owned' the customer, and served him or her from beginning to end. This system reduced conflict among sales staff. However, it also caused other problems. The particular employee was not always available and the customers did not always remember the employee's name. Many employees also refused to serve customers when the responsible person was not available, because they would not earn commission.
>
> **A ball-bearing plant**
> At this plant employees received incen-

tives when they exceeded the standard rate of production. All but four of the 320 employees in the plant performed at 40 per cent above the expected level, while the four performed at 100 per cent above the required level. These four employees were union officials. It turned out that the ordinary employees felt that if they worked harder, performance standards would be raised. The union officials acknowledged (and it was apparently true) that their standards would not be raised due to their union status. At a meeting with management, union officials indicated that the performance of the entire plant could be increased by a further 20 to 30 per cent if management would agree to freeze standards. Management did not agree. They were worried that employees would 'make too much money'.

SOURCE: Lawler, E.E. (1966:207).

According to Kreitner and Kinicki (1998:239) pay should only be linked to performance goals when:
- goal attainment is under the control of the employee;
- goals are quantitative and measurable; and
- payments are frequent and substantial.

The critical point that organisations and their managers should remember from Maslow's theory and related theories is that human beings are motivated by internal feelings of accomplishment, capability, and competency, not just by extrinsic rewards such as food, water, acceptance, and financial well-being. Money is a motivator, but it is not the only or most powerful source of motivation. Organisational designs that do not emphasise the role of intrinsic rewards, fail to tap a very powerful source of motivation that can lead individuals to perform at extraordinary levels (Lawler, 1996:55).

14.6 Motivating contingent employees

Part-time jobs attract a full range of employees – students, retirees, working mothers and fathers needing an extra income, people wanting to earn while searching for 'the right job', and even professionals who prefer the freedom that comes with flexitime. Downsizing, rightsizing, and outsourcing also create fewer opportunities for full-time employment and more for part-time. The ratio of part-timers to full-timers is expected to increase in the next few years.

Organisations need to consider the motivation and performance standards of

Encounter 14.3 Microsoft South Africa

Consider what is done at Microsoft to facilitate worker motivation. In the words of Terry Annecke, marketing director at Microsoft in South Africa: 'Microsoft succeeds because we hire great people and because we create an environment in which employees can create, have control and make a positive contribution every day. We encourage decision making at all levels. This ensures that we have the ability to meet and exceed customer needs.'

SOURCE: Management Today (2000:19).

part-timers. Nelson (1999) suggests the following guidelines for the motivation of part-time employees.

- Appreciate part-time employees for the job they do. Recognition and appreciation are only achieved if goals are set, performance measured, and feedback given.
- Treat part-time employees the way you want them to act. If you want them to have a long-term perspective, talk about their relationship with the organisation, their goals, and the skills they need or are interested in learning.
- Provide new challenges through job rotation. Provide a choice of assignments where possible.
- Assign a mentor to the part-timer. This will ensure that the part-timer internalises the values and attitudes of the organisation.
- Encourage part-timers to take initiative in providing better products and services to customers.
- Provide the right training and resources. Provide orientation as well as training related to the successful execution of jobs.
- Communicate. Part-time employees are easily excluded from meetings and discussions that concern their jobs. Allow ample opportunities for communication. Encourage part-timers to initiate communication.
- Make part-timers feel part of the team. Part-timers also have affiliation needs and want to feel accepted in the organisation. Invite part-timers to attend formal and informal meetings.
- Make it fun. Create an enjoyable work environment. Labour turnover is very high with part-time employees. High labour turnover is not only disruptive, but also affects customer satisfaction.

14.7 A holistic approach to motivation

In a holistic approach, the assumption is that a person is an organised whole, functioning in totality through the interaction of various needs, expectations, beliefs, personality traits, skills, and abilities. People are also perceived as unique beings, with a dynamic nature. From this approach the question should not arise as to which motivational theory is the best; rather, all of the theories should be used to understand human motivation in the workplace. The different theories on motivation complement each other and provide a framework for the understanding of human behaviour.

When a performance problem arises in the organisation, it should not immediately be ascribed to a lack of motivation. The cause might lie in poor material, machinery, or work processes. When a motivational problem is evident, the inter-relatedness of the individual, the job characteristics, the job context, and the organisational culture should be considered. The various approaches to motivation should be considered and utilised in analysing and rectifying the situation.

14.8 Motivation and quality assurance

An organisation cannot compete successfully without a motivated workforce. Total quality management (TQM) implies a continuous improvement in products and services through the active learning and participation of all employees. It is, therefore, imperative that a culture is established within an organisation where all human potential is realised. Motivating employees should not be the isolated initiative of one or a few managers; instead, it should become a well-planned and carefully monitored intervention driven jointly by the human resources department or consultant and management. First-line supervisors and managers can empower their employees only if they, themselves, are empowered by their managers. An organisational culture of achievement, self-actualisation, and continuous learning is conducive to quality products and service.

14.9 Conclusion

Organisations exploit various resources in order to compete successfully. These resources include material, machinery, money, methods, and manpower. Few people realise that in comparison to other resources, human resources are the only resources that increase in quality and capacity the more they are utilised. Employees who actively participate in decision-making and problem-solving learn and develop in the process, and are then progressively able to handle more complex and challenging situations. The potential of people is unlimited. Organisations cannot afford to ignore this valuable resource. Motivation is a calculated technique that managers can use to explore human potential and talents. A positive, self-enhancing organisational culture is more likely to render higher motivation and commitment than a culture dominated by power, punishment, and suspicion.

Summary

Motivation is defined as intentional and persistent behaviour aimed at achieving a goal. A motivated employee is one who willingly and enthusiastically works towards achieving the organisational goal.

The content theories of Maslow and Herzberg attempt to explain specific things that motivate people at work. They identify people's needs and the goals they pursue in order to satisfy these needs.

The process theories attempt to identify the variables that impact on motivation. These theories are concerned with how behaviour is initiated, directed, and sustained. The emphasis is placed on the actual process of motivation.

The various motivational theories provide a framework for understanding employee behaviour and performance in the workplace. It is important that a holistic perspective of motivation is taken rather than isolating one theory as the best.

Theorists differ on the impact that money has as a motivator. Money only serves as a motivator if it is directly linked to performance. However, it is agreed that intrinsic rewards have a powerful impact on motivation.

Managers should also consider the motivation of part-time employees, as they will increasingly form a significant part of the future work force.

Quality cannot be separated from motivation. By building motivation into the job content and job environment, employees will be enabled to produce quality products and services.

Related websites

This topic may be investigated further by referring to the following Internet websites:
Microsoft South Africa – http://microsoft.com/southafrica/
South African Breweries – http://www.SAB.co.za
Ritz Carlton Group – http://www.workforceonline.com

Case study
Motivating a low-wage workforce

An Internet survey done in 1997 on human resources professionals' thoughts about motivating a minimum-wage workforce, revealed that 62 per cent of respondents had a problem retaining minimum-wage workers strictly because of pay; 69 per cent made use of incentives such as bonuses, prizes, or promotions to motivate employees; and 53 per cent indicated that they had to give benefits because they were unable to retain employees with pay alone.

Two human resources experts have provided tips for motivating low-wage employees. Tony Bryant, human resources associate of Irving Co., a producer of fine leather products suggested the following:
- Connect employees to the bigger picture. Let them see how their jobs impact on the final product. When employees see that their hard work is valuable, they will feel good.
- Involve employees in decisions that affect their jobs. When making changes in policies and benefits, ask the workers their opinion.
- Encourage personal growth. Educational benefits, training, and internal promotions are good for both workers and organisations.

Laura Parsons, director of field human resources for Miami-based Burger King Corporation, offered these tips:
- Treat people well and with respect.
- Make the work environment a fun place to work. Burger King celebrates birthdays and anniversaries, and recognises outstanding performance with a party. Some store employees organise softball teams and bowling leagues. Encourage activities that bring unity and teamwork.
- Offer flexible work schedules.
- Offer bonuses. Burger King offers an anniversary bonus to employees for completing each year of service. The amount depends on the employee's years of service.
- Offer benefits. Burger King offers a benefit programme for full-time employees who average thirty hours of work a week. The plan includes health care after six months of service and dental care after five years.
- Offer management opportunities and communicate the opportunities clearly and often.

SOURCE: Laabs, J. (1998:57).

Questions

1 Using Maslow's needs hierarchy, indicate which needs of employees these two companies attempt to satisfy.

2 From Herzberg's perspective, how successful do you think these two companies will be in motivating their employees?

3 What is the effect of a service bonus on an employee's behaviour and performance?

Experiential exercise 1

Purpose
To evaluate the extent to which employees in diverse jobs are motivated.
To recommend ways in which the motivation levels of employees can be improved.

Introduction
The various motivational theories provide a framework for the understanding of motivation in the workplace. It is short-sighted to believe that one theory will provide all the answers to motivational problems.

Task

Step 1 (1 hour)
Form groups of five students each. Each group will be allocated a specific motivation theory (excluding Maslow's need hierarchy). In your groups, compile a questionnaire, based on the allocated theory, that can be used to determine how motivated an employee is. Make provision for a short job description.

Step 2 (done outside scheduled periods)
In your own time, ask three diversely employed people to complete the questionnaire as honestly as possible. Your study facilitator will provide advice on how to conduct this task in a professional manner.

Step 3 (30 minutes)
Analyse and compare the completed questionnaires. How motivated would you say each person is? What would you recommend should be done to increase their motivational levels?

Step 4 (5 minutes per group)
The groups get the opportunity to share their findings and recommendations with everybody.

Experiential exercise 2

Purpose
To debate the impact money has on the motivation of South African employees.

Introduction
Well-known theorists disagree about the impact of money on the motivation of employees. Most management theories originate from America, and their applicability to the South African context is not conclusive. Many organisations use financial incentives to increase productivity.

Task
Step 1 (30 minutes)
Form groups of five learners each. Half of the groups will prepare an argument for, and the others an argument against the use of money as a motivator in the South African workplace.

Step 2 (3 minutes per group)
Each group offers their argument in a debate presentation.

Step 3 (5 minutes)
The facilitator (or designated person) summarises the main arguments and draws conclusions.

To make this exercise more meaningful, the groups could be granted an opportunity to do additional research and also interview managers and employees on their experiences with financial incentives, before presenting their arguments.

Self-assessment 14.1 Interpretation

Physiological needs: Add up the total for items 2, 10 and 14.
Security needs: Items 5, 11 and 13.
Social needs: Items 1, 6 and 15.
Esteem needs: Items 4, 7 and 9.
Self-actualisation needs: Items 3, 8 and 12.

Which needs are the most important to you?
Which needs are the least important to you?

Compare your needs profile to that of another learner. Do you have similar needs? If you do have similar needs, is the strength of these needs the same? In which ways do you try to satisfy your most important needs? Considering the needs profile of your fellow learner, what would you suggest he or she does to satisfy his or her needs?

Chapter questions

1. Whose responsibility is it to motivate employees?
2. What behaviours distinguish a motivated employee from one who is not motivated?
3. How will you respond to a person who says that it is impossible to motivate certain employees, such as machine operators, mechanics, cleaners, or security officers?
4. Use the concepts in Vroom's expectancy theory to explain how motivated you are in terms of your studies.
5. Considering all of the motivation theories discussed in this chapter, what general guidelines will you provide to managers for motivating their employees?

Bibliography

BERGH, Z.C. & THERON, A.L. 1999. *Psychology in the work context.* Thomson, Johannesburg.

FINANCIAL MAIL CORPORATE REPORT. 22 October 1999. SA Breweries. The glass that cheers.

GERBER, P.D., NEL, P.S. & VAN DYK, P.S. 1998. *Human resource management.* 4th edition. ITP, Johannesburg.

GREENBERG, J & BARON, R.A. 1995. *Behavior in organisations. Understanding and managing the human side of work.* 5th edition. Prentice-Hall, New Jersey.

HAYS, S. 1999. Exceptional customer service takes the 'Ritz' touch. *Workforce Journal.* http://workforceonline.com.

IVANCEVICH, J.M. & MATTESON, M.T. 1999. *Organisational behaviour and management.* 5th edition. Irwin/McGraw-Hill, USA.

JEFFRIES, M & LEWIS, G.A. 1992. Smithmark, New York.

KREITNER, R. & KINICKI, A. 1998. *Organisational behaviour.* 4th edition. Irwin/McGraw-Hill, USA.

LAABS, J. 1998. Motivating a low-wage workforce. *Workforce Journal.* http://workforceonline.com.

LAWLER, E.E. 1996. *From the ground up.* Jossey-Bass, San Francisco.

MASLOW, A.H. 1954. *Motivation and personality.* Harper & Row, New York.

MICROSOFT – IT'S A PEOPLE'S BUSINESS. 2000. *Management Today.* Volume 16, No 2, pp18-22.

MOL. A. 1990. *Help! I'm a manager.* Tafelberg, Cape Town.

MULLINS, L.J. 1996. *Management and organizational behaviour.* 4th edition. Pitman, London.

NELSON, B. 2000. Top 10 ways to motivate part-time employees. Http://www.workforceonline.com/00/04/13/005284.html.

PLUNKET, W.R. 1996. *Supervision: diversity and teams in the workplace.* 8th edition. Prentice-Hall, Upper Saddle River, New Jersey.

ROBBINS, S.P. 1989. *Organisational behaviour: concepts, controversies and applications.* Prentice-Hall, Englewood Cliffs, New Jersey.

ROBBINS, S.P. 1998. *Organisational behaviour.* 8th edition. Prentice-Hall, New Jersey.

15

Leadership

A Werner

Learning outcomes

At the end of this chapter the learner should be able to demonstrate the following outcomes:
- Define leadership.
- Compare and contrast leadership and management.
- Discuss the task and people dimensions of leadership.
- Explain how power and authority influence leadership.
- Discuss and apply various leadership theories to organisational situations.
- Provide an overview of transformational leadership.
- Discuss leadership challenges in a virtual workplace.
- Indicate the importance of quality assurance in leadership.

Key words and concepts

- emotional intelligence
- empowerment
- quantum leap change
- self-fulfilling prophecy
- situational leadership
- transformation
- virtual leadership

Illustrative case
The Welch revolution

Jack Welch is known as the person who changed General Electric forever. As CEO of this world-renowned company which was founded by Thomas Edison, he revolutionised the way business was done. His leadership example still serves as a valuable lesson for business leaders all over the world who have to steer their companies into an uncertain future. He pushed for change long before anybody else deemed it necessary. He sensed the danger of lagging productivity and global competition and acted proactively to prevent a crisis. He ultimately transformed the very nature of General Electric by not only reshaping its businesses but also its culture. He instituted radical, fundamental changes by breaking away from the doctrine of scientific management, and changed a military-style hierarchy into a value-based organisation by involving employees in the decision-making processes. He eliminated the company's unviable businesses, and created a logical organisation by concentrating on core businesses.

Physically, Welsh is not a big person. However, the power and intensity of his personality has a magnetic effect on others. He is open, honest, straightforward, enthusiastic, passionate, emotional, and appreciative. His success as a leader is less a consequence of his personality than his quality of thought. He is intelligent, creative, analytical, and disciplined. The remarkable story of General Electric's revitalisation has served as an excellent example to leaders and business people all over the world.

Source: Tichy & Sherman (1993: 3-11).

15.1 Introduction

In a world that is becoming more and more complex through the accelerated development and application of information technology, organisations have to respond much quicker to challenges. Bill Gates of Microsoft urges that it is now necessary to 'operate at the speed of thought'. Globalisation is forcing organisations to become competitive and to operate according to international standards. These challenges require quantum leap change, rather than adaptive change from organisations. Quantum leap change becomes necessary when environmental changes make traditional ways of operating organisations redundant and, thus, demand fundamentally different approaches to ensure ongoing survival and future success. In order to cope in a new world, a new breed of leader is required. What the leaders of today have learned in the past may not be applicable to the future. The way in which organisations respond to new challenges is unmistakably tied to the values, attitudes, styles, and responses of their leaders. It is, therefore, imperative for leaders to unlearn old habits and beliefs, and engage in ongoing learning and personal development.

In this chapter we will explore what leadership is, dimensions of leadership, power and authority in leadership, and different approaches to leadership. We will also discuss transformational and charismatic leadership. We will consider the leadership challenges in a virtual workplace, and the importance of quality assurance in leadership.

15.2 What is leadership?

A generally accepted definition of leadership is: the process whereby one individual influences others to willingly and enthusiastically direct their efforts and abilities towards attaining defined group or organisational goals. According to this definition, leadership involves the exercise of influence and not coercion. The leader attempts to change the attitudes and actions which are related to specific goals, and not attitudes or actions which are not related to the goal. Leadership is very much a two-way relationship; not only does the leader influence the followers, but the followers also exert influence over the leader.

15.3 Leadership versus management

In everyday speech, the terms leader and manager are often used interchangeably. There is, however, a clear distinction between the two. Figure 15.1 demonstrates some of the important differences between leadership and management.

Leadership focuses on vision, strategic development, and initiative, whereas management deals with the implementation of the vision. Humphrey Walters (1999: 10), co-founder and chief executive of the Mast International Organisation, writes the following: 'Most people realize that the art of leadership is a learned craft. Management, on the other hand, is a science.'

Managers are more concerned with short-term problems in the organisation, whereas leaders take a much broader perspective and concern themselves with the environment, internal and external to the organisation. Leaders have a long-term perspective and anticipate the future needs of the organisation. It is often said that leaders do the right things, while managers do things right. Leadership in an organisation, unlike management, is not restricted to people in specific positions or roles, but is related to all people with the ability to influence and inspire others to attain a goal. To enhance innovation and teamwork in the organisation, leadership must be present at all levels. Managers will also become much more effective if their leadership skills are developed and utilised. The fact that South Africa maintains a very low position in the World Competitive Survey, indicates a need to identify and develop more leaders, and to create an organisational culture that encourages and supports leadership initiative.

15.4 The qualities or traits approach to leadership

A question often asked is whether leaders are born or not. Many studies have been done to identify common characteristics of leaders. Although some of these studies have found common characteristics in leaders, no universal set of characteristics has been confirmed. However, these studies underline the fact that leaders are different to other people and that they possess outstanding characteristics. Leadership is a very demanding, unrelenting job with enormous pressures and grave responsibilities.

Humphrey Walters (1999: 10) identifies the following characteristics of leaders:
- Leaders have the ability to create a vision and to excite people to try and achieve the impossible.
- Great leaders have an external energy and an inner strength that see them through tough times.

Figure 15.1 Leadership versus management

Criteria	Leadership	Management
Change	Provide a vision and initiate change	Implement changes as suggested by leader
People	Inspire and develop	Control
Power derived from	Ability to influence others	Authority
Task	Do the right things	Do things right
Commitment to goal	Passionate	Impersonal

- Leaders have a mental agility that enables them to make effective decisions much faster than most other people.
- Leaders allow their team members to grow, and to carry out tasks without interruption. They delegate power to others.
- Leaders have the ability to tap into people's souls. They are emotionally intelligent, and enhance people's confidence by understanding and dealing appropriately with their emotions and concerns. This reflects the ability to adapt to the needs of different situations and people.

Ultimately, one has to accept that even if a person has certain inborn characteristics which provide the potential for good leadership, these natural talents need to be encouraged and developed.

15.5 Participative versus autocratic leadership behaviours

In the late 1940s, researchers began to explore the idea that a leader's behaviour determined effectiveness. The Ohio State Leadership Studies (Kreitner & Kinicki 1998: 499) identified two clusters of behaviour:
- *Consideration*, which includes behaviours such as helping subordinates, communicating, listening, and explaining. Consideration involves creating mutual respect and trust and having a concern for group members' needs and desires.
- *Structure initiation*, such as clarifying rules and procedures, maintaining performance standards, and explaining to employees what their roles are. Structure initiation focuses on what the group should do to achieve results.

Subsequent studies have produced the concepts of employee-centred and job-centred behaviours, which are parallel to consideration and structure initiation. The original idea of these studies was to determine which behavioural approach was more effective.

Contemporary leadership theories, such as the leadership grid of Blake and Mouton, and the situational leadership theory of Hersey and Blanchard (which are dealt with later in this chapter) also distinguish between task behaviour and people behaviour. However, these theories do not suggest that there is one best leadership style. Rather, they argue that the effectiveness of a given leadership style depends on situational factors.

15.6 Power and authority

Every leader possesses a certain influence and power over others. Managers, on the other hand, have the ability to influence subordinates due to the authority vested in them. Leaders are not always associated with a specific position, yet still have the ability to influence people towards the attainment of organisational goals. The power to influence is awarded to the leader by his or her followers. The exercise of power is a social process that helps to explain how different people can influence the behaviour of others. The ability to influence people is based on various sources of power.
- *Reward power:* the extent to which the follower believes that the leader has the ability and resources to provide rewards for behaviour that meet the expectations of the leader. Examples of rewards are recognition, praise, money, privileges, and allocation of challenging tasks.
- *Coercive power:* the extent to which the follower believes that the leader has the ability to punish or disadvantage followers. Examples of punishment include withholding information, privileges, or growth

Encounter 15.1 Leadership at South African Breweries

In the executive corridors of South African Breweries Ltd people whisper that if, for some reason, all other employees of the company were suddenly to disappear, Norman Adami could keep your favourite beer flowing. The only limitation would be that there is only one of him.

Adami is 45 years old and has been the MD of SAB since 1994. His energy and passion for the business, his strategic insight as well as his relentless attention to detail are all legendary. He personifies the company's collective can-do attitude and lack of complacency. It's a mind-set that has made SAB into one of very few SA firms that can hold their own against the best in the world. For a company that has built formidable capabilities in such areas as marketing, distribution and production, you'd think an occasional corporate nap might be forgivable. But Adami won't have any of it. He is continually moving the goal-posts by which success is measured. Adami's objective for SAB Ltd is that it should be a globally competitive and growth-orientated business, with pride in its products, people, customers, brand and reputation.

SOURCE: Furlonger & Sikakhane (1999: 6).

opportunities, withdrawal of emotional support, formal reprimand, or ostracism.
- *Legitimate power:* the extent to which the followers believe that the leader has the right to influence them, by virtue of the leader's role or position in the organisation. Legitimate power is based on authority.
- *Referent power:* the extent to which a follower identifies with and respects the leader. The leader attracts followers due to perceived attractiveness, charisma, or reputation.
- *Expert power:* the extent to which the follower believes that the leader is an expert in a specific field, is competent, and has special abilities.

Leaders may have more than one source of power. These sources of power are based on the perceptions of the followers, and may not be based on objective evaluation of the leader's ability or strength.

Before reading further, complete Self-assessment 15.1. The interpretation is discussed at the end of the chapter.

15.7 McGregor's X and Y theory

McGregor's X and Y theory is based on the following self-fulfilling prophecy: A manager's assumptions about the nature of human beings impact on the manager's behaviour towards employees. The manager's behaviour then influences the employees' behaviour, which again serves to reconfirm the manager's assumptions.

Let us first explore the different assumptions managers could have about employees and then consider how these assumptions influence the manager's and employees' behaviour.

McGregor identified two sets of assumptions managers have about employees, and he called these Theory X and Theory Y. Theory X assumptions are negative, and include the perception that people are lazy, dislike work, require close supervision, do not want responsibility, and have little ambition. Since people act according to what they believe, a manager with these outdated beliefs will give detailed instructions, supervise employees

Self-assessment 15.1 Are you an X or Y person?

Answer TRUE or FALSE.
1. Most people will do less if the supervisor is not present.
2. The average person can be trusted with the valuables of an organisation.
3. Employees want to improve themselves.
4. Punishment is the best way to ensure that employees do not disobey rules.
5. Most people work only for payday.
6. Employees will work hard if they set their own goals.
7. People don't like to be told how to do things.
8. Employees are willing to accept responsibility for a task.
9. Employees feel motivated if they receive detailed instructions on how to do their jobs.
10. Most people will disobey rules when nobody is watching.
11. If a person had a choice, he or she would choose the easiest task.
12. Punishment is an ineffective way to control employees.
13. Most employees prefer the manager to make decisions.
14. People are only interested in how much they get at the end of the month.
15. Employees feel proud when managers show trust in them by giving them moderately difficult tasks.
16. Most people are willing to learn new things.
17. People want to show others how well they can do things.
18. People are lazy by nature.
19. Knowledge of progress (feedback) motivates employees.
20. Employees will always complain about management.

---

closely, and use threats of punishment to control behaviour. Employees treated in such a way tend to do just what is required of them to stay out of trouble, abuse sick leave, and stay uncommitted to the organisation or its goals. Theory X managers will observe these behaviours and allow them to reconfirm their original beliefs about people. A vicious circle of negativity is created. South Africa is notorious for its low levels of productivity. Is the answer to this problem to be found in McGregor's theory? Why do some companies, such as South African Breweries, manage to compete successfully despite tough international competition?

Theory Y is a modern and positive set of assumptions about people. Theory Y managers believe that employees are hardworking, want to make a positive contribution, seek responsibility, and can control their own performance. They view employees as self-energised, committed, responsible, and creative. Such managers provide employees with opportunities, positive guidance, and recognition. Employees working under them feel respected, acknowledged, and proud. They become responsible and hardworking. The subsequent performance of the employees reconfirms the original beliefs of the manager. Figure 15.2 illustrates leaders' assumptions about people according to McGregor's theory.

McGregor's theory has exerted a major influence on modern day management, especially since it underlines a humanistic perspective.

Figure 15.2 Leaders' assumptions about people

X beliefs	Y beliefs
People are inherently lazy and avoid work whenever they can.	People perceive work as natural as play.
Most people are only interested in money.	People want to make a worthwhile contribution.
People do not want responsibility.	Most people are keen to demonstrate their ability.
The average person does not have much ambition.	People are creative and strive for self-actualisation.
Most people are not capable of solving problems.	People are problem-solvers by nature.

15.8 Schein's theory of human assumptions

The human assumptions identified by Schein (1980:53) reflect the historical course of human assumptions. Each assumption is briefly discussed below.

The rational-economic assumption, underpinned by hedonism, claims that people's behaviour is aimed at obtaining the greatest advantage for themselves. Assumptions of the rational-economic approach can be summarised as follows:
- people are motivated mainly by economic incentives, such as money and bonuses, and their behaviour is directed towards actions that will result in the greatest economic gain;
- since economic incentives are controlled by the organisation, people are a passive factor that can be manipulated, activated, and controlled by the organisation;
- people's feelings are irrational, therefore an attempt must be made to prevent these irrational emotions from interfering with their work; and
- organisations must be designed in such a way that people's feelings are controlled.

A supervisor who holds rational-economic assumptions will exercise control over subordinates by means of direct authority. The rational-economic assumption relates to McGregor's X theory.

The social assumption is a result of the well-known Hawthorne experiments done by Elton Mayo and his colleagues. Mayo found that work negates people's social needs. In this respect Schein (1980:59) says that 'industrial life had taken the meaning out of work and had frustrated man's basic social needs'. The following assumptions are typical of this approach:
- people are motivated by social needs and acquire their basic identity in relationships with others;
- the meaning of work has been reduced by the Industrial Revolution and the rationalisation of work and, therefore, people must find meaning in their social relationships at work;
- people will react to the social influence of their immediate colleagues (peer group) rather than to incentives and control from management; and
- subordinates will only react to management influence to the extent that a supervisor can satisfy their social needs.

The conduct and attitude of a supervisor with a social assumption towards subordinates will differ considerably from that of one with a rational-economic approach. Such a supervisor will pay much more attention to meeting the needs of subordinates, especially the need for social acceptance.

The self-actualisation assumption, according to Schein (1980:68), supports the view of several researchers, including Argyris, McGregor, and Maslow, that the meaning of work has been lost in organisational life: Many jobs in modern industry have become so specialised or fragmented that they neither permit workers to use their capacities nor enable them to see the relationship between what they are doing and the total organisational mission.

He emphasises the role of self-actualisation (1980:76):

The following assumptions are typical of the self-actualisation approach:

Even the lowliest untalented man seeks self-actualisation, a sense of meaning and accomplishment in his work, if his other needs are more or less fulfilled.

- Human needs form a hierarchy, namely:
  - the need for survival, safety, and security;
  - social needs;
  - the need for esteem (ego needs);
  - the need for independence and autonomy; and
  - the need for self-actualisation.
- People strive towards maturity in their work and they can experience growth in the context of their work. This implies that they have to have independence and autonomy, accept long-term perspectives, and develop special skills and greater adaptability.
- People are primarily self-motivated and can exercise self-control. External control measures and strict supervision are likely to make them feel threatened and reduce their maturity level in their work.
- There is no inherent conflict between self-actualisation and effective organisational performance. If an individual is given the opportunity, he or she will voluntarily integrate his or her own needs and goals with those of the organisation.

A supervisor who follows the self-actualisation approach will act in the same way as one who follows the social approach, except for a few important differences. According to the self-actualisation assumption, the supervisor will concentrate on making the work intrinsically more meaningful and challenging, rather than considering the social needs of subordinates.

The complex person assumption postulates that humans are much more complex than assumed by past organisational theories. Schein (1980:80) states:

Not only is he more complex within himself, being possessed of many needs and potentials, but he is also likely to differ from his neighbour in the patterns of his complexity.

The complex person assumption may be summarised as follows:
- People are not only complex, they are also highly changeable.
- Employees can develop new needs as a result of their experience in an organisation.
- Employees' needs may differ from one organisation to the next, and even in different departments of the same organisation.
- People may productively join in the activities of an organisation to satisfy different needs; ultimate need satisfaction and the ultimate effectiveness of the organisation are only partially dependent on the nature of employees' motivation.
- People may react positively to different management strategies (or leadership

styles), depending on their own needs, goals, abilities, and the nature of their work; in other words, there is no one correct managerial strategy that will work for all people at all times (Schein 1980: 80).

For managers, the most important implication of the complex person assumption is that they must, firstly, be good diagnosticians and, secondly, be adaptable.

15.9 The leadership grid of Blake and Mouton

The leadership grid of Blake and Mouton was first published as the Managerial Grid in 1964 and republished in 1991 as the Leadership Grid (Mullins 1996: 439). The grid is illustrated in Figure 15.3. The grid provides a basis to compare different leadership styles in terms of two dimensions:
- concern for production; and
- concern for people.

Concern for production is the extent to which the leader emphasises production, profit, deadlines, task completion, and results. This is represented on the horizontal axis of the grid.

Concern for people is the extent to which the leader emphasises the needs and expectations of employees, and fosters employee satisfaction. This is represented on the vertical axis of the grid.

"Concern for" is not a specific term which indicates the amount of actual production or actual behaviour toward people. Rather it indicates the character and strength of assumptions present behind any given managerial style (Blake & Mouton 1978: 9).

Both dimensions of leadership behaviour are presented on the grid, in nine point scales from low (point 1) through average (point 5) to high (point 9). The different scale points do not allocate absolute values to leadership behaviour, but merely indicate varying degrees of concern for people and for production.

The following leadership styles are identified:
- *The authority-compliance leader* (9,1) shows maximum concern for production (scale point 9) and minimum concern for people (scale point 1). Production is achieved by means of formal authority, and subordinates are controlled by enforcing submissiveness. Decisions are made unilaterally and communication is mainly one-way.
- *The country club leader* (1,9) is a democratic leader who will show minimum concern for production (scale point 1) and maximum concern for people (scale point 9). Cultivating and maintaining sound interpersonal relationships with colleagues and subordinates will therefore be most important. This leader maintains that the job will be done automatically if interpersonal relationships are sound. Communication is aimed at maintaining a pleasant working atmosphere, and conflict is avoided at all costs.
- *The impoverished leader (1,1)* has a laissez-faire approach. This person shows little concern for production and little concern for people (both at scale point 1). A laissez-faire leader does the absolute minimum required, in both the job and interpersonal relationships, to stay on as a member of the organisation. The impoverished leader avoids commitment to decisions. This style is often associated with managers who are close to retirement or managers who have emotionally withdrawn from the organisation.
- *The middle-of-the-road leader (5,5)* tries to maintain a balance between production and interpersonal relationships. Blake

Figure 15.3 Blake and Mouton's Leadership Grid

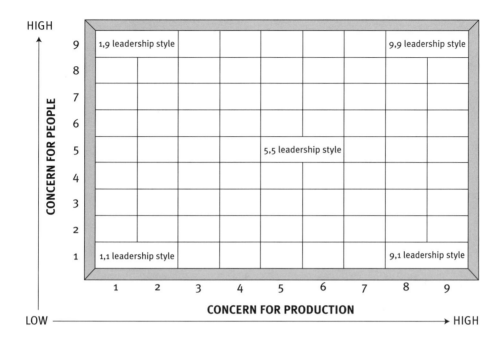

SOURCE: Blake and Mouton (1978: 11).

and Mouton (1978:12) describe this style as 'the 'go-along-to-get-along' assumptions which are revealed in conformity to the status quo'. Such leaders try half-heartedly to pay attention to both aspects (both at scale point 5) but do not succeed. They assume that it is impossible to integrate the needs of employees with organisational goals.

- *The team leader (9,9)* integrates concern for production and concern for people at a high level (both at scale point 9). This style emphasises teamwork, is goal-orientated, and strives for excellent results through participative management, involvement with people, and conflict management. The 9,9 rating provides the ideal that leaders should strive for.

In the 1991 edition of the grid (Mullins, 1996:441) two additional styles were added:
- *9+9 paternalistic leadership.* Here, reward and approval are exchanged for loyalty and obedience, and punishment is threatened for failure to comply. It is also called 'father knows best' leadership.
- *Opportunistic leadership.* Here, the leader utilises a style that will benefit him or her the most. It is also called 'what's in it for me' leadership.

By knowing the styles of other leaders and their own leadership style, leaders will be better equipped to appraise themselves and others more objectively, communicate better, understand where differences originate, and to assist and lead others in being more productive. Blake and Mouton developed a self-assessment questionnaire which gives an indication of the leader's dominant style. Responses can be compared to those of typical leaders who are considered as generally successful. Blake and Mouton (1978: 6) describe the usefulness of their approach as follows:

> Learning grid management not only makes people aware of the assumptions under which they operate but also helps them to learn and to embrace scientifically verified principles for effectiveness in production under circumstances that promise mentally healthy behaviour.

15.10 The leadership continuum of Tannenbaum and Schmidt

Tannenbaum and Schmidt (1958) advocate a leadership continuum which illustrates the situational and varying nature of leadership. Figure 15.4 illustrates this continuum. This approach identifies four main styles of leadership: tells, sells, consults, and joins.

- *Tells.* The leader identifies a goal, decides how the goal should be achieved and instructs employees without providing an opportunity for participation.
- *Sells.* The leader still decides what should be done and how it should be done, but expects resistance and therefore convinces employees of the validity of the decision.
- *Consults.* The leader chooses a decision only after the views and proposals of employees are considered.
- *Joins.* The leader defines the problem and the decision parameters, and leaves the decision to the group, with the manager acting as a group member of equal status.

The continuum illustrates that leadership varies according to the distribution of influence among the leader and his or her subordinates. The leadership style changes from left to right, from leader-centred to subordinate-centred, as the leader exercises less control (authority) and allows subordinates more influence and freedom to take decisions on their own. Leadership behaviour and the leadership style used by a leader will therefore depend on how much authority he or she delegates to subordinates.

Three types of forces determine which style is practical and desirable: forces in the leader, forces in the subordinates, and forces in the situation. An effective leader is aware of these forces and acts according to them.

- *Forces in the leader.* A leader's behaviour is influenced by his or her personality, background, knowledge, and experience. Other internal forces are:
  - the leader's value system;
  - the leader's confidence in subordinates;
  - the leader's own leadership philosophy; and
  - the leader's feeling of security in an uncertain situation, especially when he or she is operating towards the right of the continuum.
- *Forces in the subordinates.* Before a leader can decide how to guide subordinates, he or she must consider the forces affecting these subordinates. Each subordinate is affected by personality variables and expectations of how the leader will act towards him or her. A leader can allow subordinates more freedom and involvement in decision-making if they:
  - have a relatively high need for independence;
  - are prepared to accept responsibility for decision-making;
  - are interested in the problem and feel that it is important;
  - understand the goals of the organisa-

Figure 15.4 The leadership continuum of Tannenbaum and Schmidt

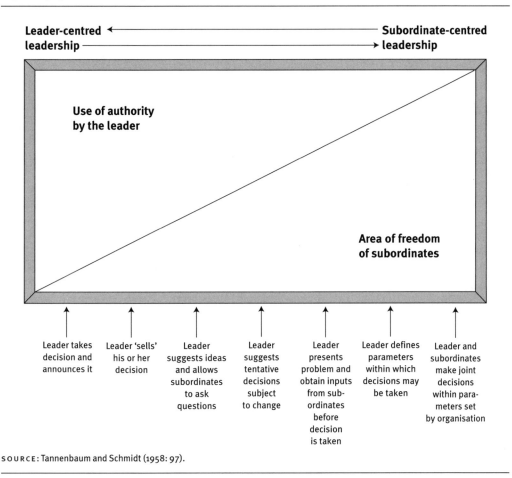

SOURCE: Tannenbaum and Schmidt (1958: 97).

tion and can identify with them;
- have the knowledge and experience required to deal with the problem; and
- understand that they are expected to share in decision-making.
- *Forces in the situation.* Apart from the forces present in the leader and the subordinates, the general situation may also affect a leader's behaviour. Important factors include:
  - the type of organisation, and the people's values and traditions;
  - group effectiveness, including previous experience, group cohesion, mutual acceptance, and commonality of purpose;
  - the complexity of the problem; and
  - time pressure which may result in others not being involved in decision-making.

Although the leadership continuum is a logical concept with practical application value, it does have some shortcomings, the most important of which is the lack of instructions on exactly how a situation is to be diagnosed. Furthermore, it is not clear how leadership behaviour must be judged.

Little empirical research has been conducted about the leadership continuum.

15.11 The situational leadership theory of Hersey and Blanchard

Hersey and Blanchard devised a leadership model based on the maturity or readiness level of employees. This is represented in Figure 15.5, which illustrates the following important concepts.
- *Task behaviour*, according to Hersey and Blanchard (1982:96) implies the degree to which leaders are likely to organise and spell out the tasks of group members by indicating who should do what, when, where, and how. Task behaviour is also characterised by a leader instituting well-defined organisational patterns, channels of communication, and procedures for the execution of tasks.
- *Relationship behaviour* implies the degree to which leaders are likely to maintain interpersonal relationships between themselves and group members by providing open channels of communication, socio-emotional support, psychological stroking, and facilitating of subordinates' behaviour.
- *Maturity levels*, four of which are identified:
  - M1 (low maturity) refers to subordinates who are unwilling or unsure how to execute a task, and do not have the necessary ability to do it;
  - M2 (low to average maturity) refers to subordinates who do not have the ability to execute a task, although they are willing and confident enough to do it;
  - M3 (average to high maturity) refers to subordinates who have the ability to execute the task, but are unwilling or unsure how to do it; and
  - M4 (high maturity) refers to subordinates who have the ability and confidence to execute the task, and are willing to do it.
- *Leadership styles*, of which there are also four, derived from the combination of task and relationship behaviour:
  - S1 (telling) involves high task behaviour combined with low relationship behaviour. The leader explains by means of task behaviour to his or her subordinates what to do and how, where, and when to do it. Such a leader describes his or her subordinates' tasks thoroughly, without explaining to them why a task has to be done or why certain procedures are to be followed. Communication is mainly one-way.
  - S2 (selling) involves high task behaviour with high relationship behaviour. The leader provides guidance to subordinates and tries, by means of two-way communication and socio-emotional support, to persuade his or her subordinates to accept decisions.
  - S3 (participating) is characterised by high relationship behaviour with low task behaviour, meaning that the leader and subordinate take decisions together by means of two-way communication. Subordinates can participate in decision-making because they have the required abilities, and are encouraged to participate by means of high relationship behaviour.
  - S4 (delegating) is characterised by low relationship behaviour with low task behaviour, implying that the leader allows subordinates to take completely independent decisions by delegating authority to them. Therefore, supervision is of a general nature, which means that subordinates' work is not checked continuously as they are fully capable of executing their tasks, they have the necessary confidence, and are willing to do so.

Figure 15.5 Hersey and Blanchard's situational leadership theory

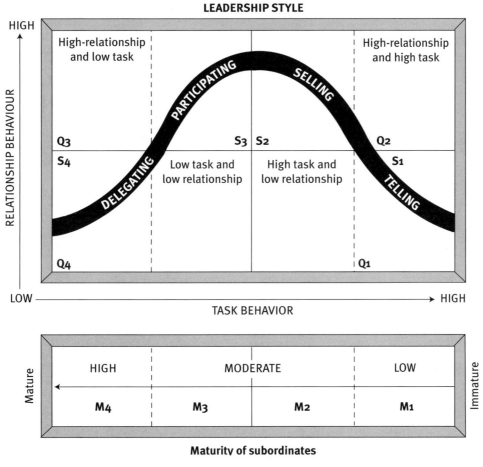

SOURCE: Hersey and Blanchard (1982:152).

According to Hersey and Blanchard, leadership behaviour is a function of subordinates' maturity. The leader first determines the maturity level of the subordinates, either individually or as a group, with regard to the particular task to be carried out, and then assumes the appropriate leadership style. The appropriate leadership style can easily be determined by drawing a perpendicular on the continuum from the identified maturity level to where it crosses the bell-shaped curve in Figure 15.5. The appropriate leadership style is indicated by the quadrant in which the lines cross.

According to Hersey's and Blanchard's situational leadership theory, a leader whose subordinates have a low maturity level (M1) should maintain a high level of task behaviour and a low level of relationship behaviour (the S1 leadership style: telling). As the maturity level of the individual subordinate or group of subordinates increases (to level M2) the leader should reduce task behaviour and increase relationship behaviour (the S2 leadership style: selling). When subordinates become even more mature (M3) both task behaviour and relationship behaviour must be reduced (the S3 leadership style: participating). When the individual subordinate or group of subordinates reaches a high level of maturity (M4), the leader should maintain a low level of both task behaviour and relationship behaviour (the S4 leadership style: delegating). An effective leader is one who is able to adjust his or her style accurately, according to the maturity level of the employee.

A subordinate does not have a fixed maturity level; it depends on the task at hand and the experience and confidence of the employee in relation to the specific task. A person might have a high maturity level in terms of one task, and a low maturity level in terms of another task. Leaders should, however, at all times keep the development of subordinates in mind, and help them to increase their maturity levels.

15.12 Revised model of situational leadership by Nicholls

The validity of Hersey's and Blanchard's basic model has been challenged by Nicholls (in Mullins 1996:273) who claims that the model violates three logical principles: consistency, continuity, and conformity.

Nicholls suggests a corrected model (Figure 15.6) which no longer violates the principles of consistency, continuity, and conformity, and which presents a completely new model for situational leadership.

Mullins (1996:273-4) explains Nicholls's situational leadership model as follows:
- For groups at a low development level, that are both unable and unwilling, the leader acts in the same role as a parent who wishes to develop simultaneously

> The basic model is inconsistent in the way it connects concern for task/relationships with ability/ willingness. The development level continuum lacks continuity since it requires willingness to appear, disappear and reappear as the development level increases. Finally, it runs counter to conformity in that it does not start with a style of high task and high relationship for a group which is simultaneously unable and unwilling.

the ability and the social skills of a child. As both ability and willingness increase, activity connected with both task and relationships can be reduced. This allows progression from 'tell', through 'consult', to the role of a developer (bottom left quadrant).
- The developer role of leadership continues with a light touch to use 'participation' and 'delegation' in order to develop further the ability and willingness of the group.
- However, if willingness develops more quickly than ability, the leader will have the opportunity to act more in the role of a coach who is anxious to improve ability.
- If, however, ability develops more quickly than willingness, the leader may have to revert to the role of driver in order to push the group to achieve results up to its potential and to prevent unwillingness causing a shortfall in performance.

To summarise, the model requires a smooth progression of the leader from parent, using a high task and high relationship leadership style (following the usual progression 'tell-sell', or consult – participate – delegate) to the leader as developer, using a low task and low relationship leadership style.

But if ability and willingness do not develop in harmony, the leader may find it

Figure 15.6 Nicholls's revised model of situational leadership

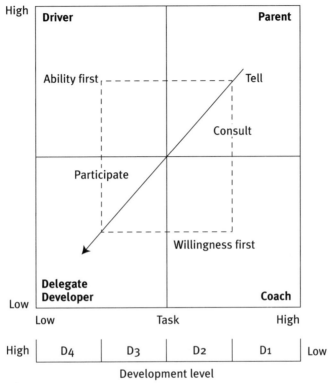

SOURCE: Mullins (1996:273).

appropriate to act more like a coach to develop ability, or more like a driver to overcome unwillingness.

In the latest edition of their work, Hersey and Blanchard appear to make reference to the points raised by Nicholls.

Some people have difficulty understanding the development of followers from M1 to M2 to M3. How can one go from being insecure to confident and then become insecure again? The important thing to remember is that at the lower levels of maturity, the leader is providing the direction – the what, where, when and how. Therefore, the decisions are leader-directed. At the higher levels of maturity, followers become responsible for task direction, and the decisions are follower-directed. This transition from leader-directed to self-directed may result in apprehension or insecurity. As followers move from low levels of maturity to higher levels, the combinations of task and relationship behaviour appropriate to the situation begin to change.

The situational leadership theory provides for contingency and flexibility. The leader is not restricted to one specific leadership style, but adjusts his or her style after a careful evaluation of the situation. The leader and follower can jointly determine the follower's maturity or readiness level and the most appropriate leadership style. This will provide a greater chance that the follower will respond positively to the leader's style and expectations.

15.13 Transformational leadership

Various macro and micro environmental factors have made it necessary for South African organisations to adapt or renew their basic structures, systems, organisational culture, and management practices. These factors include international competition, emphasis on information technology, and socio-political and socio-economic changes.

Transformation is a difficult and long-term process. It is only possible to institute meaningful change if credible and capable leaders guide the process. Unless top management support and guide change, it is likely to be fragmented. Strategic leadership is required for systematic, planned and controlled change. Leaders of change help to define the vision of the organisation, and establish the link between that vision and the type of management and organisational principles that are introduced. A 'vision' is the ability to perceive something not actually visible. It is an impossible dream which the transformational leader or leaders communicate to others. Transformational leaders influence others to believe that the dream can become reality. Even though change in certain organisations is associated with a single 'transformational hero', change is normally led by a group of leaders who provide ongoing leadership and direction. The transformational leader acts as a coach, role model, and inspirational figure to create conditions under which employees and all other stakeholders enthusiastically contribute towards achieving the stated organisational goals.

What do transformational leaders do? They:

- establish a sense of understanding of the need and urgency for change;
- articulate a dream or vision for the organisation;
- provide a systematic plan and clear objectives for attaining the vision;
- formulate structures to foster the full participation of everybody involved in the organisation;
- remove constraints that hinder the accomplishment of the new vision, and provide capacity for successful goal attainment;
- evaluate the process on a periodic basis; and
- sustain and reinforce the new culture continuously.

The following characteristics are associated with transformational leaders:
- credibility, the ability to foster trust by acting fairly and honestly in all relationships;
- sense of mission and purpose;
- ability to communicate a vision;
- ability to perform at high levels;
- a result orientation;
- ability to inspire others;
- emotional intelligence;
- ability to participate fully with people on all levels;
- strength to resist peer pressure and confidence to stand up for what is right;
- ability to detect positive qualities in others, and the willingness to share responsibility in a measure appropriate to those qualities; and
- willingness to learn, adapt, and grow, since change is often a step into the unknown.

Since leaders provide a model of attitude, direction, and action, which is usually reflected in the workforce, the success or failure of transformation rests squarely on the shoulders of those who lead the process.

15.14 Charismatic leadership

There are numerous examples of charismatic leaders who, through their unique and charismatic personal characteristics, have reached high positions in organisations and societies. This view of leadership gives rise to the question of 'born' or 'natural' leaders. Charismatic leaders have very strong referent power. They always have a very strong vision, and an exceptional ability to communicate that vision with passion and conviction. According to Bergh and Theron (1999:232) a charismatic leader is characterised by behaviour that is out of the ordinary, novel, unconventional, and counter to norms. They are also perceived as mavericks who initiate and support radical change. In an organisation, charismatic leaders are useful in the sense that they can convince and inspire people to support changes. Charismatic leaders instil trust and reduce resistance to change. According to Francesco and Gold (1998:150) charismatic leadership is more appropriate in situations that require drastic change, while other leadership styles are more appropriate in situations where gradual change is required.

15.15 Leadership in a virtual workplace

With the new paradigm of a virtual business environment, the need to define and redefine leadership is becoming more important. Leadership lessons learned in the past may not apply to the future. Leaders of the present and future need to become receptive to new ideas on how to improve the effectiveness of virtual teams who operate in an environment that constantly changes.

Virtual leadership gives rise to the following questions:

- Can inspirational leadership be attained in a situation where physical contact is minimal?
- What communication processes and tools can be used in an atmosphere of constant change?
- How are teams formed and maintained in cyberspace?

In a virtual environment, where the leader cannot keep visual tabs on team members, motivation cannot be sustained through verbal encouragement and personal attention. The leader of the virtual team mostly influences the behaviour of group members by the way the work is designed and allocated, and by monitoring the group's functioning. Fundamental to the virtual working environment is a workforce that is dynamic and knowledgeable, and able to function relatively independently. Virtual team systems and work designs enable individuals to act anywhere, at any time. The success of the virtual team depends to a large extent on the design of the organisation, the team, and the job, as well as the state and use of technology. The work design in the new knowledge-based and results-orientated organisation encourages high involvement, provides job enrichment, is process-based, and allows individuals to control how the work is being done. The virtual era is an era of partnerships, where work and work relationships are based on equality and competence. Leaders in this environment do not fear that they will lose control, and they allow high levels of participation in decision-making.

In a virtual team, one of the leader's main functions is to proactively manage potential problems that can harm the effectiveness of the team. Specific issues that need the leader's attention are:

- *Trust.* Employees from different locations, cultures, and technical backgrounds may mistrust the way their information will be used, presented, or

valued. They may also doubt the quality of other members' contributions.
- *Expectations.* A virtual team is not continuously exposed to the organisational culture and may not know exactly what is expected of them or what behaviours are allowed. The leader must explicitly discuss norms and expectations.
- *Cultural differences.* Virtual team members often represent different organisations or departments, each with its own distinctive culture. These cultures may represent different views on commitment, participation, or values, which may cause conflict in the virtual team.
- *Work-coordination.* Virtual team members cannot collaborate or react timeously if they are not equipped with up-to-date computer and communication technology, or do not have access to adequate technical support.
- *Group dynamics.* It can be difficult to build good relationships among group members who are not in face-to-face interaction. Some members may easily feel neglected or isolated. It is suggested that virtual teams do spend some time together in order to establish a working relationship.

Virtual teams add a whole new dimension to organisational structure, performance, and customer satisfaction. The effectiveness of the virtual team depends to a large extent on how well it is composed and managed.

15.16 Quality assurance in leadership

The success of outstanding organisations is almost always associated with the efforts of one or more unique individuals who are identified as leaders. These leaders did not achieve fame through their own efforts, but through their ability to inspire others to work towards the attainment of organisational goals. Leaders have a tremendous influence on the behaviour and attitudes of others. Leaders articulate the vision of the organisation and inspire others to direct their efforts and skills at realising the vision. Without quality leadership, an organisation cannot become a significant role player in the economy or in society. Leadership is not restricted to specific positions or roles in the organisation, and different people can serve as leaders in different situations. Quality in leadership is only achieved if potential leaders on all organisational levels are identified, developed, and provided with opportunities to exercise their skills. The human resources manager has a vital role to play in the development of organisational leaders.

15.17 Conclusion

Many South African organisations have produced leaders of outstanding quality who have made a name for themselves and their organisations. However, when we consider South Africa's poor rating on the World Competitiveness Survey, it remains an indisputable fact that we do not have sufficient quality leadership in our organisations. It is, therefore, imperative that people with leadership potential are continuously identified, trained, and developed to become effective leaders. The dynamic environment in which organisations operate necessitates the ongoing development of all leaders. It is also imperative that a culture within the organisation is established where employees from all levels are encouraged to take initiative and assume leadership when the situation arises.

Summary

Leadership is the ability to influence others to enthusiastically work towards organisational goals. Leaders derive their ability to influence from a variety of sources of power.

Leadership differs from management. Leaders are visionary, and concerned with the organisation's long-term success. Managers are more concerned with everyday problems and decisions.

The quality or trait approach to leadership assumes that leaders are born, not made. However, no common set of leadership characteristics or traits has been agreed upon.

Two important dimensions of leadership behaviour have been identified: structure initiation (task dimension) and consideration (people dimension). The extent to which the leader exercises these dimensions gives rise to autocratic or participative leadership.

According to McGregor, a leader's assumptions about the nature of human beings influence the leader's as well as the employee's behaviour.

Schein provided a historical perspective of the different assumptions about human nature.

Blake and Mouton developed the Leadership Grid which identifies five leadership styles based on the amount of concern the leader has for the task and people.

Both Tannenbaum and Schmidt, and Hersey and Blanchard proposed a situational approach to leadership. Hersey and Blanchard's theory was adjusted by Nicholls to provide for continuity, consistency, and conformity.

Transformational leadership is imperative in a changing and dynamic business environment. Charismatic leaders have a unique ability to influence people to accept a new order and support changes.

The virtual work environment provides new challenges for leadership. Leaders must carefully consider the composition of the virtual team and its job design, and also monitor the virtual team's effectiveness by anticipating potential problems.

Quality leadership cannot be compromised in a competitive business world.

Related websites

This topic may be investigated further by referring to the following Internet websites:
General Electric – http://www.ge.com
SA Breweries – http://www.sab.co.za
Leadership – http://leadershipmanagement.com

Case study
Rainbow comes out of hiding

Rainbow's new boss is changing the company and opening up communication with staff, the media and shareholders. Rainbow Chickens has broken years of silence with the media and, under newly appointed CE, Yannick Lakhnati, has opened its doors to explain the radical management style changes intended to save SA's largest chicken producer.

Rainbow has also increased communication with employees, a move aimed at restoring pride and identifying and removing problems.

Until 1996, Rainbow's slide into the red appeared unstoppable, culminating in an attributable loss, to March that year, of R2 684m. This was despite revenue growing about R100m annually, as sales of chicken, the cheapest source of protein, increased in line with population growth.

Attempts to ascertain from senior executives and management what policies were being implemented to redress the situation resulted only in unanswered telephone calls and speculation from analysts fighting the same stony silence as the media. This was until Lakhnati took over the leadership at Rainbow in April 1998.

The chapter on management non-communication seems to have been closed. The first indication that Rainbow was lifting the veil of silence was when the year-end results were released with extensive commentary and explanations on the losses incurred, as well as directions for the current year.

This was followed by a five-page report to shareholders in the annual report, extensively detailing the results and balance sheet, operations, controls, and prospects of the company. A footnote to the report boasted contact telephone numbers for Lakhnati and Thys Visser, who was appointed chairman, with an invitation to shareholders to direct their enquiries to either executive.

Lakhnati spent a day with invited media, showing them the chicken business and then opening himself to answer questions. Since arriving at Rainbow, he has instilled a vastly changed management style. Lakhnati not only shows the business community how he plans to restore the company's fortunes, but also communicates with the 8 400 employees across three processing and distribution regions.

In-house newsletters are distributed weekly, monthly and quarterly, while the company has been divided into mini-businesses, each with its own team leader to manage the operation. Rainbow has created 350 mini-businesses and aims to extend this to 500. Each identifies customers and suppliers, and records volumes, attendance, and performance.

Each team has its own board displaying the team name and photograph as well as the record for daily, weekly, and monthly targets, and general information.

Lakhnati said this empowerment is rebuilding pride among Rainbow employees. The system also gives accountability and management to process leaders, while identifying and removing problems at source rather than allowing them to escalate through a single supply chain.

The system was custom-designed for Rainbow following in-house surveys to establish the requirements. Extensive, company-wide staff training highlighted the natural leaders and boosted the management development programme.

The business demanded radical changes and this system gave people the opportunity to release their full potential, Lakhnati said. However, there was a very long road ahead.

Although there were guiding principles involved in returning Rainbow to profitability, there was no cast-iron strategy. It would focus on fundamentals, but Lakhnati was open to suggestions and improvements.

SOURCE: Jenvey (1998).

Questions

1 Would you describe Lakhnati as a transformational or charismatic leader? Explain.
2 What fundamental changes were made at Rainbow Chicken?
3 Identify the leadership style of Laknati, according to the leadership theories discussed in this chapter. What behaviours of Laknati underline his leadership style?
4 How does Rainbow develop the leadership potential of employees?

Experiential exercise 1

Purpose
To demonstrate all the leadership styles as presented by the various leadership theories.

Introduction
Leaders act on a continuum ranging from autocratic to participative behaviours. Different leadership styles are associated with specific leadership behaviours.

Task
Step 1 (30 minutes)
Form groups of approximately five members each. Each group is assigned a specific leadership style from a specific leadership theory without the other groups knowing which style it is. Each group prepares a role play to demonstrate their assigned leadership style. Carefully consider ways in which to demonstrate specific behaviours that are associated with the specific leadership style.

Step 2 (3 to 5 minutes per group)
Each group gets the opportunity to demonstrate their assigned leadership style. The facilitator will introduce each group by indicating which leadership theory the group represents. The other groups must try to identify the exact leadership style in accordance with the identified leadership theory.

Experiential exercise 2

Purpose
To identify the outstanding characteristics and behaviours demonstrated by successful leaders.

Introduction
Researchers who investigated the specific qualities or traits of successful leaders were not able to identify one common set of shared qualities or traits. However, we all know that leaders, especially transformational or charismatic leaders, are different from other people.

Task
Step 1 (30 minutes)
Form groups of three to five members. Each group selects a leader of their choice and writes a memo to explain why the selected leader is considered as exceptional.

Step 2 (2 or 3 minutes per group)
An assigned member of each group reads the memo to the whole class.

Step 3 (5 minutes)
The class identifies the most common characteristics or qualities mentioned, and lists them on a flip chart or white board.

Chapter questions

1 Respond to the following statement: 'You are either born a leader, or not.'
2 In your opinion, what type of leadership is most appropriate in South African organisations today? Substantiate your answer.
3 'There is no one effective leadership style in organisations.' Discuss this statement.
4 According to Blake and Mouton, the 9,9 leadership style (team leader) is the most effective. Hersey and Blanchard, on the other hand, suggest that there is no one best style of leadership. How can these two theories be reconciled?
5 What advice would you offer a person who has to monitor the performance of a project team, the members of which are physically dispersed and communicate mainly through e-mail and telephone?

Self-assessment 15.1 Interpretation

This self-assessment is based on McGregor's X and Y theory. Decide whether your answer to each statement reflects a positive or negative assumption about the nature of people. If your answer reflects a positive assumption, write a Y next to your answer. If your answer reflects a negative assumption, write an X next to your answer. How many Y's and how many X's did you get? Do you want to compare your responses to those of a fellow learner? What advice will you offer to a person who has predominantly X assumptions?

Bibliography

BERGH, Z.C. & THERON, A.L. 1999. *Psychology in the work context.* Thomson, Johannesburg.

BLAKE, R.R. & MOUTON, J.S. 1978. *The managerial grid.* Gulf, Houston.

CANTU, C. 1999. *Virtual teams.* CSWT Reports. http://www.workteams.unt.edu/reports/Cantu/html.

FRANCESCO, A.M. & GOLD, B.A. 1998. *International organisational behaviour: text, readings, cases and skills.* Prentice Hall, New Jersey.

FURLONGER, D. & SIKAKHANE, J. 1999. SA Breweries: The glass that cheers! Corporate Report. 22 October. *Financial Mail.*

GERBER, P.D., NEL, P.S. & VAN DYK, P.S. 1998. *Human resource management.* 4th edition. ITP, Johannesburg.

GREENBERG, J. & BARON, R.A. 1995. *Behaviour in organisations: understanding and managing the human side of work.* 5th edition. Prentice Hall, New Jersey.

HERSEY, P. & BLANCHARD, K. 1992. *Management and organisational behaviour: utilising human resources.* Prentice Hall, New Jersey.

JENVEY, N. 1998. Rainbow comes out of hiding. 23 July. *Business Day.*

KREITNER, R. & KINICKI, A. 1998. *Organisational behaviour.* 4th edition. McGraw Hill, New York.

LAWLER, E.E. 1996. *From the ground up.* Jossey-Bass, California.

MCGREGOR, D. 1960. The human side of enterprise. Prentice Hall, New York.

MULLINS, L.J. 1996. *Management and organisational behaviour.* 4th edition. Pitman, London.

NICHOLLS, J.R. 1985. A new approach to situational leadership. *Leadership and Organisational Development Journal,* vol. 6 (4), pp. 2-7.

TANNENBAUM, R. & SCHMIDT, W.H. 1958. How to choose a leadership pattern. *Harvard Business Review,* vol. 2 (36), pp. 95-101.

SCHEIN, E.H. 1980. *Organisational psychology.* Prentice Hall, New Jersey.

WALTERS, H. 1999. Leadership and teamwork in a hostile environment: a true inspirational challenge. *Management Today,* vol. 15 (7), pp. 10.

16

Groups and teamwork

A Werner

Learning outcomes

At the end of this chapter the learner should be able to demonstrate the following outcomes:
- Explain the importance of groups in South African organisations.
- Evaluate the extent to which a given group reflects the defining characteristics of a group.
- Contrast and compare formal and informal groups.
- Determine the extent to which a given group's development follows the progressive steps of the five-stage model and the punctuated equilibrium model.
- Outline aspects that contribute to effective group functioning.
- Explain the utilisation of quality circles and self-managed work teams in organisations.
- Provide guidelines for effective teamwork.
- Highlight criteria for successful virtual teams.
- Relate groups and teams to quality assurance.

Key words and concepts

- conformity
- gestalt
- grapevine
- group development
- group dynamics
- inertia
- networking
- norms
- role conflict
- status
- team-building
- teams

Illustrative case
A new life

December 1976. A team of professionals gather to execute a task that has been planned with the utmost precision. A life is at stake. History is to be made. Every member of the team has a specific role to fulfil. The goal is clear. Trust, timing, communication, and total devotion to the task are absolute requirements for success.

The scene is that of the first ever heart transplant operation in the world. The team is led by Dr Christiaan Barnard, senior cardiothoracic surgeon at the Groote Schuur Hospital in Cape Town, South Africa. The patient, Louis Washkansky, suffers from diabetes and an incurable heart disease. Shortly before, a woman in her mid-20s was fatally injured in a car accident, but her heart was still healthy; and now the team is going to transfer the heart of the deceased woman into the body of Washkansky.

In a five-hour operation on 3 December 1976, Dr Barnard and his team successfully replaced Washkansky's diseased heart with the healthy heart. The moment that the electrodes were applied to the heart and it resumed beating, the team knew it was a surgical success.

SOURCE: http://www.pbs.org/wgbh/aso.

16.1 Introduction

According to the Gestalt principle, the whole is worth more than its separate parts. In a very competitive environment, organisations realise that they can only achieve their goals through the combined efforts of everybody involved in the organisation. Groups and teamwork allow for greater participation and increased performance, and ultimately influence the motivation and satisfaction of employees. Some groups tend to be more productive than others and, for this reason, it is essential to investigate the factors that contribute to effective group functioning. The introduction of virtual teams into the workplace also offers new challenges for the way in which people are managed.

In this chapter we will explore the nature of groups, how they develop, and the factors that contribute to effective group functioning. We will also examine special forms of groups, namely teams, that are utilised to increase employee participation and satisfaction.

16.2 What is a group?

According to Kreitner and Kinicki (1998: 287) a group can be defined as two or more individuals interacting with each other to achieve particular goals, and who share a common identity and have common norms.

We can derive from this definition that a group consists of individuals who:
- have a mutual goal or objective;
- consciously work towards achieving this goal or objective;
- relate to each other; and
- have behavioural expectations of each other.

As the interaction between group members increases, the group becomes closer because the members of the group realise that they can help and support each other in achieving their common goal. The members of the group then begin to speak of 'us'. In other words, they develop a feeling of belonging to the group. Figure 16.1 illustrates the four sociological criteria of a group.

Figure 16.1 Sociological criteria of a group

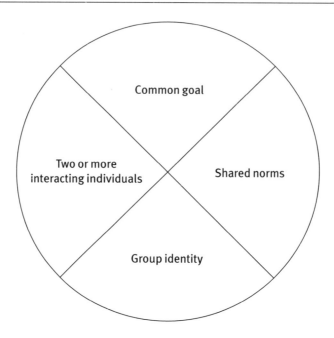

16.3 Comparing and contrasting formal and informal groups

A *formal group* is one established through the formal organisation, whose goals and activities are directly related to the achievement of the declared organisational goals. Formal groups are part of the structure of an organisation, and are formed during the organisational process. Formal groups may be departments, sections, task groups, committees, and so on. A group of employees investigating cost saving measures in the organisation is an example of a formal group.

An *informal group* is one that, as a result of the daily activities, interactions, and feelings of its members, develops spontaneously to satisfy their needs. The main goal of the informal group is social satisfaction. A group of employees working in close proximity and who develop affection for each other, is an example of an informal group. The informal group also serves as a source of identification, motivation, status, power, communication and security for its members. Any deficiency in the formal group is catered for by the informal group. If, for example, the formal group does not provide adequate and timely information, employees create information through the informal communication network, the grapevine. Although this information spreads very quickly, it is often distorted, especially when the content is more emotional in nature.

The formal and informal groups have a reciprocal relationship, which can either be positive or negative. The formal organisation often exerts a great influence on the formation and functioning of informal groups (for example, as a result of the physical layout of the work, leadership practices of the manager, or security offered in the organisation). At the same time, informal groups can also exert a great influence on the formal organisation. It often happens that employees discuss work-related problems during a social get-together outside working hours, and come up with useful solutions. On the other hand, if, for example, the manager's leadership style is unacceptable to the employees, the informal group can offer resistance to him or her by agreeing amongst themselves to lower their work output. Table 16.1 illustrates some of the differences between formal and informal groups.

Robbins (1998:240) classifies groups as command, task, interest, or friendship groups.

- *The command group.* This group is usually characterised by a formal organogram and a line of authority. Almost all businesses are formally organised into command groups, as the activities are carried out at the command of a manager. The 'command' may take the form of a request, but it still remains a command due to the line of authority within the group. For example, the training manager and his subordinates, consisting of two trainers, one course developer, one training administrator, and one secretary, form a command group.
- *The task group.* This group is created for a specific task or project. It is also a formal group. As soon as the specific project has been completed, the group disbands. A group commissioned to investigate alternative administrative systems, is a task group.
- *The interest group.* This group may be either formal or informal. The emphasis is on the needs of the group itself. There may be a line of authority and the group may have a task to fulfil, but the reason for the existence of the group is that the members all have the same interests. For example, in a specific school, five teachers have shown a special interest in children with learning problems; when they are requested to explore creative methods for teaching these children, and do a presentation on their findings, a formal interest group is formed; on the other hand, if these teachers do some reading on the topic in their own time, and discuss their findings and ideas during teatime, an informal interest group has developed.
- *The friendship group.* This group develops because the members have common characteristics. The group may be based

Table 16.1 Comparison between the formal and informal group

	Formal group	Informal group
Goal	Profit/organisational	Satisfaction of needs
Structure	Planned	Spontaneous
Basis for interaction	Task or position	Personality
Communication	Formal channels	Grapevine
Individual power base	Authority	Influence
Behaviour control mechanism	Rules and procedures	Norms
Position identification	Job/task	Role
Behavioural control mechanism	Progressive discipline	Rejection from group
Representation of relationships	Organogram	Sociogram

on similar age, ethnic heritage, support for soccer, or any other shared characteristic.

16.4 Group development

Knowledge about the development of groups is very useful to assist groups in progressing toward goal attainment. Work groups are only effective if a spirit of co-operation and combined action towards achieving goals exists. In a dynamic working environment, where quick action is required, groups cannot afford to waste time on unproductive conflict and behaviour.

Different opinions exist in terms of how groups develop. We will discuss the five-stage model of group development and the punctuated-equilibrium model.

16.4.1 The five-stage model of group development

Bruce W Tuckman proposed the five-stage model of group formation in 1965 (Kreitner & Kinicki 1998:289). The five stages of group development are forming, storming, norming, performing, and adjourning. Figure 16.2 illustrates these five stages and some of the behaviours that are associated with each stage. During each stage certain group developmental tasks must be completed successfully for the group to be effective. The development of groups does not necessarily take place in a specific order. Sometimes a group might experience two stages at once, or regress to a previous stage.

- *Forming* is characterised by uncertainty. Members do not know what is expected of them and are often scared that they will not measure up. They are also unsure of the structure, leadership, and roles in the group. Groups progress successfully through this stage once members perceive themselves as part of the group.
- *Storming* reminds one of the way in which animals fight each other to establish leadership and subordination. Human beings tend more to engage in a psychological contest, where skill, experience, authority, popularity, personality, etc., are measured and compared. This stage is characterised by interpersonal conflict, in the form of fighting, or physical or emotional withdrawal. Groups progress successfully through this stage when a leader has been chosen and accepted, and a relatively clear hierarchy exists.
- *Norming* is marked by cooperation and collaboration. During this stage members become aware of what behaviour is acceptable or not. Members share information openly and are willing to listen to others. Close relationships develop and cohesiveness increases. The group progresses successfully through this stage when the group structure is relatively established, behavioural expectations are clear, and the group is ready to function fully.
- *Performing* is characterised by full participation of all group members. Energy and effort are spent on the task at hand. In some groups performance is maintained at a constant level, while in other groups, through the process of learning and development, higher levels of effectiveness and creativity are reached continuously. The success of this stage is marked by goal attainment.
- *Adjourning* marks the end of the group's existence. Emotions vary from satisfaction with achievements to a feeling of loss of friendship.

In a strong organisational context, where goals, structure, norms, and information are provided, groups can move faster to the performing stage, and then the five-stage model might have limited applicability. However, in the modern era, where piece work and project work become more

Figure 16.2 The five-stage model of group development

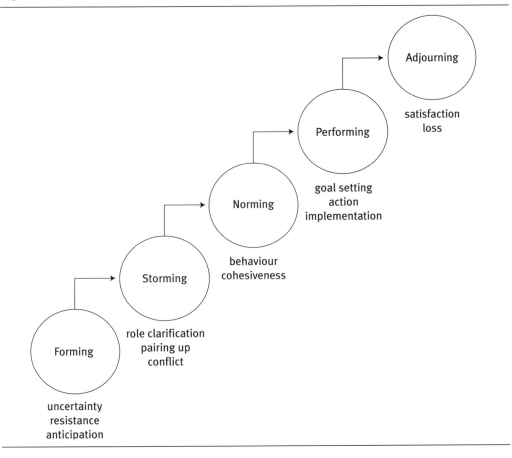

and more common, groups members might find themselves in a less familiar environment with less clear goals and undefined norms. Group members will have to establish a common ground before they will be able to function effectively.

16.4.2 The punctuated-equilibrium model

The punctuated-equilibrium model highlights a consistent time-frame, within which groups change during their existence. More specifically, the following has been found (Robbins 1998:244):

The first meeting sets the group's direction. Behavioural patterns and norms are firmly established during the first meeting. For example, when a group of students who must do a project meet the first time, their behaviour at this first meeting will set the tone for their future interaction and behaviour. If they 'goof off' a lot and concentrate little on the task at hand, this will be become the behavioural pattern for the future. If they strongly speak out against a member who is not present at the meeting, everyone will know that attendance is very important at future meetings.

The first phase of group activity is one of inertia. Behavioural patterns established during the first meeting remain firmly in place for the first half of the group's existence. The group tends to become locked in a fixed course of action.

A transition takes place at the end of the first phase, when the group has used up half of its allotted time. Exactly halfway between the first meeting and the official deadline, members of the group realise that they have used up half their time, and that they have either done very little constructive work or taken the wrong course of action. Members tend to criticise each other, and open conflict can occur.

Heightened levels of energy and activity mark this transition. New expectations are determined, goals are reviewed, new perspectives adopted, and alternative actions taken.

Phase two is a new equilibrium or period of inertia. During this phase, plans adopted during the transition phase are carried out. The group is once again locked in a fixed course of action.

The group's last meeting is characterised by a burst of energy. Consider the group of students just before they have to hand in their project. Final changes have to be negotiated, separate parts need to be integrated, and everyone is anxious that the project be completed and handed in. Figure 16.3 provides a schematic representation of the punctuated-equilibrium model.

When comparing the five-stage model with the punctuated-equilibrium model one can say that the group goes though forming, norming, and storming during the first meeting, followed by a stage of low performance, then goes through another phase of storming and norming, followed by a stage of high performance before finally adjourning.

Case-in-point
Sentry Laboratories

Sentry Laboratories is a private organisation in the medical industry that specialises in the testing of blood and tissue samples for cancer detection, development of pharmaceutical products, and research. The five managers of Sentry are respectively responsible for daily operations, marketing, finances, technology and administration/personnel. Once a year the team books into a remote holiday resort for three days. This breakaway serves more than one purpose. Firstly, it allows the group to interact in a more relaxing atmosphere, away from daily work pressures. This is a great booster for interpersonal relations and group cohesion. The group will typically engage in a physical exercise that requires teamwork, skill, and strength, such as playing soccer, snorkeling or net fishing. Secondly, the group uses this opportunity to re-evaluate and review the business environment and strategic goals for the organisation. The group decides on ways in which to achieve these objectives and work out a schedule for implementation.

Figure 16.3 The punctuated-equilibrium model

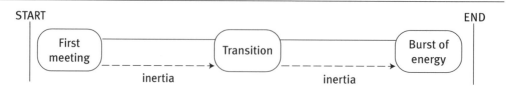

> The organisation employs 160 people and prides itself on having a well-skilled, diverse group of employees. Once a year, over a weekend, all employees, together with management, gather at a local holiday resort. This breakaway takes a similar shape to the one discussed above. Employees get an opportunity to interact in an informal way and have fun. They also divide into their natural work teams and set their own strategic goals for the next year. A number of very creative ideas have flowed from these breakaway sessions. Right at the beginning, a management consultant was contracted to facilitate these sessions, but employees became so skilled in strategic planning and goal setting that they are now able to appoint facilitators among themselves. It is not surprising then, that a number of 'organisational successes' can directly be linked to ideas originating from these weekend breakaways.

16.5 Effective group functioning

Not every collection of people satisfies the definition of a group, or functions effectively. The internal functioning of a group (i.e. its goals, patterns of interaction, etc.) develops over time and largely determines the success of the group in achieving its goals and satisfying the needs of its members. Use Self-assessment 16.1 to evaluate your team's effectiveness.

Compare your responses to those of the other team members. Do you have any suggestions for improving the way in which your team functions?

Effective groups have the following characteristics:

- the group knows the reason for its existence;
- there are guidelines or procedures for decision-making;
- there is communication between the group members;
- the members receive and render mutual assistance;
- the members handle conflict within the group in a constructive manner; and
- the members diagnose their processes and improve their own functioning.

Various factors that influence the effectiveness and performance of a group will be discussed below.

16.5.1 Group leadership

A leader is someone who has the ability to inspire group members to achieve group goals voluntarily and enthusiastically. Leadership influence depends on the type of power that a leader can exercise over followers, which vary from reward, coercive, legitimate, and referent to expert power. The most important point here is that each group has a leader at any given time, and that the person who is formally appointed is not necessarily the leader.

Effective leaders have a concern for the task, as well as for the members of the group. Task behaviours expected from leaders include planning, decision-making, organising, and monitoring. People-functions include individual functions (such as meeting the needs of individual members, giving recognition, developing skills, and providing opportunities) and group functions (such as building group cohesiveness, communication, resolving conflict, and training).

Although most of us would assume that a democratic leader is preferable and more desirable, most authors and researchers suggest that the effectiveness of a leadership style depends on the characteristics of

Self-assessment 16.1 Assess your team's effectiveness

Indicate on a scale from 1 to 5 to what extent your group meets the following requirements:
1. Team members work towards achieving a clearly stated vision.
   Seldom   1   2   3   4   5   Usually
2. Team members adhere to the agreed behavioural norms.
   Seldom   1   2   3   4   5   Usually
3. All team members participate in the decision-making process.
   Seldom   1   2   3   4   5   Usually
4. Communication is open and uninhibited.
   Seldom   1   2   3   4   5   Usually
5. A spirit of cooperation and collaboration prevails in the group.
   Seldom   1   2   3   4   5   Usually
6. Every team member makes a special contribution to the team.
   Seldom   1   2   3   4   5   Usually
7. Members provide honest feedback to each other.
   Seldom   1   2   3   4   5   Usually
8. Members are encouraged to express diverse opinions.
   Seldom   1   2   3   4   5   Usually
9. Differences are discussed in a mature and constructive way.
   Seldom   1   2   3   4   5   Usually
10. Team members assume rotating roles to foster multiskilling and personal development.
    Seldom   1   2   3   4   5   Usually

the followers and the task. A democratic approach is more effective when followers are ready to participate in the decision-making processes and can make a reasonable contribution. An autocratic approach is more effective when the followers lack knowledge and experience, and don't feel confident to participate. One important function of a leader is to facilitate the developmental process of group members so that they can make a meaningful contribution to the attainment of group goals, and experience satisfaction.

16.5.2 Roles

A role refers to a set of expected behaviour patterns associated with someone in a given position in a group. For example, the director of finance in an organisation is expected to organise and monitor the department of finance. An accountant, on the other hand, is expected to complete financial records and statements.

Each role has associated attitudes and behaviours, which create role identity. People find it relatively easy to learn new roles, and to shift from one role to another. Consider the change in behaviour and attitude of a machine operator who has been promoted to supervisory level. Most of the time such a person will adopt a pro-management attitude and orientation.

The understanding of roles is complicated by the difference between role expectation and role perception.

Role expectations are defined as how others believe you should act in a given role. Most of us have stereotyped conceptions about how certain roles should be acted out. We expect different behaviours and attitudes from a minister, manager, professor, prison warden, waitress, and soccer coach.

Role perception refers to how we believe we should act out our roles. Many women experience a discrepancy between traditional role expectations and their own perceptions of how they should fulfil their roles. This discrepancy can cause a lot of frustration and tension, both in the work place and at home. When we compare the traditional employment contract to the new employment contract, we see vast differences between what was expected of employees in the past and what is expected of them today. Previously employees were expected to be at work and deliver a decent amount of work. Today employees are expected to make a meaningful contribution to the organisation and manage their own careers. Employees' role perception should change accordingly. Conflict in groups occurs when members perceive their roles differently to what is expected of them. It is therefore important that roles are clarified through open discussion.

Role conflict occurs when a person performs multiple roles, with contradictory role expectations. A human resources manager, trying to satisfy the needs of both managers and employees, might experience role conflict. Managers might emphasise cost-cutting measures, while employees demand higher wages. When one belongs to more than one group, which places different demands on one's time and perspectives, tension occurs.

16.5.3 Group norms and conformity

Over time, the interaction within the group leads to the development of group norms. A norm is a generally accepted standard of behaviour that each member of the group is supposed to maintain. The strongest norms apply to the forms of behaviour that the group members regard as the most important.

Norms can be defined as acceptable standards of behaviour within a group that are shared by the group's members (Robbins 1998:255).

> Did you know that golf players do not talk while a fellow player putts? Why?

Norms may be formal, and explicitly stated by the group leader, for example: 'Membership cards will be produced at each meeting.' Norms can also be informal and based on interaction between group members, for example, when a cell phone rings during the first meeting and sounds of irritation are uttered, everybody knows that they should keep their cell phones switched off during meetings. Certain norms are valued more highly than others, and members of the group must adhere to them. These norms are called obligatory norms, and are unlikely to change. A student who does not attend compulsory classes will quickly find out that he or she is not granted admission to the examination: an obligatory norm.

There are also peripheral norms, and although it is not obligatory for members to adhere to them, they are regarded as sound and worth the effort. A member of a soccer team, for example, will not gain the approval of his team-mates if he misbehaves during the reception held after the match. A norm that is regarded as important by one group may be unimportant to another. A social club, for example, might prescribe that men who dine there should wear a tie and jacket, while another club might well regard this as a peripheral norm and permit its members to wear what they like.

The success and continued existence of a group may depend on whether the members adhere to the group norms. Groups that lack strong norms are unlikely to be as stable, long-lived or satisfying for their members as groups with well-developed norms that are strongly supported by the members.

Conformity refers to the acceptance of a group's norms by its members. There is consensus in the literature that a group member can react to group norms in three different ways: he or she may reject them, conform to them, or only accept the important ones and ignore the peripheral norms. When a group member rebels against the group's norms, he or she will experience considerable pressure to conform, as noticeable non-conformity constitutes a threat to the group's standards, stability, and survival. This type of pressure may be particularly strong. It has happened in organisations where workers are paid according to a piece wage system, in other words, according to the production of each individual, that the workers have a well-founded fear that if some of them were to perform at a very high level, the management would reduce the work tariff. The result is strong pressure on the workers not to exceed the group norms for work carried out.

The extent to which people conform to norms depends on a number of factors, such as their values, personalities, status, and needs. Individuals with low status in the group, for example, will tend to adhere strictly to all the group's norms so that the other group members will accept them. People with little self-confidence also tend to conform to a greater extent, because they regard the group's decisions as better than their own. Individuals who feel that the group's goals coincide with their own also tend to conform to a greater extent.

Is conformity to norms good or bad? Norms preserve a group's existence and survival; however, blind conformity may counteract innovation, as the creative ability of a member will be lost to group conformity. 'Groupthink', the tendency of a group to make a premature decision based on limited information, is the result of conformity. This happens when everyone in the group supports a decision, without considering alternatives, in order to preserve group solidarity. The ideal is probably that certain basic norms are supported, such as showing respect to other group members, but that members are encouraged to be divergent and creative.

16.5.4 Status

Status refers to the relative social position a person has in comparison to others in the group. Status is important because it is a motivational factor, and also influences the behaviour of those who experience disparity between what they believe their status is, and what they believe others perceive their status to be. Status can be formal or informal, and is awarded as follows:

- *Scalar* status refers to status obtained through one's formal position in a group. A supervisor has status due to the authority associated with his position.
- *Functional* status is earned through the task one has to fulfil in the group. A computer technician, who is on a lower level in the organisational hierarchy, might have more status than a manager due to his or her ability to solve everyone's computer problems.
- *Achieved* status is earned through hard work and effort, and is based on one's qualifications and achievements. We are all impressed when there is a professor in our midst!
- *Ascribed* status refers to inborn characteristics over which we have limited or no control, such as attractiveness, gender, build, and age.

Status differences can either facilitate or hinder group interaction. It facilitates interaction when members perceive status differences as equitable, that is they believe those with higher status rightfully deserve more status. Lower status members in this case are more willing to follow the directives of high status members. Consider the training department as a (command) group, where the training manager has more status, due to his authority, expertise, and skill. On the other hand, status differences might be inappropriately emphasised in a group where members are supposed to work as equals. It happens far too often that when a group meets to brainstorm ideas, those with lower status hesitate to share ideas, and ultimately criticise the ideas of others.

16.5.5 Group size and composition

Size influences a group's overall performance, depending on the purpose of the group. Larger groups (fifteen or more members) are generally preferred when a group has to produce divergent ideas or alternatives. A large group offers a greater range of combined experience and ideas. One negative aspect of a bigger group is social loafing, that is when some individuals lessen their input, knowing or hoping that others will unwittingly stand in for them. This has an important implication for organisations that utilise groups as a means to improve employee satisfaction and productivity. Even though an individual works in a team, his or her individual efforts must be identifiable and measurable. Smaller groups are more effective in the execution of tasks. Smaller groups work faster and responsibility is more explicitly given to individuals.

According to Bergh and Theron (1999: 269) research has shown that groups of five to seven members are preferable. An odd number prevents a tie with voting.

Groups made up of five to seven members combine the best of small and bigger groups, with the group small enough to avoid domination, the formation of cliques, and inhibited participation, and large enough to allow for a diverse input.

Group composition relates to the extent to which group members are alike. A homogenous group shares a number of similar characteristics, such as race, gender, socio-economic background, education, age, work experience, or cultural orientation. A heterogeneous group, on the other hand, is composed of individuals who have few or no similar characteristics.

In South Africa, work groups are more likely to be heterogeneous than homogeneous. A heterogeneous group will most likely be able to perform at a higher level in terms of creativity. However, in order to synergise the group to high levels of effectiveness, the group has to manage conflict constructively.

We should also consider the group demographics – the degree to which members of a group share the same demographic attributes such as age, gender, race, length of service, or qualifications. This becomes important when most individuals in the group, with the exception of one or two, share the same characteristics. Imagine being the only male or female in a group, or the only person without a remarkable qualification. People are more likely to leave a group if they are different to others in terms of any attribute that they perceive as relevant to their comfort.

16.5.6 Decision-making in groups

Groups are formed to make decisions. There are, however, advantages and disadvantages to group decision-making.

Advantages of group decision-making:
- more knowledge and experience are put into decision-analysis and alternative design;

- individuals participating in decision-making will tend to support the decision and take responsibility for its implementation;
- it stimulates communication and discussion in the organisation;
- it is in line with social and political changes and, therefore, is perceived as more legitimate; and
- it serves as a developmental tool by exposing people to each other's ideas.

Disadvantages of group decision-making:
- it is a time-consuming process and places more demands on the leader's ability to facilitate a meeting and to manage behaviour;
- pressure to seek conformity may lead to less than optimal decisions;
- the formation of cliques, and pre-meeting agreements can negate the virtue of group decision-making; and
- people often act impulsively during group meetings, and decline to take responsibility for the implementation of ideas.

In order to get the most out of group decision-making, appropriate decision-making techniques should be utilised. The following techniques are very useful to stimulate creative thinking while preventing domination by individuals.

- *Brainstorming.* This process is frequently used to provide the maximum number of ideas in a short period of time. A group comes together and is presented with a problem. Members are then encouraged to generate as many ideas as possible to solve the problem. The emphasis is on quantity and not quality, and members refrain from making any remarks about the presented ideas. Weird ideas are welcomed as a way to stimulate the thoughts of others. Once a satisfactory number of ideas has been presented, the ideas are systematically analysed and evaluated.
- *Nominal group technique.* This technique is excellent for ensuring full participation, without individual domination. Individuals meet as a group, and they silently generate ideas in writing. This silent period is followed by a round-robin procedure in which each group member presents an idea to the group, which is then recorded on a flip chart. Once all the ideas are presented, each idea is discussed for clarification and evaluation. Finally, the group members conclude the meeting by silently and independently recording their rank-ordering of the ideas. The scores are tallied and the idea with the highest ranking is chosen. This is called a nominal group, due to the limited interaction among its members.
- *Delphi technique.* This technique is used where the group members are physically dispersed. Participants never meet face to face. A facilitator presents members with a carefully designed questionnaire to provide potential solutions to a well-defined problem. The questionnaires are completed independently and returned to the facilitator, who summarises the results. These results are circulated back to the members who offer a second round of input. This process is then continued until members reach consensus. The Delphi technique can be conducted electronically, through sophisticated computer technology, to save time and expenses.

16.5.7 Communication

The only way through which we can establish and maintain relationships with other people, is through communication. The more easily people in a group communicate with each other, the more cohesion will be experienced. Cohesiveness refers to the extent to which group members are attracted to each other and vote to stay in the group.

Communication is clearly a social process. A variety of social influences affect the accuracy with which we perceive information. These include differences in status, language, frame of reference, and expectations, as well as selective listening, premature judgement, and source credibility.

Most people assume that they are good communicators; yet, most interpersonal problems stem from misunderstandings. People do not formulate their messages accurately, and do not listen attentively to what others say. Should it become evident that communication is a problem in a group, it should not be ignored, but addressed through training.

The following can serve as guidelines for effective communication in groups (adapted from Ivancevich & Matteson 1999:490):

- Follow up to determine how a message was received. A friendly gesture, such as suggesting that a person does not take on added responsibility, might be interpreted as a perception that he or she cannot handle multiple tasks.
- Regulate information-flow in terms of quality and quantity. To prevent overload, ensure that only matters of importance are discussed in the group. Prevent repetitive arguing around one specific point.
- Use feedback to check whether a message has been understood as intended.
- Show empathy towards others, especially when backgrounds and experiences differ considerably.
- Encourage mutual trust so that all members will feel confident in expressing their opinions and feelings.
- Time communication effectively to prevent barriers that result in distortions and value judgements.
- Use simplified language to convey meaning, especially in diverse groups.
- Listen effectively to others by reflecting on the content and feeling conveyed by the message.
- Use the grapevine. The grapevine is the informal network of communication that bypasses the formal communication network. It is known for its speed, also its inaccuracy. The grapevine is a useful tool to distribute information rapidly and to determine the prevailing mood and needs of a group. Ensure that information spread through the grapevine is accurate and that all group members are exposed to it.
- Promote ethical communication. Group members must be respected, treated justly and exposed to all relevant information.

16.5.8 Conflict

In all groups some conflict is inevitable. Conflict can be defined as the process in which individuals feel that other individuals have frustrated their ability to achieve their goals.

Conflict – good or bad?

Conflict in groups can be positive or negative, depending on its consequences. Positive conflict is an energising force that spurs members to better alternatives and higher goals. It stimulates creative thinking and innovation. Members agree on the goal, but disagree on how to achieve the goal. Debating the alternatives helps with the evaluation process, and a combination of ideas might prove to be the best course of action. In groups where there is little or no conflict, due to high levels of cohesion and conformity, performance tends to be low. The status quo is seldom challenged. Negative conflict, on the other hand, occurs when goal attainment is frustrated because energy is spent on highlighting or resolving interpersonal differences rather than on goal attainment. This can lead to chaos and a negative attitude that hinders constructive problem solving. Figure 16.4 illustrates the effect of various levels of conflict on performance.

Managing the different levels of conflict

Levels of conflict which are either too high or too low, lead to low performance. A moderate level of conflict leads to the optimum level of performance. Conflict (if it is too low) can be stimulated through the dialectic technique, where individuals in the group are requested to take an opposing perspective on an issue, or the devil's advocate technique, where an individual is asked to critically evaluate any proposed action. It is also useful to introduce new, diverse members to the group to offer fresh ideas and different perspectives.

When conflict levels are too high, various methods can be adopted to reduce it. These vary from setting superordinate goals, identifying a common enemy, smoothing differences, and compromising, to using authoritative command. Interpersonal conflict is best resolved through levelling, a process in which members of a group are totally open and honest with each other about their feelings and concerns.

16.6 Work teams

What is the difference between a group and a team? A team can be defined as a small number of people with complementary skills who are committed to a common purpose, performance goals, and a work strategy, for which they feel mutually accountable. We referred earlier to the five-stage model of group development. A team is considered to be a group that has matured to the performing stage. Due to conflicts over leadership and member roles during the storming and norming phases, many groups never reach this stage.

Figure 16.4 The effect of various levels of conflict on performance

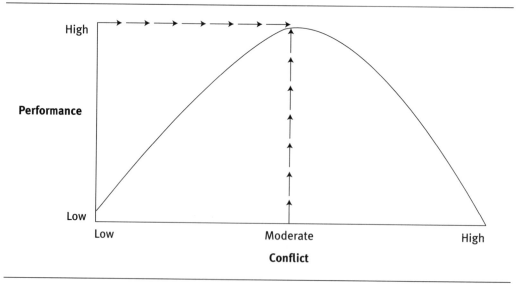

16.6.1 Characteristics of successful work teams

The following characteristics describe a high-performing work team:
- the group has a clear vision and goal, which are internalised by each member;
- the group consists of a diverse number of individuals who, due to their unique characteristics, make unique contributions to the group's success;
- disagreement is viewed as constructive, and members are willing to consider all ideas with an open mind;
- interpersonal relations are relaxed, with ample open communication and mutual support;
- group members identify strongly with the group, and feel proud of the way the group functions, as well as its achievements;
- change is not feared, but initiated;
- networking with outside individuals and groups is used to achieve excellence and to build credibility;
- even though the group might have a formal leader, leadership shifts from member to member depending on the task at hand; and
- group members evaluate their own development and performance, and seek opportunities for continuous learning.

16.6.2 Types of work teams

Examples of work teams are problem-solving teams, cross-functional teams, self-managed teams, and virtual teams. These teams differ in terms of their nature and purpose.

16.6.2.1 Problem-solving teams

Problem-solving teams comprise employees who meet on a weekly basis to discuss ways of improving the quality of products, efficiency of work methods, and work environment. The supervisor usually leads these groups. Members identify problems, brainstorm alternative solutions, and present their suggestions to management. These groups seldom have the direct authority to implement their ideas. According to Lawler (1996:147) a problem with these groups is that they are normally not informed of financial and capacity constraints and, therefore, they often suggest unrealistic and impractical interventions. If group members feel bulldozed into proposing ideas that fall within the thinking of management, they see no purpose in the group's existence, and will withdraw emotionally, if not physically, from the team. However, if these groups are well managed, and their ideas seriously considered and implemented, they can make a valuable contribution to quality assurance in the organisation. Quality circles and green areas are examples of problem-solving groups.

16.6.2.2 Cross-functional teams

Cross-functional teams are very popular in the motor manufacturing industry, where project teams comprise representatives from a cross-section of the organisation, for example manufacturing, engineering, marketing, research, development, and traders. The cross-functional team has a specific task to accomplish, such as to develop a new product. These teams allow people from diverse areas to analyse problems, exchange information, develop creative ideas, solve problems, and coordinate complex projects. It is a challenging task to build trust and cohesion in such a complex team. The group leaders should have a clear understanding of group processes and provide a sense of direction for the group.

16.6.2.3 Self-managed teams

Self-managed work teams are formed to take accountability for a complete work process, which was previously perceived to consist of separate jobs, often performed by separate departments. The ideal design for such a work team allows it to take a product through the entire production process. The team manages an entire mini-business, where the process starts from buying raw material from an external vendor, and ends with delivering a finished product or service to an external customer. The team enjoys autonomy over how they meet the customer's demands.

How a team-based design differs from the traditional functional approach, can be illustrated by the following example of a shoe factory. Previously, a work team designed, planned, and controlled the whole manufacturing process, the purchasing department obtained the raw material, and separate groups of employees cut and dyed the leather, sewed the shoes, attached fittings, packed the shoes, and delivered the finished product. Different levels of supervisors and managers managed the process, staff specialists took care of human resources, finance, and scheduling, and quality controllers checked the final product. The plant manager took responsibility for quality, costs, and productivity. In the team-based design, a team takes responsibility for the entire process and becomes accountable for cost, quality and rate of production. In the shoe factory, teams are given responsibility for a specific product, such as slippers, ladies court shoes, or sport shoes, and have to take the product through the entire process, from raw material to a finished and packed product. This leads to improvements in cost, speed, and quality.

Lawler (1996: 167) highlights a few crucial points for a team-based system to be successful:
- the work done by the team must be interdependent and relatively complex;
- team leaders must understand group processes and provide direction;
- human resources management reward and information systems need to provide the right kind of training, feedback, and recognition for teams;
- the location of the members of a team and its size are crucial to its effectiveness; and
- teams should take responsibility for satisfying their customers.

16.6.2.4 Virtual teams

Global competition, information technology, and excessive travel expenses have given rise to virtual teams that transcend distance, time zones, and organisational boundaries. To the uninformed, the perception remains that virtual team members are in one location, and that they operate in the same time zone. Examples of virtual teams are groups of individuals in different locations who develop and manage new products such as an electronic advertising board, a new financial package for women, an Internet company, or gymnasium equipment. The possibilities are endless. The members of a virtual team might not even belong to a specific organisation, but are contracted to a specific project. Virtual team members communicate mainly through electronic media. The success of the virtual team, however, depends a lot on the structure and management of the team.

The following potential problems make the management of virtual work teams more challenging:
- *Trust.* Members could mistrust each other owing to the perception that their contributions might not be adequately valued and presented by others.
- *Expectations.* Members might be unsure of what is expected of them and what they are allowed to do.
- *Cultural differences.* These differences can inhibit cohesion, participation, and open communication.
- *Work coordination.* A real danger for virtual teams is a slow response-time in

dealing with each other and environmental demands. Members might become despondent if they feel that no progress is being made.
- *Group dynamics.* Virtual teams do not have the same opportunities as other teams to build rapport.
- *Leadership.* The leader is not in physical contact with members to influence them on a daily or weekly basis. The leader must be aware of the above-mentioned factors and manage them proactively.

Planning and design are key factors to the virtual team's success, and the following should be considered in this regard:
- *Organisational design.* The virtual team's goals must be aligned with the overall organisational goals. Behavioural norms should be developed that allow for multicultural and multifunctional work, yet support basic organisational values. Infrastructure must be created to support the involvement of team members with each other and with the host organisation. The virtual team could manage their own design and support systems as a way to establish ownership for their success.
- *Job design.* A realistic description of how the member will spend his or her time, as well as the negative aspects of the job, will help the member to cope better in the virtual environment. Every member should know what he or she is accountable for and how this links up with the responsibilities of other members. The team must have authority to make decisions. Compensation must be clarified. In virtual teams, compensation is linked to contributions and end-results. Performance feedback remains an inherent part of managing a virtual team.
- *Team design.* Members are selected only after a careful study is done of the purpose of the team and the skills needed to achieve the goals. An identity for the team should be created through a team name that is descriptive and expresses the mission, such as the 'X-Generation Gym Equipment Team' for a team that designs gymnasium apparatus. The team must go through the exercise of creating a vision or mission statement; the value of this lies more in the exercise than in the framed version. The goals of the team must be clearly stated, and the team must be organised around these goals. Contact between virtual team members is enhanced if contact and location information is formally supplied; this should include names, office locations, traditional postal addresses, phone numbers, fax numbers, e-mail addresses, web-page addresses, and meeting places.
- *Coordination of work through technology.* Some face-to-face interaction is absolutely essential for the success of the team, especially during the establishment phase. All members should be present during these interactions. Electronic technology that assists the interaction of virtual group members includes video conferencing, desktop-conferencing, group software, newsgroups, bulletin boards, and electronic mail linked to Internet as well as Intranet systems. Virtual teams have the ability to revolutionise the workplace by pooling expertise in an incredibly short time to achieve organisational goals of quality products or services and excellent customer satisfaction.

16.7 Groups and teams and quality assurance

One of the cornerstones of Total Quality Management is teamwork. Teamwork is increasingly being introduced into the structures of South African organisations to increase performance levels, and employee and customer satisfaction. These goals can only be achieved if attention is first focused on the internal functioning of groups and teams. Quality within the team must first be achieved before quality in the organisation can be achieved. This can be done through team-building exercises that focus on goal setting, interpersonal relations, conflict-management, and trust building, and through continuously monitoring the performance of the group.

16.8 Conclusion

The introduction of groups and teams in the South African workplace is not only in line with political and social changes, but also with the dominant African cultural value of collectivism. Groups and teamwork do not guarantee higher performance levels. Many factors influence the effectiveness of groups. These factors should be identified and managed continuously. When groups are well managed, they do contribute to greater employee commitment and organisational effectiveness.

Summary

Groups are defined as collections of individuals who interact with each other to achieve a common goal, whose behaviour is directed by a common set of norms, and who share a common identity.

Groups and teams have become a prominent feature in organisations in the form of self-managed work teams and problem-solving teams. Many organisations have switched from a traditional assembly line to a team-based work arrangement that allows for greater employee participation and satisfaction. Virtual teams are groups of people who are physically dispersed but work towards a common goal. Virtual team members interact mostly through advanced computer technology. Leading and motivating virtual teams and team members pose a new challenge to management.

Many factors, such as leadership and conflict-management, can influence a group's effectiveness. The internal functioning of groups, as well as their performance, should be monitored continuously to identify and address problems. Moderate levels of conflict increase a group's performance, when aimed at finding the best course of action, and not focusing on personal differences.

Quality assurance in both the inputs and outputs of groups and teams will add value to the organisation and its quest to deliver top quality products and services.

Related websites

This topic may be investigated further by referring to the following Internet websites:
HR Magazine – http://www.shrm.org/docs/Hrmagazine.html
Workforce – http://www.workforceonline.com/researchcenter/
CSWT Reports – http://www.workteams.unt.edu/reports

Case study
Teamwork

Six computer technicians were requested to draw up a plan of action to upgrade all the computers used in the organisation before the end of the year. The technicians agreed to meet on the first of September. Early that morning, one of the technicians, Sipho, informed the rest that he could not make it to the meeting, since his child was sick and he had to take him to the doctor. The rest of the group indicated that they were not happy with the situation, but that they would tolerate it this one time. During the morning, Sipho decided to phone his mother and asked if she would not take his child to the doctor so that he could attend the meeting. On the way to the meeting venue, the group members talked about a variety of things such as soccer, the local news and the appointment of a new salesperson.

A while after the meeting started, Rodney spoke up: 'OK guys...hm...sorry...and girl, let's get down to work. How are we going to handle this? We must have it done before the end of November so that we can sort out any unforeseen problems during December.' Everybody talked at the same time. Everybody had a different idea. Pinky, the only female in the group, was told to keep notes. The meeting ended after an hour. They agreed to meet again after a week.

During the second meeting, they reviewed all the ideas discussed the previous week and ended the meeting. After two more similar meetings Luyanda remarked: 'Hey guys, do you realise that we have not progressed one inch with upgrading the computers. It is already the end of September.' Suddenly there was a lot of activity. Specific areas in the organisation were demarcated, each person was allocated one area and they agreed to have the computers done in three weeks.

After two more weeks, Rodney contacted each person to check the progress. Very little had been done. He urged everybody to make a move, since they were only one week away from the due date. Siyolo complained that his boss required him to attend a workshop on Wednesday. During the last week, the technicians worked voluntarily overtime, all the computers were upgraded and the team could celebrate their achievement at a local restaurant.

Questions

1. To what extent did the development of this group follow the pattern of the punctuated-equilibrium model?
2. Did this group meet the four defining characteristics of groups?
3. Name the five stages through which groups develop and identify behaviours from the case study that relate to each stage.
4. Identify all the different roles these employees fulfil.
5. Provide examples of role conflict from the case study.
6. What is interesting about the composition of this group?

Experiential exercise 1

Purpose
To identify shared values within a group.

Introduction
When groups are formed, individuals often feel that they do not have much in common with other group members and, therefore, reserve their participation. This exercise demonstrates that, regardless of how diverse the group is, group members can still find common ground.

Task
Step 1 (10 minutes)
Each individual learner lists the five people he or she admires most for what they have done or stand for. It can be a family member, community leader, political leader, teacher, lecturer, or sports person. After compiling the list, the learner describes the characteristics of each person on the list.

Step 2 (20 minutes)
Form groups of five to seven people. Each person gets the opportunity to share his or her list with the rest of the group. Once everybody has had a chance to do this, the group reaches consensus on the five characteristics that appear most often on the individual learners' lists. A new single list is compiled of these five characteristics, which represent the values that are most important to the group, and which should be used to guide their behaviour as group members.

Step 3 (10 minutes)
Each group shares its list with the rest of the class.

Experiential exercise 2

Purpose
To experience group interaction and performance. If the weather allows, this exercise can be performed outside.

Introduction
A variety of factors influence the effectiveness and performance of groups. This exercise requires each group to build a bridge. Five learners will assume the role of judges and have to reach consensus on which group is the winner.

Material
Each group should have two newspapers, two meters of string, masking tape, one box of matches, ten drinking straws and one plastic bag.

Task
Step 1 (40 minutes)
Groups of five to seven people are formed. Each group receives the same amount of material and constructs a bridge with the given material. After 30 minutes, the groups display their bridges in a communal area. During this stage the appointed judges compile a list of criteria that will be used to evaluate the bridges.

Step 2 (15 minutes)
The judges evaluate the bridges and decide on a winning team. During this stage the groups are requested to complete a questionnaire based on how they performed as a group.

Step 3 (15 minutes)
The winning team is announced and the groups get an opportunity to share their experiences in their group.

Chapter questions

1. Considering all the human resources management functions that you have studied so far, which functions would you say require a team approach? Describe the different roles of team members with regard to one specific human resources management function that you have identified.
2. Which of the two models, the five-stage model or the punctuated-equilibrium model, would you consider as being a closer description of how groups develop in reality? Explain your answer.
3. Are group norms, and conformity to group norms, a positive or negative aspect of groups? Discuss.
4. Which two characteristics of successful work teams do you consider as most important?
5. What are the positive aspects of belonging to a virtual team? What are the negative aspects?

Bibliography

BERGH, Z.C. & THERON, A.L. 1999. *Psychology in the work context.* Thomson, Johannesburg.

CANTU, C. 1999. Virtual Teams. *CSWT Reports.* http://www.workteams.unt.edu/reports/Cantu.html.

GERBER, P.D., NEL, P.S. & VAN DYK, P.S. 1998. *Human resources management.* 4th edition. ITP, Johannesburg.

HOLPP, L. 1999. *Managing teams.* McGraw-Hill, New York.

IVANCEVICH, J.M. & MATTESON, M.T. 1999. *Organisational behaviour and management.* 5th edition. Irwin/McGraw-Hill, USA.

KREITNER, R. & KINICKI, A. 1998. *Organisational behaviour.* 4th edition. Irwin/McGraw-Hill, USA.

LAWLER, E.E. 1996. *From the ground up.* Jossey-Bass, San Francisco.

MULLINS, L.J. 1996. Management and organizational behaviour. 4th edition. Pitman, London.

PLUNKET, W.R. 1996. *Supervision: diversity and teams in the workplace.* 8th edition. Prentice Hall, Upper Saddle River, New Jersey.

ROBBINS, S.P. 1989. *Organisational behaviour: concepts, controversies and applications.* Prentice-Hall, Englewood Cliffs, New Jersey.

ROBBINS, S.P. 1998. *Organisational behaviour.* 8th edition. Prentice-Hall, New Jersey.

17

Cultural diversity and change management

T Sono

Learning outcomes

At the end of this chapter the learner should be able to demonstrate the following outcomes:
- Define the role of culture in organisations.
- Explain the meaning of cultural diversity and factors that increase it.
- Understand Hofstede's dimensions of cultural difference.
- Discuss change and change management.
- Outline the impact of disengagement, disidentification, disenchantment, and disorientation in the workforce as reactions to change.
- Distinguish between managing change and managing diversity.
- Explain Chang's organisational diversity model.
- Discuss Burnes' nine-point approach to managing change.

Key words and concepts

- behavioural reactions to change
- combination strategy
- corporate-level strategy
- diversity
- harvesting strategy
- homogeneity and heterogeneity
- growth strategy
- Hofstede's dimensions of cultural difference
- managing diversity
- managing resistance to change
- power distance
- principles of managing change
- resistance to change
- scope of change
- stability strategy
- strategic management
- uniculturality, biculturality, and multiculturality
- workforce
- workplace

Illustrative case

XYZ is a food-processing company with a workforce composed of employees from different racial and religious backgrounds. XYZ is a fast-expanding company which is also popular amongst work-seekers because of good remuneration and wage scales. In its expansion it introduced a pork processing division. A sizeable number of XYZ employees come from a religious background which shuns pork.

Upon being given the responsibility of processing pork into food parcels, these employees refused to undertake the chores on the grounds that handling pork products violates their religious convictions and personal beliefs.

At first, managers of XYZ sought to enforce their decision that the employees should process pork products. When the employees threatened to undertake industrial action and strike on the grounds of management's 'violation of their religious rights', management was caught in a dilemma. As a 'cultural diversity consultant' how would you advise XYZ management to deal with this problem?

Suggestion
Provide a self-assessment task for all employees, which involves the exploration of each employee's own values, perceptions, and expectations. Members of the organisation, thus, examine their own points of view regarding people who are different. The four-step self-assessment process could be helpful (see Chang 1996:76).

Your next step may be to advise management to explore the principal forces that have an impact on diverse workforce teams. The principal forces, as in self-assessment, are values, expectations, and perceptions. Taken together, these forces represent important aspects of 'culture', through which each diverse group has its own shared experiences and rules to live by (Chang 1996: 80).

In short, to manage the diversity problems of the XYZ company, Chang's (1996:119) organisation diversity model may be the answer:
1. Create a diversity vision: create your vision; determine and define your values; promote your vision and values.
2. Build organisational awareness and commitment: assess where you are at, take action on areas for improvement, and focus on awareness.
3. Ensure workforce capability: staff for success, build team capability, and communicate effectively.
4. Reinforce on an ongoing basis: formalise norms and establish ground rules, track and measure your success, and emphasise involvement.

17.1 Introduction

Workplaces and organisations are becoming global in orientation and outlook, and companies are, thus, becoming more diverse in the composition of their workforce. A homogeneity of workforce backgrounds is giving way to heterogeneity; a homogenisation of the human race, in terms of technological culture, is taking place. Unicultural groups, in which virtually all members come from the same background, are no longer the norm in workplaces. This is a paradox, though, because a 'world culture' is simultaneously also evolving.

Biculturality and multiculturality, not only of the workforce in general, but of workforce management in particular, are now the trend, unlike the previously predominant unicultural workforce management. Technology is rendering human culture similar paradoxically, even as workforces are becoming bicultural or multicultural. In a bicultural workforce more members represent one or other of two distinct cultures, whereas in a multicultural workforce, members represent three or more ethnic backgrounds (Adler 1991).

For the past decade, businesses and other organisations have been facing crises because of the pressing requirement to change the composition of their workforces. Diversity and change are central to today's companies and both require management. The consequence is a diverse workforce. But what is diversity?

17.2 Diversity: a definition

Diversity encompasses all forms of difference among individuals, including culture, gender, age, ability, religious affiliation, personality, economic class, social status, military attachments, and sexual orientation (Nelson & Quick 1997: 39). In South Africa, we may add political affiliation, which is a subtle but powerful force in the diversity stakes. It now plays a critical role in affecting the composition, and thus the diversity, of the workforce in both the public and private sectors.

Diversity is the opposite concept to universality, a generalisation which may be made about all cultures. Certain activities occur across cultures; that is, they are common to all cultures, but their manifestation may be unique to a particular society (Harris & Moran 1979: 65 – 66). Workforce diversity is a powerful force for change in organisations, and change itself is a force to be reckoned with in companies. As already indicated, diversity encompasses various forms of difference, the most pressing being:

- culture;
- ability;
- gender;
- age; and
- sexual orientation.

This chapter will confine itself to one form of diversity, namely culture. A brief word on culture and its role in organisational behaviour is appropriate, before we examine the complex of cultural diversity.

17.2.1 Role of culture

Diversity of cultures is becoming a common occurrence in the workforce. Many companies no longer appear familiar regarding their workforce's cultural background. As a result, diversity is receiving increasing attention. The importance of cultural diversity should not be minimised, since an organisation's culture, as a system of shared values and beliefs, leads people, decision-making processes and procedures, and control systems to interact so as to produce behavioural norms. A strong culture guides behaviour and gives meaning to activities and, thus, contributes significantly to the long-term success of organisations. Strong cultures attract, reward, and hold the allegiance of people performing essential roles and meeting relevant goals (Kast & Rosenzweig 1985: 680).

'Culture impacts on every aspect of life, from the way people behave toward one another to their natural environment' (Harris & Myers 1996:7). Beliefs and values, assumptions and perceptions, all are cultural influences on behaviour. Culture, in other words, is 'communicable knowledge for human coping within a particular environment that is passed on for the benefit of subsequent generations' (Harris & Moran 1979:32).

Culture can be an asset, because shared beliefs ease and economise communications and facilitate decision-making. Motivation, cooperation, and commitment may also be facilitated by shared values. Organisational efficiency is achieved as a result. However, a strong culture can also be a liability, because if it is not appropriate to an organisation's environment and overall strategy it would be ineffective. Congruence between culture, strategy, and managerial style is important because it facilitates organisational efficiency.

Culture is, without question, an important dynamic in the organisation. An appropriate recognition of cultural diversity in modern companies cannot, therefore, be over-emphasised.

17.2.2 Cultural diversity

We know what causes cultural diversity, i.e. differences in cultural values, customs, beliefs, and practices, as well as ethnic or racial backgrounds. Companies today do not only have employees around the world, they also have employees from distant and different places. In other words, their human resources managers, especially, are faced with the difficult task of supporting a culturally diverse workforce.

Companies face crises because of pressing requirements to change the composition of their workforces from monocultural (of similar backgrounds) to polycultural (of diverse backgrounds). The requirement to accommodate diversity implies that human resources mangers must avoid unfair discrimination in hiring.

Managers must help expatriates understand the cultures of the countries their companies are located in. They have, thus, to facilitate inter-cultural understanding in diverse workforces. But do cultural differences translate into differences in work-related attitudes? Using many case studies, Harris and Moran (1979) authoritatively conclude that they do. A more comprehensive work, undertaken by a Dutch researcher, Geert Hofstede and his colleagues, also emphatically answered the question affirmatively. They studied workers from the same company in the same jobs, but working in different countries. Hofstede found that national culture explained more differences in work-related attitudes than did other diversity issues (such as age, gender, profession, or position within the organisation).

Hofstede also found five dimensions of cultural difference that formed the basis of work-related attitudes (See Figure 17.1).
- *Individualism versus collectivism.* In some cultures individualism predominates, in others it is collectivism that predominates. Individualist cultures foster loose

Figure 17.1 Hofstede's dimensions of cultural difference

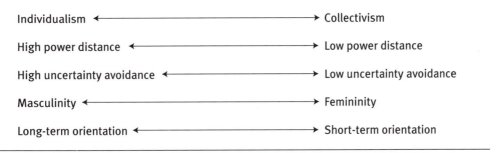

SOURCE: Hofstede (1993:81-94).

social frameworks among people, whose primary concern is for themselves and their families. The emphasis in these cultures is on individuals looking after their own interests. Personal responsibility is highly valued and individual decision-making is cherished.

Collectivist cultures, on the other hand, have different social frameworks which are tightly knit. Group cohesion and group decisions are valued and practised. Loyalty and unity, and a group approach to life and work, colour and influence personal conduct in collectivist cultures. The United States of America is an example of individualist society, whereas Japan is an example of a collectivist culture.

Individualist cultures encourage initiative, flexibility, and experimentation. Individual achievement is valued. Collectivist cultures, on the other hand, cherish a harmonious fit within the group. Members of the group are characterised by conformity. Team unity is the norm.

- *Power distance*. This cultural dimension deals with the degree of unequal distribution of power. In cultures with a high power distance, managers and supervisors have more powers precisely because they are supervisors and managers. This is a high hierarchy; formality is the norm and titles are valued and used. Many Afrikaner organisations and businesses, for instance, display this cultural trait. Authority is not easily bypassed. Those who hold power are entitled to their privileges. Bosses are bosses, and subordinates are juniors. The twain hardly ever meet, other than in a superior-inferior relationship.

  In low power distance cultures there is a strong belief that social inequality should be reduced to a minimal role. There is more trust among people at various power levels. There is a relaxed regard for the seniority-juniority dimensions. Superiority is based on merit. Managers without expertise cannot be such. Employees easily bypass bosses in order to get the work done.
- *Uncertainty avoidance*. Some cultures easily accept uncertainty and ambiguity; others are intolerant of such conditions. Cultures with high uncertainty avoidance are concerned with security and tend to avoid conflict. There is a need for consensus. The inherent uncertainty in life is a threat against which people in such cultures struggle constantly.

  Cultures with low uncertainty avoidance are more tolerant of ambiguity. Here people are risk-takers and are not perturbed by individual differences. Conflict is not a threat, but is seen as constructive. There is no fear of dissenting views. Such cultures place a premium on job mobility, unlike those of Japan and Italy which place a premium on high uncertainty avoidance and, thus, emphasise career stability.

17.2.2.1 Factors that increase cultural diversity

Many factors lead to growing cultural diversity in the workplace. These are dealt with below.

- *Globalisation* of business affects all aspects of an organisation, especially its human resources management. With companies having employees around the world, human resources managers, as we have already seen, are confronted with a culturally diverse workforce. Not only managers, but employees in general, must learn to deal with their work colleagues of different cultural backgrounds. Both local and global workplaces today are affected by a culturally diverse workforce. Globalisation inevitably leads to a culturally diverse workforce.

Even though our world is undergoing 'planetization' (Harris & Moran 1979:3) global transformation requires an understanding and appreciation of cultural diversity which, in turn, requires new organisational models, more appropriate management styles, and new paradigms. The transformation of countries and organisations is an ongoing process today, and as culture becomes dynamic its character also becomes diversified.

- *Changing demographics* of the working population is another factor that has led to the increase in diversity. More women have entered the workforce. In the United States of America, for example, more businesses are run by women. There is also the phenomenon of more people retiring later in their work lives in places such as North America, the European Union, and Japan.
- *Age-diversity*, thus, has increased in the workplace. This diversity also brings along with it cultural diversity. Older workers do not necessarily come from a monocultural background; they also come from different cultures and, with this diversity, age differences constitute a complex cultural diversity issue.

Some countries have low birth rates, to the extent that they have a shortage in their economically active population. This requires importation of workers from other countries. Japan is a classic example, but the United States and Western Europe also display similar characteristics.

- *Labour migration,* as well as *company migration*, increases diversity. In North America there is the well-known movement of work-seekers from Latin America (especially Mexico, Nicaragua, El Salvador, Honduras, and Guatemala) to the United States. These migrations have come to change not only the composition of the workforce, but its colour, culture, and of course its diversity.

The movement of people from the Caribbean islands to North America has come to have the same impact, especially in companies on the eastern seaboard of the United States and Canada. Western Europe, similarly, has been flooded by citizens of former communist countries. This is in addition to people from former European colonies. There is the flood of Asians, Africans, and Caribbeans from their respective homes to resettle in Great Britain. All these movements of people affect the cultural colours of companies, because they bring with them diverse cultural backgrounds. Migration of labour is, thus, an important factor that influences the increase of diversity.

- *Competition* is both a source of change and a force of diversity. The economy is characterised by the intense competition of companies which seek to gain an edge over their rivals and, thus, to increase profitability. To be competitive, companies employ skills from diverse sources, cultures, backgrounds, etc. Competition drives change in the economy and workplace. Corporate competition requires a multiplicity of skills if performance, productivity, and profitability are to be created. Competition, thus, requires diversity not only of abilities but of cultural backgrounds as well.

17.2.2.2 Advantages of managing cultural diversity

Diversity, like change, is a challenge that has the potential to be a source of either positive or negative influence on an organisation. For diversity to have a positive effect, knowledge must be combined with action. The existence of diversity must be acknowledged and capitalised upon (Chang 1996: 7). Cultural diversity, like change, needs to

be managed if its positive influences are to be harnessed. The advantages of this management are that it will:
- stimulate, rather than stifle, individual participation and creativity;
- increase the flow of ideas;
- attract and retain the best skills;
- improve employer-employee relations;
- increase the morale of the workforce, rather than create suspicion and hostility amongst employees;
- reduce tension, confusion, and counter-productivity in the workforce; and
- lead employers to view differences as valuable assets rather than unwanted liabilities.

Since individuals differ, these differences will also be felt in the workforce of organisations. Management of differences become important if managers are to motivate diverse workforces. It is also important for managers to learn to communicate effectively with employees who have different values and language skills (Nelson & Quick 1997:39). Because workforce diversity is increasing, its management requires close attention.

17.3 Change management

Change is now as powerful a factor in organisations as productivity is a permanent requirement in companies. Change occurs because new realities in the workplace or organisation replace old ones. Simply defined, change means to make things different (Robbins 1989:527). Change, to be successful, requires unfreezing the status quo, a movement to a new state, and re-freezing the new change to make it permanent (Lewin 1951). Too much change, however, leads to chaos, and too little change leads to stagnation (Nelson & Quick 1997:15).

17.3.1 Forms of change

Two basic forms of change are found in organisations: planned and unplanned change.
- *Planned change.* This occurs when a change results from a deliberate decision to alter the organisation. A company may wish to move from one structure to another and, thus, engage in a carefully constructed or orchestrated approach to alter the structure or functions of the organisation. However, change is not always planned.
- *Unplanned change.* Alterations may occur as a result of imposed conditions. Such change may be unforeseen. Unplanned changes may be environmental, e.g. natural disasters. Government regulations and economic conditions may lead to abrupt and unexpected changes for organisations.

Whether forced or planned, but especially in the latter instance, change needs to be managed, because change can either be disruptive or constructive.

17.3.2 Scope of change

Planned change has three scopes.
- *Incremental change.* This is change of a relatively small scope, such as making a small modification in a work procedure; it is change involving minor improvements.
- *Strategic change.* This is change on a larger scale, such as the restructuring of an organisation. In strategic change, the organisation moves from an old state to a known new state during a controlled period of time (Nelson & Quick 1997:544). Strategic change usually involves a series of transitional steps.
- *Transformational change.* This is the most massive scope of change. With this change, the organisation moves to a

radically different and, at times, unknown future state. In this change, the organisation's mission, culture, goals, structure, and leadership may all change dramatically (Jick in Nelson & Quick:544).

Those who introduce or manage change are known as a change agents. Managers or employees who oversee the change process are internal change agents. Change agents can also be external, such as outside consultants.

Change management, simply put, is managing change. Once a company has made a decision to change, a careful management of the change is imperative if the goals of the desired change are to be attained. Change management is, thus, a challenge because diverse individuals in the organisation will invariably hold diverse views of change, and their energy will need to be harnessed in order to meet the goals of change.

Change is its own challenge, and is driven by many factors and forces. In turn, it unleashes many reactions among affected individuals. Change is a big challenge that faces many managers today. Organisations continually evolve, and thus change, which in turn makes managing change a complex issue.

Change has to be managed so as to control it. Managing change, in effect, is also management of the reactions and resistance to change.

17.3.3 Resistance to change

Change has to be managed because people generally fear and resist change. They perceive change as a threat to their self-interest. 'Reactance' is a negative reaction that occurs when people feel that their personal freedom is threatened (Brehm in Nelson & Quick 1997:546). But change is not always a threat; in some cases, it is palpably beneficial, such as an increase in one's salary. Hardly anyone would resist such a change.

Change is often resisted because it is perceived as leading to some loss. According to Nelson and Quick (1997:546–547) change induces the following fears.

- *Fear of the unknown.* Whether planned or not, change often brings with it a great deal of uncertainty. It creates ambiguity, sometimes anxiety. Employees facing technological changes, such as the introduction of new computer systems, may resist the change simply because it leads to a situation of uncertainty and ambiguity where, before, there was certainty and comfort.
- *Fear of loss.* An impending change generally leads some employees to fear for the security of their jobs or positions. The introduction of advanced technology, like robotics, for instance, will lead some to fear losing not only their status but also their jobs.
  When new user-friendly computer systems are introduced, for instance, computer experts may feel threatened, as they may feel that their expertise is eroded by the introduction of the new systems. When experts perceive an erosion of their expertise, they perceive their status to be lowered and their jobs, ultimately, to be at stake.
- *Fear of failure.* One of the greatest factors inducing fear of change is fear of failure. New workplace systems arouse a sense of self-doubt about the workers' ability to interact with the new systems, especially computers. State-of-the-art systems may arouse a great sense of insecurity and inability to deal with them.
- *Fear of disrupted relationships.* Changes at the workplace may lead to disrupted interpersonal relationships. Often employees develop meaningful, long-term interpersonal relationships at the workplace. Introducing changes may affect these relationships. Some may be

relocated to other buildings, floors, plants, or cities. Change, however positive, does not necessarily lead to positive feelings as it may lead to disconnected or disrupted relationships.

Computerisation has also led to fewer interpersonal relationships developing in the workplace because it leads to a closer person-machine interactions.

- *Fear of conflict.* Some fear change because it may introduce new situations where employees may have to deal with new colleagues with different attitudes in the workplace. Conflicts may result as a consequence of a changed workplace situation; this may lead to conflict because employees may feel that their concerns and needs no longer receive the attention they once did.
- *Fear of loss of power or influence.* One of the greatest fears of organisational change is the disturbance of the settled balance of power. Those who hold power, or have great influence under the prevailing arrangement, will feel threatened by the prospects of losing their political advantage or influence with the advent of change.

17.3.4 Managing resistance to change

The traditional view treated resistance to change as something to be overcome, but many organisational attempts to reduce the resistance have only served to intensify it. The contemporary view holds that resistance is simply a form of feedback, and that this feedback can be used very productively to manage the change process. One key to managing resistance is to plan for it, and to be ready with a variety of strategies to help employees to negotiate the transition.

Three key strategies for managing resistance to change are communication, participation, and empathy and support (Cummings & Huse in Nelson & Quick 1997:547).

- *Communication* about impending change is essential if employees are to adjust effectively. The details of the change, but equally important, the rationale behind the change, should be provided. Employees want to know why change is needed. If there is no good reason for it, why should they favour the change?

  Providing accurate and timely information about the change can help prevent unfounded fears and potentially damaging rumours from developing. It is also beneficial to inform the people about the potential consequences of the change. Educating employees on new work procedures is often helpful.
- *Participation* in the change process is very important. Studies have shown this importance. For instance, in a garment factory study, employees were introduced to change in three different ways:
  – one group was simply told about the new procedure;
  – one group was introduced to the change by a trained worker; and
  – one group was allowed to help in the implementation of the new procedure.

  The third group, those who participated in the change, adopted the new method more quickly, was more productive, and experienced no turnover. It accepted the changed environment more readily and positively.

  Participation helps employees to become involved in the change and to establish a feeling of ownership of the process. When they are allowed to participate, they are more committed to the change.
- *Empathy and support* is critical for employees who have trouble dealing with the change. Active listening is an excellent tool for identifying the reasons behind resistance and for uncovering fears. Expressions of concern about the

change can provide important feedback that managers can use to improve the change process. Emotional support and encouragement can help an employee deal with the anxiety that is a natural response to change.

17.3.4.1 Typical reactions and interventions (Nelson & Quick 1997:550–551)

Change can lead to a series of negative reactions which would, in turn, trigger managerial interventions. Corporate change constantly needs appropriate husbandry. Some of the negative reactions and the managerial interventions they call for are dealt with below.

Disengagement

Disengagement is a psychological withdrawal from change. The employee may appear to lose initiative and interest in the job. Employees who disengage may fear the change, but take on the approach of doing nothing and simply hoping for the best. Disengaged employees are physically present but mentally absent. They lack drive and commitment, and they simply comply without real psychological investment in their work. The disengaged are recognised by behaviours such as being hard to find or doing only the basics to get the job done. Typical of their statements are 'no problem' or 'this won't affect me'.

The basic managerial strategy for dealing with disengaged individuals is to confront them with their reaction, and draw them out so that they can identify the concerns that need to be addressed. Disengaged employees may not be aware of the change in their behaviour, and they need to be assured of organisational intentions and plans. Disengaged people seldom become cheer-leaders for the change, but they can be brought closer to accepting and working with a change by open communication with an empathetic manager who is willing to listen.

Disidentification

Those reacting in this way feel that their identity has been threatened by the change, and they feel very vulnerable. They often cling to a past procedure because they had a sense of mastery over it, and it gave them a sense of security. Disidentified employees often display sadness and worry. They may appear to be sulking and dwelling in the past by reminiscing about the old ways of doing things. Because disidentified employees are so vulnerable, they often feel like victims in the change process. The disidentified are characterised by such verbal indications as 'my job has completely changed' and 'I used to …'.

As a manager, you can help them through the transition by encouraging them to explore their feelings, and to transfer their positive feelings into the new situation. One way to do this is to help them identify what they liked in the old situation, and to show them how it is possible to have the same positive experience in the new situation. Show them that work and emotion are separable.

Disenchantment

This is also a common reaction to change. It is usually expressed as negativity or anger. Disenchanted employees realise that the past is gone, and they are angry about it. They may try to enlist the support of other employees by forming coalitions. Destructive behaviours like sabotage and backstabbing may result. It is often difficult to reason with disenchanted employees. A particular danger of disenchantment is that it is quite contagious in the workplace. Bad-mouthing and rumour-mongering are its chief weapons of sabotage. Typical verbal signs of disenchantment are 'this will never work' and 'I am getting out of this company as soon as I can'.

The manager should bring these people from their highly negative, emotionally charged state to a more neutral state. To neutralise the reaction does not mean to dismiss it, but rather to allow the individuals to let off the necessary steam so that they can come to terms with their anger. The second part of the strategy is to acknowledge that their anger is normal and that you do not hold it against them. Sometimes disenchantment is a mask for one of the other three reactions, and it must be worked through to get to the core of the employee's reaction.

Disorientation

Disorientation is a final reaction to change. Disorientated employees are lost and confused, and are often unsure of their feelings. They waste energy trying to figure out what to do instead of how to do things. Disorientated individuals ask a lot of questions and become very detail-orientated. They may appear to need a good deal of guidance and may leave their work undone until all their questions have been answered. Disorientation is a common reaction among people who are used to clear goals and unambiguous directions. When change is introduced, it creates uncertainty and a lack of clarity. The disorientated are characterised by 'analysis paralysis'. They feel that they have lost touch with the priorities of the company, and they may want to analyse issues to death before acting on them. The disorientated employees may ask questions like 'Now what do I do?' or 'What do I do first?'

Managers should explain the change in a way that minimises the ambiguity that is present. The information about the change needs to be put into a framework or an overall vision so that the disorientated individual can see where he or she fits into the grand scheme of things. The employee needs a sense of priorities to work on.

Managers need the ability to diagnose these four reactions to change.

17.4 Principles (or the how to) of managing change

- Managers should be able to identify the forces of change. These forces come from diverse sources, external and internal.
- A shared vision for change should be developed and should include participation by all employees in the planning process.
- Top management must be committed to the change and should visibly demonstrate support.
- A comprehensive diagnosis and needs analysis should be conducted.
- There must be adequate resources for carrying out the change.

Table 17.1 Behavioural reactions to change

Reaction	Expression	Managerial
Intervention	Disengagement	Withdrawal
Confront, identify	Disidentification	Sadness, worry
Explore, transfer	Disenchantment	Anger
Neutralise, acknowledge	Disorientation	Confusion
Explain, plan		

SOURCE: Adapted from Woodward & Buchholz (1987:15).

- Resistance to change must be planned for and managed. Communication, participation, and empathy are ways of helping employees to adjust.
- Reward systems should reinforce new behaviours, not old ones.
- Participation in the change process should also be recognised and rewarded.
- Change management efforts should be undertaken in an ethical manner and should preserve employees' privacy and freedom of choice.

17.5 Strategic change management

The word 'strategy' comes from the Greek 'stratego', meaning to plan the destruction of one's enemies through the effective use of resources. The concept remained a military one until the Industrial Revolution, when it began to permeate the business world. Changing population, income, and technology brought, in their wake, an awareness of the opportunity and need to employ existing or expanding resources more profitably. Strategic management has the additional focus of winning market share from competitors.

Strategic management's perspective suggests that managers are central figures in organisational change. As decision-makers they have a proactive role in anticipating and shaping the environment, and in charting the organisation's course. According to Jemison (in Kast & Rosenzweig 1985:145) the strategist's primary task is to ensure a good strategic alignment between the organization and its environment. This alignment process involves two functions:
1 matching the organization's competencies with the demands of the environment, and
2 arranging internal structures and processes so that other people can come up with creative strategic alternatives and develop new competencies to meet the challenges of the future.

Strategic management is thus important to change management. Without it it's not easy both to legitimise change and to assess whether or not its impact has a positive or negative effect on an organisation. In Burnes' view certain basic features regarding strategic management stand out:
1 the full scope of an organisation's activities, including corporate objectives and organisational boundaries;
2 matching the activities of an organisation to the environment in which it operates;
3 ensuring that the internal structures, practices and procedures enable the organisation to achieve its objectives;
4 matching the activities of an organisation to its resource capability, assessing the extent to which sufficient resources can be provided to take advantage of opportunities or avoid threats in the organisation's environment;
5 the acquisition, divestment and reallocation of resources; and
6 translating the complex and dynamic set of external and internal variables, which an organisation faces, into a structured set of clear future objectives which can be implemented on a day-to-day basis (Burnes 1992:92–93).

Burnes goes on to identify three types of strategy, namely corporate level, business level and functional level strategies. Corporate level concerns the direction, composition and co-ordination of the various businesses and activities that comprise a large and diversified organisation. Business level strategy relates to the operation and direction of each of the individual businesses within a group of companies. Functional level strategy concerns individual business functions such as marketing or personnel.

Corporate level strategy reveals six basic types of strategy:
- *Stability strategy* is designed to keep organisations quiet and stable, and is frequently found in successful organisations. Because of their markets and products, such organisations believe they have no need to make sudden changes and have the time and position to allow events to unfold before making any response (Wheelen & Hunger in Burnes 1992:96).
- *Growth strategy* is the most common form of all strategies, and involves either concentrating on dominating one industry, or growing by diversification across a number of industries.
- *Portfolio extension* is a variant of growth strategy but is achieved through mergers, joint ventures, or acquisitions, rather than organic growth.
- *Retrenchment strategy* is usually embarked upon when an organisation is in trouble, or because it sees trouble ahead of adverse market conditions. It usually involves a process of cutting back on numbers employed and activities undertaken. The general aim is to refocus the organisation so as to be able, once again, to attain prosperity.
- *Harvesting strategy* involves reducing investment in an area of business activity in order to reduce costs, improve cash flow, and capitalise on whatever residual competencies or areas of advantage still remain. This strategy can involve fast or slow harvesting.
- *Combination strategy.* As the above strategies are not mutually exclusive they can be linked together in whatever combination seems appropriate, given the circumstances of the organisation in question (Burnes 1992:96–97).

There are different types and levels of change (the individual, the work group, and organisational levels). Since our focus is on the level of organisational change, no matter what theory or approach (and there are many theories and approaches) is applied, the process requires some person or group to intervene in the running of the organisation to effect this change. The intervention could be led by the people who are the subject of the change process itself (as has been happening in South African universities since the early 1990s). Successful intervention involves moving an organisation through several distinct states in order to achieve a higher level of performance (Bullock & Batten 1985).

Burnes (1992:257–270) details nine elements which constitute a new approach to managing change. These are:
1 Creating a vision.
2 Developing strategies.
3 Creating the conditions for successful change.
4 Creating the right culture.
5 Assessing the need for and type of change.
6 Planning and implementing change.
7 Involvement.
8 Sustaining the momentum.
9 Continuous improvement.

17.6 Conclusion

Increasing diversity in the workforce, just like change, are powerful factors in organisations that require effective management. Cultural diversity, in particular, must be recognised as an important form of diversity. The challenges posed by diversity and change demand that human resources managers intervene proactively by recognising the nature of these two forces and implementing the necessary strategies to channel them in a positive direction.

Chapter questions

1 Using Chang's organisation diversity model how would you manage diversity in the company Afri-Euro Distributors Ltd, whose middle and upper management used to be all white males?
2 Explain Hofstede's dimension of cultural differences.
3 What are the major factors that increase cultural diversity?
4 Explain the fears that are induced by change.
5 Discuss the key strategies for managing resistance to change.
6 What negative reactions flow from change and what managerial interventions may be used to counter these reactions?
7 State the principles of managing change.

Bibliography

ADLER, N.J. 1991. *International dimension of organizational behavior.* 2nd edition. PWs Kent, Boston.
BULLOCK, R.J. & BATTEN, D. 1985. It's just a phase we're going through: a review and synthesis of OD phase analysis. *Group and Organization Studies* 10, December, 383–412.
BURNES, B. 1992. *Managing change: a strategic approach to organisational development and renewal.* Pitman Publishing, London.
CHANG, R.Y. 1994. *Mastering change management: a practical guide to turning obstacles into opportunities.* Richard Chang Associates Inc., Irvine, California.
CHANG, R.Y. 1996. *Capitalizing on workplace diversity: a practical guide to organizational success through diversity.* Richard Chang Associates Inc., Irvine, California.
COCH, L. & FRENCH, J.P. 1945. *Overcoming resistance to change.* Human Relations 1: 512–532.
CONNOR, P.E. & LAKE, L.K. 1985. *Managing organizational change.* Praeger, New York.
JICK, T.D. 1993. *Managing change.* Irwin, Homewood, Illinois.
JOHNSTON, W.B. 1991. Global work force 2000: the new world labor market. *Harvard Business Review*, March–April: 115–127.
KAST, R. & ROSENZWEIG, J.E. 1985. *Organization and management: a system and contingency approach.* 4th edition. McGraw-Hill Book Company, New York, Johannesburg.
NELSON, D.L. & QUICK, J.C. 1997. *Organisational behaviour: foundations, realities and challenges.* West Publishing Company. Minneapolis/St. Paul, New York, Los Angeles, San Francisco.
ROBBINS, S. 1989. *Organizational behaviour: concepts, controversies and applications.* 4th edition. Prentice Hall, Englewood Cliffs.
SCHLESINGER, L.A. & KOTTER, J.P. 1979. Choosing strategies for change. Harvard Business Review 57: 109–112.

part six

Employee, group and organisational empowerment through human resources interventions

18

Job design and organisational design

HB Schultz

Learning outcomes

At the end of this chapter the learner should be able to demonstrate the following outcomes:
- Differentiate between the concepts of job range and job depth.
- Evaluate the specialised approach to job design.
- Discuss the use of job range, job depth, and team-based designs as a means of improving the design of specialised jobs.
- Describe the link between strategy and organisational design.
- Compare various approaches to organisational design.
- Provide an overview of emerging trends in organisational design.
- Discuss the necessity for quality assurance in job and organisational design.

Key words and concepts

- boundaryless structure
- bureaucratic structure
- doughnut organisation
- flat structure
- job depth
- job design
- job enlargement
- job enrichment
- job range
- job rotation
- job specialisation, or job simplification
- organisational design
- professional design
- reengineering
- shamrock organisation
- team-based job design
- vineyard organisation
- virtual organisation

Illustrative case
The world's most unusual workplace

Ricardo Semler is a maverick, a nonconformist. He is not only the world's most unusual CEO; his company, Semco S/A, is the world's most unusual workplace. Semler took over the reins of Semco, a company that manufactures pumps, at its headquarters in São Paulo, Brazil in 1981, when he was still a young man in his early twenties. He studied law at São Paulo University, but was drawn to the corporate business world. However, from Day One, he proved to be the most unconventional CEO Brazilian business magnates had ever known. Semco was a traditional company in every respect, with a pyramidal structure and a rule for every contingency; but today, factory workers set their own production quotas and even come in on their own time to meet them, without prodding from management or overtime pay. They help redesign the products they make, and formulate business plans. They set their own salaries, with no strings attached. Financial information at Semco is openly discussed and, when the organisation considers buying another company, everyone at Semco gets a vote.

In the last two decades, Ricardo Semler has been the driving force behind restructuring the company from twelve layers of management into a streamlined flattened structure of just three levels. He devised a new organisational structure based on fluid concentric circles instead of a rigidly hierarchical pyramid. Workers have redesigned their own jobs and work groups have been born out of diversity. New products are designed and tested, not by Research and Development teams, not by Project teams, but by 'Diversity Teams' that include factory workers, engineers, office clerks, sales reps, and executives. Policy manuals have been thrown in the dustbin and not replaced.

At the HRD 2000 Conference held in London in April 2000, Semler warned bosses to face up to radical change because most companies are still operating the same way they did centuries ago. Semler has proved his formula for success because Semco is one of Latin America's fastest-growing companies, acknowledged to be the best in Brazil to work for, and with a waiting list of thousands of applicants hoping for a place in the company.

SOURCE: Semler, R. (1993: 110–113).

18.1 Introduction

Globalised competition and technological innovation are changing the way companies are managed. In the new century, organisations must wrestle with revolutionary trends such as accelerating product change, deregulation, demographic changes, a service society, and the so-called information age. Companies that have successfully responded to these challenges have recognised the need to examine their job and organisational structures. They have not been content to retain the status quo; instead, they have tested new job and organisational designs and have acknowledged the need to accept changes that are sometimes drastic and radical.

Job design determines the content of work, how the job is performed, and the depth of responsibility associated with the job. The objective of a well-designed job is to provide job satisfaction for the job-holder, and to achieve the strategic goals of the organisation. Although a number of job designs have been around for decades, the mere fact that we now live in a 'competency-based' world necessitates that all jobholders have the opportunity to test different job designs.

Traditionally, an organisation's structure was hierarchical and based on physical location; but technology has made that obsolete and we are quickly moving to a new model that sees organisations as flatter and less linked to geography, with greater dependence on networking and personal empowerment.

We commence this chapter with a discussion on the differences between job range and job depth. Various approaches to job design are examined, including the specialised approach and team-based designs, before we proceed to investigate the link between strategy and organisational design. The bureaucratic organisation is the forerunner of organisational design, but we also turn our attention to recent adaptations such as the flatter structure and the boundaryless design. Some exciting trends in organisational design are examined, and the concept of the virtual corporation is debated. We take a brief look at reengineering before closing with some thoughts on job and organisational design, and quality assurance.

18.2 Job range and job depth

According to Swanepoel et al. (1998:237) job design refers to the way in which the different tasks and responsibilities required to carry out a job, structure the work activities of that job. For the sake of strategy, work should be organised in some specific way to obtain the required performance from the employee.

Job range is the number of different tasks that make up a particular job, and job depth refers to the extent to which a jobholder is able to influence the activities and outcomes of that job. Swanepoel et al. (1998:238) state that the greater the job depth, the more autonomy the job-holder will have; the greater the job range, the larger the variety of activities and tasks a job-holder will be expected to undertake.

Job range and depth distinguish one job from another, not only within the same organisation, but also among different organisations. Highly specialised jobs are those having only a few tasks to accomplish by prescribed means. These jobs are routine and they tend to be controlled by specified rules and procedures, resulting in low depth. A job with high range has many tasks to be accomplished within its framework; a job requiring much autonomous decision-making would be regarded as one with high depth.

Within an organisation, there are usually great differences between jobs, in both range and depth. When consideration is given to the design or redesign of jobs, the focal point is usually on the amount of range or depth associated with the job (Ivancevich & Matteson 1999:236).

18.3 The specialised approach to job design

Carrell et al. (1998:110) discuss specialisation-intensive jobs as those that are characterised by very few, repetitive tasks, which require few skills and little mental ability. These jobs display the characteristics of low range and low depth. The job specialisation approach, which is also known as job simplification, produces jobs that are designed for people with very few skills or little experience. Specialisation is a method of job creation, but overspecialisation can cause a number of problems:

- routine tasks, repeated many times during a work shift, cause employees to become bored;
- the mechanically paced speed of an assembly or production line causes those employees who find the pace too slow to divert their attention away from the task at hand;
- employees are not part of the entire process and, because they are not able to identify the end product, have little pride in or enthusiasm for the work;
- specialisation-intensive jobs are not conducive to social interaction among employees; and
- employees do not make inputs regarding how the job should be performed, the work procedures, or the tools to be used, which creates a lack of interest, because the employees are unable to change or improve anything.

Werther and Davis (1993:155) propose an interesting theory that could be used by countries with a high unemployment rate, such as South Africa. They state that the potential problem of boredom is more common in advanced industrial countries that have a well-developed work force. In less developed countries, highly specialised factory jobs may be acceptable because they provide jobs for workers with limited skills. South Africa cannot truly be regarded as a less developed country, although in many areas we teeter on the brink of third-world status. The quandary, then, is to perform a balancing act between providing jobs for the unemployed through work simplification or specialisation, and developing a multi-skilled labour force which adds value to organisations and which will not find job satisfaction where job specialisation has taken place.

18.3.1 Designing job range

Limited, uniform, and repetitive tasks yield a narrow job range. The consequences of narrow job range are job discontent, high dissatisfaction, turnover, and absenteeism. Various strategies are used in an attempt to increase job range and reverse some of these consequences (Ivancevich & Matteson 1999:239).

18.3.1.1 Job rotation

This practice involves rotating managers and non-managers alike from one job to another, in an attempt to offer more activities to the jobholders, since each job includes different tasks. The job range and perception of variety in the job content is therefore increased. Increasing task variety should increase employee satisfaction, reduce mental overload, decrease the number of errors due to fatigue, improve production and efficiency, and reduce on-the-job injuries. Many companies have had great success in using job rotation. Where there are teams, team members rotate jobs with other team members to provide task variety and cross training. Team members are also trained to do routine maintenance and repairs of their equipment and not to depend on a separate maintenance team for that support. These companies aim to give individuals as much control as possible over the conditions that govern work pace and quality. Some thoughts on job rotation are offered in Table 18.1.

Although some critics state that job rotation often involves nothing more than having people perform several boring and monotonous jobs rather than one dull and tedious job, the case-in-point provides research data indicating that rotating people from job to job can be a good corporate strategy.

Table 18.1 Eight points you need to consider about job rotation

1. Manage job rotation as part of the company's training and career-development system.
2. Ensure that there is a clear understanding of which skills will be enhanced by placing an employee in a job rotation process.
3. Use job rotation for developing employees in all types of jobs – managerial and non-managerial.
4. Plan to use job rotation with early-career, later-career, and plateaued employees.
5. Job rotation provides opportunities to develop and motivate employees without necessarily granting promotions.
6. Female and previously disadvantaged employees can receive special attention through job rotation plans.
7. Ensure that job rotation is perceived as voluntary, that the assignment is linked to predetermined outcomes, and that employees are aware of the developmental needs addressed by each job assignment.
8. Manage the timing of rotations and operating procedures to maximise benefits and minimise costs of rotation.

SOURCE: Cheraskin & Campion (1996: 36).

Case-in-point
Job rotation benefits at Eli Lilly and Company

Eli Lilly and Company is a major American corporation that researches and produces medication for treating health conditions such as endocrine diseases, diabetes, osteoporosis, infectious diseases, schizophrenia, and cancer. In 1990, a study was conducted using Eli Lilly and Company as a test case to establish exactly what relationships there are between rotating people to different jobs and their overall training and development. The study confirmed that job rotation can, and should, be used as a proactive means of enhancing the value of work experience for the goals of training and development.

Rotating employees from job to job has, for many years, been viewed as an integral part of Ely Lilly's culture of professional development. This reputation for job rotation has tended to increase overall employee satisfaction. This study focused on one particular division of the organisation, the financial department, which includes such areas as treasury, accounting and payroll. This department consists of approximately 500 workers. At the time of the study, most rotations consisted of lateral rather than vertical moves. The financial department has a planning committee comprised of executives who meet monthly to coordinate job rotations for the company. Job rotations are based on the vacancies that occur, the development needs and interests of the employees, and the staffing requirements of the business.

The study found that higher-performing employees seem to accept more job rotations. The nature of an employee's current job also influences his or her interest in rotation. However, executives in the financial department displayed a lack of interest in job rotation, probably because they have less to gain career-wise, or they may be tired of the rapid job movement involved in climbing the corporate hierarchy.

Employees value job rotation because there are measurable outcomes, such as promotion and salary growth. As a training and development tool, job rotation's primary advantage is employees' improved knowledge and skills in the technical, business, and administrative areas. Unfortunately, although much good is gained by job rotation, there are two knowledge areas where it has little impact: the external business environment, and how to develop others. The study at Eli Lilly also showed that employees who rotate more often, or who are interested in rotating, perceive greater improvement in the skills acquisition process.

Job rotation increased career satisfaction, involvement, and motivation. There was enhanced employee commitment to stay with the company, and more opportunity for development and promotion. Employees' contact networks were expanded across the organisation; they attained a better understanding of strategic issues, and were stimulated by the variety and challenges that came from new jobs.

There are, however, disadvantages associated with job rotation. Workload may increase and productivity may decrease for the rotating and other employees. There may be a disruption in work-flow, and costs incurred in the time spent learning a new job, in training, and in the errors that trainees often make. Data obtained from employees involved in this study showed that rotation sometimes takes place too fast – most people seemed to think that there should be a period of at least twelve months between rotations.

Job rotation must be integrated with the organisation's HR strategy. This method of job design creates generalists, rather than specialists, and it must not be forgotten that specialist skills are still needed in an organisation. Job rotation may replace the need for job enrichment because, if used properly, it can have a similar, positive effect on motivation by increasing job challenge, skills usage, and task variety. Eli Lilly's study proved, however, that job rotation is an HR tool that should not be overlooked in training and career development. The advice of the researchers is: 'Don't underestimate the power of a different job on employee performance.'

SOURCE: Cheraskin & Campion (1996: 31–38).

18.3.1.2 Job enlargement

An alternative design strategy to job rotation is job enlargement. Job enlargement strategies are directed at increasing the number of tasks that an employee performs. Leap and Crino (1993:157) state that the job only undergoes horizontal expansion and, consequently, a previously monotonous job remains monotonous, only on a larger scale. However, Ivancevich and Matteson (1999:240) feel that the practice of job enlargement has become increasingly more sophisticated in recent years, because effective job enlargement involves more than simply increasing task variety. Other aspects of job range, such as worker-paced, rather than machine-paced control are also taken into consideration. Job satisfaction usually increases because boredom is reduced.

Not all employees can cope with enlarged jobs because they cannot all comprehend complexity. They may also not have a sufficiently long attention span to complete an enlarged set of tasks. However, if employees are open to job enlargement and have the required ability, job enlargement should increase satisfaction and product quality, and decrease absenteeism and turnover.

18.3.2 Designing job depth

Creating opportunities for employees to gain more control in their jobs, make more decisions themselves, and solve problems on their own increases job depth. One can then say that job enrichment has taken place.

The application of job enrichment is based on Herzberg's two-factor theory. The basis of this theory is that factors that meet individuals' need for psychological growth (especially in terms of responsibility, job challenge, and achievement) must be characteristic of their jobs. Job enrichment is brought about through direct changes in job depth. Job depth can be expanded by:
- timely and direct feedback in the evaluation of performance;
- providing opportunities to learn while in the job;
- allowing employees to schedule at least some part of their own work;
- ensuring that each job possesses some unique qualities or features;
- allowing individuals to have some control over their job tasks; and
- providing employees with the opportunity to be accountable for the job.

Dessler (1997:109) agrees with the above suggestions and adds that forming natural work groups, combining tasks, and establishing client relationships will also assist in enriching jobs.

Managers have become aware that job enrichment requires numerous changes in how work is done. Employees must be given greater authority to participate in decisions, to set their own goals, and to evaluate their own and their work group's performance. Managers must also be willing to delegate authority. Ivancevich and Matteson (1999:242) believe that if these conditions are met, gains in performance can be expected, provided that the work environment is supportive.

18.4 Team-based job designs

Team-based job designs aim at providing a team, rather than an individual, with a whole and meaningful piece of work to do. The onus is on team members to decide among themselves how to accomplish their tasks. They are cross-trained in different skills, and rotated within the team. Gómez-Mejia et al. (1998:61) state that team designs work best within a flat or boundaryless organisational structure. These structures are discussed in Section 18.6.

A self-managed team (SMT) represents a job enrichment approach to redesigning jobs at the group level. SMT members are empowered to perform certain activities based on procedures established and decisions made within the group, with minimum or no outside direction. SMTs include task groups, project teams, quality circles, and new venture teams. Team members are, typically, responsible for an entire process from inception to completion. They often select their own members and evaluate their own performance (Ivancevich & Matteson 1999:245). Worldwide, the automotive industry has been particularly interested in the use of SMTs. Varying degrees of success have been experienced, based predominantly on workers' acceptance of the team concept.

There is no one best approach to job design. However, with the different approaches at our fingertips, we possess the tools for making an informed choice. The various approaches to job design are displayed in Figure 18.1

18.5 Strategy and organisational design

Dessler (1997:15) states that new paradigms of organising and managing have meant the introduction of innovative modes of structure and design. The traditional, pyramid-shaped organisation is giving way to new organisational forms. Employees are being empowered to make more and more decisions, and experts argue for turning the typical organisation upside down. Flatter organisations are the norm and work is increasingly being organised around teams and processes rather than specialised functions.

Organisational design is the macroscopic term that includes an organisation's structure and its processes for decision-making, communication, and performance management. Organisational structure can limit the freedom of individuals to achieve their goals. This is one of the reasons why strategists never cease in their attempts to find the most acceptable and feasible structures for their organisations (Benton 1995:217).

Torrington and Hall (1995:110–111) agree that new forms of organisation are needed for the future. Their view is based on the following reasons:

- *Big is no longer always beautiful.* In the past organisations were established on the assumption that the business would expand. This is no longer the case as diversification and change are sometimes wise alternatives.
- *Business is not always directed towards permanence.* The notion that companies are established to continue indefinitely no longer holds true. There is now greater emphasis on projects and ventures that run for a time and are then terminated or sold.
- *The customer is king.* The service culture of the new century demands that organisations become less concerned with internal affairs and organisational

Figure 18.1 The approaches to job design

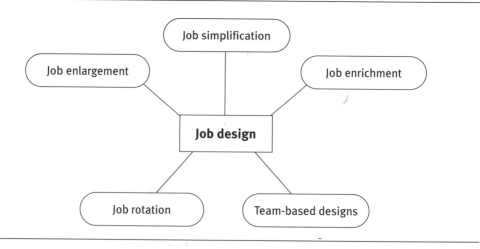

politics, in order to meet the customer's needs.
- *The proliferation of expertise.* Successful businesses rely on an increasing variety of skills and diverse expertise, much of which has to be bought in on a temporary basis from consultants or contractors.
- *Information technology.* Computerised environments depersonalise the management process to a great extent. Individual and departmental objectives can be quantified and performance can be measured.

18.6 Approaches to organisational design

In complex organisations, there are usually several levels of management, but only one or two levels of workers. Supervisors interact with the employees, and monitor and control their work closely. The more management levels there are, the taller the structure will be, and the longer it will take for messages to reach desired levels. Benton (1995:218) therefore suggests the axiom: the taller the structure, or the more numerous the levels of management, the poorer the communication; the flatter the structure or the fewer the levels of management, the better the chances that accurate information is being transmitted.

18.6.1 The bureaucratic organisation

Bureaucracies are usually thought of in negative terms; inefficient structures with many layers of management and huge amounts of red tape that frustrate creativity. There is a great deal of truth to this view, but this type of design has served organisations for over a hundred years. The organisation chart is the symbol of a bureaucratic structure and depicts an organisation broken down or decentralised into component parts and operations. Each operation is linked to others in a fixed rank order of control. The concept of division of labour simplifies jobs and makes them more specialised. Responsibility or authority for each operation is delegated downward through the hierarchy and communication flows upward through the same channels (Schultz & Schultz 1994:298).

A major problem with a bureaucratic organisation is that employees do not always accept or abide by its structure, because bureaucracies ignore human needs and values. Bureaucracies also harm themselves by fostering stability, rigidity, and permanence, and do not adapt quickly or well to changing social conditions and technological innovations. Lundy and Cowling (1996:144) believe that this type of structure provides us with an orderly, well-regulated organisation, where there are clear career structures and where top management has a clear overview of the whole structure. However they also agree that these structures can become inflexible and unable to respond to changes in the environment. In the rapidly changing scenario of the 21st century this can only spell disaster. The typical organisational chart of the bureaucratic structure is shown in Figure 18.2.

18.6.2 The flat organisation

Flatter organisational structures, with sometimes as few as three or four levels are becoming more prevalent. Benton (1995: 218) describes a flat organisational structure, with widely distributed authority and fewer strict controls, as a good environment for people who like to work independently.

According to Swanepoel et al. (1998: 250) a flat organisational design emphasises aspects like adaptability, responsiveness, and development, through limiting the use of rules, regulations, and procedures. It emphasises decentralisation of authority

Figure 18.2 The bureaucratic structure

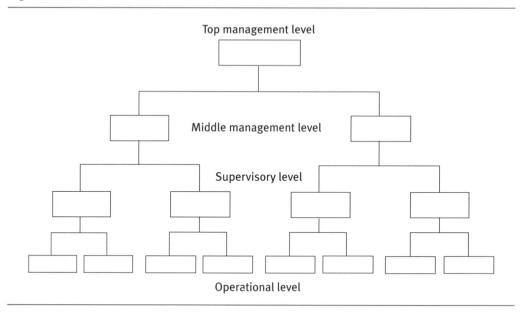

and lower degrees of specialisation. Jobs are generally more broadly defined, with greater overlaps and more flexible boundaries. Figure 18.3 is an example of a flat organisational structure.

18.6.3 The boundaryless organisation

According to Torrington and Hall (1995: 112) the boundaryless organisation eliminates barriers that separate functions such as marketing and manufacturing, domestic and foreign operations, different levels of work, such as managerial and blue-collar, and between the organisation and its customers and suppliers.

Ivancevich and Matteson (1999:584) maintain that as traditional organisational boundaries crumble, a new set of psychological boundaries must be managed. These new dimensions can be identified as authority, task, political, and identity boundaries. Psychological boundaries pose questions that do not always have ready-made answers in the dynamic organisational milieu of the new century:

- The authority boundary asks, 'Who's in charge of what?'
- The task boundary asks, 'Who does what?'
- The political boundary asks, 'What's in it for us?'
- The identity boundary asks, 'Who are we?'

A more fluid, boundaryless organisation will create more blurred roles for workers, and senior executives will require new types of management skills in order to deal with these psychological boundaries. A boundaryless organisational structure is depicted in Figure 18.4.

18.7 Emerging trends in organisational design

Ivancevich and Matteson (1999:583) state that never before did so many enterprises

Figure 18.3 A flat organisational structure

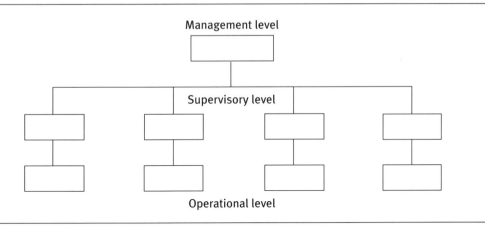

question the fundamental principles of traditional organisational structures as during the 1990s. Pressure to become more customer-driven, to manage horizontally and to pay greater attention to core business processes created the need to be able to adapt quickly to changing circumstances, or be left behind by the competition. New organisational designs have become more the norm than the exception as we enter the new millennium. Some of these designs will be fleeting, but some have a great deal of merit. We shall examine some of the more feasible designs proposed by Charles Handy, Europe's best known and most influential management thinker, and D. Quinn Mills, who regards himself as an 'architect of future organisations'.

18.7.1 Shamrocks, doughnuts, and vineyards

In an interview on the Australian Broadcasting Corporation's programme Lateline, Charles Handy, the British human resources philosopher and author stated:

> In the future your working life will span twenty-five years, not forty-five years; most of your education will take place outside the classroom; corporate retirement funds will become a thing of the past; and half of all jobs available will be part-time, not full-time.

Is this fact or fantasy? You can listen to Handy's entire interview, lasting thirty-five minutes, on the Internet website http://www.morganbanks.com.au/handy.htm and decide for yourself.

The shamrock organisation

Handy's metaphor of a shamrock, or four-leaf clover, which he uses to illustrate his predicted organisational structure, is depicted in Figure 18.5. The first leaf contains core workers who are essential to the existence of the firm – qualified professionals, technicians, and managers. The second leaf contains contract workers who carry out non-essential, but specialised work at low cost. The third leaf contains the flexible work force – part-time and temporary workers who are contracted and terminated according to customer requirements. The fourth leaf features the external customers. This radical departure

Figure 18.4 A boundaryless structure

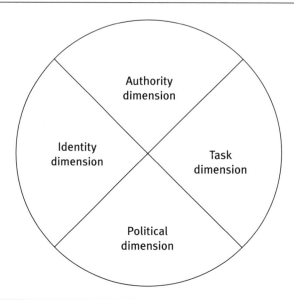

from traditional structure views the customer as an integral part of the organisation and not a separate entity.

It is only the professional core that will be relatively permanent. The other leaves of the shamrock will be adaptive and flexible. The new worker will have a work portfolio made up of wage or fee work, homework, gift work, and study work. Portfolio people will continually contract their skills where there is the greatest demand and will move on when the assignment is finished (Ivancevich & Matteson, 1999:585).

Handy (1994) identifies three concepts crucial to the survival of organisations in the future. He believes that organisations must be aware of, and react to the sigmoid, or S-shaped curve, the doughnut principle should be considered as an organisational design for the future, and Chinese contracts must become part of organisational systems. Each of these concepts will be discussed below.

Figure 18.5 The shamrock organisation

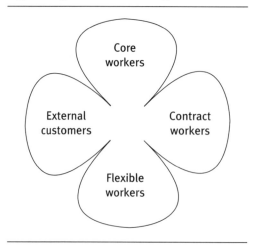

The sigmoid curve

The sigmoid curve (depicted in Figure 18.6) plots the path of every successful human system, including organisations. A period of experimentation is followed by one of growth and development, before the curve reverses its trajectory and enters a declining phase. To be successful, organisations must develop and initiate a new curve before the old one starts its downward slope. This very often entails a complete turnaround in mindset, culture, product development, and strategy. Many organisations fail to start a new curve because top managers see the company in a period of growth and success, and are afraid to change the status quo before it is absolutely necessary. They really only wake up when it is too late.

Change on the curve results in great confusion, represented by the shaded areas. This is due to the two contrasting, and often competing cultures existing side-by-side. However, continued success and survival depend on the development of new curves, which will provide the foundation for a learning organisation.

The doughnut principle

Handy's doughnut organisation is an inside-out one, inasmuch as the usual hole one would find in the middle of a doughnut has become a solid core surrounded by an empty but bounded space. The core of the doughnut represents the place for essential business and offers scope for initiative. The space around the core is filled by a flexible band of subcontractors, advisers, and part-time workers.

In the past, jobs were tightly designed, leaving little room for discretion. Handy proposes that jobs should also be designed in the form of his inside-out doughnut, with a specified essential core having outer limits of discretionary and expandable authority.

Handy goes on to describe organisations as comprising groups of doughnuts, for example, a doughnut group responsible for the development and marketing of a particular product. This group would have its essential core of permanent 'community members' (no longer referred to as employees) with an outer space providing flexible support in the way of researchers, suppliers, and service contractors. Doughnut groups are continuously evolving and declining as their life span comes to an end, but the sigmoid curve should be brought into play before the curve starts to dip. A simple depiction of the doughnut organisation is shown in Figure 18.7.

The Chinese contract

Handy maintains that partnerships must be based on a win-win situation, where both sides benefit equally, reinforcing trust

Figure 18.6 The sigmoid curve

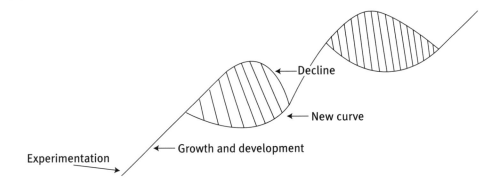

Figure 18.7 The doughnut principle

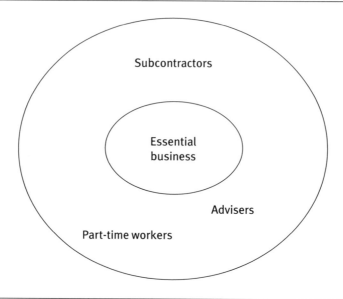

rather than enforcing legal sanctions. True partnerships prefer mutuality rather than competition, and look for shared benefits. Parties should know each other well enough to share information, common goals, and ambitions for the enterprise. This philosophy is contrary to Western traditions, where the principle of competition has always been foremost. However, Handy believes that a successful future for our organisations, and society as a whole, depends on the adoption of Chinese contracts.

The professional design

In a similar vein to Charles Handy, but perhaps less metaphoric, Torrington & Hall (1995:113) propose a new approach to organisational design, called the professional design. Fundamental to its operation is the core/periphery type of split in the workforce. The core contains all those activities that will be carried out by employees, while the periphery contains activities that will be put out to tender by contractors or moved elsewhere in the supply chain. The crucial decisions relate to which activities should be in which area. The core should of necessity contain those skills that are specialised to the business and the periphery contains all the other activities. Many organisations have already opted for this type of design, believing that they should concentrate their expertise on what they do best.

The vineyard organisation

D. Quinn Mills (in Ivancevich & Matteson, 1999: 586) suggests that the organisation of the future will be a 'cluster'. This concept portrays groups of people around a common vine, like bunches of grapes. The vine is the organisational vision; the employees are the grapes. The vine and the clusters produce the wine of the business. Mills sees people drawn from different disciplines working together on a semi-

permanent basis. The six types of cluster (illustrated in Figure 18.8) are:
- a core team, comprised of top management;
- business units, conducting their own business and dealing directly with customers;
- staff units, providing accounting, personnel, and legal services;
- project teams, assembled for a specific project;
- alliance teams, involving participants from different corporations, involved in marketing, sales, and product development; and
- change teams, created for the purpose of reviewing and modifying broad aspects of the firm's activities.

18.7.2 The virtual organisation

Wright and Oldford (1995) point out that the norms of organisational culture dictate the tradition and values held by the organisation. For centuries, the centre of the work environment has been the workplace itself. Recently, the trend has been towards the decentralisation of organisations; telecommuting is seen as the ultimate extension of decentralisation, paving the way for the birth of the virtual organisation.

The virtual corporation does not necessarily adopt a new structure, but is a company that adapts its design to make maximum use of technology. A virtual organisation is one where there are far fewer employees to be found in their corporate offices than was the norm in the past. Where are these people now? They are still on duty, only now their offices are where they choose to set them up: in a corner of the company cafeteria, in their own homes, on a train or in an airport, in a hotel room, at the client site, or even in a secluded park somewhere. As long as the nature of their jobs allows them to link up to the corporate head office by means of a personal or laptop computer, with access to electronic mail (e-mail) and the Internet, fax-modem, and cellular telephone, a virtual office can be set up almost anywhere. It can be permanent, semi-permanent, or transient. According to a 1997 Watson Wyatt Worldwide survey, 51 per cent of organisations in the United States with more than 5 000 employees on the

Figure 18.8 The vineyard organisation

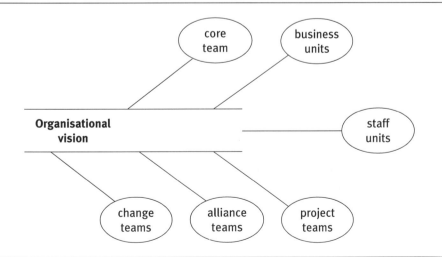

payroll, and 63 per cent of all companies surveyed, offered virtual facilities to their workers (Micco 1997).

Sometimes the virtual workplace combines the efforts of people in diverse venues or different corporate entities. Crandall and Wallace (1997:27) believe that survival will depend increasingly on people from two or more companies working together in a virtual environment. They identify three successive stages in the development of the virtual workplace:

- the telecommuting model, in which individual employees work from remote locations and commute most of the time on an electronic basis;
- the front-line model, which involves placing sales and service locations in the field and close to the customer; and
- the cyber link model, which represents the greatest level of 'virtuality' an organisation can hope to achieve; teams of employees and customers work together in a flexible, virtual environment, remaining virtually linked, sometimes never even meeting face-to-face, until business opportunities have been fully realised.

Encounter 18.1 paints a picture of how conventional corporate offices are being transformed to fit into today's mobile environment.

Advantages and disadvantages of the virtual organisation

Greengard (1994:66-79) believes that the virtual workplace is creating tremendous opportunities, but is also generating a great deal of stress and difficulty as many organisational changes are required to make it work. Not everyone is suited to working in a virtual office environment. Workers have to learn how to use technology effectively, and must also adjust their work style and lifestyle. Working at home blurs the structure of having 'working hours', and some people can easily become workaholics without the discipline of having to start and stop work at certain times. Maintaining an office at home also poses problems, as productivity drops if the employee is surrounded by noisy children, loud music, or a demanding spouse.

A major concern of a virtual organisation is how managers should evaluate their workers. Many managers believe that only face-to-face interaction is meaningful, and may pass over mobile workers for promotions. Performance reviews in a virtual environment should be conducted informally every quarter, and formally every six months. The final analysis of performance can no longer measure good citizenship and attendance, but how much work people actually get done, and how well they do it. The following, according to O'Connell (1996), are the attributes of a successful remote employee:

- familiar and comfortable with the job;
- a strong work ethic and self-motivated;
- discipline and skills for self-management;
- effective communication skills;
- adaptable and able to compromise;
- knowledgeable about organisational procedures;
- technical self-sufficiency; and
- results-orientated.

According to Wright and Oldford (1995) several elements must be present if the virtual organisation is to stand a chance of success:

- top-level management support;
- careful choice of management and subordinates;
- no forfeiture of benefits, training, and career advancement opportunities;
- employee evaluation based on output or results;
- good communication links; and
- fixed commuting days to the main office.

Encounter 18.1 Telecommuting centres provide an alternative to the corporate office

Corporate offices are expensive to build, furnish and maintain, and more often than not they are located in areas that are inconvenient for commuters. These days, many companies are turning to smaller telecommuting centres, places that offer a fully equipped office, secretarial aid, and facilities such as photocopying, e-mail, and fax-modems.

In the United States, companies such as IBM, Pacific Bell, and Panasonic, are creating their own telecommuting centres, and independent firms are sharing centres. In Valencia, California, a city that is close to Los Angeles, the Newhall Land and Farming Company has converted a 30,000 square foot warehouse into a centre with state-of-the-art offices, conference rooms, free parking, and convenient freeway access. Barely a year after it was opened the centre showed 100 per cent occupancy rates. All office suites are separate and secure. Furnished and unfurnished offices are available and the overall environment has been designed and laid out by consultants who specialise in alternative worksites and technology issues.

How does the concept work? Companies lease space at the centre, and certain categories of workers, mainly administrative, marketing and sales, and human resources personnel, use the offices whenever they need the facilities provided. They are even able to drop off and collect their business mail at the centre. Because companies have realised that not all employees utilise their offices all of the time, these shared facilities are much more cost-effective for organisations. Staff members reserve time in the offices through a centralised reservations office, thus overcoming problems of too many people and too little space. The centre is open twenty-four hours a day, seven days a week. Employees have unique contracts with their organisations, laying out the ground rules of face-to-face contact time with their managers.

Jim Backer, director of marketing for commercial and industrial real estate at Newhall Land and Farming says, 'People find they no longer have to spend hours on the freeway getting to and from the office. It has improved their productivity and the quality of their lives.'

SOURCE: Greengard, S. (1994: 66–79).

Proponents of virtual organisations list a wide range of benefits:
- personal scheduling of hours;
- less commuting time;
- fewer interruptions;
- less absenteeism; and
- retirees can continue to contribute to the organisation.

18.8 Reengineering the organisation

Reengineering is the basic rethinking and radical redesign of business processes to achieve dramatic improvements in critical organisational areas such as cost, quality, service, and speed. It has little or nothing to do with downsizing, restructuring, automation, or software reengineering. It must also not be confused with reorganising, delayering, or flattening an organisation, although reengineering may produce a flatter organizational structure (Hammer & Champy 1993:32).

Gómez-Mejía et al. (1998:52) discuss Hammer and Champy's concept of re-engineering by stating that it is not a quick fix, but rather a fundamental rethinking and radical redesign of business processes involved in producing a product or delivering a service to the customer. Process engineering uses work flow analysis to identify jobs that can be eliminated or combined to improve company performance.

18.9 Job and organisational design and quality assurance

Job design strategy focuses on jobs in the context of individuals' needs for economic well-being and personal growth. Ivancevich and Matteson (1999:247), however, state that the issue of quality in job design cannot be separated from the technical demands of jobs and the social demands of people doing the jobs. They maintain that too great an emphasis on the technical system or too great an emphasis on human relations will lead to poor job design. This socio-technical approach to job design is compatible with total quality management, and designers must take both issues into account for the sake of quality assurance.

In the field of organisational design, organisations must be aware that quality losses are inevitable when implementing a new model. For this reason it is imperative that decision-makers investigate very thoroughly the implications of proposed changes before finalising radical departures from the established structure.

18.10 Conclusion

Playing around with job designs and organisational structures is of no use without consideration of the purpose of the organisation, the nature of the demands being placed on it from outside, the types of operation it carries out, and the people available. The bottom line is that organisations of the 21st century must be adaptable and flexible enough to consider departure from established structures in order to maintain equilibrium in the future.

Summary

Job design is the way in which the different tasks and responsibilities required to carry out a job, structure the work activities of that job. Job range is the number of different tasks that make up a particular job. Job depth is the extent to which a jobholder is able to influence the activities and outcomes of that job.

The greater the job depth, the more autonomy the job-holder will have; the greater the job range, the larger the variety of activities and tasks a job-holder will be expected to undertake.

Specialisation-intensive jobs are those that are characterised by very few, repetitive tasks, and which require few skills and little mental ability. Over-specialisation can cause a number of problems.

The consequences of narrow job range are job discontent, high dissatisfaction, turnover, and absenteeism. Some of the strategies that are used to increase job range and reverse some of these consequences are job rotation, job enlargement, job enrichment, and team-based job designs.

The traditional, pyramid-shaped organisation is giving way to new organisational forms. Flatter organisations are the norm, and work is increasingly being organised around teams and processes rather than specialised functions.

Organisational design includes an organisation's structure and its processes for decision-making, communication, and performance management. The more management levels there are, the taller the structure will be, and the longer it will take for messages to reach desired levels.

Bureaucracies usually have many layers of management and huge amounts of red tape that frustrate creativity. Employees do not always accept this structure, because bureaucracies ignore human needs and values. They encourage stability, rigidity, and permanence, and do not adapt quickly or well to changing social conditions and technological innovations.

Newer organisational designs are the flat structure, the boundaryless structure, and the shamrock, doughnut, and vineyard structures. The professional design has a core-periphery type of split in the workforce. The core contains those skills that are specialised to the business and the periphery contains all the other activities.

A virtual organisation is one where there are far fewer employees to be found in their corporate offices than was the norm in the past. As long as the nature of their jobs allows them to link up to the corporate head office electronically, a virtual office can be set up almost anywhere. The virtual workplace creates tremendous opportunities, but also generates a great deal of stress and difficulty, as many organisational changes are required to make it work.

Reengineering is the rethinking and radical redesign of business processes to achieve dramatic improvements in critical organisational areas such as cost, quality, service, and speed.

Too great an emphasis on the technical system or on human relations will lead to poor job design. Organisations must be aware that quality losses are inevitable when implementing a new model. It is thus imperative that decision-makers thoroughly investigate the implications of proposed changes before finalising radical departures from established structure.

Related websites

This topic may be investigated further by referring to the following Internet websites:
Interview with Charles Handy – http://www.morganbanks.com.au/handy.htm
Strategy and Business – Thought Leaders: Charles Handy –
   http://www.strategy-business.com/thoughtleaders
What will HR look like in 2020? –
   http://www.workforceonline.com/archive/article/000/79/64
Four key forces shaping the future –
   http://www.workforceonline.com/archive/article/000/64/68
The future calls for change –
   http://www.workforceonline.com/feature/00/00/68/index
Do you understand the new workforce? –
   http://www.workforceonline.com/archive/article/000/16/26
Workflow and Reengineering International Association (WARIA) - http://vvv.com/waria/

Case study
A company is only as strong as its weakest link

In 1995, a personal computer franchise called The Link was established in Johannesburg, South Africa. The Link originated in the United States, where the franchise had become exceptionally successful during the eight years prior to setting up operations in South Africa. The rapid growth of The Link was attributed by many to the dynamic management team, who had been particularly skillful in obtaining financing, and marketing the franchise throughout America. The Link was already established in the United Kingdom, Australia, and New Zealand, and it was presumed that the exercise would run smoothly in South Africa.

There was no shortage of applicants as franchise-holders and very soon plans were in place to open up branches in Pretoria, Durban, Cape Town, Port Elizabeth, East London, Bloemfontein, and Kimberley, in addition to the existing 'main franchise' in Johannesburg. Top management emphasised decentralisation, in which the franchise managers were given as much freedom as possible to fulfil their responsibilities in whatever way they thought best. This decentralisation was accompanied by the understanding that the individual manager must 'deliver'. This policy was conveyed and reinforced through letters, memoranda, and personal conversations. Branch managers who increased sales, or reduced costs, or made their operations more efficient, were rewarded with financial bonuses and praise.

However, during the third year of franchise operation in South Africa, it became apparent that profits were not nearly as good as they should have been. The Link was always the first PC company in the country to make new software applications available to the public, and top management made sure that there were very exact procedures to be followed in the marketing and selling of these packages. Senior managers were dismayed when time and again they found sales were not going well and large quantities of merchandise were left standing on the shelves, unsold. They couldn't understand it.

The franchise holders could have told them that by the time they received instructions from senior managers at head office, other PC companies had passed them in sales to the public. What was the cause of this delay? Information and instructions were passed through the various levels of management starting at the Managing Director, who authorised every memorandum relayed to the franchisees. From the managing director, memoranda were passed to the Sales Director, who forwarded information to the District Sales Managers. Once the information left the District Sales Managers' offices (one in every province where a franchise branch was situated) it found its way to the Regional Branch Managers, who were the franchisees.

In the franchise, salespersons and cashiers reported to a Floor Manager, and warehouse staff and shelf packers reported to the Receiving Manager. Both Floor Manager and Receiving Manager reported to the Regional Branch Manager.

Questions

1. Evaluate the firm's organisational structure and design in terms of the information provided in the case study.
2. What kind of changes do you think should be made to the current organisational design?

Experiential exercise 1

Purpose
To show that many types of organisation exist, all have a certain type of structure and design, and that you can find a place for yourself in numerous organisations.

Introduction
To the majority of people the word 'organisation' is typically associated with some kind of business. However, many organisations are not associated with the business concept. From school-going age, individuals are tied to organisations long before they enter the business world.

Task
Draw the organisational chart (hierarchy) for your organisation (it may be a student organisation, your temporary job, a social organisation, or even your church or soccer club).

1. Show job titles of two or three organisational levels above you.
2. Show your job title, or place in the organisation, as well as others on your organisational level (circle your job title).
3. Show job titles of two or three organisational levels below you.

Is this organisation bureaucratic, tall, flat, or boundaryless?

Experiential exercise 2

Purpose
To investigate the viewpoints of management in various types of organisation, regarding the most feasible organisational design for their companies.

Task
Make contact with one of each of at least five of the following types of organisation. In most cases you might be able to speak to a representative of the HR department. In some cases, the organisation will not have a HR department, and you will have to make a decision on who would be the most likely person to share the information with you.

- a hospital
- library
- a university/technikon/college faculty
- a shopping mall
- a primary/high school
- a hotel
- a trade union
- a municipality
- a manufacturing organisation

Present a short overview of the organisational designs discussed in this chapter, and ask your contacts which of the designs they feel would be most feasible for their organisation. Try to obtain answers to the following questions:

- Why did they select the specific design?
- What type of design describes the organisation at the present moment?
- Is the current organisational design successful?

Chapter questions

1 Explain the difference between job enlargement and job enrichment. Under what circumstances would an organisation not wish to enlarge or enrich a job?
2 How could the range and depth of the following jobs be increased: a postman or postwoman, shop assistant in a clothing store, pharmacist, and legal secretary?
3 'Self-managed teams are simply an attempt by management to get more productivity out of employees without paying them more.' Do you agree or disagree with this statement? Motivate your answer.
4 If you were responsible for the daily management of a busy airport, which of the following activities would you locate in the core and which on the periphery of your business?
   - baggage handling
   - airport information
   - the fire service
   - car park attendance
   - catering
   - maintenance of premises
   - news agency
   - cleaning
5 An increasingly important organisational design is the virtual corporation. Various adaptations of the virtual workplace are finding favour all over the world, but before decision-makers rush into making use of the concept, they should weigh up the pros and cons. If you were a human resources manager making a recommendation to the top executives of your company concerning the implementation of the virtual organisation concept, how would you present the advantages and disadvantages of the model from the point of view of both the organisation and its employees?
6 Changes in organisational size affect design. In what ways might growth (increasing size) and decline (decreasing size) affect an organisation's design?

Bibliography

BENTON, D.A. 1995. *Applied human relations: an organizational approach.* 5th edition. Prentice-Hall, Englewood Cliffs, NJ.
CARRELL, M.R., ELBERT, N.F., HATFIELD, R.D., GROBLER, P.A., MARX, M. & VAN DER SCHYF, S. 1998. *Human resource management in South Africa.* Prentice Hall, South Africa.
CHERASKIN, L. & CAMPION, M.A. Nov. 1996. Study clarifies job-rotation benefits. *Personnel Journal.* 75(11), 31-38.
CRANDALL, N.F. & WALLACE, JR, M.J. Jan/Feb. 1997. Inside the virtual workplace: forging a new deal for work and rewards. *Compensation and Benefits Review.* 29(1), 27-36.
DESSLER, G. 1997. *Human resource management.* 7th edition. Prentice-Hall, Upper Saddle River, NJ.
GÓMEZ-MEJÍA, L.R., BALKIN, D.B., & CARDY, R.L. 1998. *Managing human resources.* 2nd edition. Prentice-Hall, Upper Saddle River, NJ.
GREENGARD, S. Sept. 1994. Making the virtual office a reality. *Personnel Journal.* 73(9), 66-79.
HAMMER, M. & CHAMPY, J. 1993. *Reengineering the corporation: a manifesto for business revolution.* Nicholas Brealey Publishing, London.
HANDY, C. 1994. *The doughnut organization. A management resource on video.* Melrose Film Productions, London.
IVANCEVICH, J.M. & MATTESON, M.T. 1999. *Organizational behavior and management.* 5th edition. Irwin McGraw-Hill, Boston.
LEAP, T.L. & CRINO, M.D. 1993. *Personnel/human resource management.* 2nd edition. MacMillan, New York.
LUNDY, O. & COWLING, A. 1996. *Strategic human resource management.* Routledge, London.

MICCO, L. 1997. Employees may prefer pajamas in new workplace trend. *HR News Online.* http://www.shrm.org/hrnews/articles.

O'CONNELL, S.E. Mar 1996. The virtual workplace moves at warp speed. *HR Magazine.*

SCHULTZ, D.P. & SCHULTZ, S.E. 1994. *Psychology and work today.* 6th edition. MacMillan, New York.

SWANEPOEL, B.J. (ED.), ERASMUS, B.J., VAN WYK, M.W. & SCHENK, H.W. 1998. *South African human resource management.* Juta, Kenwyn.

TORRINGTON, D. & HALL, L. 1995. *Personnel management.* 3rd edition. Prentice-Hall, London.

WERTHER, JR, W.B. & DAVIS, K. 1993. *Human resources and personnel management.* 4th edition. McGraw-Hill, New York.

WRIGHT, P.C. & OLDFORD, A. 1995. Telecommuting and employee effectiveness: career and managerial issues. Reading from *International Journal of Career Management.* Internet conference. 15 May 1995 to 15 August 1995.

19

National level skills development issues

G D Haasbroek

Learning outcomes

At the end of this chapter the learner should be able to demonstrate the following outcomes:
- Explain the macroeconomic context within which training policies are developed.
- Critique the education and training challenges faced by South Africa.
- Explain the role of governments in shaping training policies.
- Express an opinion on possible training policy options to be considered by South African authorities.

Key words and concepts

- certification of training
- cost and benefit of training
- demand for labour
- Education and Training Quality Assurance (ETQAs) bodies
- funding mechanism for training
- global markets
- learnerships
- National Qualifications Framework (NQF)
- National Skills Authority
- National Skills Fund
- National Standards Bodies (NSB)
- new world economy
- Sector Education and Training Authorities (SETAs)
- Skills Development Act
- Skills Development Levies Act
- South African Qualifications Authority (SAQA)
- South African Qualifications Authority Act
- Standards Generating Bodies (SGBs)
- supply of labour
- training levy-grant scheme
- unemployment
- vocational education and training

> **Illustrative case**
>
> Eastern Enterprises is an international conglomerate with subsidiaries in twenty countries. Its main line of business is the manufacturing and distribution of domestic appliances. South Africa has been listed in a report of Smith and Smith, a business consultancy firm, specialising in identifying emerging markets worldwide, as one of four countries in which Eastern Enterprises could consider investing. The Board of Eastern Enterprises commissioned Q-Consulting to conduct a feasibility study into the prospects of opening a manufacturing plant in South Africa with special emphasis on the regulatory framework regarding human resources development and the level of competence and flexibility of the labour force.
>
> What do you believe are the major issues Q-Consulting needs to include in its study to be able to establish the feasibility of doing business in South Africa, bearing in mind the relevant legislation, funding arrangements for training, certification of training outcomes, and the level of commitment amongst all role players, including the government, to make it an attractive option for Eastern Enterprises to invest in South Africa?

19.1 Introduction

Skills development through education and training has always been the most powerful lever for improving both individual opportunity and the institutional competitiveness of countries worldwide. Governments and employers recognise the critical role a skilled and knowledgeable workforce can play in securing competitive advantages in international markets. There is consensus amongst forward-looking countries that the quality of their human resources will be the determining factor in their continuing progress and prosperity.

National vocational education and training systems form an integral part of the socio-economic environment of most countries, particularly advanced industrial countries. Vocational education and training, in the first place, is a political issue because of its relationships with economic growth, levels of unemployment, productivity, and industry competencies, and should therefore not be approached in the narrow context of being only an economic or human resource issue.

The Australian government's national strategy for vocational education and training for 1998-2003 clearly demonstrates the importance progressive countries attach to education and training. The Australians believe that forces arising from complex economic, technological, and social changes will influence the education and training environment and, therefore, have to be catered for in their vocational education and training strategy (Australian National Training Authority, 1998). Some of these forces are:

- the growth in global markets, accompanied by intensified international competition and the lowering of tariffs in Australia;
- the emergence of service and knowledge-based industries as important sources of employment;
- changes in the geographical and regional distribution of employment opportunities;
- the impact of new information and communication technologies on the community in general, and on Australian enterprises in particular;
- the growth in small business and changes in working arrangements, such as increasing part-time and casual employment, and the use of outsourcing arrangements and labour-hire firms;

- changes in the ways in which work is organised within enterprises, such as the use of flatter business structures and an emphasis on teamwork and multi-skilling;
- demographic changes such as the ageing of the Australian population, the ethnic diversity of the population and the feminisation of the labour force;
- social changes, such as those brought on by changes in family structures, lifestyles, sources of income, and personal aspirations;
- community expectations that all Australians, including those who are most disadvantaged, should have the opportunity to realise their full potential, for example through education and employment opportunities;
- the continuing need to reduce the level of unemployment;
- increasingly sophisticated consumer expectations about the range and quality of products and services; and
- changes in the roles of governments, away from direct service provision to the purchasing of services, with an increased focus on competitive processes and purchasing output.

The approach of the Australian government is indicative of many industrially developed or newly industrialised countries that address the challenge of skills development from a strategic point of view. This chapter explores a number of macro-strategic issues impacting on skills development policies, gives a national perspective on the policy environment influencing skills development, provides an overview on the funding and certification of training, touches on the legislative framework regulating and facilitating skills development, and speculates on possible policy options available for South Africa in its quest to compete internationally and to introduce social equity in society.

19.2 Macroeconomic context

To be successful, and to yield the necessary returns, requires education and training policies shaped within the prevailing macro-social and economic circumstances as well as the national strategic vision of a particular country. In the following paragraphs, macro-issues impacting directly or indirectly on the formation of training policies are discussed.

19.2.1 The new world economy

The world economy finds itself on a path of rapid globalisation. The new world economic environment is changing the structure of labour markets by increasing the level of competitiveness and, thereby, creating a need for improved labour productivity and a more flexible workforce. In this environment of rapid and fundamental change, the education and training of human resources has become the driving force for meeting the demand for the highly skilled workers and technical staff needed to manage the new social and economic challenges.

19.2.2 The changing working environment

The working world is currently undergoing radical change. The impact of economic, technological, social, and political factors is transforming it fundamentally. The movement of technology, goods, capital, the location of production and, to a lesser extent, labour across national borders, is leading to the rapid globalisation of the world economy. The result is that national economies are becoming interdependent and integrated. The liberalisation of trade, and the development and universal availability of rapidly evolving information technology are among the major driving forces behind the globalisation of the economy.

International trade is also becoming more market-orientated as a result of deregulation and the transition of former socialist economies to market economies. In the process, labour markets are being restructured to meet the challenge of being competitive, thereby creating a need for increased productivity and continuous innovation in the business environment. This leads, in turn, to restructuring, privatisation, the relocation of production, the redeployment of workers, and change in job content, work processes, and organisation, which eventually affects skill requirements (Mitchell 1995).

New technologies are being developed and introduced across all industry sectors and areas of work, boosting productivity and creating demands for new and different skills. Electronic commerce is creating more business opportunities, and is expected to sustain economic and employment growth. It is expected that online technology will create a mayor shift from people employed by large organisations to people working for themselves.

Case-in-point
The Fiat website

When Italian Automation Fiat wanted to test a new design concept for its Punto, it invited potential customers to visit the Fiat website and select from an array of features. More than 3 000 people participated. As a result, Fiat was able to capture valuable insight into the likes and dislikes of a targeted consumer group, test different design concepts of low cost, and design a car far more reflective of customer preferences. For their part, customers got a car closer to what they actually wanted.

SOURCE: Andersen Consulting (1999).

19.2.3 Productivity and flexibility

Middleton et al. (1993: 1) do not beat about the bush: 'Both common sense and economic research support the idea that the quality of a nation's workforce is important to economic growth and social development.' According to Middleton et al. (1993: 6) two factors are generally considered to be prime determinants of the quality of a workforce; one is labour productivity and the other is the flexibility of the workforce.

These two factors become increasingly significant to countries seeking to expand their economies and to improve the welfare of their citizens in a highly competitive and changing world economy. The higher a country's labour productivity and the more flexible its workforce, the better that country is able to acquire and adapt the technology needed to produce better quality goods and services, at lower costs, and to shift the structure of production to new markets and products.

Productivity and flexibility depend on a number of factors, such as the level of capital investment, the technology of production, and the quality of management. All these factors are, however, dependent on the skills of workers at all levels, from senior level to semiskilled operators. Sound management alone is not enough for improved productivity and flexibility. Of equal importance is the competence of skilled workers and technicians who occupy the middle level of the workforce. In modern economies, these workers facilitate the adaptation and use of new technologies, enhance the efficiency and quality of production and maintenance, and supervise and train workers with lesser skills (Middleton et al. 1993).

19.2.4 Investment in training

Improving the job skills of the workforce has attracted considerable funding in developing and developed countries, either by governments themselves or from donors. Unfortunately, the results of much of the investment in skills training have been disappointing, according to Middleton et al. (1993). The causes of the poor returns in training investment are complex, and vary from country to country. In some cases, expectations regarding the power of training programmes, especially those aimed at young people making the transition from school to work, have been unrealistic, largely because of the slow growth in skilled wage employment. In other cases, inefficient administration has reduced the returns in public training investments, and governments are not always mindful of economic policies that distort the incentives, to firms and individuals, to invest in skills.

A hard but important lesson countries have learned over the years, is that economically and socially disadvantaged citizens do not benefit from training unless the skills learned improve their productivity in employment. The effectiveness of investment in training is highly dependent on the nature of employment in society.

19.2.5 Economic and social policies

A nation's economic and social policies not only affect patterns of economic and employment growth, but also determine the market signals and incentives that guide individuals, employers, and trainers in making decisions about investments in training. It is, therefore, important for policy-makers to understand the relationship between the economic environment and the incentive structure for skills development that individuals and enterprises face. The record suggests that training policies are more effective if they are adapted to the nature of the economy, and that these policies should evolve as the economy changes. Government's role in vocational and technical education and training can be made more effective through more dynamic planning, encouragement of employer and private training and improved responsiveness and efficiency in public training programmes.

19.2.6 State intervention

Middleton et al. (1993:105) address the fundamental question of why and when governments should intervene in skills training. They argue that traditional private training markets proved too limited in meeting the broad skills needs associated with economic development and growth. The result was that governments started to emerge as the leading actors in the training market.

There are two main reasons that justify government intervention in training markets. Firstly, there is the issue of external benefits. The focus of individuals and enterprises is on higher productivity, profits, and wage earnings which come from training and which affect them directly. Government, on the other hand, representing society at large, is likely to capture the largest share in tax from a flexible and competitive economy, which may accrue from a better-trained workforce. Secondly, there is the issue of social equity. Public subsidisation on equity grounds for the disadvantaged, women, and marginalised youth is justified, provided it is carefully targeted to ensure that only those in need benefit.

19.3 A national perspective

19.3.1 The broad political, social, and economic scene

South Africa finds itself at a critical juncture of its political, economic, and social history after the first ever democratic election in 1994. The government of the day, besides the challenge of bringing about peace and political stability, has the enormous task of developing policies aimed at the promotion of economic growth and social development.

Much of the debate in South Africa today is about policies and programmes to facilitate job creation, to narrow income differentials, and to redress inequalities in access to wealth. General consensus exists between the main role-players that South Africa's future hinges on a sound and vibrant economy that can fulfil all the needs and aspirations of its people. Political stability, a policy that encourages economic growth largely through private initiative, fiscal discipline, exposure to foreign competition, and sound labour relations are seen by experts as prerequisites for sustainable growth and for tackling the problems associated with unemployment, poverty, and socioeconomic backlogs.

Great emphasis is placed on a supply-side approach in the new economic order to be adopted in South Africa, including supply-side measures such as education and training, and job creation through national public works programmes. Reconstruction and development are currently high on the national agenda and are seen as a process of empowerment through which each and every citizen is entitled to active participation in the economy, not only to help create wealth and prosperity, but also to share in its fruits.

19.3.2 Human resources development

The country's human resources hold the key to solving many of its economic and social problems. It is the country's human resources, and not so much its material resources, that will eventually make the difference. Historically, South Africa has invested heavily in first stage processing industries for export and domestic markets, under high protection. The tide of international trade has, however, turned against primary products and low-technology manufactured goods over the last decade. In the process South Africa has lost most of the competitive edge that, in the past, was provided by its natural resources. These changing circumstances leave the country with no option other than to invest much more in its people. In its quest to establish a competitive economy, South Africa is faced with the challenge not only of developing its people in order to allow them to make a meaningful contribution towards economic growth and, eventually, wealth creation, but also of allowing them to share in the wealth created by participating in the economy

For South Africans to meaningfully participate in economic and social development, as well as in their own advancement, they need not only general capabilities, such as the ability to read and write, to communicate effectively, and to solve problems in their homes, communities, and workplace. Given the demands of a complex and changing economy, characterised by increasing use of information, and the more complex and greater skills required of jobs, people must also have rising levels of applied competence (Department of Labour 1997).

19.3.3 Tertiary education

According to the Foundation for Research and Development (1996: 70) one of the critical issues facing the tertiary education sector is a need for models linking information and dynamics pertaining to tertiary education with statistics and trends relating to the workforce, especially with regard to the demand for, and supply of, skilled human resources.

These models will inform decision-making on issues such as the correct mix between the output required in the natural sciences and engineering, as opposed to the social sciences and humanities, as well as that between university and technikon graduates. Universities produced over 44 000 graduates in 1993, compared to technikons with just over 14 000 diplomats. The Foundation for Research and Development (1996:28) found that South Africa produces too few students with technical and career-orientated qualifications, relative to those with university qualifications. The demand for human resources should, therefore, inform the debate as to whether the ratio of university-technikon output should not be reversed or, at least, the more career-orientated output from technikons increased.

An international comparison for 1991 reported South Africa as having 15 per cent of its 20- to 24-year-olds enrolled at tertiary education institutions, which placed it on par with the Czech Republic (18 per cent), Mexico (15 per cent) and Brazil (12 per cent). In the UK, 28 per cent of the same age-cohort was enrolled for tertiary education, in Germany 36 per cent, and in France 43 per cent. The US reported 76 per cent of its 20- to 24-year-olds enrolled in tertiary education (Foundation for Research and Development 1996: 28).

The National Commission on Higher Education (1996) proposes a comprehensive transformation of higher education and envisaged a system which should be able to:
- offer access and the possibility of success to all talented individuals, irrespective of race, colour, gender, creed, age, or class;
- meet as many as possible of the high-skill vocational and employment needs presented by a growing economy, which aspires to global competitiveness;
- support the culture of critical discourse and experimental thinking, human rights, and intercultural communication and respect, to help bring about a free society with a creative and innovative leadership, with a firm commitment to a humane, non-racist, and non-sexist community life; and
- contribute, in keeping with internationally recognised standards of academic quality, and sensitive to the specific problems of the African and Southern African context, to the advancement of all forms of knowledge and scholarship that can make a difference to the social, cultural, and economic development of the country and all its people.

19.3.4 Science and engineering

Any nation that wishes to compete in the international arena today cannot do so unless it possesses the necessary skills in science and technology. The level of technological development in any country depends largely on the size and skills-level of the science and engineering workforce.

The Foundation for Research and Development (1996:76) reported an increase of 2,4 per cent per annum between 1988 and 1990, and a decrease of 1,9 per cent per annum between 1990 and 1992 in the South African science and engineering workforce.

There is a growing concern about the relatively low numbers of entrants into this workforce. South Africa has 938 scientists and engineers engaged in research and development (R&D) per million people, which does not compare favourably with most of its economic competitors (refer to Table 19.1). At the top of the scale is Japan with 6 309 scientists and engineers per million (UNESCO 1998) engaged in research and development.

19.3.5 School education

A sound general education is an essential foundation for all subsequent training. This is currently an area of great concern in South Africa. Not only is the percentage of illiterate adults unsatisfactory, but the

Table 19.1 Numbers of scientists and engineers engaged in R&D in various countries, per million people

Country	Latest data available	Number of scientists and engineers
Japan	1994	6 309
Canada	1993	2 656
UK	1993	2 417
Australia	1994	3 166
US	1993	3 732
Brazil	1995	168
South Africa	1993	938
India	1994	149
South Korea	1994	2 636
Malaysia	1992	87
Nigeria	1987	15

SOURCE: UNESCO (1998).

school system has not yet stabilised to the extent that it ensures a sound and solid general education for the youth. The result is that new entrants to the labour market lack the literacy, numeracy, and intellectual skills necessary to contribute to productivity in the workplace. What complicates the solution to South Africa's education problems is that an increase in expenditure on education is not going to solve the problem. Education expenditure is the single largest item of public expenditure in the country, representing about 28 per cent of total non-interest expenditure. Education expenditure increased from R34.1 billion in 1995/96 to R45,2 billion in 1998/99, reflecting an average annual growth rate of 9,8 per cent. Education spending accounted for 6 per cent of GDP in the 1998/99 financial year (Department of Finance 1999: 104). Measured against international norms, South Africa's spending on education is among the highest in the world. Unable to solve the problem with more funds, the authorities are left with basically only two measures to improve the education situation: to instil a culture of learning in the schools (in both children and teachers) and to ensure that schools are managed much more efficiently.

The Department of Education (1999: 8) has identified the following urgent problems in education:
- the dysfunctional state of many educational institutions;
- continuing inequalities in terms of basic facilities and learning resources;
- unacceptably high levels of illiteracy amongst the youths and adults;
- sexual harassment and violence, including crime and drugs; and
- the scourge of HIV/AIDS.

19.3.6 The labour market

19.3.6.1 Supply of labour

The economically active population (EAP) comprises the number of people, over the age of fifteen years, whether employed or not, who present their labour for remuneration on the labour market for the production of economic goods and services. Barker (1999:46) estimates that the South African economically active population was in the order of 14,2 million in 1996. More than 70 per cent of the EAP are African and about 46 per cent are women. According to Barker (1999) between 300 000 and 400 000 persons are entering the labour market annually looking for work. Standing et al. (1996:63) found that the size of the African working-age population and overall population have been growing much faster than the size of the African employed labour force. This apparently implies that a substantial portion of those entering the labour market will not find work.

19.3.6.2 Demand for labour

The total employment in the non-agricultural formal economy is expected to increase by 45 000 between 1998 and 2000 (HSRC 1999). By far the most jobs are expected to be created at the professional level. The HSRC (1999) estimates that the employment of professionals will rise by 93 000, and the employment of managers and artisans will rise by 16 000 and 12 000, respectively. An estimated 71 000 semi-skilled and unskilled positions are expected to be lost over the five-year period.

19.3.6.3 Level of literacy of the labour force

From the point of view of economic growth and development, and of material standards of living, it is the quality of the labour force, and not just its size, that really counts. Barker (1999:215) found that the education level of the labour force has improved substantially over the last two decades, but that there is still a large number of illiterate people in the country. Of the economically active population, 29 per cent are regarded as functionally illiterate, i.e. have an educational level representing less than seven years of schooling. There has, however, been a sharp increase in education levels over the past few years, 24 per cent of the economically active population having reached Grade 12 and higher in 1991, compared to only 9 per cent in 1970. Barker (1999:225) further found that there has been a rapid increase in high-level personnel (with at least two years of education and training after Grade 12) from 9 per cent of non-agricultural employment in 1985, to 21 per cent in 1994. However, some observers are of the opinion that labour shortages in certain skilled occupations are likely to place a ceiling on economic growth and development in South Africa.

19.3.7 Vocational education and training

The school-to-work transition in South Africa is not up to standard with its trade partners. There is very little linkage between school-based vocational training and in-company training. The level of enterprise-based training is low by international standards. The apprenticeship system has been declining for over a decade, and technical college education and training has, on average, produced poor outcomes. The training of unemployed persons through special training programmes is limited and has failed to provide meaningful work opportunities. Although the private training market (Department of Labour 1997) is relatively well developed, it specialises mainly in short courses, tailored to very narrow industry demands, or focuses on communication and service-related skills. The new training legislation recently introduced by the Department of Labour is an attempt by Government to correct the deficiencies in the South African training market (refer to Paragraph 19.6 in this regard).

19.4 Funding of training

19.4.1 Who is responsible?

Historically, the role of governments, worldwide, in training has been a limited one. Private training markets were far more important. Small enterprises assumed the dominant role in skill creation. Informal apprenticeships in craft trades were the primary training venue (Middleton et al. 1993: 105).

It has always been, in general terms, the view of the government in South Africa that employers are responsible for the funding of the training of their employees, while government should be responsible for the funding of education. Government did, however, during the 1980s, make a significant contribution to the funding of training through the tax concession scheme for approved training. The scheme was, however, phased out in 1990. During the nineties, the government's financial contribution to training was mainly in the areas of training of unemployed persons and the subsidisation of trade tests.

Against this background the question is: What kind of policies should be introduced that would, on the one hand, place an obligation on employers and, on the other hand, encourage employers to contribute to the development of the country's workforce? The notion of training as an investment in human capital, and that it should be a key part of an enterprise's human resources development strategy, should ideally be strengthened by national economic and training policies. Policies on funding mechanisms should also be based on fundamental principles that ensure the most productive application of scarce funds.

19.4.2 Cost and benefit of training

19.4.2.1 Economic policies and incentives for skills development

There is a direct relationship between the economic environment and skills development. Quite often this relationship is overlooked in planning and policy development.

It is important for policy-makers to understand the relationship between the economic environment and the incentive structure for skills development that individuals and enterprises face. Education planners and policy-makers should take this incentive structure into account in anticipating the mix of public and private funding in skills development and the demand for training places. On the other hand, economic planners and policy-makers should also consider the market signals a country's economic policies send to individuals and enterprises with regard to training and skills development, and the consequences of these signals for labour supply, economic growth, and wage and price stability.

In the following paragraphs an outline is given of the influence of the economic environment on the cost and benefit of training.

19.4.2.2 Individuals, enterprises, and government

The cost and benefit of training applies to individuals, enterprises and the government.

Individuals

For individuals, training is at the cost of lower earnings, but could also be regarded as an investment, in the sense of higher future earnings, career opportunities, and personal fulfilment. Resources used for schooling and training yield net benefits of greater value than alternative uses. Economic policies that would alter this stream of benefits and its value, in relation to the value of alternative uses, are expected to change an individual's incentives to acquire skills. If no jobs are available, for example, the incentive to acquire skills is reduced. Economic policies that distort relative capital and labour costs affect employment growth and eventually the pace of skills development.

Enterprises

Training is perceived by enterprises as an investment but also as a cost, which must be measured against potential profitability and productivity gains. The fact that training competes for an enterprise's resources with other investments, including capital investment, means that it needs to offer a greater productivity improvement than alternative uses of those resources. Like any other form of investment, training can only be seen as a nett contributor to improved efficiency if it leads to an enhancement in an enterprise's performance, which outweighs its cost.

The economic environment influences not only the incentive to acquire skills but also the incentive to provide training. Government interventions that distort competitive markets can also affect the willingness of enterprises to train. Because enterprises are the most efficient providers of skills training, economic policy-makers must guard against policies that are detrimental to skills development by enterprises. According to Middleton et al. (1993: 116) general economic policies, such as a minimum wage, may actually discourage enterprises from skills training. The requirement to pay minimum wages may restrict the ability of an enterprise to shift the cost of general skills training to the worker in the form of lower wages. Enterprises are quite often also reluctant to invest in general skills training because of the risk that their investment will be lost through labour turnover. The individual worker can capture all the benefits of investment in training, but still leave the employer for higher wages elsewhere.

Benefits of training to enterprises should, however, not be viewed strictly in mechanistic terms. Research studies show consistently that those production systems which treat management, capital investment, workplace consultation, and training as an integrated whole, lead to superior outcomes than a piecemeal approach to these issues.

Government

Governments in many developing countries are faced with pressure to stabilise spending on social programmes, including education and training. At the same time, rapid population and labour force growth are expanding the demand for these services.

The question may arise why governments should be involved in the financing of training. According to Middleton et al. (1993: 107) there are two main conditions that justify government intervention in the financing of training: external market benefits and the striving for social equity.

- *External market benefits.* The focus of individuals and enterprises is on higher productivity, profits, and wage earnings which come from training and which affect them directly. Government, on the other hand, representing society at large, is likely to capture the largest share from a flexible and competitive economy, which may accrue from a better-trained workforce.
- *Social equity.* Public subsidisation of training, on equity grounds, for the disadvantaged, women, and marginalised youth is justified when carefully targeted to ensure that only those in need benefit.

19.4.2.3 Regulation and certification of training

A cost-benefit analysis with regard to training should not only be applied in the case of the provision of training, but also in the case of the regulation and certification of training. Care should be taken to ensure that the development and implementation of qualification structures do not become a cumbersome and expensive process that eats too deeply into funds that are actually earmarked for the provision of workplace education and training. The investment made in certification systems must eventually be offset by the benefits, which government, employers and individuals eventually gain from the certification of training.

19.4.3 Sources and application of training funds

Funds earmarked for training usually come from four sources: government, enterprises, individuals and donors and are usually applied in three areas, namely regulation and quality assurance; training of employees; training of unemployed persons and those in pre-employment programmes.

19.4.3.1 Government

Government's involvement in the funding of training can take a variety of forms, such as:
- vocationally orientated education and training through the technical college system, e.g. apprentice training;
- tax credits for approved training;
- assistance to industry through incentives encouraging employers to employ, for example, apprentices;
- grants for training innovation and infrastructure;
- offset of interest in terms of loans granted to individuals;
- training of unemployed persons and other labour market programmes;
- pre-employment training programmes; and
- covering the cost of the regulation of training and measures to ensure quality of training.

19.4.3.2 Enterprises

Training funded by enterprises can be divided into two broad categories:
- Enterprise-specific training that is offered by individual enterprises to its employees. The training can be conducted either according to a structured plan and format, designed to develop job-related skills and competence, or unstructured on-the-job training, whereby employees are shown how to do things as the need arises and learn by doing a job.
- Industry-specific training that could be funded either through sectoral payroll levy schemes or through a national levy scheme.

19.4.3.3 Individuals

Training expenditures by individuals include:
- fees payable to training-providers;
- loans that have to be repaid; and
- indirect contributions, made through the acceptance of lower income during the period of training.

19.4.3.4 Donors

The contribution of donors should be guided by the national human resources development targets of a country, and not by the initiatives of the donors themselves, as these may not necessarily respond effectively to national goals and needs. Donors are likely to focus their contributions on research, policy design, and the implementation of training and skills development systems.

19.4.3.5 Mix of funding sources and the application of funds

Donors have already pledged funds for human resources development in South Africa. The Reconstruction and Development Programme (RDP) served as an ideal vehicle for donors to target their funding towards economic and equity strategies. Research leading to the implementation of the National Qualifications Framework is an area where donors made a valuable contribution.

The mix of sources of funding and areas of application of funds earmarked for workforce education and training is outlined in Table 19.2.

The different levels of contributions indicated in the matrix are arbitrary, and do not necessarily reflect the views of the authors. Ideally, such contributions should be established through negotiation, on the one hand, and the meeting of national targets, on the other.

19.4.4 Alternatives for generating training funds

In the discussion above, reference was made to government intervention in training as a means of obtaining the external benefits, which come from producing a skilled workforce that is able to adapt quickly to changing economic conditions in a global economy. Reference was also made to government intervention in order to address social disparities in access to training.

How can stable funding be secured for vocational education and training? The three main sources of revenue, according to Middleton et al. (1993:125) that could be applied in this regard are now discussed.

19.4.4.1 General taxation

The generation of training funds through general taxation constitutes a vulnerable source of finance, due to budgetary constraints, as well as other social concerns that need to be addressed. Funds raised through general taxation are mainly for the training of the unemployed, and less is used for the funding of training for the employed.

19.4.4.2 Levies on payroll or turnover

The principle that those who benefit should be those who pay, implies that the financing of entry-level training and skills upgrading for the employed should come from employers and the workers themselves.

Payroll levies, if not planned and applied correctly, may increase the cost of labour, and possibly discourage employment creation. Where this occurs, employers quite often respond by substituting capital for labour, or engaging in informal-sector activities, outside the scope of government

Table 19.2 Mix of sources of funding and areas of application of funds earmarked for workplace education and training

Source of funds → Areas of application ↓	Government	Industry	Donors	Individuals
Regulation and quality assurance	High	Low	Medium	Low to zero
Training of employees	Low	High	Low to zero	Low
Training of unemployed persons and pre-employment	High	Low	Medium to high	Zero

regulations and taxes. If the training is, however, productivity-orientated, there is less reason for resistance to such a levy on the grounds of its possible negative effects on employment. Not only can improved labour productivity help to lower the unit costs of goods produced, but it can also expand output and increase employment and wages.

There are basically three types of levy system:
- levy-exemptions, which allow enterprises to prove that they have paid for approved training, and avoid paying the levy;
- levy-grant systems, which require the payment of levies, but funds may be returned to enterprises to pay the cost of approved forms of training; and
- levy income, which is turned over to state-recognised organisations to provide training (labour and business are usually part of the governance structure of these organisations).

19.4.4.3 Private expenditure

Governments can also intervene, via the tax system, by introducing tax exemptions or credits for enterprises' and individuals' training expenditure. Experience, however, shows that for small enterprises and low-income populations, cash transfers in the form of tax rebates are more effective instruments for expanding private spending on skills training. Other alternatives are vouchers that entitle individuals to purchase approved training, or loans that are either subsidised or not.

19.4.5 Funding mechanisms in South Africa

19.4.5.1 Background

Funding mechanisms for training in South African have taken on various forms during the last three decades. A national tax incentive scheme for employers was in place from 1974 to 1990. The Manpower Training Act, which was introduced in 1982, provided for industries to establish a training levy scheme. Approximately fifteen industry-based levy schemes were registered up to the time that new legislation, namely the Skills Development Levies Act, was introduced in 1999, making provision for the funding of training. Some of the serious deficiencies of the industry-based training levy schemes were the inefficient collection of levies, inadequate coverage of the workforce, and a weak linkage between training and labour market skills needs.

A study into the funding mechanisms for training in South Africa (Department of Labour 1995) was conducted during the course of 1994/95 under the auspices of the National Training Board and the National Economic and Development Labour Council (NEDLAC). Seven main conclusions were drawn from the findings, which served as the basis for subsequent policy proposals for funding mechanisms to be considered by government, namely:

- *The training system is not well co-ordinated.* There are no agreed national targets and priorities for training in South Africa; formal sector funding mechanisms, the Industry Training Boards (ITBs) do not cover all sectors; and training programmes rarely link the unemployed (and the youth) with employers.
- *Employer expenditure on training is low and there is limited external pressure to train.* Mechanisms need to be found to increase the activities of individuals (and their trade unions) to pressurise employers to train and to provide portable qualifications; government may wish to intervene with financial incentives to increase employer investment in training.
- *Individual attitudes to training are restricting investment.* Individuals need to change their attitudes regarding their contribution towards the investment in

training, beyond obtaining their initial pre-employment qualifications (especially if portable qualifications are provided by employers); government could encourage cost-sharing arrangements through suitable incentive programmes.
- *There are gaps in the provision of training.* Significant gaps exist in the provision of training for school leavers, rural people, the long-term unemployed, and emerging businesses; mechanisms are needed to encourage greater provision of technical skills training.
- *The introduction of a qualification and accreditation framework is required.* Mechanisms are needed to encourage portability of training, and for government to link the provision of public funds for training to a proper qualifications framework.
- *Competition in the training supply market is constrained.* Many issues are currently adversely affecting the supply market; in many cases, government and donors are determining demand on insufficient information and research regarding market demand; rural areas are under-provided, and ITBs have control over certain sectors of the market; government policy needs to address these issues.
- *Barriers prevent suppliers entering the market.* In addition to the above issues, investment costs for technical vocational training are high and restrict the entry of new suppliers; shifting allocation of government funds also creates uncertainty and consequently a lack of investment.

In terms of the formal sector, the following policy options were eventually identified by the above-mentioned study:
- Option 1
  - retain the voluntary system of ITBs;
  - retain industry-based levies; and
  - no central coordinating body.
- Option 2
  - introduce compulsory ITBs;
  - introduce compulsory industry-based levies;
  - allow escape clauses for certain industries; and
  - consider a national tripartite coordinating body with limited funding from ITB levies.
- Option 3
  - introduce a national training levy; and
  - establish a national coordinating body to collect and disburse funds.
- Option 4
  - introduce a national tax incentive scheme for employers; and
  - establish a national collection agency.

19.4.5.2 Levy-grant scheme

The government eventually opted for a national levy-grant scheme when it introduced the Skills Development Levies Act in 1999. The Act establishes a compulsory levy scheme for the purpose of funding education and training, as envisaged in the Skills Development Act. Paragraph 19.6 provides more detail on the Skills Development Act.

The government decided on the levy-grant scheme because it is easier to monitor, and because the levy-grant relationship establishes a closer link between the cost and benefit of training. This improves the market discipline acting on the training undertaken by firms, which is not present in either tax incentive or subsidy schemes. In short, the levy-grant scheme provides the following benefits.
- *It ensures core levels of training.* The levy-grant scheme serves as a platform for revenue allocated to training, as an active labour market policy, to enable the provision of a core level of training, consistent with the skill requirements of the labour market. It locates the funds for training directly with the main bene-

ficiaries, namely, the employers and unions. It will, further, require employers to consider their training needs more seriously, and providers to offer training that meets the needs of the workplace.
- *It alleviates the free-rider problem.* The levy will ensure that all firms contribute to the cost of training and, therefore, successfully address the free-rider problem.
- *It improves collection efficiency.* The collection of the levy by the South African Revenue Service will improve compliance, and reduce the administrative costs of collection.
- *It balances development and equity.* The levy scheme serves as a mechanism to redeploy resources consistent with economic needs. Training resources will be shifted to expanding sectors and sectors that are targeted for strategic development. It will, further, balance regional and social needs within the country and redistribute training resources within established parameters to respond to strategic development needs and social equity.
- *It promotes training effectiveness and efficiency.* Resources, on the demand side of the labour market, will be assembled to promote effectiveness and efficiency from training providers in the market system. Grants will be linked to the National Qualifications Framework, which will allow for the purchase of outcomes, in the form of skills acquisition, rather than focusing on the cost of inputs.
- *It ensures multipartite participation.* The responsibility of employers and workers in the governance of training funds changes the psychology of funding, in the sense that it develops a culture amongst employers and workers of accepting the necessary accountability for the productive utilisation of training funds.
- *It allocates revenue to address social equity needs.* The levy-grant scheme will allow for the training of unemployed persons and groups in the informal sector, as well as allocating revenue for the purpose of social equity.
- *It emphasises competitive procurement.* Training will be moved from a supply-driven to a demand-driven system. This will be achieved by awarding training grants to providers on a competitive basis.
- *It ensures proper monitoring and evaluation.* The levy-grant scheme also has the potential for the establishment of monitorable performance indicators to evaluate the performance of the various role-players in the system.

19.4.5.3 Sector Education and Training Authorities

Sector Education and Training Authorities (SETAs) established in terms of the Skills Development Act, play a significant role in the collection and disbursement of levy funds. The Skills Development Levies Act stipulates that employers must pay the levy to the Commissioner for the South African Revenue Service. However, the Act also makes provision for SETAs, if they are able to meet certain criteria, to collect levies.

Of all levy funds collected, 80 per cent is paid into the bank accounts of SETAs and 20 per cent into the National Skills Fund (NSF). The levy funds paid over to SETAs are utilised to defray their administrative cost within prescribed limits and to allocate grants to employers who meet the eligibility for grant recovery. Paragraph 19.6 provides more detail on SETAs and the NSF.

19.5 Certification of training

19.5.1 A qualifications structure

Certification of training brings with it the notion of a qualifications structure. A qualifications structure could be regarded as the driving force behind a vocational education and training (VET) system. Besides the general objective of providing training that leads to recognised qualifications, it also facilitates accessibility towards further learning experiences. A qualifications structure is, therefore, not aimed exclusively at obtaining a qualification at the end of a training programme, but also aims to promote admission to courses that are already under way, as well as to make it easier for candidates to switch over to other education programmes, if they so wish. Besides access to training opportunities, a qualifications structure will also allow, for example, for different learning pathways leading to the same qualification.

Stewart (1999) refers to five key principles that should inform and guide the design and operation of any national system of education and training, namely:
- removing barriers to access to development opportunities and qualifications;
- recognising current ability, achieved through means other than formal education and training;
- being flexible in practice in terms of both development and assessment;
- responding to the different needs of occupations at different levels, from foundation to professional; and
- being relevant to vocational practice.

The lack of uniformity in qualifications offered in the VET market is usually owing to the absence of a national approach. Various bodies, including education departments, industry-training organisations, employers, and private providers, develop occupational profiles and standards according to their own needs and insights. This method results in a wide variety of content, that is of limited use for educating the country's workforce in a coherent way, and is considered to be aimless and inefficient.

Such a situation gives rise to several shortcomings:
- a wide discrepancy exists between the standards of the various courses offered in the VET-market;
- harmonisation problems occur between initial training and further training;
- the plethora of training courses and pathways that are available make it increasingly difficult for employers to determine the value of the qualifications achieved by trainees;
- trainees find it difficult or even impossible to continue with further learning, based on the results they have already achieved; and
- those who leave the education system before completion of the whole course or programme cannot show any proof of a marketable qualification.

19.5.2 Certification in South Africa

19.5.2.1 National Qualifications Framework

The HSRC (1995:5) identified three major challenges which face South Africans in the field of education and training:
- An equitable system of education and training, which serves all South Africans well, will need to accommodate those people who are in conventional schools, colleges and training programmes. It will also need to find ways to include the learning needs of the many South Africans who have not enjoyed formal education and training.
- The quality of education and training is inadequate for achieving significant levels of economic growth and for becoming internationally competitive.

- The perception has to be removed that education and training are not linked. Education and training have been separated, both by the way they are organised and by the way society thinks about them. For example, academic study is generally perceived to be more valuable than training for useful occupations.

These challenges prompted interested parties to find solutions that would enable the country's education and training systems to provide a productive and skilled workforce, matched to the needs of employment. The answer was found in an approach that makes education and training more flexible, efficient, and accessible. Eventually this led to the National Qualifications Framework (NQF).

The NQF is a framework on which standards and qualifications, agreed to by education and training stakeholders throughout the country, are registered. Registered unit standards and qualifications are structured in such a manner that learners, on successful completion of accredited prerequisites, are able to move between components of the delivery system; it further allows for multiple pathways to the same learning end. The principles underlying the NQF are cited in Table 19.3.

Table 19.3 Principles underlying the NQF

Principle	Definition: Education and training should...
Integration	form part of a system of human resources development which provides for the establishment of an integrated approach to education and training
Relevance	be and remain responsive and appropriate to national development needs
Credibility	have national and international value and acceptance
Coherence	work within a consistent framework of principles and certification
Flexibility	allow for multiple pathways to the same learning ends
Standards	be expressed in terms of a nationally agreed framework and internationally acceptable outcomes
Legitimacy	provide for the participation of all national stakeholders in the planning and coordination of standards and qualifications
Access	provide access to appropriate levels of education and training for all prospective learners in a manner which facilitates progression
Articulation	provide for learners, on successful completion of accredited prerequisites, to move between components of the delivery system
Progression	ensure that the framework of qualifications permits individuals to move through the levels of national qualifications via different appropriate combinations of the components of the delivery system
Portability	enable learners to transfer their credits or qualifications from one learning institution or employer to another
Recognition of prior learning	through assessment, give credit to learning which has already been acquired in different ways, e.g. through life experience
Guidance of learners	provide for the counselling of learners by specially trained individuals who meet nationally recognised standards for educators and trainers

The NQF consists of eight levels, providing for General, Further, and Higher Education and Training bands. The NQF structure is outlined in Table 19.4.

19.5.2.2 Development and implementation of the NQF

The South African Qualifications Authority (SAQA) which came into being through the SAQA Act (refer to Paragraph 19.6.5 for more detail) is responsible for overseeing the development and implementation of the NQF.

All learning, in terms of the NQF, is organised into twelve fields and a number of sub-fields. A National Standards Body (NSB) exists for each field. Members of a NSB are drawn from six constituencies, namely state departments, organised labour, organised business, providers of education and training, interest groups, and community/learner organisations. The prime task of NSBs is to recommend standards and qualifications for registration on the NQF to SAQA.

The fields of the NQF are as follows (SAQA 1999):
- agriculture and nature conservation;
- culture and arts;
- business, commerce, and management studies;
- communication studies and language;
- education, training, and development;
- manufacturing, engineering, and technology;
- human and social studies;
- law, military science, and security;

Table 19.4 The NQF structure

NQF Level	Band	Qualification type
8	Higher Education and Training	• Post-doctoral research degrees • Doctorates
7		• Masters degrees • Professional qualifications
6		• Honours degrees • National first degrees
5		• Higher diplomas • National diplomas • National certificate
Further Education and Training Certificate (FETC)		
4	Further Education and Training	National certificates
3		
2		
General Education and Training Certificate (GETC)		
1	General Education and Training	Grade 9 ABET Level 4

SOURCE: South African Qualifications Authority (1999).

- health science and social services;
- physical, mathematical, computer, and life sciences;
- services; and
- physical planning and construction.

National Standards Bodies (NSBs) operate on the basis of Standards Generating Bodies (SGBs), established by the NSBs, which are responsible for developing standards and qualifications. SGBs are established according to sub-fields and members are drawn from the sub-field in question. The SGB for Teacher Education, for example, is made up of schoolteachers, professional teacher bodies, and university, college, and technikon teaching staff. NSBs do not generate standards or qualifications, but rather oversee these activities at sub-field level. To ensure that the education and training offered in terms of the NQF is of high quality, and in accordance with the registered standards and qualifications, SAQA accredits Education and Training Quality Assurance (ETQA) bodies.

ETQAs do not set standards, but are primarily responsible for accrediting education and training providers, and for the certification of learners. In doing so, they assure the quality delivery and assessment of registered standards and qualifications. In seeking accreditation from ETQAs, providers need to fulfil inter alia the following criteria:
- be registered as providers in terms of the applicable legislation;
- have a quality management system;
- be able to develop, deliver, and evaluate learning programmes which culminate in NQF qualifications or standards;
- have the necessary financial, administrative, and physical resources; and
- have the ability to achieve the desired outcomes using available resources and procedures.

19.5.2.3 Compliance and quality assurance

The NQF is a qualifications system which makes provision for the hallmarking of qualifications. In essence, this means assuring employers, learners, and providers that learning outcomes are relevant, market-related, and in terms of nationally recognised standards.

It further makes provision for a recognised assessment process through which learners are certificated to be competent in terms of recognised standards, which serves as an assurance for the employers and the learner that a qualification earned in terms of the NQF system is valid and nationally recognised.

To ensure general acceptance of, and confidence in, the NQF, a comprehensive quality assurance process has been put in place. The development and registration of qualifications and standards on the NQF are, for instance, subject to the participatory and representative structures and processes of the NSBs and SGBs. The quality of provision of education and learning, and the legitimacy of the certification of learners, are ensured through the ETQA system. In essence, the NQF is a system of assuring and continually re-assuring learners and other users of the education and training systems, that credits, awards, or certificates, issued during the learning process, adhere to the standards registered on the framework, and that all forms of provision are geared to deliver learning to the same standards for accreditation purposes. The inclusive nature of the quality assurance cycle ensures that the responsibility for setting standards, and for delivery of quality education and training, rests with the education and training stakeholders who participate in the SAQA processes (SAQA 1999: 13).

19.5.2.4 NQF qualifications

In terms of the SAQA Act, a qualification is defined as the achievement of a certain number of credits, embodied in a coherent number of unit standards. A qualification is a nationally agreed statement of learning achievements. The achievement of a qualification serves as proof that a learner has achieved an outcome on one of the eight levels, irrespective of when, how, and where it was achieved.

All qualifications are made up of three elements:
- *fundamental elements*, being competencies needed to successfully undertake the learning contained in the qualification, for instance functional literacy and numeracy;
- *core elements*, being the contextual elements to the relevant qualification; and
- *elective elements*, being optional elements from which learners may choose.

To satisfy the minimum requirements, a qualification must:
- represent a planned combination of learning outcomes, which has a defined purpose and which is intended to provide qualifying learners with applied competence and a basis for further learning;
- add value to the qualifying learner by providing status, recognition, and enhancing marketability and employability;
- provide benefits to society and the economy;
- comply with the objectives of the NQF by enhancing access to learning, mobility and progression, and national recognition;
- embody specific and critical cross-field outcomes that promote life-long learning; and
- be internationally comparable, where applicable.

Qualifications are made up of unit standards, which are clustered in a systematic and coherent way. Unit standards are nationally agreed and comparable statements supported by specific outcomes and assessment criteria. Unit standards are packaged according to specific criteria to establish a qualification (SAQA 1999).

19.6 Training legislation

19.6.1 Introduction

The training environment, as emphasised in previous chapters, should not be viewed in isolation, but against the background of current economic, technological, social, and political factors that are in the process of transforming the working world. In Paragraphs 19.2 and 19.3, it was shown that the responsibility of reforming the training system in response to changing demands rests with the state. In fulfilling this core function, the state is faced with the dilemma of increasing the relevance, effectiveness, efficiency, equality, and sustainability of the training system to meet new requirements, at a time of reduction in public spending. The training system in South Africa, as in many other countries, is receiving severe criticism for lacking relevance to market demands. It is a universal problem of training systems being trapped in tradition and bureaucracy, and unable to respond to rapidly changing labour markets. Government in South Africa is faced with the challenge of balancing, on the one hand, the demand for a skilled and flexible labour force to make industries in the country more competitive and, on the other hand, of ensuring equal access for all citizens to training opportunities, as well as redressing disadvantages faced by particular groups.

To influence the training system and bring about the necessary changes to meet new challenges, the state is compelled to take the lead in developing policy that is supportive of the economic and social changes the country is facing. Hand in hand with policy, goes legislation that should make provision for enabling mechanisms, but that will also regulate the actions and inputs of those involved in the training market.

In this chapter the focus falls on the legislation which governs training and skills development in South Africa.

19.6.2 The background to the current training legislation

South African training legislation has gone through different stages, each characterised by the political climate of the day. Prior to 1981, racial discrimination was still entrenched in training legislation, making it illegal for Blacks to be indentured as apprentices. Arising from the Wiehahn Commission's report, in which it was recommended that industrial relations be de-racialised, the Manpower Training Act was passed in 1981. For the first time, training legislation did not specifically refer to racial categories. The Act also introduced, for the first time, a tripartite forum, namely the National Training Board, to advise the relevant Minister on training matters. In 1991 the Manpower Training Act was amended to make provision for the establishment of Industry Training Boards (ITBs). ITBs were made responsible for the training of all workers, the management of apprenticeships, and trade testing in their respective industries.

The foundation for the current training legislation was laid by the work of a representative Task Team, under the auspices of the then National Training Board, consisting of four constituencies, namely business, trade unions, the state, and providers of education and training. The Task Team conducted its work in terms of the following vision: 'A human resources system in which there is an integrated approach to education and training and which meets the economic and social needs of the country and the development needs of individuals.'

Arising from the Task Team's report, three totally new pieces of training legislation were developed and enacted by Parliament, namely the Skills Development Act, Skills Development Levies Act and the South African Qualifications Authority Act.

19.6.3 Skills Development Act

19.6.3.1 Rationale for the Skills Development Act

South Africa has a poor skills profile as a result of the poor quality of general education for the majority of South Africans, the inappropriateness of much publicly funded training, and the low level of investment by firms in training. This profile inhibits productivity growth in firms, new investment prospects, and the employability of the young and unemployed. The sustainability of small and medium-sized enterprises is similarly impaired.

The Skills Development Act seeks to develop the skills of the South African workforce and, thereby, increase the quality of working life for workers, improve the productivity of the workplace, and promote self-employment and the delivery of social services. The Act also seeks to encourage employers to use the workplace as an active learning environment, and to provide opportunities for new entrants to the labour market to gain work experience.

A special focus of the Act is to improve the employment prospects of previously disadvantaged persons through education and training. The employment services are to focus on helping work-seekers to find work, retrenched workers to re-enter the labour market, and employers to find qualified employees.

The alignment of the Skills Development Act and the South African Qualifications Authority Act is ensured to promote the quality of learning in and for the labour market. The Act also gives organised employers and workers greater responsibility for ensuring the relevance of training, which will enhance quality (Republic of South Africa, 1998).

19.6.3.2 Objects of the Skills Development Act

The objects of the Act, as well as the Skills Development Levies Act (refer to Paragraph 19.6.4) are to be achieved by establishing a stronger institutional and financial framework than that which previously existed under the Manpower Training Act. The National Training Board is replaced by a National Skills Authority (NSA). The NSA is an advisory body to the Minister of Labour, with the responsibility for ensuring that national skills development strategies, plans, priorities, and targets are set and adhered to. ITBs are replaced by SETAs, responsible for developing sector skills plans which are aligned to the national skills strategies and targets. The sector skills plans will be presented to the National Skills Authority and approved by the Minister of Labour.

The functions of the NSA are:
- To advise the Minister of Labour on:
  - a national skills development policy;
  - a national skills development strategy;
  - guidelines on the implementation of the national skills development strategy;
  - allocation of subsidies from the National Skills Fund; and
  - any regulations to be made.
- To liaise with SETAs on:
  - the national skills development policy; and
  - the national skills development strategy.
- To report to the Minister on progress made in the implementation of the national skills development strategy.
- To conduct investigations arising out of the Skills Development Act.

Two learning programmes are identified in the Act: learnerships and skills programmes. These incorporate traditional apprenticeships. They include structured learning and work experience that leads to nationally registered, occupationally linked qualifications in areas of skill, need, or opportunity in the labour market. These assist young, unemployed people to enter employment, as well as existing workers to improve their skill levels. Skills programmes are not learnerships, but should also meet quality and relevance criteria to qualify for grant payments from SETAs or the National Skills Fund (the latter is defined in Paragraph 19.6.4).

A learnership is a mechanism to facilitate the linkage between structured learning and work experience, in order to obtain a registered qualification which signifies work readiness.

The decline in traditional apprenticeships over a decade has prompted the relevant role-players to seek a new mechanism to facilitate more flexible learning arrangements that are linked to the NQF.

A learnership consists of combined structured learning and work experience components. The structured learning component includes fundamental learning, core learning, and specialisation. The work experience component relates to the structured learning and prepares the learner for competence assessment.

The functions of SETAs are:
- To develop a sector skills plan within the framework of the national skills development strategy.
- To implement its sector skills plan by:
  - establishing learnerships;
  - approving workplace skills plans;
  - allocating grants to employers, education and training providers, and workers; and
  - monitoring education and training in the sector.
- To promote learnerships by:

- identifying workplaces for practical work experience;
- supporting the development of learning materials;
- improving the facilitation of learning; and
- assisting in the conclusion of learnership agreements.
• To register learnership agreements.
• To collect and disburse the skills development levies in its sector.
• To liaise with the NSA on:
  - the national skills development policy;
  - the national skills development strategy; and
  - its sector skills plan.
• To liaise with the employment services of the Department of Labour and any education body to improve information:
  - about employment opportunities; and
  - between education and training providers and the labour market.

19.6.4 Skills Development Levies Act

19.6.4.1 Rationale for the Skills Development Levies Act

The rationale for a national levy scheme for skills development is premised on the assumption that effective skills formation requires a strong link between occupationally based education and training and the workplace. The Skills Development Levies Act provides a regulatory framework to address the current low level of investment by firms in training. The Act establishes a compulsory levy scheme for the purpose of funding education and training as envisaged in the Skills Development Act (Republic of South Africa 1999).

19.6.4.2 Objects of the Act

The Act introduces a levy, equivalent to 0,5 per cent of an employer's payroll per month, with effect from 1 April 2000, and equivalent to 1,0 per cent thereof, with effect from 1 April 2001.

Employers must pay the levy to the Commissioner for the South African Revenue Service. However, where the Minister of Labour and Minister of Finance are satisfied that sufficient grounds exist, and where certain criteria are met, they may grant permission for employers within the jurisdiction of a particular SETA to pay their levies directly to that SETA. Twenty per cent of the funds collected will be allocated to the National Skills Fund established by the Skills Development Act. Together with the money received from the fiscus, this money will be used to fund national skills priorities. The remaining 80 per cent of the levies must be paid into the bank accounts of the various SETAs, to fund the performance of their functions and pay for their administration within the prescribed limit. Where there is no SETA, funds for that sector will be paid into the National Skills Fund.

The Skills Development Levies Act requires national and provincial government departments to budget at least 0,5 per cent of personnel costs for skills development from 1 April 2000 and 1,0 per cent from 1 April 2001. The same applies to national and provincial public entities, where 80 per cent or more of their expenditure is defrayed directly or indirectly from funds voted by Parliament. All public service employers in the national and provincial spheres of Government, and the said national and provincial public entities are, therefore, exempted from the payment of the levy.

Those employers not required to register for employees' tax purposes in terms of the Fourth Schedule to the Income Tax Act No. 58 of 1962, and whose total annual wage bill is less than R250 000, are also exempted. The Act further makes provision that the levy is not payable by any religious or charitable institution contemplated in section 10(1)(f) of the Income Tax Act, or any fund contemplated in section 10(1)(a) of the Act, established to provide funds to any such institution (Republic of South Africa 1999).

19.6.5 South African Qualifications Authority Act

19.6.5.1 Rationale for the South African Qualifications Authority Act

The plethora of training qualifications and pathways that are available on the training market make it increasingly difficult for learners to judge the credibility and market value of a course, and for employers to determine the value of the qualifications achieved by trainees. The South African Qualifications Authority Act successfully addresses this problem by providing for a comprehensive national recognition framework consisting of national standards to improve the quality and relevance of training. The Act establishes the South African Qualifications Authority (SAQA) whose function it is to oversee the development and implementation of the National Qualifications Framework (NQF). The NQF serves as a vehicle to create an integrated national framework for learning achievements and to enhance access to, and mobility and quality within, the components of the education and training delivery system (Republic of South Africa 1995).

19.7 Possible training policy options for South Africa

South Africa's future economic and social challenges will inevitably influence national and sectoral policies and strategies in the medium to long term. The country's economic challenges will come from a competitive global economy requiring a world-class workforce. Its social challenges, on the other hand, will come from the quest to build a democratic, non-racial, non-sexist future. The quality of South Africa's human resources is central to both challenges, and is the prime factor in determining the country's continuing progress and prosperity.

With the advent of the new political era, which will eventually have a major impact on the economy and civil society, a window of opportunity has opened that, from a strategic management point of view, provides excellent opportunities to create a policy environment with the potential of steering the country, within the next twenty to thirty years, towards becoming one of the world's developed nations. Judging from various policy documents and initiatives, human resources development has shifted to the centre stage of the strategic management environment. Conceptually, this is a major victory for the country on its road to prosperity and social equity. The vital question, however, is: What types of investment in the country's human resources will eventually yield the returns that are vital for sustainable growth and development?

This section, as indicated in the introduction, reflects only the training aspect of the human resources development policy environment. The following areas will be touched on briefly: strategic partnerships between stakeholders; an education system that is supportive of economic growth; a vocational education and training system that is flexible and responsive to market demands; and interventions in the informal sector to stimulate employment creation and public training programmes for the unemployed.

19.7.1 Policy option 1

Align human resources development policies with economic and social development policies to ensure that:

- the education and training systems are responsive to the skill needs of the economy and society;
- education and training initiatives are supportive of business activity and the improvement of the national quality of life; and
- in the face of global competition, South Africa's industries are competitive.

The lessons from the successful newly industrialised economies indicate that there is no quick-fix solution to achieving the sustainable growth and development that would enable the country to provide for the basic needs of its citizens. A long-term vision, supported by effective growth and development policies, is needed to achieve the desired results. The prerequisite for growth and development is empowered people, who are skilled and motivated to create wealth, as well as to share in it by means of participation in the economy and society. Against this background, it is essential for South Africa to align its human resources policies with policies that are aimed at the stimulation of industrial and economic growth.

19.7.2 Policy option 2

Introduce measures to turn around the current enrolment ratio of universities to career institutions (technical colleges and technikons) to ensure that:
- educational institutions provide for the envisaged needs of the economy; and
- the science and engineering workforce is improved, quantitatively and qualitatively.

From international comparisons (see Table 19.1) it is apparent that South Africa is sadly lacking in engineers and scientists, and would be faced with a dilemma were the economy to improve. Add to this the unfavourable enrolment ratio of universities to technikons, and it becomes evident that market-orientated education and training policies are vital for South Africa in its quest to achieve higher economic growth rates and greater social equity. Policy-makers, in the field of tertiary and further education and training, should seriously consider implementing policies that would stimulate growth in the science and engineering workforce by turning around the current enrolment ratio of universities to career institutions.

19.7.3 Policy option 3

Establish strategic partnerships between the state and enterprises, which are based on mutual trust, co-determination, and the sharing of responsibility.

Public-private collaboration takes place at both the macro and micro levels in a wide range of areas. The value of these partnerships lies not only on the operational level, but in that they could also be directed towards priority areas for national and local development, which have a strategic impact on functional areas such as the provision of skilled human resources for the economy. Critical areas for collaboration in skills development are the following:
- *Training policy development.* Policies give specific signals to different stakeholders. They also influence decisions, and can be instrumental in building commitment among enterprises to invest in skills development. Policies could also exert influence on decisions made by individuals to acquire skills, and on the provision of training by private providers. One of the values of public-private partnerships, in the training policy environment, is that policies stand a better chance of being market-driven. Another benefit, from the state's point of view, is the commitment of enterprises and private providers to actively support the implementation of training policies. From the private sector's point of view,

the value of a partnership is that it could influence policy to suit or benefit their own interests, provided they are aligned with the national interest.
- *Financing.* Collaboration in this area includes the exploitation of new sources of financing from the various stakeholders; incentives for investment in training with a view to encouraging voluntary initiatives; and the joint management of funds by social partners.
- *Delivery of training services.* Collective arrangements between the state and the private training market, for the delivery of training, have the benefit of leading to the improvement of the performance of public training institutions, in terms of relevance, effectiveness, and efficiency of training, when enterprises are involved in its design, delivery, and quality control. A further value is that it encourages the private sector, particularly enterprises, to share their experience and infrastructure with a view to increasing the training capacity of the country in the most cost-effective way.

19.7.4 Policy option 4

Institute a world-class education system that has the potential to:
- instil a culture of learning and a sense of discipline;
- provide for the basic learning needs of all citizens;
- respond to the needs of the economy; and
- equip students with the desired knowledge, understanding, and attitudes.

There is no doubt that the current deficiencies in South Africa's education system constitute a major threat to future growth and development. The system not only lacks a culture of learning and a sense of discipline, but also struggles to prove its relevance. The education system seems unable to meet the requirements that employers expect of their employees. Education also seems to trail behind the technological developments experienced by industry. The end result is a wide discrepancy between the competence of workers and the requirements necessary to fulfil certain functions within the employment system.

19.7.5 Policy option 5

Revitalise the current vocational education and training system for it to be able to:
- respond quickly to changing skill needs;
- provide the critical interface between the general education system and the working world; and
- create opportunities for workers to upgrade their skills on a continuous basis.

A dynamic vocational education and training (VET) system not only serves as the critical interface between the general education system and the working world, but is also regarded as the decisive factor determining the competitive strength of South Africa's economy. The following essentials are fundamental to a VET system that would respond sufficiently to the needs of individuals, the community, and the economy.
- It should be based on sound initial education. Employers and training providers expect trainees to, at least, possess basic literacy and numeracy skills, in order to be able to react positively to education and training programmes.
- It should be able to respond quickly to market demands. In this regard it is critical who is in control of policy design and implementation. International experience has proved that VET systems which are mainly teacher-controlled, tend to have a very strong supply-driven character. In an attempt to move the

centre of gravity of the VET system from a supply-driven to a demand-driven system, South Africa should take the option of the full involvement of industry (social partners) in the design and execution of VET programmes.
- It should be underpinned by a national qualifications structure. A qualifications structure should not serve, exclusively, as a mechanism to award a qualification at the end of a training programme, but should also promote admission to courses that are already under way and make it easier for candidates to switch over to other education and training programmes if they so wish.
- It should provide for key actors in the labour market to be involved. The active role to be played by the social partners in designing policy and training specifications, establishes the notion of co-responsibility for a skilled and flexible workforce, one of the essentials for competitive industries.
- It should provide for a broad-to-specific approach. It is essential that a broad-to-specific approach should be followed. Within similar learnerships, training should start with vocational foundation training, which is the same for all trainees. In the second stage, learnerships within similar trades should be grouped together, before the training becomes highly specialised in the final stage.
- It should provide for initial work-based training. As there is currently very little linkage to school-based vocational training, consideration should be given to bringing work-based training, provided by enterprises, into the ambit of the VET system.
- It should complement occupational skills with transferable life-skills. Besides occupational competence, emphasis should be placed on personal, social, and methodological competence. The ability to plan, execute, and monitor one's work in a self-reliant manner should serve as a guideline in the structuring of the training curriculum. Personal and social competence consists of skills related to motivation, decision-making, and the ability to work in a team. Methodological competence consists of abstract and logical reasoning, and problem-solving strategies.

19.7.6 Policy option 6

Target the informal sector as an area for intervention, using training as an instrument to transfer knowledge, skills, and attitudes by focusing on:
- areas in the informal sector that have the potential for sustainable growth;
- the real needs and problems of the target group; and
- the possibility of integrating training with other interventions.

There is a growing awareness of the small, medium, and micro-enterprise (SMME) sector's potential for job creation. It is generally accepted among planners that the formal economy will not generate sufficient employment for the expanding labour force in South Africa. Those who cannot be absorbed by the formal economy, turn to the informal sector as a means of survival. The records show that more than three-quarters of the working population in developing countries eke out a meagre living in the informal sector. Training is an intervention that has stood the test of viability and cost effectiveness worldwide, and is seen as an instrument to transfer knowledge, skills, and attitudes to ensure that business activities in the informal sector are more than just a means of subsistence. However, in order to yield returns, training must ensure greater efficiency and minimise the risk of informal sector operators ignoring the most basic business principles. The following are prerequisites for

training to be successful as an intervention in the informal sector:
- training should not be seen as a means to create jobs, apart from those for trainers and support staff, and should, therefore, not be designed and implemented in isolation but should be integrated with other interventions;
- training interventions should be based on knowledge of the people, their environment, and their major problems and aspirations; and
- training should not be offered as a social service but rather as a response to market stimuli; it should correspond to national training policies and fit in with national training practices and the prevailing labour market situation.

19.7.7 Policy option 7

Training provided to the unemployed should form an integral part of active labour market policies, by ensuring a linkage between training, job placement, unemployment benefits, and growth industries.

Active labour market policies portray a progressive shift of resources from passive income-support for the unemployed to active measures. Training should not be a goal in itself, but should improve access to jobs, develop job-related skills, and promote efficient labour markets by establishing an interface between the supply and demand of qualified labour. The training of the unemployed is justified from a social equity point of view, as well as in terms of the government's commitment to fight unemployment. To improve cost-effectiveness, policy-makers should seriously consider linking the current training programme with other measures, such as job placement and employment benefits, in order to minimise the risk of trainees not accessing the labour market. Although training of the unemployed is regarded as of great importance, broad training programmes, aimed at large groups, have proved not to be cost-effective. To ensure that training pays dividends, the following policy issues should be considered:
- target and diversify training programmes for the unemployed, based on thorough assessment of labour market needs;
- purchase training for the unemployed on a competitive basis in the private and public training markets; and
- involve all key players at local level (employees, trade unions, educational institutions, provincial and local governments) in a combined effort to develop training programmes that respond to local needs.

19.8 Conclusion

The new world economy, characterised by global markets and fierce competition by countries in an attempt to secure maximum market share, has given rise to the emergence of service and knowledge-based industries as an important source of employment. This forces countries to approach education and training from a strategic point of view, to be able to respond to the need for improved labour productivity and a more flexible workforce. The notion of training as an investment in human capital, raises the question of who should be responsible for training, and what the respective roles of governments, employers, and individuals are in this regard. This chapter addresses the cost and benefit of training, alternatives for generating training funds, and the funding mechanism adapted by the South African government. The issue of certification is fundamental to recognised and quality training. The South African Qualifications Authority (SAQA) is responsible for the development and implementation of the National Qualifications Framework (NQF) which makes provision for national standards and qualifications. The role and functions of SAQA and its supporting structures are discussed and explained in this chapter. Attention is also given to the legislative framework governing training, in general, the funding of training, and the certification of training. The chapter concludes with a reflection on training policy options for South Africa, against the background of prevailing socio-economic circumstances and the challenges facing the country in the face of global competition.

Case study

Global Consulting, a consultancy firm, has won the contract to develop a human resources development strategy for one of South Africa's neighbouring countries. The particular country's vision is to become a leading business hub in the New Economy. Through tax incentives and an investment-friendly industrial environment, the country is committed to attracting international investment to stimulate economic growth and employment. One of the constraints identified by the government of the country in question, is the lack of a skilled and flexible workforce. To overcome this problem, the government decided to develop a human resources development strategy which is aimed at generating sufficient skilled workers for the envisaged economic growth and business activity. The frame of reference of the project to be executed by Global Consulting makes special reference to the alignment of the human resources development strategy with the economic and social development policies of the country, funding arrangements for vocational education and training, and the recognition of training outcomes through a certification process.

Assume you are a senior partner at Global Consulting, and have been appointed as project manager for the said project. Your first task is to assemble a team of experts and to draw up a plan of action to be approved by the country in question. In preparation thereof, you need to attend to the following:

1 Identify the disciplines you would cover when selecting the team of experts.
2 Formulate terms of reference for the project team, and a business plan indicating the objectives, key performance indicators, and activities you believe are critical for the success of the project.
3 Draw up an operational plan indicating, inter alia, the nature of the investigations and studies that would support the outcome of the business plan.
4 Describe in broad terms the most important elements you believe should form part of the human resources strategy you need to develop, taking into account the unique circumstances of the country, current training legislation, and the level of participation of the social partners in the training environment.

Chapter questions

1 Discuss the macroeconomic context against which training policies are developed worldwide.
2 Express an opinion on whether South Africa has a sufficient skills base in the face of global competition. If not, explain how this could be rectified.
3 Discuss the cost and benefit of training from the employer's and Government's points of view.

4 Should workers also contribute financially to their own training? Motivate your answer. If your answer is yes, explain the form in which workers should contribute.
5 Why is certification of training necessary, and what benefits could employers and workers derive from certification?
6 Do you think the current training legislation is sufficient to develop a skilled and flexible workforce? Motivate your answer.
7 Do you believe the state should regulate skills development to a greater extent? Motivate your answer by referring specifically to the responsibilities of the various social partners.
8 Critique the various training policy options listed in this chapter.

Bibliography

ANDERSEN CONSULTING. 1999. *Outlook*, vol. XI, no. 2, June. Andersen Consulting.
AUSTRALIAN NATIONAL TRAINING AUTHORITY. 1998. *A bridge to the future – Australia's national strategy for vocational education and training*. 1998–2003. Brisbane.
BARKER, F. 1999. *The South African labour market – critical issues for renaissance*. Van Schaik, Pretoria.
DEPARTMENT OF LABOUR. 1997. *Green paper: skills development strategy for economic and employment growth in South Africa*. Department of Labour, Pretoria.
DEPARTMENT OF LABOUR. 1995. *South African funding mechanism research, industry training – supply and competition*. Department of Labour, Pretoria.
DEPARTMENT OF EDUCATION. 1999. *Implementation plan for Tirisano*. Department of Education, Pretoria.
DEPARTMENT OF FINANCE. 1999. *Intergovernmental fiscal survey*. Department of Finance, Pretoria.
FOUNDATION FOR RESEARCH AND DEVELOPMENT (FRD). 1996. *SA science and technology indicators*. FRD, Pretoria.
HUMAN SCIENCES RESEARCH COUNCIL (HSRC). 1999. *SA labour market trends and future workforce needs*. HSRC, Pretoria.
HUMAN SCIENCES RESEARCH COUNCIL (HSRC). 1995. *Ways of seeing the national qualifications framework*. HSRC, Pretoria.
MIDDLETON, J., ZIDERMAN, A. & ADAMS, A.V. 1993. *Skills for productivity*. Oxford University Press, New York.
MITCHELL, A.G. 1995. *Strategic training partnerships between the state and enterprises*. Paper delivered at the ILO/APSDEP seminar, 12–21 December, 1995. Chiba, Japan.
NATIONAL COMMISSION ON HIGHER EDUCATION. 1996. An overview of a new policy framework for higher education transformation. National Commission on Higher Education, Pretoria.
REPUBLIC OF SOUTH AFRICA. 1998. Skills Development Act 97 of 1998. Government Printer, Pretoria.
REPUBLIC OF SOUTH AFRICA. 1999. Skills Development Levies Act. Government Printer, Pretoria.
REPUBLIC OF SOUTH AFRICA. 1995. South African Qualifications Authority Act. Government Printer, Pretoria.
SOUTH AFRICAN QUALIFICATIONS AUTHORITY (SAQA). 1999. *The national qualifications framework: an overview*. SAQA, Pretoria.
STANDING. G., SENDER, J. & WEEKS, J. 1996. *Restructuring the labour market: the South African challenge*. International Labour Office, Geneva.
STEWART, J. 1999. *Employee development practice*. Financial Times Management, London.
UNESCO. 1998. *Statistical yearbook*. UNESCO Publishing and Bernan Press, Paris.

20

Training and development of employees and career management at organisational level

P S Nel

Learning outcomes

At the end of this chapter the learner should be able to demonstrate the following outcomes:
- Explain the difference between education, training, and development.
- Compile a strategic training and development model for his or her organisation.
- Explain the different elements of a training programme, and the contribution it can make towards effective training and development.
- Identify and apply appropriate training methods to a particular training situation.
- Design and apply an evaluation model to assess the training and development employees have undergone.
- Explain the difference between training, development, and career management.
- Distinguish between career planning and career development.
- Draw up a programme to establish a career path for an employee.

Key words and concepts

- apprenticeship training
- adult learning
- career management
- career stages
- competency
- development
- diversity training
- education
- human resources development (HRD)
- job analysis
- management development
- managerial obsolescence
- needs assessment
- on-the-job training (OJT)
- outcomes-based education and training
- performance gap
- recognition of prior learning
- sensitivity training
- training
- training and development methods
- training and development models
- training and development evaluation

Illustrative case

Byham Kiate has been the senior salesperson for ten years at Eezy Walk Shoe Wholesalers in Soweto. Last week, Byham was called in by the general manager, Mohapi Rkaolojane, and given the good news that he is in line for promotion to the position of manager. He was, however, reminded of the company's promotion policy: he would only be promoted if a suitably qualified and experienced person was available to replace him.

Byham thinks that Jeandia Phadan is a suitable person to replace him as senior salesperson. Jeandia has been with the company for a number of years and has been one of the top salespeople during the last few years. Jeandia is a very likeable and competent employee, and is eager to learn more about his job. Byham thinks that Jeandia has the potential to be the next senior salesperson. This is enhanced by the fact that Jeandia had been involved in shoe manufacturing at Eddils Shoe Manufacturers in Pietermaritzburg, before joining Eezy Walk. Furthermore, Jeandia has a friendly attitude with regard to the job and is always willing to assist and train other salespeople, should the situation call for it. Jeandia is committed to the company, and is always prepared to strive towards the achievement of the company's goals, under the guidance of Byham.

Jeandia's only problem is that he is unsure of himself when placed in a supervisory position. Byham discovered this when, on various occasions, he had been away on leave or on management development courses, and Jeandia had been placed in charge of sales, as acting senior salesperson. Jeandia would then be unsure of himself, become stressed, and fail to achieve sales targets. As a result, he would unleash his frustration on the other salespeople and, occasionally, on representatives of retail outlets coming to do bulk purchases of shoes from the company. During such periods of uncertainty, he would refuse to listen to his sales staff, and even unilaterally take decisions, which he would autocratically force on them.

Byham thinks that these problems can be overcome by properly directed training, in such a manner than Jeandia's good qualities can be utilised to the company's benefit. Byham is sure that adequate training techniques and courses exist to enhance Jeandia's ability to supervise the other sales staff effectively.

Consider what possible training and education needs are at stake, and how Jeandia's ability and potential to be successful in this business could be enhanced.

20.1 Introduction

In the previous chapter, the macro environment regarding human resources training and development was discussed. Aspects such as the macroeconomic context, training legislation, funding of training, certification of training, the South African Qualifications Authority (SAQA), and the National Qualifications Framework (NQF) were focused on. The national training strategy was also outlined, providing the context within which the development of employees at organisational level takes place.

This chapter focuses on operational issues relating to training and development at organisational level, which are of vital importance for the human resources staff in fostering a learning culture that will eventually contribute meaningfully to the bottom line of the organisation. The chapter concludes with a focus on career management, as an additional intervention to develop employees and to prepare them for upward mobility in an organisation, once they are adequately skilled in the required facets of the business.

20.2 Clarification of concepts

20.2.1 The concept of education

Education is regarded as those activities directed at providing the knowledge, skills, moral values, and understanding required in the normal course of life. The approach thus focuses on a wide range of activities, rather than on providing knowledge and skills for a limited field or activity. Education is, therefore, concerned with the development of sound reasoning processes, to enhance one's ability to understand and interpret knowledge. De Cenzo and Robbins (1994:265) define it as the deliberate, systematic, and sustained effort to transmit, evoke, or acquire knowledge, attitudes, values, skills, and sensibilities, and any learning that results from the effort, intended or unintended. Education, therefore, refers to a process of deliberately and purposefully influencing and shaping the behaviour of children and adults.

Education, in essence, creates a general basis that prepares the individual for life, without any specific job-related skills being developed. The concepts of training and development, on the other hand, guide an individual and prepare him or her to perform specific activities, as directed by the job they occupy or aspire to.

20.2.2 The concept of training

According to De Cenzo and Robbins (1994:255):

Training is a learning experience in that it seeks a relatively permanent change in an individual that will improve his or her ability to perform on the job.

Training can, therefore, be regarded as a planned process to modify attitude, knowledge, or skills behaviour through learning experience, in order to achieve effective performance in an activity or range of activities. Its purpose, in the work situation, is to develop the abilities of the individual and to satisfy the current and future needs of the organisation. Training brings about behavioural changes required to meet management's goals for the organisation. It is, thus, a major management tool in developing the full effectiveness of the organisation's most important resource, its people.

Training is executed to ensure that a task is performed correctly and, therefore, the behavioural change brought about by training must be measurable in terms of an organisation's requirements. Consequently, training must be result-orientated, it must focus on enhancing those specific skills and abilities needed to perform the job, it must be measurable and it must make a real contribution to improving both goal achievement and the internal efficiency of an organisation.

Erasmus and Van Dyk (1999) state that training standards for a specific job are primarily derived from the job description or task requirements of a particular job. Training is, therefore, directed at improving an employee's job performance. Training is executed when current work standards are not maintained, and when this situation can be ascribed to a lack of knowledge and/or skills, and/or poor attitudes among individual employees or groups in an organisation. Training is also presented as a result of technological innovation in an organisation. (See also Chapter 8 in this regard.)

20.2.3 The concept of development

Development is aimed at employees serving in a managerial capacity, or preparing for managerial posts within an organisation. It is essentially directed towards preparing supervisory and managerial staff for subsequent levels of management. It can be seen as a process by which managers obtain the necessary experience, skills, and attitudes to become or remain successful leaders in their organisation.

De Cenzo and Robbins (1994:255) maintain that development focuses on future jobs in an organisation. As the individual's career progresses, new skills and abilities are required, e.g. for management positions. Development, thus, refers to development possibilities within a job or position for a specific employee, with reference to the employee's personal growth and personal goals.

Should every manager be appointed in an organisation solely for aspiring towards its objectives, one might conclude that considerable demands are made on management. To fulfil their tasks efficiently, managers must keep abreast of new developments in the technological, economic, political, legislative, and social fields, as well as in personnel-management practices. Due to pressure of work, this is not always possible, and management often becomes obsolete in its outlook. This affects an organisation detrimentally, since it pervades the whole organisation and results in stagnation. One of the general objectives of development is the prevention of obsolescence. Obsolescence occurs when a person in a particular post lacks the current skills and knowledge, generally considered by other managers as vital for that person to remain effective in performing his or her work (Van Dyk et al. 2000).

For an organisation to survive in a highly competitive and developing market, it is essential to prevent obsolescence, and to develop managers who are able to keep abreast of new challenges. Management development is, therefore, an organisational development intervention at the individual level, to strategically align an organisation's management potential according to the demands that flow from a proactive business strategy.

20.3 Outcomes-based education and training

In terms of the National Qualifications Framework and the Skills Development Act, the current national approach followed by the Department of Labour with regard to education and training is outcomes-focused.

The re-engineering of the South African learning system is aimed at enabling South Africa to play a significant role in the world economy. This means a change from the traditional systems of learning, to an outcomes-based approach. According to outcomes-based learning, the only way to get to a goal is to know how to get there. As soon as the goal is identified (e.g. a product or service) strategies and techniques can be developed as to how to get there (Olivier:1998).

The outcomes-based approach differs from the traditional approach to education and training in that it focuses on the mastering of processes, knowledge, and skills needed to achieve certain outcomes. Outcomes-based education and training, however, also integrates the traditional approaches, such as Trainer-Centred, Learner-Centred, Mentor-Centred (Sit-by-Nelly), Criteria-Referenced Instruction, and Competency-Based Training (Strydom 1998:5–6).

An outcomes-based education and training system has, as its starting point, intended outputs (outcomes) as opposed to the inputs of traditional curriculum-driven education and training. An outcome is regarded as what a person can do and understand; a competence is what a person is able to combine regarding the use of skills, information, and understanding necessary in a particular situation. An essential outcome is a competence which a learner has acquired at a required level of performance. According to Erasmus and Van Dyk (1999:4):

> An outcome is not simply the name of the learning content, or a concept, or the name of a competence, a grade or score, but an actual demonstration in an authentic context. The basic approach is thus that if learning were based on outcomes, the starting point would be with the intended outcome – the end result. Once this is established, the curriculum processes (learning programmes) such as design, instructional planning, teaching, assessing and the development of learning according to the outcome can commence. Outcomes-Based Education is a results-orientated approach to learning and is learning-centred.

Outcomes-based education and training is, therefore, a radical departure from the previous system used in South Africa. This is illustrated in Table 20.1, which compares outcomes-based education to the traditional approach.

Outcomes-based training methods focus on two important aspects, according to Strydom (1998:10): firstly, the end result of the learning process, where learners must be able to demonstrate that they are competent with regard to prescribed outcomes; and secondly, the learning process and the transfer of information. This must guide the learner to the end result.

Outcomes-based training is a learner-based and result-orientated approach to learning, founded on the following principles:

- All learners are allowed to be able to learn to their full potential. Both trainer and learner must, therefore, have high expectations of being able to learn successfully.
- Success breeds success. Every success a learner achieves motivates the learner to strive for greater success.
- The environment must be learner-friendly, and encourage a culture of learning.
- All parties concerned, such as the community, the State, and learners must share in the responsibilities of learning. In outcomes-based training, all stakeholders should, therefore, co-operate in the development and implementation of learning processes.
- Learning achieves much more than mere memorising of knowledge and rote learning of skills.

According to Van Der Horst et al. (1997:27) the characteristics of an outcomes-based training are as follows:

- active learners;
- regular assessment of learners;
- critical thinking and reasoning are encouraged;
- the integration of knowledge which is relevant, and linked to life experience;
- a learning-centred approach – trainers are merely facilitators, and group-work and teamwork are important;
- learning-programmes merely provide guidelines, because creativity in the establishment of learning-programmes is encouraged;
- learners take responsibility for their own learning;
- learners are motivated by regular feedback and recognition of their learning efforts;
- the emphasis is shifted to outcomes, which the learner understands and is competent in;
- flexible time allocation, for learners to work at their own pace; and

Table 20.1 Comparison of the outcomes-based approach and the traditional approach

Traditional approach	Outcomes approach
• Rote learning.	• Critical thinking, reasoning.
• Syllabus is content-driven and broken down into subjects.	• Learning is a process, outcome-driven, and connected to real-life situations.
• Textbook/worksheet-bound.	• Learner- and outcome-centred.
• Teacher-centred.	• Teacher is facilitator.
• Syllabus is rigid and non-negotiable.	• Learning programmes are seen as guides.
• Emphasis on what teacher hopes to achieve.	• Emphasis on outcomes, what learner achieves.
• Curriculum development process not open to public.	• Wider community involvement is encouraged.

- recommendations and inputs into the process by the community are encouraged.

From this information, it is clear that outcomes-based education and training constitutes a radical departure from the traditional approach to training and development in South Africa.

20.3.1 Distinguishing between objectives and outcomes

It is essential to distinguish between objectives and outcomes, when education and training is being executed. According to Swanepoel et al. (2000:503) the differences between objectives and outcomes are as follows:
- objectives focus on what the teacher does, whereas outcomes focus on what the learner will do;
- objectives describe the intent of teaching, and outcomes describe the results of learning;
- objectives focus on the opportunities provided for learning, and outcomes emphasise how learning is used and can be applied in new areas; and
- objectives estimate how much can be learned in a given period of time, and outcomes require the flexible allocation of time.

According to Erasmus and Van Dyk (1999: 14) objectives are viewed as input-driven, whereas outcomes are viewed as output-driven. An argument against the use of objectives is that they are knowledge-driven, giving rise to a static form of learning and, thus, promoting rote learning. The outcomes approach encourages the use of an end result, which is a product of a learning process in which knowledge is obtained through participation and transparency.

An outcome statement should:
- describe the learner's performance in terms of observable, demonstrable, and assessable performance;
- contain action verbs, be clear and unambiguous;
- involve more than mere isolated tasks or skills; and
- refer to knowledge, skills, and attitudes or values (abilities).

An outcome must indicate:
- who is to perform;
- what task is to be performed;

- what conditions apply (if any); and
- the minimum response that will indicate mastery of the task.

The outcomes to be achieved regarding training and development in an organisation are to:
- improve the quality of an enterprise's output;
- reduce costs incurred through wastage and the maintenance of machinery and equipment;
- reduce the number and cost of accidents;
- restrict labour turnover and absenteeism;
- promote job satisfaction and motivation;
- reduce or overcome obsolescence in management;
- qualify employees for their jobs;
- provide present employees with further training;
- rectify poor performance resulting from poor knowledge and skills;
- reduce learning time and cost;
- improve job performance;
- foster the right attitudes;
- improve recruitment and selection;
- meet manpower needs; and
- increase customer satisfaction.

20.4 The place and role of the training function in an organisation

According to Erasmus and Van Dyk (1999: 39-41) an organisation consists of various sub-systems that pursue the achievement of organisational objectives by means of different organisational processes. These sub-systems are organised according to the unique needs of each enterprise, and usually include the marketing, production, financial, and human resources functions. Each of these sub-systems can be divided into smaller systems or sub-subsystems, such as the planning, provision, maintenance, training, and development of human resources, and labour relations.

The training and development function is regarded as a sub-system of the human resources management function, based on the following assumptions:
- The training function is a processing system that determines training needs, applies training technology and expertise, and transforms untrained employees into trained employees who can make productive contributions to the organisational objectives.
- The primary input into a training system (training needs and untrained employees) is transformed into an output (trained employees) by means of training processes, such as analysis, design, development, and the evaluation of training.
- As a sub-system of an enterprise, the training function is exposed to the same influences as the other systems in the enterprise. These influences include politics, the economy, and legislation.

The training function should be viewed as part of the human resources function as a whole, but should operate as a separate training department if this is affordable, because training takes place at various levels in an enterprise, and provides a support service to the entire enterprise. To ensure success, it is critical that training practitioners continuously monitor the training input that is made available in order to achieve the organisational objectives. This will increase the credibility of the training department in the enterprise.

The key roles that should be present in all training departments are:
- achievement and need analysis;
- development of curricula;
- development and acquisition of training resources;

- training per se;
- advancement of training efficiency; and
- administrative management of learners.

Training departments often take on the following additional duties:
- marketing training courses and learner registration systems;
- the supply of training materials for on-the-job training;
- the supply and management of training facilities and equipment;
- organising achievement conferences;
- representing the enterprise on professional bodies; and
- trading training programmes and training material with other enterprises.

20.5 Strategic human resources development

Due to the importance and cost of training and development to an organisation, it must be effectively managed. Over and above this, Erasmus and Van Dyk (1999: 48–50) state that a human resources development manager faces a wide range of challenges, namely:
- The human resources manager must ensure that all programmes are presented in a purposeful and effective manner. Organisations must, therefore, ensure that its training and development programmes are not offered merely for the sake of presenting a programme.
- Imbalances exist between traditionally advantaged managerial personnel and historically disadvantaged personnel, and these must be addressed and rectified via accelerated programmes.
- Management must realise that attitudes towards employment equity programmes cannot change organisations overnight, and must be carefully addressed via training and development programmes.
- Human resources development managers and practitioners ought to be carefully selected, since the success of programmes largely depends on their quality and knowledge of training and development.

From this point of view, it is essential to adopt a strategic approach to human resources development to ensure that it has the maximum benefit to an organisation. Strategic human resources development is geared to the strategic business plan and to implementing the human resources strategy, by improving the knowledge and skills of employees of the organisation and the knowledge and efficiency levels of interest groups outside the organisation. (See Chapter 23 for more detail in this regard.)

According to Rothwell and Kazanas (1994:19–21) the key assumptions in executing strategic human resources development (SHRD) are as follows:
- there should be an overall purpose statement for the organisation, and the human resources development (HRD) effort should be related to it;
- every major plan of the organisation should be weighed in terms of the skills available to implement it, and alternative ways of obtaining those skills;
- people at all levels in the organisation's chain of command should share responsibility and accountability for HRD; and
- there should be a formal, systematic, and holistic planning process for the corporation, personnel department, and HRD.

20.6 A strategic training approach

Arie de Geus (in Swartz 1992) made the observation years ago that learning faster than your competitors is the only sustainable competitive advantage. Every organisation learns; some just learn faster than others, do it more deliberately, and use their new knowledge more rapidly. Nicky Opperheimer, chairman of the Anglo American Corporation, emphasises the strategic role of training when he refers to the contribution of the HR-manager as a bottom line issue, because it is only those businesses with human resources policies that are sustainable and that enhance the company's capacity to create wealth, which will be successful into the twenty-first century.

Strategic training requires an approach in which the primary thrust is to create an environment in which learning for all the members of the organisation is encouraged, rather than seeing the establishment and maintenance of a training department as a major strategy to only influence the development of people in organisations.

When referring to strategic training, the concept virtual training in organisations comes to mind. The virtual organisation is the ultimate results-centred enterprise. By using Future Work principles, it is able to produce results that are at least equal to those of its traditional competitors but leveraged from a smaller asset base. The results of the virtual organisation are real and will show up in the bottom line, but if one starts searching for the traditional means of achieving these results – massive office buildings, work restricted to fixed times and locations, and the madness of large-scale commuting – one will not find them because they are not there.

Virtual organisations are, according to McIntosh (1995) becoming a virtual reality. They are organisations that forge alliances with other firms to streamline processes, cut costs, and crack new markets. For virtual organisations to evolve, they need support from virtual training organisations (VTOs). VTOs devise flexible structures and systems so that they can respond rapidly to their organisation's needs. Three principles dictate VTO operations:
- individual employees, and not their organisations, have the primary responsibility for their own personal growth;
- the most powerful learning takes place on the job, not in a classroom; and
- improved performance hinges not on the relationship between a trainer and a class participant, but on the relationship between the manager and the employee.

Table 20.2 illustrates a VTO model that incorporates five competencies: strategic direction, product design, structural versatility, product delivery, and accountability for results. McIntosh (1995) illustrates each of the five competencies in detail, and compares the characteristics of a traditional training organisation with those of a virtual training organisation.

By re-orientating traditional training approaches to enable learners to anticipate the future and prepare for it, training departments will not only justify their existence but also contribute to meaningful growth and development of their organisations.

20.7 Training and development policy

A training and development policy is based on certain assumptions and principles, which manifest themselves in the form of a philosophy. This can be described as the managerial attitude (either proactive or reactive) or perception of the importance of its human resources potential to enhance company goal achievements by means of investments in the training and development efforts of the organisation. The policy should reflect, from a strategic as well as an operational point of view, the reasons why an organisation is willing to invest in the development of its employees.

Table 20.2 Comparing a traditional training department with a virtual training organisation

Strategic direction

A traditional department:
- leaves objectives unstated or vague
- assumes that class participants are its only customers
- limits offerings to predetermined list
- continues to supply products that are no longer useful
- organises its offerings by courses

A virtual training organisation:
- broadly disseminates a clearly articulated mission
- recognises that its customer base is segmented
- provides customised solutions to its client's needs
- understands product life cycles
- organises offerings by competencies
- competes for internal customers

Product design

A traditional department:
- uses rigid and cumbersome design methodologies
- views suppliers as warehouses of materials

A virtual training organisation:
- uses benchmarking and other innovative design strategies to develop products quickly
- involves suppliers strategically

Structural versatility

A traditional department:
- employs trainers who serve primarily as facilitators and classroom instructors
- operates with a fixed number of staff
- relies solely on training staff to determine the department's offerings

A virtual training organisation:
- employs professionals who serve as products managers and internal consultants
- leverages resources from many areas
- involves line managers in determining direction and contents

Product delivery

A traditional department:
- distributes a list of courses
- offers courses on a fixed schedule at fixed locations

A virtual training organisation:
- offers a menu of learning options
- delivers training at the work site

Accountability for results

A traditional department:
- believes that the corporation manages employee development
- ends its involvement with participants when courses end
- considers the instructor the key player in supporting learning
- relies on course critiques as its primary source of feedback
- vaguely describes training outcomes

A virtual training organisation:
- believes individual employees must take responsibility for their personal growth
- provides follow-up on the job to ensure that learning takes place
- considers the manager the key player in supporting learning
- evaluates the strategic effects of training and its bottom-line results
- guarantees that training will improve performance

SOURCE: McIntosh (1995).

It is essential for an organisation to base its training and development policy on an integration of job content, management skills, and leadership training, in accordance with the various career levels. A theoretical basis for a training and development policy is depicted in Figure 20.1.

This conceptualisation indicates that all employees of an organisation should receive job content training throughout their careers. Initially, job content training (at a low level) enables employees to gain basic skills, which are required in the execution of their tasks. Later, job content training enables employees to know more about their functional area, in order to be promoted in accordance with those newly learned skills and to be promoted above others. Job content training at the highest level implies that senior personnel are kept up to date with the latest technology in their functional areas to enable them to become better decision-makers.

Because members at lower levels of the organisation work more with people (as one of the factors of production) than top management, it is essential that these members receive a greater measure of training in leadership behaviour, team building, and group utilisation. This explains the decreasing tendency towards this type of training as career promotion takes place and the employee moves up the organisational ladder. Conversely, top management has a larger management task than the middle and lower levels and, therefore, the relationship between management skills and leadership skills is reversed, although the job content training at all levels remains practically the same. Training in leadership behaviour must be directed at the establishment of a situational diagnostic approach to the practice of leadership.

According to Erasmus and Van Dyk (1999:61) the attitude of an organisation towards the training and development of employees is reflected in its policy, and this policy governs the priorities, standards, and scope of its training activities.

Training policies are developed for four main reasons:
- to define the relationship between the objectives of the organisation and its commitment to the training function;
- to provide operational guidelines for management;
- to provide information for employees; and
- to enhance public relations.

According to Reid and Barrington (1997: 259) the policy for training and development of an organisation is influenced by a number of variables, such as:
- size, traditions, and prevailing culture;
- products or services;
- economic and social objectives;
- obligations to provide continuing professional updating training, e.g. for nurses;
- top management's view of the value of training;
- the availability of information about the training needs of the organisation;
- the labour market, and alternative means of acquiring skilled and qualified staff;
- past and current training policies and practices;
- the training experience of its managers;
- the calibre of its specialist training staff;
- resources that can be allocated to training;
- the expectations of employees and their representatives; and
- legislation, e.g. on health and safety, and government-funded schemes, such as youth training.

Figure 20.1 A theoretical basis for a training and development policy

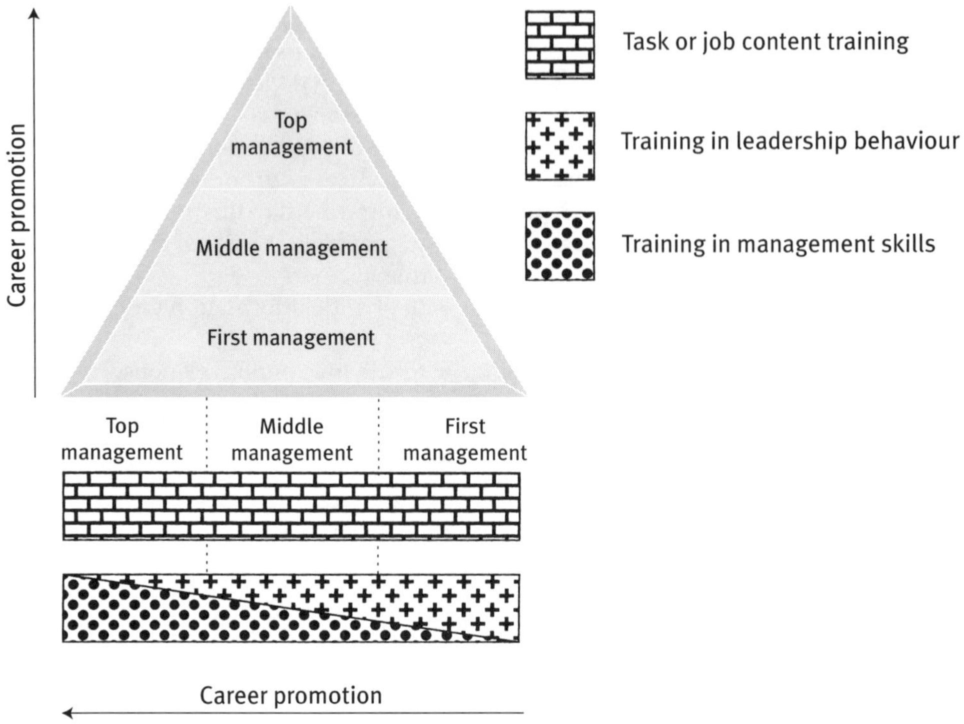

SOURCE: Van Dyk et al. (2001).

20.8 Training and development models

Training and development can only take place effectively if it is executed within the context of a logical and systematic process. This can be via the application of a training model, which would include steps such as determining training needs and job analysis, programme design, and presentation and evaluation of training. Various models exist which broadly follow this approach. Examples of some of the popular models follow.

Nadler's model (1980) views the training process in holistic terms and is referred to as the critical events model. In this model, nine steps are outlined, namely:
- Step 1: Identifying the needs of the enterprise.
- Step 2: Evaluation and feedback.
- Step 3: Specifying performance.
- Step 4: Identifying training needs.
- Step 5: Formulating training objectives.
- Step 6: Compiling a syllabus.
- Step 7: Selecting instructional strategies.
- Step 8: Acquiring instructional resources.
- Step 9: Presentation of training.

The training model of Camp et al. (1986) broadly coincides with Nadler's, and has the following steps:

TRAINING AND DEVELOPMENT

- Step 1: Gather/diagnose data.
- Step 2: Establish objectives.
- Step 3: Identify resources.
- Step 4: Develop curriculum.
- Step 5: Plan logistics.
- Step 6: Perform training.
- Step 7: Facilitate transfer of learning.
- Step 8: Gather/evaluate data.

A further model, which has gained popularity due to its simplicity and effectiveness, is the so-called high impact model, a six-phase process which focuses on providing effective and targeted training which was developed by Sparhawk (1994). In this model, each phase moves the training and development effort forward; in other words, the one phase is the input for the next.

The model's use and application can be illustrated in terms of the activities which ought to take place in each phase, and the product that is to be produced as a result thereof.

20.9 Application of various models to training and development

A sound approach to training and development ought to take cognisance of the models outlined above to be successful; but it should first ensure that the macroenvironment has been scanned and assessed (see Chapter 19) and that the strategy and policy of the organisation concerning training and development has been observed or re-evaluated.

It must also be borne in mind that the process of executing training and development requires two major aspects prior to the training itself. Firstly, the standards against which job performance must be measured, i.e. the job content of the post must be clearly defined; and secondly, the performance of the individual (the actual state of affairs) must be measurable. The

Figure 20.2 The high impact training model

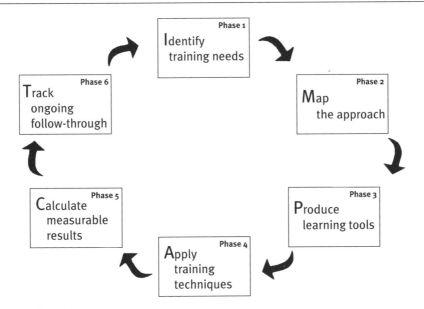

SOURCE: Sparhawk, S. (1994:13).

Table 20.3 Action and product phases of the high impact model

Phase		Action	Product
1	Identify training needs	Gather and analyse appropriate information	A description of the specific training needed to improve job performance
2	Map the approach	Define what needs to be learned to improve job performance. Choose the appropriate training approach	Detailed objectives for the training programme. A design plan for the training program
3	Produce learning tools	Create the actual training materials	Training manuals; Facilitator's guide; Audio-visual aids; Job aids, etc.
4	Apply training techniques	Deliver the training as designed to ensure successful results	Instructor-led training. Computer-based training. One-on-one coaching, etc.
5	Calculate measurable results	Assess whether your training/coaching accomplished actual performance improvement; communicate the results, and redesign (if necessary)	An evaluation report. A redesigned course (if necessary)
6	Track ongoing follow-through	Ensure that the impact of the training does not diminish	Ongoing suggestions and ideas that support the training

SOURCE: Sparhawk (1994:14).

difference between the standards and the current performance constitutes the performance gap and, therefore, represents the training need to be executed to achieve the desired outcome.

The job content must also be analysed before the determination of training needs can commence. The process of job analysis to determine training standards and improve job performance must be undertaken (see Chapters 9 and 21).

The steps which follow should be included in an effective approach to training and development.

20.9.1 Identify training needs

Whenever a comprehensive needs analysis is undertaken, it will usually address one or more of the following three key areas: the organisation, the job, and the individual concerned (Fisher et al. in Swanepoel et al. 2000:500–502).

Organisational assessment

This considers the proposed training within the context of the rest of the organisation. The following are some of the questions which should be asked:

- What are the training implications of the organisation's strategy?
- What will the result be if training is not undertaken?
- How does this training programme fit in with the organisation's future plans and goals?
- Where in the organisation is training needed?

- How are various departments performing in relation to expectations or goals?
- In which departments is training most likely to succeed?
- Which departments should be trained first?
- Can the organisation afford this training?
- Which training programmes should have priority?
- Will this training adversely affect untrained people or departments?
- Is this training consistent with the organisation's culture?
- Will this training be accepted and reinforced by others in the organisation, such as the trainees' superiors, subordinates, and clients?

It must also be borne in mind whether the training is synchronised with an organisation's mission, strategy, goals, and culture. Today, corporate culture, in particular, is important when training and development is to be executed in an organisation.

The job

This entails a thorough task analysis of an incumbent, the purpose of which is to find out if a person's task is of importance to an organisation and whether training is to be executed.

The individual

Training can only be executed if it has been determined which employees should receive training and what their current levels, knowledge, and skills are. The assessment of the individual will indicate the range of skills and knowledge to be acquired.

Training is based on one or more needs, as outlined above, defined as gaps or discrepancies between an ideal and an optimal stage. Needs arise from the job, from a comparison between desired and actual work methods, or between desired and actual work results. Rothwell (1994) refers to three methods of identifying needs: the generic method, performance analysis, and competency assessment. Where performance analysis focuses on deficiencies or problems, competency assessment focuses on opportunity for improvement. Trainers identify how they believe people should perform and then design the training programme to give the workers the skills they need.

20.9.2 Devise instructional objectives

An instructional objective is a description of a performance you want learners to be able to exhibit before you consider them competent. It describes an intended result of instruction, rather than the process of instruction itself. According to Mager (1975) there are three parts to any objective:

- *Performance* – what learners will be capable of doing after the instructional experience is completed;
- *Conditions* – what content and what tools will be necessary for performance to occur; and
- *Criteria* – how well the performance will be exhibited.

Rothwell (1994) categorises objectives by type and scope. He also distinguishes between three types of objective:

- *Cognitive*, which has to do with knowledge and information;
- *Affective*, which has to do with feelings and beliefs; and
- *Psychomotor*, which has to do with the ability to manipulate objectives.

There are also two ways of thinking about the scope of objectives, namely:

- *Terminal* – what learners will be able to do upon the completion of a course or programme; and
- *Enabling* – behaviours that contribute to mastery of terminal objectives.

20.9.3 Prepare test items based on the objectives and desired outcomes

Test items enable the trainer to establish whether the learner has mastered behaviours that a training programme has been designed to teach. There are generally two types of test items:
- *Norm referenced*. Achievement is assessed relative to other learners and compares each learner to others; and
- *Criterion referenced*. Achievement is assessed relative to individual success, and compares a learner's progress to pre-established measures.

20.9.4 Select or design instructional content

The selection or design, in other words, the decision what to teach, is based on the test items and instruction objectives. In this process (Rothwell:1994) it is important to consider whether the content should be obtained from existing sources, such as text books, other training courses, or published articles, tailor-made for the purpose at hand, or prepared from a combination of externally available and internally produced content. Figure 20.3 provides a useful algorithm for making this decision.

20.9.5 Choosing delivery methods

The method of teaching is dependent on what is to be taught. Teaching methods depend heavily on the preference of the trainer. Table 20.4 provides a list of different delivery methods. (Refer also to paragraph 20.10, where training techniques are discussed in more detail.)

20.9.6 Offering instruction

Training can be offered either on the job by the supervisor, off the job by in-house trainers, or outside the organisation. The latter is commonly associated with formal instruction, while on the job is usually informal and rarely distinguishable from regular work activities.

20.9.7 Transferring learning back to the job

The main purpose of off-the-job training is to give employees the knowledge and skills they need to perform effectively on the shop floor. According to Rothwell (1994) there are factors on the job that prevent transfer of learning. They include:
- *The individual (learner)*. If learners see no value in applying new skills, believe no rewards will result from doing so, or do not value the rewards, then the transfer of learning from classroom to the job will not occur.
- *The job*. If individuals have little or no latitude to change what they do because the job tasks are tightly controlled, then training can never be applied unless the job itself is changed first.
- *The supervisor*. If a learner's supervisor is not in favour of training, then there is little likelihood that a learner will apply newly acquired skills. Supervisors exert powerful influence over the behaviour of subordinates because they control rewards and punishment.
- *The work group*. If a trainee returns to the shop floor only to find that fellow workers greet new ideas with scepticism, then training will not transfer successfully.

The literature suggests that the assumptions on which current training and development models are based need to be re-examined. Human resources training and development practitioners are expected to bring about organisation-wide change while confined to their classrooms. McIntosh (1995) suggests a recognition of aspects such as virtual training organisations,

Figure 20.3 Algorithm for deciding whether to produce your own instructional material

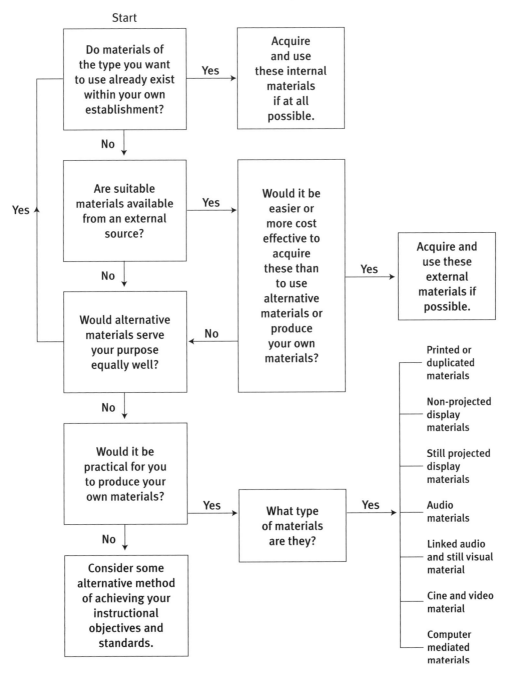

SOURCE: Ellington (1985).

Table 20.4 Training delivery methods and strategies

Method	Description	Appropriate for
Lecture	• A structured presentation, usually lasting an hour or longer	• Group presentations • Orientating employees to policies, introducing topics, providing information
Tutorial	• A one-on-one, structured instructional experience	• Individualised presentation • On-the-job training • Building skills, demonstrating how to use equipment
Case study	• A narrative description of a situation, real or fictitious, prepared for instruction purposes, usually written	• Stimulating discussion, especially in a small group setting • Identifying problems in realistic situations • Weighing alternative solutions
Critical incident	• A very short narrative description of a problem situation, usually only a sentence or paragraph in length	• The same purposes as case study
Role-play	• Trainees are assigned parts to play in a dramatised version of a case study or problem situation	• Groups of two or more • Dealing with instruction about interpersonal situations
Game	• A ritualised representation of a job duty	• Group instruction • Especially useful for developing cooperation or assessing leadership in a team setting
Simulation	• An extended role-play or game	• Same purposes as game
Buzz groups	• A small group of people, assembled to identify a problem or problems, consider and select alternative solutions	• Use with case study, critical incident • Taking advantage of the ability of small groups to deal with unstructured problems more effectively than individuals
Panel discussion	• A structured or unstructured presentation on a topic, problem or issue by a group of from three to ten people to a larger group	• Stimulating insight • Posing problems • Clarifying issues and problems
Computer-based instruction	• The use of a computer, usually a microcomputer, to present instructions	• Communicating information very efficiently but not necessarily cheaply
Videotape	• The use of a televised presentation to provide instruction, often in a form that mixes instruction with entertainment	• Demonstrating effective interpersonal skills • Conveying information in an interesting (but not necessarily cheap) manner

as opposed to the traditional approach followed by training and development departments.

20.9.8 Evaluation

Training and development can never be effective if it is not properly assessed. The expression that 'to measure is to know' is acutely apt in this context. It also forms the last link in the loop of the systems approach to training and development, since it determines whether the training need (the difference between the required performance and the actual performance of the trainee) has been satisfied. Without measuring what has happened, the training department and its efforts cannot be effectively assessed. It also forms the starting point for the next round of training and development, if need be.

According to Erasmus and Van Dyk (1999:192–3) the following aspects regarding the evaluation of training and development are of cardinal importance if it is to be successful:
- the evaluation of training is a continuous process and not something that occurs only at the end of the training period;
- training evaluation must be well planned, with its objectives clearly indicated, and not conducted on an ad hoc basis;
- accurate and applicable measuring instruments must be used to obtain information for the purposes of decision-making;
- training evaluation is a form of quality control; and
- evaluation is not directed only at testing students, but also at testing the entire training system.

The principles of assessment proposed by Meyer (1996:90–1) are the following:
- Assessment must be reliable and valid. Reliability refers to the consistency of assessment results for equal performance of individuals, which are independent of time or the assessor. Validity refers to whether the assessment method tests the behaviour which it is supposed to test.
- Assessment must be practical, cost-effective, and create a minimum of disruption in the workplace.
- Access to assessment should not be subject to artificial barriers, e.g. prescribed educational qualifications, prescribed learning times, and age restrictions.
- An appeals mechanism should be established for those dissatisfied with their assessment.
- The process of setting assessment criteria and procedures should be open to all stakeholders.
- Those involved in assessment should be competent in both the performance being assessed and in assessment techniques and principles.
- Where practical, multiple assessment methods should be used to gather evidence from a variety of contexts or situations.
- Where it is only practical to assess a sample of the required performance, it is essential that the performance measured provides sufficient evidence of competence and the achievement of the required outcome.

Evaluation therefore serves the purpose of:
- making decisions regarding the performance of individual employees (for example, their needs, the syllabus, and feedback);
- making decisions on course improvement, for example, the most suitable training methods and content;
- making administrative decisions on the effectiveness of the training function; and
- determining, during the course of the development process, whether set objectives are achieved, to ensure that feedback can be provided in this regard.

Various types of evaluation exist, but according to Rothwell and Kazanas (1994: 480–482) the two main types are formative and summative.

Formative evaluation requires that a learner's performance be evaluated to:
- determine the extent to which the course content has been mastered;
- provide feedback to students; and
- assist students in correcting errors which still occur, and in improving future learning performance.

Summative evaluation requires a human resources training and development practitioner to execute the following in order to be effective:
- Examine all instructional materials after they have been revised in the light of formative evaluation results. Do they appear to do what they are supposed to do?
- Observe an instructor delivering the material. Do learners respond as expected? Does the instructor present the material adequately?
- Administer a post-test to measure trainee achievement of objectives.
- Administer an attitude survey to find out how well participants liked the course and to what extent they felt that it met their needs.
- Compare the subsequent job performance of:
  - those who received training, and
  - those who did not receive training (or who benefited from a different kind of performance improvement strategy).

The evaluation of training can also be executed by considering why training fails, in order to correct it. Based on empirical research by the American Society for Training and Development, Rothwell and Kazanas (1994:475) list the reasons in Table 20.5 for the failure of training in the United States of America. There is little doubt that this applies equally in South Africa.

The issue of written or oral examinations is of particular importance in South Africa. Where an outcome does not necessarily require reading or writing ability, oral assessment should be permitted. It is essential, in this case, that the assessor records the questions asked and notes the correctness or otherwise of responses. A checklist is an important tool in oral assessment.

20.10 Training and development methods

Various methods can be applied, which are used either off the job or on the job. These are discussed below.

20.10.1 Off-the-job training

Off-the-job training is exactly what it says. It is training that is done in a classroom, vocational school, or any other place, except for the shop floor.

Organisations apply off-the-job training in varied ways and do not only stick to the most obvious method, i.e. for the trainer to give a lecture of the material to be learned. Besides the lecture method, a number of other ways of applying off-the-job training are briefly discussed below.

Case studies

The trainees read, study, and analyse a hypothetical business problem that contains elements of a real-life situation. They are then required to choose the best solution and implement it. Learning is best if there is interaction between the learners and the instructor, because the role of the instructor is that of catalyst and facilitator. The method gives learners an opportunity to apply the knowledge and principles they have learned previously, and to test their ability to deal with a simulated real-life

Table 20.5 Why training fails

Reason for failure	Respondents (%)
• No on-the-job rewards for behaviours and skills learned in training	58
• Insufficient time to execute training programmes	55
• Work environment does not support new behaviours learned in training	53
• Lack of motivation among employees	47
• Inaccurate training needs analyses	40
• Training needs changed after programme had been implemented	35
• Management does not support training programme	30
• Insufficient funding for training programme	21

SOURCE: Rothwell & Kazanas (1994:475).

situation. It also provides trainees with an opportunity to develop independent thinking and to exchange ideas. The experience is a trial run for business activities in the real world.

The incident method

This is a variation on the case study method. In this method, trainees are given the bare outlines of a problem and are each assigned a role. Each trainee must then view the problem from the perspective of his or her role. Additional information is made available according to the questions they ask.

According to Ivancevich and Glueck (1986:484):

Each student 'solves' the case, and groups based on similarity of solutions are formed. Each group then formulates a strong statement of position, and the groups debate or role-play their solutions. The instructor may describe what actually happened in the case, and the consequences, and then everyone compares their solutions with the results. The final step is for participants to try to apply this knowledge to their own job situations.

Role-play

This is another variation on the case study method, in which trainees act out a specific role, applying the theory instead of merely thinking passively about it. It becomes a dynamic learning process, particularly if closed-circuit television, which films the trainees playing their roles, is used to assess them. In role-play there are no rehearsals, because situations must be spontaneously acted out. A realistic representation should be allowed to develop, particularly when the topic deals with human relations. The instructor should first explain the human relations problem in a formal lecture. He or she then stipulates the roles that learners are to play, but not how they should play them. Learners then use their initiative and play the role as they perceive it ought to be played. The role-play starts with a given passage of dialogue and ends when the stipulated problems have been solved and the situation has been brought to a conclusion. At the end, the instructor comments on the observed actions. Role-play can be effectively used to give learners insight into interpersonal problems. It makes them aware of their attitudes towards others and it creates opportunities for them to improve their ability to deal with human relations issues. It is important for trainees to understand that this method involves serious learning and that each participant needs to be positive towards change, otherwise the exercise will not be successful.

In-basket training

This is also called the in-tray exercise. The trainee is given a number of letters, messages, reports, and telephone messages that would typically come across a manager's desk. These items range from urgent to routine handling. The trainee must act on the information contained in these items. He or she has to analyse each item and decide how to carry out the tasks. Afterwards, the decisions are analysed and evaluated by the instructor. Trainees are normally not allowed to communicate with one another during this type of exercise; they are thus compelled to undertake independent thinking and problem solving.

The method can be effectively used to analyse trainees' decision-making abilities in order to identify further training needs. It can also be used to develop their managerial skills and provide them with practice in decision-making. This method is often used in assessment-centre training.

The Kepner-Tregoe technique

This variation on the in-basket method resembles case studies in that material about an organisation is provided in writing ahead of time. It also involves role-play, and each trainee is assigned one, two, or even five roles which he or she is required to play in the hypothetical organisation. Each trainee plays a role for approximately ninety minutes and then switches roles. Trainees are then evaluated on their performance in each role. Once again, some problems are more urgent than others, and trainees have to distinguish the important from the unimportant in order to make decisions. This method claims to make trainees better aware of the managerial decision-making process, and it also improves problem-solving skills if teams work together on the exercises.

Management games

Management games, also called business games, are a development of the in-basket and role-play methods. Trainees play various roles in an imaginary business situation over a period of time. A business game usually involves two or more hypothetical organisations competing against each other in a given product market, and participants are assigned the roles of managing director, marketing manager, etc. They are required to take decisions on price levels, production volume, and inventory levels. Their decisions are manipulated in a computer to give results as in an actual business situation. The participants are then able to see how their decisions affect other groups, and vice versa. A lengthy business phase of five to ten years can be played in three to five hours. There are usually six to eight participants in a group representing a specific organisation. Two to five organisations can compete against each other simultaneously. The groups normally start off by controlling identical shares on the market and they then have to react to various stimuli presented to them.

The feedback session by the trainers is an important aspect of this method because it enables individuals and groups to evaluate their performance. Participants' performance and decision-making abilities are compared with those of other groups representing other hypothetical organisations. The advantage of this training is that if a group makes a mistake that costs their hypothetical organisation a few million Rand, they do not lose their jobs. They will, however, learn to exercise caution when making decisions in a real-life situation.

Syndicate training

This is also a variation on the case study method, and combines lectures and group work in small groups of about five to ten trainees. Instructors formulate points that should be considered by their groups. After the groups' deliberations, each trainee writes a report which is then criticised and discussed by other members of the group. Finally, group decisions are arrived at and discussed by the instructor and the other groups. This method gives each trainee a chance to participate in group discussions, especially about complex tasks. Problem-solving ability is improved by deciding what is relevant and what is irrelevant. This form of training can also bring about changes in attitudes and behaviour in individuals and groups.

Conference method

Group discussions are conducted according to an organised plan in which the trainer seeks to develop knowledge and understanding by obtaining verbal participation from all the trainees. This method has advantages over the lecture method, because each trainee plays an active role. Learning is achieved by building on the ideas contributed by the various participants. Thus, one trainee learns from another. Groups should be limited to fifteen to twenty participants, who should sit facing one another around a conference table, rather than in rows as in a classroom. The responses of trainees are recorded on a chalkboard, and the discussion is summarised by the instructor. Interest tends to be high because this method stimulates talk about problems and issues which can be examined from different points of view. It can also be used to reduce dogmatism and to modify attitudes, because trainees participate in finding solutions and reaching conclusions, and because many different points of view are heard and expressed.

Brainstorming

This is also sometimes called 'free wheeling'. Brainstorming seeks creative thinking rather than practical analysis. Small groups of participants meet, with or without conscious knowledge of the subject, and submit any solution or idea that occurs to them, no matter how strange or impossible it may sound. Trainees do not consider the practicality of ideas. They list all ideas generated and place the list where all the participants can see it. Later all the ideas or solutions are examined and assessed to determine how practical or acceptable each might be. The time period for such an exercise is usually five to twenty minutes. Brainstorming is primarily used to develop novel ideas to solve problems, and to encourage creativity and participation among trainees. Note that the number of ideas is more important than their quality, because the prerequisite for this method is the suspension of all judgement and of all evaluative or analytical discussion until the group has drained itself of ideas. To ensure the success of this method, participants should represent a variety of disciplines and management functions in the organisation. Brainstorming is a form of synergism because it produces a result that is better than the members could have achieved had they been working on the project individually.

University programmes not for degrees

University programmes give managers a new perspective on their organisations, helping them to change their outlook on events around them. Courses of this nature are ideal for middle and top managers with the potential to broaden their perspective, to prepare them for the highest positions in their organisations. Such programmes are aimed at adapting a manager's attitude to changing circumstances and providing him or her with up-to-date information on a broad front. Examples are the Management Development Programme (MDP) and the Senior Management Programme (SMP) of the University of Pretoria's Graduate School of Management. In these programmes, the teaching staff act as equals rather than superiors, and serve as moderators and discussion leaders rather than teachers. In this way, executives gain maximum benefit from these courses in an adult teaching environment. Managers expand their knowledge and learn about theories and procedures that they would not encounter on the job. University programmes are also popular for career development.

Sabbaticals

Sabbaticals provide managers with the opportunity for mind stretching, particularly those who have been in business for a number of years. Managers should be granted one academic year (sabbatical) in every ten years of employment. The sabbatical should be planned well in advance, to give an assistant the opportunity to understudy the superior's position and gain experience in it while the superior is away. A variation is to allow top managers who are experts in certain fields to be assigned to academic institutions for a time to teach. This gives such managers an opportunity to refresh their knowledge, update facts in a different environment, and advance their own development. It provides students with an opportunity to learn practical know-how from seasoned business people. Such an exchange programme could be of great benefit to South African students who need practical knowledge of the business environment, since many students are rapidly moved into managerial positions because of the dire shortage of managerial personnel the country is experiencing.

Programmed instruction

In this method, the material is presented in small, carefully sequenced fragments, usually called 'frames'. Each frame elicits a response from the learner, who immediately finds out whether or not the response was correct. If the response was correct the trainee can proceed to the next frame. This method can be used at odd times and in odd places. Trainees use books because machinery is not necessary and, consequently, the learners can study either at home or at work. A high degree of learner motivation is, however, necessary for this method to succeed, because progress depends on the learner. The greater the learner's motivation, the faster and more effective the learning will be.

Programmed instruction provides knowledge rather than skills. The method is useful for learning concepts, particularly in relation to interpersonal behaviour.

The advantages of programmed instruction are as follows:
- the learner is presented with instruction in small incremental steps requiring frequent responses;
- there is an overt participation interaction, or two-way communication, between the learner and the instructional programme;
- the learner receives immediate feedback, informing him or her on progress;
- reinforcement is used to strengthen learning;
- the sequence of lessons is meticulously controlled and consistent; and
- the instructional programme shapes and controls behaviour.

Computer training

This is an extension of programmed instruction and uses computers as a tool. The speed of presentation and the limited dependence on an instructor are major

advantages of this method. Various methods can be utilised, namely:
- computer-assisted instruction (CAI);
- computer-managed instruction (CMI);
- computer-based training (CBT);
- computer-mediated education (CME);
- computer-based multimedia (CBM); and
- interactive video training(IVT).

The method a trainer selects will depend on the cost of the method, the number of trainees, the availability of skilled trainers, and whether the desired training result warrants the method.

Lectures

Lectures remain an essential method for supervisory and management training and hold considerable advantages, particularly flexibility and economy. A good lecturer can achieve excellent results within a short space of time, provided lectures are carefully structured and presented. Lectures are seldom presented on their own; they are usually accompanied by a variety of audio-visual aids and tools. Some of these can also be used on their own. The most common training aids are:
- *Films and video-tape recordings.* These can be used to good effect in training, in particular to explain principles and theories, and to present case studies, etc. They should, however, be used in combination with other methods. For example, slides, tapes, flip charts, and the chalkboard can enhance lectures and films.
- *Closed-circuit television.* Videotape recordings of role-play situations are often used to give trainees direct feedback on their behaviour. They are often used in interpersonal skills training and team building exercises because they let trainees see a recording of their own behaviour. Trainees can use videotape recordings to make detailed analyses of their skills.
- *Overhead projectors, magnetic boards, and flip charts* are other tools that can be used to supplement a lecture.

Action learning

Managerial development has become important for organisations to remain competitive, since their original training quickly becomes outdated.

Action learning is a way to give managers challenging jobs with support systems to help them learn, because it is the study of real-life problems and solutions provided within a real-life environment. It, therefore, provides challenges for managers and demands the transformation of problems into opportunities. Action learning is clearly demonstrated in Table 20.6, where it is compared with traditional learning.

20.10.2 On-the-job training

On-the-job training methods usually fit the needs of a particular employee and suit his or her background, knowledge, and skills. Trainees learn by doing; they learn continuously and over a long period. Their immediate superiors extensively influence trainees; superiors are usually directly responsible for the training of their subordinates. According to Ferrell and Hirt (1993:322) on-the-job methods are regarded as allowing workers to learn by actually performing the tasks of the job. New employees work under the guidance of an experienced employee, who can offer advice and suggestions for performing the job efficiently and effectively.

On-the-job training can, however, prevent trainees from acquiring a broad perspective and can adversely influence their perception of their job and how it fits into the activities of the organisation.

Table 20.6 Comparing action learning with traditional learning

Traditional learning	Action learning
• Individual-based	• Group-based
• Knowledge emphasis	• Skills emphasis
• Input-orientated	• Output-orientated
• Classroom-based	• Work-based
• Passive	• Active
• Memory tested	• Competence tested
• Focus on past	• Focus on present and future
• Standard cases	• Real cases
• One-way communication	• Interactive
• Teacher-lead	• Student-lead

SOURCE: Swanepoel et al. (2000:516).

The methods below are generally used for on-the-job training or development.

Coaching

This is also called counselling. It entails the instruction of a subordinate by his or her superior with the purpose of developing the subordinate's potential. It includes daily guidance by the superior to develop the subordinate in his or her present position and to prepare him or her for promotion. It is a continuous process of learning, based on the face-to-face relationship between superior and subordinate.

Coaching is a low-cost means of improving employees' performance. Solutions to problems can be found, and subordinates can be given the opportunity to make suggestions to superiors regarding the work they do. It enables a superior to set tasks and to check the standard of work done. It is, however, only effective if the subordinates understand the relevance and value of their work and if the coaching is systematic and purposeful. The relationship between the superior and subordinates must be based on mutual trust if the method is to succeed.

Although many organisations use coaching and counselling as either a formal or an informal management development technique, it is not without its problems. Coaching and counselling fail when inadequate time is set aside for them, when subordinates are not allowed to make any mistakes, if rivalry develops, or if the dependency needs of the subordinate are not recognised or accepted by the superior.

Job rotation

Job rotation is a method whereby trainees receive training and gain experience, in turn, under close supervision. According to Skinner and Ivancevich (1992:383) job rotation means that 'managers are transferred from job to job on a systematic basis. Job assignments can last from two weeks to six months'. It is used to develop generalists, with wide experience of the organisation, to enable them to make high-level decisions later in their careers. By rotating through various jobs, learners cultivate a fresh approach, which will enable them to establish new procedures and make changes in their existing jobs. Trainees are moved into new jobs for short periods of time. They need to be extensively briefed as to what is expected of them, and their progress must be carefully checked. This method enables trainees to acquire specific practical experience quickly, instead of having to wait for opportunities to present themselves over a period of time through transfers and promotions. Job rotation is also an invaluable method of inducting a young graduate.

Junior boards

This method, also called multiple management, is usually employed to give promising managers experience in analysing the overall problems of the organisation. These managers are given assignments by top management to study problems identified by top managers and to propose solutions. The members of junior boards, mostly promising middle and junior managers, usually rotate to ensure the continuity of the board's work in the organisation. This is an effective development method only if the problems assigned to the junior board are genuinely company-wide and cut across all departmental lines. Junior boards are not usually granted authority to take decisions, but merely to investigate and analyse problems and propose solutions to top management.

Job instruction training

This is a precise method for teaching a trainee to do a specific job. It compels all trainees to learn in a standard fashion. It is a way of quickly expanding manual and psychomotor skills, and is particularly applicable to lower-level workers. A number of steps are followed. The trainer decides what the employees are to be taught and ensures that the right tools, equipment, supplies, and materials are ready, and the workplace is properly arranged. Once this is done, trainees are instructed by means of the following four steps:

- *Preparing the workers.* The trainer puts the workers at ease, explains what the job is, and finds out what they already know about it. He or she gets workers interested in learning the job.
- *Presentation of the operation.* The trainer now describes, demonstrates, and illustrates the new operation. He or she questions the learners to be sure that they have grasped the facts. Only one step should be given at a time, and key points should be stressed. The operation should be summarised in a second practical demonstration.
- *Performance try-out.* The learners are asked to perform the task while the trainer asks them the why, how, when, and where of the job. Instruction continues until the instructor can see that the trainees have mastered the job.
- *Follow-up.* Trainees now work on their own but their work is checked to ensure that they follow instructions. The learners work under close supervision until they are qualified to work under normal supervision.

Understudy

This method resembles coaching and job rotation in some respects. Understudy is the temporary assignment of a manager to a more senior manager, in order to broaden his or her managerial viewpoints by exposing him or her to various aspects of managerial practice. During a short period of time, the subordinate manager closely observes the activities of the senior manager and helps him or her to perform duties and, at the same, time is given the opportunity of being coached. The method usually provides a trainee with a broader perspective, because during training the senior manager carries out the work he or she normally does. Giving junior managers understudy assignments, provides the organisation with a pool of potential managers who have been carefully observed and evaluated and who could, if they were successful as understudies, be promoted at a later date to a higher level of authority in the organisation. It is also a popular career development method. It is, therefore, a practical and fairly quick way of preparing chosen junior managers for greater management responsibility. The motivation to learn is usually high because 'learning by doing' is emphasised.

Learner-controlled instruction

This method allows trainees to decide on the pace at which they choose to learn, as well as the specific methods used and the sequence of learning steps. They also evaluate their own learning. Methods that could be used are, for instance, case studies, simulations, group discussions, books, and films. The instructor only acts as facilitator and offers assistance to the trainees. There are no set lesson plans and no examinations. The instructors set learning objectives with the learners' participation. The learners themselves are expected to be accountable for meeting these agreed-upon objectives. This method is usually used in conjunction with other methods.

20.10.3 Learnership training (previously apprenticeship training)

This type of training dates back to biblical times. It is used to train workers in trades such as tool-making, armature-winding, electronics, and diesel mechanics. The major characteristic is that the learner works under the guidance of a skilled artisan. Trainees receive training mainly at two sites – on the shop floor and at vocational schools. One of the main characteristics of learnership training is its inter-linkage with the production process. Not only is it a more cost-effective way of training, but it also enables the trainee to make contact with the working world right from the start. A learner enters into a contract, which can be registered only if the trade has been designated, and the conditions of the learnership have been prescribed. These designated trades and conditions vary in South Africa, since they depend on the needs of a particular industry. Contract conditions include qualification requirements for a learnership, periods of apprenticeship, remuneration, technical studies required, centralised technical training, and the use of logbooks, all of which are covered by Chapters 4 and 5 of the Skills Development Act No. 97 of 1998.

20.10.4 Vestibule training

In vestibule training the trainee learns the job in an environment that simulates the real working environment as closely as possible; an example is the simulated cockpit of an aircraft used to train airline pilots in operating a specific aircraft type.

Vestibule training is especially appropriate when the job to be learned involves the operation of a new machine, repetitive processes, or is performed in an area too full of distractions to permit effective learning. An advantage of this style of training is that there are none of the production requirements and pressures of the real work situation. The trainee is not under stress to maintain a standard of production from the outset, nor is he or she held accountable for high reject rates in the early stages of training. Once employees meet the standards, they move on to the job itself.

20.11 Issues inherently applicable to training and development in the South African context

Owing to the peculiarities of the South African situation, which are legacies of the past, various other factors impact on training and development, and need to be borne in mind when executing training.

20.11.1 Adult learning

Workplace training and development programmes in South Africa must take particular cognisance of the fact that learners are adults (quite often illiterate or semi-literate) who require different teaching methods to children. Adults and children learn in fundamentally different ways. Androgogy is the study of how adults learn, as opposed to pedagogy, which investigates how children learn.

While children are more often characterised as learning for curiosity's sake or just for the sake of learning, adults are more oriented towards learning for application in the near future. The reasons most frequently mentioned for adult learning episodes are problems on the job, in preparing for an occupation, at home, personal responsibilities, and improving some area of competence related to recreation or hobbies.

The literature suggests the following characteristics of adult learners, and different training approaches which facilitate adult learning:
- Adults prefer to plan their own learning projects and to adopt a self-directed approach towards learning. This is derived from a desire to set their own pace, establish their own structure, and keep open the option to revise the learning strategy.
- Adults possess a vast reservoir of experience, which can greatly facilitate the learning process. Adults approach learning with a fairly well-defined cognitive map. This map is based on their experience in the world, and the older they are the more detailed their map is likely to be. Adults should, therefore, be made aware of how the newly-acquired knowledge will supplement their existing knowledge and what benefits they stand to derive from it.
- Adults act from internal motivation, which originates from the need to grow and develop to self-realisation. The lecture material should, accordingly, be meaningful to learners and should relate to their objectives and work situation.
- Adults are problem- and task-orientated in their approach to the learning process. They learn best if learning is built around their practical living and working environment. Instead of presenting subject matter to be memorised, the trainer should present it as problems that have to be investigated and solved.

Table 20.7 is a summary of the differences between the child and adult in the learning situation.

20.11.2 Diversity training

The changing demographics and socio-political scene in South Africa are having a significant impact on communities, organisations, society, and the nation. Employee morale, productivity, and success will depend on the way organisations manage the changing demographics of their current and future workers. (See also Chapter 17 in this regard.)

Theories on training usually assume that the workforce is homogeneous. In South Africa that may be counterproductive if they do not take into account the diverse

Table 20.7 Summary of learning characteristics

Characteristic	Child	Adult
1 Need to know	Need determined by teacher	Needs to know why before learning
2 Learner's experience	Little or no experience	Great volume and quality of experience
3 Concept of learner	Dependent on teacher	Self-directing
4 Readiness to learn	Ready when told to learn	Ready when need is experienced
5 Orientation to learning	Activities are subject-centred	Activities are life- or task-centred
6 Motivation to learn	Largely extrinsic	Largely intrinsic
7 Authority	Dependent on teacher	Self-dependent and self-responsible
8 Responsibility	Little or no responsibility	Co-responsibility

SOURCE: Van Dyk et al. (2001).

composition of the South African workforce. To assist organisations to retain productive workers, maintain high employee morale, and foster understanding and harmony among culturally diverse workers, diversity training presents one solution.

To be effective, diversity training must be designed to change the myths of diversity (such as affirmative action training), to educate participants about the realities of diversity, and to offer ways to respond to the challenge of valuing and managing diversity in the workplace.

20.11.3 Recognition of prior learning

The identification of training needs should take cognisance of the realities which exist in South Africa, and include the recognition of prior learning (RPL) although it often has no documented or certificated proof. The RPL approach has become popular in South Africa over the last number of years because of its informal evolution and the restricted access to education and training for historically disadvantaged groups. The high profile RPL is enjoying is because it brings hope for many people, especially those from historically disadvantaged communities, who have acquired capabilities outside the formal learning system for which they receive no formal recognition.

RPL is the verification of skills, knowledge, and abilities obtained through training, education, and work and life experiences (Meyer 1996:89). Put another way, it is the verification of competence no matter how it was achieved. According to Meyer, RPL must be managed according to certain principles, namely:

- sound assessment principles must be applied;
- competence should be evaluated against defined unit standards;
- a variety of assessment methods should be used; and
- a procedure should be applied enabling a learner or employer to have access to RPL evaluation processes.

20.11.4 The training of supervisors in South Africa

Supervisors control the activities of lower-level employees and, through those employees in their charge, they are responsible for carrying out the policy and achieving the objectives of management. Supervisors not only act as a model and example to subordinates but also form the link between higher-level management and lower-level employees. For this reason, it is essential that supervisors fulfil their role effectively.

Supervisors' jobs can be divided into two parts: supervisory work, which deals with planning, organising, directing, and controlling a subordinate's work; and technical work, which covers everything else in the job. For the technical part of the job the supervisor will need on-going technical training for the job that he or she was initially employed for. Technical training, however, falls outside the scope of supervisory training, which is concerned only with the non-technical or supervisory part of a supervisor's job.

The Institute of People Management (Fact Sheet 14) suggests the following questions to check whether a supervisor is doing his or her job effectively. The supervisor requires assistance if the answer to any of the following questions is 'yes', and he or she should receive training in the identified area.
- Does the supervisor fail to get the best out of the workers?
- Has he or she failed to tell them what they are doing and why they are doing it?
- Is absenteeism among people under his or her supervision high?
- Is discipline poor?
- Are workers often late?
- Is the labour turnover in his or her department high compared with other departments?
- Do new employees working under the supervisor leave within the first three months?
- Is the accident rate high?
- Does it happen regularly that management hears of accidents under his or her supervision too late to take effective action?
- Is the supervisor often overloaded with work while his or her subordinates are under-utilised?

The three most common weaknesses of existing supervisory staff are, according to Wood (1995) a lack of assertiveness, unwillingness to make decisions, and lack of planning skills. Against this background the question can be asked whether the successful supervisor displays attributes that distinguish him or her from the unsuccessful supervisor. Wood (1995) detected the following attributes among successful supervisors in the footwear industry:
- a willingness to teach others;
- self-control;
- advice-seeking skill;
- understanding of individual psychology;
- self-planning skill;
- motivation skill;
- quality orientation;
- positive expectations;
- assertiveness;
- productivity;
- self-organising skill;
- accurate self-perception;
- manager-assisting skill;
- loyalty to the company;
- idea-generation skill;
- role understanding; and
- conceptualising skill.

An analysis of these traits in those individuals who were promoted to supervisors found that the majority of the attributes are related to self-management and describe the behaviour of the individual before promotion, and that six of these attributes are relevant to the actual work of a supervisor.

Building on the personal attributes that are vital for any supervisor to be effective, a training programme for supervisors should also concentrate on the knowledge and skills that supervisors need to manage their jobs successfully. The Institute for People Management (Fact Sheet 217) lists

a number of knowledge and skills areas for supervisory training:
- an understanding of their role in the organisation;
- problem-solving and decision-making;
- planning;
- organisation;
- time management (their own time and that of others);
- delegation;
- giving instructions;
- the empowerment of subordinates;
- control;
- leadership;
- effective communication (both verbal and written);
- the bridging of communication barriers;
- teamwork and the initiation of team leader strategies;
- the effective chairing of meetings;
- the management of change;
- an understanding of how the organisation functions;
- understanding employee behaviour;
- handling conflict;
- implementing quality procedures;
- giving effective feedback;
- effective cooperation with workers, peers, and managers; and
- carrying out recruitment and making appointments.

These aspects will give supervisors an overall grasp of their work, which means that they will have a holistic understanding of their job. There are also broad organisational and socio-economic factors that directly influence supervisors in their work environment, and that should also be covered in training.

- *Understanding and implementation of the organisation's policies and rules.* Supervisors may be expected to know and understand the policies and practices relating to, for example, job evaluation, grading, and wage deductions. However, many supervisors lack a basic understanding of policies, practices and structures. Training should, therefore, focus on these issues.
- *Human resources policy.* Concepts such as the NQF and the RPL should also be explained as part of a training programme; not only as a matter of interest, but also as to how they can benefit supervisors and the employees working under them.
- *Employment relations.* The recognition of trade unions through legislation has brought about changes in the power and authority of supervisors. Their authority has been modified, and often even eroded. Supervisors need to be trained to deal with trade union officials and shop stewards, as well as with workers who are trade union members. Unacceptable behaviour on the part of the supervisor in dealing with these workers cannot be tolerated, as the consequences for the organisation are too great. Therefore, training in employment relations is of great importance in South Africa's work environment. (See Chapter 5 for more detail in this regard.)
- *Inter-group conflict in the work situation.* Supervisors have long been recognised as key figures in socio-political problems and problems related to cultural diversity in South Africa. This is because the relationship between themselves and their subordinates is so significant. Supervisors' values and attitudes often shape the attitudes and behaviour of their co-workers and subordinates. Therefore, if supervisors received interpersonal relations training at this level, they could contribute significantly to peace and stability in the workplace. The effectiveness of a supervisor in minimising inter-group conflict depends on his or her values and knowledge of company policy and of other management aspects (see Chapter 6).

- *Interpersonal contact and social interaction.* It is well known that inter-group stereotyping and prejudice can be alleviated by contact between members of the different groups. Frequent informal social events should be organised within the organisation. Diversity training to develop an understanding between different race groups and training to develop interpersonal skills could promote better relations in the working environment.

Various challenges face illiterate supervisors in South Africa in order to do their job well, as discussed in Encounter 20.1.

20.11.5 Benefits of training and development to an organisation

Now that training and development have been discussed, it should be easy for the reader to identify with the following benefits to an organisation. Rothwell and Kazanas (1994:398) present these as follows.
Training and development:
- lead to improved profitability and/or more positive attitudes toward profit orientation;
- improve job knowledge and skills at all levels of the organisation;
- help people identify with organisational goals;
- help create a better corporate image;
- foster authenticity, openness, and trust;
- improve the relationship between boss and subordinate;
- aid in organisational development;
- help prepare guidelines for work;
- aid in understanding and carrying out organisational policies;
- provide information for future needs in all areas of the organisation;
- lead to more effective decision-making and problem-solving;
- aid in development for promotion from within;
- aid in developing leadership skill, motivation, loyalty, better attitudes, and other aspects that successful workers and managers usually display;
- aid in increasing productivity and/or quality of work;
- help keep costs down in many areas, e.g. production, and personnel administration;
- develop a sense of responsibility to the organisation for compence and knowledge;
- improve labour-management relations;
- reduce outside consulting costs by utilising competent internal consulting;
- stimulate preventive management, as opposed to putting out fires;
- eliminate sub-optimal behaviour (such as hiding tools);
- create an appropriate climate for growth and communication;
- aid in improving organisational communication;
- help employees adjust to change; and
- aid in handling conflict, thereby helping to prevent stress and tension.

Benefits to the individual, in turn, should benefit the organisation. Here, training and development:
- help the individual in making better decisions and effective problem-solving;
- internalise and operationalise the motivational variables of recognition, achievement, growth, responsibility, and advancement;
- aid in encouraging and achieving self-development and self-confidence;
- help a person handle stress, tension, frustration, and conflict;
- provide information for improving leadership, knowledge, communication skills, and attitudes;
- increase job satisfaction and recognition;

Encounter 20.1 Illiterate supervisors: the South African challenges

Once organisations are convinced that immediate training is vital and agree to go ahead, they discover a critical obstacle. In order to participate in supervisory-level workshops and training programmes, supervisors must be literate.

Out of a population of 43 million, English is the mother tongue of only 8,7 per cent of South Africans, while 43 per cent can speak it as a second or third language, yet it is the most common language for supervisory training.

Three forms of literacy can be identified:
- Traditional literacy, the ability to read and write in an academic setting;
- Functional literacy, the ability to comprehend and use information that people need to participate effectively in society; and
- Workplace literacy, encompassing basic communication and computation skills required to successfully perform the day-to-day operations of a job. This is the form of literacy that employees are most concerned with, because of its direct connection to work, to quality and to job performance.

With the advent of new thinking, many organisations embarked on training programmes for their workers, including supervisors. The typical question that came to the fore was, 'How am I expected to teach these people when they can't read?' Possible solutions to this problem are to:
- Minimise the written work by designing exercises for small-group discussion.
- Simplify the language by rewriting text books to make them easier to read, use short simple questions, short paragraphs, lots of white space, and replace difficult words with easier to read synonyms.
- Build into the programme the major principles of adult learning, such as:
  - participants should see the immediate practical value of what they are learning;
  - the curriculum should include materials and tasks that apply to the specific needs of supervisors;
  - experimental learning situations should be created with exercises relating to on-the-job uses;
  - participants should be given ample opportunity to succeed and be treated as intelligent adults, learners should be addressed and the learning process should be enjoyable; and
  - the programme should be highly interactive, with participants realising that the focus of the training is not directed at the trainer but that the students are leading the training themselves.
- Use competent trainers who can 'switch gears' between the literate and illiterate supervisors.
- Select a highly visual format for transferring knowledge and skill. Rely on the old adage 'a picture is worth more than a thousand words'.

SOURCE: Kats (1994). Adapted by the authors.

- move a person toward personal goals, while improving interaction skills;
- satisfy the personal needs of the trainer and the trainee;
- provide the trainee with an avenue for growth, and a say in his or her own future;
- develop a sense of growth in learning;
- help a person develop speaking, listening, and writing skills; and
- help eliminate fear in attempting new tasks.

Benefits in human relations, intra- and inter-group relations, and policy implementation impact positively on the organisation.

Training and development:
- improve communication between groups and individuals;
- assist in the orientation of new employees and those taking new jobs through transfer or promotion;
- provide information on equal opportunity and affirmative action;
- provide information on other laws and administrative policies;
- improve interpersonal skills;
- make organisational policies, rules, and regulations viable;
- improve morale;
- build cohesiveness in groups;
- provide a good climate for learning, growth, and co-ordination; and
- make the organisation a better place in which to work and live.

20.12 Career management

Career management is part of the throughput process and occurs in the job context environment. The interaction of career management in the various environments has a direct influence on the development, status, and recognition of workers in the job content environment. In the job context environment it has an influence on management philosophy, leadership, working conditions, and inter-group and intra-group relations.

It is to the advantage of any organisation to retain productive employees for as long as possible. Earlier in this chapter, the use of training and development to make employees more productive in an organisation was discussed. A further means, closely linked to training and development, is for the organisation to invite employees to treat their relationship with their employer as a career. Ideally, there should be sufficient opportunities and promotion possibilities to enable employees to remain with their employer for the duration of their working lives.

The long-term interests of employees should be protected by the organisation, and employees should be encouraged to grow and realise their full potential for the benefit of the organisation. If the career planning and development of employees is effective, they will realise their full potential and will probably be prepared to remain with their present employer till retirement. This trend is, however, decreasing and more and more employees change jobs more frequently than before, not only in their own country, but literally from country to country. The world is really starting to become a global village in terms of the international job market, as international barriers fall away and the mobility of professionals, in particular, increases rapidly.

Succession planning in an organisation is essential to ensure that suitably qualified and experienced employees are available when vacancies arise, and to fill human resources needs that result from the growth and reorientation of the organisation in the economic environment in which it operates. Employee succession and filling of new jobs, particularly management jobs, are therefore essential for the survival of any organisation.

Career management has become a crucial issue in South Africa, and one reason is that many organisations are controlled by their founders, or the families of the founders. The success of a number of organisations listed on the Johannesburg Stock Exchange is attributed, at least in the public mind, to the continued good health and leadership of a single founder-owner. However, with the rapid development of the South African economy, organisations of this nature will jeopardise their position if they do not implement career planning and development or succession in posts.

Scores of small and medium-sized organisations in South Africa are in this position, and they will suffer losses if the founder-owner should die suddenly.

In South Africa, it is more important than ever before that large organisations draw up five-year career management plans, medium-sized organisations draw up three-year plans, and small organisations plan to implement career management within a year to meet changed market demands for human resources.

A career can be defined as a series of jobs that follow a hierarchy of levels or degrees of difficulty, responsibility and status (Graham & Bennett 1993:389).

Career planning may be defined as the process by which an individual analyses his or her work situation, specifies his or her career goals, and plans various means to achieve these goals.

To plan a career, an employee must set certain career priorities, evaluate the behaviour and attitude of other people who have successfully achieved such a career, choose a type of work that makes use of his or her strong points, undergo the necessary training and, where possible, get a good mentor to guide him or her. The individual must then regularly monitor his or her progress against the goals that have been set, investigate shortcomings and, where necessary, re-plan.

A *career path* is regarded, from the organisation's point of view, as flexible lines of progression through which an employee typically moves in his or her career. By following an established career path, the employee participates in career development with the assistance of the organisation.

Career development is defined as a formal approach taken by the organisation to ensure that employees with proper qualifications and experience are available when they are needed by the organisation.

An important question is who is responsible for career planning and development. The answer is that it normally requires effort from three sources – the organisation itself, the employee's immediate manager, and the employee.

- *The organisation's responsibilities.* An organisation cannot and should not bear the sole responsibility for planning and developing an employee's career. The organisation has to furnish career opportunities for its employees and advise employees about the various career paths that are available in that organisation to enable them to achieve their career goals. The human resources department is generally responsible for relaying this information to employees and informing staff when new jobs are created and old ones are phased out. The human resources department, therefore, needs to work closely with individual employees and their superiors to ensure that their career goals are realistic and are followed within the constraints of the organisation.
- *The employee's immediate superior.* This person, although he or she is not expected to be a professional counsellor, can and should take part in facilitating his or her immediate subordinate's career planning. The superior should act as communicator, counsellor, appraiser, coach and mentor, ensuring that the subordinate employee gets the information necessary for furthering his or her career. It is unfortunate that many super-

iors do not see it as part of their duties to assist in the career development of their subordinates. Either they do not know how to go about it or they see every subordinate as a potential threat to their own positions, so they give no assistance, and may even exert a negative influence.
- *The individual employee.* The final responsibility for career planning and development rests with individual employees because they know what they want from their careers and how hard they are prepared to work.

Successful career planning and development is, therefore, a joint effort by the individual employee, his or her immediate superior, and the organisation: the employee does the planning, the immediate superior provides the resources, and the organisation provides the means and structure for development.

The rest of this section is devoted to the importance of career management, career choices employees should make, the various career stages of employees, legislation that assists employers with career choices for employees in South Africa, a more detailed analysis of career planning and development itself, and a practical five-step approach that employers and employees can use for career management.

20.12.1 The importance of career management to employers and employees

For the organisation the major purpose of career management is to match the employee's needs, abilities, and goals with the current or future needs of the organisation. This is intended to ensure that the organisation places the right employee in the right place at the right time, and so to offer the employee the opportunity of achieving personal fulfilment in the job. Matching the employee with the job is the first step, which entails matching the employee's potential with the requirements of the job, and the employee's needs with the job reward, as discussed in the chapters on recruitment and selection.

The reasons for implementing career management in organisations include the following:
- To cope with global competition and the threats of highly increased mobility of professional employees, in particular.
- Employees wish to have control over their own careers, and the new generation of younger employees wants greater job satisfaction and more career options. Being given the ability to advance increases the quality of work life of employees.
- It is necessary today for organisations to avoid obsolescence by encouraging employees to learn new skills. This is because rapid changes in technology and changes in consumer demand cause skills to become outdated. With career development programmes, employees can gain new skills when their old skills are no longer in demand.
- Career management reduces staff turnover in the organisation. Employees experience less frustration and greater job satisfaction because they know they can advance in the organisation.
- When employees' specific talents have been identified, they are given the opportunity through career planning to perform better and to be placed in jobs that fit their ambitions and personal talents.

Career management integrates the objectives of the individual and the organisation in such a way that both will gain. The employee will experience satisfaction and personal development, while there will be increased productivity and creativity within the organisation.

The end result of career management is an organisation staffed by committed employees who are well trained and productive.

20.12.2 Career stages and choices

South Africa has a vast unskilled and semi-skilled population and small numbers of qualified personnel. Organisations, therefore, need to identify skills and talents quickly and embark on effective career development programmes, so that employees can contribute to the productivity of the organisation. The Human Sciences Research Council does research into the aptitudes, career choices, personalities, and so on, of employees. The various needs and the career and life stages of employees need to be taken into account when career planning and development programmes are being designed. Employees also need to analyse how a career choice should be made and developed.

Figure 20.4 shows that all people go through different but interrelated stages in their lives and careers. Depending on the stage they have reached in their lives and their careers, they have different needs. This should be borne in mind when careers are planned and developed. Most people prepare for an occupation in some formal educational institution like a high school, and then take their first job. They will eventually move to other jobs within the same organisation or join other organisations. Although the stages may vary, most employees go through all the stages indicated in Figure 20.4.

Analysis of the various career and life stages of people shows that the most important decision a person makes is what career to follow. It is generally accepted that what employees accomplish and derive from their careers will depend on the congruence between their personality

Figure 20.4 The relationship between people's most important needs and their career and life stages

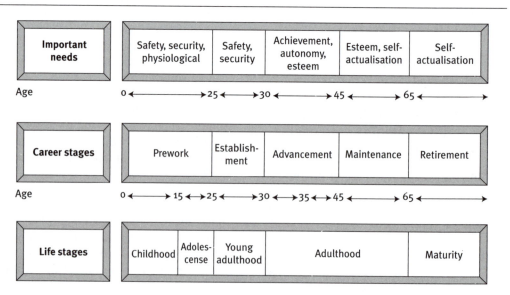

SOURCE: Adapted from Ivancevich (1995:494).

and the job environment. Each individual resembles one of six personality types, to some extent, and people choose their occupations in accordance with their personality, in order to follow a career that generally matches it. People sometimes have a combination of these personality characteristics. The personality types are:

- *Realistic:* individuals who prefer activities involving the use of machinery or tools; for example artisans, tool and die makers, farmers, engineers, and carpenters.
- *Investigative:* individuals who are analytical, curious, methodical, and precise; for example medical technologists, teachers, biologists, and astronomers.
- *Artistic:* people, who strive for self-expression, are non-conformist, original, and introspective; for example artists, musicians, photographers, sculptors, and actors.
- *Social:* individuals who enjoy helping and working with others, and who avoid systematic activities such as working with tools or machinery; for example police officers, social workers, and guidance counsellors.
- *Enterprising:* individuals who enjoy activities that permit them to influence others to accomplish their goals; for example computer salespeople, life assurance agents, estate agents, business managers, and lawyers.
- *Conventional:* individuals who enjoy the systematic use of data or reproduction of material; for example credit managers, office workers, accountants, and supermarket managers.

Depending on the personality type, alternatively referred to as 'career anchors' by some writers, an employee could find an occupation that suits his or her personality or combination of characteristics, and it would be a satisfactory career. Organisations should be flexible enough to provide alternatives for satisfying employees' varying career needs. Organisations should also recognise that not every employee is or wants to be the enterprising type.

20.12.3 Career planning

20.12.3.1 Career planning by the individual

We have stated that career planning is a process whereby an individual sets career goals and identifies the means to achieve them. The responsibility for career planning rests primarily with the individual, but he or she will need support from superiors and the organisation in general. Career planning begins with understanding oneself; each individual needs to identify his or her personality characteristics, as described above. Career planning is as important to a new job-seeker as it is to an adult worker already in employment. Adult workers planning their careers need to establish their present life stage and career stage (see Figure 20.6). As a person progresses through life, his or her priorities usually change. People also have different priorities in different life and career stages.

By introspection, individuals should decide what kind of person they are, what skills they possess, their values and interests, likes and dislikes, and strengths and weaknesses. They should draw up a balance sheet, listing their strengths on the left-hand side and weaknesses on the right. It may be necessary to make several lists because such repetition forces a person to discover more about his or her characteristics. On the basis of these lists a person might decide on a career in, say, a technical field instead of in the arts or management.

An employee should identify job opportunities in his or her organisation by asking:

- What are my prospects for promotion and transfer from my present job?

- What positions have my peers reached within the last year or two?
- What are the compensation ranges for various jobs in the organisation?
- Which division in the organisation has the fastest growth and, therefore, provides the best promotion opportunities? The employee might even consider changing jobs and accepting a lower grade job in the organisation to obtain a position that is an avenue for moving up faster in the organisation.

Employees should also study trends in the economy, for example where there are human resources shortages in various skills, what technological developments are taking place, and how government policy could shape the future job market. In South Africa, there is a particular shortage of managerial talent and technically competent artisans (see Chapter 19). These issues should be taken into consideration when career decisions are made and opportunities investigated.

The next step, after job trends and specific opportunities in the employment market have been analysed, is to set goals in terms of the personal strengths, weaknesses, interests, and values identified. Then short-term, medium-term, and long-term goals must be set in order to monitor growth in the chosen career. Goals should be consistent with a person's capabilities and compatible with his or her self-image, because unrealistic goals lead to frustration and disillusionment.

Once the goals have been set, the employee needs to prepare a plan to meet them. In drawing up this plan the employee needs to have discussions with superiors in the organisation and with members of the human resources department. They will assist him or her to implement the plan.

20.12.3.2 Career planning by the organisation

If an organisation is to be successful, it needs to ensure that sufficient numbers of qualified employees are available when vacancies occur or expansion takes place. Recruitment and selection is one means of ensuring this; on the other hand, an organisation can implement training and development and have recourse to promotion from within to achieve this goal. What is essential is that people must be groomed for posts, and planning must be instituted so that the right people are available for vacant positions when other people retire or resign or when the organisation expands. This process is a technique that outlines specific progression from one job to another by employees, according to the goals and needs of the organisation. It includes plans for a sequence of development activities which will give an individual job experience, enabling him or her to step into more advanced jobs in the future. The major aim of career planning programmes, therefore, is to ensure that the goals of the organisation are smoothly achieved through the utilisation of human resources.

To help employees with their career planning, employers should make information available about jobs and should create career options; they should help employees to set realistic career goals and to plan their careers.

Employers traditionally developed career paths for upward mobility because if a person could not move upward he or she had to leave the organisation. Today, enlightened organisations recognise that not everybody wants to follow a vertical career path and become the top executive; career paths can be developed with lateral, diagonal, and even downward career progression (for example, as a person nears retirement). In other words, when an employee's career is planned, the career path can be built in accordance with his or her goals, ensuring that the employee's job satisfaction remains of paramount importance. If the organisation synchronises its career planning activities with the career planning of the individual, the result is bound to be a positive response on the part of employees, and the organisation will have sufficiently qualified and motivated staff when vacancies occur.

In the modern era organisations have also come to the realisation that careers alone are not sufficient to retain employees, since a plateau can often jeopardise an employee's future career development. Consequently, the idea of a two-ladder-career approach has evolved; one being the traditional managerial ladder, and the other a professional ladder. The latter implies that an employee (e.g. an engineer, advisor, or legal specialist) who has not had the opportunity to move up the managerial ladder may move up a technical or professional job ladder. This can be substituted for the steps in the managerial career, and the employee may remain in the organisation instead of resigning in order to move up in his or her career elsewhere. This approach has been adopted in various semi-governmental organisations, such as the military service, police, and correctional services where doctors, lawyers, social workers, etc. can follow their own professional ladders, instead of the rank-orientated managerial structures. Such staff often attain remuneration and fringe benefit levels which are higher than those they would occupy in the managerial structure.

20.12.4 Career development

As we have mentioned, career development is a formal approach by the organisation to ensure that employees with proper qualifications and experience are available when needed. To realise this goal, the organisation needs to support career development and be committed to it. The immediate superior of the employee is of cardinal importance in providing support, advice and feedback, but the employee is ultimately responsible for his or her own career development. Employees proceed from one job to another in a certain sequence. It is generally accepted that the right sequence of jobs contributes materially to career development. Firstly, career development starts with the job itself. Each day the employee faces different challenges and different tasks to be mastered. What is learned at work often has a greater influence than formally planned development activities. Secondly, different jobs demand different skills: a supervisor needs human relations skills, and a training specialist needs teaching skills and technical knowledge. Development can take place when a person is assigned a job for which he or she has not yet developed the necessary skills, and he or she would learn the skills while doing the job. Thirdly, a transfer might help an employee to acquire the skills and knowledge needed for a further promotion. Fourthly, a rational sequence of job assignments can reduce the time required for an employee to develop the necessary skills for a chosen target job. If particular jobs teach particular skills, a series of job assignments should be selected that will provide the best means of development over the course of an employee's career.

Career development programmes can use both formal and informal means. Informal means would, for example, be on-the-job training or off-the-job training, but within the organisation. Alternatively, the trainee can participate in off-the-job programmes away from the organisation; for example, seminars and short courses provided by technikons, universities, and the Institute of People Management. If employees want to be successful in their careers, they must be on the constant lookout for the best career opportunities. In addition, they must keep their options open; not waste time working for a manager who procrastinates; ensure that they are vital subordinates to a proactive superior; strive for exposure and visibility in the organisation; be prepared to present themselves when jobs become vacant; leave the organisation if their career development slows down too much; be ready to resign if necessary and not let success in their present job jeopardise their career plan, because it would reduce their upward mobility.

20.12.4.1 Career development methods

The most important methods used in carrying out career development are outlined below.
- *Performance appraisal.* The organisation can use performance appraisal as a valuable tool for career development, because the strengths and weaknesses of employees are assessed.
- *Workshops.* Through workshops lasting two or three days, employees can be actively assisted with the planning and development of their careers.
- *Career counselling.* The human resources department or outsiders can assist employees by counselling them on their careers.
- *Tailor-made materials.* Some organisations provide material that has been specifically developed to assist employees in their career development and planning, for example company brochures showing future plans and expansion. Assessment-centre material is devised which portrays a specific organisation's activities and needs.
- *Management by objectives.* This could be an excellent means of assisting employees with career development, because superiors and subordinates jointly agree on ways to achieve the organisation's goals, while also taking employees' personal goals into account. When goals are not achieved, new development needs may be identified and included in employees' career development.

20.12.4.2 Career development for retirement

Career development for retirement is the last logical step in the career management process.

Employers should not retrench or dismiss staff lightly, but rather focus on retraining employees for a new career. Retirement via retrenchment has become so widespread in South Africa during the last few years, that employees under the age of forty are given the option to retire voluntarily. This means that a second or even a third career will have to be embarked upon before an employee reaches genuine retirement, which normally occurs at age sixty-five or older. Organisations, therefore, have a wider responsibility to not only retire employees but, if they are younger, to assist them with career development for a new and sometimes vastly different career from what they previously had.

For many employees, retirement is a bitter experience because many organisations do not prepare employees for it, particularly if they are retrenched for operational reasons. Some employees look forward to retirement as the culmination of their career, providing an opportunity to relax. Yet, often it is a disappointment and a bore. Where life was once busy and full of incident it has become dull and unexciting. Furthermore, retirees sometimes struggle to maintain their sense of identity and self-worth without a fulfilling job. This is particularly the case when an employee is retired before the normal retirement age, due to restructuring, unbundling, retrenchment, and so on. Organisations, therefore, need to devote attention to this

stage of career development for employees, and start by asking the following questions:
- When does the employee plan to retire?
- Who is considering early retirement?
- What does the employee plan to do during retirement?
- Will he or she attempt a second career outside the organisation?
- Can the organisation assist him or her in preparing for such a career?
- Can the retiree be approached by the organisation to help new employees learn the job?

The human resources department, in particular, should provide counselling for those about to retire, helping them to accept their reduced role, to live a less structured life, and to make adaptations in their family and community life. Other subjects for counselling are how the pension scheme operates and how lump sum payments will be made, how leisure time can be spent, health issues, accommodation arrangements, financial arrangements and investments.

20.12.4.3 Career management for dual-career couples

Career management has evolved dramatically over the last three decades. It is a fact of life today that with many couples, both parties actively pursue careers. Sometimes both work for the same organisation, which requires even more fine-tuning between the two spouses than would otherwise be the case. It is also in the interests of the organisation employing them to view them jointly with regard to career development.

In general, however, where both spouses pursue a career, working for different organisations, it is in their interests to synchronise their career-pathing and personal lives in conjunction with the organisations' human resources departments. The result will be enhanced relationships in their private and business lives, since conflict can easily arise out of their employment activities. This aspect must be focused on by the human resources department, as part of its human resources development activities.

According to Guterman (1991:169) a dual-career couple can be defined as: 'any two people in an ongoing, committed relationship, where both partners work, where there may or may not be children, and where decisions (family and work) are influenced by the working situation of each partner'. Dual-career couples often experience work and family conflict, which does not occur where only one member of a family works.

According to Swanepoel et al. (2000: 453) conflict between work and family roles can be created by the following work-related factors:
- number of hours worked;
- lack of control over the decision to work overtime;
- an inflexible work schedule;
- irregular starting time; and
- psychologically demanding work.

Schreuder and Theron (1997:152) however, suggest the following action to balance family and work needs:
- more organisational sensitivity for home life;
- the introduction of flexible benefits to assist employees with family needs, such as child care and the care of sick children;
- the introduction of flexible work hours and work-at-home programmes;
- the revision of relocation policies to make provision for the needs of the modern worker; and
- the introduction of alternative career paths – not all employees want to climb the corporate ladder.

Should an approach of this nature be followed, it will also have a positive effect on the organisation.

20.12.5 A practical approach to career management

As already stated, employee career development is the joint responsibility of the employee and employer. If there is to be sound employee career development, a structured strategy should be followed. A practical five-step strategy that employers can use to ensure effective career development in their organisations is given below.

Step 1: Match the goals of the individual with those of the organisation

It is essential that each employee involves himself or herself in a career planning exercise to determine what he or she wants to do now and in the future. This means that the organisation must also have very clearly defined strategic and tactical plans, i.e. careful organisational planning is undertaken.

In addition, the employer should undertake human resources planning, which will indicate exactly what the demand will be for particular employees in the organisation at any particular time, and whether there will be sufficient people to meet the demand. Job analysis is also important, because it indicates what the personal requirements are for a job and what the job entails. It is then easy to determine whether a specific employee is capable of doing a particular job. Recruitment and selection are also easier if career planning is done, because employers are able to fill specific vacancies internally. Career development will identify internal staff when capable outside employees cannot be recruited. The reward system could motivate employees to develop themselves in a particular direction. It can also gauge how successful an employee's career development programme has been. Performance appraisal also plays a role in employee career development in that it can be used to determine an employee's development potential.

An individual who is already in the employ of the organisation must go through a specific procedure related to his or her career before he or she can participate in career development. The steps are as follows, and the employer should help the employee with each step:
- self-assessment by the employee;
- crystallisation of work values in the organisation as the employee sees it;
- advice on how the employee can decide on a career;
- a connection workshop, where employee and employer are sensitised to future labour needs and availability thereof;
- a discussion between the employee and the relevant supervisor or manager to ensure understanding exists regarding jobs to be performed;
- supervisors and managers should be trained to counsel subordinates about their future career opportunities; and
- the writing of an individual development plan by the employee, in conjunction with his or her superior and the human resources department.

Step 2: Link career development with the human resources department and with management

Management, and particularly the human resources department, needs to ensure that all key supervisors and managers are fully conversant with the career development programmes in the organisation and actively support them. Top management could circulate a letter expressing support for career development and praising supervisors and managers who direct such programmes. Such support is essential if career development programmes are to succeed in an organisation.

Career development should fit in with the organisation's management system to ensure that career development programmes do not clash with the organisation's long-term philosophy, strategy, and goals.

Step 3: Link career development with environmental trends and values

The whole process of career development needs to be refined in terms of future trends. The organisation's goals, production methods, and demographic shifts should be considered.

It is commonly accepted that technological changes occur so rapidly today that an employee's skills should be comprehensively updated every five years if he or she is to remain abreast of technological developments. These factors should be taken into account in career development. Employees should start working on a bridging qualification long before it is actually required, so that they can adjust their careers and move to more suitable jobs if necessary. It may be necessary, for example, to put some employees on flexitime so that they can undertake part-time study in case they need to change their jobs.

Step 4: Have regular communication between the employer and employees

All affected parties should communicate regularly on the drawing up of career development plans, and should be kept up to date on the actual progress made.

These parties are the human resources department, heads of sections and departments, trade union representatives, and the affected employees. Interactive meetings should be held where career development plans are updated, and employees should receive feedback on their progress.

Should employees discover that their career development takes place at a faster pace than their actual progress in the organisation, consideration should be given to lateral moves within the organisation. If upward movement is out of the question and the employee insists on it, he or she should be assisted by the employer to find alternative employment, either in another plant or in a different organisation. This is important, since a major impediment in the career development path of an employee could lead to frustration and a decrease in productivity.

Step 5: The employer's responsibilities in effective career development for employees

The employer's commitment to career development should be evident in the creation of opportunities and provision of the means required by an employee to carry out his or her career development. The participation of employers should be apparent in the following areas:
- periodic review of employees' progress;
- opportunity for self-study;
- establishment of support teams; and
- provision of counselling by the employer.

20.13 Conclusion

Factors such as global competition and the socio-economic challenges to enterprises have brought a new dimension to workplace training and development. The days are gone when enterprises could regard the equipping of their workers as a 'nice to have' or an add-on activity just because everybody else is doing it.

For enterprises to survive in a highly competitive marketplace, the decision to invest in the development of their human resources must be a business decision. To maximise their investment, enterprises will have to adopt a strategic training approach and, in doing so, move away from the notion that training is an activity run by trainers somewhere in a lecture room. This chapter gives training managers as well as operational managers insight in how to adapt traditional training approaches to a much more strategic approach.

The various training delivery approaches are also discussed briefly in this chapter to give readers a feeling for the wide variety of methods available to transfer knowledge and skills in the workplace setting.

Effective training requires much more than an instructor, a lecture room, and learning material. To become managers of learning, training people must be informed on the broad contextual issues related to workplace training and development. This chapter deals with a number of these contextual issues, such as competency-based training, recognition of prior learning, adult learning, diversity training, and the National Qualifications Framework.

Since the role of supervisor is becoming more and more vital in assisting management in achieving the organisation's objectives, this chapter also touches on some of the challenges faced by enterprises with regard to the training of supervisors.

There is also a close relationship between training and development and career development, since training and development are means that enable employees to achieve their own career goals. It is of cardinal importance, however, that employees know what they want and how they want to spend their working lives. They need to plan their careers in terms of their own talents and limitations.

Career planning and development need to be painstaking if an employee is to gain the maximum benefit from his or her endeavours. Career management by organisations should be broad enough to meet the specific career needs of individuals, yet specific enough to afford employees flexible job experience.

Case study
Training for the sake of training

Peter Rathumbu manages the Administration Department of Zecso Appliance Manufacturers (Pty.) Ltd. One of the eight supervisors reporting to him is Pricilla Modiga. Pricilla oversees the Accounting Procedures Unit. She has been in that position for two years, after working in the unit as a clerk for four years. While she was a good performer as a clerk, she has had real problems as a superintendent. Her attitude as a superintendent has been that employees had better do what they are told to do, because she thought they ought to get on with the job without her meddling in it.

There were, however, regular mistakes made by her subordinates, which required her attention. Morale was low and resignations regularly occurred. The high staff turnover was ascribed to a high market demand for people with accounting experience and qualifications and, therefore, Pricilla's superiors paid little attention to this.

Peter suggested that she needed training, and enrolled her for an Advanced Administration Management course which was also designed for superintendents' advancement. The course was presented at the Cum Laude College which was ten kilometres from Zecso Appliance Manufacturers (Pty.) Ltd. When Pricilla received the course attendance memo from the Training and Development

Department, she enquired from Peter why she was to be sent on the course. He replied that he thought she might like to attend it, that the company needed to jack up their accounting systems, and that she might find the course valuable as well. A week later, Pricilla received some advance-reading for the course. During the next day, Peter saw her reading some of the course notes, and told her to carry on with her work instead, and not to read course material during work time.

Pricilla arrived at the Cum Laude College, where the Advanced Administration Course was to be held, in a rather apprehensive state of mind. She did not know what the course would cover and felt uncertain about her ability to cope with it. She, however, stayed for the five days, which was the duration of the course. Unfortunately, the facilitator was less than enthusiastic about the course, and lectured all day every day, without making much use of instructional aids such as videos, the overhead projector or case studies, let alone interactive class participation. The course, however, included a few topics that dealt specifically with Pricilla's work problems. At the end of the course, she felt that she had learned a lot and was confident enough to try out some of the things she had learned in the work situation.

Peter asked how her 'holiday' was when she got back to work, and she found this insulting, to say the least. Her first day was primarily spent on getting back on track, by clearing up the backlogs which had built up. After a few days, she was ready to try out some of the things she had learned at the college. However, each time she did something she had learned, Peter made comments that demoralised her. Pricilla asked Peter why he made the non-supportive remarks. He then told her that she needed to deal with her work in the way it was always done, and not be 'hyped up' by all the untried training theory the wise guys at the College dished out.

Pricilla was very upset and decided to return to her old style of doing her job and, from then on, primarily minded her own business. However, two long-serving employees in her department resigned shortly thereafter. Pricilla then thought that the training was no good and that the company, in particular, was wasting its money. She decided that she would never go on another course, since Peter did not seem enthusiastic or supportive about it either.

Questions

1 Compile a human resources development strategy, which would encapsulate the promotion of positive attitudes to training at Zecso Appliance Manufacturers (Pty.) Ltd. as a primary element of the strategy.
2 Identify the factors relevant to the training result, in this case.
3 You are a lecturer at the Cum Laude College and have a friend who works with Pricilla, and who gives you feedback on the result of the course experience. Devise a programme that would successfully empower Pricilla to positively transfer what she and other students have learned to their work situation.

Chapter questions

1. Explain, in one page, the difference between strategic and traditional training approaches.
2. Assume the human resources manager provides you with a challenge to draft a training programme, aimed specifically at achieving the organisation's strategic objectives. Concentrate on issues such as a training and development philosophy, training policy, training intent, and the various steps in the training process.
3. Explain the difference between norm- and criteria-referenced test items. Elaborate on the latter, with special reference to competency-based training.
4. Write an essay on adult learning.
5. List the various methods that could be used to equip a worker on the shop floor with the necessary knowledge and skills.
6. Express a view on the challenges faced by enterprises with regard to supervisory training, and discuss how these challenges can be met.
7. Describe the relationship between training and development, and career development.
8. What benefits do you see from managing your own career? Discuss.
9. Who should be responsible for managing an employee's career – the individual or the organisation? Discuss critically.
10. What are your career goals? Draw up a balance sheet of your strengths and weaknesses, and decide whether you are in the right job at present.
11. In the light of the rapid changes facing South Africa since the election of April 1994, does career planning still make sense, given employment equity programmes in terms of Act No. 55 of 1998, on the one hand, and the staff shortages in many organisations, on the other? Present a career plan taking cognisance of these issues.

Bibliography

ARMSTRONG, M. 1984. *A handbook of personnel management practice*. 2nd edition. Kogan Page, London.

BIRCHALL, D. & LYONS, L. 1995. *Creating tomorrow's organisation – unlocking the benefits of FutureWork*. Pitman, London.

BIRKENBACH, B & HOFMEYR, K. 1990. New imperatives for human resource development. *IPM Journal*, vol. 9, no. 4, November.

CAMP, R.C., BLANCHARD, P.M. & HUSZCZO, G.E. 1986. *Towards a more organisational effective training strategy and practice*. Prentice-Hall, New York.

CHAMBERLAIN, G. 1995. Competency based training enhances productivity. *Human Resource Management*, vol. 11, no. 3, April.

DE CENZO, D.A. & ROBBINS, S.P. 1994. *Human resources management concepts and practices*. John Wiley & Sons, New York.

DEPARTMENT OF EDUCATION. 1995. South African Qualifications Authority Act No. 58. Pretoria.

DEPARTMENT OF LABOUR. 1999. *Career guide*. October. Government Printer, Pretoria.

DEPARTMENT OF LABOUR. 1995. *1994 Annual Report*. RP 136–1995. Government Printer, Cape Town.

DUBOIS, D.D. 1993. *Competency based performance improvement*. HRD Press, Amherst.

ELLINGTON, H. 1985. *Teaching materials: a handbook for teachers and trainers*. Nichols Publishing, New York.

ERASMUS, B.J. & VAN DYK, P.S. 1999. *Training management in South Africa*. 2nd edition. International Thomson Publishing (Southern Africa) (Pty) Ltd, Halfway House.

FERRELL, O.C. & HIRT, G. 1993. *Business: a changing world*. Homewood, Boston.

INSTITUTE FOR PEOPLE MANAGEMENT. *IPM Journal*. Fact sheets 14, 47, 71, 137, 141, and 142.

GRAHAM, H.T. & BENNETT, R. 1993. *Human resources management*. Business Handbooks, London.

GUTERMAN, M. 1991. Working couples: finding a balance between family and career. In Kummerrow, J.M. (ed.) *New directions in career planning and the workplace*, 167–193. Davies

Black Publishing, Palo Alto, California.

IVANCEVICH, J.H. & GLUECK, W.F. 1986. *Foundations of personnel: human resource management.* Business Publications, Plano, Texas.

IVANCEVICH, J.M. 1995. *Human resource management.* Irwin, Chicago.

KATZ, M. 1994. Illiterate supervisors: a home-grown solution. *People Dynamics.* November/December.

KINLAW, D. 1996. *The ASTD trainer's sourcebook: coaching.* McGraw-Hill, New York.

KINLAW, D. 1996. *The ASTD trainer's sourcebook: facilitation skills.* McGraw-Hill, New York.

MAGER, R. 1975. *Preparing instructional objectives.* 2nd edition. Fearon-Pitman, California.

MCINTOSH, S.S. 1995. Envisaging virtual training organisations. *Training and Development Journal.* May.

MEYER, T. 1996. *Creating competitiveness through competencies.* Knowledge Resources, Randburg.

MIDDLETON, J., ZIDERMAN, A. & ADAMS, A.V. 1993. *Skills for productivity.* Oxford University Press, New York.

MOBLEY, M. & PAYNE, T. 1992. Backlash! The challenge to diversity training. *Training and Development Journal.* December.

MUCHINSKY, P.M., KRIEK, H.J. & SCHREUDER, A.M.G. 1998. *Personnel psychology.* International Thomsons Publishing, Midrand.

NADLER, D. 1980. Defining the field: Is it HRD or OD, or ...? *Training and Development Journal,* vol. 34, no. 12, pp. 66–68.

OLIVIER, C. 1998. *Outcomes-based education and training programmes.* OBET. Pro:Ifafi.

REID, M.A. & BARRINGTON, H. 1997. *Training interventions managing employee development.* 5th edition. IPD, London.

ROTHWELL, W.J. & KAZANAS, H.C., 1994. *Human resources development: a strategic approach.* Massachusetts HRD Press, Amherst.

SCHREUDER, A.M.G. & THERON, A.L. 1997. *Careers: an organisational perspective.* Juta & Co. Ltd, Kenwyn.

SENGE, P.M. 1993. *The fifth discipline.* Bantam Doubleday Dell Publishing Group, London.

SILBEMAN, M. 1995. *101 ways to make training active.* Pfeiffer & Company, San Diego.

SKINNER, M.S.J. & IVANCEVICH, W.F. 1992. *Business for the 21st century.* Irwin, Homewood, Illinois.

SPARHAWK, D. 1994. *Identifying targeted training needs: a practical guide to beginning an effective training strategy.* Richard Chang Associates, California.

SWARTZ, P. 1992. Peter Swartz' long view. *People Dynamics.* August.

VAN DER HORST, H. & MCDONALD, R. 1997. *Outcomes-based education. A teachers manual.* Kagiso Publishers, Pretoria.

VAN DYK, P.S., NEL, P.S., LOEDOLFF, P. VAN Z. & HAASBROEK, G.D. 2001. *Training management. A multidisciplinary approach to human resources development in Southern Africa.* 3rd edition. Oxford University Press, Cape Town.

21

Performance management

H B Schultz

Learning outcomes

At the end of this chapter the learner should be able to demonstrate the following outcomes:
- Discuss the achievement of organisational effectiveness through performance management.
- Debate the objective of 'adding value', as opposed to that of achieving pre-determined goals in performance management.
- Examine the elements of performance management, including launching the process, coaching for improvement, and evaluating performance.
- Discuss who should perform the evaluation.
- Compare relative and absolute performance evaluation methods.
- Explain common rater-errors.
- Provide guidelines for an effective feedback interview.
- Consider the influence of legislation on performance management systems.
- Discuss the necessity for quality assurance in managing employee performance.

Key words and concepts

- 360-degree appraisals
- absolute and relative evaluation methods
- actor/observer bias
- added value
- behaviourally anchored rating scales (BARS)
- bias
- central tendency
- computerised appraisals
- critical incidents
- customer appraisal
- essay method
- forced choice
- forced distribution
- graphic rating scales

- halo effect
- knowledge worker
- leniency and strictness
- management by objectives (MBO)
- paired comparisons
- peer review
- ranking
- rational and political perspectives
- recency
- reverse appraisals
- self-appraisal
- team appraisals

Illustrative case 'The world's favourite airline'

When Sir Colin Marshall took over as CEO of British Airways in early 1983, the company was the laughing stock of the industry. Comedians referred to the company, known by its initials BA, as 'Bloody Awful'. Employee morale had hit rock bottom; thousands of employees had just been laid off, and those remaining were embarrassed to work for the worst airline in the world. Colin Marshall changed the company from one that seemed to disdain customers to one that strives to please them. Marshall's first challenge was to restore pride. To send a clear message to both employees and potential customers, he ordered newly designed uniforms for all personnel. The fleet of planes was also repainted with bright stripes and the motto, 'To fly, to serve'. With this motto, the service era was born at British Airways.

Dull, tasteless food, poor cabin service, and cramped leg room were remedied immediately. But Marshall also scrutinised the less obvious details, such as calling passengers by name and scheduling flights for the convenience of customers, not the airline. Today, British Airways' marketplace performance unit tracks some 350 measures of performance, including aircraft cleanliness, punctuality, technical defects on aircraft, customers' opinions on British Airways check-in performance, the time it takes for a customer to get through boarding procedures, and customer satisfaction with in-flight and ground services.

But none of this will make any difference if the performance of the ground and cabin staff is not top-notch. How does BA achieve this class of performance? By using 360-degree appraisals. In fact, BA was a ground-breaker in this area in the United Kingdom, way back in the late 1980s and early 1990s. Since then, external customers have continuously been asked what they wanted by way of service, and the customers (the airline's passengers) are the first to be asked to rate the performance of whoever has interacted personally with them. Passenger ratings are followed by peer ratings, managers' ratings, and subordinates' ratings, if relevant. This holistic approach to performance appraisal resulted in the airline being dubbed 'the world's favourite' and incorporating this into their marketing strategy.

SOURCE: Ivancevich et al. (1997:446–7).

21.1 Introduction

Individual performance in organisations has traditionally centred on the evaluation of performance and allocation of rewards. Organisations are increasingly recognising that planning and enabling individual performance have a critical effect on organisational performance. Contemporary approaches to performance in the workplace emphasise the importance of a shared view of expected performance between manager and employee. Many organisations are grappling with a process of self-renewal as a result of constant pressure for enhanced competitiveness. However, comparatively few have simultaneously overhauled their outdated performance management systems. Strategic success lies in focusing attention at all levels on key business imperatives, which can be achieved through effective performance management (Bennett & Minty 1999:58).

This discussion commences with some thoughts on how performance management can contribute to organisational effectiveness. The performance management process is introduced in detail; the debate covers the inception of the process, coaching the employee to better performance, and the evaluation of performance. Possible rater-errors are described and the feedback interview is examined. Some guidelines are offered for the avoidance of legal problems, and the chapter closes with an overview of the link between performance management and quality assurance.

of performance appraisals. The total management of employee performance, when handled properly, should thus be a welcome alternative to merely measuring an employee's actions (Schultz & Schultz 1994:146).

Torrington and Hall (1995:327) state that performance management systems are increasingly seen as the way to manage employee performance rather than relying on appraisal alone. When performance management systems are tied into the objectives of the organisation, the resulting performance is more likely to meet organisational needs. They also represent a more holistic view of performance.

In order for performance management to be effective, it must be line-driven rather than personnel department-driven. Development of a performance management system should be a joint effort between line and human resources managers. This will offer line managers ownership of the system and ensure stronger commitment. Lundy and Cowling (1996:306) point out that ownership should be taken a step further in that subordinates should play an active role in the management of their own performance, linked to organisational performance as a whole.

21.2 Achievement of organisational effectiveness through performance management

Performance appraisal programmes hardly ever enjoy full support from employees in general. Managers who have had unsatisfactory experiences with poorly designed or inadequate appraisal programmes are often sceptical about their usefulness; some managers are loath to play the role of judge, or to provide negative feedback. Few employees enjoy being tested or evaluated, few welcome criticism, and most react with suspicion or hostility to the idea

21.3 The performance management process

Bennett and Minty (1999:59–60) state that there are generally three major purposes of performance management:
- it is a process for strategy implementation;
- it is a vehicle for culture change; and
- it provides input to other human resources systems, such as development and remuneration.

According to Sloman (1997:167) performance management systems are considered to be operating when the following conditions are met:

- a vision of objectives is communicated to employees;
- departmental and individual performance targets are set within wider objectives;
- a formal review of progress towards targets is conducted; and
- the whole process is evaluated to improve effectiveness.

An example of an organisation engaged in creating a new model of performance management is offered in the Case-in-point.

Case-in-point
Southern Californian Edison creates a bright glow

In the early 1990s restructuring programmes and attempts to redefine a corporate culture had left the staff at Southern Californian Edison (SCE) feeling very insecure. SCE's new values emphasised empowerment but the current performance management system was counterproductive in all respects. Corporate HR left it up to each operating department to design the performance management system that suited its business strategy best. There were only two stipulations:
- each system should include a way of encompassing employee and team goals, evaluating individual contributions to strategic priorities, and building commitment to corporate values; and
- three milestones should be observed – filing a performance plan at the beginning of the appraisal year, conducting a mid-year review, and producing a final evaluation at year's end.

Ron Juliff, head of health care and employee services, used interviews and focus groups to collect in-depth data on the existing performance management system. The results confirmed the current negative attitude. The department decided to create a completely new performance system. The first step was to call for volunteers from across the board to form the nucleus of a task force to determine key problems and define parameters for the new system.

At first, it was difficult to convince the task force that they were really driving the process. This was the first time they had had an opportunity to influence how they and their colleagues would be assessed. Nevertheless, they were soon working enthusiastically, meeting once a month as a group and working in subgroups on issues such as programme structure. The task force offered ownership of the performance programme to the departmental workforce by soliciting supervisors' and employees' opinions. The latter were continuously encouraged to provide input, and slowly a new performance paradigm took shape. After about six months, the task force had finalised their proposals, founded on the following philosophy:
- employees as well as supervisors assume responsibility;
- both supervisors and employees learn new skills so that they can work better;
- the steps are 'doable' for both;
- the focus is on values and future growth, not past problems;
- both parties are honest and candid; and
- the discussion is not a control tool, but rather supports a partnership between employee and supervisor.

> The new programme was given the title 'Performance Enhancement Process (PEP)' and it has rewritten productivity levels in the healthcare and benefits department at SCE. The department continues to fine-tune the programme, but employee surveys reveal that departmental staff are content with what they have achieved. Supervisors and employees feel energised by moving from being passive recipients to active participants, and by the continuous improvement in candidness that pervades the department. Staff have learnt to work together to plan performance and have become true partners in improving their business.
>
> SOURCE: Moravec et al. (1995:104–108).

In the following section an attempt is made to provide a holistic approach to managing performance, incorporating some traditional processes and offering some newer approaches and trends for consideration.

Figure 21.1 places the performance management process in perspective.

21.3.1 Launching the process

A new paradigm is emerging in the way that performance is managed in an organisation. The trend is away from the prescriptive mode towards collaboration in the workplace. In a recent study, Kemske (1998:52) points out that organisations will focus more on performance and results in the future. The study also forecasts a number of other trends that will alter the way that managers approach the facilitation of their subordinates' performance:

- the role of human resources practitioners will change to that of creator of overall values and direction;
- lifelong learning will be a requirement;
- the focus of learning and training activities will be on performance improvement and not only on skill building;
- practical work problems will serve as the training medium for problem-solving and decision-making;

Figure 21.1 The performance management process

Launching the process
- Alignment with business strategy
- Alignment with departmental goals
- Determining employee goals to add value
- Defining parameters of an action plan

Coaching
- Interim checking of progress
- Exploring causes of poor performance
- Counselling and mentoring

Evaluation
- Measuring performance
- Determining amount of value added
- Allocating results of evaluation to HR systems
- Reviewing new business strategy, and departmental and employee goals

- performance appraisal will measure the value of employees' contributions to the business, and not the fulfilling of predetermined objectives;
- successful human resources departments will focus on strategic performance management, with an emphasis on human capital development and organisational productivity; and
- a key human resources role in the future will be multidisciplinary consulting around individual, team, business unit, and corporate performance.

What is evolving, therefore, is the management of performance through the amount of value the subordinate's performance adds to the overall organisational performance. The traditional way of managing performance, by measuring whether the employee has achieved prescribed objectives, is no longer adequate. Crossley and Taylor (1995:11) state that managers are being pressurised to rediscover competitive advantage, and the only way to achieve this is by developing the core competency of becoming a 'knowledge worker' and encouraging subordinates to become knowledge workers as well. Knowledge workers are those who can use their hands and minds to organise and deal with information and technology. They possess the skills to analyse and problem-solve complex issues and tasks, and they are far more independent than employees of the past.

Must managers stop involving their subordinates in determining the goals they wish to achieve? The answer is 'No!' Organisations must still set strategic goals, which must be filtered down to departments and individuals. But the new paradigm goes further. Top managers must decide how much value will be added to the organisation if the goals are achieved. Value can be financial, developmental, competitive, or knowledge. The individual can add value in the form of knowledge, skills, abilities, competencies, and innovation.

The first stage of the performance management process therefore involves the following steps:

1. Manager and subordinate meet to jointly discuss how the organisation's strategic goals must be adopted and adapted by the department and the individual.
2. Manager and subordinate jointly decide on an action plan to achieve the individual's goals.
3. Manager and subordinate agree on specific times for formal checks to be made on progress towards the goals.
4. Manager and subordinate agree on the type of value, and the amount of value that will be added if the goals are achieved.

If the outcomes of the above four steps are incorporated into a written document, which is signed by both the manager and the subordinate, it becomes a contract that should encourage the participation of both parties. It is also useful in checking the progress made towards the achievement of added value.

21.3.2 Coaching and mentoring

The astute manager is always aware of the level of his or her subordinate's performance. Whether the organisation's objective in managing performance is to achieve goals or to add value, performance problems must be noticed and analysed at an early stage. Informal day-to-day performance management is much more important than an annual review. Katz (1995:38) states that interim progress reviews and coaching meetings are key elements in monitoring an employee's performance. The manager uses coaching skills to help the employee to improve, offers advice on changing behaviours and approaches, and encourages progress

towards achieving goals and adding value. According to Gómez-Mejía et al. (1998: 219–223) supervisors who manage performance effectively generally share four characteristics:
- they explore the causes of performance problems;
- they direct attention to the causes of problems;
- they develop an action plan and empower workers to reach a solution; and
- they direct communication at performance and emphasise non-threatening communication.

Exploring the causes of performance problems

Exploring the causes of performance problems is often quite challenging. Many factors are beyond the worker's control. In most work situations, however, observers tend to attribute the causes of poor performance to the worker, while workers tend to blame external factors. This tendency is called actor/observer bias. There are three reasons why the causes of performance deficiencies must be determined accurately:
- determination of causes can influence how performance is evaluated;
- causal determination can be an unspoken and underlying source of conflict between supervisors and their workers; and
- causal determinations affect the type of remedy selected.

Directing attention to the causes of problems

After determining the causes of problems, the next step is to take control of the problems. Factors that affect performance positively should be encouraged, and constraining factors should be eliminated or at least reduced. Different tactics are required depending on whether the cause of the performance problem is related to ability, effort, or situational characteristics.

Developing an action plan and empowering workers to reach a solution

Traditionally supervisors gave orders and workers followed them but this did not usually lead to maximum performance levels. The empowerment approach requires supervisors to take the role of coach instead of director or controller. The 'supervisor coach' is an enabler who creates a supportive, empowered work environment, clarifies performance expectations, provides immediate feedback, and strives to eliminate unnecessary rules, procedures, and constraints.

Directing communication at performance

Communication must be directed at the performance and not at the person. An evaluative or judgemental approach during communication is likely to evoke a defensive reaction. What is communicated and how it is communicated can determine whether performance improves or declines.

21.3.3 Performance evaluation

Employee performance can be measured on the basis of whether the type of judgement called for is relative or absolute.

Relative judgements require supervisors to compare an employee's performance to the performance of other employees doing the same job. Relative judgements force supervisors to differentiate between their workers. However, relative judgements do not make it clear how great or small the differences between employees are. Relative systems do not provide any concrete information, so managers cannot determine how good or bad the performance of workers is.

Absolute judgements ask supervisors to make judgements about an employee's performance based solely on performance standards. Feedback to the employee can be more specific and helpful because ratings are made on separate dimensions of performance. Absolute rating systems also have their disadvantages. All workers in a group can receive the same evaluation if the supervisor is reluctant to differentiate between workers. Also, different supervisors can have different evaluation standards. Nevertheless, absolute rating systems avoid creating conflict among workers, and are generally easier to defend than relative systems when legal issues arise (Gómez-Mejía et al. 1998:205).

The objectives of performance evaluation

There are two perspectives that can be taken when evaluating an employee's performance: the rational perspective and the political perspective. The rational perspective assumes that the value of each worker's performance can be estimated. The political perspective assumes that the value of a worker's performance depends on the agenda, or goals, of the supervisor. The political approach holds that performance measurement is a goal-oriented activity and that accuracy is seldom the goal (Gómez-Mejía et al. 1998:215). The distinction between the rational and political approaches is depicted in Table 21.1.

21.4 Methods of performance evaluation

The success of performance evaluation depends on two decisions: the person, or persons, designated to carry out the evaluation, and the method or technique chosen to measure the performance.

21.4.1 Who should evaluate performance?

Cascio (1995:290) states that the fundamental requirement for any rater is that an adequate opportunity is made available for performance to be observed over a reasonable period of time. This offers the possibility of several different choices of rater.

The immediate supervisor

This is the most popular and easiest choice for a rater. The supervisor is probably most familiar with the subordinate's

Table 21.1 The difference between the rational and the political approaches to performance evaluation

Rational approach	Political approach
• The goal of appraisal is accuracy. • Supervisors and workers are passive participants in the process. • The focus of appraisal is measurement. • A worker's performance should be clearly defined. • Supervisors make dimensional and overall assessments based on specific behaviours they have observed.	• The goal of appraisal is utility. • Supervisors and workers are motivated participants in the measurement process. • The focus of appraisal is management. • What is being assessed is left ambiguous. • Appropriate assessment of specifics follows the overall assessment.

SOURCE: Gómez-Mejía et al. (1998:215).

performance and has the best opportunity to observe actual job performance on a daily basis. The disadvantage in using the immediate supervisor as a rater is that he or she may be too lenient in rating an employee in an attempt to curry favour.

Peers

Logistics may preclude the immediate supervisor from rating some jobs, such as outside sales, law enforcement, and teaching. Although objective criteria could be used in these cases, the judgement of peers often provides a perspective on performance that is different from that of immediate supervisors. However, the potential of friendship bias skewing the feedback value of the information provided is always present, and it is important to specify exactly what the peers are to evaluate. Even when peer evaluations are done well, it is best to consider them as part of a system that includes input from other raters as well.

Subordinates

So-called 'reverse appraisals' can be a useful input to the immediate supervisor's development. Subordinates know how well a supervisor delegates, communicates, plans and organises. Considerable trust and openness is a prerequisite if subordinate appraisals are to be valuable. They can work well in a large organisation where a manager may have a large number of subordinates and anonymity of the subordinate is assured.

Self-appraisal

Cascio (1995:291) believes that the opportunity to participate in the performance management process, particularly if appraisal is combined with goal setting and the chance to add value to the organisation, improves the ratee's motivation and reduces defensiveness during the evaluation interview. However, self-appraisals tend to be more lenient and more biased, and are probably more appropriate for counselling and development than for employment decisions.

Customer appraisals

In some situations an individual's internal customers, or the organisation's external customers can provide a unique perspective on job performance. Although the customer's objectives cannot be expected to correspond entirely with those of the individual or the organisation, the information that customers provide can serve as useful input for promotion, transfer, and training decisions.

Computerised performance appraisals

Many employers are using computerised appraisal systems, generally with good results. Several inexpensive software packages are on the market, most of which function within the Windows operating system. Computerised appraisal systems enable managers to log notes on their subordinates during the year, and to rate employees on a series of performance traits. The programme generates written text to support each part of the appraisal (Dessler 1997:359).

360-degree appraisals

Katz (1998:42) discusses the relatively new 360-degree, or multi-rater, system of carrying out employee evaluation. It is a questionnaire that asks many people (superiors, subordinates, peers, internal and external customers) to respond to questions on how well a specific individual performs in a number of behavioural areas. An example of the statements found in a 360-degree questionnaire is offered in Table 21.2.

Table 21.2 Typical statements found in a 360-degree feedback

He/she is someone who is open to questions.
He/she tries new ideas first with his/her employees.
He/she keeps firm in difficult matters.
He/she tries to be as independent as possible.
He/she has a large social network.
He/she is easy to understand.

SOURCE: Jansen, P. & Vloeberghs, D. (1999:455–476).

The combination of these multiple perspectives offers a more balanced point of view on the employee's overall performance. 360-degree feedback can be valuable if it complies with the following requirements. It should:
- be thoroughly tested for reliability and consistency;
- measure what it says it measures;
- be easy to use, straightforward, and simple;
- be clearly focused on a specific set of skills, competencies, or behaviours;
- generate clear, detailed and personalised feedback; and
- guarantee confidentiality.

According to Jansen and Vloeberghs (1999:456), multi-rater feedback requires 'bystanders' to assess a multitude of work situations which are controlled or managed by the person who is the focus of the feedback. This circle of bystanders indicates the degree to which, in their view, specific behaviours apply to the focal person. The focal person also rates himself or herself in terms of the questionnaire. Bystander ratings are averaged and compared with the self-ratings of the focal person. Negative differences provide data that indicate potential areas for personal development and performance improvement.

Certain undesirable reactions that could occur are:
- the employee completely neglects the feedback;
- the employee only takes positive feedback into account;
- the employee is only motivated by negative feedback; and
- the employee is only interested in feedback that is given by someone who is considered 'really important' (such as a supervisor).

Nevertheless, there have been many successes in the 360-degree system of performance evaluation. The experiences of human resources representatives at Federal Express are reported in Encounter 21.1.

Team appraisals

The growth of self-directed work teams has created a need for a new way of managing and appraising group performance. Team evaluations require a combination of two approaches: a measure of how well each member contributes to the team, and a measure of how well the team accomplishes its goals. Individual member contributions are usually measured through peer evaluation. The focus of this appraisal is usually developmental. Team performance is most often measured against specific team objectives. Cherrington (1995: 300) states that teams are usually created to increase organisational flexibility. Members often rotate assignments and, therefore, a team must be evaluated as a unit and rewarded as a unit with team incentives. The team evaluation process is relatively easy if specific and measurable objectives are in place.

21.4.2 Performance evaluation techniques

In section 21.3.3 performance evaluation was categorised into relative and absolute

Encounter 21.1 Customer service drives 360-degree goal setting

---

Federal Express (FedEx) is a global organisation specialising in worldwide courier and overnight delivery services. The head office is in Memphis, Tennessee and this is where the 360-degree evaluation process was first tested in the company. Representatives of the HR department wrote the goals of their customers into an internal customer-service guarantee. The guarantee specifically stated what services HR (the supplier) would provide in the next year to a given department (the customer). It included items such as timely response, 24-hour turnaround for feedback, and semi-annual training sessions.

The HR department at FedEx linked its goals to performance feedback by identifying six items for a customer-satisfaction survey. The evaluation was scored on a one-to-five scale – from strongly disagree to strongly agree. These issues were then evaluated by a sampling of the customer's employees at year-end. The 360-degree goal-setting process helped to explicitly state goals in terms of the customer's (rather than the employee's) words and language. The connection between customer-developed goals and customer-driven performance appraisals made employees accountable for their performance, and motivated them to work toward the company's desired behaviour.

FedEx learnt that there were advantages and disadvantages to 360-degree performance evaluations.

Advantages
- They provide a more comprehensive view of employee performance.
- They increase credibility of performance appraisal.
- Feedback from peers enhances employee self-development.
- They increase accountability of employees to their customers.

Disadvantages
- They are time consuming and more administratively complex.
- Extensive giving and receiving feedback can intimidate some employees.
- They require training and significant change effort to work effectively.

SOURCE: Milliman, J.F. et al. (1995:136–142).

---

judgements. Rating techniques can be categorised in a similar manner (Swanepoel et al. 1998:415–422).

21.4.2.1 Relative rating techniques

Ranking

Ranking entails the ordering of individuals according to overall merit or selected performance factors, from the best to the worst performer. It is a very simple technique and is usually very subjective. It should only be used when small numbers of employees are to be rated. The ranking method compares performance amongst a group of employees, but is not directed at personal development – the employee ranked best may only be a mediocre performer.

Paired comparisons

In this technique, each worker is compared with every other worker in a selected group. The final ranking of each individual is then determined by the number of times he or she was judged to be better than the others. This measurement instrument becomes cumbersome when large numbers of employees are involved. The disadvantages are similar to those of the ranking technique. Figure 21.2 compares four employees by means of the paired comparison rating method.

Figure 21.2 The paired comparison rating method

Nomfuso	Harrison √
Nomfuso	Thanduxolo √
Nomfuso	Lisolomzi √
Harrison	Thanduxolo √
Harrison √	Lisolomzi
Thanduxolo √	Lisolomzi

NUMBER OF FAVOURABLE COMPARISONS

Nomfuso	0
Harrison	2
Thanduxolo	3
Lisolomzi	1

RANKING

Thanduxolo	1
Harrison	2
Lisolomzi	3
Nomfuso	4

Forced distribution

Categories are chosen to which a certain percentage of workers in a group are assigned. These categories usually range from poor performance through to superior performance. The forced distribution of percentages does not have to comply with the requirements of a normal distribution curve. Thus, the specified categories, and assigned percentages, could easily be as follows:

Performance	
Poor	5%
Below average	15%
Average	60%
Above average	10%
Superior	10%

In the above example, if 200 employees were evaluated: 20 were rated as superior, 20 as above average, 120 as average, 30 as below average, and 10 as poor.

21.4.2.2 Absolute rating techniques

Essay method

The essay method requires the rater to write a report in the form of an essay, usually describing the strengths and weaknesses of the employee. It is a time-consuming method, dependent on the writing skill of the rater and reliant on comprehensive reporting. It can, however, be a valuable feedback tool.

Critical incidents

This technique focuses on the continuous recording of actual job behaviours that are typical of success or failure. Incidents reflecting good and bad performance are noted. It is a time-consuming method and can be influenced by incidents that are recorded towards the end of the review period, or by incidents that may have been omitted.

Forced choice

The rater is provided with a list of paired job-related descriptions from which he or she is forced to choose the description that best fits the employee in each case. It is a partly objective method of evaluation, but the rater may be forced into making a choice between two descriptions, neither of which may fully describe the employee's performance.

Graphic rating scales

These rating scales are one of the most popular absolute evaluation techniques. A rating scale is developed by selecting various characteristics that relate to the specific job. The rater makes a choice across a continuum between two poles, usually ranging from strong agreement to strong disagreement, or from exceptional to poor. Graphic rating scales are popular because they are easy to understand and apply, they are standardised, acceptable to users, are less time-consuming, and provide a high degree of consistency, provided that all raters are trained to avoid rater-errors. Figure 21.3 presents an example of a graphic rating scale.

Behaviourally anchored rating scales (BARS)

The BARS technique combines graphic rating scales with examples of critical incidents. These rating scales are job specific and require a high level of participation from supervisors. The complex development procedure of the BARS technique makes it time-consuming and expensive.

Management by objectives (MBO)

The MBO technique provides for an initial goal-setting phase, based on the formation of long-range organisational objectives that are cascaded through to departmental goals, and finally individual goals. The latter goals are set mutually by the employee and his or her manager. The aspect of joint participation in goal-setting is one of the major strengths of the MBO technique, provided that the goals are measurable and achievable.

The manager pursues an open-door strategy, inviting the employee to discuss performance problems on an informal basis at any time. Periodically, the manager will measure progress towards the goals, and will coach the subordinate if progress is lacking or slow. The final evaluation is carried out at the end of the review period. The regular interaction between subordinate and manager provides opportunities for building good relationships, but the popularity of the MBO method has declined somewhat due to the fact that it only addresses results, and not how the performance should be managed.

Figure 21.3 A graphic rating scale

	5 EXCEPTIONAL	4 HIGH	3 AVERAGE	2 LOW	1 POOR
Reliability		√			
Initiative			√		
Dependability	√				
Accuracy			√		
Interpersonal skills			√		
Quality of work			√		

OVERALL RATING: Average

Assessment centres

Many South African organisations make use of the assessment centre concept to assess an employee's potential for future advancement. The assessment centre is discussed in Chapter 20.

21.5 Rater-errors

Performance evaluations are fraught with danger, mainly because many human agendas can come into play. Managers can unwittingly 'play God', and employees can be overly optimistic or 'put on a good show', knowing that increases, career progress, and peace of mind may well rest on how they are rated. Several issues must be borne in mind by whoever is undertaking the measurement of employee performance (Dessler 1997:360).

Unclear standards

Whether performance is evaluated according to goal achievement, or value added, an ever-present problem is inconsistency of standards between raters. The problem lies in the way that different people define standards; 'good', 'average', and 'fair' do not mean the same things to everyone. The solution is to develop and include descriptive phrases that define the language the rater is required to use. This specificity results in performance evaluations that are more consistent and more easily explained.

Halo effect

The halo effect occurs when a manager's rating of a subordinate on one characteristic biases the way that other characteristics are rated. For example, if the employee has successfully added value to the organisation through the development of higher skills, he may be rated satisfactory overall, even if he has not added value in other areas that were agreed upon. Likewise, failure in one area may negatively influence an overall rating. This is known as a negative halo, or the 'devil's horns' effect. Being aware of this problem is a major step toward avoiding it.

Central tendency

Some raters find it difficult or unpleasant to evaluate individual employees higher or lower than others, even though their job performance may reflect substantial differences. In this case, they may tend to rate everyone as average, resulting in a central tendency. This problem can also occur if supervisors are unfamiliar with the work of the subordinate, if they lack supervisory ability, or if they fear a reprimand for rating too leniently or too strictly. The solution to this problem lies in ascertaining the reason for applying a central tendency, and then counselling the supervisor.

Leniency or strictness

Inexperienced supervisors often appraise performance too leniently and rate an employee highly because they feel it is the easiest route to follow. In some cases, the employees may not deserve the rating. In addition, some supervisors may feel that they could gain in popularity if they use a lenient approach. However, there could be individuals in the department whose performance has been above average and who do deserve a high rating. This could result in feelings that the evaluation has been unfair.

Strictness is the opposite of leniency, and could occur if the supervisor believes that no one has achieved the standards required. In both the above cases, counselling is probably the best method of dealing with the problem.

Recency

Raters can easily be influenced by recent incidents in the employee's performance. This tends to influence the supervisor's overall perception of the individual's performance. One way of combating this would be to hold more frequent and regular performance evaluations.

Bias

Supervisory bias may occur when the rater is influenced by characteristics such as the age, gender, race, or seniority of the employee. Bias may be conscious or unconscious, and can be difficult to overcome because it is usually hidden.

On the whole, proper rater training and specific development of the appraisal system by means of job analysis can improve performance evaluations. In fact, many rater-errors can be dealt with in this way.

21.6 The feedback interview

21.6.1 The nature of the feedback interview

The appraisal interview should be both evaluative and developmental. Goals that have been met do not warrant long discussion, except for the praise that must accompany these achievements. The evaluators should consider the guidelines contained in Table 21.3.

Cascio (1995:298) suggests a framework of activities that should be used by the person conducting the feedback interview. These activities should take place before, during, and after the interview.

Before the interview, the rater must:
- communicate frequently with employees about their performance;
- get training in performance appraisal interviewing;

Table 21.3 Guidelines for conducting the feedback interview

The evaluator must
- strive for internal consistency
- treat employees fairly
- make meaningful comments.
- focus on employee behaviour, not on the employee
- focus on employee actions, not on intent
- focus on deficiencies, not their causes
- focus on organisational expectations, not legalisms

The evaluator must not
- make comments that are inconsistent with numerical rankings
- criticise indirectly
- offer excuses for the subordinate's poor performance
- make comments that are either too general or too specific

SOURCE: Segal, J. (1995).

- plan to use a problem-solving approach rather than 'tell-and-sell'; and
- encourage subordinates to prepare for the interview.

During the interview, the rater must:
- encourage ratee participation;
- judge performance, not personality;
- be specific;
- be an active listener;
- set mutually agreeable goals for future improvement; and
- avoid destructive criticism.

After the interview, the rater must:
- communicate frequently with ratees about their performance;
- periodically assess progress toward goals; and
- make organisational goals contingent on performance.

Gómez-Mejía et al. (1998:219) mention the two schools of thought regarding the discussion of salary matters during the feedback interview. In the past, many organisations believed that if performance and salary discussions are combined, employees don't listen to their performance feedback because their interest is focused on salary decisions. However, human resources practitioners now widely believe that discussion of salary in an evaluation session has a positive impact on the success of the interview. Reasons for this are that managers and employees are much more likely to take the evaluation session seriously when money is at stake, and discussion on salary can energise the performance discussion.

21.6.2 Scheduling the feedback interview

It is difficult to prescribe how often feedback interviews should take place. The structure of the performance management system will determine when an interview should be scheduled. However, if the system is cyclical, formal feedback should occur at least twice a year. Often new recruits to an organisation, who are still in training for their jobs, have feedback interviews scheduled more regularly. In addition, the very nature of performance management systems that add value to the organisation, demand continuous feedback, even if it is not on a formal basis.

21.7 Legal considerations in performance management

With the enactment of new labour legislation all over the world, and especially in South Africa, human resources professionals and those in charge of performance management programmes must take into consideration how every aspect of such a programme is implemented. Dismissal on the grounds of poor performance is justifiable in terms of the Labour Relations Act No. 66 of 1995, but the process must be legally sound to avoid litigation. Carrell et al. (1997:264) suggest several guidelines that will help protect a company from legal problems in performance management:
- written appraisals must be conducted at all levels in the organisation, and must never be backdated or altered later;
- all raters, whether supervisors, subordinates, peers, or customers must be trained in evaluation procedures;
- standards must be job-related and must be consistent, explicit, and objective;
- rater-errors must be guarded against;
- problem areas must be identified;
- timetables and specific goals for improvement must be established when substandard performance is identified;
- employees must be given clear opportunities to respond to negative feedback;
- written evidence must be provided that the employee received the performance evaluation;
- access to performance evaluations must be restricted to those with a need to know; and
- past performance evaluations must be checked for evidence of poor performance, especially if there are grounds for dismissal.

21.8 Performance management and quality assurance

Studies conducted by the Institute of Personnel Management, United Kingdom, as reported by Fletcher and Williams (in Lundy & Cowling 1996:308) found that there were major weaknesses in the manner in which performance management was being conducted. Firstly, there was little indication of a real sense of ownership of performance management among line managers. This resulted in little depth of commitment, as too many managers perceived it as a top-down process with no feedback loop. There was also a widespread perception that performance management systems were 'owned' by the human resources departments. Finally, a lack of thought and imagination had been shown in tackling the issue of rewards. Lundy and Cowling (1996:309) maintain that if these issues are addressed, the quality of performance management systems will be improved and maintained. South African organisations have no other options – performance management systems must be made to work.

W. Edwards Deming, the father of Total Quality Management, argues that everything in an organisation is done within the framework of a system – if the system itself prevents good work, individuals will not be able to improve their performance, even if they want to. It all boils down to the fact that the quality of a performance management system will only be assured if workers have significant control over the variables that affect their individual performances (Cascio 1995:295). Meyer (1998:32) maintains that the most important criterion in performance management should be the measurement of an individual's contribution towards customer satisfaction. It is, thus, imperative that performance systems are adapted to support quality management implementation.

21.9 Conclusion

This discussion on performance management has seen the introduction of some contemporary viewpoints and also the elaboration of some traditional schools of thought. It is obvious that the performance evaluation process can no longer stand on its own, and must become an integral part of a holistic performance management system that adds value to the organisation. Human resources practitioners and senior managers are beginning to realise that the management of employee performance must take place within the pursuit of strategic business goals. This is one of the major reasons why many organisations are starting to favour a multirater, or 360-degree approach to performance evaluation. The next decade should prove whether this is a viable method of appraisal.

Summary

The philosophy of participation and added value should encourage all employees to welcome the idea of total performance management. When performance management systems are tied into the objectives of the organisation, the resulting performance is more likely to meet organisational needs. Ownership of performance management systems must be vested in both line managers and subordinates.

Performance management is a process for strategy implementation, a vehicle for cultural change, and it provides input to other HR systems. It involves communicating a vision of objectives to employees, setting departmental and individual performance targets, and conducting a formal review of performance.

Performance management is evolving around the amount of value the subordinate's performance adds to the overall organisational performance. Managers and subordinates meet to jointly discuss and agree to the adoption and adaptation of organisational goals, an action plan to achieve the individual's goals, specific times for formal checks to be made, and the type and amount of value that will be added if the goals are achieved. The manager uses coaching skills, offers advice on changing behaviours and approaches, and encourages progress towards achieving goals and adding value. Either relative or absolute judgements are made when measuring employee performance. Several different choices of raters can be made: the immediate supervisor, peers, subordinates, self-appraisal, customers, computerised, 360-degree, and team appraisals.

Rating techniques can be categorised into relative and absolute methods. There are advantages and disadvantages to all of them, but rating scales are still the most popular. Rater-errors such as unclear standards, the halo effect, central tendency, leniency or strictness, recency, and bias must be eliminated or at least minimised.

The appraisal interview should be both evaluative and developmental. Certain guidelines must be followed when planning and conducting the feedback interview.

The performance management process must be legally sound to avoid litigation. The quality of a performance system will only be assured if workers have significant control over the variables that affect their individual performance.

Related websites

This topic may be investigated further by referring to the following Internet websites:
Society for Human Resources Management, HR Magazine – http://www.shrm.org
Personnel Journal, Research Center – http://www.workforceonline.com
Performance Management Associates, Inc. – http://www.pmassoc.com
Performance-by-design – http://www.performance-by-design.com/human
Performance Management Resources – http://www.zigonperf.com/performance.htm
360-Degree Feedback – http://www.360-DegreeFeedback.com

Case study
Explosions in the chemical industry

During the 1990s the chemical industry in South Africa underwent extensive restructuring due to the expiry of patents, competition for resources to support existing products, and a highly competitive market. A major company in the chemical industry acquired Hazardline Chemicals Ltd. The result of this merger was a retrenchment exercise that reduced the original staff complement by 30 per cent. Within Hazardline Chemicals Ltd. a survey revealed a task-orientated culture in which employees felt disconnected from the business, people management skills were undervalued and underdeveloped, and decisions were taken at a high level. Although top management had assured the workforce that there would be no more retrenchments, the staff was still extremely apprehensive, as deployments were taking place on a regular basis. This major upheaval had a grave impact on employee motivation and productivity.

The holding company initiated a performance improvement strategy, based on a new performance management system. The new system aimed at achieving better communication of company objectives, developing individuals to help them achieve agreed targets, and fostering closer relations between staff and line managers. The goal of the new performance system was to offer the following benefits to all individual staff members:

- clear understanding of the job;
- a basis for regular discussion of tasks;
- agreement on development needs;
- feedback on performance; and
- the adding of value both to the employee's work-life and the organisation as a whole.

The workforce at Hazardline could be grouped into three major divisions: senior management and administrative staff, research and development chemists and project engineers, and operators. Most of these people had never really been part of a performance management system before, and prior to the merger performance appraisal had been perfunctory to say the least. Heads of department were sceptical about the new performance management system, mainly because of the lack of information available.

If you were a human resources consultant employed to drive the performance management process, how would you answer the following questions?

Questions

1 Compile a brief report containing an explanation of the performance management process. The report must not be longer than 500 words, and you should be able to present the report to all levels of workers in Hazardline.
2 Debate who should undertake the responsibility of carrying out the evaluation process in Hazardline.
3 Recommend a performance management technique, or techniques, that could easily be applied in the company.
4 Explain how raters should go about giving feedback on performance.

Experiential exercise

Purpose
To role-play a feedback interview.

Introduction
The latest performance evaluation of an employee has just taken place and the supervisor has scheduled an interview where the results of the evaluation can be discussed. The rating was done by means of a graphic rating scale that covered the following elements: quality of work; quantity of work; work attitudes; relationships with others; reliability; initiative; cooperation; and dependability.

Task
The class is divided into two groups: everyone in one group plays the role of the supervisor. Everyone in the other group plays the role of the employee.

Each person in the group playing the role of the employee must choose an occupation they want to role-play (secretary, human resources officer, salesperson, administrative officer, etc.).

Each employee finds a partner from the other group so that pairs are formed, comprising an employee and a supervisor. Each employee and each supervisor spends a few minutes getting used to their roles in terms of the information provided.

Everyone then role-plays his or her parts to each other. The supervisor should do his or her best to defend the evaluation and at the same time encourage the employee to persevere with future performance. This should take about fifteen minutes.

After the role-play, the supervisor rates himself/herself by completing Form A. The employee rates the supervisor by completing Form B. Thereafter, they compare forms in terms of similarities and differences.

Role-play (Employee)

You are worried about your performance evaluation because you are sure your supervisor will rate you down in the areas of 'relationships with others' and 'dependability'. A few weeks ago you were absent from work for two days because your spouse was ill and there was no one to look after her or him. You didn't tell your supervisor the real reason for your absence; instead you merely phoned in and said you were not feeling well. In your company, an absence of two days does not require a doctor's certificate. When you returned to work, your supervisor was very angry because your department had fallen behind with its tasks, and he had to provide his manager with an explanation. He blamed you, and you felt this was unfair. Eventually the discussion turned into a shouting match. You haven't heard any more about the incident but you are sure the supervisor will find some way of paying you back.

Role-play (Supervisor)

You have tried to be honest in your subordinate's evaluation, but you have had to rate him or her below average in the areas of 'relationships with others' and 'work attitudes'. You feel sure that your subordinate will link these ratings to an event that took place a few weeks ago, when he or she was absent from work and you felt the absence was not really justified. However, this is not the reason for the low rating. You have documented a number of other occasions when you have had to intervene between the employee and co-workers, when arguments have brought their work to a standstill. You want to prevent this feedback interview from turning into another shouting match.

Form A
Supervisor's appraisal of own interview technique

	Yes	No
1. Did I put the employee at ease?		
2. Did I ask the employee how he/she feels about his/her own performance?		
3. Did I praise good performance?		
4. Did I give the employee a chance to ask questions?		
5. Did I allow the employee to make suggestions?		
6. Did I help the employee to establish future goals?		
7. Did we clarify any disagreements?		

Form B
Employee's appraisal of the supervisor's interview technique

	Yes	No
1. Did the supervisor make me feel at ease?		
2. Did the supervisor ask me how I feel about my own performance?		
3. Did the supervisor praise my good performance?		
4. Did the supervisor give me a chance to ask questions?		
5. Did the supervisor allow me to make suggestions?		
6. Did the supervisor help me to establish future goals?		
7. Did we clarify any disagreements?		

Chapter questions

1 Many employees dislike performance evaluations, just as many students dislike tests and examinations. What would happen if employers discontinued managing and evaluating their subordinates' performance? What would happen if everyone received the same rating?

2 Is involving someone besides the immediate supervisor a realistic approach to evaluating performance? Consider the advantages and disadvantages of input from more than one source in performance evaluation.

3 How would you discuss negative information with an employee if you were a supervisor? How would you want your supervisor to handle negative information if you were the employee?

4 Discuss common rater-errors and indicate how these errors can be reduced or minimised.

5 Almost all organisation members will have contact with a variety of internal customers. Contact someone who has a

permanent job and ask him or her to identify his or her internal customers. With the help of your contact, design a short questionnaire to collect feedback that would be important in performance evaluation.

6 'My subordinates depend on me for instructions and guidance on how to do their jobs.' Do you think the manager who said this would use the rational or the political approach to performance evaluation? Motivate your answer by comparing the two approaches.

Bibliography

BENNETT, K. & MINTY, H. 1999. Putting performance management on the business map. *People Dynamics.* Nov./Dec., 17(11), 58–63.

CARRELL, M.R., ELBERT, N.F., HATFIELD, R.D., GROBLER, P.A., MARX, M. & VAN DER SCHYF, S. 1998. *Human resource management in South Africa.* Prentice Hall, South Africa.

CASCIO, W.F. 1995. *Managing human resources: productivity, quality of work life, profits.* McGraw-Hill, New York.

CHERRINGTON, D.J. 1995. *The management of human resources.* 4th edition. Prentice-Hall, Englewood Cliffs, NJ.

CROSSLEY, T. & TAYLOR, I. 1995. Developing competitive advantage through 360-degree feedback. *American Journal of Management Development.* 1(1), 11–15.

DESSLER, G. 1997. *Human resource management.* 7th edition. Prentice-Hall, Upper Saddle River, NJ.

GÓMEZ-MEJÍA, L.R., BALKIN, D.B., & CARDY, R.L. 1998. *Managing human resources.* 2nd edition. Prentice-Hall, Upper Saddle River, NJ.

IVANCEVICH, J.M., LORENZI, P., SKINNER, S.J. & CROSBY, P.B. 1997. *Management: quality and competitiveness.* Irwin, Chicago.

JANSEN, P. & VLOEBERGHS, D. 1999. Multi-rater feedback methods: personal and organizational implications. *Journal of Managerial Psychology.* 14(6), 455–476.

KATZ M. 1995. Performance management. *People Dynamics.* Jan. 38.

KATZ, M. 1998. 360-degree evaluation. *People Dynamics.* March, 16(3), 42.

KEMSKE, F. 1998. HR 2008: A forecast based on our exclusive study. *Workforce.* January, 77(1), 46–60.

LUNDY, O. & COWLING, A. 1996. *Strategic human resource management.* Routledge, London.

MEYER, M. April 1998. Quality management: the essential component is teamwork. *People Dynamics.* 16(4), 30–35.

MILLIMAN, J.F., ZAWACKI, R.A., SCHULZ, B., WIGGINS, S. & NORMAN, C.A. 1995. Customer service drives 360-degree goal setting. *Personnel Journal.* June, 74(6), 136–142.

MORAVEC, M. JULIFF, R. & HESLER, K. 1995. Partnerships help a company manage performance. *Personnel Journal.* Jan., 74(1), 104–108.

SCHULTZ, D.P. & SCHULTZ, S.E. 1994. *Psychology and work today: an introduction to industrial and organizational psychology.* 6th edition. MacMillan, Englewood Cliffs, NJ.

SEGAL, J. 1995. Evaluating the evaluators. *HR Magazine.* Oct.

SLOMAN, M. 1997. Relating human resource activities to business strategy. In Tyson, S. (ed.) *The practice of human resource strategy.* pp. 155–173. Pitman, London.

SWANEPOEL, B.J. (ED.), ERASMUS, B.J., VAN WYK, M.W. & SCHENK, H.W. 1998. *South African human resource management.* Juta, Kenwyn.

TORRINGTON, D. & HALL, L. 1995. *Personnel management: HRM in action.* 3rd edition. Prentice-Hall, London.

22

Organisational renewal

T Sono

Learning outcomes

At the end of this chapter the learner should be able to demonstrate the following outcomes:
- Understand the claims and strategies of organisational renewal.
- Assess the renewal strategies of the Kitty organisation.
- Understand the distinctions between organisational renewal, organisational development, and organisational change.
- Understand the nature of organisations.
- Discuss critical factors for organisational renewal.
- Explain Waterman's key corporate renewal factors.
- Distinguish the relationship between environmental factors and organisational renewal.
- Know the role of globalisation in organisational renewal.
- Discuss the role of technology in organisational renewal.

Key words and concepts

- adaptation/adaptiveness
- affirmative action
- behavioural change
- change
- corporation/company
- corporate renewal
- customisation
- development
- employment equity plans
- environmental factors
- flexibility
- friendly facts
- goals
- goal-directed behaviour
- globalisation
- informal organisation
- informed opportunism
- innovation
- knowledge resources
- learning
- lessons in organisational renewal
- marketplace

- means
- new norms
- organisational change (OC)
- organisational development (OD)
- organisational renewal (OR)
- renewal processes
- responsiveness
- stability in motion
- technology
- transformation

Illustrative case

The Kitty Group is a company that was founded in the early 1950s in South Africa. It specialised in the production of knowledge and the dissemination of information. For decades since its formation, it preferred to employ persons of a particular racial, cultural, and gender background.

Of its more than a thousand employees, 90 per cent were from one racial group. The remaining 5 per cent were from another racial group. The latter occupied only menial positions and performed servile roles. The lowest ranks in the organisation were entirely staffed by women.

With the changes that occurred in South Africa since 1994, the Kitty Group saw its chances of survival greatly reduced because a large source of its revenue was from Government, either through grants or contracts.

The senior management of the Kitty company came to the conclusion that in order to survive, the organisation had to renew itself, not only in order to be competitive in a suddenly open market, but also to be politically legitimate in a changed environment.

From 1995, the Kitty Group undertook to implement renewal strategies, such as the following:
- recruitment;
- selection and appointment;
- promotion;
- training and career development;
- accountability; and
- targets and time frames.

Recruitment. The old recruitment policy was eliminated, and in its stead a new one prescribed that, should a post become available, every possible effort must be made to attract suitably qualified and/or experienced candidates from the previously excluded groups. Advertisements for a vacancy should also state that suitable experience should receive a higher consideration. Posts should also be advertised internally and externally, simultaneously.

Selection and appointment. Candidates from the previously excluded group should be selected, as far as possible, to meet the renewal goals. The criteria employed were as follows:
- preference should be given firstly to any suitable candidate from the designated group who is an employee of the Kitty organisation;
- should no suitable candidate be available, preference should be given to a candidate from outside the organisation who meets the requirements;
- should no suitable candidate be available, then all other Kitty employees who qualify for the post should be considered; and
- should no suitable candidate be available internally, then all other suitable candidates may be considered.

Promotion. This procedure would follow the recruitment strategy outlined above, the essence of which is that candidates from designated groups should be considered first for any promotion in an existing vacancy.

Training and career development. Appropriate opportunities for training and career development would be extended first to the staff from the designated groups, and then to the rest of the staff equally, regardless of race, colour, or gender.

Accountability. The chief executive of the Kitty group would bear responsibility for the policy, but line management would be responsible for its implementation. Clearly stated objectives regarding the efforts and process used to support and implement this policy, would form part of their critical performance areas.

Targets and time frames. To ensure that representation was effected throughout the organisation, the aim was to have members of the previously excluded groups forming at least 55 per cent of its staff complement by June 1999. The organisation set the following targets:

Kitty's renewal strategies
(All figures reflect percentages)

Category	Current (1994)	1996	1999
Management	7,8	33,3	50
Researchers	22,6	36	50
Professional support	23,3	45	50
Technical support	46,9	50	60
Clerical/secretarial	29,9	50	60
General assistants	100	on merit	on merit
TOTALS	26,6	43,8	54,6

Learning task

Comment on and discuss the Kitty Group's renewal strategy.
- How successful was it, given the above table?
- Was this form of organisational renewal necessary?
- Explain how human resources management is part of organisational renewal.
- Comment on the ethics of the above renewal strategies.

22.1 Introduction

New organisational possibilities have constantly appeared in the late twentieth and early twenty-first centuries. Organisations renew themselves. Organisational renewal is a form of change and learning, where improvement processes in the organisation have become widespread and are part of the culture of the workforce and management. In organisational renewal, new norms must be communicated and understood throughout the organisation (Kast & Rosenzweig 1985:618). In the renewal of the organisation, new approaches become an integral part of the basic planning, control processes, and communication procedures of the organisation. Organisational renewal, thus, is a behavioural change by an organisation. That is to say, organisational renewal involves organisational change and development.

Organisational renewal is actually adaptation and development. This requires organisations to invest some resources in activities that will enhance the nett worth of the organisation in the future (e.g. in research and development investment). Without renewal efforts, 'organisational survival is often threatened by short-term shifts in market demands, resources, etc.' (Steers 1988:28). Human resources managers are an integral part of renewal processes. In some studies, the terms organisational renewal (OR), organisational change (OC), and organisational development (OD) are interchangeable. The following definition of OD identifies the three interchangeable elements of renewal, change, and development:

> The term 'Organizational development' ... implies a normative, re-education strategy intended to affect systems of beliefs, values, and attitudes within the organization so that it can adapt better to the accelerated rate of change in technology, in our industrial environment and society in general. It also includes formal organizational restructuring which is frequently initiated, facilitated and reinforced by the normative and behavioural changes (Winn in Gibson et al. 1985: 676).

French and Bell (1973:15) see organisational renewal and development thus:

> Organizational development is a long-range effort to improve an organization's problem-solving and renewal processes, particularly through a more effective and collaborative management of organization culture – with special emphasis on the culture of formal work teams – with the assistance of a change agent, or catalyst, and the use of the theory and technology of applied behavioural science, including action research. But organizational development is not exactly one and the same thing with organizational renewal.

Organisational development is a planned, systematic process of organisational change, based on behavioural science technology, research, and theory. To the extent that organisational development is characterised by the following, it is not different from organisational renewal:

- seeking to create self-directed change to which people are committed;
- being a system-wide change effort;
- placing equal emphasis on solving immediate problems and long-term development of an adaptive organisation;
- placing emphasis on collaborative efforts of data collection, diagnosis, and action planning; and
- often leading to new organisational structures and relationships (Hellriegel et al. 1983:451).

Thus both organisational development and organisational renewal involve organisational change. The elements of one are involved in the processes of the other. Waterman (1987:6) refers to renewal and change in the following terms:

> Somehow there are organizations that effectively manage change, continuously adapting their bureaucracies, strategies, systems, products and cultures to survive the shocks and prosper from the forces that decimate their competition... They are masters of renewal. The fact is that managers are going to have to become masters of change and renewal to be effective in the future.

Burnes' book (1992) has the subtitle 'organisational development and renewal', yet nowhere in the book, neither in the contents page, nor in the index, let alone in the body of the text, is there any reference to organisational renewal. Organisations, however, do need to renew themselves if they are to stave off being grounded in a rut.

Organisations, like individuals, undergo changes in both ends and means, i.e. the goals they strive for and the methods they use. Some goals remain stable, such as survival, profitability, market share, service to clients, and growth. The means to achieve these goals, however, vary from time to time because of various factors, internal and external, such as the environment, government regulations, competitive conditions, and technological innovations and advancement.

In some cases, the means stay the same, while the ends are adjusted. In other cases, simultaneous adjustments to both ends and means are made in order to attain, for instance, racial balance in companies. Affirmative action and employment equity plans may be introduced so as to increase workforce diversity (see Chapter 17). Introducing diversity in the workforce is to introduce change; it is to renew the organisation. Another example may be the corporate responsibility for the control of water, ground, or air pollution, which may introduce new and significantly different production processes and management focus and direction. These are the new processes that give impetus to the renewal of organisations. Failing to change, when change is required, may lead to the demise of the organisation. To understand renewal requires that we first understand what an organisation is.

22.2 What is an organisation?

The human race could be traced through the history of the development of social organisations. Families and small nomadic tribes came first; then came permanent villages and tribal communities. These were followed by the feudal system and nation-states (Kast & Rosenzweig 1985:3). Organisations are entities that enable society to pursue accomplishments that cannot be achieved by individuals acting alone. Organisations are characterised by their goal-directed behaviour (Gibson et al. 1985:7).

The corporation, or company, is the current dominant organisational form in the Western world. When we refer to organisational renewal in this chapter, it should be understood as a reference to the renewal of a corporation. The organisation however, is a dynamic system, constantly changing and adapting to internal and external pressures, and is in a continuous process of evolution.

There are essentially two forms of organisation, the formal and the informal. A formal organisation is a rationally structured system of interrelated activities, processes, and technologies within which human efforts are coordinated to achieve specific objectives. We are accustomed to observing such organisations in business, schools, hospitals, government, etc. Informal organisations, on the other hand, spontaneously develop whenever people interact closely for a period of time (Williams & Huber 1986:268–269). Informal organisations exist in cliques, gangs, and cooperative work groups. Another view sees a formal organisation as that part of a corporation that has legitimacy and official recognition; and an informal organisation as the unofficial part of the corporation (Nelson & Quick 1997:11).

Because of overlapping membership of formal and informal organisations, the latter play a significant role in the life of the former. The term organisation should, nevertheless, be understood to mean formal organisation. Organisations may produce goods or deliver services; they may manufacture products such as automobiles, candles, computers, and food, or provide services, such as insurance and banking. Organisations are, thus, open systems (Perrow 1973:11). They are also viewed as sub-systems of a broader suprasystem – the environment. They have identifiable but permeable boundaries that separate them from their environment (Kast & Rosenzweig 1985:131). Others see an organisation as a consciously coordinated social unit, composed of two or more people, that functions on a relatively continuous basis to achieve a common goal or set of goals (Robbins 1989:4).

22.3 Critical factors for renewal

Although organisations are not necessarily destined for a life cycle of birth, growth, maturity, decline, and death, many aspects of such a cycle are apparent (Kast & Rosenzweig 1985:620). Adaptation and innovation are critical for organisational survival, especially if traumatic experiences such as bankruptcy are to be avoided. These factors are also essential for renewal. While stability and continuity are important attributes to the basic function of organisations, other factors that give impetus for renewal continually play upon these attributes.

The importance of organisational renewal cannot be overemphasised, because it can make the difference between the success and the survival of the organisation. This means that an organisation must continuously adapt to its environment; without renewal, management will not maintain efficiency, excellence and, thus, sustained productivity. Organisational renewal is an on-going process of building innovation and adaptation into the organisation (Eisenhardt in Harvey & Brown 1996:31).

Stability and change often vie with each other in organisational processes, precisely because both are essential in an organisation; yet, at the same time, they obstruct each other. Effective and successful organisations tend to resist change. They see no need to change what they see as successful. This is the 'if it ain't broke don't fix it' mindset. Organisational renewal, nevertheless, is an approach to preventing organisational ossification. Waterman (1987:8) suggests eight key factors for corporate renewal:

- *Informed opportunism.* Renewing organisations set directions, not detailed strategy. These companies treat information as their main strategic advantage, and flexibility as their main strategic weapon.
- *Direction and empowerment.* The renewing companies treat everyone as a source of creative input. They give up some control over subordinates to gain what counts: results.
- *Friendly facts.* The renewing companies treat facts as friends, and financial controls as liberating. They love facts and information that remove decision-making from mere opinion.
- *A different mirror.* The leaders of renewing organisations seem to get their determination from their singular ability to anticipate crises. This stems from their willingness to listen to all sources – to look into a different mirror.
- *Teamwork and trust.* Renewers constantly use such words as teamwork and trust. They are relentless at fighting office politics.
- *Stability in motion.* The renewing companies know how to keep things moving. Renewing companies undergo constant change against a base of underlying stability.
- *Attitudes and attention.* In renewing companies, visible management attention gets things done. Action may start

with words, but must be backed by behaviours.
- *Causes and commitment.* Renewing organisations seem to run on causes. Commitment results from management's ability to turn grand causes into small actions so that everyone can contribute.

22.4 Characteristics of organisational development and organisational renewal

Organisational development (OD) shares certain distinguishing characteristics with the renewal process. According to Margulies and Raia (1978:25):
- *It is planned.* OD is a data-based approach to change that involves all of the ingredients that go into managerial planning. It involves goal setting, action planning, implementation, monitoring, and taking corrective action when necessary.
- *It is problem-orientated.* OD attempts to apply theory and research from a number of disciplines to the solution of organisational problems. It is taking problem to method, and not method to problem.
- *It reflects a systems approach.* OD is both systemic and systematic. It is a way of more closely linking the human resources and potential of an organisation to its technology, structure, and management processes.
- It is an integral part of the management process. OD is not something that is done to the organisation by outsiders. It becomes a way of managing organisational change processes.
- *It is not a 'fix-it' strategy.* OD is a continuous and ongoing process. It is not a series of ad hoc activities designed to implement a specific change. It takes time for OD to become a way of life in the organisation.
- *It focuses on improvement.* OD's emphasis is on improvement. It is not just for 'sick' organisations or for 'healthy' ones. It is something that can benefit almost any organisation.
- *It is action-orientated.* The focus of OD is on accomplishments and results. Unlike approaches to change that tend to describe how organisational change takes place, the emphasis of OD is on getting things done.
- *It is based on sound theory and practice.* OD is not a gimmick or a fad. It is solidly based on the theory and research of a number of disciplines.

22.5 Environmental factors and renewal

Organisational renewal is often stimulated by alterations in the environment. The environment may be both general and specific. The general environment for any organisation includes economic, ecological, demographic, informational, political, and cultural factors. We may also speak of an external, or market, environment which is made up of customers, competitors, suppliers, government, etc. (Steers 1988:68). That is, within the general environment, each organisation has a more specific set of factors (i.e. its task or market environment) that is pertinent to its decision-making processes. Each has an influence on an organisation's goal-directed activities. Change in these spheres has been taking place at an accelerating pace, especially in the last decade of the last century, and will continue to do so in the new century.

Managers of organisations have historically been concerned with reacting to changes in the marketplace. Competitors introduce new products, increase their advertising, reduce their prices, or increase their customer service; in each case, a response is required unless the managers are content to permit the erosion of profit and market share (Gibson et al. 1985:682). Simultaneously, changes occur in customer tastes and incomes. The firm's products may no longer have customer appeal; customers may be able to purchase less expensive, higher quality forms of the same product. A human resources manager would, in such an event, be alerted to the dearth of management ability to make the organisation efficient and viable. Intervention would be required to renew the organisation. There is, thus, a correlation between efficiency in organisational productivity and efficient human resources management responses.

The most important of the general environmental factors are globalisation and technology.

22.5.1 Globalisation

Globalisation implies that the world is free of national boundaries and that ours is really a borderless world (Ohmae 1990). The globalisation phenomenon is a challenge that spurs renewal in organisations. The increased movement across borders of people, products, services, and capital are some of the driving forces behind the globalisational processes. All these forces are greatly aided by the rapid evolution of information technology (IT) and other technologies. Just as boundaries between industries are blurring, boundaries between nations are becoming fluid in our globalised era.

The pressure of globalisation has rendered the national state less important, and the global organisation ever more important. Countries have become like companies; they are all engaged in competition. Organisations are in search of optimal operating environments. They, thus, engage in self-renewal. Without renewal, organisations soon ossify and become less competitive. Many simply die off.

In the global organisation there are no mental distinctions between domestic and foreign operations. Global organisations are constantly engaged in renewing themselves, because they constantly meet new environmental situations and complex cultural demands. Demands for organisational change increase at a rapid pace. Organisations, like their workers, are buffeted by these demands.

Workers, like companies, are of the world. Companies, like their workers, are now competing across nations, across borders. They are involved in a continuum of renewal. They are compelled to become innovative, inasmuch as they renew themselves on a constant basis. In organisational renewal, adaptiveness, flexibility, and responsiveness are critical. These are vital qualities for organisations, especially global companies, to succeed in meeting the competitive challenges that they face today. Change and renewal have been the norm in the globalisation era (Verespey 1992: 35–38).

It is no longer enough, as it was in the past, for organisational success to be based on excellence in one area, such as quality, reliability, or cost (Nelson & Quick 1997: 540). To be truly global, organisations must have capability and efficiency in all areas. The concept of customisation is fast becoming a leading indicator in terms of organisations positioning themselves locally and globally. To meet the needs of customers, companies (and other organisations) both locally and globally, are placed on good relationships with customers. Customer intimacy is becoming an important factor in the renewal of global companies. The basic ingredients of globalisation are increased trade and the use of IT, and these demand the global company to continually renew itself in order to stay competitive. The growing power of IT reinforces the idea that we live in a global village.

22.5.2 Technology

In a general sense, technology refers to the application of knowledge for the more effective performance of certain tasks or activities (Kast & Rosenzweig 1985:208). By organisational technology is meant the techniques used in the transformation of inputs into outputs. Both human resources managers and production managers employ technology in the transformation and renewal of their organisations. The effects of technology on organisational structure and behaviour are today more pronounced than ever before. The actions managers take to make some change, improvement, or development in the organisation are referred to as technology impacts. A compatible, but broader, definition of technology is that 'technology is the application of knowledge to perform work' (Rousseau 1979:531). Thus, organisational structures reflect technology in the ways that jobs are designed (the division of labour) and grouped (departmentalisation).

Technology improves the range of choices that managers have in increasing organisational efficiency and renewal. Even though technology can also be constraining in the range of such choices, managers have considerable discretion within those constrains. Technology affects people in organisations in diverse ways. It is now a key factor in determining the tasks and degree of specialisation required, even in human resources management. It often determines the size and composition of the immediate work-group and the range of contacts with other workers and supervisors (Kast & Rosenzweig 1985:220). Its impact on management systems is even more dramatic than on other organisational sub-systems.

22.6 Failure of organisations to renew themselves

Parliament was recently warned of an impending collapse of university and technikon education as a result of drastically falling student numbers. The Council on Higher Education informed Parliament that in the year 2000 there were at least 100 000 fewer students at tertiary education institutions than was predicted in 1995. Initial calculations in 1995 estimated an annual 4 per cent increase in student numbers, from 570 000 to 710 000 in the year 2002. Instead numbers dwindled to 560 000 in 1999.

University and technikon institutions fail to undertake renewal strategies that would enhance and sustain their viability. Their problems are:
- large reductions in student enrolments;
- government grants drying up, and tertiary institutions lacking innovative ways and means to garner replacement funds;
- white students emigrating in larger numbers than anticipated; and
- large numbers of black students being ineligible for entry into higher education.

Of the 500 000 grade 12 students who wrote final examinations in 1999, 272 000 passed, but only 69 000 obtained the exemption that allows entry into higher education. It is Afrikaans universities, however, which show better adaptive strategies, as they have attracted increasing numbers of black students, particularly since 1995.

The major failure of tertiary institutions is one of lack of self-renewal and appropriate transformation. Many mistook affirmative action programmes to be the real transformation that was required. These institutions are now gradually ossifying and a few will no longer be in place within five years.

What the higher education sector failed to fully grasp are the patterns of successful and unsuccessful change.

22.6.1 Conditions for successful change

Hellriegel et al. (1983:451) identify the following conditions for successful change:
- people in the organisation must feel pressure in order to be ready for change;
- the participation and involvement of people in re-examining problems and practices is necessary to build commitment for change;
- new ideas or concepts must be brought in from the outside to help people in the organisation find new approaches to improve its effectiveness;
- to ensure early success and prevent major failures that can slow down the momentum of change, an organisation should limit the scope of early change efforts; and
- an organisation often needs a skilled leader, or change agent, to bring in new ideas and to support individuals in the process of improving its effectiveness.

22.6.2 What to avoid

- Change efforts are often characterised by poorly defined goals and poorly defined problems.
- Renewal strategies must not be assumed to be understood by all in the management. There has to clear communication about the need for such renewal, its purpose, and what the consequences of failure may be.
- Faulty assumptions about organisational learning should be avoided.

22.6.3 What is organisational learning?

The simple answer is that it is the main process by which innovation and adaptation by management occurs. As the question suggests, two concepts are matched in organisational learning: organisation and learning. An organisation, as we have seen, is a dynamic system that is constantly changing. It, thus, has the capacity to learn as if it were a subject. It processes information and knowledge; it has skills, expertise, and the capacity to store, retrieve, and communicate data and information.

Organisations have a close relationship with the process of learning and, thus, with knowledge and information and its transmission. Since organisations can be seen as systems that learn, learning is intrinsic to organisational renewal. The father of the learning organisation, Senge (1987:5–9), sees five new 'component technologies' of the learning organisation:
- system thinking;
- personal mastery;
- mental models;
- shared vision; and
- team learning.

A learning organisation continuously expands its capacity to create its future; it constantly renews itself to overcome organisational entropy.

22.6.4 In summary: organisational renewal strategies

These strategies are not separate and independent of other organisational processes, but are intertwined with organisational development, organisational change, organisational transformation, and the learning organisation.
- *Organisational development* poses the following questions:
  - Where are we?
  - Where do we want to be?
  - What must we do to get there?
- *Organisational change* is more constant than stability. Change occurs because of external and internal forces impacting

on the organisation. Change is constant, or organisations atrophy.
- *Organisational transformation* is not simply a search for a new organisational identity, but rather a positioning of the organisation in response to new forces so as to stave off obsolescence.
- *Learning organisation:* an organisation that does not learn cannot renew itself. Self-renewal of an organisation demands the learning of new approaches, new understandings, and new alignments.

22.7 Goals and values

These are a further impetus for renewal and change. Modifications to the goals of the organisation require modifications to the organisation itself. Changes in what is good and desirable (values) are also important because they lead to changes in goals; or, if the goals remain constant, changes in values can lead to changes in what is considered appropriate behaviour.

Organisations depend on the basic values that underline goal setting and decision-making. In the renewal of organisations, values and goals, thus, play an important role, especially as regards the future operations of the organisation. But what, then, are goals and values?

'Goals represent the desired future conditions that individuals or organizations strive to achieve' (Kast & Rosenzweig 1985:179). They, thus, include missions, purposes, targets, and deadlines. Values are normative views, held by individuals, of what is good and desirable (Kast & Rosenzweig 1985:178). Value issues affect organisations in a variety of ways, such as group dynamics, organisation, pursuit of goals, and the entire management of the organisation. Values and goals are integral to the process of renewal.

The goals of an organisation influence its interactions with the environment; but goals are, themselves, shaped by the unique tasks or problems an organisation emphasises, since organisations are contrived goal-seeking systems.

We have seen the environmental influences on organisational renewal, but the environment also has an impact on organisational goal-setting, which is a product of specific interactions, namely competition, bargaining, co-option, and coalition (Katz & Rosenzweig 1985:181–182).

Thompson and McEwen (in Kast & Rosenzweig 1985:183) show that a competitive relationship exists where two organisations are competing for the support of a third party: for instance, companies compete for customers, material resources, and labour inputs; universities compete for funds, students, and faculties; and hospitals for paying patients. Competition, thus, drives organisations to renew themselves, and leads to goal-attainment which, in turn, is a renewal agency.
- *Bargaining* involves direct negotiations between organisations. In the bargaining situation, each party must modify its own goals in response to the needs of the other party. In the joint ventures that have occurred in the last decade, bargaining has featured prominently, and companies have modified their goals and, thus, advanced their renewal prospects.
- *Cooptation* is defined as 'the process of absorbing new elements into the leadership or policy-determining structure of an organization as a means of averting threats to its stability or existence' (Thompson & McEwen in Kast & Rosenzweig 1985:182). This is an action of giving 'outsiders' positions of responsibility in the organisation. For instance, businesses may have representatives of banks on their boards, and university managements may have student representative councils on their councils or administrative boards. Cooptation influences goals in this fashion.

- Coalitions between organisations require a further modification of the goals. 'The term coalition refers to a combination of two or more organisations for a common purpose. Coalition appears to be the ultimate or extreme form of environmental conditioning of organizational goals' (Thompson & McEwen in Kast & Rosenzweig 1985: 182). A coalition suggests organisational modification of goals to accommodate other parties or interests.

22.8 Conclusion

Organisational renewal is the purposeful effort to alter the structure and processes of an organisation in order to make it more effective and productive. There can, thus, be no renewal by the organisation as a whole, unless individuals and groups in the organisation are willing to alter patterns of behaviour.

Organisational renewal is usually stimulated by changes in the environment. The general environment of any organisation in society includes technological, economic, ecological, demographic, legal, political, and cultural factors. Change in these spheres seems to be occurring at an accelerating rate (Kast & Rosenzweig 1985: 621). However, within this general environmental constellation are the specific, powerful forces of globalisation, technology, and information and knowledge management. These factors are already, to a large extent, shaping organisational renewal. Other pressures for renewal stem from rapid product obsolescence, the changing nature of the workforce, and demands for a higher quality of work life (Hellriegel et al. 1986:595).

Factors that spur renewal are not new, however. Some are as old as human history itself. Technological beginnings coincide with the first hominidal use of a stone to crack a nut, just as globalisation is as old as Marco Polo's adventures or Prince Henry the Navigator's exploits. Knowledge, said the Athenian Hellenic more than 2 000 years ago, is power. Data leads to information, information to knowledge, and knowledge to action which, in turn, leads to results. There is, thus, nothing new about information-based businesses, much of whose organisational renewal is based on information and knowledge strategies.

Organisational renewal is a process in which an organisation is engaged so as to attain or retain a competitive edge. In an attempt to gain competitive advantage, organisations and their managers actively engage themselves in a process where speed is increasingly seen as a key to this advantage. Renewal affords organisations the ability not only to be competitive but to become global players as well. Organisations, thus, attempt to marry their global reach and resources with the speed and adaptability of small, start-up enterprises.

Speed is a form of technology which is essential for organisational renewal. An indicator of an organisation's ability to retain its competitive edge, is the rate at which it renews itself. Increasingly, this rate lies not only in the skills the people in the organisation have, but also in the innovations and technologies the organisation is willing to introduce.

Together with these innovations and technologies, are goals and values which are essential for organisational renewal. Goals and values represent the primary determinant of behaviour (Steers 1988: 192). In human resources management, the focus on renewal, as we have seen, expresses itself in such processes as change, transformation, development, learning, and adaptiveness.

Case study

The Telco vs. Siza battle for supremacy: renewal or die.

Telco Distribution Company (Pty.) Ltd. was founded in 1969 to distribute electrical and electronic equipment to the up-scale markets of the urban areas of SA's major cities. Telco had a virtual monopoly in the distribution services for its products.

In 1994, a rival company, Siza Distribution Company (Pty.) Ltd., was founded to distribute similar products but to a fast-growing clientele in the townships and the same up-scale markets that Telco monopolised for years. The demographics of the up-scale markets underwent great changes between 1991–1997. Siza thus made considerable inroads into the client-base of Telco.

Telco began to seek new strategies because its competitive edge was fast eroding. What do you think were its renewal strategies to counter the competitiveness of Siza?

Telco renewal strategies, amongst others, were the following:

- It increased its 'empowerment' profile by expediting affirmative action, increasing managers from previously disadvantaged backgrounds in its managerial pool, formed joint ventures with companies with credible PDI status, and even put a woman on its board of directors.
- It began to include townships and other rural areas that it did not previously include in its market strategies.
- It also diversified its products by including those of cheaper qualities to cater for the lower economic classes.

Question

1 If you were the managing director of Siza what new strategies would you devise to counter the renewal strategies of Telco?

Chapter questions

1 What do you understand organisational renewal to be?
2 What role may affirmative action play in organisational renewal?
3 What role may employment equity plans play in organisational renewal?
4 Discuss Waterman's key factors for corporate renewal.
5 Discuss environmental factors and their relationship to organisational renewal.
6 What are the conditions for successful renewal as outlined by Hellriegel et al?
7 What role do goals and values play in organisational renewal?

Bibliography

BURNES, B. 1992. *International dimension of organizational behavior.* 2nd edition. PWs Kent, Boston.

FRENCH, W.L. & BELL, C.H., JR. 1973. *Organizational development.* Prentice-Hall, Englewood Cliffs.

GIBSON, J.L., IVANCEVICH, J.M. & DONNELLY, J.H., JR. 1985. *Organizations: behavior, structure, process.* Business Publications, Inc. Plano, Texas.

GRAY, J.L. & STARKE, F.A. 1977. *Organizational behavior: concepts and applications.* Charles E. Merrill, Ohio.

HARVEY, D.F. & BROWN, D.R. 1996. *An experiential approach to organization development.* Prentice-Hall, Englewood Cliffs.

HELLRIEGEL, D., SLOCUM, J.W. & WOODMAN, R.W. 1986. *Organizational behavior.* 4th edition. West Publishing Company, St. Paul, New York, Los Angeles, San Francisco.

KAST, R. & ROSENZWEIG, J.E. 1985. *Organization and management: a system and contingency approach.* 4th edition. McGraw-Hill Book Company, New York, Johannesburg.

MARGULIES, N. & RAIA, A.P. 1978. *Conceptual foundations of organizational development.* McGraw-Hill, New York.

NELSON, D.L. & QUICK, J.C. 1997. *Organizational behavior: foundations, realities and challenges.* West Publishing Company, Minneapolis/St. Paul, New York, Los Angeles, San Francisco.

OHMAE, K. 1990. *Borderless world: power and strategies in the interlinked economy.* Harper & Row, New York.

PERROW, C. 1973. The short and glorious history of organization theory. *Organizational Dynamics,* Winter.

ROBBINS, S.P. 1989. *Organizational behavior: concepts, controversies, and applications.* 4th edition. Prentice-Hall Inc., Englewood Cliffs.

ROUSSEAU, D.M. 1979. Assessment of technology in organizations: closed versus open systems approaches. *Academy of Management Review,* October.

STEERS, R.M. 1976. When is an organisation effective? A process approach to understanding effectiveness. *Organisational Dynamics,* Autumn.

STEERS, R.M. 1988. *Introduction to organizational behavior.* 3rd edition. Scott, Foresman and Company, Glenview, Illinois, Boston, London.

VERESPY, M.A. 1992. When change becomes the norm. *Industry Week,* 16 March, 35–38.

WATERMAN, R.A. 1987. *The renewal factor.* Bantam Books, New York.

WILLIAMS, J.C. & HUBER, G.P. 1986. *Human behavior in organizations.* 3rd edition. South-Western Publishing Company, Cincinnati, Chicago, Dallas.

part seven

Strategic and international human resources management

23

Interdependency between organisational strategy and strategic human resources management

P S van Dyk and P S Nel

Learning outcomes

At the end of this chapter the learner should be able to demonstrate the following outcomes:
- Explain the basic concepts that constitute strategy.
- Explain the concept of strategic human resources management.
- Define strategy and identify the elements of the strategic process.
- Explain the relation of decision making to the strategy formulation process.
- Demonstrate the integration of a human resources management strategy with the overall organisational strategy.
- Explain the relation between organisational strategy and human resources development.

Key words and concepts

- functional level strategic planning
- human resources planning
- human resources management development
- levels of planning
- long-term planning
- mission
- operational planning
- organisational environment
- organisational values
- strategic business planning
- strategic business unit
- strategic human resources management
- strategic management
- strategy
- vision

> Illustrative case
> Nirvana Commercial Property Leasing and Estate Agents (Pty.) Ltd.
>
> The company has been in existence since 1964 and started in Gauteng as a

one man estate agency headed by Johnny Bigbucks, assisted by his wife, Brenda; it was established after an argument with his family concerning his position and share in the family business. He came from a stock of estate agents and property developers who had been in this business since starting in Cape Town in 1907. Johnny followed in his grandfather's and father's footsteps, and built up his own business over the last few decades into a large, thriving property leasing and estate agency business. By 1985, the company had regularly won national awards as the best estate agency, with the top sales people (having exceeded R200 million property value sales per annum) as well as being one of the largest commercial property leasing agencies in Gauteng. The company was one of the three largest businesses of this nature in the eastern part of the country and had a staff of over 500. The company's nett worth was more than R25 million and its turnover ran into billions by 1990. The two sections of the business have been in constant competition and a spirit of healthy rivalry exists.

In the early 1990s, Johnny decided to consolidate the business and to concentrate its activities more. He gradually reduced the operations in major centres like Durban, Port Elizabeth, and Bloemfontein, and relocated them to Cape Town, in particular, and Mitchell's Plain became a focus area. National fears of instability in Gauteng, and forecasts of doom and gloom in most other provinces, encouraged him to relocate most of the staff and business activities to Cape Town, although he felt a little uneasy about this concentration of his business. He also moved his head office to Green Point in Cape Town. By early 1998, 70 per cent of the business activities were concentrated in the Cape Peninsula and adjacent areas; 20 per cent of the business was located in Gauteng, and the remainder scattered across the country.

Since 1998, business has taken a turn for the worse and Johnny's financial situation has deteriorated to a nett loss for the 1999/2000 financial year. Johnny fears that this situation may continue. The loss was mainly because staff refused to work in the Cape Peninsula owing to violence, bombings, attacks on staff, and a general lack of confidence with regard to personal safety. Large numbers of people have sold property and moved back to Gauteng. Property available for leasing has also mounted to thousands of square metres in Cape Town and vicinity, and has left Johnny with two empty buildings on his books, for which he signed leasing rights for ten years, starting on 1 January 1998.

The high incidence of car and pipe bombings in Cape Town, and the Golden Arrow Bus drama which left four of his staff members wounded and two killed, has resulted in a major exodus of staff from Nirvana Commercial Property Leasing and Estate Agents (Pty.) Ltd. Various robberies of staff collecting rent have also taken their toll. To make matters worse, most of his staff in the Cape Town area were recruited by the Property and General Workers' Union of South Africa (PGWUSA). The union has insisted on better safety for employees, and a significant increase in pay and overtime rates.

Johnny is now desperate and realises that he has to do something about his staff situation urgently or else he will soon see his empire collapse. He is also thinking seriously about relocating the whole business back to Gauteng.

> You are a consultant from Property Dynamics (Pty.) Ltd., who has been approached by Johnny to advise him on a new business strategy and human resources management strategy for Nirvana Commercial Property Leasing and Estate Agents (Pty.) Ltd. You also have a human resources specialist on your team. What advice would you give to Johnny with regard to his situation?

23.1 Introduction

Every organisation should have a strategy, subdivided into sub-strategies such as marketing, finance, human resources, and production. Of all the sub-strategies, the human resources sub-strategy has thus far been mostly neglected by management in organisations the world over.

With the recurring low productivity that characterises South African organisations, and the great shortage of professional and highly skilled employees, management has finally accepted that people are the only sustainable competitive advantage of an organisation. This shift in focus is welcomed by human resources practitioners in South Africa, but the ball is now in their court to meet the expectations of top management in this regard.

This book deals with basic aspects of human resources management; strategic aspects are regarded as advanced subject matter. For this reason, strategy will only be briefly discussed on the basis of the principal learning components as shown in Figure 23.1.

Figure 23.1 Principal learning components of strategic human resources management

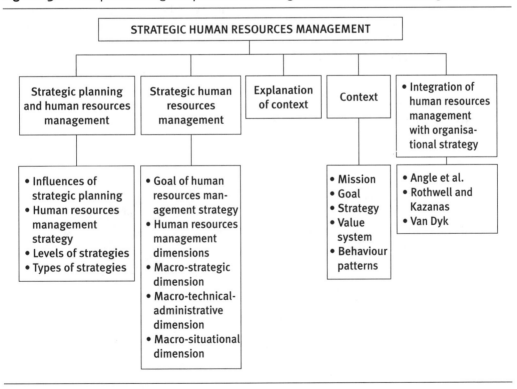

23.2 Explanation of concepts

The general concepts used in describing any organisational strategy are given in Figure 23.2.

Only the concepts in the centre of Figure 23.2 are briefly discussed here.

Any talk about 'vision', 'mission', and 'strategy' is nothing more than rhetoric unless the employees make it their own and learn to live with it (Plevel et al. 1994:62).

- *Vision.* This represents the goal or raison d'être of the organisation.
- *Mission.* This refers to the business in which the organisation is involved and represents a general plan of how the organisation aims to achieve its objectives, as is explained in more detail elsewhere in this chapter.
- *Values.* These are expressed in the manner in which the organisation and its people handle customers, suppliers, and each other.
- *Objectives.* The end result that the organisation wants to achieve is derived from its mission. Objectives generally represent the task that the organisation wishes to carry out.
- *Strategy.* This refers to the long-term plans developed by top management, usually for periods of two to ten years or even longer. These plans are used to evaluate and seize opportunities as well as to allocate resources. Strategy includes plans to create new products, to purchase other organisations, to sell unprofitable sections of the business, to make shares available, and to enter international markets. Anthony et al. (1999:10) adds an additional dimension by defining it as follows: 'The formulation of organizational missions, goals, and objectives, as well as action plans for achievement, that explicitly recognize the competition and the impact of outside environmental forces.'
- *Tactical business plan.* Short-term plans to implement the activities and objectives contained in the strategy. These plans usually cover a period of a year or less. They keep the organisation on the course determined by its strategic plan. Tactical plans enable the organisation to react to changes in the environment, while at the same time concentrating on the overall

Figure 23.2 A pyramidical framework for strategic management

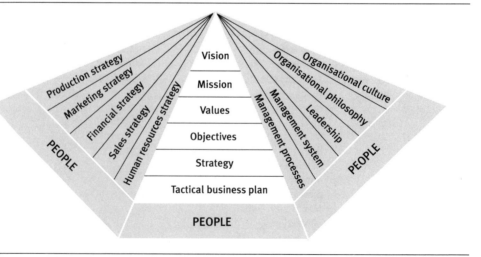

strategy. Management should regularly review and adapt the tactical business plan.
- *People.* These are all the employees of the organisation – from top management to the lowest level. They may be regarded as the power base for all the components of the pyramid. Plevel et al. (1994:59) rightly remark that people are an organisation's only sustainable competitive advantage. This confirms the main theme of this book, i.e. that the basic building block of organisational success is individual performance-orientation.

23.3 The relation between strategic planning and human resources management

Organisations recognise that there is a critical relation between an organisation's human resources and their contribution to the achievement of its objectives. Managers are often confident that they will find human resources when business activities dictate it and the existing staffing appears to be insufficient. Key personnel in organisations tend to concentrate on financial and marketing strategies, often at the expense of human resources. Human resources managers are often not informed of future business activities and expansions, and the critical relation between strategic business planning and human resources planning is ignored.

The need for a strategic perspective on human resources management is realised as an organisation grows larger and more complex. Systematic planning is required for the people needed to staff the organisation. A lack of adequate talent may be the single major constraint in the ability to sustain future company growth. Strategic human resources management is a practical step towards more comprehensive employee planning and development.

The following are the advantages of integrating strategic planning and human resources management:
- improved understanding of the implications of strategic organisational planning for human resources;
- proactive recruitment of the required and experienced human resources;
- improved human resources development activities; and
- improved analysis and control of costs related to human resources, by providing more objective criteria for payroll, labour market, training, and other expenses.

Strategic management and planning should also include strategic human resources planning from the outset, due to the benefits it has for an organisation. Anthony et al. (1999:16) fully supports this view by stating that:

The key idea behind overall strategic management is to coordinate all of the company's resources, including human resources, in such a way that everything a company does contributes to carrying out its strategy. If all the resources are integrated within an overall, appropriate strategy, additional value to the company is generated by the effective combination of integrated forces.

It is, therefore, obvious that synergy is obtained whereby extra benefit or value is realised when resources have been combined and coordinated effectively. This is the focus of this chapter.

23.4 Strategic business planning

Authors writing about strategic business planning usually make some assumptions about it, as it is difficult to pinpoint all its detail. This is usually derived from a SWOT (strengths, weaknesses, opportunities, and threats) analysis. Although strategic planning is usually complex, it does operate as a sequential process.

According to Rothwell and Kazanas (1994:3) strategic business planning is a process in which decision-makers have to focus their attention on the following:
- *Clarify purposes.* What is the purpose of the organisation? What should it be?
- *Select goals and objectives.* What is the organisation trying to achieve? How can achievement be measured?
- *Identify present strengths and weaknesses.* What is the organisation doing well? Not so well?
- *Analyse future threats and opportunities.* What opportunities or threats will the external environment pose to the organisation in the future?
- *Compare strengths and weaknesses to threats and opportunities.* How can the organisation take advantage of future opportunities and avert future threats posed by the environment, considering its present internal strengths and weaknesses?
- *Decide on long-term strategy.* What should be the long-term direction (strategy) pursued by an organisation so that it can take advantage of opportunities and avert threats posed by the environment?
- *Implement strategy.* What changes need to be made inside the organisation so that its chosen strategy can be pursued with the greatest likelihood of success?
- *Evaluate strategy.* How well do decision-makers think the strategy will work? How well is it working? How well has it worked?

Mondy et al. (1999:144) however, claim that strategic planning in organisations can logically be divided into four steps. These are discussed below.

23.4.1 Step 1: Determination of the organisational mission

It is important to determine an organisation's mission, because it forms the totality of its purpose. It also answers the questions of what the organisation's management is trying to do, i.e. should it maximise profits or pursue stability of earnings, etc. This process, however, also includes management decision-making to determine which direction it is to take, e.g. a competitive compensation strategy, improving diversity, or being a market leader or innovator.

A purpose statement can also be the economic rationale for an organisation's existence (Rothwell & Kazanas 1994:4). To address this issue, decision-makers should ask:
- In what areas of business activity should the firm operate?
- How much opportunity does a business activity offer the organisation in terms of growth? Flexibility? Stability? Return on investment?
- What does it take to succeed in the business?
- What are the organisation's capabilities?
- How well do the organisation's capabilities match up to what is needed to succeed in the business?
- What is the organisation's likelihood of success in the business activity?
- What methods of doing business can be considered?
- How do these choices compare on the basis of feasibility?
- How do these choices compare on the basis of potential profitability?
- What business activities should the organisation enter in the future? What should its purpose be?

These questions can only be effectively answered if various strategies and levels of business strategy and planning are analysed.

Campbell and Tawadey (1990:2) have developed a different approach to the concept of 'mission' which is much wider than the traditional one. They identify four elements:
- goal;
- strategy;
- organisational values; and
- standards of behaviour.

The goal of an organisation is the most philosophical part of the mission. It provides an explanation of the raison d'être of the organisation; in other words, for whom or for whose benefit the effort is made. Campbell and Tawadey (1990:2-3) state that 'some chief executives dedicate their companies to the shareholders, arguing that the company exists to create wealth for the shareholders'. This is probably true for small and medium-sized organisations but, according to the authors, is not necessarily applicable to very large organisations.

Strategy is the second element of the definition of a mission. It is the business rationale of an organisation's mission. It relates behaviour and decisions to the goal of the organisation. In order to formulate a strategy, management has to describe and define the domain in which the organisation intends to operate and compete. A strategy serves no purpose unless it is transformed into behaviour patterns and decisions. A strategy should spell out what action and behaviour it requires if it is to have an influence on the organisation.

Organisational values are beliefs that support the organisation's management style, and determine its attitude towards employees and shareholders, as well as its ethics.

Behavioural standards are part of the organisation's way of doing business. They refer to how managers have come to feel as to what is important to effectively run the organisation. These behavioural standards are defined not only by the organisation's strategy, but also by its values. There are, therefore, two reasons for doing something in an organisation. The first is a strategic or commercial reason; the second, a moral or value-based reason.

The mission will be healthy if all the previously mentioned components form a tightly knit whole. The question, thus, arises as to how important a mission is for human resources management. Campbell and Tawadey (1990:6–8) identify three advantages for employees who identify with the mission of the organisation. Firstly, employees are more motivated and will work more intelligently if they believe in what they are doing and trust the organisation for which they are working. Secondly, staff selection and training. Organisations with strong values find it easier to recruit, select, promote, train, and develop employees of the right calibre. It is implicitly a self-selection process, since prospective employees whose values and outlook on life do not agree with those of the organisation, will prefer not to join the organisation, or will resign at a very early stage. Thirdly, and most important, is better cooperation and mutual trust. Employees with a sense of mission find it easier to work together, to respect each other, and to search for solutions that will benefit the organisation as a whole, and not just individual departments.

23.4.2 Step 2: Assessment of the organisation and its environment

After the mission has been determined, an organisation must assess its position in the external environment. This will also identify what the organisation must do to retain or improve its competitive position regarding its products or services. This process must also be linked with the organisation's internal competencies, to assess where it should be going. Consequently, the organisation's strengths should be maximised and weaknesses minimised.

According to Prinsloo (2000:30) the process should involve a strategic analysis which takes the following factors into consideration:

- *Internal environment*
  - people (management and employees, capacity, skill, morale, etc.);
  - capital (gearing availability, cash flow management, investment);
  - systems (reliability);
  - product (brand, price, specialisation, quality, differentiation);
  - plant/equipment (capacity, technology fit);
  - spread of infrastructure;
  - service;
  - market segments;
  - customers (profile, perceptions, etc.); and
  - suppliers (terms, reliability, bargaining power).

- *Client needs/wants*
  - products (range, quality, quantity);
  - service (availability, backup, distribution);
  - price (discount, credit, cash, affordability);
  - trends; and
  - sensitivity (push all factors).

- *Competition*
  - market share;
  - growth rate;
  - profitability;
  - technology fit;
  - product range;
  - flexibility;
  - customers;
  - suppliers;
  - infrastructure; and
  - tactics/weapons.

- *External environment*
  - social;
  - economic;
  - technological;
  - political/legislative;
  - stakeholders (shareholders, unions, suppliers, financiers); and
  - global trends.

Once this is undertaken, the organisation's decision-makers would know where they stand vis-à-vis the environment and competitors, in terms of their own position.

23.4.3 Step 3: Setting of specific objectives or direction

These activities are aimed at attaining a common approach regarding what the organisation aims to achieve. They, therefore, improve the process of management in focusing on what it must do to achieve objectives.

In order to determine the organisation's position, gap analysis takes place to move it from the current to the desired situation. This means that various scenarios should be compiled, which would include a worst, best, and most likely scenario. The decision-makers then have to take decisions to pursue the objectives they have decided upon.

23.4.4 Step 4: Determination of strategies to accomplish objectives

Specific strategies would include financial budgets and the communication to the relevant parties of how these are to be accomplished. The strategies decided upon would probably bring about change in one or more of the following: leadership ability, organisational structure, human resources utilisation, etc.

This entails an execution framework to achieve the decisions which have been taken, by compiling appropriate strategies at the appropriate levels in the organisation. This is outlined in more detail below.

23.5 Strategy and levels of planning

Strategic planning should be followed up by considering at which level what occurs. This would be dependent on what the organisation regards as its core business. For example, if a business produces a single product, then a single strategic plan would cover all aspects. However, where multiple activities are applicable, various levels exist which need to be addressed. There are, consequently, several levels of planning required to roll out the various strategies of the organisation. Functions such as production, finance, marketing, supply chain, and human resources have their own strategies, each related to a business strategy and supportive of it, if multiple activities and products exist.

The various levels are discussed below.

23.5.1 Grand strategy

According to Swanepoel et al. (2000:201) a grand strategy can be described as a comprehensive general approach that guides an organisation's major actions. Mondy et al. (1999:143) call it the corporate level strategic plan and see it as defining the overall character and purpose of the organisation, the businesses it will enter and leave, the way resources will be distributed amongst those businesses, the way it competes, and the means by which the organisation's goals and objectives are to be achieved.

The responsibility to compile it is that of the corporate chief executive and the corporate board of directors. This grand strategy of an organisation thus ties together all other plans so that they do not work at cross-purposes.

23.5.2 Business strategy

This is the plan for a single business within an organisation, which its top management adopts to be competitive and to manage that particular business. This is important because many organisations have interests in different businesses, and top management has a difficult time organising the varied activities. A way to deal with this is to create a strategic business unit to emphasise its relative autonomy.

23.5.3 Strategic business unit

Any part of an organisation that is treated separately for strategic planning purposes, is regarded as a strategic business unit (SBU). It can either be a single business or a collection of related businesses. At the SBU level, decision-makers focus on questions such as:
- What specific products or services does the SBU produce?
- Who are the SBU's clients?
- How can the SBU best compete in its particular product or service segments?

These questions are quite different from those considered at the corporate level, where grand strategy necessarily focuses on the overall corporate mission and on methods of tying together distinct SBUs into a corporate portfolio of businesses.

Many organisations nowadays set up SBUs as separate profit centres, which gives them practically full autonomy. In practice, SBU operations are the responsibility of a Deputy Managing Director of the organisation.

23.5.4 Functional strategy

This is the plan for one activity within an enterprise. It is, therefore, a narrow area of activity which is focused upon. Functions include finance, marketing, logistics, production and operations, and human resources. Any major department is also a function. Functional strategies are, in a sense, secondary or 'down stream' to corporate or business strategy but, nevertheless, form an integral part of strategic management. Functional strategy means the planned direction for key activity areas within an organisation.

> **Example of strategies**
> A large university will have a grand strategy that defines its overall purpose and desired relationships with such key external stakeholders as government, community, alumni, business, and other segments of society; each faculty within the university has a business strategy that defines its purpose, its services, and groups whose needs it is intended to serve; each department within the faculty has its own functional strategy that defines a segment of the enterprise, its purpose, its services, its programmes, its service users, and its relationship to the faculty and university.

The functional strategy is also part of a planning hierarchy that reflects differing concerns and time periods. There are three levels of planning in this regard namely strategic, coordinative, and operational.

Strategic planning is chiefly the concern of top-level managers. It is directed towards achieving long-term goals and objectives over several years. Strategic plans are uncertain and involve high degrees of risk. They help decision-makers anticipate changes in a largely uncontrollable external environment and play a high-stakes game in organisational success or failure. In practice, it entails the following:
- the concern of top management;
- long-term time horizon;
- encompasses the entire organisation; and
- primary focus is external.

Coordinative planning is intermediate-term. It is primarily the concern of middle-level managers. Less risky than strategy-making, coordinative plans 'determine how certain areas of a business will deploy resources to reach objectives by following the policies and strategies that have been established in the strategic planning process' (Huse 1982:144). In practice, it entails the following:
- the concern of middle managers;
- intermediate-term horizon;
- encompasses only part of the organisation; and
- primary focus is internal.

Operational planning is short-term. It is the primary concern of first-line supervisors. Annual budgets are expressions of operational plans. Less risky than strategic or coordinative plans, operational plans involve scheduling and moving needed resources. These plans are tied to their longer-term strategic and coordinative counterparts. In practice, it entails the following:
- the concern of supervisors;
- short-term time horizon;
- encompasses only a small segment of an organisation's full range of activities; and
- primary focus is internal.

It must, however, be borne in mind that due to the reciprocal interdependence between the various strategies, they must be integrated, and this forms the major challenge of strategic management for an organisation's decision-makers and top management.

23.6 Strategic management

According to Swanepoel et al. (2000:202) strategic management is a process at the top level of the organisation which entails planning, organising, leading, and control. At this level, the focus is on the success of the organisation as a whole, over the long run. Strategic management is, therefore, regarded as the process of examining both the present and future environments, formulating the objectives of the business and making, implementing and controlling decisions focused on achieving the objectives of an organisation in the present and future environments.

Strategic management, however, cannot be regarded as comprising rational decisions and related behaviour. Unfortunately, issues such as the socio-organisational side of management become important and, therefore, the ideology of managers and their motivations as well as their perceptions of their organisations play a significant role in what they do. It is clear that these issues also impact on how an organisation's strategic human resources management evolves. Let us now focus on strategic human resources management.

23.7 Strategic human resources management

In view of what has been discussed, Swanepoel et al. (2000:204) state that strategic human resources management is:

> those long-term, top-level management decisions and actions regarding employment relationships that are made and performed in a way that is fully integrated with the overall general strategic management of organisations.

It entails synchronising and integrating the organisation's strategic business needs and plans with all those aspects stemming from and relating to the management of its employees.

Anthony et al. (1999:51) also clearly state that, by involving human resources considerations when the overall strategy is formulated, human resources management contributes to the achievement of a strategic advantage for the organisation, because of the synergy which is achieved throughout the organisation's activities. It is, consequently, obvious that strategic human resources management cannot be viewed as separate from, or subordinate to, the formulation and implementation of business or corporate strategy. If, for example, human resources requirements are compiled for a strategy of innovation, these will be vastly different from those required for a relocation or start-up section of the business in a neighbouring country. Innovation will entail that the competition must be beaten, and that improved products or services must be provided. The strategy can only be considered, and be effective, if management is willing to employ and train workers who would be creative and flexible in their employment endeavours.

According to Anthony et al. (1999:14) the characteristics of a strategic approach to human resources management are that it:
- explicitly recognises the impact of the outside environment;
- explicitly recognises the impact of competition and the dynamics of the labour market;
- has a long-range focus (three to five years);
- focuses on the issue of choice and decision making;
- considers all personnel, not just hourly or operational employees; and
- is integrated with the overall corporate strategy and functional strategies.

23.7.1 Formulating human resources management strategy

This process involves top management decisions and actions regarding appropriate strategies for the management of human resources within the context of the internal and external environment. According to Swanepoel et al. (2000:205) strategic choices must be made within the context of environmental constraints. This is because an organisation's success is dependent upon its ability to match or fit the variety in the environment in which it operates. Anthony et al. (1999:59) however, point out that all strategies are situational, and that a proper strategy for any particular organisation will depend on the unique situation it faces. What works for one organisation may not necessarily be applicable to another. There must, however, be a fit between the organisation and its environment for any particular organisation to make it work for it, and this entails:

- a scanning of the environment to create the necessary fit;
- considering the organisation's mission in terms of its human resources management approach;
- deciding on an appropriate human resources management strategy; and
- establishing a human resource management business plan.

The aforementioned is essential because the human resources management strategy and the human resources management business plan must fit into a particular organisation's grand strategy. In other words, the human resources management business plan's purpose should basically be to operationalise, or bring about, the concept of fit between general business strategy and the human resources management strategy. Although the selection of an appropriate human resources management strategy must, itself, ensure that there is an alignment between business and human resources management, the various elements of the business plan must clarify how the necessary fit will be achieved.

These issues clearly demonstrate the link between the various strategies in ultimately ensuring that human resources utilisation contributes to the goal achievement of the organisation, which means that key areas and strategic priorities must consistently be revisited and redesigned where necessary. It may, for example, be necessary to rewrite job descriptions, to recruit new employees with different characteristics, or to update the employment equity plan for the further transformation of an organisation. These aspects are discussed in preceding chapters but, in summary, involve:

- individual level considerations, e.g. job redesign, horizontal work redesign, vertical work redesign, ergonomic work redesign, and flexibility in work;
- group level considerations of work organisation, e.g. restructuring work teams;
- organisational level considerations, e.g. changing the organisation structure, or focusing on different types of structure; and
- structural considerations regarding human resources management functions, e.g. redefining the job of the human resources specialist, or changing the reporting position of the human resources department in an organisation by doing away with a corporate human resources department and relocating it to a SBU.

Various other views also exist with regard to strategic human resources management and are presented below.

23.7.2 The view of Cascio

A different view which can also be used is that of Cascio (1995:42) who states that strategic human resources management simply means getting everybody from the top of the company to the bottom to do things to implement the strategy of the business as effectively as possible. People, as a resource, must be used to fit the strategic needs of the company. The relationship between strategic business needs, people as a resource, and human resources management has led to the development of a framework, which he terms the 5-P model. Cascio's (1995:42) strategic business needs set the 5-P model in motion. Organisations define (or redefine) such needs during times of turbulence. These needs reflect management's overall plan for survival, growth, adaptability, and profitability. The strategic human resources management activities are listed as follows:

- *Philosophy* expresses statements defining business values and culture. It will express how to treat and value people.
- *Policies* express shared values (guidelines). They will establish guidelines for action on people-related business issues and human resources programmes.
- *Programmes* are articulated as human resources strategies. They will coordinate efforts to facilitate change, to address major people-related business issues.
- *Practices* for leadership, managerial, and operational roles. These will motivate needed role behaviours.
- *Processes* express the formulation and implementation of other activities. They will define how these activities are carried out.

23.7.3 The view of Van Dyk

South African organisations cannot successfully compete in the labour market for scarce human resources in all fields of specialisation, owing to a general lack of availability of skilled human resources. Furthermore, certain skills will be required that will not be available on the open labour market. This is due to the emigration of skilled people, poor education policy, lack of funding, and the legacies of apartheid, to name but a few. This poses a great challenge to human resources management and – more than ever before – there will be a need for interaction between human resources managers and other functional and line managers in organisations. Figure 23.3 shows some of these interfaces, the most important of which are briefly discussed below, as well as the types of interaction and information that human resources managers will have to obtain at a strategic level.

It is clear from Figure 23.3 that management of human resources, with a view to successful human resources development, is a comprehensive task. From a systems and quality assurance point of view, the macro-variables (mega-trends) that have an effect on organisational strategy also have a profound effect on human resources. A proactive strategic approach implies that an analysis of the strengths and weaknesses of the available human resources must be done in order to adapt the strategy agreed upon for every sub-strategy (such as logistics), both qualitatively and quantitatively. This must be done in the form of a human resources audit for every functional department and its sub-strategy, to determine the current state of affairs and to extrapolate the figures for future requirements in the various labour categories (managers, professionals, skilled workers, semiskilled workers, and unskilled workers) for the various functional departments in order to ensure future organisational success.

Another important aspect that human resources managers of organisations must develop, particularly in our times of high technology and information, is new job profiles, since it is expected that the nature of jobs will change drastically in future.

As a result of technological and other job-related innovations, many jobs will become obsolete and new ones will emerge. For this reason, it is essential for organisations to develop new job profiles and to use them as a concept for compiling a skills inventory that can serve as a basis for

Figure 23.3 A strategic human resources management model

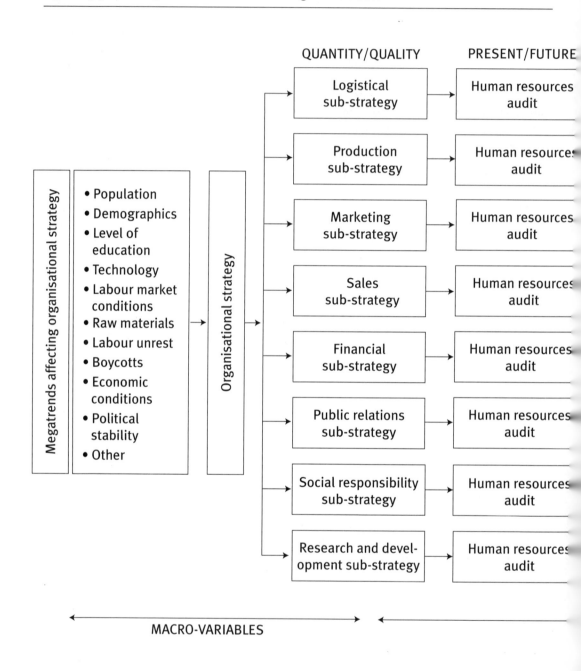

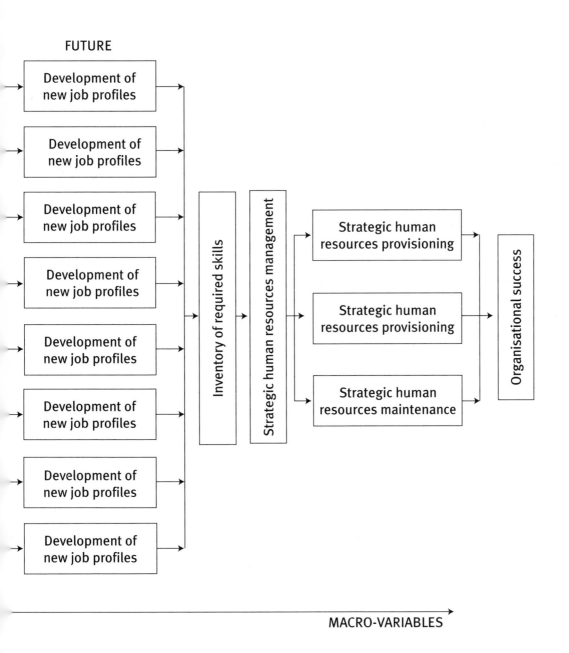

the strategic human resources management of the organisation.

It is certain that the success of future human resources activities will depend on integrating human resources strategies with the overall organisational strategy, as well as on the interaction between the managements of the various business units to determine what inputs are required for sound human resources management.

Let us now focus on the critical element of skills development, from a strategic human resources development point of view.

23.8 Strategic human resources development

Strategic human resources development (SHRD) means the process of changing an organisation, stakeholders outside it, groups inside it, and people employed by it, through planned learning, so that they possess the knowledge and skills needed for the future. There is a critical shortage of skilled human resources in South Africa which must be addressed if the country is to become globally competitive. Strategic human resources development helps implement strategic business plans and human resources plans by cultivating the skills of people inside the firm or changing the knowledge and skills of stakeholders outside it. According to Rothwell and Kazanas (1994:17) the possible relationship between strategic business plans, human resources plans, and strategic human resources development can be presented as follows:

- The point of departure is the mission and grand strategy, which indicates the longterm direction of an organisation.
- From this, the other functional plans of the organisation flow, which would include marketing, finance, supply chain, products, etc. A simultaneous flow is of the human resources plans and strategy which determine the long-term human resources direction of the organisation, and which indicate the nature of skills which ought to be required.
- From the human resources strategy, the human resources development strategy flows, which is aimed at the development of human resources over time. Again, more specific plans flow from this, such as recruitment, promotion policy, and particular training and development issues.
- The cycle is completed by evaluating whether human resources development departmental plans are contributing to the achievement of the organisation's objective, by having developed human resources which are available as and when required.

Strategic human resources development is, therefore, more holistic than traditional human resources development. The growth of strategic human resources development is an organisational strategy for the human resources development effort which guides the direction of an organisation. In strategic human resources development, the focus of planning centres around the roles and responsibilities of everyone – human resources development practitioners, line managers, and participants. This focus on human resources development effort – a broad undertaking in which many people have roles to play – differs from mere human resources development department planning.

A further distinction between traditional and strategic human resources development concerns experience. Experience denotes awareness based on participation in past problem solving. It occupies a central place in most human endeavours. Everyone has heard the old saying, 'Experience is the best teacher'. Many people believe that 95 per cent of all learning occurs through experience. The trouble is, however, that experience is not always appropriate in preparing for the future. There are many reasons why this is so. New knowledge is created faster today than it was in the past. Computers increase the speed with which information can be processed – but not the speed at which human beings can absorb or use it. Organisations face more competition, and must anticipate competitive challenges if they are to survive. The same principle applies to individuals who are competing with others for career success.

A new approach to human resources development is, therefore, needed to cope with a future that, in many respects, is not like the past. This approach should help individuals anticipate the knowledge and skills needed in the future, rather than react after problems become apparent. Strategic human resources development does this.

This is not to say that strategic human resources development always differs from its traditional counterpart. Traditional human resources development and strategic human resources development coincide when the external environment of the organisation, individual or job is relatively stable. If the future is likely to be like the past, then traditional and strategic human resources development intersect; but if the future is likely to be utterly unlike the past, due to external environmental change, then strategic human resources development is appropriate for equipping people with new knowledge and skills.

By applying strategic human resources management development effectively, organisations will certainly be better equipped to face the challenges of the future of global competition, and simultaneously be more productive locally.

23.9 Conclusion

In this chapter, an overview is given of the essential elements of strategy. Strategy is a prerequisite for any effective human resources management. It is also pointed out that organisational strategy, with all its facets such as business strategy and functional strategy, including the various levels of planning, is an all important prerequisite to embarking on any human resources management activity. It is, furthermore, highlighted that vision, mission, organisational values, and standards of behaviour form the nucleus of elements which impact on decision-makers in deciding on the direction an organisation is to take to achieve and retain a competitive edge.

It is, therefore, clear that an interdependent relationship exists between an organisation's grand strategy and its approach to managing human resources strategically. If either is poorly formulated or executed, the chances of an organisation being successful decrease rapidly. The synergy between human resources management and organisational effectiveness should never be underestimated.

It is also evident that the development of human resources should be undertaken from a strategic point of view, as this would be the optimal way for the organisation to have the right quality and quantity of human resources available to achieve its objectives in the most competitive way. The fact remains that human resources, particularly if managed strategically, are the greatest asset any organisation can have, because effective knowledge management of its human resources will be the ultimate core success weapon of any organisation in the decades to come.

The detail presented in this chapter clearly shows how necessary interaction between macro- and micro-variables is. The effectiveness of this interaction ultimately determines the effectiveness and efficiency of the human resources function as a sub-strategy of the overall organisational strategy.

Case study
Drought and transformation blues at the co-op

Agricultural activity and related businesses have never been easy in South Africa. Climatic conditions, which often result in droughts or flooding (and sometimes catastrophic floods like the 2000 disaster in the North Eastern parts of South Africa), provide major risks for farming. This makes it a very risky economic activity out of which to make a living, and to remain in business. Changed land tenure legislation, the role of the Land Bank, changed interest rates, and more foreign competition have led to the deterioration of the financial position of farmers. The situation is not much different for the Tropical Grain and Fruit Growers Co-op (TGFGC) situated in Eastern Mpumalanga.

The co-op's business primarily comprises servicing farmers who grow maize, sunflowers, beans, bananas, oranges, sugarcane, etc. The co-op has been in existence for forty-two years, and has assets of just over R31 million and an annual turnover of R495 million. Three cousins with the surname Jackson, who come from a large farming family, have run the co-op for most of its forty-two years. They are also farmers in the area and their family have lived in the region since the Waterval Boven railway tunnel was built a hundred years ago, when their grandfather made his start-up money to buy farm land.

The co-op has sixty-five employees who are mainly semiskilled. There is also very little formality between the managing director and supervisors. Recently the co-op experienced varying degrees of fluctuation in its business, mainly owing to droughts. To cure these pains, the co-op altered its strategy somewhat to diversify; and the focus of human resources management has changed, in turn.

The co-op was founded on the principle of having farmers as lifelong customers. The co-op employees were empowered to operate on the principle that the customer is always right and to make sure that the customer is always happy. The co-op staff, especially the Jacksons, built close, personal relationships with the farmers, many of whom recognised that the co-op and the Jacksons had helped them get their farms on a sound footing. The farmers were charged reasonable prices and given personal attention when they did business at the co-op. The staff knew most of the farmers and dealt with them on a personal basis. This approach was sound and contributed to the co-op's profits.

This approach remained a major factor in the co-op's growth in recent years. Customers of other co-ops in nearby communities began to recognise the value of doing business with the co-op. In the past eleven years, the Jacksons implemented a growth strategy to enhance the co-op's reputation for personal service. The co-op did nothing differently, but encouraged new business through word-of-mouth advertising and expanding the shop, which provided for all the farmers' needs, on the basis of being a 'farmers' supermarket'. The strategy also included an expansion of services into the financial sector, by running a soft loan system like micro lenders do. The employees were the reason for success, because the primary emphasis continued to be the co-op's customer orientation. When new customers came into the co-op, they were there to stay. The co-op had high growth during the late 70s and early 80s.

The last of the Jacksons retired from the co-op early in 1994, and Mr. Lucky Dlamini took over as managing director. The growth continued, as it became evident that Lucky Dlamini would continue to subscribe to the co-op's customer-orientated philosophy.

A number of factors, however, combined to result in several serious problems for the co-op. The rapid growth resulted in the need for new employees, but meeting this need quickly with qualified people was difficult.

Employees recognised the importance of giving customers their complete attention. As a result of attempting to provide personal service to an increasing number of customers, details were often overlooked on such things as credit from the supermarket and interest rates on tractors and other farming equipment. In many cases, the histories of loan applicants were not adequately investigated and necessary supporting documentation often was completed hastily, if at all. The number of new farmers who acquired land and applied for assistance from the co-op, but who had limited security, exacerbated this situation.

During this time, employees did not keep Dlamini sufficiently up to date on the overall health of the co-op. In a number of ways, the growth made Dlamini feel that he no longer controlled the co-op's operations as he had when he took over. No real departmentalisation existed, so delegation of duties was problematic.

The growth problems were exacerbated by a large number of regulatory changes brought on by the deregulation of the farming industry in the mid-1990s. A number of economic factors also presented real problems for local businesses and, consequently for the co-op. Droughts and changing governmental policy on tenure rights for farm workers also caused unforeseen difficulties for farmers. As a result, the economic health of the rural area deteriorated somewhat during the 1990s and drastically influenced the co-op's profitability.

In early 1999, the number of overdue accounts increased steeply. A record number of loans, characterised by management as 'poor performers', negatively affected the co-op's profitability as well. The co-op's overdraft increased during much of 2000. By the end of 2000 the co-op made a large loss.

Dlamini recognised the problems the co-op was experiencing and decided to revise its strategy somewhat. The revised strategy continued to emphasise the personal approach to customers, but also recognised the slow growth in some of the fruit growing sectors, in particular. He realised that the size of the staff was inadequate to implement the strategy. For example, the current staff members were unable to provide personal service, while following procedures completely and correctly. He also recognised that staff members needed training in areas related to regulatory maters, loan assessment, and debt collection.

Overall, the co-op's strategy emphasised the following of procedures and processes in an orderly manner, correcting existing problems, and preparing adequately for future growth. Growth and market development were no longer major parts of the strategy. The new strategy was designed to maintain current business, to retrench staff, and to extensively re-train staff.

Questions

1. What overall strategy and human resources management strategy would you follow under these conditions to revitalise the co-op and to safeguard its position?
2. Compile a strategic human resources development programme for the co-op, which would specifically focus on uplifting historically disadvantaged employees to participate in first line supervisory and management tasks within five years.
3. Do you believe that Lucky Dlamini adequately changed the co-op's strategy to remedy the problems discussed? Present your view of the problems he is facing.

Chapter questions

1. Define the concepts on the front panel of the strategic framework (Figure 23.2).
2. Describe human resources management strategy.
3. Motivate the necessity of strategic human resources planning.
4. Use a diagram to explain the integration of human resources management strategy with the overall organisational strategy.
5. Draw up a list of examples to differentiate between the following concepts in your organisation:
   - organisational strategy;
   - grand strategy;
   - strategic business unit strategy; and
   - functional strategy.
6. Describe organisational level considerations of work organisation you would adjust in your organisation to achieve its objectives.
7. From a strategic management perspective, how would you go about integrating decisions concerning employment relations management to promote harmony in the workplace (also use Chapter 6 in this book for the purpose of your answer).

Bibliography

ANTHONY, W.P., PERREWÉ, P. & KACMAR, K.M. 1999. *Human resource management. A strategic approach.* 3rd edition. Dryden Press, New York.

BIRCHALL, D. & LYONS, L. 1995. *Creating tomorrow's organisation – unlocking the benefits of Future Work.* Pitman, London.

CAMPBELL, A. & TAWADEY, K. 1990. *Mission and business philosophy: waning employee commitment.* Billings, London.

CARRELL, M.R., ELBERT, N.F., HATFIELD, R.D., GROBLER, P.A., MARX, M. & VAN DER SCHYF, S. 1998. *Human resource management in South Africa.* Prentice Hall South Africa (Pty.) Ltd., South Africa.

CHARLTON, G. 2000. *Human habits of highly effective organisations.* Van Schaiks, Pretoria.

DOWLING, P.J., WELCH, D.E. & SCHULER, R.S. 1999. *International human resource management. Managing people in a multinational context.* 3rd edition. South Western College Publishing (an International Thomson Publishing Company), Melbourne.

IVANCEVICH, J.M. 1995. *Human resource management.* Irwin, Chicago.

MONDY, R.W., NOE, R.M. & PREMEAUX, S.R. 1999. *Human resource management.* 7th edition. Prentice Hall, New York.

OGILVIE-THOMPSON, J. 1993. People management critical for business. *Human Resources Management*, vol. 9, no. 5, June.

PLEVEL, M.J., NELLIS, S., LANE, F. & SCHULER, R.S. 1994. Linking HR with business strategy. *Organizational Dynamics*, Vol. 22, No. 3, Winter.

PRINSLOO, R. 2000. Strategic planning model. *People Dynamics*, vol.18, no.1, pp.30–31.

ROTHWELL, W.J. & KAZANAS, H.C., 1994. *Planning and managing human resources:*

strategic planning for personnel management. Massachusetts HRD Press, Amherst.

ROTHWELL, W.J. & KAZANAS, H.C., 1994. *Human resources development: a strategic approach.* Massachusetts HRD Press, Amherst.

SWANEPOEL, B.J. (ED.), ERASMUS, B.J., VAN WYK, M. & SCHENK, H. 2000. *South African human resource management: theory and practice.* Juta & Co. Ltd., Cape Town.

TAYLOR, T., BEECHLER, S. & NAPIER, N. 1996. Toward an integrative model of strategic international human resources management. *Academy of Management Review,* Vol.21, No.4, p.959, Oct.

TYSON, S. 1995. *Human resource strategy. Towards a general theory of human resource management.* Pitman, London.

VAN DYK, P.S., NEL, P.S., LOEDOLFF, P. VAN Z. & HAASBROEK, G.D. 2001. *Training management: a multidisciplinary approach to human resources development in South Africa.* 3rd edition. Oxford University Press, Cape Town.

Websites

American Department of Labour: http://stats.bls.gov
International Business Machine (IBM): http:/www.ibm.com
American affirmative action register: http://aar-eeo.com
Fortune magazine: http://www.fortune.com

24

Human resources information systems

A Werner

Learning outcomes

At the end of this chapter the learner should be able to demonstrate the following outcomes:
- Appreciate the role of a human resources information system.
- Discuss the myths that surround the use of human resources information systems.
- Discuss the components of a human resources information system.
- Discuss the areas in human resources management where information systems are utilised.
- Explain how human resources information systems can be used as a diagnostic and decision-making tool with regard to selected organisational variables.
- Discuss quality assurance in human resources information systems.

Key words and concepts

- business intelligence
- decision support system (DSS)
- enterprise resources planning (ERP)
- human resources information system (HRIS)
- management information system (MIS)

Illustrative case
Time travelling

1822: Charles Babbage develops and partially builds a steam-driven mechanical computer. Before his death in 1871, he develops the world's first general-purpose, stored-programme digital computer, which was never built owing to the lack of technology. Babbage was a strong advocate of the division of labour and specialisation.

1937: Howard H. Aiken develops a computer at Harvard University in the United States. He combines the punch card input method with the electrical and mechanical technology of the time.

24.1 Introduction

There is no question about it: we are in the electronic and information age where systems, software, and databases manage vast reservoirs of data. In this environment, business intelligence is taking on a new meaning. Organisations use modern technology to find the most profitable customers, identify the best marketing techniques, identify parts and equipment that need replacement, control production, manage finances and sales, and fulfil a vast number of other functions. The human resources information system (HRIS) forms part of the organisation's larger management information system (MIS). A HRIS is used to collect, record, store, analyse, distribute, and retrieve data concerning the organisation's human resources.

It has become increasingly important for the human resources department to fulfil a bigger role in the strategic direction of the company and to effect internal and external change. The strategic value of human resources management lies in the ability to distribute relevant and accurate information to key decision-makers in the organisation, and to ensure that the respondents are able to interpret and utilise the information. This function is called the decision support system (DSS).

Advances in computing technology always present a paradox: the promise of well-managed information, time and cost savings, and the threat of an inability to handle the technical maintenance or application of the system. However, for a company to be dominant in today's markets it must be able to react to change, successfully participating in and managing events and turning them into competitive advantage. Although the information technology (IT) department is responsible for assembling and maintaining the technology, it is hardly able to determine the information needs within a business. The driving force

---

In 1944 he develops the MARK 1 electromechanical calculator. It is 15 metres long, 2,5 metres high, and uses 800 kilometres of wiring. It takes the MARK 1 almost 4,5 seconds to multiply 2 numbers, each comprising 23 digits.

1960: The human resources software industry is born with the introduction of payroll and accounting systems. These systems do not cater for non-accounting information, such as education, skills, dependants, and beneficiaries, which is becoming increasingly important for workforce planning, and benefits-cost planning.

1970: Full-featured human resources information systems are installed at large organisations with thousands of employees.

1980: Personal computers are introduced. Human resources software becomes available to smaller organisations. Functions are more specialised and include recruitment automation and training registration.

1990: Integrated solutions (which combine personnel, payroll, benefits, recruitment, career development, training, etc.) deliver more value by sharing common information, simplifying multi-system updates, and providing a more complete view of each employee. Integration with financial, manufacturing, and supply-chain systems results in the 'enterprise resources planning' (ERP) systems. The Internet and Intranet are becoming increasingly part of the organisational information system.

SOURCES: Jeffries & Lewis (1992:58); La Pointe (1999:90–92).

behind a HRIS is the human resources department, which must provide a conceptual framework of what is required. Putting all the pieces into place is not an easy task. It is, by nature, complex and sometimes very frustrating to ensure that the data is correct, that it flows correctly, and people know how to use the analytical tools sitting on their desktops. Once it is working, however, success becomes more of a reality than a gamble.

In this chapter, we will explore the myths surrounding the use of HRISs. We will investigate the areas in which they are generally applied, and the way they can be used as diagnostic and decision-making tools with regard to absenteeism, labour turnover, job satisfaction, and job equity. Quality assurance in HRISs will also be considered.

24.2 Components of a human resources information system

A HRIS consists of four distinct components: hardware, software, data, and the users. These components are interrelated, and defects in one can affect one or more of the other components.

- *Hardware* refers to all the physical, tangible parts of a computer, such as the central processing unit, keyboard, display screen, printer, disks, and compact disks.
- *Software* refers to the instructions that are built into a computer or computer programme to make it work. Software enables a computer. Software is divided into two categories: system and applications software. System software includes the operation system and all the utilities that enable the computer to perform. Windows is an example of system software. Applications software includes actual programmes used for a specific purpose. Examples of software are word processors, such as Word Perfect, MS Word, or Apple Works, and spreadsheets and database management-systems, such as payroll and employee record systems.
- *Data* are distinct pieces of information, usually formatted in a special way. Examples of data include: employee's name, number, job title, job skills, educational level, performance rating, and attendance status.
- *User* refers to anyone who uses a computer. Users of HRISs include human resources practitioners, data-entry specialists, managers, and employees. The users have access to designated information components, and not the total HRIS.

24.3 Myths of human resources information systems

Human resources practitioners and other key decision-makers within organisations often have misconceptions about the installation and use of information technology in the human resources department. According to Witschger (1999) these misconceptions lead to the slow introduction of HRISs into organisations, and include the following.

HRISs will solve all human resources information problems

HRISs automate existing processes. If the manual systems used are of high quality, then software will speed up the operation, make it more vital, visible, and timely. If the manual system is not well managed, the software will expose these shortcomings. For example, HRISs cannot produce a well-presented absenteeism report with missing or incorrect information. However, it can produce this bad report at a very high speed.

HRISs will eliminate jobs in the human resources department

HRISs seldom result in job losses owing to automation in the human resources department. Staff members, who previously had the mundane task of recording or filing information, can now direct their efforts to what they are supposed to be doing: serving management as is appropriate, and contributing more effectively to the strategic goals of the organisation.

HRISs are complex and therefore expensive

HRISs are much less complex than accounting systems. A key factor, however, is the amount of information that is tracked for employees, applicants, jobs, etc. The storing, reporting, and calculation process is basic.

HRISs take a long time to implement

A well-managed, manual human resources function in a small to mid-size organisation can be implemented within a week or two. Automation implies the conversion of existing programmes into computerised ones. The same historical data is used. It is possible that the current procedure has to be adjusted to the computerised system, but the basic elements of the process will stay the same.

HRISs require expensive and intensive training

A well-designed software programme merely automates tasks that are already performed. Intensive training will only become necessary if the human resources function was not performed well before. In this case, the introduction of the programme can only benefit the organisation, and the costs and time spent on training will be justified.

Customising HRISs requires very expensive consultants

The human resources department must analyse their information system needs carefully before making a decision about what system and software to acquire. It is important to choose a system that is very close to the identified needs. Most programmes have customisation options that allow for flexibility.

HRISs require constant involvement from the information technology (IT) department

A well-designed and well-implemented system does not require constant IT department involvement.

Technical support is not readily available for HRISs

Information about the quality of after-sales technical support from the supplier can be obtained from other customers, and from the quality of pre-sales efforts. It is best to negotiate after-sales technical support for a defined period, as well as a retainer fee.

From the above discussion it is clear that a decision regarding a specific HRIS should only be made after a thorough study of the human resources information needs, and the products and services of reputable suppliers. Introducing a computerised system provides an organisation with the opportunity to simultaneously upgrade their existing processes and procedures.

24.4 Application of human resources information systems to human resources management

HRISs are built on a modular basis to allow flexibility. These modules or components

are interrelated and use the same basic database. 'Best practice' for human resources software is founded on:
- an extensive database for a wide range of employee and employer information;
- a significant 'data-sensitive' historical capacity; and
- an easy-to-use reporting and analysis capability, with a broad user community.

Employee data maintenance

Employee data collection, capturing and maintenance form the core of the information system in human resources management. Employee data includes information such as the employee's name, personnel number, identity number, address, family particulars, date of employment, job information, salary comparison data, qualifications, competencies, and other basic information required by the organisation. The employee data component supports all other human resources information. Any change made in the information in this component is immediately reflected in all other components that use the same data.

Payroll processing

The payroll component handles the entire payroll process, including regulations, tax considerations and deductions. It can also

Table 24.1 Examples of human resources software available in South Africa

Application area	Package	Description
Data maintenance	Vision	Provides a totally integrated HR management system. Supplied by Educos.
Payroll	UniQue	A fully integrated modular human resources and payroll system. Supplied by Q Data Dynamique.
Equity management	Employment Equity Software	Makes provision for a workforce profile, skills development report, analysis of employment policies, practices, and procedures, work environment, equity plan, and benchmarking. Supplied by Van Zyl Rudd and associates.
Competency management	Peodesy	Supports all HR tasks through a modular system. Supplied by FSA-Contact.
Recruitment and selection	Assist	A fully integrated staff recruitment system. Supplied by CPS-Computerised Personnel Systems.
Time and attendance	Paywise	An integrated personnel/administration system that combines accounting and time recording functions. Supplied by Paywise Software.
Human resources planning	Third Foundation Manpower Planning	Provides a comprehensive package, covering affirmative action, employee development, performance management, post profiling, and related functions. Supplied by Third Foundation Systems.
Self-help desk	PWA Empower	An Internet/Intranet workflow-enabled solution with a manager and employee self-service function. Provided by EmSoft.

be used to develop appropriate compensation and benefits systems, and to track individual employees, as well as groups of employees, in order to identify compensation trends in the organisation. It can also handle stock purchase and stock option plans. Information about salary grades, job classification and salary ranges form the basis of this component.

Equity management

This component enables employers to formulate an employment equity plan, in line with the new regulations published by the Department of Labour in 1999. It provides a profile of the workforce and the skills development of employees, and handles the development of an equity plan.

Competency management

A competency system package tracks the skills levels of employees, and develops compensation and training to match employee and organisational needs. Both the manager's and the employee's evaluations of training needs can be entered. This component contains information about internal and external training courses, training course evaluations, instructors, costs, and enrolment facilities. It also provides individual profiles, containing information on qualifications, training received in-house and outside, results of courses, financial reimbursements, and training needs.

Recruitment and selection

This component keeps record of vacant positions and of candidates for those vacancies. It tracks résumés and matches candidates with the requirements of the vacant positions, records the length of time vacancies have existed, and compares the offer-to-acceptance ratios. Information kept on applicants includes personal details, educational background, work experience, etc. This component allows the organisation to locate the most successful interviewer, recruitment source, and recruitment area.

Time and attendance

This component tracks the number of hours worked by using magnetic-strip-cards or PC-based systems, instead of a time clock or handwritten timecards. This information is also used in the wage and salary administration component. It can further provide information on the amount of time lost due to absenteeism, the causes, costs involved, personal absence profiles, and group records.

Human resources planning

This module is used to estimate future human resources management needs, by analysing current job occupation, turnover, transfers, promotions, and retirement, as well as the related skill levels.

Self-help desk

This is a relatively new addition to the HRIS, which provides many new opportunities for the employer-employee relationship. Traditionally, the human resources department has been viewed as a 'query office'. This component frees the human resources department from this function, allowing more time to be spent on strategic or organisational issues. The employee self-help desk is linked to the organisation's Intranet, and allows employees to have instant access to information relevant to the user.

The self-help desk can be used for the following purposes:
- *Personal information.* The employee has the opportunity to review, confirm, and

Figure 24.1 A typical advertisement for an HRIS found in professional magazines

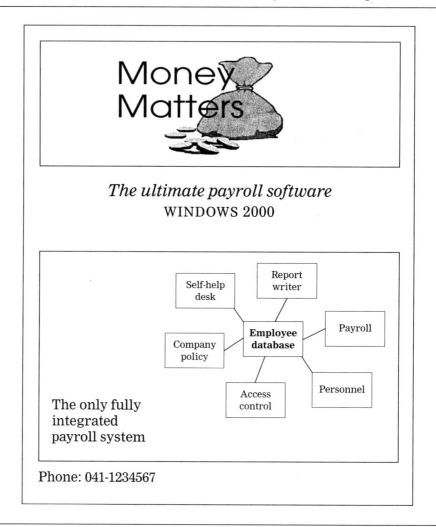

change personal information, such as marital status, dependants, emergency contacts, and beneficiaries.
- *Suggestions.* The self-help desk provides employees with an outlet for their ideas and complaints.
- *Organisation bulletin.* Employees can access the bulletin or submit their creative contributions.
- *Company policies.* Employees have instant and permanent access to all relevant policies and procedures, such as those for grievances and discipline, sexual harassment, benefits, and other rules governing the workplace.
- *Financial benefits.* Benefit statements, investment modelling, stock and other options may be accessed.
- *New forms.* Information can be collected quickly and efficiently, for example in cases where employees have to exercise an option.

- *Socialisation.* The corporate culture is reinforced by exposing employees to the mission, goals, expectations, behavioural norms, and results of the company.

The self-help desk allows both the human resources department and the employee to spend their time more productively, by reducing time spent on requesting information, filling out forms, and following up on them. It reduces paperwork and provides an anonymous and equal service to everyone.

24.5 The human resources information system as a diagnostic and decision-making tool

A statistic often quoted by the IBM Corporation in New York, indicates that the average company only uses 2 to 4 per cent of the data that resides in its system. The rest of the information never sees the light of a computer monitor (Greengard 1999: 103–4).

Organisations vary in the extent to which they utilise human resources information. The ideal is that the organisation will exhibit a high competency and capability to handle information, and make use of human resources software to support well-articulated and aligned business goals across all human resources disciplines. The dynamic environment in which organisations operate necessitates a learning culture. Calculated decision-making and constructive problem-solving are based on accurate and timely information which generates knowledge and understanding.

> The human resources department is continuously under pressure to prove that they add value to the organisation. In one such an organisation the HR data is used to identify every employee who is connected to sales in the organisation. By linking sales and commission statistics to these employees, the best performers can be identified. The information is used to develop competency and skill characteristics, which form the basis for a sales-performance knowledge base that can be deployed across the Internet, and around the world. The link between HR software and the improvement in sales is compelling.
>
> SOURCE: La Pointe (1999:90–92).

24.5.1 Areas of human resources related research

The ability to conduct research and utilise the findings appropriately is critically important to human resources practitioners and managers. In contrast to basic research, which has the aim of generating theoretical knowledge to create a greater understanding about a given subject for future use, applied research is aimed at solving a particular practical problem immediately. Basic research is mostly done under the guidance of an academic or research institution, while applied research is done within organisations.

Research in organisations can be planned and conducted on human resource aspects such as:
- the equity status of the organisation in accordance with the Employment Equity Act;
- the absenteeism status within various sections or departments, and the main causes of the problem, if it exists;
- the labour turnover rate and the nature of a labour turnover problem;
- the job satisfaction of employees;
- the current organisational culture in comparison to the desired culture;

- the reasons for the slow implementation of a mentoring programme;
- training needs analysis;
- the alignment of individual performance management applications with organisational goals; and
- competency assessment of employees.

24.5.2 The application of human resources information

What follows will focus on the application of human resources information with regard to the management of employment equity, absenteeism, labour turnover, and employee satisfaction.

24.5.2.1 Employment equity

The Employment Equity Act requires that employers prepare and implement an employment equity plan that complies with the new regulations published by the Department of Labour in 1999. These regulations stipulate the exact manner in which designated employers must analyse their workforce, and the relevant information that must appear in their equity reports. Chapter 7 covers employment equity and affirmative action.

The introduction of various software programmes has made the procedural application of the Employment Equity Act easier. Some of these programmes enable the employer to:
- compile a profile of the workforce, in terms of designated groups, non-designated groups, occupational categories, occupational levels, and permanent and non-permanent employees;
- compile a report on the skills development of employees;
- analyse the organisation's employment policies, practices, procedures, and the working environment;
- compile the organisation's equity plan; and
- benchmark itself against similar organisations.

24.5.2.2 Absenteeism

A search on the Internet for information on absenteeism revealed more than 10 000 absence-related websites, an indication of the magnitude of this problem. On the other hand, the new, logical organisation is result-driven and not behaviour-orientated. In an emerging virtual environment, absenteeism is becoming less and less important. Before management embark on a programme to control and reduce absenteeism, they should first consider whether attendance is linked to performance outcomes or not.

Absenteeism is defined as the non-attendance of an employee when scheduled to work. Research on absenteeism is important, owing to the potentially disruptive effect it has on operations within the organisation, as well as the related costs involved. Absenteeism is regarded as withdrawal behaviour when it is used as a way to escape an undesirable working environment. Figure 24.2 illustrates the cost of absenteeism in small businesses, as established by a survey done in America. It plainly shows that absenteeism can be expensive.

Factors contributing to absenteeism

The human resources practitioner must stay sensitive to the fact that people do get sick and that they do encounter problems that might prevent them from attending work. However, it is also a fact that, for various reasons, people do abuse the sick leave that they are granted by the organisation. The same cold that would not prevent us from attending a social meeting, becomes a convenient excuse not to attend work. These reasons can be explained as follows:

Figure 24.2 Costs related to absenteeism

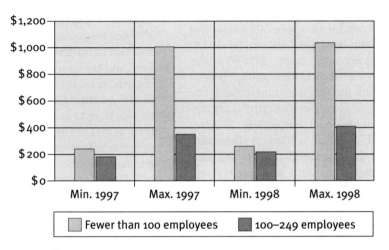

SOURCE: Business owner's toolkit.

- *Unmet expectations.* New employees enter an organisation with certain expectations relating to the opportunities of applying their skills and abilities, equal treatment, receiving respect, or satisfactory working conditions. If the employee's expectations are not met, the employee could abuse sick-leave as a mechanism to withdraw temporarily from the job or the job situation.
- *Job–person match.* If an employee's personality, abilities, and skills are not congruent with the job requirements, the person becomes either bored or stressed and withdraws from the situation by being absent. If there is a good match between the job characteristics and personal characteristics of the employee, the person will rather accept responsibility and stay committed to his job.
- *Organisational culture.* If a permissive culture exists within an organisation regarding absence, employees will consider sick-leave as a benefit that needs to be utilised, or it will be lost. On the other hand, if unnecessary absence is frowned upon by either management or co-workers, the employee will think twice before abusing sick-leave.

Absence categories

For the sake of accurate recording and analysis, absenteeism is divided into three categories: sick, authorised, and unexcused absence.

- *Sick absence* occurs when a person is absent owing to a reported illness, genuine or not. The company policy will state at what stage a medical certificate is required.
- *Authorised absence* occurs when the employee is absent for any reason other than illness, and it is accepted by management. Employees should be encouraged to seek permission beforehand if the situation allows for it.
- *Unexcused absence* is considered unacceptable and should not be tolerated. Progressive discipline is used to handle this problem.

Recording absenteeism

The HRIS makes it very easy to record individual absences. The most basic information required is the person's name and employee number, days absent, and reason for the absence. Some HRISs make provision for further information, such as the name of the doctor who issued the medical certificate. The contemporary approach is to counsel employees as soon as a trend of absenteeism is detected. Employees are reminded that their attendance is important, and assistance is offered in dealing with any problem. Once individual absence information is entered, group records and trends can be followed. Group records include absenteeism measurements per section, department, race, gender, skill level, etc. These distinctions allow for more effective problem-detection and problem-solving.

Measuring absenteeism

Measuring absenteeism allows us to determine the extent and nature (reasons) of absenteeism in order to take appropriate corrective action if necessary. Two measures are generally used: Total time lost and absence frequency.

- *Total time lost* gives the percentage of work time lost owing to absenteeism. The international norm is 3 per cent. However, the question is raised whether organisations that compete in world markets should be content with an absenteeism norm of 3 per cent. The total time lost index is calculated as follows:

$$\text{Total time lost} = \frac{\text{Total number of days lost due to absence over the period}}{\text{Average number of employees} \times \text{total workdays over the period}} \times 100\%$$

- *Absence frequency* gives an indication of the number of absence incidents per employee. An incident is one spell of absence, irrespective of duration. A high absence frequency rate suggests that absence incidents are of a shorter duration, and thus more disruptive to the organisation. It is easier and less costly to make contingency plans when it is known that an employee will be absent for a longer period than it is for short, unexpected absence incidents. The absence frequency rate is calculated as follows and expressed as a ratio:

$$\text{Absence frequency} = \frac{\text{Number of absence incidents over the period}}{\text{Average number of employees employed over the period}}$$

The total time lost index and frequency ratio are determined for every group of employees and every category of absence, namely sick absence, authorised absence and unexcused absence.

Analysis of absenteeism measurements

The recording and measurement of absenteeism figures is of absolutely no value if not interpreted and acted upon. The measurement of absenteeism should be used as a diagnostic tool to identify organisational problems. A comparison between different departments and worker groups can pinpoint trends. If most days are lost due to sick absence and a large number of employees is involved, it might be an indication of withdrawal behaviour. If authorised absence is a problem, the organisation's policy and the involvement of supervisors should be considered. Lastly, unexcused absence is unacceptable under any circumstances, and can be reduced by properly communicated and applied disciplinary procedures. Figure 24.3 illustrates some of the options available for the analysis of absence by means of an absence software program.

24.5.2.3 Labour turnover

Labour turnover is the movement of employees in and out of the boundaries of the organisation. Transfers are, thus, not considered as labour turnover. Labour turnover is considered to be permanent withdrawal from the working situation. Labour turnover can be disruptive and costly to an organisation. The stability of the work group is influenced, and new employees must be recruited, employed, and trained. A certain amount of labour turnover can be beneficial, however, if it provides the organisation with new, enthusiastic employees who bring creative ideas with them. Labour turnover is influenced by the prevailing economic climate, the nature of the organisation, and the type of employee.

Causes of labour turnover

As in the case of absenteeism, unmet expectations and the person-work relationship will also influence labour turnover. Individual factors that have an effect are age, education, background, and personality. Employees sometimes remain in an organisation for a long period because they have built up a good relationship with co-workers.

Controllable and uncontrollable labour turnover

Labour turnover is divided into controllable and uncontrollable turnover, depending on management's ability to prevent it or not. Voluntary resignations (V) and dismissals (D) are regarded as controllable. Voluntary resignations can be controlled if management provides better leadership, wages, opportunities, working conditions, etc. Dismissals can be prevented through proper employment, training, policies, and procedures. Only controllable labour turnover is included in the measurement of labour turnover. Uncontrollable labour turnover includes death, permanent illness, pregnancy, retirement, and retrenchment. These are recorded, yet not included in the measurement of labour turnover, as no reasonable action from management can reduce or prevent them.

Recording of labour turnover

Information required for the measurement of labour turnover includes the employee's name and personnel number, dates of entry and departure, and reasons given for leaving.

Figure 24.3 Group trends menu of an absence software program

Absenteeism program – group trends

- ▶ Department/section
- ▶ Age
- ▶ Gender and race
- ▶ Marital status
- ▶ Education
- ▶ Length of service
- ▶ Residential area
- ▶ Go to main menu

Measurement and analysis of labour turnover

Labour turnover is measured by calculating the labour turnover rate (LTO), median length of service (MLOS) and percentage of voluntary resignations (% V). The labour turnover rate indicates the percentage of people who left the organisation due to controllable reasons. The LTO is calculated as an annual figure to make comparison possible. The norm for labour turnover is dependent on the type of worker and industry, the economic conditions, and geographical area. It is suggested that labour turnover be compared with the organisation's turnover rate over a period of time, and with similar groups or organisations.

$$LTO = \frac{V + D}{\text{Average number of employees}} \times \frac{100}{1}$$

$$\% V = \frac{V}{V + D} \times \frac{100}{1}$$

$$MLOS = \text{median length of service (middle figure)}$$

The MLOS indicates at what stage of employment employees have left. The MLOS differs from the average length of service in the sense that a median refers to the middle figure. The MLOS is indicated in months. Should the length of service of employees who have left be 1, 2, 2, 3, 4, 5, and 6 months respectively, the MLOS will be 3 months. A short MLOS indicates problems with employment, induction, training, and mentoring. A long MLOS indicates problems with advancement opportunities, or resistance to change in the organisation.

The % V indicates the percentage of leavers who left voluntarily, as opposed to being dismissed. A high % V indicates employee dissatisfaction with the organisation, whereas a low % V indicates a high rate of dismissals, thus dissatisfaction on the part of the organisation. The MLOS and %V must be interpreted together.

The above analysis is an indication of the course of action that should be taken in order to reduce labour turnover. If a high percentage of employees leave the organisation voluntarily soon after employment, the employment, induction, and placement practices should be re-evaluated. If many employees are dismissed, employment practices and training should be reconsidered.

Employees who leave after a reasonable time period often feel that they have started to stagnate, and leave for better opportunities or more challenges. If many employees leave after a long service with the company, it will be an indication that changes have taken place that they found difficult to cope with. Resistance to change should be managed by informing and involving employees, in advance of change.

24.5.2.4 Job satisfaction

High absenteeism and labour turnover figures might be an indication of dissatisfaction in the organisation. Greenberg and Baron (1995:169) define job satisfaction as individuals' cognitive, affective, and evaluative reaction to their jobs. Although a direct relationship has not been found between job dissatisfaction and performance, it is generally agreed that job satisfaction influences absenteeism, labour turnover, commitment, and organisational citizenship. Research has found differences in the levels of satisfaction of white-collar personnel (e.g. managerial and professional people) and blue-collar workers, older people and younger people, more experienced and less experienced people, women and men, and people belonging to minority and majority groups.

Factors contributing to job satisfaction

Two main groups of factors contribute to job satisfaction, namely personal factors and organisational factors. Personal factors refer mainly to personality, status and seniority, general life satisfaction, and the extent to which the job characteristics are congruent with personal characteristics. Organisational factors refer to the following:

- *Pay and benefits.* People perceive their remuneration as an indication of what they are worth to the organisation. The principle of equitable pay is very important. People compare what they put into the organisation with what they get out, and with what other people put in and get out. Inequity leads to job dissatisfaction.
- *The work itself.* People have a preference for interesting and challenging tasks that provide opportunities for self-actualisation and recognition.
- *The supervisor.* Job satisfaction is influenced by the amount of technical and social support extended by the supervisor.
- *Relationship with co-workers.* Whereas the first three factors have a strong influence on job satisfaction, the relationship an employee has with co-workers only influences job satisfaction moderately. People with a strong career orientation may place less emphasis on social relations.
- *Working conditions.* People become dissatisfied if they work in an overcrowded, dark, dirty, or noisy place. Adequate working conditions are taken for granted, and not noticed.

Measurement of job satisfaction

Various reliable and valid instruments are available to measure job satisfaction systematically. These include the following:
- *Rating scales.* A rating scale is a questionnaire in which people report their reactions to their jobs. The Job Descriptive Index (JDI), for example, is a questionnaire in which employees describe whether or not each of several adjectives describes a particular aspect of their jobs. Questions deal with the work itself, pay, promotional opportunities, supervision, and co-workers. The advantage of a rating scale is that it is easy and quick to fill in, and norms are usually available for comparison.
- *Critical incidents.* Here employees are given an opportunity to describe situations or events in their jobs that made them either very satisfied or very dissatisfied. For example, employees might indicate situations where they received special recognition or situations where they were treated rudely. The researcher will examine the replies in order to identify underlying themes.
- *Interviews.* Structured interviews are preferable, since they provide a basis for comparison, and ensure that important aspects are covered. On the other hand, an unstructured approach allows the employee to express any thought on his or her mind that might not be covered by a structured interview.

Conducting a job satisfaction survey in an organisation tends to create expectations in employees that positive changes will be instituted. Not attending to obvious problems, may aggravate any existing dissatisfaction.

24.6 Human resources information systems and quality assurance

HRISs provide the human resources department with an excellent opportunity to contribute constructively to the strategic goals of the organisation, by providing timely and accurate information to support key decision-making. The ultimate purpose of HRISs is not to collect an intensive database of information, but to use the information to assist the organisation in adapting to internal and external environmental changes.

The distinguishing, best-practice characteristics of a HRIS are highly integrated and complete databases, broad self-service access by employees and managers, harnessed Intranet and Internet connectivity, and a tightly aligned link between the goals of the business and human resources activities.

24.7 Conclusion

It is impossible to make informed decisions in an organisation without timely and accurate information. The human resources department is responsible for maintaining a user-friendly database relating to all human resources issues and information. Although the advent of computers has made this function easier, it has also created greater expectations. The human resources department has to prove that it does contribute directly to the strategic vision of the organisation.

Summary

The function of a HRIS is to collect, record, store, analyse, distribute, and retrieve data concerning the organisation's human resources.

Various myths surround the implementation and utilisation of HRISs in organisations. These myths cause resistance to change and lead to the slow introduction of such systems into organisations.

HRISs consist of hardware, software, data, and users. HRISs can be applied in every aspect of human resources management, such as recruitment, salary administration, skills development, equity management, and performance management. A new addition is a self-help desk that is linked to the Intranet to assist employees with personal inquiries, and to allow them to communicate their ideas and suggestions to either the human resources department or other users in the organisation.

The HRIS serves as a diagnostic and decision-making tool in the organisation. Specific areas where it can be utilised as a data-bank and research tool include absenteeism and labour turnover control, employment equity management, and the monitoring of job satisfaction.

Quality assurance in HRISs is crucial. Effective decision-making is only possible if it is based on accurate, complete, and timely information. Managers must be trained in the use of technological decision-making tools.

Related websites

This topic may be investigated further by referring to the following Internet websites:
Q Data DynamiQue – http://www.dynamique.co.za
Department of Labour – http://www.labour.gov.za
Employment equity software – http://www.equityact.co.za
  – http://www.emsoft.co.za
  – http://www.vanzylrudd.co.za

Case study

Fresh Flour Products (Pty.) Ltd. is a bakery in the Western Cape. In line with most other big producers in the country, the organisation makes use of a computerised system to control the production process. The exact ingredients for each batch of bread are measured, mixed, poured into baking tins, and baked; all of this with very little human intervention. This automated process enables the company to deliver 15 000 loaves of bread per day, all of the same quality, all of the same size.

Fresh Flour employs highly qualified technicians to maintain the production process. Lately, the company has experienced a high labour turnover among these employees. As the human resources practitioner in the organisation, you decide to investigate.

Questions

1 Why does labour turnover need to be controlled?
2 How will you measure the extent of the problem?
3 Suppose you determine that the high labour turnover is linked to job dissatisfaction, how will you find out what aspects of their jobs the technicians are dissatisfied with?

Experiential exercise 1

Purpose
To get an overview of the human resources related software that is commercially available and the specific services that are offered.

Introduction
Human resources practitioners have to consider very carefully what software they introduce into the organisation to assist with the management of information relating to employees and management practices.

Task
Step 1 (10-15 minutes)
Divide into groups of three to five learners. Make a list of the criteria that human resources practitioners should consider when deciding on which software to introduce into the organisation.

Step 2
Study human resources software advertisements obtained from professional magazines, and make a list of which specific human resources functions they address. What advantages of each product are emphasised in the advertisements?

Experiential exercise 2

Purpose (debate topic)
To debate the importance of absenteeism-control in the organisation.

Introduction
Various opinions exist about the importance of absence-control in the work situation. Many people maintain that it has a negative effect on the organisation, while others use the virtual work environment as a departure point to debate against excessive focus on attendance.

Step 1 (30 minutes)
Form groups of five learners each. Half the groups will prepare an argument for,

and the others an argument against, absence-control in the workplace.

Step 2 (3 minutes per group)
Each group offers its argument in a debate presentation.

Step 3 (3 minutes)
The facilitator or designated person summarises the main arguments and draws conclusions.

Chapter questions

1 How can the realisation of the myths surrounding the introduction of HRISs into organisations be prevented?
2 What factors should one consider when buying human resources information software from a vendor?
3 How can information regarding absenteeism be used to pinpoint more specific problems in the organisation?
4 How will you respond to a person who says: 'Labour turnover is good for an organisation. It brings new blood into the organisation.'
5 Which method will you select to collect information about the job satisfaction levels of employees?

Bibliography

BERGH, Z.C. & THERON, A.L. 1999. *Psychology in the work context.* Thomson, Johannesburg.
BUSINESS OWNER'S TOOLKIT. Http://www.toolkit.cch.com.
GREENBERG, J. & BARON, R.A. 1995. *Behavior in organisations. Understanding and managing the human side of work.* 5th edition. Prentice-Hall, New Jersey.
GREENGARD, S. 1999. Mine your corporate data with business intelligence. *Workforce,* 78 (1), 103–104.
IVANCEVICH, J.M. & MATTESON, M.T. 1999. *Organisational behaviour and management.* 5th edition. Irwin/McGraw-Hill, USA.
KREITNER, R. & KINICKI, A. 1998. *Organisational behaviour.* 4th edition. Irwin/McGraw-Hill, USA.
LA POINTE, J.R. 1999. HR software products are rarely finished. *Workforce,* 78 (10), 90–92.
MULLINS, L.J. 1996. *Management and organizational behaviour.* 4th edition. Pitman, London.
ROBBINS, S.P. 1998. *Organisational behaviour.* 8th edition. Prentice-Hall, New Jersey.
VAN DER MERWE, R. & MILLER, S. 1988. *Measuring absence and labour turnover.* Lexicon, Johannesburg.
WITSCHGER, J. 1999. Eight myths of HRMS software. http://www.workforceonline.com

25

International human resources management

H B Schultz

Learning outcomes

At the end of this chapter the learner should be able to demonstrate the following outcomes:
- Describe factors affecting human resources management in global markets.
- Explain the stages of corporate international involvement.
- Compare the approaches to managing an international subsidiary.
- Discuss the problems faced by the expatriate.
- Examine the difficulties faced by the repatriate and offer guidelines for dealing with these problems.
- Provide a brief overview of international human resources management policies.
- Outline the predictions for global business at the start of the twenty-first century.

Key words and concepts

- ethnocentric
- expatriate
- geocentric
- global corporation
- host or local country
- parent or home company
- polycentric
- regiocentric
- repatriate

Illustrative case
Living in the Lion City

At the forefront of the bustling Pacific Rim economies is Singapore, the romantic island city-state known as the Lion City. Though only twenty-four miles wide, with a population of approximately three million, Singapore is aggressively leading the region in the level of trade, commerce, and high-tech industry that will characterise the twenty-first century. The locals speak English as a national language, the country has one of the cleanest, most transparent systems of business and government, and it offers a safe, comfortable lifestyle. One of the attractive, mysterious lures of Asia, however, is that things are rarely as simple as they appear.

Expatriates quickly learn that networking is critical for survival and prosperity in Singapore. Westerners often fail to realise that, in a culture like Singapore's, every relationship can be important. It is important to learn the proper behaviour and mannerisms that bring respect in Singaporean society. Relationships in Singapore are based on favours, or *guanxi* in Chinese. Singaporeans might ask for a small favour; this is an indication that they want to build a relationship with you. Westerners are quick to grant the favour, but fail to request a reciprocal favour out of an unwillingness to impose; this is regarded as a strong signal that a relationship is not uppermost in the Westerner's mind.

Singaporeans are open and friendly. They are willing to discuss things more openly than other Asians, and they welcome outsiders, but expatriates and visitors would be wise to learn about the core values of Singapore. Relationships, proper behaviour, and a polite demeanour mean a lot, and practising these manners will carry the expatriate a long way.

SOURCE: Cucullu, G. (1998:10-11).

25.1 Introduction

Human resources management is part of business which, at present, is experiencing an expansion of its environment into global markets. It is becoming more and more commonplace for companies to export their products, to establish plants or subsidiaries in other countries, or to enter into alliances with other companies in foreign markets. The main reason for this phenomenon is that companies attempt to gain a competitive advantage by exploiting new markets with a large number of potential new customers, or by capitalising on the lower labour costs for relatively unskilled jobs in the new country.

We have excellent examples of current global changes, which illustrate how human resources management is now forced to contribute towards gaining a competitive advantage in a global economy.

The European Economic Community (EEC)

The EEC, which began in 1992, is a confederation of most of the European nations, which agreed to enter into free trade with one another. Because of their close proximity, these countries experienced their economies as very much intertwined. The European Commission (EC) is the regulating body which oversees trade between these countries. Under the EC, the legal regulations between these participating countries have become almost uniform, which was somewhat of a problem before. The regulations in Germany, for example, were vastly different from those of a country such as Italy. These differences have, to a large extent, disappeared. The EEC is now the largest free market in the world.

The unification of Germany

After World War II, from 1949 until 1989, Germany was divided into East Germany, under Soviet influence and with a socialistic economic system, and West Germany with a capitalistic economy. In 1990, steps were taken to reunify East and West Germany, thereby entering the two countries as a unity into the global market. The East German integration into a capitalistic economy posed tremendous human resources management problems. Under the socialistic government in East Germany, every citizen was guaranteed a job, causing overstaffing, low motivation, little incentive to maximise profits, and a general lack of competitiveness. The fact that wages were relatively low compared to high skills, to a large extent compensated for these problems, making former East Germany a viable proposition for investment by foreign companies. The unification process remains a constant challenge to human resources management to merge two very diverse workforces.

The North American Free Trade Agreement (NAFTA)

The United States of America and Canada entered into a free trade agreement in 1989. NAFTA, however, brought Mexico into this agreement, which will probably open a free market larger than the EEC. This will lead to an increase of US investment in Mexico, resulting from the lower labour cost for low-skilled employees. On a macro level, it may result in a large portion of low-skilled jobs being moved to Mexico, lowering employment opportunities for low-skilled Americans.

The Soviet Union

After the unification of Germany and the fall of the Berlin Wall, there was a move by countries controlled by the Soviet Union to convert their economies to the capitalist system. This movement resulted in an opening up of markets and the privatising of government-owned enterprises. For the previous few decades these countries had been deprived of private or foreign investment; this has now changed completely. These major changes offer interesting challenges to human resources management, ranging from training, to culture management and the normal activities of human resources management, which were absent in the communist past.

In this chapter attention will be given to:
- factors affecting human resources management in global markets, including culture, education/human capital, the political/legal system, and the economic system;
- the stages of international involvement;
- the mix of host-country and expatriate employees;
- problems faced by the expatriate;
- problems faced by the repatriate;
- international human resources management policies; and
- international human resources management in the twenty-first century.

25.2 Factors affecting human resources management in global markets

Various authors, such as Noe et al. (1994) and Gomez-Mejia et al. (1998) have identified certain factors which impact upon human resources management in global markets. They include diverse cultural, educational, economic, political, and legal environments.

25.2.1 Culture

The ability to understand and balance cultural values and practices regarding things such as the importance of work, how status is determined, the relationship of work to the whole person and the group, the perceived value of experience versus training and development, the desire for change, and how people from different cultures view what is happening in the world, form an important part of the task of the international manager.

Different cultures cultivate different beliefs. A general overview reveals the following. German managers, more than others, believe that creativity is important for career success, and focus on preparations for functional careers. British managers, on the other hand, believe that the ability to create the right image and to get noticed for what they do is essential for career success. French managers view an organisation as an authority network, where the power to organise and control originates from their positioning in the hierarchy. Cultures such as those in Singapore and Jamaica socialise individuals to accept uncertainty and take each day as it comes. People from these cultures tend to be more easygoing and flexible regarding different views. Cultures in Greece and Portugal socialise their people to seek security through technology, law, and religion, in the process providing clear rules on how to behave. In Japan and Germany strong roles are given to males; performance, success, and competition are emphasised. In contrast, Sweden and Norway focus more on the female roles of putting relationships before money, helping others, and protecting the environment. Japan and China have a long-term orientation, with a focus on the future and values such as saving and persistence. Countries with a more short-term orientation include the United States of America, Russia, and West African countries (Gomez-Mejia et al. 1998:531–535).

Trompenaars and Wooliams (1999:33) explore seven major dimensions in which cultures differ. Five of these dimensions relate to solving problems in human relationships. They look at how different cultures balance the everyday dilemmas of dealing with rules and relationships, the individual within the group, how status is given and earned, how emotions are expressed, and what is considered private and what public.

The sixth dimension deals with how cultures relate to their environment – do they seek to control it, or to accept and adapt to it? The seventh looks at how different cultures relate to time, how they perceive the relative importance and degree of integration of the past, the present, and the future, and how they organise time within this.

It is important to emphasise that culture is closely intertwined with, and has a strong impact upon, the other three factors (education/human capital, the political/ legal system, and the economic system). If a culture values education highly, it is obvious that members of a community will strive to improve their knowledge and skills. Laws are a direct result of how the inhabitants of a country view right and wrong. Culture and the economic system are closely intertwined, as cultural values will determine, to a large extent, which economic system will be adopted.

25.2.2 Education/human capital

It is significant that the Pacific Rim countries such as Japan, Taiwan, Singapore, Korea, and Hong-Kong, which lead the world in productivity and quality, despite limited natural resources, have gained their competitive edge through their people. Their heavy investment in education and training are providing the rewards.

Human capital can be described as the productive capabilities of individuals, i.e. the knowledge, skills, and experience that, in themselves, have economic value. Different countries have different levels of human capital. The shortage of human capital in the USA results from jobs being created which require skills beyond those of most of the new entrants into the labour market. In West Germany a shift in types of production has taken place, requiring highly skilled workers, and resulting in a human capital shortage for high-skill jobs.

Where free education is offered, as in the Netherlands and the former Soviet Bloc, a high level of human capital becomes available. In contrast, a low level of human capital is available in Third-World countries, as a result of a low investment in education. From a practical point of view, countries with low human capital levels manage to attract investment in facilities that require low skills and low wage levels. On the other hand, companies in developed countries like USA, currently locate unionised, low-skill/high-wage manufacturing and assembling jobs in Mexico. They manage to obtain low-skill workers in Mexico for substantially lower wages. Japan ships its low-skill work to neighbouring countries, while maintaining its high-skill work at home.

25.2.3 Political/legal system

The political/legal system, by its nature, is closely linked to the culture in which it operates. Norms and values are usually reflected in legal regulations which, again, are directly manifested in the practices of human resources management regarding training, employment, lay-offs, compensation, industrial relations, etc. Norms and values in a specific country will, through legislation, indicate clearly in what direction that country is moving. The United States of America was, for example, the first country to eliminate discrimination based on sex or colour in the workplace. Employees in Germany have been granted the legal right to co-determination at the company plant and industrial level. The implication of this is that employees who serve on the supervisory council have a direct influence over important decisions that affect them directly. Another good example of the influence of the political/legal system is the European Economic Charter of 9 December 1989, which provides for the social rights of workers, including freedom of movement, freedom of choice of own occupation, the right to be fairly compensated, the guarantee of social protection via social security benefits, freedom of association and collective bargaining, equal treatment for men and women, and a safe and healthy work environment.

Finally, an important concern for multinational corporations is whether human resources policies will be created at corporate headquarters and transplanted to local companies, or created by local companies in accordance with local laws and customs. Employment policies, such as conditions of employment, retirement, termination, discrimination, and workers' rights differ greatly from country to country (Cherrington & Middelton 1995:130).

25.2.4 Economic system

The economic system can broadly be described as the manner in which society produces and distributes its goods and services. The world is, to a large extent, divided into capitalistic or socialistic blocs. This demarcation, together with economic factors such as exchange rates, availability of raw material, labour cost, technology, and level of innovation, play an important role in the decision as to where a corporation will conduct its business.

It is obvious that the economic system operating in a country has a very definite impact upon the profitability of a company and, more specifically, on the human resources management of the organisation. The tax system, as part of the economic system, for example, has a profound influence upon profitability. In capitalistic countries, attempts are made to reward the individuals by allowing them to keep as much of their earnings as possible. The higher taxes in socialistic countries provide for services, which the employee receives 'free'. In capitalistic countries the individual's salary is a reflection of the quality of human capital. The highly skilled worker will receive more than his less skilled counterpart. The investment in human capital will, thus, be a fairly accurate barometer of the level of economic development in a particular country, which will be valuable information for a corporate head-office to consider when doing business in a foreign country.

25.3 The stages of international involvement

Before we examine how an organisation becomes involved in international business, it is important to understand what the term 'international company' means. Pitfield (1996:12) categorises international companies as:
- *traditional*, or 'colonial' companies which were established as the result of international commercial activity and followed the political models of their national states;
- *modern*, or domestic 'high-fliers' which developed from a sound national base and expanded their operations into the international market in the face of local competition; and
- *fast-movers*, resulting from mergers and acquisitions, which moved from a strong home or regional base to acquire complementary organisations in other parts of the world.

A further model has emerged in recent years: the international company resulting from alliances in order to achieve the benefits of global operation. One of the most prominent examples of alliances in this region is South African Airways, which has forged alliances with many powerful international airlines.

Gomez-Mejia et al. (1998:516–518) indicate how firms progress through five stages as they internationalise their operations and adapt their human resources practices to diverse cultural, economic, political, and legal environments.

Stage One

At this stage, the firm's market is exclusively domestic, and primarily local and national forces dictate human resources practices such as staffing, training, and compensation. Many South African companies are still operating within this stage but, to become globally competitive, will have to consider expanding their operations.

Stage Two

Dessler (1997:671) states that exporting is often the first choice when a company decides to expand overseas. The company retains production facilities within domestic borders, and although few employees expect to be posted overseas, human resources practices should be geared towards managerial incentives, and appropriate training and staffing strategies that focus on the demands of international customers. In South Africa, the elimination of trade barriers is contributing to the number of firms that fall into Stage Two. Besides exporting, companies can also enter into franchising and licensing agreements, which place them in this stage of internationalisation.

Stage Three

Many firms move some of their operations out of the home-country, particularly for parts-assembly. These facilities tend to be under close control of corporate headquarters, and most top managers are expatriates (citizens of the home country). Human resources practices must emphasise the selection, training, and compensation of expatriates, and the development of personnel policies for local employees.

Stage Four

When an organisation reaches Stage Four, it has a parent firm based in the home country to coordinate a fully-fledged multinational corporation, which operates manufacturing and marketing facilities in several countries. Although many personnel decisions affecting foreign branches are made at corporate headquarters, foreign operations are still managed by expatriates, resulting in complex human resources practices dealing with diverse ethnic and cultural groups in multiple countries.

Stage Five

Marketing experts believe that the multinational corporation is facing its demise, as the new global transnational corporation becomes more prominent. These corporations have weak ties with any given country, operations are highly decentralised, and each business unit makes personnel decisions with little or no control from corporate headquarters. They sell the same products (such as the Sony Walkman) in the same way everywhere, and the organisation freely hires employees from any country.

Human resources practices at Stage Five attempt to create a shared corporate culture, rather than a national identity. Managers are usually trained in the home country and may receive some exposure at corporate headquarters, before being sent on international assignments.

Pitfield (1996:6) notes that the traditional expatriate manager is rapidly declining in status, as the speed of international travel and communication renders the opportunity for developing local nationals to run local operations more obvious. In addition, 'third-country nationals' demonstrate their ability in an overseas operational area, and are then posted to other parts of the world to broaden and build their experience.

Organisations are increasingly using troubleshooters to perform the interface role between headquarters and local operations. They are highly mobile and able to solve problems in a wide variety of cultural environments, and then to move on to the next international assignment.

The advent of trustworthy and efficient phone, fax, video, Internet, and electronic mail links has also brought about the rise of the stay-at-home international manager, who is rarely called upon to travel abroad, but who has significant contact with, and responsibility for, the international operation.

25.4 The mix of host-country and expatriate employees

When a firm opens a foreign branch, thus passing into Stage Three of internationalisation, issues of control between the parent company and its international subsidiary become important, as do concerns about management and human resources issues (Beardwell & Holden 1997:702).

25.4.1 Approaches to managing an international subsidiary

There are four main approaches to managing an international subsidiary.
- *The ethnocentric approach.* In this approach, parent-company nationals fill all key positions. Direct control over the host-country subsidiary is established and is common in the early stages of internationalisation. The approach may also be used if there is a lack of qualified host-country nationals.
- *The polycentric approach.* This approach to managing international operations uses personnel from the host country to manage and staff subsidiaries.
- *The geocentric approach.* The use of the

geocentric approach involves the parent company deliberately searching on a worldwide or regional basis for the best staff to fill key positions. Transnational firms at Stage Five tend to follow this approach, as it enables the development of an international executive team.
- *The regiocentric approach.* The regiocentric approach allows for the movement of staff within the geographic operations of a multinational corporation, and offers the opportunity for development of management succession programmes.

25.4.2 Using parent-company and host-country employees

Expatriates usually hold key positions, but it makes little financial sense to pay high salaries (usually based on the home country's pay systems) and to finance relocation costs, if foreign nationals can competently

---

Encounter 25.1

When Tellabs, Inc., a Chicago-based designer and manufacturer of telecommunications products decided to open a German branch in 1994, a major task was to impart Tellabs' corporate culture before handing over the office to host-country nationals. Tellabs' culture is informal and flexible, their global policy underlining the conviction that host-country nationals know the marketplace as well as they know the business. Hiring German nationals, however, was not easy in a society where cultural values differ in many areas to those of the American parent company.

Tellabs used the lessons learnt when opening their branches in Ireland, the Netherlands, and Finland. In Ireland, there was no cross-pollination of resources and Irish nationals did not always manage the business in the manner anticipated by the Americans. Problems with cross-cultural sensitivity became apparent when an American marketing representative addressed a company president in the Netherlands by his first name, midway through a sales presentation. The stony silence that ensued was underlined when he lost the sale and local salespeople informed him that it was rude to call company presidents by their first names.

This led to the implementation of cross-cultural counselling at the startup of the Finnish operation. The focus was placed on how to conduct business meetings, the components of the supervisory relationship, and how to communicate effectively. For example, Tellabs learned that employees in Finland prefer written communication to verbal interaction. These interventions had a positive impact on the establishment of relationships between the Finnish operation and the parent company.

In Germany, Tellabs used the same approach to dealing with cultural differences, coupled with a readiness to adapt to local conditions. In the area of recruitment, they realised that Germans wanted to be assured of the transfer of leadership when a host-country national heads the facility. Germans also seek specific and detailed information regarding benefits, because German companies are very paternalistic and offer great security. Tellabs has achieved profitability in their overseas operations, because they have adopted the principle of doing things the way the host country does, as long as they achieve the required business results.

SOURCE: Solomon, C.M. (1995:60–67).

fill these positions. In addition, many countries require that a certain percentage of the workforce be local citizens. The use of expatriates generally increases when:
- sufficient local talent is not available, as in developing countries;
- an important part of the firm's overall business strategy is the creation of a corporation-wide global vision;
- international units and domestic operations are highly interdependent, for example, in certain production processes that require all divisions of a corporation, both international and domestic, to work closely with one another;
- the political situation is unstable; and
- there are significant cultural differences between the host country and the home country, demanding cross-cultural sensitivity.

25.5 Problems faced by the expatriate

Before discussing the problems facing expatriates, it is necessary to distinguish between the various types of international employee. Expatriate is the term used for an employee sent by a company in one country to manage operations in a different country. There are, however, different types of expatriate. Parent-country nationals are employees who were born and live in the parent country. Host-country nationals are those employees who were born and raised in the host country. Third-country nationals are employees born in a country other than the parent country or host country, but who work in the host country.

Apart from the above distinctions, companies are referred to as multinational or international companies when operating globally. International companies become multinational when they build facilities in a number of different countries, in an attempt to capitalise on lower production or distribution costs in different locations. A third type of organisation, the global organisation, competes in state-of-the-art, top-quality products and services, on the basis of the lowest cost possible. The global company emphasises flexibility, and wants customisation of products to meet the needs of particular clients. The global company will, thus, proactively consider the cultures, human capital, political/legal systems, and economic systems to determine where production facilities can be located to provide a competitive advantage. This will result in less hierarchical structures, emphasising decentralised decision-making.

The compensation package of an expatriate manager is obviously very high. Likewise, the cost of an unsuccessful expatriate returning early will be significant. It is, therefore, important not to underestimate the impact of such assignments on a company's profitability. The major issues that contribute towards effective management of expatriates include selection, training and development, compensation, and their reacculturation (re-entering of their home country).

Understanding the reasons why many international assignments end in failure can assist in reducing the high failure-rates of expatriates. Gómez-Mejía et al. (1998: 522) mention six factors that account for most failures.
- *Career blockage.* International companies usually believe that the career planning of their expatriates is well taken care of. However, after the initial excitement of moving abroad has worn off, many employees perceive their careers to be stagnating while their counterparts at home are climbing the corporate ladder. This perception is owing to the fact that the majority of firms do not identify the technical, managerial and interpersonal competencies required by expatriates,

- nor do they link international competencies and experiences to career planning.
- *Culture shock.* Expatriates who cannot adjust to a different cultural environment experience the phenomenon called culture shock, and try to impose the home country's values on the host country's employees, instead of learning to work within the new culture. Escalating cultural clashes and misunderstandings may then force the expatriate to return to more familiar surroundings.
- *Lack of pre-departure cross-cultural training.* Only about one-third of multinationals provide any cross-cultural training to expatriates, and this tends to be rather cursory. Many expatriates, especially women, feel that they are not accorded proper respect when having to undergo business rituals they do not understand in the host country. Advance knowledge of what to expect could pre-empt embarrassing situations.
- *Overemphasis on technical qualifications.* Often, expatriates who have impressive credentials in the home office are regarded as natural choices for starting up a new international facility or for troubleshooting when technical difficulties arise. However, these same traits may not be perceived as relevant in the host country, and the latter's workplace practices may be regarded as unacceptable to the expatriate. It appears that cultural sensitivity is more important than technical skill in an overseas assignment.
- *Getting rid of a troublesome employee.* In some cases, organisations see an international assignment as an easy way of resolving difficult interpersonal situations or political conflicts at the home office. This can have disastrous effects, especially if the expatriate is not selected according to the competencies required to carry out the assignment.
- *Family problems.* Very often, the expatriate's spouse and children are unable or unwilling to adapt to life in another country. Coupled with the stress experienced when trying to function in unfamiliar surroundings, this problem can easily result in an aborted international assignment. Surprisingly, very few companies provide any type of counselling programme for the families of expatriates, especially when one spouse in a dual-career couple is asked to make a career sacrifice in order to allow the other's development. Torrington and Hall (1995: 663–664) add that economic development and geographic location, especially if the host is a Third-World country, exacerbate the problem of the expatriate's family adapting to a new lifestyle.

25.6 Problems faced by the repatriate

Dessler (1997:687) explains that repatriation is the process of moving back to the parent company and country from the foreign assignment. Many companies do not anticipate the problems which may be faced by the repatriate and, consequently, do not adopt a proactive approach to making the transition as smooth as possible.

25.6.1 Common repatriation problems

Even if the expatriation phase has proceeded smoothly, there are three common problems that many repatriates have to deal with.
- *Lack of respect for acquired skills.* In many cases, the repatriate who has gained a wealth of information and valuable skills on a foreign assignment is not accorded the recognition and appreciation he deserves. If the international assignment has lasted several years, the repatriate may be regarded as out of touch with the situation at corporate headquarters. Very

few repatriates believe that overseas assignments enhance their career development and, as Gómez-Mejía et al. (1998:524) report, most companies do not take advantage of what their expatriates have learned overseas.
- *Poor planning for return position.* Often, the home office repatriates an employee without giving much thought to what his or her new career assignment will be. The repatriate may suffer much anxiety regarding the uncertainty of the position he will hold on his return.
- *Reverse culture shock.* Extended international assignments can result in internalisation of the host country's norms and customs. Expatriates are usually unaware of how much psychological change they have undergone, until they return home and experience a culture to which they have been unaccustomed for a long time. This may result in reverse culture shock, leading to alienation, a sense of uprootedness, and even disciplinary problems. The repatriate's family may also suffer when having to re-establish old friendships and habits.

25.6.2 Guidelines for dealing with the repatriate

Repatriation problems are common, and Dessler (1997:687) offers a number of steps that progressive multinational companies can take to reduce their frequency.
- *Write repatriation agreements.* These agreements guarantee that the expatriate will not spend longer than a stipulated period abroad and that, on return, a mutually acceptable job will be made available.
- *Assign a sponsor.* A senior manager at the parent company can be assigned to keep the expatriate informed of significant corporate changes, monitor the expatriate's career interests, and ensure that he or she is considered for key openings on return.
- *Provide career counselling.* Formal career counselling sessions provide the opportunity to ensure that job assignments meet the expatriate's needs, on return to the parent company.
- *Keep communications open.* Parent companies can keep expatriates informed of home office business affairs by holding management meetings abroad, frequent home leave, and regularly scheduled meetings at headquarters. Rapid advances in technology also allow frequent and interactive communication by means of faxes, email, and video conferencing sessions.
- *Offer financial support.* Companies with the financial means can assist the expatriate in maintaining his or her residence in the home country, which can alleviate settling-in problems when the family returns.
- *Develop reorientation programmes.* Adjustment back into the home culture can be facilitated through reorientation programmes, which the repatriate and his or her family can attend.

25.7 International human resources management policies

If the parent company carefully plans and executes its international human resources management policies, many of the problems that face expatriates when undertaking an overseas assignment can be alleviated. Research undertaken by Henley Management College in the United Kingdom indicates that certain, specific competencies are required if managers are to operate successfully in the international area (Pitfield 1996:9–12). These competencies include:
- *Familiarity with a variety of cultures.* Multicultural exposure, longish periods

abroad, and frequent working visits to overseas operations contribute significantly to the ability of the international manager to operate successfully.
- *Real experience of different cultures.* Genuine cultural contact, perhaps staying in the home of one of the host country's local managers and obtaining firsthand information of the pervading culture by using local transport systems, contributes to an awareness of cultural differences.
- *Acceptance of mobility.* The Henley studies reveal that managers are much less willing to move abroad than in the past, especially when considering issues relating to property prices, children's schooling, overseas allowances, and foreign exchange controls. The extent of company support for families and personal circumstances can be a deciding factor in deciding to move, particularly if there are dual-career difficulties.
- *Cultural sensitivity and flexibility.* Successful international managers have acquired sensitivity and flexibility in different management cultures, before they arrive in the host-country. Some of the issues that they may face include:
  - recognising that the purpose of meetings can differ in different countries;
  - understanding that the use of first names may not be acceptable;
  - realising that attitudes towards time and punctuality may differ;
  - accepting that demonstrations of hospitality are often required before business can be conducted;
  - recognising that the balance of work and social relationships can differ markedly between different cultures; and
  - cultivating an awareness that ethical issues such as 'bribery' may be viewed in a different light in the host country.
- *Knowledge of languages.* Although the international language of business is English, it is wise to have a social knowledge of other languages, to express thanks, gratitude, and admiration, and to demonstrate that an effort has been made to move towards the culture of the host country.
- *Information technology communication skills.* The mobile international manager requires high-level IT skills, in order to be able to communicate effectively with headquarters and other subsidiaries.

Based on the above competencies, the focus of human resources management policies is directed towards the areas of recruitment and selection, training, remuneration, performance management, and labour relations.

25.7.1 Recruitment and selection

Although necessity may demand that an organisation, which has little experience of overseas operations, use external recruitment, people within the organisation may already possess some of the required competencies. These employees should be identified, and development activity should be based on those skills that are lacking. Although recruitment for overseas assignments should include both employees identified by the company, and internal and external applications, Dessler (1997: 681) recommends that adaptability screening be used in all recruitment efforts, to assess the potential expatriate's ability to handle the foreign transfer. A psychologist or a psychiatrist usually conducts this process.

Realistic previews of what to expect in the new job and a different culture are essential, as is an evaluation of the extent to which the future expatriate possesses those qualities perceived to contribute to the success of an international assignee. According to Dessler (1997:681) the qualities are:
- job knowledge and motivation;
- relational skills;

- flexibility and adaptability;
- extra-cultural openness; and
- family situation.

25.7.2 Training

A crucial question, when preparing expatriates to take up their new assignments, is what sort of special training overseas candidates need. Dessler (1997:683) prescribes a four-step approach:
- Level One, where training focuses on the impact of cultural differences;
- Level Two, which aims at an awareness of how attitudes influence behaviour;
- Level Three, where training provides factual knowledge about the target country; and
- Level Four, which introduces skill-building in language, and adjustment and adaptation skills.

Gómez-Mejía et al. (1998:528–9) also stress the importance of a cross-cultural approach to training, which provides the skills required to deal with a wide range of people with different values. Gómez-Mejía et al. identify three approaches to cross-cultural training:
- *the information-giving approach*, which lasts less than a week and provides indispensable briefings, and a little language training;
- *the affective approach*, which lasts from one to four weeks and provides the psychological and managerial skills needed to perform effectively during a moderate-length assignment; and
- *the impression approach*, which lasts from one to two months and provides the manager with field experiences and extended language training.

Coupled with the above readiness training, the parent company must also give attention to the career development opportunities offered to the expatriate. Gómez-Mejía et al. (1998:528–529) state that headquarters should, at least, position the international assignment as a step towards advancement within the firm, and should provide support for expatriates by maintaining contact through a mentor at the home office, or by allowing the employee to visit the home office occasionally to foster a sense of belonging and to reduce re-entry shock.

25.7.3 Remuneration/benefits issues

Pitfield (1996:29) mentions that some of the most stressful aspects of overseas assignments relate to the financial implications of spending a period abroad. Areas which must be addressed by the home office are: a removal allowance, salary structure, pension arrangements, tax issues, overseas allowance, home visits, family arrangements and a local or home-based compensation package. Gómez-Mejía et al. (1998:529–530) believe that planning compensation for expatriates requires management to follow three important guidelines:
- provide the expatriate with a disposable income that is equivalent to what he or she would receive at home;
- provide an 'add-on' incentive for accepting an international assignment; and
- avoid having expatriates fill the same jobs as those held by locals, or lower-ranking jobs.

25.7.4 Managing the performance of expatriates

One of the complications of managing and appraising the expatriate's performance is the question of who will undertake this responsibility. Allowing only host-country management to conduct the exercise may result in distorted cultural differences. On the other hand, parent-company managers may be so geographically distanced from

the expatriate that their input would not be valid. Dessler (1997:685–686) provides five suggestions for improving the performance management of expatriates:
- stipulate the assignment's difficulty level, and take difficulty-level differences into account during the appraisal period;
- weight the evaluation more towards the on-site manager's appraisal than towards the home-site manager's distant perceptions;
- allow home-site managers to use a former expatriate from the same overseas location to provide background advice;
- modify normal performance criteria to fit the overseas position; and
- encourage the expatriate to offer relevant insights into the functioning of the operation and the interdependencies of the domestic and foreign operations.

Case-in-point

The Monsanto company is a billion-dollar food, chemical, and pharmaceutical firm with 30 000 employees, based in St. Louis in the United States. Monsanto is often referred to in business journals for its exemplary strategic international human resources policies. Back in 1992, John Amato, manager for human resources in international assignments, decided to tackle the high rate of attrition of repatriates, but he did not stop there. Amato said: 'We were doing a good job on the front end in preparation for the assignment, and we were doing a pretty good job on the back end of the assignment (in repatriation), but we wondered what was happening in the middle.'

What was happening in the middle, formed the basis for the creation of their overseas performance management plan.

International assignees of Monsanto speak with both the parent-country and host-country managers before they leave for overseas. The three parties jointly produce an action plan for development that includes not only the business goals, but also the cross-cultural competency they need to achieve on-site.

Before employees attend cross-cultural training, they develop a job description from the action plan and identify what they are supposed to accomplish while on assignment. When the expatriate arrives in the host country, he or she asks the host manager to buy into the action plan and assist with its achievement. In this way, the home manager and the host manager are jointly accountable for the development and progress of the action plan.

SOURCE: Solomon, C.M. (1994:96–108).

25.7.5 International labour relations

Substantial differences in labour relations practices are to be found among the world's countries and regions. Labour relations policies should focus on answering the following questions in order to prepare the international manager for his or her assignment abroad:

- Does collective bargaining take place industry-wide or regionally, or does it occur at plant level?
- What degree of autonomy and decision-making power do unions in the host country possess?
- To what extent is collective bargaining undertaken by employer organisations?
- How formal are recognition agreements

in the host country?
- Does the host country practice closed-shop or open-shop agreements?
- Are labour-management contracts legally binding, or 'gentlemen's agreements'?
- What is the content and scope of bargaining issues?
- How are grievances, disciplinary offences, and strikes handled in the host country?
- What is the local government's role in labour relations?
- To what extent is worker participation encouraged?

25.8 International human resources management in the twenty-first century

Cascio (1995:28) emphasises the global focus that is needed in the worldwide economy of the twenty-first century. Even small companies, such as the Loctite Corporation in the United States, have realised that their markets cannot be narrowly defined within the borders of their own countries. Customer preferences and buying patterns are tracked and merchandise is discontinued immediately if it does not sell. The focus is on providing what the customer wants, even if the customer is not located in the home country. Many companies have found that even a single change poses new challenges to management and has implications that impinge directly on the concept of quality assurance. Quality is now regarded not as a competitive advantage, but as a competitive necessity.

In a recent study, Kemske (1998:46–60) compiled a number of predicted trends that will influence the way that global corporations and human resources managers conduct their business in the future. These predictions must be borne in mind by global corporations, when planning and implementing international assignments for their employees:
- mega-global business alliances will grow in number and scope;
- there will be an explosive growth of companies doing business across borders;
- technology, especially the Internet, will enable more businesses to enter the global marketplace;
- the continued emergence of a world marketplace will require the development of an international workforce;
- the role of corporate human resources management will change to that of creator of overall values and direction, which will be implemented by local human resources departments in different countries;
- human resources professionals will have advanced acumen in international business practices, international labour laws, multicultural sensitivities, and multiple languages; and
- small teams of human resources professionals will focus on providing performance improvement consulting services to a variety of locations around the world.

Bennis and Mische (1995:23–26) had previously identified similar trends, but offered some cautionary predictions, which the international human resources manager must consider when planning strategies:
- global markets will become saturated because of the price and quality parity of products;
- any competitive advantage that is held through technology will soon be neutralised because information technology can be replicated quickly;
- in order to be competitive, an organisation will have to be technologically enabled;
- service will be critical, as consumers are more knowledgeable, better educated, and more discriminating;

- organisations will have fewer full-time workers with core competencies, and more highly specialised contract personnel; and
- the only way to generate the kind of performance that will carry an organisation to success, will be through the use of intellectual assets.

It goes without saying that corporate success in the global arena depends on the extent to which quality assurance is an underlying philosophy in the way international human resources management is practised.

25.9 Conclusion

It is clear that companies embarking on international business initiatives must have a clear knowledge of global trends and the ways in which international assignments can be managed effectively. To do this, problems facing expatriates and repatriates must be obviated by means of the proactive planning, implementation, and maintenance of the exercise. Distinct international human resources policies must be formulated to ensure that quality standards are upheld.

Summary

The impact of future global business trends must be considered when planning the management of international assignments.

An international company can follow the traditional, modern, fast-mover, or alliance model. Companies progress through various stages of international business, expanding from a purely domestic market, through the export stage, to an extension of operations out of the home country, before a multinational corporation undertakes manufacturing and marketing in several countries. The global transnational corporation has weak ties in any given country, and its operations are highly decentralised.

Parent companies must decide whether to follow an ethnocentric, polycentric, geocentric, or regiocentric approach to managing an international subsidiary. These approaches dictate the mix of host-country and expatriate employees.

Some of the problems that expatriates may experience include career blockage, culture shock, a lack of pre-departure cross-cultural training, an overemphasis on technical qualifications, being sent on an overseas assignment to resolve difficult interpersonal situations or political conflicts, and family problems experienced by the expatriate's spouse and children.

On return to their home country, repatriates often face a lack of respect for the skills they have acquired, a loss of status, poor planning for their position when they return, and reverse culture shock.

International managers need a familiarity with a variety of cultures, real experience of different cultures, acceptance of mobility, cultural sensitivity and flexibility, knowledge of languages, and IT communication skills. International human resources policies must focus on recruitment and selection, training, remuneration and benefits issues, performance management, and international labour relations.

Quality assurance in international human resources management is a prerequisite for competitive success.

Related websites

This topic may be investigated further by referring to the following Internet websites:
Thunderbird School of International Management – http://www.t-bird.edu/
Across Frontiers International – http://www.acrossfrontiers.com
Craighead Global Knowledge – http://www.craighead.com
Kroll Associates – http://www.krollassociates.com
Society for Human Resource Management Global Forum –
   http://www.shrmglobal.org

Case study
Glass problems at Millennium

In 1996, Millennium Glassworks signed a contract with a Chinese firm to manufacture motor car windscreens for the Chinese market. The contract provided for windscreens to be manufactured in South Africa for the first year, and to be exported to the Chinese mainland until a subsidiary factory was built and staffed in China. A South African expatriate would then be appointed as general manager of the subsidiary, and ten South African technicians would assume responsibility for production and quality control in China.

Since 1997, two South African general managers and six technicians have returned home before the end of their agreed international assignments. These early repatriations, and resulting lost production in China, have cost the South African parent company at least two million Rand.

This state of affairs could not be allowed to continue as the Chinese government threatened to terminate this lucrative contract. This was Millennium Glasswork's first excursion into an overseas market, and the human resources director, Andile Yiko, decided to find out first hand what was happening at the Chinese plant. During the course of his two-week stay in China, he interviewed the local production manager, four local supervisors, and ten shop-floor workers. Although he had the service of an interpreter, it was still extremely difficult to obtain the whole picture. Eventually, after comparing the results of all the interviews, he discovered that the Chinese employees were all agreed on the following issues:

- the South Africans were perceived to be very demanding and set unrealistic targets and deadlines;
- they felt that the South African general managers exercised too strict a policy when it came to disciplining Chinese workers for absenteeism (in many cases, these workers were absent due to celebrating local religious festivals);
- the Chinese believed that there was a language barrier, and they did not always understand the instructions issued by the South Africans; and
- the South African expatriates enjoyed a much more affluent lifestyle than their Chinese counterparts, which was indicative of inequity in salary structures.

Andile also interviewed the repatriates when he returned to South Africa. Their perceptions were the following:

- The Chinese did not know the meaning of achieving production targets and deadlines. Their philosophy was 'Tomorrow is another day'.
- They felt that the Chinese used their religious festivals as an excuse to stay away from work. The South Africans were not familiar with Chinese religious holidays and found it difficult to dispute this as a reason for absenteeism. Therefore, all cases of unauthorised absenteeism were disciplined.
- The South Africans found it difficult to communicate in Chinese, and did not trust the interpreters to convey correct instructions.
- There were great differences between the Chinese and South African cultures and customs, and their spouses and children were very unhappy in the foreign country. In addition, all the repatriates and their families have found it very difficult to adjust to their work and home situations on their return to South Africa.

Andile was in a quandary. He did not have any ready answers, so he decided to call an international consultant for advice.

Questions

1 If you were hired to advise Andile, what do you think would have contributed to the current state of affairs?
2 Based on what you have learned in this chapter, what recommendations would you make to Andile? These recommendations should include advice on how to develop an international human resources policy so that these problems never occur again.

Experiential exercise

Purpose
To indicate the wide cultural differences that can influence the success of an international assignment.

Task (20 minutes)
Divide into groups of three or four. Half of the groups must identify typical South African characteristics or cultural traits. The other groups must identify typical Chinese characteristics or cultural traits. Bear in mind that China follows the principles of communism.

The feedback received from the class will enable the instructor to compile a list of South African characteristics and another list of Chinese characteristics. In comparison, similarities and differences between the two cultures will become evident.

How could these differences and similarities affect the development of international human resources policies?

Chapter questions

1 Various predictions have been made concerning the way in which global corporations will conduct their business in the future. How do you think human resources managers should react to these predicted trends?
2 Describe the stages through which firms progress as they internationalise their operations. At what stage of international involvement are the majority of South African companies currently operating?

3 What specific conditions would determine an ethnocentric, polycentric, geocentric, or regiocentric approach to international staffing?
4 What recommendations would you make to human resources managers to alleviate the problems faced by expatriates?
5 Develop a programme that a company can use to reduce the repatriation problems of returning expatriates.
6 Compare the management of an expatriate's performance with that of a home-office manager. Provide some recommendations for dealing with the unique problems of appraising the expatriate's performance.

Bibliography

BEARDWELL, I. & HOLDEN, L. 1997. *Human resource management: a contemporary perspective.* 2nd edition. Pitman, London.

BENNIS, W. & MISCHE, M. 1995. *The 21st century organization: reinventing through reengineering.* Pfeiffer & Co, San Diego, DA.

CASCIO, W.F. 1995. *Managing human resources: productivity, quality of work life, profits.* 4th edition. McGraw-Hill, New York.

CHERRINGTON, D. & MIDDLETON, L.A. 1995. An introduction to global business issues. *HR Magazine.* 40(6), June.

CUCULLU, G. 1998. Living in the Lion City. *GlobalWorkforce.* 3(6).10–11.

DESSLER, G. 1997. *Human resource management.* 7th edition. Prentice Hall, Upper Saddle River, NJ.

GÓMEZ-MEJÍA, L.R., BALKIN, D.B. & CARDY, R.L. 1998. *Managing human resources.* 2nd edition. Prentice Hall, Upper Saddle River, NJ.

KEMSKE, F. 1998. HR 2008: forecast based on our exclusive study. *Workforce.* 77(1), 46–60. January.

PITFIELD, M. 1996. *Developing international managers.* Technical Communications, Herts.

SOLOMON, C.M. 1995. Learning to manage host-country nationals. *Personnel Journal.* 74(1), 60–67, February.

SOLOMON, C.M. 1994. How does your global talent measure up? *Personnel Journal* 73(10), 96–108, October.

TORRINGTON, D. & HALL, L. 1995. *Personnel management: HRM in action.* 3rd edition. Prentice Hall Int. (UK), Herts.

TROMPENAARS, F. & WOOLIAMS, P. 1999. First-class accommodation. *People Management,* 33, April.

26

The future of human resources management

H B Schultz

Learning outcomes

At the end of this chapter the learner should be able to demonstrate the following outcomes:
- Describe the employee and organisation of the future.
- Debate the evolving role of the human resources professional.
- Discuss how the human resources department can add value to the organisation by cultivating knowledge workers.
- Explain the contribution of the human resources professional to achieving strategic customer orientation.
- Briefly discuss the need for superior quality assurance in the future role of human resources management.

Key words and concepts

- continuum
- deliverables
- doables
- heterogeneous workforce
- intellectual capital
- just-in-time
- knowledge workers
- mindset
- paradigm
- phoenix leader
- strategic
- value chain
- value proposition
- visionary

Illustrative case
Will the HR deparment still exist when there are no more jobs?

David Pearce Snyder, the lifestyles editor for The Futurist magazine, believes there is a major change coming to the world of human resources. Snyder forecasts that very soon there will be no more jobs as we know them. He says, 'The list of fixed skills and responsibilities we call a job will be a thing of the past in the age of the unbundled enterprise. Jobs are going away because the large bureaucracies that require them are going away.'

In an interview in 1998, Snyder stated that by the year 2008 there will be a two-thirds reduction in the ranks of permanent career employees, owing to the downsizing and outsourcing trends we are faced with. He believes that the twenty-first century organisation will see the workforce split – 35 per cent of workers will be a core of permanent employees engaged in the essential business of the company, 25 per cent will be outsourced suppliers of components and support services, 25 per cent will be contingent workers, and 15 per cent will be contract specialists.

Snyder maintains that this will have profound implications for human resources professionals. He predicts the emergence of a free-standing, or freelance human resources industry. Practitioners will become agents of workers instead of serving organisations as a whole. People won't have jobs, they will have careers, and individuals will need help in managing their careers, help that organisations will not be in a position to provide.

There will be many more human resources specialists than generalists in the next decade, geared primarily to providing individual customer service, and thereafter to providing organisational service. Snyder exhorts human resources experts to prepare themselves for the demise of the HR department.

SOURCE: Kemske (1998:56).

26.1 Introduction

Laabs (2000:56) cites a recent KPMG Management Consulting study conducted in Europe, North America, and in Asia Pacific, which indicates that more than half the companies surveyed believed that change is necessary if the human resources management function is to become truly viable and successful. Respondents agree that human resources professionals need to practice being creative, strategic, and visionary. Laabs also reports the following statement published by the American-based Society for Human Resource Management (SHRM) in 1999:

> The next few years represent a critical period for the human resources community as new roles and responsibilities in organisations are being renegotiated. So far, HR as a whole is significantly behind the change curve. Clearly, HR professionals will not only have to fulfill their traditional roles, but assume critical new roles that focus on adding value to operational excellence.

These rather serious viewpoints introduce our debate on the future of human resources management. If one had a crystal ball to predict future scenarios with any certainty, it would make this discussion a great deal easier. However, there are definite areas where the demands of the future are already making themselves felt, and where human resources practitioners can continue to play an important role in making organisations more effective and competitive.

With this in mind, this chapter opens with an envisaged picture of the employee and organisation of the future. The role of the human resources professional must evolve in order to meet the challenges of change, and this is discussed in depth. The information age has brought with it the requirements of so-called knowledge workers. The way in which the human resources department can add value to the organisation through knowledge workers is also debated. Finally, we turn our attention to the survival of human resources professionals through the development of strategic customer orientation.

26.2 The employee and the organisation of the future

Rapid changes and advances in technology, medicine, and new mindsets since the Second World War have resulted in a worldwide heterogeneous workforce that has diverse approaches to the way in which work is regarded. The employee and organisation of the future is pictured in the following paragraphs.

26.2.1 Employee values

According to Noe et al. (2000:22) the workforce is predicted to become more diverse in terms of age, ethnicity, and racial background. It is, therefore, unlikely that one set of values will characterise all employees. For example, 'traditionalists', born between 1927 and 1945, tend to be uncomfortable challenging the status quo and authority; 'baby boomers', born between 1946 and 1964, view work as a means to self-fulfilment; and 'baby busters', born between 1965 and 1975, value unexpected rewards for work accomplishments, opportunities to learn new things, praise, recognition, and time with the manager. Fostering these values requires companies to develop human resources management practices that provide more opportunity for individual contribution and entrepreneurship.

26.2.2 Drivers for change

Ulrich (1998:87–91) has definite views on the employee and organisation of the future. He believes that all companies are global, now that technology has made information more accessible and has joined people electronically in ways that impact on organisations and work relationships. A knowledge-based workforce will turn many employees into 'volunteers' in the future, because they could choose to work elsewhere for equal or more money. This means they work in an organisation by choice, not by obligation. The challenge is to turn worker knowledge into productivity and to leverage intellectual capital.

26.2.3 Forces shaping the future

Tulgan (2000:1) maintains that organisations must be completely flexible in the new century because markets are chaotic and resource needs are unpredictable. Individuals must be correspondingly flexible and self-reliant as there is no one way to think about or do anything any more. The only relevant time frame of the present and the future is just-in-time. According to Vincola (2000:12) employees of the future will increasingly consider the work/life issue and will expect on-line services, telecommuting, excellent child-care facilities, well-constructed employee assistance programmes (EAPs), and organisations with a social conscience.

Blair (1999) in his web site 'The Goals Guy', offers ten rules for success in the new millennium:
- Rule 1: Organisations must expect volatility in the velocity, complexity, and unpredictability of change.
- Rule 2: Organisations must invent new rules if they wish to transcend the existing parameters of competition.
- Rule 3: Organisations and employees

must develop conscious strategies and mechanisms to promote consistent innovation.
- Rule 4: Twenty-first century companies must dismantle the internal barriers that separate people, departments, and disciplines, and the external boundaries between firms and their outside suppliers, customers, and competitors.
- Rule 5: Implementation of all organisational issues must be fast.
- Rule 6: Organisations and employees must think like an entrepreneur, allow for failure, and improve because of it.
- Rule 7: Organisations must become accustomed to shopping in a single global supermarket for everything from groceries to staff.
- Rule 8: Organisations and employees must sustain their competitive advantage by developing the ability to learn faster and better than competitors.
- Rule 9: Organisations must measure performance on the key strategic and profitability drivers of the business.
- Rule 10: Organisations and employees of the twenty-first century must leave behind the image of the unpleasant manipulators of the past and become the 'nice guys' of the future.

In his third annual 'Lessons in Leadership' conference in November 1998, Tom Peters emphasised that today's economic environment requires that a fresh look be taken at the individual, the job, the department or dimension, and the organisation. Innovation of organisations and individuals in the manner in which products and services are provided to the client is essential. Peters conveyed a strong message that the overwhelming majority of white-collar workers will lose their jobs in the new economic revolution. Trade on the Internet doubles every few months and the Internet trader makes much more profit than a supermarket owner.

Peters warns that the generation who grew up on Sony's Playstation and other computer games will, in future, experience what they see on the computer screen as reality, and the people and employees around them as virtual. In this new environment the message to the employee is clear – be excellent in what you do, learn new skills, be special to your organisation, create your own personal trade mark, keep on growing in your job, be innovative, and keep on marketing yourself and your skills. The message to the organisation is to do research, talk to clients, innovate, appoint highly talented people, pamper diversity, reward active success, and evaluate the ongoing projects to establish whether they are creative, revolutionary, and evoke passion and enthusiasm.

Tom Peter's ideas on 'The New World of Work' are available on his website http://www.tompeters.com and provide dynamic insight into the requirements for business survival in the new millennium.

26.3 An evolving role for human resources management

Gibson et al. (2000:451) believe that the future role of human resources professionals will be greatly influenced by the forces for change at work in our organisations. Comprehending the implications of these forces requires organisational learning processes, which involve the capacity to absorb new information, process that information in the light of previous experience, and act on the information in new and potentially risky ways. Only through such learning experiences will organisations survive in the twenty-first century.

Numerous authors (Ulrich 1998:87–91, Brewster et al. 2000:216, and Noe et al. 2000: 566, for example) agree that a new model for the role of human resources management is necessary. The new model must emphasise the strategic function of human resources professionals as business partners. To become a full-fledged partner in business, the human resources department must evaluate its role, practices, and effectiveness. In the past, human resources managers have concentrated on transactional and traditional activities. These activities are still necessary, but transformational activities now assume their rightful place.

Transactional activities are the day-to-day transactions, such as benefits administration, record keeping, and employee services, and are low in strategic value. Traditional activities can be classified as performance management, training, recruiting, selection, compensation, and employee relations functions. These activities have moderate strategic value. Transformational activities create long-term capability and adaptability for the firm, and they include knowledge management, management development, cultural change, and strategic redirection and renewal. These activities have the greatest strategic value for the organisation.

The time allocation for the various human resources activities now becomes the most important element of this model, and the rapid pace of change dictates that time allocation must be flexible, with the activities taking place on a time continuum such as depicted in Figure 26.1.

Ulrich (1998:87–91) takes the idea of continua further and uses the concept to describe what the future role of human resources management might be. These continua are depicted in Figure 26.2.

- *Administrative versus strategic roles.* The human resources function has evolved from administrative to strategic, but if the administrative work is not done efficiently, accurately, and timeously, strategic roles will suffer. The ongoing challenge is to balance these roles.
- *Existing versus transformed versus disappearing human resources departments.* Some practitioners argue that the department should rediscover values and administrative processes; some believe that the department should be transformed into an elite strategic corps of business partners, while others believe that human resources departments should disappear and be outsourced.
- *Human resources professional versus line manager versus staff.* Who should do human resources work? Role and accountabilities will be discussed for the next few years but will almost certainly persist along a continuum.
- *Metaphors for human resources professionals.* Multiple roles will exist for practitioners, and behaviour will be shaped according to the descriptions of leaders, architects, stewards, partners and players.
- *Aggressiveness of human resources professionals.* The debate will rage as to when practitioners should become more assertive and take a stand. Their roles will at different times require advocacy, acquiescence, and proactive and reactive approaches.

Figure 26.1 A continuum of human resources activities

Transformational activities (50–60%)

Transactional activities (20–30%)   Traditional activities (20–30%)

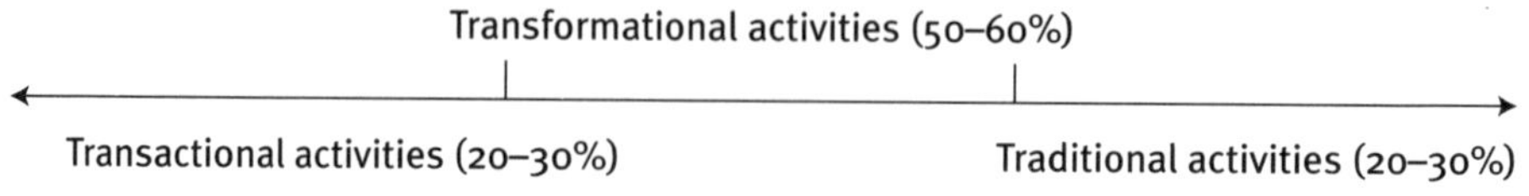

Figure 26.2 The role of the human resources professional

What are the competencies that human resources professionals, themselves, believe they will need in the future? Table 26.1 indicates, in rank order, the feelings of current practitioners in a Workforceonline (2000) survey.

Wheatley (1997) states that human resources professionals who know who they are and mean what they announce, ensure that people are free to create and contribute. This is, perhaps, the most important role in future human resources management.

26.4 Adding value in the knowledge-based economy

Despite the rather radical changes in the environment of the human resources management function, where human resources activities have become decentralised, outsourced, insourced, or even absorbed by line managers, there has been a stronger recognition of the links between how people are managed and the bottom-line. Human resources managers recognise that they are accountable for business results

Table 26.1 The role of the human resources professional

1	Communication skills	7	Technology
2	Problem solving	8	Forecasting
3	Leadership	9	Compensation design
4	Recruiting/staffing	10	Benefits design/administration
5	Employment law	11	Accounting/finance
6	Training and development	12	Record keeping

through effective management practices. The softer side of competitiveness reflects the shift towards a knowledge-based economy. In the industrial world today, roughly 15 per cent of the active population physically touch a product in the production process. The other 85 per cent add value by the creation, management and transfer of information. A modern economy, thus, depends heavily on the human factor as a key to success.

With this in mind, the human resources management function will continue to play an important role in making organisations more effective and competitive. The changing image of human resources management as a bureaucracy to a strategic partner, by integrating business issues with human resources solutions, is evident. Fitz-enz (2000) states that knowledge is not a technical issue, it is a human issue, and offers human resources managers the chance to be at the heart of the most important force in the twenty-first century – information.

According to Laabs (2000:52–56) human resources professionals of the future will add value by becoming 'phoenix' leaders. Phoenix leaders are defined by their ability to make five essential contributions:
- they surface issues that confront the organisation;
- they engage the people in resolving those issues;
- they prioritise and allocate resources to address those issues;
- they unleash ownership so everyone accepts responsibility for dealing with those issues; and
- they energise learning.

Ulrich (1998:87–91) emphasises that a new human resources management is emerging, and that the future will be characterised by understanding and mastering the following challenges:
- *Focusing on deliverables more than on doables*. Ulrich proposes a new paradigm with less focus on what human resources does and more on what it delivers. Deliverables will include a focus on globalisation, customer intimacy, operational excellence, operating margins, and other business strategies.
- *Human resources theory*. Theoretical research in the field of human resources management is needed to stop mindless benchmarking and to set expectations regarding standards of performance.
- *Realising that human resources management is not just for human resources managers*. In the future, human resources management will be accomplished not only by those within the human resources management function, but also by line managers, other management, and strategic partnerships with outside vendors. The challenge for human resources managers is to articulate effectively when each member of the human resources community can add value to an external customer, such as line managers

Encounter 26.1 What will the human resources arena look like in 2020?

Answering this question, Roger E. Herman, of The Herman Group, Greensboro, North Carolina, USA, states that one area that will continue on its current path is that of outsourcing. Although several generalists will manage the corporate and strategic human resources function, recruitment, selection, record-keeping, and compensation and benefits administration will be outsourced, mainly on an electronic basis.

A major portion of the workforce will be contingent labour, and human resources professionals will require a substantially different set of skills for recruiting, negotiating, managing, and servicing a very flexible workforce. Many workers will be free agents, and a large number will sell their services through an international network of brokers.

Benefits will be self-designed and self-managed, relieving employers from carrying out this administrative burden. Most employment arrangements will be established though individual negotiation, and wage and salary specialists, together with employee relations specialists, will play a much different role in the future.

SOURCE: Workforceonline (February 29, 2000).

---

teaching executive programs, and strategic partners dealing with the outsourced work of human resources management, such as administration.
- *Human resources tools.* New human resources tools will emerge, dealing with areas such as global human resources, cultural change, technology, defining competencies of the future, and the transfer of knowledge. Mastering these new tools will require that old human resources tools be more automated, be completed by others in the human resources community, and/or be discontinued completely.
- *Human resources value chain.* Human resources work is shifting across boundaries and in the future will focus on the value chain, where suppliers and customers take part in the design and implementation of human resources practices. Different companies may share a training centre, staffing centre, administration centre, and career development programs. An existing example is the Motorola University where 50 per cent of the attendees are suppliers and customers of Motorola.
- *Human resources value proposition.* Human resources management and its contribution must be measured. The relationship between investment in human resources practices and business results must be determined. The human resources management legacy of being soft and non-business should be removed. It should be able to determine how human resources practices affect the market value of the organisation and impact upon the intellectual capital of the organisation.
- *Human resources careers.* The human resources management career will not be linear, but rather a mosaic of experiences inside and outside the function. The mosaic career emphasises what the human resources professional knows and is able to do. The mosaic career is characterised by employees being able to take risks. Human resources professionals are seen as business partners more than functional experts.

- *Human resources competencies.* Human resources professionals are emerging from common clusters of competencies:
  - business knowledge – finance, strategy, marketing, and operations;
  - state of the art – theory and leading edge practices for human resources tools;
  - change and processes – a model of change and the ability to apply the model to a specific situation; and
  - credibility – personal credibility through accurate work and intimacy of relationships.
- *Human resources and intellectual capital.* Intellectual capital refers to the collective insights, knowledge, and commitment of the organisation's employees. Intellectual capital as an asset means ensuring that competence is added annually. Depreciating intellectual capital takes place through burnout, stress, or demoralisation of employees. The challenge should be to experience intellectual capital as an ongoing investment, where employees add value through ongoing learning, changing, challenging, and reinventing both themselves and their organisations.

26.5 Strategic customer orientation

Global environments and organisational strategy will govern the future of human resources management. Organisational strategy refers to the way the organisation positions itself in its setting in relation to its stakeholders, given the organisation's resources, capabilities, and mission. Strategic choice refers to the idea that an organisation interacts with its environment instead of being totally determined by external forces (McShane & Von Glinow 2000:585).

Noe et al. (2000:569) state that a customer orientation is one of the most important changes in the human resources function's attempts to become strategic. A customer orientation entails three defining steps:
- firstly, human resources practitioners must identify their customers in the form of line managers, the strategic planning team, and all employees;
- secondly, the products of the human resources department must be identified in the form of high-quality employees, information and recommendations for the planning process, and fair compensation and benefit programmes and decisions; and
- thirdly, human resources professionals must identify the technologies required to satisfy customer needs.

This customer orientation is essential in creating the organisation of the future. Wheatley (1997) says that if we are to develop organisations of greater and enduring capacity, we have to turn to the people of our organisation. Human resources professionals must learn how to encourage the creativity and commitment that they wanted to express when they first joined the organisation, and they must figure out how to re-engage people in the important work of organising. This is what strategic customer orientation is all about.

26.5.1 Developing strategic customer orientation

What are some of the ways in which the human resources department can aim for the goal of strategic customer orientation? Laabs (2000:52–56) believes that the challenge is to discover which areas of a company need human resources leadership and which need human resources management, and at what times. Caudron (1999:30–33) adds that if you want your organisation to be perceived as more strategic, more valuable, and more reliable, you need to think about what customers want from you, how well you deliver it, and how to improve your overall brand image. This implies that human resources practitioners must think like business partners, with a product to be developed, marketed, and reliably delivered to the customers who need their services. These ideas are summarised in Table 26.2.

Table 26.2 Eight steps to developing strategic customer orientation

1. Identify your customer's needs and perceptions.
2. Craft an identity based on customer needs.
3. Develop a mission statement to guide you through change.
4. Align human resources practices with the goals of customer service.
5. Improve the image of the human resources department.
6. Market the achievements of the human resources department.
7. Validate the improvements of the human resources department with customers external to the organisation.
8. Subject the human resources department to self-scrutiny.

Fitz-enz (2000) maintains that human resources professionals must begin to think in terms of human capital business management, rather than concentrating on a human resources programme. Human resources programmes are tools to assist in managing expensive human capital. It is imperative to move from mechanical to electronic distribution channels, and to think in terms of the external customer. The objective of human resources departments should be to help managers cut costs, move more quickly, produce more with less, and improve quality.

Caudron (2000:30–32) declares that if human resources practitioners wish to prevent their own jobs from being outsourced, they must understand what work is required for their company to be successful, and then determine the most efficient way to accomplish that work. As Roger Herman, management consultant and president of The Herman Group in Greensboro, North Carolina, explains: 'We're moving into a much different world and we cannot survive tomorrow using the same approaches we used yesterday, let alone today.'

26.6 Quality assurance in the future role of human resources management

The identification and quantification of intellectual capital and its relationship to the company's current and future plans and goals is of utmost importance. The recognition of intellectual capital acknowledges that the future of an enterprise mainly depends on the uniqueness, abilities, and experience of the company's employees. Butteriss (1998:49) believes that many organisations have realised the need to reorganise their human resources functions to obtain the quality results required in the area of intellectual capital. This reorganisation for the sake of quality assurance is intensifying the trend for organisations to have small corporate human resources functions, whose role is to provide overall strategy and policy advice, and to decentralise all other aspects of the department.

The decentralisation of the human resources function involves having some staff reporting to line managers, who draw specialist advice and consulting skills in areas such as compensation, recruitment, and organisational development. Human resources staff at the business-unit level are becoming like account executives, as they identify business and human resources needs, contract for the required help, and charge for services they have provided. The business of adding value is inextricably linked to the business of providing quality service.

26.7 Conclusion

The new world-class management scenario requires that organisations take their competitors seriously in order to determine in what area they can obtain a competitive advantage. The three areas that stand out are an obsession with quality, the client, and technology. Within this new world-class scenario the management of human resources has also undergone a significant transformation. Like all business activities, human resources management should focus on making a significant contribution towards the bottom line.

In 1871 the noted English artist and writer John Ruskin (1819–1900) wrote:

> In order that people may be happy in their work, these three things are needed: they must be fit for it; they must not do too much of it; and they must have a sense of success in it.

Throughout this book a constant reminder to this basic approach is signaled. The new millennium will require human resources management to manage its human capital in such a manner that value is added to both the organisation and the employees involved. Developments in globalisation, technology, the social environment, and quality requirements will have to be monitored very carefully in order to be flexible in meeting the challenges arising in these fields. The fact that improved employee performance is a key to improved business results, sends a clear message to management: People are a bottom line priority.

Summary

The employee and organisation of the future will emerge from the values that employees hold, depending on whether the worker is a 'traditionalist', 'baby boomer', or 'baby buster'.

Drivers for change in the form of technology and a knowledge-based workforce are shaping the future of all employees and the organisations in which they work.

Organisations must be completely flexible and the only relevant time frame of the present and the future is just-in-time.

Organisational learning processes are needed to be able to contend with the forces of change.

The new model for the role of human resources management emphasises the strategic function of human resources professionals as business partners, allowing transformational activities to dominate. The future role of the practitioner will probably be found along numerous continua.

The image of the human resources department will change from that of a bureaucracy to a strategic partner, intent on adding value to the organisation by integrating business issues with human resources solutions.

Human resources professionals of the future will add value by becoming 'phoenix' leaders who understand and master the challenges of delivering as opposed to doing.

Human resources professionals must develop a strategic customer orientation by identifying their customers, their products, and the technologies required to satisfy customer needs.

Many organisations have reorganised their human resources functions to obtain the quality results required in the area of intellectual capital.

The trend has intensified for organisations to have small corporate human resources functions, whose role is to provide overall strategy and policy advice, and to decentralise all other aspects of the department.

Related websites

This topic may be investigated further by referring to the following Internet websites:
The fifth discipline – http://www.wbur.org
Lessons in Leadership conference – http://www.lessonsinleadership.com
Thought leaders – http://www.gwsae.org
The leader's new work – http://home.nycap.rr.com/klarsen/learnorg/senge2
The HR value chain – http://tigger.stthomas.edu/mccr

Case study
HP Labs – turning inventors into entrepreneurs at Hewlett-Packard

Hewlett-Packard (HP) is one of the world's largest computer companies and is well known for its printers that set the standard for technology, performance, and reliability. HP has 125 000 employees worldwide and is consistently recognised as one of the best companies to work for.

This chapter has focused on the future of human resources professionals – a future that is dependent on a working knowledge of technology. In keeping with this philosophy, the information for this case study is not presented in 'hard copy' form. Instead, to be able to work through the Hewlett-Packard case you will need to visit the website at http://www.hp.com, click on 'South Africa' in the list of countries, 'Company information', and 'About HP'. Review HP's corporate objectives by clicking on 'Corporate objectives and the HP Way'; and the company's commitment to diversity and work life, by clicking on 'Diversity and Work Life'.

Answer the following questions:
1 Evaluate the information on HP's home page and hyperlinks and identify HP's corporate objectives.
2 What human resources practices help HP reach its corporate objectives? Are these practices in line with the future role of the human resources function?

Experiential exercise

Purpose
To analyse the roles of human resources professionals in a selected organisation and to determine whether these roles conform to the anticipated roles of HR professionals in the future.

Introduction
Many human resources departments are still engrossed in performing transactional and traditional functions, while business initiatives and strategies are calling for transformational activities. This experiential exercise will allow the learner to gain a better understanding of the nature of human resources practitioners' jobs, and to gain insight into the interface between human resources and line managers.

Task
This assignment may be undertaken individually or by groups of learners.
Locate a human resources manager to interview. You may select a human resources generalist or specialist. After the manager understands the research project and agrees to cooperate, conduct the interview, which should take about 45 minutes to one hour.

Also interview a line manager in the same organisation to gain his or her views of human resources management. Your objective is to prepare a report of 8–10 pages indicating the results of the interviews. The report will culminate with recommendations regarding areas where the human resources department should be concentrating on intensifying its transformational role.

The report will use the following framework:
- A description of the overall operations and role of the human resources department.
- The type of interaction between human resources and line managers.
- The extent to which the organisation's human resources management practices conform to theoretical prescriptions. If differences are found, discuss why they exist.

Chapter questions

1 In 1996, *Fortune* columnist Thomas A. Stewart suggested that the human resources function as we know it should be blown up. Do you agree with this statement? Motivate your answer. If there are certain parts of the function that you feel should be eradicated, how would you do it? If you feel that you do not have enough knowledge to answer this question, approach a human resources professional for an expert opinion.

2 Why have the roles and activities of the human resources department changed over the last twenty years, and how effectively do you think practitioners have responded?

3 Various forecasts have been made regarding the probability of a predominance of contingency workers in the future. How do you think the human resources function should handle the needs of this nucleus of workers?

4 What recommendations would you make to human resources managers to develop a strategic customer orientation?

Bibliography

BLAIR, G.R. 1999. Ten rules for success in the next millennium. *Workforceonline*. http://www.workforceonline.com/archive.

BREWSTER, C., DOWLING, P. GROBLER, P., HOLLAND, P. & WARNICH, S. 2000. *Contemporary issues in human resource management: gaining a competitive advantage.* Oxford, Cape Town.

BUTTERISS, M. (ed.). 1998. *Re-inventing HR: changing roles to create the high-performance organization.* John Wiley & Sons, Toronto.

CAUDRON, S. 1999. Brand HR: why and how to market your image. *Workforceonline*. (78)11, 30–33.

CAUDRON, S. 2000. Jobs disappear when work becomes more important. *Workforceonline*. (79)1, 30–32.

DAVIDSON, L. 1999. Top 12 future HR competencies. *Workforceonline*. (78)2, 73.

FITZ-ENZ, J. 2000. Blueberries from Chile. *Workforceonline*. http://www.workforceonline.com/archive/

GIBSON, J.L., IVANCEVICH, J.M. & DONNELLY, JR., J.H. 2000. *Organizations: behavior, structure, processes.* 10th edition. Irwin/McGraw-Hill, Boston.

KEMSKE, F. 1998. Will HR go free-lance by 2008? *Workforceonline*. (77)1, 56.

LAABS, J. 2000. Strategic HR won't come easily. *Workforceonline*. (79)1, 52–56.

MCSHANE, S.L. & VON GLINOW, M.A. 2000. *Organizational behavior.* Irwin/McGraw-Hill, Boston.

NOE, R.A., HOLLENBECK, J.R., GERHART, B. & WRIGHT, P.M. 2000. *Human resource management: gaining a competitive advantage.* 3rd edition. McGraw-Hill, Boston.

SULLIVAN, J. 2000. 10 Tenets of 21st century HR. *Workforceonline*. (79)1, 54.

TULGAN, B. 2000. Four key forces shaping the future. *Workforceonline*. http://www.workforceonline.com/archive.

ULRICH, D. 1998. The future calls for change. *Workforceonline*. (77)1, 87–91.

VINCOLA, A. 2000. Get ready for work/life change. *Workforceonline*. http://www.workforceonline.com/archive.

WHEATLEY, M. 1997. Goodbye, command and control. In Drucker, P. (ed.) *Leader to Leader.* Chapter 16. http://www.druckerfoundation.com/leaderbooks.

WORKFORCEONLINE. http://www.workforceonline.com/archive/article/64

http://www.tompeters.com.

Index

absenteeism, 582–585
   software program 585
absolute performance rating techniques 525–527
accident process 315
acculturation 259, 264
Action Learning 489, 490
added value 514, 519, 529
adult learning 465, 493
affirmative action 66, 167–168, 174
   according to the Employment Equity Act 180–182
   arguments against 183
   definition 176–178
   discrimination 174
   international 183–186
   measures/strategies 174
   view of Business South Africa 186–187
   weakness of 183
African National Congress (ANC) 177
appointment letter 251, 253
appraisals
   360-degree 514, 522–523
   computerised 514, 522
   customer 514, 522
   reverse 515, 522
   self 515, 522
   team 515, 523
associate personnel practitioners 14
attachment 28
   to the organisation 37–39

bargaining councils 91, 109–110, 148–149
basic conditions of employment 91, 97–103
Basic Conditions of Employment Act No. 75 of 1997 97–103, 135, 169
behaviorally anchored rating scale (BARS) 514, 526
benefits, employee 66, 292–294, 603
   calculating the cost 296
   mandatory 279, 292–293
   planning 295–296
   voluntary 279, 293–294
bias 514, 528
   actor/observer 514
British Institute for Personnel Management 17
broadbanding 279, 291–292
buddy 259, 262, 275
burnout 301, 305
business intelligence 574, 575

candidate personnel and associated personnel

practitioner 14
career
  development 505–506
  development for retirement 506–507
  development methods 506
  importance 501–502
  management 465, 499–501, 510
  management for dual–career couples 507–508
  planning 503–505, 510
  practical approach 508–509
  stages 465, 502–503
central tendency 514, 527
change 394, 400–406, 536
  behavioural reaction to 394, 404
  conditions for successful 545
  drivers for 612
  environmental stress factor 303–304
  forms of 400
  managing resistance to 394, 402–404
  management 400–404
  principles of managing 394, 404–405
  resistance to 394, 401–402, 405
  scope of 394, 400–401
  strategic management of 394, 405–406
  strategic 400
  typical reactions to 403–404
changing demographics 399
closed shop agreements 91, 109
coaching and mentoring 519–520
collective bargaining 106–109
collective agreements 91, 107–108
collective dimension 134
collectivism 397–398
Commission for Conciliation, Mediation and Arbitration (CCMA) 91, 102, 114–115, 147–151
Commission for Employment Equity 97
communication
  about change 402
  employer/ employee 131, 143–145
  group 384–385
compensation management 24, 66
compensation 131, 163
  compensable factors 284–285
  for injuries and diseases 91, 124
  Fund 124
  job grades 285
  survey 279, 285–287
  total 279, 281–282
  value–chain 279, 282

Compensation Commissioner 124
Compensation for Occupational Injuries and Diseases Act no. 130 of 1993 123–124
Compensation Fund 124
compensation system
  design of 281–283
  objectives 280–281
  quality assurance and 296
competency 465
competency management 579
competition 399
competitiveness 4–8
compliance costs/orders 174, 182
compressed workweeks 217, 234
conflict and violence in the workplace 311
contingent workers 217, 232–233
continuum 543, 610, 614
corporate renewal 536, 540
corporation / company 536, 538–540
critical incidents 514, 525, 587
cultural diversity 397–400
  advantages of managing 399–400
  factors that increase 398–399
Cultural sensitivity and flexibility 602
culture
  role in diversity 396
customisation 536, 543

decision support system (DSS) 574, 575
deliverables 610, 616
demotion(s) 259, 273
development 66, 468, 536, 539–540
discrimination
  fair/unfair 174, 178–179
  prohibition 180
  societal 175
  specific 175
dismissals, 274
  Code of Good Practice 118
  unfair 91, 116–120
dispute
  resolution 91, 114–116, 148–151
  handling procedures 131, 147–151
diversity training 465, 493–494
diversity 394
  definition 396
doables 610, 616

economic system 595–596
education 465, 467
  human capital 594–595

Education and Training Quality Assurance (ETQA) bodies 434, 453
emotional intelligence 348, 351, 364
employee assistance programmes (EAPs) 301, 309
employee
  attachment to the organisation 37–39
  benefits and services 66, 292–296
  contract with employer 33–37
  handbook 259, 266–267, 268
  human being, as a 29–31
  induction of 261–271
  involvement with organisation 39–40
  leasing 217, 233
  organisation of the future, and the 612
  personal goals of 37
  staffing decisions 271–274
employers' association 131, 147
employment
  codes 165
  contract 131, 134–136
  discrimination law 174, 177–179
  equity 66, 91, 167–168, 174, 178–180, 582
  equity plan 174, 181
Employment Equity Act No. 55 of 1998 95–97, 167, 174, 178, 180–181, 240, 581, 582
employment relations 66, 95
  components 143–158
  monitoring 166–167
  policy 131, 141–143
  system 104
employment test 240, 249–251
empowering workers 520
empowerment
  economic/political 174, 183
enterprise resource planning (ERP) 574, 575
environmental factors 536, 542–543
equal employment opportunity 174, 176, 179
equality before the law 174, 187
equity management 579
essay method 514, 525
ethnocentric 591, 597
European Economic Community (EEC) 592
expatriate 591, 597
  managing the performance of 603–604
  problems faced 599–600
expectancy 325
expectancy theory 334–338
  Porter and Lawler's theory 336–338
  Vroom's theory 335–336
expectations 28, 34–37

extrinsic motivation 66

flexibility 536, 543
flexitime 217, 233
forced choice 514, 525–526
forced distribution 514, 525
forecasting techniques 217, 222–223
formal dimension 134
Foundation for Research and Development 439–440
freedom of association 91, 105
friendly facts 536, 541
fringe benefits 131, 163
Functional Job Analysis (FJA) 195, 202–203
functional level strategic planning 553, 561–562

geocentric 591, 597–598
global corporation 591, 596–597
globalisation 398–399, 536, 592
goal-directed behavior 536, 546, 547
goals 536, 546–547
graphic rating scale 514, 526
grievance and discipline 131
  handling 153–158
group
  biculturality 394, 395–596
  communication 384–385
  conflict 385–386
  conformity 372, 381–382
  decision-making 383–384
  definition 373
  development 372, 376–379
  dynamics 372, 389
  effective functioning 379–386
  formal and informal 374–376
  gestalt 372, 373
  grapevine 372, 385
  leadership 379–380
  multiculturality 394, 395
  networking 372, 374, 387, 385
  norms 372, 381–382
  punctuated equilibrium model 377–378
  rights 174
  role conflict 372, 381
  roles 380–381
  size and composition 383
  sociological criteria 373–374
  status 372, 382–383
  uniculturality 394, 395

halo effect 515, 527
health and safety 24, 66, 120–122, 163–164
Herzberg's two–factor motivation theory 331–332
   hygiene factors 25, 60, 325
   motivators 25, 58, 325
heterogeneous workforce 610, 612
hierarchy of work activities 198
HIV/AIDS 131, 160, 169, 301, 311, 441
Hofstede's dimensions of cultural difference 394 397–398
holistic health care 301, 308
host or local country 591, 597–599
human resources
   activities 614
   intellectual capital 618
   aggressiveness of professionals 614
   competencies for professionals 615, 618
   decentralisation 619–20
   definition 3, 46
   department 45, 48–49, 50, 579–581
   development 45, 66, 439, 465, 468, 568–569
   functional mix 23
   functions 15
   information 575, 582–587
   maintenance 45, 48
   planning 65, 553, 556, 557–558, 579
   policy 131, 140–141
   processes 64–67
   provisioning 45, 48
   registration categories 3, 14–15
   role of the professional, the 615, 616
   software 578
   strategic development 472
   theory 616
   tools 617
   value chain 617
   value proposition 617
human resources information system (HRIS) 574, 575–576
   application 577–581
   areas of human resource related search 581–582
   components 576
   diagnostic and decision-making tool 581–587
   employee data maintenance 578
   myths 576–577
   quality assurance 587–588
human resources management
   a process in itself 77–81
   an evolving role for 613–615
   careers 3, 15–16, 617
   challenges 22–24
   components 3, 19–22
   definition 16, 19, 46, 69
   department 48–49
   effectiveness 78
   efficiency 78
   evolution 11
   functional perspective 46–48
   future challenges 616–618
   global markets 593–596
   growth 11, 12
   historical perspective 8–12
   international, in the twenty–first century 605–606
   international involvement 596–597
   interventions 7–8
   micro–aspects 4
   model of the individual as an employee 25–26
   objectives 46–48
   profession 12–15
   quality assurance in the future role 619–620
   quality assurance approach 76–78, 78
   responsibilities and functions 48–49
   role and functions 46–48
   systems approach 50–71
   systems model 55–67
   traditional functions 48
human resources manager
   functions 49

incentive pay systems 279, 290–291
individual and group performance 45, 69–71
individual dimension 133
individual interaction 28, 35
individualism 397–398
induction 65, 161, 259, 274
   follow–up and evaluation 270–271
   kit 259, 266
   model 262–264
   objectives and benefits 261
   planning, designing and implementing the programme 264–270
   responsibility for 262
   stages of 262–263
Industry Training Boards (ITB's) 455, 456
informal dimension 134
information technology (IT) department 575
informed opportunism 536, 541

Institute of People Management of South
    Africa 12–13, 495
intellectual capital 610, 618
    identification and quantification 619
international human resources management
    policies 601–602
International Labour Organisation (ILO) 96,
    126
international labour relations 604–605
international subsidiary, approaches to
    managing 597–598
interpersonal and group relations 63
interviews 246–247
    competence–based 240, 247–248
    group 240, 249
    mistakes 249
    panel 240, 249
    semi–structured 240, 248
    stress 240, 249
    structured 240, 248
    traditional 247–248
    unstructured 240, 248
intrinsic motivation 65
involvement 28
    with the organisation 39–40

job 196
    components 198
    content environment 45, 58–60
    context environment 45, 60–64
    creation 23–24
    description 195, 204–208
    evaluation 162
    satisfaction 58, 582, 586–587
    specification 195, 208–209
job analysis 195, 196–198, 284, 465, 479
    methods 200–203
    problems 203–204
    process 198–200
    uses 197
job and personal stress 301, 303–305
    reduction mechanisms 306–308
job characteristics model 332–334
job depth 411, 413
    designing 417
Job Descriptive Index (JDI) 587
job design 411, 412, 418
    specialised approach 413–414
    team–based 411, 417–418
job enlargement 411, 416–417
job enrichment 411, 417

job evaluation 279, 283–287
job hierarchy 279, 285, 286
job–orientated approach 195, 200–202
job range 411, 413
    designing 414–417
job rotation 411, 414–416, 490–491
job simplification 411, 413–414, 418
job specialisation 411, 413–414
just–in–time 610, 612

karoshi 301, 306
key performance areas (KPA's) 79
key performance indicators (PKI's) 79
knowledge–based economy 611–612
    adding value 615–618
knowledge, skills and abilities (KSA's) 195
knowledge worker(s) 515, 610, 612

labour
    demand 217, 222, 434, 442
    level of literacy 442
    net turnover 585–586
    supply 217, 434, 441–442
labour appeal court 116, 148–149
labour court 115–116, 148–149
Labour Relations Act No. 66 of 1995 97,
    103–120, 155–158, 529
layoff 259, 274
leadership 66
    Blake and Mouton's grid 356–358
    Charismatic 365
    continuum of Tannenbaum and Schmidt
        358–360
    definition 349
    McGregor's X and Y theory 352–354
    participative versus autocratic behaviours
        351
    power and authority 351–352
    quality assurance 366
    quality or traits approach 350–351
    revised model of situational leadership by
        Nicholls 362–364
    Schein's theory human assumptions
        354–356
    situational leadership theory of Hersey and
        Blanchard 360–362
    situational 348, 360
    style 61
    transformational 364
    versus management 350
    virtual 348, 365–366

learnership training 492
learning 480, 489, 490, 493, 494
learning organisations 546
leniency and strictness 515, 527
line function (authority) 45, 50

management by objectives (MBO) 515, 526–527
management information system (MIS) 217, 223, 574, 575
management philosophy 61
Maslow's needs hierarchy 327–329
   higher order needs 25
   lower–order needs 25
McWhirter Thesis 174, 182
medical check 251
Mine Health and Safety Act No. 29 of 1996 316
migration 399
mission 553, 556
money as motivator 340–341
motivating potential score (MPS) 333–334
motivating contingent employees 341–342
motivation
   definition 326–327
   holistic approach 342
   quality assurance 342–343
   role of goal setting 338–340
motivational theories 327–338
multiple goals 45, 53, 67

National Economic and Development Labour Council (NEDLAC) 447
National Occupational Safety Association (NOSA) 301, 316–317
National Qualifications Framework (NQF) 122, 434, 450–454, 458, 462, 466
National Standards Bodies (NSB) 434, 453
new world economy 434, 436
North American Free Trade Agreement (NAFTA) 593

occupational health and safety 91, 120
   Advisory Council 121
Occupational Health and Safety Act No. 85 of 1993 120–122, 135, 301, 314–315
occupational injuries
   ergonomic approach 314
offer of employment and appointment 251, 253
off-the-job training 484–489

on-the-job training (OJT) 465, 489–492
organisation 3, 21, 35, 395
   as employer 33–37
   assessment of its environment 559–560
   boundaryless structure 411, 420, 422
   bureaucratic structure 411, 419, 420
   conditions for successful change 545, 536
   definition 540–541
   doughnut 411, 421, 423–424
   failure to renew 544–546
   flat structure 411, 419–420, 421
   forces shaping the future 612–613
   goals 37–38
   human resources input 32
   human resources management function 47
   informal 536
   open system 53–55
   place and role of the training function 471–472
   shamrock 411, 421–422
   successful 39
   the Sigmoid curve 422–423
   the Chinese contract 423–424
   vineyard 411, 421, 424–425
   virtual 411, 425–427
   virtual training 473
organisational
   approaches 419–420
   assessment 478–479
   change 537, 545–546
   characteristics of renewal 542
   characteristics of development 542, 545
   climate 61
   critical factors for renewal 541–542
   culture, 61, 263–264, 581
   definition of learning 545
   design 411, 412, 418–419
   determination of mission 558–559
   development 537, 539
   effectiveness 45, 54, 68, 516
   efficiency 45, 54, 68
   environment 553
   expectations 28
   goals 28
   lessons in renewal 537
   renewal strategies 545–546
   renewal and environmental factors 542–543
   renewal and technology 544
   renewal and globalisation 543
   renewal 537, 538, 539
   renewal goals and values 546–547

renewal 538
rights 91, 106
strategic planning 219–220, 557
success 45, 54, 67–71
transformation 546
values 553, 559
orientation 259, 260–261, 263
outcomes-based education and training 465, 468–417
approach 470
traditional approach vs outcome 470

paired comparisons 515, 524–525
parent or home company 591, 597–599
pay for competencies 279, 288–289
pay for knowledge and skills 279, 287–288
payment of remuneration and deductions 100, 603
pay policy 287
payroll processing 578–579
peer review 515, 522
performance
 appraisal 66, 519
 appraisal programmes 516
 evaluation 515, 520–521
 evaluation methods 521–527
 evaluation techniques 523–527
 feedback interview 528–529
 management 516
 management process 516–521
 management and quality assurance 529–530
 management system 516, 518
 problems 520
 rater–errors 527–528
performance-based pay 279, 289–290
personal goals 28
 integration with those of organisation 37
personality 28, 29–33
 major factors 30, 31
personnel practitioner 14
personnel management 3, 10, 11
 definition 17
planning
 levels 553
 long-range 217
 long-term 553
 middle-range 217
 short-range 217
political democracy 91, 94
portfolio extension 406
polycentric 591, 597

Position Analysis Questionnaire (PAQ) 195, 202
power distance 398
process management
 continuous improvement 83
 external customer 83
 external supplier 83
 human resources operations 84–86
 internal supplier 82
 internal support chain 84
 internal customer 82
 internal supply chain 82, 84
 organisational structure 84
 process symbols 83
 process flowchart 83
 process 82
 professional staff chain 84
productivity and flexibility 434, 437
productivity ratio 4
professional design 411, 424
promoting safety 312–313
promotions 259, 272–273
psychological contract 28, 33
 cooperative contract 33–37
 types 33

quality assurance
 and job analysis 208–209
 definition 76
 process approach 82–86
 workforce planning and recruitment 234–235
quality of work life and social investment 165–166
quantum leap change 348, 348

ranking 515, 524
rational and political perspectives/approaches to recency 515, 528
realistic orientation programs for new employee stress (ROPES) 259, 263
realistic job preview (RJP) 259, 262
recognition of prior learning 465, 494
recruitment 65, 131, 160–161, 579, 602–603
 current and future trends 232–234
 factors influencing 226–227
 legal considerations 234
 policy 226
 sources and methods 227–232
re–engineering 411, 427–428
reference check 240, 251

regiocentric 591, 598
relative performance rating techniques 524–525
repatriate 591
  guidelines 601
  problems 600–601
resignation 259, 273–274
retirement 259, 274
retrenchment 164, 259, 274
rights and duties of employers and workers 137–140
rule of law 175, 183, 187–188

safety and first aid training 316
school education 440–441
science and engineering 440
select or design instructional content 480
selection 65, 131, 161, 579, 602–603
  decision 240, 242–243, 252
  definition 241
  methods 243
  process 243–251
  quality assurance 252–253
self-actualisation 325, 328, 355
self-fulfilling prophecy 348, 352
self-help desk 579–582
self-managed team (SMT) 417
skills development 91
  Authorities (SETAS) 123, 434, 449
  Sector Educational and Training
  Skills Development Levies Act 123, 434, 457–458
  Skills Development Planning Units 123
  National Skills Authority 123, 434
  National Skills Fund 123, 434
Skills Development Act No. 97 of 1998 122–123, 434, 455–457
skills inventory 217, 223
smoking policy 301, 310
social Darwinism 9
socialisation 259, 262, 581
Sono Thesis 175, 183
South Africa's National Competitiveness Balance Sheet 5–7
South African Board for Personnel Practice 13–15
South African Qualifications Authority Act No. 58 of 1995 122, 123, 434, 458
South African Qualifications Authority (SAQA) 434, 452–453, 462, 466
South African Constitution Act No. 108 of 1996 (The Constitution) 91, 94, 178
Sowell Thesis 175
spirituality in workplace 301, 307–308
stability in motion 537, 541
staff function (authority) 45, 50
  authority of human resources department 51
staffing 65, 161, 259
  importance 271–272
  quality assurance 274
  strategies 259, 272
staffing model 219
standard application blank 240, 244–246
Standards Generating Bodies (SGBs) 434, 453
standards of behaviour 559
strategic business planning 557–560
  determination of strategies to accomplish objectives 560
  setting of specific objectives or direction 560
strategic business unit 553, 561
  functional strategy 561–562
strategic customer orientation 618
  developing it 618–619
strategic human resource management 553, 555, 563–568
  a model 566–567
  formulating human resources management strategy 563–564
  view of Cascio 564–565
  view of van Dyk 565–568
strategic human resources development 568–569
strategic management 405–406, 553, 562–563
  pyramidical framework 556
strategy 553, 555, 556, 559
strategy and levels of planning 561–562
  business strategy 561
  grand strategy 561
strikes and lockouts 91, 109–112
  handling 131, 151–153
structures and personnel policy 62
substance abuse 301, 309–310
Sullivan code 176
systematic activity log 195, 202

teams (work) 372
  characteristics 387
  definition 386
  types 387–389
telecommuting 217, 234
termination procedures 131, 164–165

tertiary education 439–440
Trade Unions and Employers' Organisations 113
training 65, 467, 603
  apprenticeship 465, 492
  certification 434, 445, 450–454
  cost and benefit 434, 443–445, 497–499
  delivery methods and strategies 482
  economic and social policies 438
  funding 443–449
  funding mechanism 434, 447–449
  high impact model 477, 478
  investment 437–438
  needs 478–479
  policy options 458–462
  sources and application of funds 445–446
  strategic approach 472–473
  supervisors 494–497
  vestibule 492
training and development 131, 162
  application of various models 477–484
  evaluation 465, 483–484
  models 465, 476–477, 484–493
  policy 473–476
training levy–grant scheme 434, 448 449
transfer 259, 273
transformation 348, 364, 536

uncertainty avoidance 398
unclear standards 527
undertaking 11
unemployment insurance 91
  benefits 126
  Commissioner 125
  employers' duties 125
  Fund (UIF) 124–125

Unemployment Insurance Act No. 30 of 1966 124–126
unfair labour practice 119
unsafe acts 301, 312
  reducing 313
unsafe conditions 301, 312
  reducing 313

vision 553, 556
vocational education and training 434, 435, 442, 450

wellness 301, 308–309
work
  overload 301, 303, 304
  underload 301, 303, 304
work time and rules 91, 98–100
workaholism 301, 305
worker-orientated approach 195, 202–203
workforce 394, 395
  biculturality 394, 395–396
  diverse 91, 175, 178
  harassment 175, 179
  multiculturality 394, 395–396
  plan implementation 223–224
  planning steps 222–224
  planning 217, 218–222
  uniculturality 394, 395–396
working conditions 62
workplace 394, 395
workplace forums 91, 112–113, 131, 158–160
World Competitive Report 6, 86
World Competitiveness Organisation (WCO) 5

ZelnickThesis 175, 183